P9-CFC-674

Childhood Education in the Church

Childhood Education in the Church

Edited by
Roy B. Zuck, Th.M., Th.D.
and Robert E. Clark, M.S., Ed.D.

moody press
chicago

All scripture quotations are from the King James Version, unless otherwise noted. The use of selected references from various versions of the Bible in this publication does not necessarily imply publisher endorsement of the versions in their entirety.

All scripture quotations taken from *The Living Bible* by Dr. Kenneth Taylor, © 1971 by Tyndale House Publishers, Wheaton, Illinois, are used by permission.

All scripture quotations taken from the New American Standard Bible are used by permission of The Lockman Foundation, © 1960, 1962, 1963, 1971, 1973.

Library of Congress Cataloging in Publication Data

Main entry under title:
Childhood education in the church.
Includes bibliographical references and index.
1. Religious education of children.
I. Zuck, Roy B. II. Clark, Robert E.
BV1475.2.C47 268'.432 74-15350
ISBN 0-8024-1249-1
Fourth Printing, 1978

Printed in the United States of America

CONTENTS

Part V—ADMINISTRATION OF CHILDREN'S WORK

Part VI—WORKING WITH EXCEPTIONAL CHILDREN

Part VII—WORKING WITH CHILDREN BEYOND THE CHURCH

Part I

THE CHALLENGE OF TEACHING CHILDREN

1

Why Teach Children?

Donald M. Joy

A "TROUBLE SO DEEP and pervasive as to threaten the future of our nation" has gripped the United States of America, according to documents drawn up at the White House Conference on Children, late in 1970. That trouble is the "national neglect of children and those primarily engaged in their care—America's parents." The final report of the children's committee included sweeping proposals, which, if implemented, would reorder national priorities. The chairman, Dr. Urie Bronfenbrenner of Cornell University, noted with obvious urgency that "the actual patterns of life in America today are such that *children and families come last.* Our society expects its citizens first of all to meet the demands of their jobs and then to fulfill civic and social obligations."[1]

In the churches, we may hope that we have done better, but since we all are caught, whether we like it or not, under the magnetic spell of our culture and its social dynamics, the matter deserves our scrutiny. Where, really, do children stand in our churches? Are they at the center of our concern, or only at the focal point of our extravagant display?

CHILDREN NUMBER ONE?

Americans may idolize their children and imitate their teenagers, but evidently they do not place them first in their affections. History stands witness to the fact that no tribe or nation survives for long when it neglects to pass along its values—that store of treasured beliefs and practices which it holds dearer than life. And the long history of man is chiefly the account of families, tribes, and nations who have patiently and persistently loved and protected their young. Contrary to popular opinion, this is the con-

---

DONALD M. JOY, Ph.D., is Associate Professor of Christian Education, Asbury Theological Seminary, Wilmore, Kentucky.

struction placed on human history even by some "survival of the fittest" anthropologists. Loren Eisley noted that man's history is not one which is dominated by tooth and claw, that "man has not really survived by his toughness in a major sense . . . [but] by his tenderness." Eisley notes particularly the long childhood in the human species, the lengthy helplessness and dependence of children, and the survival based on affection and care.[2]

If there is wide agreement that children need our central attention, it is not so easily demonstrated that they are getting our best. We may spend ludicrous sums of money to feed, clothe, and entertain them, but these expenditures hardly make them human. And it is this humanizing energy which they need most, since children derive their genuine character as human beings chiefly through learning rather than through heredity. The frightening effects produced by isolation and sense starvation, found in deserted and abused children, remind us of their need for tenderness, intimacy with adults, and teaching.

But Dr. Bronfenbrenner reminds us that modern technological society has conspired to cut children off from adults—their reasonable source for learning the store of treasured beliefs and ways of living. First, we isolated children from the tribe by moving out of clans and into suburbia. Then, we cut them off from ourselves by stratifying the lonely, nuclear family—each member living virtually to himself and associating only with his peers.[3]

The net result is that children know increasingly fewer adults. Children are transported from the front door to schools where they mill around in ever larger buildings with literally mobs of peers. After school, they study, club, or roam in packs of peers as they wait for parents to provide dinner and to hand over the keys to an automobile, so they can continue the narrow age-level segregation into the night. It would be easy to suggest that our children have invented this kind of life-style. But, the fact is, we did it. We invented baby-sitters and the thousand things that conspire to keep our children out of our lives. They have accurately read our arms-length-and-no-more relationships as indifference and neglect. Today's climate in North America is such that children have few alternatives but to cling to the available sources of attention and security: their age mates and television. Neither is a particularly helpful source of values nor a suitable model from which to conclude what is human about humans. Peers have only their own impoverished experience to share. Television, easily a powerful influence, is a suspicious custodian of the nursery, with dubious morals and lack of principles.

So the generations, having sensed their own neglect, quickly gather their isolation about themselves and set their feet against all others. It is as if a malignant nodule had exploded in our society to set every horizontal age group against every other. The college student confesses that he cannot communicate with his younger brother. The high school student looks with contempt on the fourth grader, and the junior high youngster would not bother with a preschool child—except for baby-sitting money. To put it plainly, affection across the generations has gone out of our lives; we live as strangers under the same roof with our own children.[4]

God's Design for Childhood

Jean Piaget, that remarkable Swiss psychologist who has spent most of a very long life observing children and studying their ways of thinking, is confronted often with what he calls "the American question." The question goes like this: "If there are stages that children reach at given norms of ages, can we accelerate these stages?" To such efforts to speed up everything, Piaget answers by pointing out that it takes, for example, from nine to twelve months before a human baby develops the sense that an object is still there when you place a blind between the baby and the object. Kittens go through the same stages as children, but they do it in three months. "In this an advantage or isn't it?" Piaget asks. Then he answers: "We can certainly see our answer in one sense. The kitten is not going to go much further. The child has taken longer, but he is capable of going further, so it seems to me that the nine months probably were not for nothing."[5] This attitude of Piaget seems appropriate in any study of ourselves, and especially so when we seek to unravel a theory of man, based upon what we can observe from Holy Scripture and from history.

The opening chapters of Genesis suggest that our first parents came from the hand of God fully grown. Created in the "image of God," they were fully formed spiritually, emotionally, and physically. The account is plainly set down to illustrate their intimate fellowship with God, their acceptance of themselves and of each other in maturity and poise, and their obvious physical capability. These priceless endowments, which all other human beings would derive from heredity and environment, were God's direct gift to Adam and Eve.

All other humans, however, have been the product of another sort of formation process—that of "parenting." Only a tiny fraction of the human race ever has had a course in child psychology or in "marriage and the family," yet the race has survived. The quality of family relationships is probably more related to faithfulness to a handful of unchanging principles which may be observed in a biblical view of man and family than in much of today's theorizing.

The book of Genesis underscores the importance of both male and female in the creative process of producing children and in the home environment where children grow. Intimacy and interdependence in the household made both parents equally available to the child, a clue which speaks to today's concern over the learning of sex-appropriate behavior and resolving the frustrations of young males who are deprived of male models, many for most of their waking hours and some for their entire childhood.

Learning to "have dominion" and to honor the living God are learned undoubtedly most efficiently by walking in the shadow of a parent who lives out his teaching. If one had to choose between formal schooling and informal learning from parents, even in the total effects on today's parent-starved children, the schools would lose. The most difficult learning task in all of life, the learning of one's native language, is accomplished chiefly during the preschool years, by use of informal and indirect methods, and under the tutelage of parents. The best language laboratories and intensive instruction can never match what parents did without tapes, films, or earphones.

We get only glimpses of childhood training and teaching patterns through the Old Testament. The affirmation of faith in the Shema recorded in Deuteronomy 6:4-5 is followed by directions which call for believers to keep God's commandments in their own hearts and to repeat them to their children. The instruction was to be in the form of speaking both indoors and outdoors, visual reminders bound to foreheads and wrists, and written text on the doorposts of the houses and on the gates. Such education was comprehensive in scope and made virtually all of life a school. It acknowledged that children are immersed in a total curriculum of experience, and it detailed fundamental teaching-learning modes as contemporary as Jerome Bruner's "action, image, and language" forms of representation.[6]

The Hebrew pattern for transmitting values and beliefs consisted especially of handing on the treasured store from father to son. It has been suggested by modern observers that the male conscience develops differently from that of the female. The male is both more ruggedly committed to his father's values and more rigidly and inflexibly formed in those values than the female, thus making the male particularly well suited for transgenerational transmission of values and for applying them in the tough situations of marketplace and government.[7] It is almost universally observed that in clashes of ideologies and values, males more violently defend their own, battling to death in wars of varying dimensions. Women and children have been spared and taken captive from time immemorial, but men seem always to have been more fiercely welded to their values, hopeless of reformation or reindoctrination, hence better conservators of value systems.

This transgenerational communications system is clearly displayed in Psalm 78:5-6 (NASB):

> For He established a testimony in Jacob,
> And appointed a law in Israel,
> Which He commanded our fathers,
> That they should teach them to their children;
> That the generation to come might know,
> even the children yet to be born.

A similar pattern, clearly set within family life, shows up also in Proverbs 4:1-4 (NASB):

> Hear, O sons, the instruction of a father,
> And give attention that you may gain understanding,
> For I give you sound teaching;
> Do not abandon my instruction.
> When I was a son to my father,
> Tender and the only son in the sight of my mother,
> Then he taught me and said to me,
> "Let your heart hold fast my words;
> Keep my commandments and live."

"Father" and "son" were labels somewhat larger than strict usage in North America today would allow. They had tribal overtones, and one saw his own actual offspring as the "sons" of his own father and grandfather also. As the tribal tasks were divided, formal instruction was arranged in the synagogue school, but the sense of urgency remained high for transmitting community values—beliefs of the larger family.

"No nation has ever set the child in the midst more deliberately than the Jews did," writes William Barclay.[8] He cites both Scripture and early Hebrew writings to illustrate his point. The Midrash commentary on Exodus 25:34 interprets the "blossoms" as referring to children: "And in the lampstand [there shall be] four cups shaped like almond blossoms" (NASB). The Jews were sure, says Barclay, that of all people, the child was dearest to God. "Touch not mine anointed, and do my prophets no harm" of 1 Chronicles 16:22 was regarded as referring to children, the "anointed," and to their teachers, "my prophets." Extreme writings suggested that these schools were more important even than worship: "Perish the sanctuary, but let the children go to school."[9] Josephus, too, underscores childhood instruction: "Our chief ambition is for the education of our children. . . . We take most pains of all with the instruction of children, and esteem the observation of the laws, and the piety corresponding with them, the most important affair of our whole life."[10]

Such education and such concern persists into New Testament times, and Jesus' comments about children and their importance seem in harmony with this long-term Jewish attitude toward childhood. Lest we should too quickly identify that concern and those schools with our own, let it be noted that such training (*a*) sought no commitment to God, but assumed it, (*b*) was exclusively education in holiness, (*c*) consisted of rote mastery of Jewish Scriptures and writings, and (*d*) was for boys only.

Jesus and the Child

The gospels, written by and for adults, reflect the fact that children were allowed to be children in Jesus' day. There was no preoccupation with them as objects of prophetic or salvation utterances. A certain aloofness seemed to emerge easily from a society that completely committed itself to the processes of family and synagogue education for transmitting its treasured beliefs and life-styles. So the New Testament has little to say about children. There exist occasional allusions to them, however, suggesting that they were present, and that they sometimes came playing, running into the presence of Jesus and the apostles.

Jesus was apparently never too busy for children, and we have no record of His becoming impatient with them. He took them in His arms (Mk 10:16). He set a child in the midst of a crowd to draw a lesson for the adults (Mk 9:36-37), and He at least once cited children's games as an analogy of His own unheeded ministry with adults (Mt 11:16-17). Among His sternest warnings are those against causing a little child to stumble or go astray (Mt 18:5-6). Jesus knew what we often forget—that parents, even earthly and evil ones, love their children and want to give them the best gifts (Lk 11:13).

When His disciples bickered and pushed for selfish status, Jesus called a child and set him in front of them (Mk 9:33-37). He proceeded to illustrate with the child that (*a*) entering the kingdom of God requires a humility like that of a child; (*b*) children are somehow numbered among those who believe in Christ; and (*c*) their guardian angels in heaven enjoy a privileged place, looking directly into the face of the father. Looked at as a whole instead of fragments (Mt 18:1-10), Jesus' allusions to childhood in this passage instruct us in some troubling ways: (*a*) He seems to have offered no direct instruction or summons to children, (*b*) He placed on them no evangelistic emphasis calling them to belief or repentance; (*c*) He made no effort to draw them into His following as disciples.[11]

This attitude toward children which emerges in the gospels continues through the entire New Testament. Virtually nothing is said about what or how to teach children. They are to obey their parents (Eph 6:1). Their fathers are to bring them up in the "nurture and admonition of the Lord" (Eph 6:4). Bishops, deacons, and elders are to be faithful and successful in the rearing of their own children (1 Ti 3:1-4; Titus 1:6). Fathers are to be careful not to deal so harshly with their children that they become discouraged (Col 3:21).

With this scant list, we see the entire scope of New Testament teachings about childhood education. There is no prescribed curriculum. What religious education did exist in Jewish synagogues is not alluded to, and there is not so much as a hint that Christians made any arrangements for the religious instruction of their children outside of the home.

Children in Church History

In the early centuries of the church, no provision was made for the education of children, either in basic literacy or in Christian faith. Classes were formed in the first and second centuries for new converts, and, presumably, older children found themselves in these converts classes, called "catechumenal schools." The classes were "graded," or grouped, according to the level appropriate to the individual person's commitment. "Hearers" were allowed to listen to the reading of Scripture and to sermons. "Kneelers" were allowed to remain afterward for prayers and for more instruction; they were examined as to daily Christian discipline and habits of life. "The chosen" were given intensive theological instruction and were prepared for baptism. The catechumenal schools continued for several centuries, but they deteriorated after about the fifth century.[12]

Catechetical schools appeared late in the second century and were for the training of ministers and Christian scholars. These were established throughout the Christian world; and a pattern formed by which a cluster of congregations would jointly sponsor an "episcopal" or "cathedral" school. Even so, they were not for all children or even for all boys. They admitted only those who were in preparation for the priesthood of the church.

Not until the decades following the Reformation did Christian concern focus upon basic literacy education for children in general or upon the usefulness of Bible study in the education of the young. Martin Luther was committed to a broad education of children. But it was John Amos Comenius, late in the sixteenth century, who urged a thoroughly Christian education for all children. Comenius, Philip Spener, and August Hermann Francke were the moving forces who introduced Bible study to Christian education in any large sense. The early centuries had employed a certain amount of Scripture in the rote teaching of catechumens, but the printing press now made possible the wider use of Scripture. It was to become for several centuries the chief means of teaching reading.

Robert Raikes' early Sunday schools were as much aimed at bringing basic literacy to the deprived chimney sweeps on Sooty Alley as they were to bringing them salvation. The Gloucester editor assembled his first S ınday school in Mrs. Meredith's kitchen. He paid her for teaching them, and later employed others. But he was "outside" the church, and few clergymen gave him encouragement. Among those who did were John Wesley and William Fox. Both gave Raikes early endorsement, even before Raikes revealed to the public what had been going on in Gloucester kitchens for nearly three years. The movement flourished. By the time of Raikes' death in 1811, there were nearly a half million children enrolled in his Sunday schools. William Fox founded the Sunday School Society in London in 1785, and, backed by several wealthy friends, he proceeded to spread the idea.

When the Sunday school movement leaped to America, it became less and less a literacy program and increasingly a gospel agency. By 1810, the American version of the Sunday school was permitted to come into the churches. As the churches became involved, they became more interested in the content of the teaching, and denominations formed Sunday school boards, or commissions, to supervise the educational work in local churches.

The early twentieth century ushered in more and wider programs aimed at the moral and spiritual education of children. The scout programs were founded between 1910 and 1912. Child Evangelism Fellowship began in 1923. While the scouts were relatively secular in their approach, Child Evangelism Fellowship, working chiefly through Good News Clubs, gathered children in their neighborhoods to lead them to Christ. CEF and a proliferation of other children's agencies continue. Christian Service Brigade, Pioneer Girls, Awana Youth Association, Christian Youth Crusaders, each designate growing and well-developed Christian education programs for children, each working beyond denominational lines with a concern for bringing the child to Christ and to discipleship.

Reasons for Ministering to Children Today

The sweep of history seems to trace a moving pattern in child training as follows: (*a*) all training is in the matrix of the home and is informal; (*b*) child training is shared by parents and relatives and is still informal in nature; (*c*) training is organized by the tribe or subcultural group to transmit an increasingly complex body of treasured values and is carried on in both formal and informal ways; (*d*) child training is delegated to education specialists without regard to their values, and procedures are almost entirely formal, both unrelated to the teacher's values and related only with difficulty to the real world.

The church is caught in the magnetic field of education in general, especially with regard to the separation of teaching from active living. In any consideration of the responsibility of the church for the child, the obligation is surely upon us to note carefully what our opportunities and what our motivations are in ministering to the child. Here follow a series of observations about the importance of keeping faith with children in our trust. The sequence may have significance in terms of logic but not necessarily in terms of importance.

1. *Children are our gift from God.* There is some mysterious sense in which the creation is reechoed in the birth of every child. Whatever intrinsic marks original sin may have transmitted to children, they are uniquely beautiful in their early years. The children of every culture are alike in this way. Their laughter and games, even in the most perverse societies, are reminders that God speaks of His own holiness in the gift of life bestowed on human children. As such, they are at once a rebuke to us and a reminder that God has grand things in mind for the human race. We begin our ministry with children with a vision of helping bring them to fulfillment of God's design for them—a design glimpsed in embryo in the free, creative, joyous beauty of early childhood.

2. *Children are open to God.* The typical child does not need arguments to prove the existence of God; nor does he need to be convinced that prayer and other acts of worship are important. Beyond this, the evidence is overwhelming which suggests that young children are capable of religious experience.[13] Children are especially capable of such experiences because of the very nature of the development of the human mind. All children pass through growth patterns carefully described by Jean Piaget as "motor" and "egocentric" stages, running from birth up through about age eight. During this time, children have difficulty distinguishing between reality and fantasy. They are creative and imaginative and indulge in magical explanations, inventing a wide range of supranatural persons and events. This capacity makes them highly susceptible to belief both in Santa Claus and in God.[14] We cannot unravel the mystery of this particular stage of development, nor can we separate the child's orthodox religious belief from his unbridled fantasy. It will be important that his religious environment be stable during these years and that he have wide exposure to authentic adult faith. Where these conditions exist, he will separate fantasy from faith naturally and easily as his mind grows.

3. *Jesus placed a high value on children.* Jesus attributed faith and belief to the children who played in His presence and found themselves on His lap and in His stories. Their open credulity became the analogy of commitment to His discipleship. Yet He did not call them to discipleship or chide them for unbelief or draw the net for their conversion. He accepted them at their stage of development for what they were, but saw beyond that to their potential as full grown creatures made in the image of God.

So He went about seeking to change the life-molding environment of those children. In our ministry, we will do no better than to imitate Him. When we do, we will provide an environment for children in which we (*a*) show respect for their value to God, accepting them at their various stages of development and ministering to them in appropriate ways; (*b*) affirm their childlike faith, and (*c*) develop a rich display of faithful adherence to the traditions, values, beliefs, and life-styles which are thoroughly and honestly Christian.

4. *The church is the "family of God."* The disintegration of family life, which we are presently experiencing in North America, will affect us less if we remember that the true bond of relationship among Christians is faith, not blood. Jesus suggested as much when He posed the question about the identity of His "mother" and His "brothers" (Mt 12:48-50). Both He and the New Testament writers affirm that the new fellowship of faith is the successor to the old line of Abraham. The congregation, then, ought to be an extended family, a tribe, or a network of intimate circles of mutual concern, sharing, and faith. This feature of congregational life is no doubt the most attractive of the authentic hallmarks of Christian faith. We are created for fellowship, not isolation and loneliness, and fulfillment at the personal level is somehow contingent upon rich interpersonal relationships. If a congregation does not find ways of developing this kind of warmth and support, it cannot hope to nurture its children well. For the very dynamics of relationships in the nuclear family make it imperative that the "tribe" furnish some of the models and reinforce the parental values if they are to prevail. The congregation, through its informal and formal ministries, is uniquely prepared to contribute significantly to the child's Christian decision making and growth because it is transgenerational in character, relational in essence, and has abundant resources for both didactic and modeling instruction.

5. *Christian faith is never more than one generation from extinction.* Christian faith is not a matter of genes and chromosomes; nor is it transmitted by birthright or inheritance. "God has no grandchildren," someone has quipped, "only children." We must make no assumptions, therefore, about what children know. They know nothing about the acts of God in history unless we share that knowledge. We will carefully plan the learning exposures of our children to unfold to them the mighty acts of God in such a way as to help them arrive at the same sound faith that we possess—if we are wise.[15]

6. *The early years set the tone for lifelong values.* It is sometimes argued that we should invest our energy in reaching children because we can reach them more easily than adults and because "they have their whole life before them." Both observations are accurate, but a deeper

motive should move us. Life's earliest experiences profoundly shape all of life, for this world and the next. Empirically, this axiom is well established by studies on identification and child rearing[16] and in the growing literature on father-absence.[17] A theoretical base is constructed in the model of "satellization."[18] Poetically, the sentiment is underscored by Dorothy Law Nolte's "Children Learn What They Live."[19] The evidence is rather overwhelming that early sources of consistent value influence are essential if the child is to be formed in such a way as to be an effective, functioning person as an adult.[20] The entire array of church ministries to children must be seen as a major part of this early value influence which has long-range formation goals in mind.

7. *Children deserve to be helped to moral and spiritual maturity.* Just as children pass through cognitive stages in the development of the mind, they also move through identifiable stages of moral thought. Indeed, it seems plausible that the growing mind sets the limits on moral perception. In experiments with children in Christian education settings, Doug Scholl of Harvard University found that there is an upward yearning in the child's mind for more mature modes of moral thought. Using the basic research fabric of Lawrence Kohlberg,[21] he contrived learning experiences using what he called a "plus-one-match." In this strategy, the level of moral thinking predominating in the group was noted, then a child with advanced ways of thinking, usually one level above the majority, was used as the model to which other children's thought was elevated.[22] Kohlberg generalizes from his extensive cross-cultural studies that (*a*) each of the six stages he defines is a typology, not an airtight stage, since no person operates exclusively within one typology; (*b*) the stages form an invariant sequence through which all persons pass—the early stages, at least—in relation to age; (*c*) all movement is forward; one never arrives at stage four thinking by way of stage six, but vice versa; and (*d*) a person may stop within any of the typologies or stages; hence, biological maturity does not assure moral development. The Kohlberg observations and his model of typologies may be instructive to evangelical Christians not only because of the profound insights they may stimulate about our effectiveness in promoting growth and maturity in Christian faith, but also in understanding how believers may become arrested at immature levels and fail to grow in Christian faith and behavior. With children, his model may be particularly helpful in assessing a child's actual way of viewing moral events and in thereby coming to his aid in moving to more mature, that is, more fully Christian, ways of thinking and behaving.

8. *Early, consistent saturation in a warm, Christian nurture environment helps children respond personally to Christ's call to salvation.* During the years from birth to age ten, plus or minus two, a child's need is for a warm

identification environment in which he may develop a strong sense that he is loved by God and by the Christians around him. All the while, he will be interpreting, likely incorrectly, what he sees by reducing it to concrete, external, legalistic images and modes. Nevertheless, as the child approaches the almost simultaneous arrival of sexual awakening, of formal/abstract thinking powers, and of his own identity awareness, he will sense a deep personal need of God's grace in forgiving, fulfilling ministries, if life is to have meaning. Whatever rich childhood experiences a child may have enjoyed in his relationship with God, he must eventually come to a distinctly personal response, if meaningful discipleship is to take root.[23] We cannot stress too much the importance of an early, positive religious environment for the child, encouragement to respond to God's grace, and provision of abundant models whose life testimony affirms the validity of the gospel being verbalized in classes, clubs, and worship.

9. *The child's emerging life needs are best met in the Christian fellowship.* If we hold that Christian faith and life is the means whereby God restores fallen men to fellowship with Himself and to life of highest possible human fulfillment, then we must affirm other truths which derive from that hypothesis. One of these is that Christians are able to take the most honest and realistic view of human needs and that they possess the most useful tools for use in bringing human beings to fulfillment. In the hands of Christian educators, then, any helpful research or models which describe the human condition become torches for lighting our way in identifying persons' needs and in developing ways of meeting those needs. Christians might rightly hold that to the extent that educators and therapists operate from sub-Christian bases, they will be less able to be fully helpful in meeting human need. For example, Erik Erikson makes several announcements: that the infant wavers in the balance between an orientation of trust versus basic mistrust; that he then proceeds to the dilemma of autonomy versus shame and doubt; that by school age, he is caught between the tension of a life-orientation of initiative over against guilt; that the elementary years are predominantly fought out pitting industry against inferiority; and that when pubescence strikes, he will be wavering between positive identity discovery and role diffusion.[24] Christians ought, of all people, to apply his model to their work and ask whether such life crises are occurring before their eyes. If the model is helpful, as a majority of thoughtful persons now believe it is, we must certainly see that the first named option in each of the crisis pairs is the one Christian growth would opt for. And if one would dare to take the social science approach to Christian education,[25] he would affirm that God has so designed man and human relations that whatever one sows will be reaped—that there are methodical means of getting desired results through training and child-

hood education programs in the church. Likewise, even the most superficial glance at Abraham Maslow's hierarchy of human needs, delineated in chapter 3 of this book, will help set the agenda for our Christian education agencies and home ministries.[26] These are only two of today's dominant models which become a mandate to us as those whose highest objective is to meet human needs—needs which culminate in self-realization as they find themselves recreated in the image of righteousness and true holiness (Eph 4:24) in Jesus Christ.

10. *Child development is best understood, appreciated, and ministered to in the loving environment of the family of God.* We have noted the distinct opportunity to minister to children across their development of cognitive powers (item 2), their development of moral thought (item 7), and their unfolding developmental needs (item 9). But the church and its children's ministries are capable of responding in superior ways to the physiological-psychological-social development needs of the child as well. Children, for example, who find regular support in the church's programs from birth tend to enter school well ahead of homebound children of similar endowments. The social exchanges, the wider sources of affection, and the regular movement into larger social spheres combine to furnish our children with the benefits eagerly sought for all children through newly launched "early childhood intervention" programs. In our society, children are learning to read earlier than in the past, many reading even before they start kindergarten. The impact of television is largely responsible for the reading acceleration, no doubt. But for reasons not so clearly understood, sexual maturity is also accelerated. It is urgent, therefore, that the church adapt to these accelerations and find ways of meeting the needs which they represent. For example, the onset of puberty (legally, age fourteen for boys and age twelve for girls) seems to be moving down steadily into childhood years. The rate has been estimated to be roughly at six months per generation. The effects for those who minister to children become obvious: (*a*) identity needs which accompany biological transition may be expected to strike as early as the middle elementary years; (*b*) awakening moral sense which produces personal guilt and which needs the work of God's grace in healing and forgiveness must be anticipated in some cases well ahead of the prime junior high school years; (*c*) the drop-out rate which seems to be directly related to the onset of puberty, perhaps related to emerging discomfort, embarrassment, or even guilt over sexual feelings and activity, will be striking earlier than ever before.

11. *The educational technocracy obligates us to effective ministry with children.* Never before have we had at our disposal such an array of educational theory and educational hardware to accomplish our tasks in

ministering to children. Serious attention to the learning process, still a youthful science, was introduced among the higher concerns of man only in this century. Even now, there is no one satisfactory theory of learning on the horizon. There are tentative theories of instruction now being offered, well after earlier theories of learning which had been thought to contain all that was necessary to observe about instruction. But teaching is not merely learning theory standing on its head; the two seem to have distinctly different characteristics.[27] Beyond the methodologies involved in teaching and learning, loom our advanced understanding of how content may be packaged for efficient subsumption in the learner. The intricate steps involved in programming basic packages of information, for example, have formed a new science in itself.[28] This is not even to attempt to profile the arsenal of audiovisual and printed media which is now at our disposal. But finally, and perhaps most hopefully of all, we have now been provided with a detailed analysis of the steps necessary for learning to become internalized and valued. A veritable road map to the transmission of value-laden knowledge and beliefs now exists in an awesome sounding work called a taxonomy of the "affective domain," that is, a classification of teaching objectives based on what pupils should acquire by way of feelings, attitudes, and appreciation.[29] Jesus once sounded a warning and announced a principle to the effect that those who have wide resources at their disposal will be held accountable for equally impressive results (Lk 12:48).

12. *The secularism of our times increases the urgency of providing a rich corrective in the Christian nurture and evangelism ministries.* It is said that Viscount Bryce was once asked what would be the effect of removing Christian ideals and the Bible from public schools. He answered, "I can't answer that until three generations have passed."[30] Public education has been, by any measure, the gift of the Christian heritage to children of the Western world. It is ironic that in our time, Christian expressions have been banned from public school classrooms by judicial processes which have stressed "fairness." It may now be fairly stated that the official state religion of the United States is that of an agnostic secularism—a religion with its own host of priests and temples. While some of those priests still articulate value systems obviously rooted in the Judeo-Christian vision,[31] they are prophets in a culture whose values are sure to erode. Such erosion, as is evident in United States public morality, its tastes in entertainment, its virtually entirely expediency-oriented political climate, and its Playboy philosophy of man, sketches the pervasive and perverse conditions of our secular domain. The child of the late twentieth century is surfeited with value influences which contradict the fundamental values of Christian faith and life. Never, since the days of the young church in

the pagan Roman empire, has so much depended on the effectiveness of the family of God in infusing the life of Christ and His values into their young.

Goals with Children

Given sufficient reasons, then, for committing our resources to the effective nurture and evangelism of children, let us conclude our overview by identifying appropriate goals which will mark our achievement of the substantial task ahead.

ULTIMATE GOAL

As ministers to the child, we seek to meet fully his present and unfolding needs, to the end that we bring him to self-fulfillment and maturity in Christian faith characterized by (*a*) personal acceptance of Jesus Christ as Saviour and Lord; (*b*) mature decision-making and behavior reflecting the internalized Christian values; and (*c*) righteousness, true holiness, and the fullness of the stature of Jesus Christ.

INTERMEDIATE GOALS

The ultimate goal will necessarily require attention to specific subtasks whose accomplishment will be prerequisite to achieving the larger objective, as follows:

1. Reaffirm the primacy of the home as the chief agency of value development, articulation, and transmission.
2. Disciple heads of families, who in turn will use the leverage of position and sex-role patterning to bond the household to Christ and the church.
3. Heighten the congregation's awareness of itself as the "family of God," an extended family consisting of clusters of intimate networks or tribes of faith whose values are shared around a common commitment to Christ, and among whom there is openness and sharing of treasured beliefs, standards, and values.
4. Provide learning and sharing experiences for transgenerational groups composed of entire families, such that children may hear discussions about Christian concerns and expressions of Christian faith from their parents and other adults within the fellowship of the congregation.
5. Arrange for young children to have a wide, systematic, balanced exposure to biblical material, especially narrative accounts which stimulate positive or negative identification responses, as appropriate. It will be important that the teaching stop short of traditional moralistic interpretations, but that the child be allowed to form his own moral conclusions

based upon the Word of God through consistent teaching at home and at church.

6. Diagnose persistently the levels of moral thought which are represented in any children's ministry setting, then gear instruction and class activity to minister realistically within that level of thinking. It will be important to advance levels of thought by means of introducing ways of thinking immediately above those most common to the children involved, but short of advanced, mature adult moral thought levels.

7. Make satellization models available to children passing into puberty. Staff members should understand clearly the importance of bringing the young person to Christ. This goal can only be reached in sensitive interplay with the workings of the Holy Spirit in the life and development of this emerging autonomous, identity-seeking, sexually awakened person.

Conclusion

There is no question, then. We must effectively "set the child in our midst." In our time, we must resolve not to idolize the child, but to see him as next in line beyond us as the custodian of our treasured values, beliefs, and life-styles. It is appropriate that we hesitate in the face of such a task to inquire, How? With this glimpse into some of the opening windows of the world of childhood, of human development, and of the mysterious development of conscience and a moral sense, this volume now turns to explore evidences and strategies that will move us forward in meeting our responsibilities.

NOTES

1. Urie Bronfenbrenner, et al., "And the Last Shall be First," Report of Forum 15: Children and Parents Together in the World, White House committee document, unpublished, p. 1.
2. Loren Eisley, "An Evolutionist Speaks His Mind," in *Adventures of the Mind*, ed. Richard Thruelsen and John Kobler (New York: Random, Vintage Books, 1958), 1:6.
3. See Urie Bronfenbrenner, "The Unmaking of the American Child," in *Two Worlds of Childhood* (New York: Russel Sage, 1970), pp. 95-119.
4. See also Bronfenbrenner's more elaborate version of the above as "The Split Level American Family," *Saturday Review*, 50, no. 37 (Oct. 7, 1967): 60-66.
5. Jean Piaget, quoted in Frank Jennings, "Jean Piaget: Notes on Learning," *Saturday Review*, 50 (May 20, 1967):82.
6. See Jerome S. Bruner's discussion of "modes of representation" in *Toward a Theory of Instruction* (Cambridge: Harvard U., 1966), pp. 44-46, passim.
7. See, for example, R. S. Lee, *Your Growing Child and Religion*, (New York: Macmillan, 1963), pp. 67-68, 97, 203.
8. William Barclay, *Train Up a Child* (Philadelphia: Westminster, 1959), p. 11.
9. *Babylonian Shabbat* 119 *b*, cited in Barclay, p. 12.
10. Josephus, *Against Apion* 1. 12, cited in Barclay, p. 12.
11. We might dismiss these observations by concluding that Jesus merely reflected the attitudes of His own culture toward children. But we dare not indulge in the unbiblical practice of reading our own children's programs back into the passage and making it support what we have come to think is proper with children.

12. For more detailed information on children in the church, see Charles B. Eavey, *History of Christian Education* (Chicago: Moody, 1964), and Barclay, *Train Up a Child.*
13. See, for example, the classic study by Edwin D. Starbuck, *The Psychology of Religion, An Empirical Study of the Growth of Religious Consciousness* (New York: Scribner, 1906), especially chaps. 3 and 15. Strong emphasis to this second of my reasons is given in Frank G. Coleman, *The Romance of Winning Children* (Cleveland: Union Gospel, 1948, 1967), and in Lois E. LeBar, *Children in the Bible School,* (Westwood, N.J.: Revell, 1952), especially chap. 1.
14. Jean Piaget, *The Moral Judgment of the Child* (New York: Free Press, 1932, 1965). See also David Elkind, "How the Mind Grows," in his *Children and Adolescents: Interpretive Essays on Jean Piaget* (New York: Oxford U., 1970); and Robert P. O'Neil and Michael A. Donovan, "The Magic Years," in *Sexuality and Moral Responsibility* (Washington: Corpus Books, 1968). Both Elkind and O'Neil are deeply rooted in Piaget.
15. This mandate is eloquently put by Dora P. Chaplin, *Children and Religion* (New York: Scribner, 1948, 1961).
16. Robert R. Sears, et al., *Identification and Child Rearing* (Stanford: Stanford U., 1965). See also his *Patterns in Child Rearing* (New York: Harper & Row, 1957).
17. See E. Mavis Hetherington and Jan L. Deur, "The Effects of Father Absence on Child Development," *Young Children* 36 (March 1971):233-42.
18. David Ausubel develops the satellization model essentially out of dependency, and identification clues common to the Sears citations above. See Ausubel's *Theory and Problems of Adolescent Development* (New York: Grune & Stratton, 1954), pp. 167-216. I elaborate on his satellization model in exploring the formation of the young conscience in "How Are Values Formed," chap. 9 of *Meaningful Learning in the Church* (Winona Lake, Ind.: Light & Life, 1969), pp. 110-25.
19. Dorothy Law Nolte, "Children Learn What They Live" (Los Angeles: American Institute of Family Relations, n.d.).
20. Cf. the film, *The Conscience of a Child,* in the Focus on Behavior series (National Educational Television, Bloomington, Ind.: Indiana U., 1963). It chronicles the experiments of Robert Sears and shows resistance-to-temptation experiments with children who come from different qualities of home relationships. Especially significant are the apparent differences in resistance as related to the warmth of boys' relationships to their fathers.
21. For a casual introduction to Lawrence Kohlberg, see "The Child as a Moral Philosopher" *Psychology Today,* 1 (Sept., 1968):25-30. A more comprehensive orientation is available in "The Development of Children's Orientations Toward a Moral Order" in M. and L. Hoffman, *Child Development Research* (New York: Russel Sage, 1964) 1:383-431, or in "Stages of Moral Development as a Basis for Moral Education," in *Moral Education: Interdisciplinary Approaches,* ed. C. M. Beck et al. (Toronto: Toronto U., 1971), pp. 23-92.
22. Doug Scholl, "The Contributions of Lawrence Kohlberg to Religious and Moral Education," *Religious Education,* 66 (Sept.-Oct., 1971):364-72.
23. For an elaboration of these issues, see my "Children, Salvation, and Drop Out," *Asbury Seminarian,* 26 (Oct., 1972):20-35. The Southern Baptists are facing up to issues of early childhood conversion and its attendant baptism and membership, some issues of which are defined and explored in William Hendricks, "The Age of Accountability," in *Children and Conversion,* ed. Clifford Ingle (Nashville: Broadman, 1970), pp. 84-97. Those who have interest in the Anglo-Catholic-Wesley tradition will find rich exploration of the accountability issue in "The Magic Years," and "Sin as Orientation," the opening chapters of Robert P. O'Neil and Michael A. Donovan, *Sexuality and Moral Responsibility* (Washington: Corpus Books, 1968), pp. 1-60.
24. Erik Erikson, "Eight Stages of Man," in *Childhood and Society* (New York: Norton, 1950), pp. 219-34.
25. See the provocative work of James Michael Lee of Notre Dame University Graduate School, especially his books, *The Shape of Religious Instruction* (1971) and *The Flow of Religious Instruction* (Dayton, Ohio: Pflaum/Standard, 1973).
26. Abraham H. Maslow, *Motivation and Personality* (New York: Harper & Row, 1954), chap. 5. I explore his hierarchy of human needs for implications for Christian education in *Meaningful Learning in the Church* (Winona Lake, Ind.: Light & Life, 1969), pp. 25-36.

27. See James Michael Lee, "Learning Theory and Teaching Theory," in *The Flow of Religious Instruction* (Dayton, Ohio: Pflaum/Standard, 1973), pp. 39-57. Jerome S. Bruner offers help on teaching in *Toward a Theory of Instruction* (Cambridge: Harvard U., 1966).
28. Take seriously, for example, and complete a small programmed sequence to teach a selected body of information using Sivasailam Thiagarajan, *The Programming Process: A Practical Guide* (Worthington, Ohio: Jones, 1971).
29. David R. Krathwohl, et al., *Taxonomy of Educational Objectives: Affective Domain* (New York: McKay, 1964).
30. Viscount Bryce, cited in a larger discussion of this issue by Dora P. Chaplin, *Children and Religion* (New York: Scribner, 1961), p. 8.
31. John W. Gardner, former presidential cabinet member, is an illustration. See his *Excellence* (1961) and his *Self-Renewal* (Harper & Row, 1964). Both read like extensions of the Christian gospel; yet, when he was pressed during a question period at an eastern university to state the foundation on which his expressed values rested and from which they were drawn, he is reported to have hung his head and answered, no doubt honestly, that he did not know.

FOR FURTHER READING

Anderson, Robert H., ed. *Education in Anticipation of Tomorrow.* Worthington, Ohio: Jones, 1973.

Bolton, Barbara J. *Ways to Help Them Learn: Children, Grades 1 to 6.* Glendale, Calif.: Gospel Light, Regal Books, 1972.

Bronfenbrenner, Urie. *Two Worlds of Childhood.* New York: Russel Sage, 1970.

Bull, Normal J. *Moral Judgment from Childhood to Adolescence.* New York: Russel Sage, 1969.

Goldman, Ronald. *Readiness for Religion.* New York: Seabury, 1968.

———. *Religious Thinking from Childhood to Adolescence.* New York: Seabury, 1964.

Ingle, Clifford, ed. *Children and Conversion.* Nashville: Broadman, 1970.

Kohlberg, Lawrence. "The Child as a Moral Philosopher." *Psychology Today* 1 (Sept., 1968): 25-30.

LeBar, Lois E. *Children in the Bible School.* Westwood, N.J.: Revell, 1952.

Lee, R. S. *Your Growing Child and Religion.* New York: Macmillan, 1963.

Maier, Henry W. *Three Theories of Child Development.* New York: Harper & Row, 1969.

McCandless, Boyd R. *Children: Behavior and Development.* New York: Holt, Rinehart & Winston, 1967.

O'Neil, Robert P., and Donovan, Michael A. *Children and Sin.* Washington: Corpus Books, 1969.

Piaget, Jean. *The Moral Judgment of the Child.* New York: Free Press, 1965.

Smith, Charles T. *Ways to Plan and Organize Your Sunday School: Children, Grades 1 to 6.* Glendale, Calif.: Gospel Light, Regal Books, 1971.

2

Social Influences on Children

Oscar E. Feucht

THE SOCIOLOGICAL ENVIRONMENT of many American children is described by Emma White as follows:

> Children are all around us. Some live in crowded, deteriorating city blocks. Others live in isolated rural areas far from neighbors. Many live on quiet streets of small towns or villages. Children are living in the spreading suburbs and in mid-town apartment buildings. Other boys and girls are growing up on farms, ranches, and reservations. Still others are constantly on the move with their families.
>
> All of these children learn through firsthand, day-by-day living. They experience riots, looting, and crime on the streets. They learn the quiet beauty of the natural world near their farm homes, and on occasion, the fury and devastation of floods, tornadoes, and storms. They learn geography as they travel or move to new places. Some know real hunger, while others possess personal TV's or transistor radios.
>
> Some children attend excellent schools; others struggle and fail because of poor opportunities for education. Both rich and poor boys and girls feel great emptiness and loneliness because they have no families or friends. Yet many, many children know security and love through happy home lives and rich community experiences.
>
> Some inner-city children may have difficulty visualizing a green meadow, and some rural children may not understand what a busy city is like. All these children know a jet plane as it flies overhead. Today's children learn through split second impressions flashed before them on the television screen. They are aware of peoples, places, events, animals, and objects they have never actually seen. They are aware, in varying degrees, of tensions among groups and nations. These children live in the day of

---

OSCAR E. FEUCHT, D.D., served as Secretary of adult education for the Board of Parish Education of the Lutheran Church (Missouri Synod) from 1946 through 1968 He is now a consultant in adult and family life education for his denomination.

communication satellites and space exploration. Above all, they live in a day of constant and rapid change.

These are today's children!

These are the children the church must serve![1]

Products of our Environment

Each child is born a unified person who acts as a whole, integrated individual in every experience. Through relationships of many kinds, every person undergoes some kind of growth, mentally, socially, morally, and spiritually. Of great significance are the first intellectual and emotional experiences of early childhood. Values learned almost automatically become the integrating factors in a child's personality. This takes place as a person internalizes the values which he perceives. These values, psychologists assert, become his conscience.

A child closely related to the faith, thinking, and way of life of a conscientious Christian mother will absorb more of lifelong significance from this source than from any other single source. One pastor put it in these words: "My Christian mother was my real seminary." He absorbed a mass of theological data in college and seminary, but his basic life goals and inner strengths came from his mother. Every child is the product of his most intimate environment. Nothing less than the total life climate makes people what they are.

Too often, we equate education almost completely with the teaching-learning process in a class, a school, or some other institution. Actually, however, people are the products of many experiences in their total environment. Their basic orientation to life is learned before going to school.

No one lives in a vacuum. Children are surrounded daily by dozens of factors—both good and bad—that affect and influence their lives. Ultimately, these sociological, political, and economic factors all have their effect on our nation's morals.

Bettelheim, a distinguished child psychologist, wrote the following regarding the effect of situation ethics not on youth but on *children:*

> The big problem with situation ethics is the havoc it has wreaked in child rearing. We foolishly hope our children will grow up having mature controls when they have never been subject to a stringent morality. The situation ethic view neither equips the child to control his violent desires nor prepares him to act on a basis of long-range goals. The more refined morality that can make distinctions profitably cannot exist unless it has *at its base* a rigid belief in right and wrong, that permits no relativity.[2]

Being Loved Is Vital

Problem persons usually reflect inadequate love received from parents, siblings, teachers, or an environment of one or more negative influences.

Psychologists have observed that young children deprived of genuine parental love suffer character difficulties and fail to achieve their potential growth emotionally and intellectually.

Someone must give children more than shelter, food, and nice clothes. Every person needs a proper self-esteem and a sense of worth and direction. To develop such self-esteem, self-confidence, and sense of security, a child needs a happy, hopeful outlook on life. These prevent the aggressiveness and recessiveness of problem children.

Erich Fromm, a distinguished social psychologist, asserts that love for others and love for ourselves are *not* mutually exclusive.[3] Jesus implied the same in His command to love God with all your heart and your neighbody *as yourself* (Mt 22:37-39). Love includes feeling deeply for others. It shows concern for the welfare, happiness, and development of the one loved.

This kind of love reaches out to all humanity. Like Christ's love, it is universal. Love is not rooted primarily in sexual dynamics, as modern literature erroneously assumes. The finest love of a marriage partner flows from the larger springs of true, unselfish, *Christian* love (Eph 5:25-30).

Genuine love provides basic security; helps us love ourselves and others, interpret and constructively use our culture, and adjust to unpleasant situations; develops group fellowship; fosters warm identification with parents, relatives, teachers, and peers; and works toward alleviation of evils in society.

The Family as a Social Influence

Many moderns are predicting the dissolution of the family and the disestablishment of marriage. Some current university courses openly advocate not only trial marriage but a series of unions with different persons as people tire of each other. However, no society of the past has been able to operate indefinitely with such a system. Children—as well as youth and adults—need a more stable arrangement, if life is to be secure and generations are to contribute to society as a whole.

Sociologists point to seven functions that are most effectively carried on within the family. Though they are no longer *exclusively* carried out in the family, yet they still find their *greatest* fulfillment within the home.

1. Biologically, the home provides procreation, concern for, care of, and feeding of children and other family members.
2. Educationally, the family is the basic school of life, where we continue to learn from each other from infancy to old age.
3. Religiously, all kinds of beliefs have been taught and perpetuated in the family.

4. Economically, gainful employment by various members of the family is necessary to provide the resources for housing and housekeeping.
5. Socially, no one can long live in isolation. The warmth, mutual support, and fellowship of family members are necessary to healthy growth.
6. Recreationally, more than before, families are doing things together: recreation, sports, travel, entertaining, celebrating.
7. Affectionally, children need the ties of love which only the family can give. Without this home base, children suffer emotional deprivation. The love between husband and wife, parents and children, brothers and sisters, relatives and friends is essential for our well-being.

We cannot, without considerable loss, relinquish any of these functions exclusively to outsiders. The new policies of foster parents and adoptions, rather than maintaining orphanages, bear witness to the basic need for children to be incorporated into a family. Science has not given us a substitute.

Within the family, the child learns physical skills, customs, a language, basic housekeeping, and standards of conduct that fit him for society. He also learns religion or irreligion. In this realm there is no neutrality. The decline of family worship and Bible reading in the home is an irreplaceable loss. The absence of personal and family worship further secularizes the home. The welfare of society and the stability of the family are so interrelated that a decline in one almost always involves a decline in the other.

IMPORTANCE OF EARLY CHILDHOOD EXPERIENCES

The child's personality grows out of all the relationships that touch his life. This makes parents, brothers, sisters, teachers, and classmates, with their personalities and value systems, part of the child's environment. They give him his mind-set, sense of direction, life-purpose and goals. In early childhood, we take over the loves and hatreds of our social environment. Children learn what they are exposed to. We adults set the stage for what we call a "rehearsal," which however turns out to be the real "play." What is more, the child selects many of the lines of that "play."

Some of our greatest educators have helped us formulate a more adequate concept of education. They are telling us that a child's life-style is, to a large degree, set by the time he enters kindergarten or the first grade; that learning to respond both physically and verbally in preschool days is actually more important than learning to read and count. Pestalozzi, an influential educator of the past, has stated that the basic principle of education is not teaching, but love.

Haim Ginott says, "Only those who communicate daily with children can prevent mental disturbances."[4] In his books,* he explains how child care and discipline can be positive. Instead of blaming and shaming, we must convey caring. He warns against humiliating the child and suggests that an ounce of prevention is worth a pound of punishment. Parents can convey to their children that there is no need to lie. They can invite cooperation and teach responsibility, even without rewards or prizes. By the way they handle the child, they can remove harmful fears. Even minor mishaps can create golden opportunities to demonstrate love and better understanding. "To communicate love parents need a language of acceptance: words that value feelings, responses that change moods, replies that radiate respect. The world talks to the mind. Parents speak more intimately—they talk to the heart."[5]

SIGNIFICANT CHANGES IN MARRIAGE

Children in more recent times live in very different environments from children at the turn of the twentieth century. Gesell and Ilg describe the contrast vividly:

> In the more olden times, the world of nature and of human relationships expanded in a rather orderly manner, keeping pace with the maturity of the child. The home was large, the membership of the family numerous, and usually there was yet another child to be born. Someone was always near to look after the preschool child and to take him by graduated stages into his widening world, step by step, as his demands gradually increased. There was free space around his home, a field, a meadow, an orchard. There were animals in barn, pen, coop, and pasture. Some of these fellow creatures were young like himself. He could feast his eyes on them, touch them, sometimes even embrace them.
>
> Time has played a transforming trick with this environment. The apartment child, and to some extent even the suburban child of today, has been greatly deprived of his former companions, human and infrahuman. Domestic living space has contracted to the dimensions of a few rooms, a porch, a yard; perhaps to a single room, with one or two windows.[6]

Changes have also taken place in family living and marriage relationships. The following trends in marriage undoubtedly influence children in today's homes.[7]

1. Marriage is moving from a legal institution to a closer companionship arrangement.

2. The roles of husband and wife, once quite fixed, are more fluid for

*See Haim Ginott, *Between Parent and Child* (New York: Avon, 1972); *Between Parent and Teenager* (New York: Macmillan, 1969); and *Teacher and Child* (New York: Macmillan, 1972).

both partners. In many cases, there are now two incomes, as the wife works inside and outside the home.

3. The large, extended family of Oriental tradition (China, Japan, India), is rapidly giving way to the nuclear family (father, mother, children), often far removed from relatives and much more self-reliant.

4. The emphasis on companionship in marriage makes modern families more unitive centered than procreative centered. Many children now see their grandparents only occasionally, whereas in years past, many grandparents lived with one of their married sons or daughters and their grandchildren.

5. Contrary to opinion, divorce is not as prevalent as is generally supposed. One American study showed only one divorce for every 113 existent marriages. Actually, marriages are moving from short-spanned to long-spanned unions, as longevity and living conveniences increase.

6. In America and elsewhere, suffrage has been given to women and men alike, along with greater participation of women in civic and political affairs and a broader educational base for most Americans.

7. Marriages are now taking place across all frontiers—national, racial, and religious—due to a more democratic social structure, more ecumenical thinking, and broader world travel.

8. Fortunately, we are recovering a saner, more biblical view of sex (alongside its distortion). For 1500 years, the church, with its many negative views, has kept sex in a tunnel. We are witnessing the opposite in the current "sexplosion," not yet controlled. But the positive view is replacing the negative.

Other factors which have affected marriage relationships and family living are also evident. More mothers are working than ever before. Day-care centers, nursery schools, and prekindergartens are contributing what the average mother could not provide in child care and educational leadership.†

Shorter working hours make it possible for the father to spend more time with his children. Family outings and vacation trips keep the family together more than in former days.

More and more services have been transferred out of the home: teaching to schools, medical services to clinics or hospitals, care of the disadvantaged to social agencies, and care of the old to nursing homes.

The number of children per family is somewhat smaller. James W. Reapsome reports the following statistics on this trend:

> Couples today are getting married later in life than they have at any time since 1950. In 1971, the median age for brides was 20.9 years, compared

†For more on this subject, see chap. 24, "Child Care Programs in the Church."

> with 20.3 in 1950. A growing trend among young couples is to have no children at all. Census Bureau figures indicate that one of every 25 wives between 18 and 24 years of age now expects to have no children. In 1967, the ratio was one of every 100. The number of couples who want only one child also has grown—from 6% in 1967 to nearly 10% in 1972. Overall, the Census Bureau says that in the past 15 years young women have sharply reduced the number of children they want—from an average of 3.77 per family in 1957 to an average of 2.05 in 1972. As a result, the estimated population of the U.S. for the year 2020 has been cut from nearly 400 million to 300 million.[8]

Another interesting development reflecting the modern trend are new organizations that encourage couples not to bear children.

> "None Is Fun" is the slogan of a new organization, the National Organization for Non-Parents" (NON). Its goal: to make being child free a respectable, attractive, even fun alternative to parenthood. "We're not going around saying people shouldn't have children," says Mrs. Ellen Peck, one of the founders. "But we say people shouldn't automatically assume they should have children. Parenthood is a matter to be thought over quite carefully—for both the parents' sake and the children's."
>
> The group thinks society is prejudiced toward parenthood. "Everything in our society—from the tax laws to television shows to women's magazines to the most casual conversation—is oriented toward parenthood. It's very difficult to even consider whether you shouldn't have children when everyone is pressuring you to have kids and find out what you're missing."
>
> Two basic questions the group says should be asked before deciding to have children: (1) Are we qualified—emotionally and intellectually, not just physically—for the important job of parenthood in today's complex society? (2) Is a child-centered life what we choose for at least 20 years of our life?[9]

FOUNDATION FOR CHRISTIAN NURTURE

The family is the primary place of Christian nurture. The New Testament summarizes the task of Christian teaching in one comprehensive term: *Christian nurture.* The word *nurture* in Ephesians 6:4 is the Greek word *paideia.* The Revised Standard Version translates this word "discipline." J. B. Phillips's phrasing is "Christian teaching," and *The New English Bible* uses "instruction." *Good News for Modern Man* renders this verse, "Raise them with Christian discipline and instruction." The word for "raise" (bring them up) in the Greek is *ektrepho.* It means "to nourish up to maturity." It includes all the environmental factors collectively to which the individual is subjected *from conception onward.*

Note that this directive is given to Christian fathers. The passing on of the Christian faith is to take place in all the interactions of life in the family. William Barclay, in one of his commentaries, remarks that this assignment is given to the family as a major function, because in no other place and under no other set of related functions could full nurture of the total personality really be adequately given.

It is in the home that the "colors are coded" and that the "strands," woven together, form the warp and woof of life. From their own experience, parents can give important insights their children need: words of encouragement and direction, approval and support, love and esteem; and visions of greater goals yet to be achieved.

Samuel Hamilton describes the task of parents in the following words: "All individual personal growth is interpersonal. At every stage of life, from birth to death, the family in the home can provide the setting, the occasions, the atmosphere, the inspiration, the behavior patterns, the controls, and the dynamic of the most profoundly forming and transforming interpersonal relationships in human existence."[10]

The Church as a Social Influence

The relationship between the church and the home was succinctly stated by Hamilton:

> The Christian church and the Christian home as institutions are closely bound together. They are like Siamese twins: if you cut them apart you may sever an artery of life and cause one or both to die. The church cannot function as she should in a disordered world unless she employs the home as her main reliance in Christian nurture. And I feel certain that the family cannot be a Christian family or a happy family unless it stays in the circulation of those spiritual influences of which the church is the great custodian.[11]

While the family is not peculiar to Christianity, it is of primary concern to the church, because it is "one of the orders of creation," as Crook calls it.[12] Through the ages, the church has emphasized the Christian pattern of marriage and family living. Increasingly in the last fifty years, church bodies have engaged in biblical research and outlined a positive program of family life education. Unfortunately, many church-centered programs have *blocked* the door to a functional, practical, more relevant ministry *to* families and *through* families. Programs should be church *related* and family *centered.*

The task of the church is to make the whole ethos of the home evangelical in spirit and practice. This task will include areas of concern such as providing premarital counseling, training parents in child care and how to teach their children about sex, helping them learn to conduct family worship and inculcate Christian standards in the home, giving families a God-centered view of the world and the Christian's place in that world. One Chicago pastor made it a rule of his ministry to visit every new family at supper and demonstrate with a short devotion how meaningful family worship can be. The home is responsible for training children, but the church is responsible for training parents in how to train their children.

The influence of the church on children rises and falls as its members everywhere and in every situation live out their faith in Christ. Americans are developing a greater concern for the conservation of our natural resources. But we are equally responsible for the moral and spiritual climate in which our children are raised. Unfortunately, religious influence has declined. After a surge in church membership following World War II, membership and attendance have now slumped. This is changing the philosophy, life-style and goals of many families, and thus affecting children.

The church program must be attractive and motivating in order to hold people and encourage them to participate meaningfully.

> A well-known educator [John Holt] has suggested that public school children should be given the choice to go to class or not, and teachers should be paid according to the number of children who come to their classes. In the church school, that matter of choice has always been a factor! Both children and their parents must be convinced of the value of the sessions or sooner or later they will stop coming. It does little good to complain that they should come because it is "good for them," just as it does little good to complain that they no longer study their lessons on Saturday night. Our religion classes must have a built-in value demonstration for the learners or we will no longer have a class.[13]

Since our American separation of church and state does not permit religious instruction in public schools, churches must provide that instruction. However, will Sunday, vacation, weekday or after-school classes meet the need or be equal to the task? What can be covered in such meager time and with parental concern so limited? Let us face this fact: *The common practice in most Protestant churches with once-a-week attendance at worship services is* NOT *equal to the greater task of integrating the Christian faith into all of life!* Three things are apparent: (1) we must strengthen our Christian education ministries to children in the church; (2) churches must give more specific guidance to parents on how to nurture their children in spiritual values; and (3) we must give serious consideration to the need for Christian elementary and high schools.

The School as a Social Influence

The spirit of modern society is not overtly anti-Christian; it is merely un-Christian. This is an important change which the churches in early

America did not face except on the rough frontier, largely because the ethos of the average community was "religious" if not "Christian." Secularization confronts our children as never before.

One of the most potent social forces in America is public education from preschool to university. The quest for higher education has surpassed all previous stages of history. The thirst for knowledge is almost universal, and the things to be learned have increased on an astronomical scale. The community college has brought new learning opportunities to our own back door. However, this new wealth needs to be evaluated, not merely scientifically but ethically and spiritually. Will our spiritual and ethical growth keep pace with our scientific and psychological growth?

During the academic year, the child spends a major portion of his day at school. The role of the school is far-reaching in its social influences and may have greater effect on the child than his home. One educator has written,

> But students learn much more in school than measures of achievement can detect. The social statuses open to students, the kinds of jobs they will hold, the incomes they can expect, their mental health, their marriage and family life, and their social attitudes and values are all affected by their school experiences. These outcomes may be termed the social impact of education.[14]

In the mid-sixties, a group of elementary educators prepared a list of broad curriculum areas with detailed behavioral goals which elementary schools seek to accomplish.[15] The areas they included in the paper were: (1) physical development, health, body care; (2) individual, social, and emotional development; (3) ethical behavior standards, values; (4) social relations; (5) the social world; (6) the physical world; (7) aesthetic development; (8) communication; and (9) quantitative relationships. A study of these goals would be helpful in discovering what the schools are doing to meet social needs and to influence children.

The outstanding problem in public education is teaching moral and spiritual values. In many cases, the teacher serves as a substitute parent, especially for younger children. Many teachers have high moral standards and are eager to provide the best education for their children. On the other hand, some teachers have godless and humanistic philosophies of education which undermine the ideals and teachings of the Christian home. We recognize the need for separation of church and state, but Christian parents and leaders must assume the responsibility of spiritual teaching. It may be more appropriate for public educators not to teach moral and spiritual values, if biblical principles are so watered down that the Bible becomes nothing more than a great book of literature.

Some church bodies have set up their own Christian elementary schools and high schools at their own expense, in order to give a Christian dimension to all learning and to supply a basic sense of value to all subject areas.‡

The Community as a Social Influence

The moral climate of the neighborhood and permissiveness or tyranny of parents have great effect on children. The influence of the peer group, especially in preteen and adolescent years, cannot be overestimated. A group of delinquents can demoralize a whole neighborhood. The failure of certain housing projects in city slums is directly traceable to the mores of the occupants. This situation is a challenge to the community and has reemphasized the social and welfare ministries of the churches, often ill equipped to deal effectively with the community situation.

Though thousands of children are raised in city slums, ghettos, or rural poverty areas, the vast majority of America's youngsters enjoy the benefits of affluence. Fine homes furnished with the latest gadgets, conveniences, and luxuries—taken for granted by most of today's boys and girls—can corrode children's sensitivity to spiritual interests.

The inner city child is one of the most neglected. His parents lack education and finances to improve their standards of living. Mediocre schools often hinder the educational process. Irregular attendance, poor home conditions, and indifferent parents add frustration to the situation.

> There is a culture of poverty in the United States that is complex and self-propagating. The children of the poor grow up in squalor and filth. They are inadequately nourished, poorly clothed, and often lack adequate parental supervision. They attend inferior schools for a few years, and, under severe economic pressure, drop out as soon as they can. Lacking training, experience, and incentive, they either remain jobless or move from one casual job to another at the lowest pay. Marrying at an early age, they bring up an unrestricted number of children in the same kind of hopeless, deprived life. They may earn enough to provide some sort of food and shelter during their middle years, but in sickness and old age they fall back on relief or charity.[16]

Many inner city children learn to lie, steal, cheat, hate, and shift for themselves. They may feel they have received unfair treatment and may become rebellious toward society, and particularly toward those who have been more successful in material gain.

Some inner city children rise above their circumstances, but many continue to become more entangled and dependent on society. Family coun-

‡See chap. 29, "The Role of the Christian Day School."

seling services, welfare, and civic groups seek to meet needs, but the struggle for success is overwhelming.

Environmental changes are not sufficient to bring lasting results. Some evangelical groups have done social work in the inner city, but progress is slow and often discouraging. The answer is more than reformation from without. Until a person finds a new way of life in Christ through the gospel, little can be done in lasting value. Through genuine love and concern in practical ways, we can show we care, with the ultimate goal being to bring people to Christ as Saviour and to give them purpose for living.

Other Social Influences Affecting Children

To reach children effectively in today's society, we need to assess the world in which our generation lives—the world which is so different from apostolic times, the European culture of the middle ages, or even the frontiers of colonial America. Several other social factors affect children and how they live.

URBANIZATION

Many thousands of people in past decades have moved from rural to suburban or metropolitan areas. Because of many large cities and sprawling suburbs, most youngsters in today's society are urban rather than rural children. The way of life for rural families has changed drastically because of modernization in almost every area of life. Most Americans live in a dozen great metropolitan areas, and it is predicted that 80 percent of us will live in cities by the year 2000.

MOBILITY

It is estimated that at least one in five American families moves each year. Families are uprooted from their homes, jobs, schools, and communities to orient themselves to a new way of life. Children are probably affected more than any other group. Mobility has increased through rapid transportation. The automobile has given us freedom to go almost anywhere we like. The whole world and its way of life is open to us and our children. Many boys and girls have traveled thousands of miles with their parents in family vacations. Job transfers to other cities give families a wider experience with more places and people, and children establish many new, fine relationships.

MASS MEDIA

Newspapers, radio, and television, including telecasts from Telstar satellites, have made the world one great neighborhood. Entertainment, once expensive and limited, now streams even into the homes of the poor, via radio and television. Children have the whole wide world in their living rooms. They can get immediate reports on world happenings each day. Social, political, scientific, cultural, and religious happenings add to the vast field of knowledge confronting our children. Parental guidance can deter unwholesome influences. But where that guidance is lacking, television programs of questionable moral standards are bringing the "world" to children through the television screen.

SEX

The American emphasis on sex is described by Crook in this way.

> In recent decades Americans have exploited sex in such a way as to cheapen it and rob it of its real meaning. It is the dominant element in most of our movies and TV shows, our novels and even our jokes. It is used in advertising everything from cosmetics to bulldozers. It has been glamorized by all kinds of artificial adornment . . . Sex is virtually deified, and the beauty queen is its high priestess.[17]

To counteract this exploitation, a wholesome sex education program is needed. Parents are key participants, with the church and school having supplementary roles. Sex education must be taught with the proper spiritual and moral emphases as well as the biological. Parents are in the best position to teach their children the biblical meaning of sex in relation to the whole of life.

DRUG ABUSE

Drug abuse is a continuing and increasingly complex problem in our society. Parents are frightened with stories and reports of the results of their misuse. Drug usage ranges from glue sniffing and marijuana smoking to the use of narcotics, amphetamines, and barbiturates. The number of drug abusers among middle and wealthy classes is rapidly climbing, and the age of abusers is dropping. An estimated 20 million Americans have smoked marijuana. Users of heroin who have sought help have increased from 202 to 982 within three years in one county alone (Nassau County, New York). In 1969, 1 percent of the hard drug addicts died from overdoses.[18]

> There is no more certain destroyer of self-discipline and self-control than the abusive use of drugs. The teen-ager who has begun taking narcotics often shows a sudden disinterest in everything that formerly challenged him. His school work is ignored and his hobbies are forgotten. His personal appearance becomes sloppy and dirty. He refuses to carry responsibility and he avoids the activities that would cause him to expend

> effort. His relationship with his parents deteriorates rapidly and he suddenly terminates many of his lifelong friendships. The young drug user is clearly marching to a new set of drums—and disaster often awaits him at the end of the trail.[19]

Parts of the body, such as the heart, brain, and eyes, may be damaged by drug abuse. Thought processes and speech habits may be weakened. Emotional depression or imbalance, loss of memory, fear, and recurrence of horrifying experiences, physical exhaustion, personality disorders, mental derangement, and even death, may occur. It is evident that those who are drug users have distorted values, are incapable of coping with life and try to escape reality.

> The drug abuse tragedy occurs at all levels of society; no child is immune to the threat—neither yours nor mine. Every parent must inform himself of the facts regarding drug abuse. We should be able to recognize its symptoms and stand prepared to guide our children should the need arise.[20]

The road to rehabilitation is slow and many times ineffective, depending on the extent and use of drugs. The best treatment is prevention through a drug education program in which children are warned about drugs, their dangers, and effects.

Summary

In many ways, children are the same today as children of the past. They are also different. Eldor Kaiser has pointed out some interesting similarities and differences:

> Children are one of the few common denominators in the world. They are much the same from the Orient to Iceland and from the days of Socrates to today. They like to learn. They struggle with growing up, with liking themselves, and they need love from "significant persons." They sin. They need forgiveness. And they believe with a direct and simple faith.
>
> Kids today are different. They are less submissive and more restless. Rather than work in class, they expect to be entertained. Nothing is new to them and they quickly become bored and apathetic. What they need is a firm adult hand and stricter discipline. Kids question everything and accept nothing as "truth," not even the Bible.
>
> Kids are all the same. They need love; they need forgiveness; they need to be assured that there is a loving God who holds this crazy, changing universe together.
>
> Kids are different. No two are alike. What gets through to one doesn't work with the next. Today's kids are different from yesterday's kids—and tomorrow's.[21]

Whether or not we agree with Kaiser, the challenge is ours. We must meet the needs of children today. We cannot expect them to be like children were in the "good old days," or to behave like mature adults. The personalities of children are being shaped through many social influences, and our responsibility is to provide the kind of atmosphere and learning experiences that will enable them to accomplish all that God intended for each individual.

NOTES

1. Emma White, *Let's Do More with Children* (Nashville: United Methodist Church, 1969), p. 1.
2. Bruno Bettelheim, "Bringing Up Children," *Ladies' Home Journal,* 89 (Dec., 1972):29.
3. Erich Fromm, *The Art of Loving* (New York: Harper, 1956), p. 58.
4. Haim Ginott, "How to Drive Your Child Sane," *Reader's Digest,* 102 (Jan., 1973):89.
5. Ibid., p. 92.
6. Arnold Gesell and Frances Ilg, *Infant and Child in the Culture of Today* (New York: Harper, 1943), p. 260.
7. Adapted from points given by David R. Mace in a denominational workshop on the family. Also see Oscar E. Feucht, "The Christian Family in Today's World," in *Adult Education in the Church,* ed. Roy B. Zuck and Gene A. Getz (Chicago: Moody, 1970).
8. James W. Reapsome, *Discern the Times,* 2 (June 1, 1973):4.
9. Ibid., 2 (Jan. 15, 1973):2.
10. Samuel L. Hamilton, "The Family the Center of Religious Education," *Religion in Life,* 18 (Summer, 1949):419.
11. Ibid.
12. Roger Crook, *The Changing American Family* (Minneapolis: Bethany, 1960), p. 133.
13. Eldor Kaiser, "Kids Are Different Today—Or Are They?" *Interaction,* 13 (April, 1973):18.
14. Dorothy Westby-Gibson, *Social Perspectives on Education* (New York: Wiley, 1965), p. 357.
15. Ibid., pp. 97-98.
16. Maxwell S. Stewart, *The Poor Among Us—Challenge and Opportunity* (New York: Public Affairs Pamphlets, No. 362, 1964), p. 6.
17. Crook, p. 75.
18. Alice Shiller, *Drug Abuse and Your Child* (New York: Public Affairs Pamphlets, No. 448, 1970), p. 2.
19. James Dobson, *Dare To Discipline* (Wheaton, Ill.: Tyndale, 1970), p. 190.
20. Ibid., pp. 193-94.
21. Kaiser, pp. 13, 18.

FOR FURTHER READING

Books

Barclay, William. *Train Up a Child.* Philadelphia: Westminster, 1959.

Crook, Roger H. *The Changing American Family.* St. Louis: Bethany, 1960.

Denton, Wallace. *What's Happening to Our Families.* Philadelphia: Westminster, 1963.

Dobson, James. *Dare to Discipline.* Wheaton, Ill.: Tyndale, 1970.

———. *Hide or Seek.* Old Tappan, N.J.: Revell, 1974.

Dowdy, Edward, and Dowdy, Harriet. *The Church in Families.* Valley Forge, Pa.: Judson, 1965.
Duvall, Evelyn Millis; Mace, David; and Poperoe, Paul. *The Church Looks at Family Life.* Nashville: Broadman, 1964.
Feucht, Oscar E., ed. *Family Relationships and the Church.* Rev. ed. St. Louis: Concordia, 1970.
———. *Helping Families Through the Church.* Rev. ed. St. Louis: Concordia, 1971.
———. *Sex and the Church.* St. Louis: Concordia, 1961.
Grams, Armin. *Changes in Family Life.* St. Louis: Concordia, 1968.
Help for Your Troubled Child. New York: Public Affairs Pamphlets, No. 454.
Knutson, Melford S. *I Write Unto You Fathers.* Hayfield, Minn.: Hayfield, 1962.
May, Edward W. *Christian Family Living.* St. Louis: Concordia, 1970.
Orphans of the Living: The Foster Care Crises. New York: Public Affairs Pamphlets, No. 418.
Peterson, J. Allen, ed. *The Marriage Affair.* Wheaton, Ill.: Tyndale, 1971.
Poverty in the U.S.A. New York: Public Affairs Pamphlets, No. 398.
Shiller, Alice. *Drug Abuse and Your Child.* New York: Public Affairs Pamphlets, No. 448, 1970.
Stewart, Maxwell S. *The Poor Among Us—Challenge and Opportunity.* New York: Public Affairs Pamphlets, No. 362, 1964.
The One-Parent Family. New York: Public Affairs Pamphlets, No. 287.
Westby-Gibson, Dorothy. *Social Perspectives on Education.* New York: Wiley, 1965.
Zuck, Roy B., and Getz, Gene A., eds. *Ventures in Family Living.* Chicago: Moody, 1971.

Magazines

Childhood Education. Association for Childhood Education International, 3615 Wisconsin Ave., N. W., Washington, D. C. 20016.
Children. US Children's Bureau, Superintendent of Documents, US Government Printing Office, Washington, D. C. 20025.
Children Today. Children's Bureau, Office of Child Development. US Department of Health, Education, and Welfare, P. O. Box 1182, Washington, D. C. 20402.
Nation's Schools. McGraw-Hill, Inc., 230 West Monroe, Chicago, Ill. 60606.
Teacher. CCM Professional Magazines, Inc., 22 West Putnam Ave., Greenwich, Conn. 06830.
Today's Child. Edwards Publications, Inc., School Lane, Roosevelt, N.J. 08555.

Part II

THE NATURE AND NEEDS OF CHILDREN

3

Personality Development of Children

Mary L. Hammack

Children's workers in the church are involved in a divine program of helping to shape young lives. This makes it imperative that those leaders understand how the personalities of children develop. Scripture makes it very evident that our Lord is concerned about each person as an individual, unique from any other individual. Likewise, each teacher must know his pupils individually—their personalities and characteristics—if he is to tailor his teaching and counseling to their personal needs.

Authorities differ in their theories and definitions of personality. To the sociologist, personality is the expression of one's culture; to the scientist and those concerned with medicine, personality is a part of one's physiological and constitutional makeup. The psychologist, on the other hand, emphasizes the behavioral aspects of personality.

In this chapter, *personality* refers to those combined characteristics which make a person unique and different from all other individuals. This includes not only his spiritual characteristics but also his physical, mental, emotional, and social attributes, and congenital and environmental influences.

Though some authors believe that personality development begins at birth, others point out that some characteristics tend to be inherited and that prenatal conditions may affect one's development later. According to this view, personality development begins at the time of conception.

The development of a child's personality cannot be isolated from the influence of environmental, social, hereditary, and motivational backgrounds. Each teacher has the responsibility and challenge to minister primarily to the spiritual needs of each individual. This can be done only

---

Mary L. Hammack, Ed.D., is Associate Professor of Education, Seattle Pacific College, Seattle, Washington.

in proportion to the amount known about each child, and the love and understanding of the teacher as he prays for spiritual wisdom in meeting evident needs.

Needs are determinants of behavior. The sensitive teacher soon becomes keenly aware of deeper needs, perhaps unrecognized by parents or children. Occasional visits to the pupils' homes provide insights gleaned in no other way. The wise teacher considers each child an individual case study, unique and challenging.

Teachers should also be aware of children's universal needs which the church can help meet. These include love, security, sense of belonging, significance, recognition, and interrelated influences.* In the church's educational program, teachers can express and exhibit God's love to the child. In Christ, the child can find security. In the fellowship of the church, he can find a sense of belonging. In pleasing Jesus and in serving others, he can give love and find self-esteem and recognition.

If a child's spiritual needs are being met, many other needs and aspects of his life will be cared for automatically. Learning in the church must be supernaturally motivated, as all workers pray for the children with whom they work.

The local church is in a unique position to provide opportunity to reach children with the gospel, and thereby to initiate Christian influences affecting the continuing process of personality development. Psalm 32:8, Colossians 3:16, and many other Scriptures concerned with teaching the Word of God give ample incentive to keep this concern uppermost in educational programming.

Influences on Personality

Most child specialists agree that the following factors influence the development of children's personalities.

HEREDITARY FACTORS

A number of inherited traits definitely influence personality. Most obvious among these are certain physical resemblances to parents or relatives, such as the color of eyes, hair, complexion, and one's size. Many scientists

*Abraham Maslow's well-known "hierarchy of needs" includes the following, in ascending order of importance: physiological needs (air, water, food, shelter, sleep, sex); safety and security needs (physical and psychological); affiliation needs (love and belongingness); esteem needs (self-esteem and esteem by others); and self-actualization. The latter includes these "growth needs" (which are of equal importance, not hierarchical): meaningfulness, self-sufficiency, effortlessness, playfulness, richness, simplicity, order, justice, completion, necessity, perfection, individuality, aliveness, beauty, goodness, and truth. See Frank G. Goble, *The Third Force: The Psychology of Abraham Maslow* (New York: Grossman, 1970), p. 50, and Abraham H. Maslow, *Motivation and Personality,* 2d ed. (New York: Harper & Row, 1970) pp. 35-51.

feel that certain physical conditions related to health are also transmitted genetically. Some children will accept their inherited traits without concern or desire to change them. Other children may resent the fact that they resemble their parents, brothers and sisters, or other relatives.

Teachers and counselors in the church should be well aware of these concerns and the attitudes of children about them. Prayer is needed for each child, and it would be well to pray with him that he might accept as from God those characteristics which he has inherited. Counselors may also work with parents in helping them to instill a Christian attitude in children regarding their inherited characteristics. Thus, inherited characteristics affect the child's self-concept and the continued development of his personality. Cooperation is needed by parents and relatives in order to help instill a healthy attitude in children toward their hereditary traits, desirable or undesirable.

PRENATAL AND CONGENITAL FACTORS

Various prenatal and congenital factors also contribute to an individual's personality development. A mother's physical condition during pregnancy can bring about in her child endocrine imbalance, dietary deficiencies, and poor health. Nervous instability and a number of childhood abnormalities may result from serious health problems of a mother during pregnancy. At the time the vital organs of the unborn are being formed, some infectious diseases experienced by the mother may affect her child. Deafness, blindness, malformations, and similar disorders may be the result.

In addition, it is known that a well child will have less difficulty adjusting to a normal childhood than a sick child.

Childhood diseases, accidents, and various difficulties, such as allergies, diet, rest schedules, and the like, contribute to attitudes, an important phase of personality development. How these attitudes are accepted by those working with children in the church have positive or negative effects in personality development.

As teachers and counselors better understand some of these conditions, they will be more capable of helping children who are affected unfavorably by prenatal factors. These children need special help in becoming adjusted. They need Christian love and genuine concern from their parents and other teachers.

ENVIRONMENT

The personality development of a child is certainly influenced by his environment and conditions affecting his daily life. His personality is affected by the way he is treated by his mother, father, and others about him. The attitudes of his parents and those who care for him make a deep impression on the formation of his personality and self-concept.

A child's position in his family constellation also affects his character. The youngest child differs from the oldest; an only child differs from a middle child. Dinkmeyer and Dreikurs give this explanation:

> The competition between siblings leads to fundamental personality differences. Frequently as a result of competition, where one succeeds, the other becomes discouraged and gives up; or where one fails, the other moves in. In contrast, alliances between siblings are often expressed in similarity of interests, character traits, and temperament.[1]

Churches must reach out to children from every economic level, regardless of race, color, or a multitude of environmental changes. *All* need to be brought to Christ. However, as children from such varied backgrounds are brought together and many individual needs known, the wise teacher will show equal love and understanding for each child. Realizing that these children are innocent victims of their background and environmental circumstances, special care and patience are essential. How these children are treated in the church will leave a lasting impression on their personalities and on their attitude toward the church, perhaps throughout their lifetime.

Several longitudinal research studies indicate that many personality traits are established early and remain quite persistent throughout one's life. Results of research done by the Institute of Human Development of the University of California at Berkeley "probably offer the richest collection of data ever assembled on human beings over a long period."[2] Included in "The Guidance Study" were 252 children born in Berkeley over an eighteen-month period. They were observed for eighteen years.

> The children were weighed, measured, tested, interviewed, and observed at various times through their eighteenth year. Special attention was given to their life at home during the preschool years. Information about them was obtained also from their parents, brothers and sisters, teachers, and classmates. At 30, when they were rearing children of their own, 167 of them were studied again.[3]

This report was supported by and later published by the National Institute of Mental Health. The outcome of these studies in relation to personality development was summarized in this way:

> The child who at five was either reserved and shy or expressive and gay tended to show the same characteristics at 16. The child who was either reactive and explosive or calm and phlegmatic at five was likely to be the same at 16.

> The speed of development during childhood, which presumably is determined by both genetic and environmental factors, seems to influence personality characteristics into adulthood. The early talkers (generally those who had received more than the usual amount of parental attention during infancy) were more introspective as adults, perhaps because language rather than action had always been for them the favored response pattern.[4]

The evidence is clear that many personality traits formed in early childhood do follow through for many years. This is confirmed by Maslow's statement: "people who have been made secure and strong in the early years, tend to remain secure and strong thereafter in the face of whatever threatens."[5] This should challenge children's workers in the church to provide Christian experiences that will have deep and lasting impressions on children. These may be offered through the Sunday school, vacation Bible school, the church camping program, youth activities, and various other groups throughout the church.

However, each child is more than the product of his heredity, prenatal and congenital influences, and environment. Dinkmeyer and Dreikurs explain that a child's "subjective interpretation of all that goes on both within him and around him gives meaning to his actions. The child can take a stand towards what he experiences; he has the ability to interpret and to draw conclusions."[6] They also point out that from a child's contacts with his parents and eventually with others, he "reaches certain generalizations about people and how one deals with them."[7]

Aspects of Personality

Specific areas of personalized needs definitely influence a child's personality. Because these are discussed more specifically and chronologically in chapters 4-8, these areas are used here only to point out some of the overall needs, regardless of age, which directly affect the development of children's personalities.

PHYSICAL

The physical growth and development of a child certainly affects his self-concept and attitudes. If he is unusually large or small for his age, if he is unusually active or inactive, or if he has various other deviations from whatever is considered "normal" by his parents, his personality will be adversely affected. However, if he shows about the same growth and development characteristics as those about him, this generally has a positive effect on personality, because he will likely accept himself as he is. Very young children soon become aware of whether they are different from other children, and certainly the attitudes of their parents and peers toward them affect their personalities, often permanently. The attitude of Christians about these matters will make a lasting influence.

Consideration should be given in the church to the child who is physically handicapped and thus faces a pattern of physical growth different from others. The physically handicapped include the crippled, blind, deaf, and others. The attitude a physically handicapped child has toward himself and the attitudes others have toward him affect the way his personality develops. Some churches plan special activities for physically handicapped children, including camping and sports. However, care should be taken that these children are accepted by other children and treated on an equal basis. Most healthy handicapped children want to be treated as other children and not separated or favored because of their handicap. How much can be done along this line depends on the types of physical handicaps among children in the church and the number of such children.

Planned activities for physically handicapped children can be the means of reaching unchurched children and their parents. For example, a ramp to a side door of the church can encourage children in wheelchairs to attend Sunday school, whereas they might otherwise hesitate to attend. Crippled children are delighted to be included and provided for. Sensing a church's concern for children in need can be an excellent learning situation for the other children in the church. (For more information, see chap. 27, "Teaching Other Exceptional Children.")

MENTAL

The development of a child's personality is directly related to his mental health. A child develops certain attitudes—positive or negative—toward himself, his family, friends, teachers, and the church.

> Personality is correlated with intelligence, at least in the case of boys. Adolescent boys with high I.Q.'s were generally described as friendly, social, and independent—as they had been since the age of four.[8]

Intelligence is a factor contributing to a child's interests, attitudes, and reasoning ability. Most small children are capable of learning more than is often expected of them, although their attention span in short and they have limited concepts of numbers, time, and space. An experienced teacher quickly senses whether a child is able to comprehend the teachings offered in the church. The intelligence level of the pupils certainly should affect the manner in which one presents the truths of the Scriptures.

Children need and usually welcome intellectual stimulation and challenge. Maya Pines claims that "millions of children are being irreparably damaged by our failure to stimulate them intellectually during their crucial years—from birth to six."[9]

Jean Piaget, the well-known Swiss psychologist who has researched the intellectual development of children for several decades, has indicated that children in intellectually stimulating environments advance more rapidly than others. "His theories also explained why environments that restrict children's opportunities to explore, to test their own hypotheses, to have their questions answered and other questions raised, would retard their development."[10] (Piaget's views are discussed further in chap. 9.)

Intellectual interests of children at various growth stages should be carefully considered in planning the educational program of the church. Interests reflect personality, and that makes each child unique and a real challenge to every teacher.

The mental development of a child is also greatly affected by vicarious learning experiences. Perhaps the most common are television programs and the general attitude of his parents toward the ones he is permitted to see. The planned curriculum of the church may substitute various meaningful activities to permit child participation and thereby successfully compete for experiences in mental growth and development.

Results of research also indicate that a "bibliotherapy" (therapy through reading) is an effective influence on personality. Thus, it is important that the church be able to offer books and other literature, for older children especially, which teach Christian concepts and attitudes.

A growing number of churches are recognizing the need to minister to mentally handicapped children. Some churches have found this to be a rewarding experience which has served a number of otherwise unchurched families. (See chap. 26, "Teaching Mentally Retarded Children," for more on this.)

EMOTIONAL

The love or lack of love shown to an infant by his parents indelibly influences his personality. Behavioral psychologists, such as B. F. Skinner, teach that the need for love is an acquired or learned need, whereas other psychologists believe that the love need is innate. The latter seems to be supported by clinical experiments that demonstrate that institutionalized children show psychopathological symptoms when they are not loved, even though all other physiological needs are well satisfied. Montagu writes:

> Studies of infants who lived their early lives in hospitals or other institutions have shown that the baby requires much more than routine satisfaction of his physical wants. These children were fed and bathed and

> cared for in the soundest scientific way. But they lacked the warm personal attention—the cuddling, the carrying, the physical assurance of love—that a mother ordinarily gives her child. They lacked the feeling of support and encouragement, the feeling of being wanted. In short, they lacked love.
>
> Many of these children were found to be retarded even in their physical development. They failed to gain weight properly, they slept poorly, and they suffered longer from respiratory infections than babies who were receiving the personal attention of their mothers.
>
> Moreover, children who have lacked love during their early years very frequently developed emotional difficulties. As they grow up, they may be unsocial and hostile. They usually are insecure, filled with fear and anxiety. And in most cases they are themselves incapable of giving love.[11]

Along this line, Harris comments, "We do not learn to be loving if we have never been loved. If the first five years of life consist totally of a critical struggle for physical and psychological survival, this struggle is likely to persist throughout life."[12] Goble writes:

> In a group of young children, classified from fully accepted to fully rejected, it was found that the partially rejected children behaved in a way which demonstrated their frantic need for affection, but the children who were utterly rejected from the earliest days of life exhibited not a tremendous desire for love, but a coldness and apparent lack of desire for affection.[13]

What a challenge this is to teachers in the church to demonstrate genuine love to children, even in those children's earliest years—and earliest months—of life.

The child soon learns that there are different kinds of "love" and ways of expressing it, even though his introduction to it is through the mother or someone else who cares for the infant. As he hears God's Word, he learns that God is love. Also, he learns that teachers and others in the church express love for him. Later, he learns there is also a love for one's country, neighbors, and even enemies, as well as for parents and friends. The scriptural teachings about love are many and may be applied as appropriate for the various age levels.

Individual personality is also affected by the emotions of others. Some teachers feel that certain emotional expressions are almost contagious because of the part that imitation plays in various circumstances. Children at almost every age tend to imitate others, including their emotional expressions. This is especially important in regard to the negative emotional expressions, such as fear and hate.

Because each individual is unique, he will express his emotions in different ways. If his way is negative, then the teachings of the church, personal example, correction, and prayer can help alter these undesirable personality traits.

Children with aggressive behavior and children who are withdrawn are seeking in those ways to meet their emotional needs. Children with these "behavior disorders" need special attention from their teachers. Ways to handle and help children with these disorders are suggested in many books on child psychology.[14]

Certain behavioral maladjustments among children can be helped by careful planning and the help of Christian teachers. Some children from unchurched homes may display reaction to the church program in an unusual and sometimes undesirable way simply because of their background and lack of understanding. An increasing number of child abuse cases are being reported, and some of these children may come to the church for refuge. Church leaders must accept the challenge and opportunity to help all who need help in times of emotional crisis. Dedicated teachers and counselors need to share information about individual cases and pray for spiritual wisdom in treating children's needs.

Children's emotional needs become even more evident at times of illness and death in the family, or during and after divorce. These circumstances leave lasting impressions on their personalities, but the church can come to their aid through trained counselors and teachers who can share the love of Christ.

SOCIAL

Many are the personality influences of social needs. Some children have not been taught to get along well with others. Some are selfish and cannot share toys in the church nursery, for example, without tears. Others are shy and hesitate to play with others their own age. Some prefer to play alongside others than with them.

Local churches can provide numerous opportunities for children to socialize in a Christian atmosphere and thereby make friends of lasting influence. Parents should have an active part in this, although providing for the social needs of children does not necessarily mean a round of parties. Sports events, various group activities as well as contacts outside the church may contribute to children's social needs. Christlike conduct should be dominant in these activities.

Carefully controlled activities for children in the church should encourage friendships that will have lasting influence on the impressionable personalities of the participants. Children's weekday Bible classes, held in homes, often provide excellent opportunity for sharing and becoming acquainted with those from other home situations.

SPIRITUAL

As human beings, children have more than physical, mental, emotional, and social needs. They also have spiritual needs and problems. How and when a child's spiritual needs are met can have a profound effect on the formation of his character. Evangelicals believe that the Bible teaches the personality-transforming power of the gospel (2 Co 5:17), even among children. In addition, the sanctifying ministry of the Holy Spirit can produce great changes in one's inner life and outward behavior.

The tender heart of a young child can be directed Godward by parents and others who teach him to love God, Jesus, the Bible, church, and others.

Sensitivity to right and wrong begins to develop at an early age. This enables teachers to show children the awfulness of sin and the need for turning to Jesus for salvation.

Those who teach children in the church are responsible to pray for each one individually, to teach faithfully to him the Word of God and to apply scriptural truths to daily living. After a child receives Christ as his Saviour, his role within the church shifts to learning certain concepts of the Scriptures not applicable to him before salvation. There must be appropriate follow-up for babes in Christ regardless of their physical age.

Childhood years are impressionable ones, and the Christian life is not isolated from everyday living; love and understanding must be an obvious part of the life of his peers and adults. Many children will not see Christ reflected in their parents or relatives. Therefore church workers can help encourage those children to live for Christ.

Children's Self-Concept

An important aspect of the development of personality is the child's concept of himself as an individual. What does he think of himself and why? As teachers counsel with students informally and as they see them in their classes, definite impressions of a child's attitudes toward himself become evident.

For the most part, a child forms self-concepts from those with whom he associates. Soon he learns their attitudes toward him and begins to form similar ideas. Obviously, parents play a prominent role in this matter. A child seeks protection, care, and love, and thereby learns to love those who respond with love. Many attitudes parents have for a child also reflect their own attitudes about themselves.

A child's attitudes toward himself are strongly influenced not only by his parents but also by culture, heredity, siblings, intelligence, peers, and other factors. For example, a boy who has inherited a strong body may become a capable athlete. This, in turn, builds up his concept of himself.

If the same boy had been ridiculed because of his body, he may never have developed it for use in athletics. His concept of himself, influenced by the attitude of his peers, would have prevented him from going into athletics.

Many studies have revealed that a low self-concept and poor academic achievement among children and youth are definitely related.[15] Children's workers do well to ask themselves if their own attitudes in class contribute to or hinder the development of healthy self-concepts among their pupils. "An endless number of cases can be cited where the praise and encouragement of the child by his teacher has significantly influenced his course and development in life."[16]

Summary

Children's personalities are greatly influenced by their background, environment, and the composite of their physical, mental, emotional, social, and spiritual needs. All the personal experiences which make a child unique contribute to his personality. Observing children at home, school, play, and church can help parents and teachers have a better understanding of children's personality traits, patterns, and needs.

Teachers may be tempted to stereotype individuals according to general personality patterns, but unfounded conclusions must be avoided. If indications of abnormality are evident, it may be better to make referrals to those who are trained to handle such problems.

As a teacher studies the personalities of his students, he will want to pattern his teaching in a way that will appeal to their interests and at the same time will relate scriptural truths to their lives. The better a teacher understands the personalities and needs of his children, the better equipped he will be as an instrument of the Holy Spirit to share Christ with children and to help them develop Christlike attitudes and habits.

NOTES

1. Don Dinkmeyer and Rudolf Dreikurs, *Encouraging Children to Learn: The Encouragement Process* (Englewood Cliffs, N. J.: Prentice-Hall, 1963), p. 21.
2. *The Mental Health of the Child* (Rockville, Md.: Public Health Service Publication, No. 2168, 1971), p. 131.
3. Ibid.
4. Ibid., p. 134.
5. Abraham H. Maslow, *Motivation and Personality* (New York: Harper & Row, 1954), p. 44.
6. Dinkmeyer and Dreikurs, p. 19.
7. Ibid.
8. *The Mental Health of the Child,* p. 134.
9. Maya Pines, *Revolution in Learning: The Years from Birth to Six* (New York: Harper & Row, 1967), p. 15.
10. Ibid., p. 59. See also these books on or by Piaget: Millie C. Almy, *Young Children's Thinking: Studies of Some Aspects of Piaget's Theory* (New York: Colum-

bia U., Teacher's College Press, 1966); J. McV. Hunt, *Intelligence and Experience* (New York: Ronald, 1961); Jean Piaget, *The Origins of Intelligence in Children* (New York: International Universities, 1952); and Jean Piaget, *The Psychology of Intelligence* (Paterson, N. J.: Littlefield, Adams, 1963).

11. Ashley Montagu, *Helping Children Develop Moral Values* (Chicago: Science Research Associates, 1953), p. 29.
12. Thomas A. Harris, *I'm OK—You're OK* (New York: Harper & Row, 1969), p. 103.
13. Frank G. Goble, *The Third Force: The Psychology of Abraham Maslow* (New York: Grossman, 1970), p. 75.
14. See, for example, Katherine E. D'Evelyn, *Meeting Children's Emotional Needs* (Englewood Cliffs, N. J.: Prentice-Hall, 1957), chaps. 7 and 8; and Alfred Adler, *The Problem Child* (New York: Capricorn, 1963).
15. See, for example, William P. Purkey, *Self-Concept and School Achievement* (Englewood Cliffs, N.J.: Prentice-Hall, 1970), and Stanley Coopersmith, *The Antecedents of Self-Esteem* (San Francisco: Freeman, 1967). Also see James Dobson, *Hide or Seek* (Old Tappan, N.J.: Revell, 1974).
16. Goble, p. 152.

FOR FURTHER READING

Baller, W. R., and Charles, Don C. *The Psychology of Human Growth and Development.* New York: Holt, Rinehart & Winston, 1961.

Bloom, Benjamin S. *Stability and Change in Human Characteristics.* New York: Wiley, 1964.

Borgatta, E. F., and Lambert, William. *Handbook on Personality Theory and Research.* Chicago: Rand McNally, 1968.

Byrne, D. E. *An Introduction to Personality.* Englewood Cliffs, N.J.: Prentice-Hall, 1966.

———. *Personality Research: A Book of Readings.* Englewood Cliffs, N.J.: Prentice-Hall, 1966.

Cameron, N. H. *Personality Development and Psychopathy, A Dynamic Approach.* Boston: Houghton Mifflin, 1963.

Clouse, Bonnidell. "Psychological Theories of Child Development: Implications for the Christian Family." *Journal of Psychology and Theology* 1 (April 1973): 77-87.

D'Evelyn, Katherine E. *Meeting Children's Emotional Needs.* Englewood Cliffs, N. J.: Prentice-Hall, 1957.

Elkind, David. *Children and Adolescents: Interpretive Essays on Jean Piaget.* Paperback ed. New York: Oxford U., 1971.

Gergen, Kenneth J. *Personality and Social Behavior.* Reading, Mass.: Addison-Wesley, 1970.

Gordon, Jesse E. *Personality and Behavior.* New York: Macmillan, 1963.

Gordon, Ira J. *Human Development: Readings in Research.* Glenview, Ill.: Scott, Foresman, 1965.

Haimowitz, M., and Haimowitz, N. R. *Human Development, Selected Readings.* 2d. ed. New York: Crowell, 1966.

Hakes, J. Edward, ed. *An Introduction to Evangelical Christian Education.* Chicago: Moody, 1964.

Hoagland, Joan. "Bibliotherapy: Aiding Children in Personality Development." *Elementary English* 49 (March, 1972):390-94.

Jenkins, Gladys Gardner; Shacter, Helen S.; and Bauer, William W. *These Are Your Children.* 3d ed. Glenview, Ill.: Scott, Foresman, 1970.

Landreth, Catherine. *Early Childhood, Behavior and Learning.* New York: Knopf, 1967.

Lane, Howard, and Beauchamp, M. *Understanding Human Development.* Englewood Cliffs, N. J.: Prentice-Hall, 1959.

Ligon, E. M. *The Psychology of Christian Personality.* New York: Macmillan, 1961.

Lyppitt, Peggy, and Lyppitt, Ronald. "The Peer Culture as a Learning Environment." *Childhood Education* 47 (Dec., 1970):135-38.

Mednick, Martha T., and Mednick, S. A. *Research in Personality.* New York: Holt, Rinehart & Winston, 1963.

Murphy, Lois B. *Personality in Your Children.* New York: Basic Books, 1960.

Mussen, P. H.; Kagen, J.; and Conger J. *Child Development and Personality.* 2d ed. New York: Harper & Row, 1963.

———. *Readings in Child Development and Personality.* New York: Harper & Row, 1965.

Rappoport, Leon. *Personality Development: The Chronological Experience.* Glenview, Ill.: Scott, Foresman, 1972.

Stith, Marjorie. *Understanding Children.* Nashville: Convention, 1969.

Stott, L. H. *Child Development: An Individual Longitudinal Approach.* New York: Holt, Rinehart, & Winston, 1967.

Thorpe, L. P., and Schmuller, A. M. *Personality, An Interdisciplinary Approach.* Princeton, N.J.: Van Nostrand, 1958.

4

Understanding Infants and Toddlers

Valerie A. Wilson

SOFT, SLEEPY, red, wrinkled, cuddly, fragile, small: choose any word you want to describe them. Who does not love one of these little people? And to hear proud, happy parents and relatives talk, *their* baby is the most beautiful, the most lovable of all. Indeed, a baby is a miracle. From a fertilized egg (about the size of the dot over an *i*) emerges—about nine months later—a fully developed human being. Only the God of creation could have designed such a masterpiece.

It is equally as wonderful to contemplate the fact that God has given to this tiny person an immortal soul which is capable of knowing God. This, then, is the challenge which confronts us: to guide the growth and development of the infant in such a way that one day he will respond to the claims of God upon his life. In order to do this, we must understand the little life which we are seeking to shape, and we must also understand some of the methods which can be used to influence that life.

THE IMPORTANCE OF THE EARLY YEARS

Just as the foundation of a house determines the stability of the superstructure, so the foundation years of life determine the overall direction and characteristics of a life. No period in one's life is as important as the first two years. This is not to say that change and development cannot take place at any other time. Indeed, they must, and they do. But psychologists and educators agree that never again during his whole life will a person learn as fast or as much as he does in these first two years. One educator has written, "I think it can be said conservatively that a college student in four years does not make proportionately a fraction of the

---

VALERIE A. WILSON, M.R.E., is Editor of vacation Bible school materials and writer of the Sunday school nursery curriculum, Regular Baptist Press, Des Plaines, Illinois.

progress the well-trained infant does in his first two years."[1] Another educator is quoted as saying, "If the sensitive years are ignored, they pass like *dropped stitches,* never to be picked up during the rest of a child's life."[2]

To those who are involved in the Christian education of children, this means these first two years of life dare not be neglected or slighted in the church's program. These early years demand the *very best* the church can provide. Neither should these years simply be endured or viewed as unproductive by Christian parents. The basic values and concepts which are communicated to the infant and toddler are the very ones that will determine the course of his life. Horace Bushnell is credited with saying that when their child is three years of age, the parents have done more than half of all they will ever do for his character.

Because these first two years are so vital, it behooves us to understand them as fully as possible.

Understanding the Infant

The term *infant* is used to refer to a child during the first twelve months of his life. The understanding of the infant—or any other age child—involves two areas. First, there are those characteristics which are common to all children of approximately the same age. Second, there are those characteristics which are unique to a particular child. The effective worker will seek to know the general characteristics of the age group with which he works, but he or she will also do everything possible to know the individual child. Both areas are important. But it is within the scope of this chapter to deal only with the general characteristics.

It is readily evident that no two infants are alike. Each baby is an individual in his own right, with his own pattern and rate of growth and development. However, "Babies grow and develop in certain ways which are fairly uniform. The challenging fact is that they pass through similar stages of growth, but each one grows at a different rate of speed."[3] We need to understand these basic patterns in order to understand individual children. In seeking to understand the infant, we shall look at his life in three-month periods.

Birth through three months

The infant "is a bundle of joy and potential. He is a God-given spiritual trust."[4] But he enters the world through a shocking experience—the birth process! He leaves the calm, protected, warm atmosphere of his mother's womb in a traumatic way. And he is encountered at once with the need to function on his own. The advances of modern medicine can provide assistance if life processes, such as breathing, do not function satisfactorily.

But eventually, if he is to survive, the infant must take over for himself. The qualifications he brings with him for this momentous task are weakness, helplessness, and complete dependence!

The full-term newborn baby weighs between six and nine pounds and is eighteen to twenty-two inches long. (He has grown 3500 times in length since conception!) The male infant is usually slightly heavier and a bit longer than the female. The baby is surely a tiny little bit of humanity, but "The chief business of the infant is to grow."[5] And grow he does! His birth weight is usually doubled by the end of six months and tripled by one year.

The newborn baby often appears top-heavy, for his head is one-fourth of his body length. His arms and legs are relatively short, and his abdomen protrudes. His little hands are clenched into fists much of the time, and his legs are often drawn up toward his body. The skin of the newborn infant is red, wrinkled, and thin. In many ways, he resembles an old man more than the cute baby which most people picture in their minds.

Physical needs dominate this period of the infant's life. Eating and sleeping are all-important. Sleeping occupies as much as twenty hours of the infant's day. When he does awaken, he cries. These early cries are distress signals, reflex responses to discomfort. He cannot tolerate anything that bothers him; so he responds by being irritable—the only response he can register. The cry of the infant says to the adults around him, "Something is bothering me. I have a need. Meet it."

The baby is capable of giving only nonverbal messages, so nonverbal messages are what he picks up best. How an adult responds to his cry will teach the baby something about the world he has entered. Each day has its routine of simple acts which meet the physical needs of the baby. "But each simple act carries its own underlying lesson about this world—a lesson the child confronts for the first time."[6]

The sensory system of the baby is not fully developed. He can feel sensations of pain, heat, and cold over his entire body; but his brain cannot sort out these sensations. His eyesight is not good, but his hearing seems to be quite keen. The baby learns much through touch. For instance, he knows different adults by the way he is held. Much of his sensual gratification comes through his mouth. If he does not receive enough gratification at mealtime, he may suck vigorously on a thumb or pacifier. Eventually he begins to explore the world around him, and everything seems to find its way into the baby's mouth!

By the second and third months of life, the infant is attracted by bright, hanging toys and mobiles. He develops the ability to follow moving objects with his eyes. He will sleep more easily if his times of wakefulness are made interesting. By the end of this first three months of his life, the infant may begin to gurgle and coo—sounds which bring delight to those around him!

FOUR THROUGH SIX MONTHS

In his second three months of life, the baby becomes much more active. He rolls and wiggles, and it is not safe to leave him alone on a raised, flat surface for even a moment. During the fifth or sixth month, a baby will begin to enjoy a playpen. He is eager and bold in his approach to new things. By the sixth month, he usually rolls from his back to his tummy—his first big achievement!

The baby begins early to recognize his mother's face from others; and by six months, he knows his family members from other people. With this new recognition may come tears when family members leave.

Learning to pick up an object is mastered during this time, and a baby will grasp his plaything tightly. He must also learn to let go intentionally. It is frustrating to adults to pick up a dropped object time after time, but the developing infant is enjoying the exercise of this new skill—the ability to let go.

As the infant increases in size, his body undergoes the necessary changes which make for maturity and strength. This is development.[7] Both growth and development are evident during this three-month period, as the world and experience of the infant enlarge.

SEVEN THROUGH NINE MONTHS

Perhaps the most notable "first" of the seven-through-nine-month period is the appearance of the first tooth. This usually occurs after six months, though occasionally, a baby will have one earlier, and in rare instances an infant is born with teeth. In the process of teething, the baby is often fretful and fussy; his gums are red and swollen; his appetite may decrease; and he may sleep for shorter periods of time. Adults who care for him must keep these physical discomforts in mind and continue to provide tender, loving care for a fussy, cranky, "runny-nosed" baby.

The growing, developing infant is working on his coordination; and he enjoys exercising his muscles. In this period, he struggles to sit up and to pull himself into an upright position.

Toys for this age baby should stimulate his curious mind: small blocks; bright, wooden beads; large spools; nesting toys; bells and balls; large plastic or rubber rings; soft plastic spoons; soft, cuddly toys. Toys should be free of rough edges and tiny detachable parts. Nontoxic paint should be used on any surface which a child might chew.

Duing this time the infant may develop (as Dodson says) "stranger anxiety."[8] He may be very suspicious of people other than his mother or immediate family. He usually does warm up to people who give him time to become friendly. But these "outsiders" must evidence love and gain his confidence; they cannot force themselves on him. The baby finds increasing amusement in pleasant social contacts, and he enjoys the opportunity to explore. By the time he reaches nine months, he will begin to show active resentment if his interests are thwarted. His own distinctive nature and personality are becoming more and more evident.

TEN THROUGH TWELVE MONTHS

A ten-month-old is usually eating solid foods and drinking milk from a cup, though a bedtime bottle may still be given. He sits up without support and is probably crawling quite well. How he loves to explore! He should be kept safely out of trouble, but he needs opportunities for adventure. He needs an environment in which he can maneuver with ease and investigate the world around him.

The baby is able to respond more and more to adult attention. Now he enjoys games such as pat-a-cake and peek-a-boo. His mind needs the challenge of things such as simple pull-apart, put-together toys; several blocks instead of one; boxes, spoons, and nonclip clothespins. This is the time to introduce the child to the world of books. Books with a simple picture and one word on a page help the youngster learn about his world.

The development of nerve and muscle control during infancy starts at the head and moves downward and from the upper part of the arms and legs outward to the fingers and toes. By the end of the first year, the baby can use his thumb and forefinger together—a distinctly human trait, and he shows increasing evidence of coordination. The twelfth month of his life (sooner for some babies, later for others) will find him pulling himself upright, maintaining a standing position and perhaps taking a few steps.

At one year of age, the average child measures from twenty-eight to thirty-one inches in length, and weighs, unclothed, from seventeen to twenty-four pounds. He has as few as two or as many as six teeth. He is leaving the world of infancy to embark on a new adventure—the life of a toddler.

MEETING THE NEEDS OF THE INFANT

The needs of the infant can be summarized rather easily: his physical needs must be met, and they must be met in an atmosphere of love and by those who love him. "Spiritual, mental, emotional, and social development hinge upon the ways physical needs are met."[9] As physical needs are met in a loving way, the infant gains a basic security and a sense of trust which he will carry with him through life.

The implications are clear for those who work with infants in the church program. This worker cannot look on his job as routine. He must see it as an avenue of service to the Lord who cared deeply for little children. The worker must have for each little child a love which manifests itself in the way in which he cares for the child. The worker in the crib nursery has the awesome responsibility of helping the infant form his first and most lasting impression of the place called church. Long before he knows anything about what is *taught,* he will know how he *feels.* And how he feels *now* may influence to a large extent how readily he will expose himself to other aspects of the church's program when he is old enough to decide for himself.

The person who works with infants must be calm and gentle and not easily disturbed. This type of person exerts a calming influence on a baby. He should speak in a calm, gentle voice and in simple, short sentences. Baby talk is not necessary; simple songs and rhymes, soothing tunes, and gentle humming are much more pleasing and effective.

The role of men in the care of infants is becoming more noticeable. More and more churches are recruiting men for work with young children. James Hymes suggests that a "child's life is richer when, from the beginning, he has the benefit of both a masculine and a feminine approach to the world . . . Children of both sexes need to feel a hairy hand, a more muscular hand, a bigger hand, a calloused hand."[10] If, from his earliest experiences at church, the child has the awareness of the loving care of a man, he will find it easier to realize and trust the loving care of the Lord Jesus. The church's provision for the infant includes not only personnel but also a place. The crib nursery must be spotlessly clean and adequately equipped.* No parent wants to leave his child in a messy, cluttered, or dirty room. The church which wants to minister to parents as well as infants must do its utmost to provide clean, responsible, efficient, friendly, and loving service to the infant and his parents. Such a church is making an investment in a life. No other investment has such rewarding or eternal dividends!

Understanding the Toddler

Toddler describes the child thirteen to twenty-four months old. This designation is a natural one, since some time around twelve months, a child begins to toddle. His early adventures in walking are shaky and insecure at best; and they are filled with many tumbles. But little by little, he gains ability, momentum, and courage. Before long, he is into everything. Perhaps at no other period is so much energy and endurance, insight and courage required of adults. The toddler can make life fun or

*See chap. 22, "Leadership and Materials," for equipment needed in a crib nursery room.

frustrating. Adult frustrations, however, can be relieved somewhat if this important year of the child's life is better understood.

In infancy, a child learns basic trust or basic distrust. In toddlerhood, he learns self-confidence or self-doubt.[11] How a child learns to think of himself has far-reaching consequences in the years ahead. We can best understand the toddler by considering the various aspects of his life: physical, mental, social, emotional, and spiritual. (See chap. 28 for more description of children in this age group and how to handle them.)

PHYSICAL CHARACTERISTICS

Physically, the toddler is characterized by his newly acquired ability to walk. At times, especially while walking is still new to him, he may resort to crawling. He is quite proficient at this means of navigation, so it is easy to revert to it when the need arises to get someplace quickly. Some children never do much crawling; others do a great deal. But regardless of how much crawling does or does not precede it, walking is achieved when the child is ready. He cannot and should not be forced to walk. He will master this feat when he is ready, commonly between twelve and fifteen months.

The toddler is also gaining ability and dexterity with his hands. He has better coordination in the use of his fingers. He can pull off his cap and socks, open boxes, unscrew lids, put pegs into holes, scribble, turn book pages one at a time, and build a tower with four or five blocks. Dodson has characterized toys as the "textbooks of toddlerhood."[12] Playthings should be chosen carefully, and play activities should be directed toward purposeful ends.

A change is noticeable in the toddler's sleeping habits. He will usually cut down on daytime sleep, needing only one nap a day. He may sleep two or three hours during the day and eleven to twelve hours at night. But he does get weary; so church programs for toddlers need to include opportunities for rest.

As a child approaches age two, the parents begin toilet training him. Those who work with the child at church should be aware of this and cooperate with parents in this regard. (It should be noted, however, that it is unusual and perhaps even unwise to have a child trained before his second birthday.)

By the time he reaches the age of two, a child is usually thirty-two to thirty-four inches long and weighs thirty-three to thirty-six pounds. He has come a long way since the time he was only the size of the dot over an *i*.

MENTAL CHARACTERISTICS

The mental horizons of the toddler are enlarging even as his physical body is growing. One such area is that of language development. The toddler adds many new words (mostly nouns and verbs) to his vocabulary. He is able to name objects or pictures in a book. He begins to use words in combination and forms simple sentences. He understands commands and prohibitions and comprehends simple questions. By his second birthday, the toddler has a vocabulary of 250 to 300 words.

Of all the words he either uses or understands, the toddler's favorite word is undoubtedly *no*. He is seeking autonomy, independence; and *no* is one way to exert himself. The adult should not try to pit his will against that of the toddler. The parent or church worker should let the child know certain things are expected regardless of his response. Negative responses can be reduced by avoiding questions that invite *no* for an answer. If there is, in reality, no choice, the child should not be offered one. Rather than asking "Do you want to stop playing with the blocks?", the fact should be stated, "When you finish building the tower, we will put away the blocks. Then we will go to the story rug." (Notice that this statement also contains a time element. The toddler is given time to finish an activity before a new one is begun.)

The toddler has a brief attention span and also a short memory. Stories for toddlers must be very short, but they can be repeated often. (A teacher tires of the same thing far more quickly than the child does.) His short memory means that directions will have to be repeated several times. Furthermore, they may have to be repeated every week (in a church situation), for the child has forgotten since the last time he was there.

When directions are given, they should be given positively so that the child knows what to do. Negative directions do not tell him what is expected. Rather than saying, "Do not put the book on the floor," the parent or teacher should give a positive directive: "Tommy, let's put the book back on the table."

SOCIAL CHARACTERISTICS

The toddler's world is confined to *me* and *mine*. He has little concept of *you* and *others*. His play is solitary. He has little or no interest in others and has no ability to play with them. But as he nears his second birthday, he gains an interest in being near others. He wants to do the same thing as another child, but he does not want to do it with him. Hence his play is characterized as being parallel but not cooperative.

The church is a good place for the toddler to begin to learn to share, to take turns, and to be kind. But the young child should not be expected to make great gains in these areas. His emotional and nervous systems are not developed to the extent that he can understand or tolerate social demands. Enough toys and books should be on hand so that a toddler can engage in solitary play.

The toddler treats people in much the same way he treats things—feeling, pushing, trying to manipulate. Many times, his actions are misunderstood. An adult may think the child is misbehaving when he is actually only trying to learn about his world. Since he does not have much concept of *person,* he does not realize that one does not poke another child in the same way that one can poke a stuffed animal. When such actions occur, it is usually best to pick up a child and move him to another part of the room. As the child is being moved, the worker should say, "Timmy is our friend. We don't want to hurt Timmy. Here is a book just for you." Such a course of action does several things: (1) it separates the two children; (2) it reinforces the teaching that the other child is a friend; (3) it suggests how not to treat a friend; (4) it diverts the child's attention to something more acceptable.

EMOTIONAL CHARACTERISTICS

Insecurity characterizes the toddler emotionally. Adjustment is difficult. He gets along best in a familiar routine, in a familiar room, and with familiar faces. When toddlers are cared for at church, therefore, it is helpful to keep the room arrangement, the schedule, and the personnel the same from week to week. This will help the child feel secure when he comes to church. The person who works with toddlers needs the same characteristics as those suggested for workers with infants—calmness, stability, and gentleness. The toddler needs and responds to the calming influence of an adult.

A child's perception of a situation will vary with his physical and emotional states. His reactions are based on whether he is fatigued, insecure, and hungry, or rested, safe, and content. If a child's behavior varies from that which he usually exhibits, such physical and emotional factors may be the explanation.

Often a toddler will act out his feeling in play. The alert worker will watch for indications of how the child feels by the way he treats the dolls, plays with the blocks, and even in the books he chooses.

SPIRITUAL CHARACTERISTICS

Openness and *receptivity* aptly describe the toddler. No walls of doubt or suspicion have yet been raised; no questions concerning rationality or reasonableness have been voiced. The little child will listen with wide-eyed wonder as he is told of God who makes it rain or God who made the doggy. There will be a warm response when the toddler hears of baby Jesus, God's Son. While the toddler cannot comprehend the same depths of truth as an older child, there is no need to wait until later to begin teaching. Some basic Bible truths can be emphasized repeatedly to the open mind and receptive heart of the toddler.

The church which makes no provision for teaching toddlers is losing precious opportunities. The program for toddlers should be more than a baby-sitting service. A definite teaching program should be carefully planned. (Some publishers include helps for teaching toddlers in their curriculum materials for nursery-age children.) Anne Gilliland suggests the following "desired outcomes" which can serve as a guide in planning a program for toddlers: In regard to *God,* "experiencing happy feelings associated with God"; *Jesus,* "experiencing happy feelings associated with Jesus"; *creation,* "discovering the beauties and wonders around him"; *church,* "developing a growing sense of at-homeness in his room at church"; *Bible,* "becoming familiar with the Bible as a Book"; *family,* "associating experiences he has at home with those he has at church"; *others,* "experiencing happiness in his relationship with others"; *self,* "feeling secure in his environment."[13]

MEETING THESE NEEDS

Is a toddler really to be enjoyed and not merely tolerated? It would seem that much enjoyment can result from watching a young life grow and develop. And a sense of satisfaction should result from having a part in shaping that young life for eternity. But to accomplish this and to meet the needs of the toddler require love and patience.

The toddler must be given as much room as possible in which to move around. He must have opportunities to explore. And he must be allowed to practice, for age one is a practice year. The child will improve on everything he started to learn in the first year and will acquire new skills as well.

The church can best meet these needs by providing a separate room, trained workers, and a planned program for toddlers. The toddler-age child does not belong in the crib nursery; nor is he ready to work with two-year-olds. He needs a place, personnel, and program for his particular needs. He is full of energy, activity, and excitement. The church can cooperate with parents in molding this young life for the glory of God.

The Ministry of a Cradle Roll Department

It is impossible to discuss the church's ministry to infants and toddlers without discussing the cradle roll department. No infant or toddler just happens to be in church. He is there because he was brought there.

Therefore, the church which desires to minister to infants and toddlers must do so through a ministry to parents. And this is exactly the function of the cradle roll department. It "capitalizes on going into the home, but it also makes provisions at the church for the care of infants and toddlers."[14]

Various slogans have been used to describe the ministry of this department: "A Christian home for every baby"; "Christ-centered homes for times like these"; "Enrolling babies to reach parents for Christ." Each of these points up the fact that this department goes into homes and, in that way, reaches both parents and babies. Perhaps at no other time is a family as easy to reach with the gospel as when a new baby enters the home. The objective of the department "is not to *relieve* parents of their responsibilites for the religious training of their children, but to *help them* fulfill those responsibilities."[15]

The program of the cradle roll department has three facets. The first of these is home visitation. Cradle roll department workers (often called visitors) go to homes where there are children from birth through twenty-four months of age and seek to enroll the baby in the cradle roll department of the church. Once a baby has been enrolled, regular visits are made to the home, and literature is left with the parents.

The second phase of the cradle roll program is providing care for infants and toddlers during Sunday school and church services. The suggestions which have already been offered in this chapter regarding meeting the needs of infants and toddlers apply here. The actual implementation of them would come within the realm of the cradle roll department.

The third phase of the department's ministry focuses again on the parents. An active, vibrant, Bible class must be provided for parents when they bring their children to church. In addition to this weekly ministry, special get-togethers should be planned. Some cradle roll departments have a mothers' meeting every month; others have parents' meetings, special banquets, recognition days, or other special events. All of these things are planned to lead parents to Christ and to give them guidance regarding the spiritual training of their child.

A church cannot afford to neglect a cradle roll department and the type ministry it represents. For one thing, the future of the child is at stake. "The church that deliberately waits to enroll a child until he is three or four years old may never see that child, even though he was born to parents who are church members."[16] Habits are hard to break, especially the habit of sleeping in on Sunday because it is so much trouble to prepare the little one for his morning in the nursery.

But there is another compelling reason for having an active cradle roll department. "The place of the Cradle Roll in the church helps determine not only the future life of the child, but also the future life of the church."[17]

Many churches testify to the fact that the cradle roll department is the best of all church-building agencies. "Growths of 35 percent to 65 percent have been attributed to this one department."[18] What an open door of opportunity this presents!

Summary

No other period in one's life is as vital as the very first two years. During these first years, the patterns are established which will affect all the rest of one's life. "As the twig is bent, the tree will grow." This is the time to see that the "twig" is bent toward God. It was Gipsy Smith who said, "If we are ever to beat the devil, we must beat him with the cradle." The late J. Edgar Hoover is quoted as saying, "The cure for crime is in the high chair, not the electric chair." The church which desires to minister to the whole person and the whole family will capitalize on the unique opportunities for reaching and teaching which the years of infancy and toddlerhood provide.

NOTES

1. Bernice T. Cory, *The Pastor and His Interest in Preschoolers,* Christian Educ. Monographs, Pastors' Series, No. 8 (Glen Ellyn, Ill.: Scripture Press Foundation, 1966), p. 2.
2. Ibid., p. 3.
3. Florence Conner Hearn, *Guiding Preschoolers* (Nashville: Convention, 1969), p. 23.
4. Joan Leach and Patricia Elliott, *First Steps: Helps for Workers in the Church Nursery* (Cincinnati: Standard, 1964), p. 10.
5. J. Omar Brubaker, and Robert E. Clark, *Understanding People* (Wheaton, Ill.: Evangelical Teacher Training Assn., 1972), p. 22.
6. James L. Hymes, *The Child Under Six* (Englewood Cliffs, N. J.: Prentice-Hall, 1963), p. 6.
7. Brubaker and Clark, p. 22.
8. Fitzhugh Dodson, *How to Parent* (Los Angeles: Nash, 1970), p. 40.
9. Hearn, p. 19.
10. Hymes, p. 249.
11. Dodson, p. 53.
12. Ibid., p. 59.
13. Anne Hitchcock Gilliland, *Understanding Preschoolers* (Nashville: Convention, 1969), pp. 86-88.
14. Meryl Welch, *Cradle Roll Handbook* (Des Plaines, Ill.: Regular Baptist, 1970), p. 3.
15. Eleanor L. Doan, *It's Never Too Early* (Glendale, Calif.: Gospel Light, 1967), p. 3.
16. Leach and Elliott, p. 25.
17. Marjorie E. Soderholm, *Understanding the Pupil: Part I, The Pre-School Child* (Grand Rapids: Baker, 1955), p. 15.
18. Welch, p. 4.

FOR FURTHER READING

Books

Barnette, J. N. *The Cradle Roll Department Can Build Your Church.* Nashville: Baptist Sunday School Board, n.d.

Brubaker, J. Omar, and Clark, Robert E. *Understanding People.* Wheaton, Ill.: Evangelical Teacher Training Assn., 1972.

Cory, Bernice T. *Cradle Roll Manual.* Wheaton, Ill.: Scripture Press, 1967.

———. *The Pastor and His Cradle Roll Department.* Christian Educ. Monographs, Pastors' Series, No. 21. Glen Ellyn, Ill.: Scripture Press Foundation, 1967.

———. *The Pastor and His Interest in Preschoolers.* Christian Educ. Monographs, Pastors' Series, No. 8. Glen Ellyn, Ill.: Scripture Press Foundation, 1966.

Doan, Eleanor L. *It's Never Too Early.* Glendale, Calif.: Gospel Light, 1967.

Dodson, Fitzhugh. *How to Parent.* Los Angeles: Nash, 1970.

Gilliland, Anne Hitchcock. *Understanding Preschoolers.* Nashville: Convention, 1969.

Hearn, Florence Conner. *Guiding Preschoolers.* Nashville: Convention, 1969.

Hymes, James L. *The Child Under Six.* Englewood Cliffs, N. J.: Prentice-Hall, 1963.

———. *Enjoy Your Child–Ages, 1, 2, and 3.* New York: Public Affairs Committee, 1950.

Leach, Joan, and Elliott, Patricia. *First Steps: Helps for Workers in the Church Nursery.* Cincinnati: Standard, 1964.

Rosenberg, Edward B., and Warner, Silas L. *A Doctor Discusses the Pre-School Child's Learning Process.* Chicago: Budlong, 1967.

Rowen, Dolores. *Ways to Help Them Learn: Early Childhood, Birth to 5 Years.* Glendale, Calif.: Gospel Light, Regal Books, 1972.

Smart, Mollie Stevens, and Smart, Russell C. *Preschool Children: Development and Relationships.* New York: Macmillan, 1973.

Smiley, Palma. *Handbook for Cradle Rolls and Toddler Teachers.* Elgin, Ill.: David C. Cook, 1969.

Soderholm, Marjorie E. *Understanding the Pupil: Part I, The Pre-School Child.* Grand Rapids: Baker, 1955.

Strang, Ruth. *An Introduction to Child Study.* 4th ed. New York: Macmillan, 1959.

Tested Ideas for Nursery-Kindergarten Teachers. Elgin, Ill.: David C. Cook, 1963.

Welch, Meryl. *Cradle Roll Handbook.* Des Plaines, Ill.: Regular Baptist, 1970.

Your Baby. New York: Metropolitan Life, 1960.

Your Child . . . From Birth to Twelve. New York: Metropolitan Life, 1966.

Filmstrips

A Little Child Shall Lead Them. Des Plaines, Ill.: Regular Baptist Press. Color. Ninety-six frames. With record. No rental charge.

Teaching Babies and Toddlers. Nashville: Broadman Films. Color. Forty-five frames. With record. Rental charge.

Additional Sources

Child Study Association of America, 9 East 89th St., New York, N.Y. 10028.
Children's Bureau, Superintendent of Documents, US Government Printing Office, Washington, D. C. 20402.
Curley, Lois, ed. "Cradle Roll Tips." *Teach.* Gospel Light Publications, P. O. Box 1591, Glendale, Calif. 91209.
Public Affairs Committee, Inc. 381 Park Ave. South, New York, N. Y. 10016.
Today's Christian Mother, Standard Publishing Company, 8121 Hamilton Ave., Cincinnati, Ohio 45231.

5

Understanding Twos and Threes

V. Gilbert Beers

What is a two-year-old?

What is a three-year-old?

That depends on the way one looks at him. He is many things from many points of view.

Biologically, a two-year-old is about thirty-five pounds of bone, muscle, flesh, and blood, stretched to almost three feet in height. He is a network of plumbing long enough to reach across the country a number of times, carrying blood, water, waste materials, and various other fluids. Add another four or five pounds, pull him up another three or four inches, and you have a three-year-old.

A two-year-old is a live wire from the time he awakes until he goes to bed. His life is one of self-discovery through which he acquaints himself with the big wide world. Even a week or a month can make a significant difference in his patterns of growth in total personality development. He arrives at the age of three when he reaches thirty-six months. Life with the two- or three-year-old is never dull, but can be frustrating for those who may have limited understanding of his development.

Mentally, a two- or three-year-old child is like a sponge: he absorbs unbelievable amounts of knowledge and understanding—sometimes more knowledge than understanding. He is learning the basics of life, such as good eating habits, good sleeping habits, bladder and bowel control, following directions, getting along with others, and talking well. So much is learned during this period that by the time a child is four, the basic foundations of his life have been laid.

Spiritually, a child of this age is a bundle of trust, ready to accept what his parents or teachers tell him. He is endowed with a limitless hunger

---

V. Gilbert Beers, Th.D., Ph.D., is President of Creative Designs, Elgin, Illinois.

to learn more about the Lord and His Word. Since he has not yet learned how to read, he must depend on others, especially parents and teachers, to guide him. This trust makes him easily pliable and is both an opportunity and a responsibility to those who teach him.

Socially, the two-year-old is a loner, even when he is in a group. By the time he is three, he has begun to mingle with the group. Family ties are very strong at these ages, and it is best not to pull too hard at these ties when introducing the child to a new group. In reaching out, he will feel much more comfortable keeping a strong hold on his family, especially on mother.

Temperamentally, a two-year-old, especially about midpoint between two and three, is sometimes called a "terrible two." There is a strong reason for such a label, for he is a bundle of frustration to anyone searching for peace and quiet.

A "terrible two" may be terrible because he does "terrible" things, such as thumb sucking, bedwetting, nose picking, showing off, getting into everything, tearing up things just to see them torn up, and a number of other creative frustrations. To a child of this age, life is a two-way street on which he must travel in both directions at the same time. His powers of choice have not developed enough to show him which is best, so he often tries both ways, "shifting gears" constantly from go to stop, this way to that, pushing and pulling forward and backward, in and out, and so on.

The frustrated parent may find it easy to say "terrible two" or even "naughty child." He may even be tempted to say, "Why can't my child be like others?" not realizing that his child *is* like others of that *same age.* What he may really mean is, "Why can't my child be like an adult?"

But twos and threes are not adults. In our rational moments, we realize that we want them to behave exactly the way twos and threes should behave, not as adults. The burden of understanding is on our part, not theirs. We must understand how the child is made and how he behaves and how he learns at this particular point in his journey through life. Then we will enter with a new enthusiasm into our task of guiding him.

Recognizing Behavior Patterns

The following case studies will acquaint the reader with some of the typical behavior patterns which one might expect from twos or threes, depending on their maturity. We must recognize that some twos are more mature than some threes, so there may be a rather wide range in the maturity level among individual twos and threes.

Karen. On a rainy day, Karen comes into Sunday school with her new umbrella open. As the teacher helps her fold it and then take off her raincoat, Karen bubbles with excitement about the new umbrella.

"Mommy and I went to the store yesterday. She got me my new umbrella. Isn't it pretty?"

"Karen, that's a very pretty umbrella. Did it help to keep the rain from getting you wet?"

"Yes, and Mommy says I must not forget it. She said she won't buy me another one."

"I'll help you remember to take it home, Karen. We don't want you to get wet, do we? God made the rain so the flowers will get wet and grow. But you don't need the rain to make you grow."

"But God doesn't have an umbrella, does He? Will He get wet?"

What characteristics are evident in the conduct of twos and threes as revealed through Karen's experiences?

Karen relates herself to her mother. "Mommy and I went to the store." Even though she is growing accustomed to her Sunday school and her teacher, there is a strong tie to home and mother, and she is anxious to tell about it.

Karen seeks assurance that her umbrella is all right. "Isn't it pretty?" Children of this age need assurance that their shoes are nice or that they look pretty or that they did something good.

Karen is very candid about her home relationships. She tells the disciplines as well as the delights of her relationship with mother.

God is very specific to Karen. He is capable of having an umbrella and of getting wet. He is a personal being, and Karen shows concern for His welfare.

Ken. When Ken's cousin comes to visit, he has trouble sharing and playing with him.

That's *my* horsey. *I* want to ride it."

"Ken, why don't you let Bobby ride your horsey now?"

"No, *I* want to ride it. It's *mine!*"

"Ken, look at these pretty blankets. Why don't you put them over these chairs and make a barn with them? Bobby can ride out on the horsey to get the cows."

Ken is ready for something new and runs to put the "barn" together, while cousin Bobby quickly jumps on the horse and rides. But the two play with their "own things," doing little in playing together.

What have you discovered about Ken that indicates he may be typical of twos and threes?

Ken has trouble sharing. He feels that because his toys belong to him, he should play with them.

Ken's interest span is short. When directed to something else, he is ready to go.

Ken is a loner. Even when his cousin Bobby comes to play with him, Ken plays with his choice of toy and lets Bobby play by himself. Sometimes they play together, but often their togetherness is really each doing his own thing.

Ken and Bobby use some imagination in their play. Chairs with blankets over them can become a barn. A rocking horse can ride out to a pasture to round up some cattle.

Kevin. It is almost time for lunch and Kevin is impatient to get something to eat.

"I'm hungry, Mommy. Isn't it time to eat yet?"

"Almost, Kevin. Why don't you play awhile until we're ready."

"I don't want to play. I'm hungry."

"Kevin, you can be my helper. Then we can eat soon. Will you help me put the things on the table?"

Kevin is glad to help Mother. He is happy that he can be a helper and happy too that he can help get lunch ready earlier. He hurries back and forth, putting on the things the way Mother tells him.

What does Kevin reveal about twos and threes?

Kevin is impatient when he wants something. He is not ready to wait the necessary time to get what he wants.

Kevin resists a suggestion to "go do something" while Mother finishes preparing lunch. He insists on his wants.

When Kevin is given a new and happy experience, he is willing to give up his demands temporarily. He is happy to help Mother, especially when he realizes that his work really is helping her and indirectly is helping him too.

A Comparative Profile of Twos and Threes

The following tables will help you point out how the characteristics of twos and threes relate to each other. One must recognize that a two-year-old is technically any child from two years and zero days through two years and 364 days. There is continuous growth throughout the year toward his third birthday. Hence, when we speak of a two-year-old in this profile, we are, of necessity speaking in a rather broad sense. A child of two years and 300 days is more akin to a three-year-old because he is almost three. But the profile should help to give some orientation to the general characteristics of the age and learning levels considered here.

TABLE 5.1

PHYSICAL CHARACTERISTICS OF TWOS AND THREES

CHARACTERISTIC	TWOS	THREES
Height	About 33-38 inches	About 35-40 inches
Weight	About 25-35 pounds	About 27-40 pounds
Posture	Slightly stooped, not fully erect; knees and elbows somewhat bent, leans forward as he runs	Walks upright now, swings arms more like an adult
Sleeping habits	Needs about twelve hours at night plus a two-hour nap in the afternoon; tires easily; is upset by confusion	May begin staying awake during afternoon nap time, but he should "rest" during that time anyway
Toilet habits	Does not yet have complete control; is still subject to accidents, especially at night during sleep	Should have good control now, except he may need to be put on the toilet before he goes to bed
Eating habits	Schedule is important, adds to his security; a snack may be necessary between meals, but should be small and simple; foods may include such things as slices of fresh fruit (oranges, apples), bananas, fruit cups, milk, eggs, toast, meat or fish in easy-to-chew form, cooked vegetables (peas, beans, carrots), pudding, graham crackers, juices, small sandwiches, soups, and lettuce	Schedule is still important; the same foods could be used with some variation
Dressing ability	Is beginning to dress himself; does best with familiar clothing that pulls on or off, or buttons in front	Has learned to button and unbutton front and side but not in back; can remove shoes and can slip in and out of some boots; has not yet learned to tie shoes

TABLE 5.2

MENTAL DEVELOPMENT OF TWOS AND THREES

ACTIVITY	TWOS	THREES
Reading	"Reads" pictures by telling what is in them; likes to listen to stories or poems; interest span is three to four minutes; enjoys repetition in stories; may ask to have one story read again and again; often adds his own thoughts, especially if encouraged by parent or teacher; Bible storybooks are good because they are true and child will believe everything he hears	Still "reads" pictures by telling what is in them; enjoys rhymes, nonsense verse, and making up his own stories; likes some exaggeration; alphabet books begin to hold his interest, although he has not yet learned to read; teacher or parent should ask questions while reading to child to stimulate his thinking
Drawing	Can use crayons but does not stay within lines; likes to show off his work to parent or teacher; can make simple things from clay or sand—cakes, roads, tunnels; can begin to use finger paint but makes crude designs	Is begining to draw distinguishable objects, designs, and letters, though sizes may be disproportionate; has begun to use paint brush; crayon work is less crude than at two
Singing	Rhythm is important, especially to act out something; may be able to sing short choruses learned in Sunday school; may sing in a group but does not carry a tune; enjoys listening to records with music and stories	Some threes are beginning to stay on pitch; may sing alone but sings better in a group; still enjoys records
Playing	Simple wood puzzles, building blocks, simple construction sets, sandbox, stuffed animals, large wood beads or spools to string, clothespins, and plastic bottles are good now	Still enjoys many of the same toys; also likes dolls, punching bag, small wagon, and rocking horse; likes to play stories and act out parts; likes to imitate others

TABLE 5.3

SOCIAL RELATIONSHIPS OF TWOS AND THREES

SITUATION	TWOS	THREES
Playing with others	Is a loner and may play by himself even when with a group; needs to play with others to develop special consciousness; is extremely possessive of his toys and must be encouraged (not forced) to let even closest friends play with his toys	Has learned to take part in group activities more than at two; may also try to bully or dominate others; is more group minded; more willing to share toys and will play with others in a group
Living with parents	Gets into everything around the house; can be encouraged to help but needs supervision; if left alone, can create chaos	Is learning not to get into everything; is eager to help mother or father when asked; enjoys being appreciated for his help
Going to Sunday school	Needs contact with others and needs to hear Bible stories and music	Learns to sing with others; learns simple Bible truths; needs to share ideas with others

SPIRITUAL LESSONS FOR TWOS AND THREES

Twos and threes are ready to learn such important truths as these: God loves me. God made the world. God made me. God takes care of me. God wants to help me. God is always with me. Jesus loves me. Jesus is my best Friend. Jesus is the Saviour. Jesus is God's Son. God gave me a family. Father and Mother take care of me. Father and Mother love me. God wants me to love brothers and sisters. God wants me to help my family. I get my clothing from plants and animals which God made. I get my food from plants and animals which God made. I can talk to God. I can please God. I can listen to God's Word. My church is God's house. (Chap. 10, "Teaching Theological Concepts to Children," lists other spiritual truths children can be taught at this age.)

Twos and threes are ready to express their love to God and talk with Him. They are ready to listen to Bible stories and learn Bible facts and truths. They may at times find it hard to distinguish between God and Jesus. They will see many illustrations of God's love in their early homelife. If they have bad experiences with their father in the home, it may be difficult for them to think of God as a loving Father.

Twos and threes are happy to sing about God and things associated with God. They like to come to Sunday school and develop friendly thoughts toward God's house, God's people, and God's Book. This age level is vital for laying an early foundation for a strong Christian life.

Meaningful Experiences for Twos and Threes

One approach to the understanding of twos and threes is through an understanding of those experiences which are meaningful to them. Experiences which may have special meaning to a child of this age may often be overlooked by the adult, conditioned to a different way of life.

The experiences given here have come from actual reports by parents of twos and threes.

Twos and threes often involve themselves in parents' everyday activities. Washing the dishes, a trip to the store, a trip to the laundromat, driving the family car, filling the car with gasoline, washing the car, and taking care of household chores are all of interest for the developing child. Often they will imitate these activities and pretend that they are part of the adult world, especially the world of their father or mother.

Twos and threes have developed an interest in planting, gardening, and cultivating plants. They are usually delighted to be included in digging, watering, planting seeds, and pulling weeds. But since their interest span is short, they will soon find that this is "work" and lose interest in it. They are also curious about the color and texture of leaves and flowers and their fragrance. They may find a special delight with a plant in their room.

Twos and threes have an early interest in simple tools, such as hammers, pliers, and screwdrivers. It is not surprising to find that toymakers manufacture wood or plastic tools for the young child so that he may imitate his father in household maintenance.

Making a scrapbook is fun for a two- or three-year-old. If a parent will involve himself in this activity, helping the child go through old magazines, clipping pictures out with the child's suggestions, and helping the child mount them in a scrapbook, he will find that the child has a growing imagination in the selection and use of this material. Pictures are chosen on the basis of the child's interests at this age level, such as pets, homes, farm animals, families, and other related subjects.

The child's room and his home are of special interest to him. His world is small, compared to older children, and the room and home form a large proportion of it. Thus, experiences that center on room and home are of special interest to him.

Pets provide meaningful experiences for the two- and three-year-old. They may either be his own pets or the pets which he would like to have.

Twos and threes are interested in the care of a baby in the family or neighborhood. They learn how Mother and Father hold the baby, feed it, and care for it. This may develop a natural curiosity in the child's own time spent as a baby.

The young child develops a natural curiosity and interest in thunderstorms. He often learns fear or courage from his parents' reaction to the storm.

Men who serve the home and community, such as milkmen, mailmen, policemen, firemen, and garbage collectors, attract the interest of young children. Since these occupations touch the lives of the twos and threes more than accountants, executives, or teachers, it is understandable that they should develop an early interest in them.

The family atmosphere is an important factor in the young child's attitudes toward God and His Word. If he lives with a family suffering from undue stress, it is more difficult for him to appreciate a God of love and kindness. Parental relationships, with one another and with the children, leave lasting impressions on the young child as he forms his early concepts about spiritual things.

The world of books is an important part of the child's vicarious experiences. At this early age level, of course, he becomes acquainted with books through parents who read to him. This in itself is an important experience, bringing child and parent close together physically and mentally. Twos and threes are ready to listen to short, simple, Bible stories and react to them.

This discussion has been purposely general because no two children are alike. A parent reading this will automatically compare his child with the characteristics given and will discover that in some ways, his toddler is ahead of what has been mentioned, or perhaps, that his child is not as tall or heavy or active as the average descriptions given here. This should cause no alarm.

It would prove helpful—and certainly very interesting—for a mother to keep a diary of her child: how he spent his day, what his likes and dislikes are, how he reacts in various situations, what he eats, what toys he plays with, what gifts he receives, and many other little details. As she looks back over the previous entries, she will notice problems or needs that did not seem apparent when they occurred; she will then be able to see what areas her child is proficient in and in what areas she needs to concentrate more attention. She could also alert his Sunday school teacher or day-school worker to be aware of certain habits he may be forming or ways in which they can encourage him.

FOR FURTHER READING

Barbour, Mary A. *You Can Teach 2s and 3s.* Wheaton, Ill.: Scripture Press, Victor Books, 1974.

Better Homes and Gardens Baby Book. Des Moines: Meredith, 1951.

Brubaker, J. Omar, and Clark, Robert E. *Understanding People.* Wheaton, Ill.: Evangelical Teacher Training Assn., 1972.

Christianson, Helen M. *The Nursery School.* Boston: Houghton Mifflin, 1961.

Chukovsky, Kornei. *From Two to Five.* Berkeley, Calif.: U. California, 1963.

Cory, Bernice T. *Debby and Dan Go to the Nursery Class.* Wheaton, Ill.: Scripture Press, 1954.

———. *The Pastor and His Interest in Preschoolers.* Christian Educ. Monographs, Pastors' Series, No. 8. Glen Ellyn, Ill.: Scripture Press Foundation, 1966.

Gardner, Elizabeth C. *The 2's at Church.* Philadelphia: Judson, 1953.

Gesell, Arnold. *The First Five Years of Life.* New York: Harper, 1940.

Gesell, Arnold, and Ilg, Francis L. *Infant and Child in the Culture of Today.* New York: Harper, 1943.

Gilliland, Anne Hitchcock. *Understanding Preschoolers.* Nashville: Convention, 1969.

Heaton, Ada Beth. *The 3's at Church.* Philadelphia: Judson, 1953.

Hymes, James L. *The Child Under Six.* Englewood Cliffs, N. J.; Prentice-Hall, 1963.

Jenkins, Gladys Gardner; Shacter, Helen S.; and Bauer, William W. *These Are Your Children.* 3d ed. Chicago: Scott, Foresman, 1970.

Klein, Sara G., and Gardner, Elizabeth C. *When They Are Three.* Philadelphia: Westminster, 1956.

Langford, Louise M. *Guidance of the Young Child.* New York: Wiley, 1960.

Llewellyn, Russ. "A Man in Every Preschool Department." *Teach.* 12 (Spring, 1971):6-7, 46.

Murphy, Lois B. *Personality in Your Children.* New York: Basic Books, 1960.

Pitcher, Evelyn G., and Prelinger, Ernst. *Children Tell Stories.* New York: International Universities, 1963.

Rowen, Dolores. *Ways to Help Them Learn: Early Childhood, Birth to 5 Years.* Glendale, Calif.: Gospel Light, Regal Books, 1972.

Royal, Claudia. *Teaching Your Child About God.* Westwood, N. J.: Revell, 1960.

Salisbury, Helen Wright. *The Church Nursery School and Bible Stories for the Very Young.* Los Angeles: Cowman, 1955.

Schoolland, Marian K. *Leading Little Ones to God.* Grand Rapids: Eerdmans, 1962.

Smart, Mollie Stevens, and Smart, Russell C. *Preschool Children: Development and Relationships.* New York: Macmillan, 1973.

Soderholm, Marjorie E. *Understanding the Pupil: Part I, The Pre-School Child.* Grand Rapids: Baker, 1955.

Strang, Ruth. *An Introduction to Child Study*. New York: MacMillan, 1938.
Thompson, Jean A.; Klein, Sara G.; and Gardner, Elizabeth C. *Before They Are Three*. Philadelphia: Westminster, 1954.

6

Understanding Fours and Fives

Margaret M. Self

ALL WHO WOULD FACILITATE a child's learning must first become familiar with age-level characteristics. Having a knowledge of the stages of development within a generally predictable pattern and recognizing the developmental tasks a child needs to accomplish enables children's workers to know the kinds of behavior to expect from normal children.

While Christian educators are concerned primarily with a child's spiritual development, they dare not overlook the physical, mental, emotional, and social aspects of his total personality. Teachers who are aware of this multifaceted growth pattern have increased opportunities to relate the gospel of God's love to every part of the child's being—to relate the whole of life to the God who designed man with a physical, mental, emotional, and social, as well as a spiritual, dimension of life.

All children at different age levels follow a certain general pattern of growth and development. Specific characteristics make it possible to predict how a child will most likely respond. Although a five-year-old is generally like most other fives, he is so influenced by his environment, health, heredity, and other factors, that he proceeds through his pattern of development at his own unique pace, different from all others. The range of normalcy is wide; no two children develop at exactly the same rate and in exactly the same way. So those who guide young children need also to be aware of the specific characteristics, needs, and abilities of each individual child.

Leaders and teachers should be aware that children of a given chronological age have certain behavior in common and should make allowances for each child's own inner timetable. This knowledge encourages better

---

MARGARET M. SELF, B.A., Editor of the Early Childhood Department, Gospel Light Publications, Glendale, California.

preparation in planning activities during which children can experience success and at the same time be challenged to extend their learning. For instance, the teacher who guides a group of just-turned-fours will select puzzles with fewer pieces than he would for a group of older fives. His group time (when all the children are together on the rug) will be limited to a ten-to-twelve-minute period for young fours. As fours grow older, the teacher will increase the group time in relation to the group's maturing attention span. With his fives, for example, he will plan projects requiring the use of scissors, for he knows that five-year-olds enjoy putting their newfound cutting skill to work.

Teachers who recognize stages of development are able to deal with most behavior problems in an easy, matter-of-fact way.

The four-year-old who was seemingly well adjusted and outgoing yesterday and who turns shy today may be going through a stage. Of course, the staff member will keep his eye on the child to see if the shyness passes in a short time. If not, he will examine possible causes. A child's growth pattern is often a series of mountains and valleys, ups and downs. Very rarely does growth proceed consistently on a smoothly rising incline.

Those who work with young children need to recognize that a part of each child's growth process includes a series of developmental tasks. Each child needs to accomplish the development of a strong concept of self-worth. This task includes achieving an appropriate measure of independence, relating successfully to peers and adults, and acquiring feelings of acceptance as well as developing a measure of self-control. A knowledge of these tasks and their importance in the child's total personality development will provide guidelines for planning specific ways to help accomplish them.

In his study of age-level characteristics, the teacher of fours and fives needs to be aware of the readiness concept. He provides a variety of learning experiences at the child's level and waits for signs of readiness before beginning the next learning step. Before the idea of missions is introduced to fives, the alert teacher will observe the ability of the child to see a relationship between two events. He will watch for children's interests in others and in the world beyond home and church.

"For everything there is an appointed season, and there is a proper time for every project under heaven" (Ec 3:11, Berkeley). The right time for a child to behave like a four-year-old is during the time he is four years old. Being four is not simply a time to get ready for five!

The qualities that come with being four or five are not imperfections or flaws. Early childhood is not a disease to be endured or cured like measles or the common cold. Instead, early childhood is the "appointed season" and the "proper time" to behave like a young child.

What are the behavior traits that affect the planning and procedures of those who guide four- and five-year-old children? What makes a child thrive? What accelerates his learning, and what stunts it?

Physical Characteristics

The person of four is in a period of rapid growth. He is a whirlwind of activity, running, jumping, climbing, twisting; he is noisy and boisterous. He seems to be constantly on the go. He is using both feet going up and down stairs; he hops on one foot, turns and runs, stops and starts quickly. He is stronger and more confident than he was at three.

His rapidly developing large muscles need exercise. Leg and arm muscles are developing more than those in his fingers. His body demands movement. He actually hurts when he is required to sit still for more than five or ten minutes. Wise teachers alternate physical activities with quiet experiences so that the child is not required to sit still for long periods.

The four-year-old is gaining in his control of small muscles. Although his use of these muscles is often not dependable, he enjoys attempting activities that involve coordination. He likes to practice zipping, buttoning, and cutting, but he has difficulty coloring within lines.

Constant activity causes the four-year-old to become easily fatigued, tense, or confused. His tiredness may result in unacceptable behavior. Teachers need to be alert for the child who is becoming overstimulated in order to redirect his attention to a quiet activity.

The child of five is in a leveling off period in his physical development, but he is still full of energy and vim. He is beginning to lose his chubbiness. He is getting taller—with longer arms and legs. He is a much better coordinated person than he was at four. However, his large muscles are still developing. Although he is less restless than he was at four, he still needs exercise. He is becoming more and more skilled at all motor activities, and his activities are increasingly purposeful. A five-year-old hits the beanbag target more often now than when he was four. Eye-hand coordination is improving noticeably. He enjoys using his physical skills. Often he wants to demonstrate his physical skill. "I can stand on my toes. Want to see me do it?"

While the growth rate of five-year-olds is slowing, girls are maturing more rapidly than boys in their physical development. Boys who become restless during a large group activity might be reflecting their physical inability to sit motionless for more than a few minutes.

The child of five is increasing in his ability to sing a tune, although he often does not sing on pitch. He enjoys assembling construction toys, and he can handle small objects and tie his shoelaces. He may still have difficulty in coloring within lines or cutting accurately.

Most fives are learning to print in public school kindergarten. Wise teachers praise their accomplishments but are careful not to embarrass the child who is not yet able to write. They find other areas in the child to commend and praise.

What does this brief overview of physical characteristics imply for workers with fours and fives? First, arrange the room with open spaces, to provide for moving about without bumping into tables and chairs. When space is at a premium, remove some of the furniture. Work on the floor. A good program for fours and fives offers both large and small muscle activities. Block-building with unit blocks, puzzles, home-living play, and collage-making provide opportunity for muscle stretching. A balanced program must include frequent changes in activities, from quiet to active and then quiet again, in order to meet the children's physical needs.

Mental Characteristics

Fours and fives are hungry for stimulation! They are curious. They want to know and are eager to learn.

Four-year-olds have discovered they can put thoughts and ideas into words. And people will listen. A powerful tool, indeed! He uses his newfound language skills almost constantly, liberally punctuated with "Why?" and "How?"—sometimes to get information, sometimes to gain attention. He has discovered that experimenting with words, such as making up silly rhymes, is fun. Often he needs assistance in distinguishing between what is real and what is imaginary. He has a foot in both worlds. And the tactful adult can offer guidance that allows him to save face. When a child relates an event that is obviously a product of his imagination, the teacher can say, "That was really interesting! Have you ever seen real lions we have at the zoo? How do they look"

Limited comprehension of time and space is typical of the four-year-old. He understands "today" and "yesterday." Such expressions as "a long time ago" and "far away" are adequate for both fours and fives in Bible story settings.

Fours and fives are literal minded. They accept the words they hear to mean exactly that. Symbolism and other figures of speech are extremely confusing and misleading. When a shy child is asked, "Has the cat got your tongue?" he presumes that to be a normal occurrence! Equating misdeeds with a "black heart" is also beyond their comprehension.

Five is the age of intellectual growth. Although he is rooted in reality, he has an active imagination. He knows the difference between real and pretend in his world of "I'm the daddy and you're the mommy" dramatic play. However, he is not always sure when adults are pretending. A child of five is honestly curious about the world around him. He asks questions because he wants to know. Chatting with the five-year-old can be a delightful experience. His increasing vocabulary allows him to use complete sentences. He is beginning to understand cause-and-effect relationships.

Adults are often fooled by the five-year-old's seemingly accurate use of words. They assume that because he uses certain words, he understands their meaning. This is not always the case. A five-year-old is great at parroting what he has heard on TV or from the adults. He often thinks he understands the words. Adults too may think he understands, but they need to remember that words are not yet the best criterion of what he knows or understands.

Teachers should be especially careful in helping the four- and five-year-old learn Bible verses. The goal for these ages is to build understanding. Be certain they understand what they are repeating. Again and again, with conversation, explanation, and pictures, build a groundwork of familiarity with understanding. Memorization may then be the eventual result, but do not make it the aim.

A five-year-old is able to use equipment and materials in an increasingly varied way. Blocks become complex buildings or a launching pad. Collages take on creative designs. When he draws a picture, he usually makes the most important part the largest. The five-year-old likes to have something to show for his efforts. He demonstrates an increasing interest in letters and numbers. "What does this say?" and "How do you make a *W*?" are familiar questions he asks.

Both fours and fives enjoy stories. Fives especially thrive on answering questions and talking about the story they have just heard. Older fives like to have the teacher begin a simple story for them to finish.

Concept of time for the five-year-old is confined to the span of a day. He is likely to tell the teacher accurately what happened that morning or what he anticipates that evening. He also recalls past events quite well, but not in terms of the time that has elapsed since they occurred.

The attention span of four-and-five-year-olds is sustained when they are actively involved. Listening experiences need to include related pictures and objects to illustrate the words they hear. They learn most effectively through firsthand experiences. Since they do not read to learn, they must depend on other avenues. They look, listen, and explore. They learn by active involvement as well as by sitting still, listening.

What does this say to those who work with fours and fives? "Let me do it!" is the familiar plea of the young child. By all means let them do it. Vary the lesson-related activities in which fours and fives can discover and practice ways to know and understand God's Word, His world, and His love.

Social Characteristics

The four-year-old is making a wonderful discovery—friends! At three, he still enjoyed playing alongside others. Now, he often consciously seeks out one or two children with whom to play. He forms little groups and excludes others, often quite rudely! Sometimes fours are shy about entering a group and wait until they are invited. They feel left out if others do not accept them. Teachers need to plan activities in which fours have repeated opportunities to take turns and share materials with perhaps three or four others. Like many other concepts in Christian living, this one is not learned in a single Sunday. Fours (and fives) need repeated opportunities to practice scripture truths, such as, "Share what you have with others" (Heb 13:16, TCNT).

In spite of his newfound enthusiasm for others, the four-year-old needs guidelines on how to get along with them. A simple suggestion from a teacher to a quarrelsome group often redirects the play that has deteriorated. "I'm the mommie! You're not!" can be turned by suggesting, "This family needs a grandmother too. Here is a hat just right for Grandmother to wear shopping."

Although a four-year-old enjoys interaction with other children, he is still basically self-centered. His points of reference are highly personal: "Look at my new shoes!" "I'm going to the park after church." "My mother ironed my dress." The four-year-old uses personal pronouns overtime! Almost all his conversation turns back to himself.

One of the four-year-old's most heartfelt desires is to win the approval of those about him, particularly the adults in his life. Often he feels that the end justifies the means. Grabbing, showing off, wanting to be first, and interrupting are frequently his tools to get attention.

The four-year-old is testing his world. He is often brashly confident, and may exhibit unacceptable behavior just to see how far he can go. He finds security in the very limits he defies. Yet he needs the security of limits that do not hinder his freedom to experiment. Teachers should be consistent and positive in their guidance, emphasizing the behavior they desire. For example, they may say, "We keep the clay on the table," rather than, "Don't put the clay in the book rack."

A five-year-old is a delightful child! He is usually friendly, enjoys playing with others, is interested in taking turns and sharing, although he may not always do so. Generally, he wants to be a helpful person. He seems content with himself and those about him.

His play is still limited to small groups. His improved language skill allows him to offer suggestions and share ideas. He has fewer conflicts with others than he did at four. Often he can resolve his problems without adult assistance. However, when such assistance is necessary, the five-year-old usually understands what is fair. He is learning to respect the rights and feelings of others. With guidance, he can develop a genuine interest and concern for those about him.

The child of five exhibits a strong spirit of conformity. When one child says, "This juice tastes sour," immediately others agree. Teachers can use this "strength-in-numbers" to foster consideration for the feelings and needs of others.

Adult approval is important for the five-year-old to possess. He actively seeks praise and is willing to cooperate to get it. He identifies with the adults he most admires—feeling with those adults, wanting to be like them, and emulating their actions. When adult-child relationships are warm and friendly, identification can grow. What an opportunity for teachers to put their Christian beliefs and teachings into practice!

Although the five-year-old is becoming a friendly social being, his world still centers on himself. His authority is "my mommy and my daddy." He interprets the actions of those about him in terms of his own needs and desires.

Emotional Characteristics

The four-year-old often exhibits his emotions quite intensely. At a moment's notice, he can burst into a rage. "I'm mad at him!" he will exclaim, usually with decisive gestures. His love and hates, joy and sorrows, fears and pleasures, are all very close to the surface. But these emotional outbursts are usually fleeting. In a few minutes, all is forgotten, and he is busy with a new interest. The child of five also continues to display his emotions, but his outbursts are becoming less frequent. He is beginning to discover other ways to solve his problems.

When a child exhibits strong feelings, consider these suggestions: Help him know it is all right to have strong feelings. Help him recognize their validity. Mirror his feelings by saying, "When Timmy knocked over your blocks, you were pretty mad." Guide him to express his feelings in a nonverbal way. Pounding clay is an excellent way to give vent to emotions. Teach him that he cannot employ the "eye for an eye and tooth for a tooth" concept. Assure him that an adult nearby can be trusted to protect him from his own hostile actions.

Fear is probably the outstanding emotion fours and fives have to live with. Fear is part of a child's growing-up process. It is an unfortunate child whose teachers or parents use fear as an instrument of discipline. (Of course, a child needs to fear some things for his own protection.)

A child's fear can be lessened somewhat by a teacher's thoughtful planning. For instance, avoid the details of the crucifixion story. These awesome events tend to overwhelm the child emotionally. Emphasize the joy that "Jesus is living, and we are glad!"

Young children often reflect emotions of the adults about them. When a teacher appears worried or uneasy, children tend to mirror these feelings. Children also reflect a teacher's calm, unhurried manner.

Not all children's intense feelings are negative. They can experience intense feelings of joy and happiness and sympathy for others.

Spiritual Characteristics

Spiritually, fours and fives think of the Lord God in a personal way. These children can sense the greatness, wonder, and love of God when these attributes are translated into specific terms within their experience. Simply telling fours and fives, "God made the world," is not nearly so meaningful as displaying natural objects for them to examine. Then, "God made everything in our world, even these beautiful shells," takes on great significance.

Fours and fives can think of the Lord Jesus as a friend who loves and cares for them. Jesus' love needs to be interpreted in specific terms. Since His love is often expressed through His provision of a loving family, guide the child by saying, "Debbie, who cooked your breakfast for you this morning? . . . Did you know the Lord Jesus planned for your mother to care for you? . . . He did! The Lord loves you, Debbie."

The child of four and five has a simple trust in God, the Lord Jesus, and in the adults about him. He is ready to accept all you tell him about God and the Lord Jesus. It is imperative that information be accurate; make sure the child does not misunderstand words, attitudes, or actions.

Fours and fives can be taught to talk to God, to thank Him, and to ask Him for the things they need. Assure the child that God answers in the way that is best—with "Yes," or "No," or "Wait."

Worship experiences— a response of heart and mind to the greatness and goodness of God—can be very real to fours and fives. Worship for young children is not limited to the time designated on the morning schedule. Moments of spontaneous worship arise most often as a teacher and one or two children are involved in an activity. As Brian was stretching rubber bands over his geo board,* Mr. Ross called Brian's attention to his fingers. "Just look at what your fingers did! I'm glad God made your hands to make such an interesting picture." Brian stopped and looked at his hands as if he had never seen them before. When Mr. Ross saw Brian's expres-

*A board arranged with nails or tacks around which a child attaches rubber bands, forming a geometric design.

sion of wonder, he said softly, "Let's thank God for your hands." Together, they prayed.

Wonder, joy, and gratitude are emotions closely related to worship. But they are not in themselves worship. A teacher, sensitive to a child's feelings, can help associate those feelings with God's goodness.

Fours and fives are beginning to recognize right and wrong. Their developing conscience is not only feeling what is right and wrong for themselves, but what is right and just for others. Fours and fives can know that disobeying is doing wrong. Children need to be assured that God *always* loves them and is ready to forgive when they are truly sorry.

A child's spiritual growth is somewhat dependent on his emotional maturity. Fours and fives think in terms of the personal, as they relate to Christlike people around them. The love and care of God the Father and of the Lord Jesus become real as the child senses love from Christlike adults in their lives. Teachers who live their faith in a relationship with children are channels through which God and His love can be made known.

Development of Tasks and Needs

Some of the most important aspects of early childhood are the least obvious to the casual observer. Every young child must begin accomplishing several basic tasks, the completion of which are essential to adequate personality development. During these years of early childhood, the child must begin to develop a sense of trust, a sense of autonomy, and a sense of initiative.† He began accomplishing these tasks soon after birth; he will continue through his life span.

These tasks are not independent of each other. The accomplishment of any one of the three listed here is dependent on the successful achievement (to a degree) with each of the other two.

TRUST

Learning to trust is the child's first task in the development of a healthy personality. This task begins as a newborn. He learns to trust when he discovers he is fed when hungry, kept safe, and given attention when he wants it. By the time he nears his second birthday, he learns to trust his environment, the people in it, and himself. This sense of trust is the basis on which his Christian faith can grow. As he learns to trust the adults in his life, a foundation is being laid for trust in God.

The relationships a child has with the adults in his life at church can contribute significantly to developing his sense of trust. The presence of a

†Erik H. Erikson, *Childhood and Society* (New York: Norton, 1963), chap. 7.

different worker each week means that he and that adult must begin a new relationship. This is too much to require of a child. Trusting relationships are more easily built when the child sees the same adults regularly.

Another way for the church staff to help a child develop his sense of trust is to listen attentively to what a child has to say. Keep the secret he shares, no matter how cute or trivial it may seem to you. Be fair in settling children's disputes. Know the facts first and avoid making hasty decisions.

Love is an important tool for a child to possess in his task of learning to trust. A child needs love that is unconditional and ever available and that expresses a concern to give him what he requires for all areas of his growth and development. A child needs to know that he matters very much to someone and that someone cares what happens to him. A child can tolerate many deprivations, but never total rejection.

Help the child feel that he is loved and accepted regardless of what he does or does not do. A teacher's actions, smile, even his tone of voice can say, "I love you." A smile across the room or a friendly pat on the shoulder is often enough to let him know he is important to you. Use his name often as you talk with him. Appreciate each child for himself. Often the child who seems the least lovable is the one who needs love most. Pray for that child and ask God to show love to him through you. Offer honest praise and encouragement. Listen to the child when he speaks to you. Kneel down to his eye level. Show a genuine interest in what he has to tell you. "You are our letter of recommendation . . . written not with ink but with the Spirit of the living God, not on tablets of stone but on human tablets of the heart" (2 Co 3:2-3, Berkeley).

A child needs to feel that he is acceptable just the way he is, that he is acceptable all the time, regardless of the way he looks, the clothes he wears, or whether he is "good" or "bad." A child who feels loved and accepted for himself—not for what he does—will gain self-confidence and feel valued as a person. If he feels he must earn acceptance, he may feel insecure and unworthy. His rebellious or aggressive behavior might be a means of attracting attention to his need for acceptance.

The child who feels loved and accepted by adults will find it easier to feel accepted by God. Help the child know that he is acceptable to God at all times. Avoid giving the impression that God will not love him if he is naughty. God's love is a free, unconditional gift. God never withholds love in order to secure obedience.

The young child is taking those important first steps toward finding himself as a person. When he is five, he usually begins kindergarten and moves beyond the circle of his family. He needs to know that while he may reach out for new and exciting adventures, he can depend upon his own world to remain familiar and comforting—that he can trust what he has come to know.

Knowing and feeling he is loved is essential to a child's feeling of security. Show him through your actions that you love him. Show him that he is important to you because he is himself, not because of the way he compares with other children. It is through experiencing your love that the child begins to understand God's love. When he feels secure and comfortable in your love, he will begin to feel secure in God's love.

Because the child finds security in familiar surroundings and procedures, plan a program that follows the same general routine each session. The child finds security in limits. He needs to know what is expected of him, what he can and cannot do. Set limits for the appropriate use of equipment and material. Avoid forbidding certain behavior at one time but allowing the same behavior later under the same circumstances. Consistency helps the child to be able to predict what will happen. Consistency helps him trust his environment and the people in it. Allow as much freedom as possible with these limits.

AUTONOMY

Developing feelings of autonomy (independence) is another developmental task the child must begin accomplishing. This is an area in which he needs the assistance of understanding adults.

"Let me do it" are familiar words to those who guide young children. This plea is evidence of a child's first steps toward independence. He is attempting to discover his own abilities. He needs to know he can do things on his own but with the assurance there is an understanding adult nearby on whom he can depend if he needs assistance.

Careful, thoughtful guidance will help the child attain independence. Give him freedom in choosing materials and activities. Free choice requires that materials be readily accessible. Arrange materials so the child knows where they are and can reach materials without asking for assistance and return them when he is through.

In order to grow in independence, the child must be allowed to assume responsibility when he shows he is ready. Give the child as much independence as he can handle. Encourage his efforts and praise his accomplishments. Because children's skills vary, the teacher needs to know the ability of each child in his group.

A child is not born with the ability to control his own actions. He must develop self-control with the careful guidance of adults he trusts. Developing this self-control does not happen overnight. It takes time. A child first needs to know what adults expect of him. After he has tested these limits and found them to be consistent, he can begin to develop his own system of self-control. By adhering to a well-organized routine and enforcing a few rules of conduct, adults encourage the child in his efforts to be responsible for his own actions.

To develop self-control, the child also needs consistent, positive guidance. He needs a balance between rigid authority and total permissiveness. He needs limits but with freedom to move about within these limits. When a child has received thoughtful and careful guidance, a learning process takes place, and the child becomes responsible for his own behavior. From this responsibility grows self-control, discipline from within.

INITIATIVE

Learning to develop a sense of initiative—the desire to go ahead and discover—is the third in a young child's developmental tasks. "What will I become?" he asks himself. He wants to discover what his place in the world will be. He wants to plan and organize, to put his own ideas into practice. He is eager to "get the show on the road."

Dramatic play offers a child opportunities to "try on" different roles. It takes initiative to explore the possibilities of becoming a fireman or a doctor.

Daring to try out new ways and taking on new responsibilities requires an atmosphere conducive to experimenting. A climate in which everyone must do the same thing at the same time and in the same way stifles a child's initiative. He soon learns that attempting new ideas (the results for which he might be blamed) is too much risk for him to take. Encouraging a child's initiative helps him in healthy personality growth.

A child can usually withstand other deprivations, if only the adults in his life help him develop feelings of his own self-worth. The importance of a positive self-concept is deeply rooted in biblical teaching. Jesus taught that a good self-concept is necessary if we are to be capable of loving others. So He linked love of self and love of others in the second of His great commandments, "Thou shalt love thy neighbor as thyself" (Mk 12:31).

This kind of self-image definitely affects a child's ability and desire to learn. It allows him to give his attention to the business of learning. It encourages him to explore and experiment.

Each child needs to be assured of his own unique place in the world of people. He needs assurance of his worth as an individual. Helping a child feel good about himself is not building conceit. It is, rather, enabling him to try, to be creative, to make use of his world.

A child's recognition of his own worth depends largely on his experience of love, security, and acceptance expressed by adults. How can a child feel acceptable unless someone accepts him? When he feels secure in the love and acceptance of adults around him, he can begin to feel good about himself. When he realizes that he has certain rights and dignity as an individual, he can more readily recognize the rights and dignity of others.

Summary

Those who guide young children often become so absorbed in providing adequate materials and equipment, establishing a workable schedule, and arranging for other elements of a teaching/learning program that they overlook the initial step in planning—understanding the child himself.

Knowing the ways a child grows and how to work with each stage of his development is not something that is learned once and for all. Leaders and teachers must continually refer to age-level characteristics and needs as they evaluate programs and processes. They must be sure their plans and procedures are attuned to the God-ordained timetable the Lord has established for each little one's growth and development.

FOR FURTHER READING

Anderson, Robert H. and Shane, Harold. *As the Twig Is Bent: Readings in Early Childhood Education.* Boston: Houghton Mifflin, 1971.

Baker, Katherine Read, and Fane, Xenia F. *Understanding and Guiding Young Children.* Englewood Cliffs, N. J.: Prentice-Hall, 1971.

Beyer, Evelyn. *Teaching Young Children.* New York: Western, 1968.

Brubaker, J. Omar, and Clark, Robert E. *Understanding People.* Wheaton, Ill.: Evangelical Teacher Training Assn., 1972.

Dixon, Dorothy A. *Growth in Love.* West Mystic, Conn.: Twenty-Third Publications, 1972.

Elkind, David. "What Preschoolers Need Most." *Parents' Magazine* 46 (May, 1971):37-39, 92-94.

Fritz, Dorothy B. *The Child and the Christian Faith.* Richmond, Va.: Knox, 1964.

Gilliland, Anne Hitchcock. *Understanding Preschoolers.* Nashville: Convention, 1969.

Hartley, Ruth E.; Frank, Lawrence K.; and Goldenson, Robert M. *Understanding Children's Play.* New York: Columbia, 1952.

Heron, Frances Dunlap. "Seven Things You Should Know About Kindergarteners." *Sunday School Leader* 64 (March, 1963):25-26.

Hildebrand, Verna. *Introduction to Early Childhood Education.* New York: Macmillan, 1971.

Hymes, James L. *The Child Under Six.* Englewood Cliffs, N. J.: Prentice-Hall, 1963.

Jahsmann, Allan H. *The Church Teaching Her Young.* St. Louis: Concordia, 1967.

Kaluger, George, and Kolson, Clifford J. "The Speaking Religious Vocabulary of Kindergarten Children." *Religious Education* 58 (July-Aug., 1963): 387-89.

LeBar, Mary E. *You Can Make the Difference for 4s and 5s.* Wheaton, Ill.: Scripture Press, Victor Books, 1974.

Nicholson, Dorothy. *Toward Effective Teaching.* Anderson, Ind.: Warner, 1970.

Read, Katherine. *The Nursery School.* 4th ed. Philadelphia: Saunders, 1966.

Rowen, Dolores. *Ways to Help Them Learn: Early Childhood, Birth to Five Years.* Glendale, Calif.: Gospel Light, Regal Books, 1972.

Smart, Mollie Stevens, and Smart, Russell C. *Preschool Children: Development and Relationships.* New York: Macmillan, 1973.

Tester, Sylvia. *How to Teach Kindergarten Children.* Elgin, Ill.: David C. Cook, 1964.

Todd, Vivian, and Herreran, Helen. *The Years Before School.* New York: Macmillian, 1970.

Woodward, Carol. *Ways to Teach 3's to 5's.* Philadelphia: Lutheran Church, 1965.

Zimmerman, Eleanor. *Bible and Doctrine for 3's to 5's.* Philadelphia: Lutheran Church, 1963.

Journals

Children. US Children's Bureau, Superintendent of Documents, US Government Printing Office, Washington, D. C. 20025.

The Young Child. National Association for the Education of Young Children, 1834 Connecticut Ave., N.W., Washington, D. C. 20009.

Today's Child. Edwards Publications, Inc., School Lane, Roosevelt, N. J. 08555.

7

Understanding Primaries

Elsiebeth McDaniel

PRIMARIES ARE WONDERFUL! Why? Because these six-, seven-, and eight-year-olds come to a teacher with distinctive personalities, but with a general eagerness to learn, an unlimited curiosity, and a variety of growing skills and abilities to help them learn through what they discover themselves.

Some primaries are shy, soft-spoken, and quiet, while others are active, talkative, and outgoing. But all are in their believing years. These children believe that a teacher is to be trusted and followed.

When a teacher looks at primaries, he cannot help but think, *Look, you are important to me. I am going to do my best for you!* A public school teacher may say this to a child and mean that he will help the child acquire a great deal of factual information in the classroom and apply it to himself. However, when a Christian teacher says, "I am going to do my best for you!" he is committing himself to prayer, preparation, time, and personal interest. He is promising to give a child one of the greatest gifts that any individual can give to another. That teacher is promising to be one of the few people in the community dedicated to helping the child come to know, love, and obey the Lord.

WHO ARE THE PRIMARIES?

In our present educational system, primaries are children in the first, second, or third year grade of school. Primaries come in assorted sizes, weighing forty to eighty pounds and standing forty to fifty-two inches tall.

Thoughtless adults tend to classify them according to size. If this were a good method of classification, the tallest and heaviest children ought

---

ELSIEBETH MCDANIEL, M.A., is Editor of Pre-Primary and Primary Lessons, Scripture Press Publications, Inc., Wheaton, Illinois.

to be most mature. But size is only one way of identifying a primary. A very small boy may be intellectually ahead of a husky, tall boy. Or a seven-year-old may have more spiritual insight than an eight-year-old. Therefore, if we are to help children learn, we must realize that observable physical growth is only one way to measure maturity. Children are also growing mentally, spiritually, and emotionally. We are teaching the whole child. "Learning experiences need to involve the total child if we are to avoid fragmented learning. If we are to insure the most effective learning possible, we must be aware of all areas of growth and plan for needs in each area to be met."[1]

The whole person, or total child, makes a difference in true learning, and true learning makes a difference in the whole person. Christian educators who see children mostly in church-related activities must realize that they see only one facet of the children's lives. Is the Sunday-school Jimmy the same boy as Little-League Jimmy or playground Jimmy? How can a Christian educator discover that Jimmy is the boy with a pet dog, a fear of the dark, a protective attitude toward a younger sister, and a growing appreciation of fairness and justice?

Next to knowing the Lord and His Word, a teacher must know his pupils. It is not enough to know names and addresses. The teacher must know a child and his problems—and all children do have problems. What are a child's likes and dislikes? What are his fears, strengths, and weaknesses? How does this child think, and what skills can he perform? Answers to these questions make a difference in the teaching-learning experience.

Any list of primary characteristics is only a number of generalizations. Books about primaries will be helpful, but a teacher learns most about his pupils by becoming personally involved with each one. However, even personal involvement is not enough. Children change, and the effective teacher will be aware of this. The gullible six-year-old of September becomes the wiser and more skilled seven-year-old of June. All children are in the process of becoming: they are not finished products. Do not let your mental description of children or of a particular child become rigid. Change your thinking about a child as he changes mentally, socially, physically, and spiritually. Keep up with him!

One easy and perhaps humorous means of identifying a primary is by his teeth. Pete may have white, even, attractive teeth one Sunday and have a wide gap the next week because he has lost his two front ones. All primaries are losing baby teeth and growing permanent ones.

One can also identify primaries by their built-in need to wiggle. The growing muscles of these children must have opportunities to move. How important it is to provide a change of pace during a learning situation!

It is important too that Christian educators recognize the variation among these children in the control of smaller muscles. Some children enjoy writing, coloring, cutting, and other craft activities. Still others become impatient if their efforts fall short of the standards they set for themselves. Art and craft activities are good ways of teaching as long as the children are interested, learning, and enjoying their work. However, no child should be pushed beyond his ability and enjoyment.

Primaries are entering the "doing age," which carries them on into junior years. A first, second, or third grader will learn far more by doing than by listening to his teacher talk. He will learn more by doing than by observing. His teacher, on the other hand, will learn a great deal about a child by being both an observer and a listener. "Children tell more about themselves through their behavior than through verbalization."[2]

A primary often expresses his attitude about himself and others through his bodily movements. Notice the way a self-confident child walks and handles himself. Then study the downward glance of a shy child, and note the small, close-to-his-body movements of his hands and arms. Boisterousness and giggling are at times the result of embarrassment, but at another time, they may be cries for attention. These attitudes may indicate frustration over something that seems impossible. Or high spirits can be merely a response to another child's sense of humor and the joy of a shared joke. As you observe children, you will notice that some behavior demonstrates a child's immaturity, whereas other behavior is the warning light of an emotional need.

Based on specialized study made by educators, we can make generalizations about primaries at each age. However, teachers must realize that children are not better at something just because they are a year older. The whole child must be regarded as a different person. An effective teacher continually revises his description and understanding of each child.

Who Is Six?

Six is an age of transition. This child is moving from his preschool years of accomplishment. Probably at no period of life does a child accomplish as much as during the preschool years.[3] He is now eagerly looking forward to being recognized as a schoolchild who can read.

A six-year-old is entering a wider world. He is more eager than previously for the approval and acceptance of his peers. Educators should be aware of him as a person who is sensitive to criticism and is concerned about being left out of the group. A teacher may criticize unconsciously if he comments on one child's drawing and fails to comment on another child's work.

Many sixes are quite immature, even though they may be as tall as second or third graders. Emotions are very near the surface. A six may cry as easily as a preschooler. He still maintains a close hold on home and the familiar as he tentatively reaches out to the unknown. He vacillates between the need for security and the desire to try new experiences.

Sixes may or may not be competent readers because eyes have not attained full growth nor ease in left-to-right movement. Therefore, the Christian educator is careful not to make reading demands on sixes. He must use visuals and methods that can be understood without reading ability.

Movement is one of the outstanding traits of six-year-olds! These young children must have plenty of opportunity to move. Sixes jump, rush about, and run instead of walking. They may try hard to sit still, but it will be difficult. Many of them seem unconscious of foot-tapping, twisting a lock of hair, shifting in a chair or moving it, or making facial movements. It is well to overlook this movement unless it is a disturbing factor to other children.

Though sixes enjoy activity, it does not always have to be purposeful. They will run, push, pull, jump, skip, or walk because it is more exciting than sitting still. To run for the joy of movement is more important than running a race with other children. Sixes do not enjoy competition. They are poor losers, and it is very difficult for them not to win, be first, be the best, or be the leader. Sixes need help in getting along with others and respecting others' rights and feelings. Though first graders are trying to leave babyhood behind, it is hard for many of them.

Sixes move as quickly mentally as they do physically. Their attention span is short. Do not expect them to listen to long explanations, descriptions, or narrations. Give them one idea at a time. Keep things simple! Help them thoroughly understand one new idea at a time.

Most primaries have very little understanding of spatial distances. It is hard for them to distinguish between Old Testament and New Testament events, because anything beyond their experience is simply "long, long ago." Do not try to develop Bible chronology during primary years. Some very mature primaries may begin to grasp sequential events, but most children will not. As Dorothy Cohen says,

> The existence of this very moment in time is so strong in the consciousness of children that the existence of a time before the important now is really hard for them to conceive. Even in relation to their own growth, they feel that they are as they always were, although they take it on faith that they were indeed once babies. The future, too, seems remote. . . . The same confusion holds true of space as of time. . . . Adults take this kind of knowingness about space and time as something that has

> always existed and assume that it exists in children, too. But careful study reveals that it does not emerge until a certain amount of maturing has taken place.[4]

Sixes are trying to determine the difference between reality and fancy. Christian educators must be sure to teach the Bible clearly as reality. Television programs are a continuing influence in the lives of children, but sixes are not able to distinguish between reality and fantasy in TV programs. Furthermore, if adults on a telecast or in life do wrong acts, it is difficult for a six to believe it is wrong. Six-year-olds believe that adults are generally right!

Most sixes cannot divorce the church and goodness. If a person is in church, even though the person may not be a Christian, a six believes the person is OK. These children find it unbelievable that some Bible people (Pharisees and Sadducees, for example) could be wicked, since they knew Jesus and were closely associated with religion. Primaries tend to believe that anyone with religious connections must be good.

Who Is Seven?

Sevens are very much like sixes. Many of the same characteristics apply to both age levels. Sevens grow out of many of these characteristics as they approach eight. A second-year primary usually has a very high standard of performance. That is why seven has sometimes been called the "eraser age." A seven-year-old wants to do perfect work to earn the approval of adults, his peers, and himself. He has learned in school how writing should look, how books should be read, and how assignments should be done. Now he wants to achieve that standard. Help him accept himself and his limitations. Do not minimize his attempts at perfection by urging him to hurry or by saying, "That's good enough." See the problem from his point of view, perhaps saying, "I know you want to do good work. Why don't you finish your work the best you can? Doing the best you can is more important than doing absolutely perfect work." Do not criticize a child for taking a long time. Estimate how long an activity will take and allow time for it, or change the activity. Avoid the use of involved and intricate projects which may cause frustration. Primaries will be discouraged if they do not succeed.

Sevens worry! They worry about not being liked, being late for school, meeting new people, and not getting things done on time. Do not set impossible standards, but anticipate that in their desire for perfection, sevens will work more slowly than either sixes or eights. Be sensitive to the needs of sevens because they are sensitive people who need more praise than criticism.

Eye-hand coordination is improving at seven. If children are competent readers they will enjoy reading. Seven is a cautious age for some children. Do not shove them into new experiences until they are ready for them. Maintain a friendly, helpful attitude as you present opportunities to try writing poetry, composing a song, drawing, or using a filmstrip projector.

Seven-year-olds are more ready to fight with words than fists, though they will fight with complete physical involvement. They usually stand up for their own rights and have a growing sense of justice for themselves. Sometimes they will argue for the rights of others. Be sure Bible and other stories are fair—that behavior brings its just reward. Children love the story of Jonah because he disobeyed, was punished, received forgiveness, and did right. However, they find it hard to understand how David could be just in pouring out the water from the well of Bethlehem when his men went to so much trouble to get it (2 Sa 23:14-17).

Who Is Eight?

Eights are not little children, but neither are they big children. They resent being treated as little children, but physical and emotional maturity is still a long way off. Because eights seem much more mature than sevens, it is easy to become impatient with any immaturity they may exhibit. However, eights are growing toward being juniors, and, in the process, they will become increasingly different from the descriptions given in this text for sixes and sevens.

Organized games are for eights. Sometimes these children will make up games and rules for playing them. Children of this age enjoy a best friend, but sometimes they also want an enemy. Christian educators may need to recognize this fact and build positive values without a condemning attitude that drives children away. It will be far easier for a child to "return good for evil" to a friend who makes a mistake than to an "enemy."

At eight, there is usually some resentment of the opposite sex. Boys often find it difficult to sit near girls or to work with them. Recognize this as normal, and avoid situations that give opportunity for this resentment. No amount of arguing will persuade some boys that girls are worthwhile. Ignore the situation if you can, and give the boys an opportunity to discover the truth for themselves at a later date.

Eights are more reasonable than sevens. They are ready to accept the fact that not everyone can do the same things well. Help each child discover for himself his abilities and skills. Do not make comparisons, but ask a child what he thinks he can do well. Then perhaps remark about some observation you have made that shows an area where he does well.

Children at eight have fewer fears than they had at seven. All in all, eight is a more peaceful and serene time than seven. However, an eight-year-old will be argumentative about some things. He is beginning to sense that he is developing some of his own values, and he may be right in his convictions. Christian educators need to develop his sense of rightness on a biblical basis. There are many Bible principles that eights can understand and live, such as, "We ought to obey God rather than men"; "Overcome evil with good"; and "Even a child is known by his doings."

How to Teach Primaries

Many guiding principles for working with primaries may be found in chapters 1 through 3 and 9 through 20 of this book. Suggestions here refer directly to the characteristics of primaries and how those characteristics influence the teaching-learning process.

Children are more likely to learn from what they can experience in a concrete, physical way than from verbalization—merely talking at them. Primaries are very much aware of their physical senses, and they use them to discover new ideas and information. That is why it is very important to use visuals, tapes, records, role playing, and dramatization with primaries. A primary learns more by playing the part of a boy who must make a choice than he does from a teacher's saying, "We must all choose what God wants us to do." When a child sees a filmstrip of God's people going through the Red Sea, he learns more than from a verbal description of the event.

Primaries love stories! What an opportunity to teach the Bible which is filled with the best of stories! Be sure that primaries understand, however, that the events taught really are in the Bible. If the event is unfamiliar, a perceptive primary may say, "Is that really in the Bible?"

Because primaries are still learning what is "really in the Bible," *never* tell a story using Bible names and background, without making it very clear that your story is imaginary. It is an even better rule not to tell imaginary stories with Bible backgrounds unless it is absolutely necessary. There are many Christmas legends and myths which are interesting to an older child but which confuse the primary.

As a general rule, do not use object lessons with primaries. Primaries think in concrete, literal terms. It is impossible for them to understand that a lighthouse can represent the Bible, or rocks represent sin. Older juniors and adolescents are intrigued with symbolism, but not primaries!*

The Bible is the source book for all Christian education. Every lesson should be based on the Bible. However, unless you are planning to write curriculum (not an easy task!)—you will do well to follow the material written for primaries. Curriculum writers usually do a great deal of research before deciding what Bible lessons are suitable for primaries.

*See chap. 9, "Children and Their Theological Concepts," for a discussion on Piaget's views on children's conceptual development.

They choose Bible material that will be easily understood and effectively related to a child's experiences. There is little for a primary to apply in the story of Jephthah's vow because it is an adult situation and the consequences of the main character's actions are emotionally upsetting. Then too because a primary will learn most through stories, curriculum writers for that age group select Bible events that have a story quality about them. Principles expounded by Paul in the New Testament are generally best left for study in later years.

What do primaries need? As do other children, primaries need worship, study, expression, and Christian fellowship. Particular chapters on these and related topics must be read and related to the material in this chapter about primaries. (See chaps. 14-19.)

Primaries are ready for all the basic truths of Scripture if they are presented on the children's level and related to their lives. When they feel guilty, lonely, or frustrated, they need to understand and experience the Lord's help. When they are happy, they need to associate the Lord with the good things in this world.

What specifically should we teach primaries? We cannot teach children what we have not learned ourselves. Remember, "Religion is more caught than taught." Probably most primaries think about God in a physical form. Their understanding of Him is related to their experiences with adults. They respond readily to the idea of God as Creator, but the thought of God still at work in His creation is difficult for them to grasp. If Christian educators emphasize such attributes of God as love, kindness, wisdom, perfection, and goodness, then maturity will bring about the fuller realization that God is Spirit. When a child asks, "What does God look like?" the teacher may say, "God does not need a body as we do. The important thing to know is that He loves us and wants us to love Him."

A primary can learn that he has a personal responsibility to God. He can feel secure in God's love and forgiveness. He can understand that God sent His Son to be the Saviour. At six, seven, or eight, many children are ready to receive the Lord Jesus Christ as Saviour. At this age, a child begins to put together a connected story of the life of Jesus—from the baby in the manger to the risen Saviour.

How should we teach primaries? In the ways they learn best. We tell them Bible stories because they like stories and can easily follow the action. We ask them to answer questions in order to test their knowledge and understanding of how what they know applies to them. We ask them to express themselves through role playing, assignments, art, and writing activities, because *im*pression—our teaching— must always be followed by *ex*pression. Expressional activities help a child put into practice what he has learned. Teachers learn through these activities what a child has understood and is willing to make his own experience.

More important than a rigid schedule is the variety of experiences primaries can have in church agencies. Storytelling, filmstrips, and singing can be accomplished in a large group—up to fifty children. However, original skits (or any dramatization), creative activities such as composing a song, writing poetry, handwork, or discussion, should be used in smaller groups of five to ten pupils.

Remember that each child enters the learning experience as a total person. Some activities for primaries demand his use of seeing and hearing; but other activities demand bodily movement, creative thinking, and small muscle control. Children need a change of activity—a variety of learning experiences. It is seldom justifiable to spend an hour in any one activity. Gauge the interest of the children, and change activities to meet their needs. About twenty minutes is long enough for most activities, and sometimes, a shorter period is advisable. Some children will learn more through role playing, others through seeing a filmstrip. Vary your teaching methods to reach the interests of all primaries.

It is much easier to read a book about primaries than it is to teach them. However, working with live boys and girls in their world will be ever so much more helpful and beneficial than reading. Let your reading be a guide and a means of providing as much information as possible. But the test of teaching is teaching! Even as primaries learn through doing, so must you!

NOTES

1. Barbara J. Bolton, *Ways to Help Them Learn: Children, Grades 1 to 6,* (Glendale, Calif.: Gospel Light, Regal Books, 1972), pp. 3-4.
2. Marjorie Stith, *Understanding Children* (Nashville: Convention, 1969), p. 5.
3. Gladys Jenkins, Helen S. Shacter, and William W. Bauer, *These Are Your Children,* 3d ed. (Glenview, Ill.: Scott, Foresman, 1970), p. 81.
4. Dorothy Cohen, *The Learning Child* (New York: Random, 1972), p. 140.

FOR FURTHER READING

Baker, Dolores, and Rives, Elsie. *Teaching the Bible to Primaries.* Nashville: Convention, 1964.

Bolton, Barbara J. *Ways to Help Them Learn: Children, Grades 1 to 6.* Glendale, Calif.: Gospel Light, Regal Books, 1972.

Brubaker, J. Omar, and Clark, Robert E. *Understanding People.* Wheaton, Ill.: Evangelical Teacher Training Assn., 1972.

Chamberlain, Eugene, and Fulbright, Robert G. *Children's Sunday School Work.* Nashville: Convention, 1969.

Cohen, Dorothy. *The Learning Child.* New York: Random, Pantheon Books, 1972.

Ginott, Haim. *Between Parent and Child.* New York: Macmillan, 1965.
———. *Teacher and Child.* New York: Macmillan, 1972.
Jenkins, Gladys G.; Schacter, Helen; and Bauer, William W. *These Are Your Children.* 3d ed. Glenview, Ill.: Scott, Foresman, 1970.
McDaniel, Elsiebeth, and Richards, Lawrence O. *You and Children.* Chicago: Moody, 1973.
Phillips, Ethel M. *So You Work with Primaries.* Anderson, Ind.: Warner, 1960.
Smith, Charles T. *Ways to Plan and Organize Your Sunday School: Children, Grades 1 to 6.* Glendale, Calif.: Gospel Light, Regal Books, 1971.
Stith, Marjorie. *Understanding Children.* Nashville: Convention, 1969.

8

Understanding Juniors

Marjorie Soderholm

BUILDING CLUBHOUSES, playing football, experimenting with chemistry sets, wrestling with their friends—juniors enjoy them all. Juniors are active and noisy and full of life. And they do not leave their interests and liveliness at home when they come to the church for Sunday school, worship, or club meetings. Juniors bring all of themselves along, sometimes to the dismay of the adult leaders. But to know junior-age children is to love them. They have a keen sense of loyalty, and if they know an adult appreciates them, they identify with that adult, are loyal to him, and learn much from him.

Juniors are in the fourth, fifth, and sixth grades in school, and most juniors are from nine to eleven years old. Though there is no one junior who is average on all counts, there are some characteristics that one can expect to observe and interact with when working with juniors.

ABOUNDING ACTIVITY

Juniors are on the move. They want things to do. Suggest that the books need to be distributed, or that someone is needed to lead the next song, or that you want to send someone with a note to the office, and you will have plenty of volunteers. They like doing things that mean going places—going on a field trip, going to camp, going fishing with Dad. This is true of girls as well as boys. One girl, now a third-year college student, appreciatively recalls the times she used to go hunting with her father; and even now, recalling these experiences seems to strengthen her relationship with her father.

Juniors enjoy making things, but projects chosen must be those which will demand of the pupils what they can do. Otherwise, they will respond

---

MARJORIE E. SODERHOLM, M.A., is a consultant and instructor in Christian education and Bible study.

with "This is baby stuff," and they will do a careless job. On the other hand, a project such as making simple puzzles for younger children is not considered babyish because it is a service project for someone else. One group of juniors enjoyed making the crafts in the leftover vacation Bible school craft kits the church had purchased, knowing that these would be used as awards for attendance and scripture memory in another Sunday school. Never once did the leaders hear those juniors complain about making something too easy for them. But if the leaders had chosen those crafts for the juniors themselves, serious discipline problems would have arisen.

Juniors like Bible stories of people in action. Hero stories are among their favorites. Juniors like to have a part in telling stories they have heard before. They like to act out the stories. They like the "guess who" part of a Bible story review at the end of a series, in which each group of children acts out one of the stories for the others to identify. This is in keeping with juniors' love for action.

Hero Admiration

The foregoing leads into the characteristic of juniors called hero worship. They admire people who do things they would like to do, people who are strong, people who help others. While nine-to-eleven-year-olds admire good qualities in others, they may also identify with someone who is not of high moral character simply because that person is popular and persuasive. Juniors may be carried away by some TV drama, often along with their parents, into heroizing a person and then wanting him to reach his goal, which may even be that of taking another man's wife.

Juniors need help from parents and teachers in distinguishing between what is right and what is out of harmony with God's principles for living. Without this direction, the tolerance level of juniors for divorce, drugs, killings, defiance of authority, and so on, will stretch to accept these things as a part of normal living. Then it will be God's principles of life, rather than the violation of those principles, which will sound strange to them. It used to be said, "Many philosophies of life are in competition for the minds of high school students." But the battle for the mind is being fought earlier now. Therefore, the teacher of juniors must realize he is entrusted to use God's Word, the Sword of the Spirit, for the purpose of influencing the minds of children to follow God's principles.

Loyalty

Juniors have many loyalties. As their interests expand, they want to take part in more activities. Thus they face conflicts. If the boys' club at church meets the same time as the junior band at school, the child may want to do both, yet he must make a choice. Parents and teachers should give him principles on which to make this and other choices. It is not sufficient for adults merely to give juniors the impression that they think the best children are the ones who choose the club at the church over a school-sponsored group. Adult sponsors of junior activities need to get together to see if some schedule conflicts can be resolved in order to allow children who wish to participate in several activities.

Juniors' loyalties should be directed to the Lord. Juniors need to understand that harmony in their lives comes only if they allow the Lord to be in control of each area of their lives. It would be good for adults to reevaluate their own relationship with the Lord, for if a junior is to see the Lord's power to bring harmony within a life, he will have to see it in those adults who influence him. For instance, if a junior wants to go to summer camp, and his parents say he cannot, the club leader—or whoever is encouraging the child to go to camp—should not say, "Now, you'll have to put God first. He has to come before your parents, so we'll pray that God will let you go to camp."

Juniors need to be taught that God says they are to obey their parents, and that God uses their parents to show them what to do. If their parents say they cannot go someplace, it is not the place of other adults to stimulate friction between the children and their parents.

If friction exists in a home between parents and children, the church worker who can help bring harmony to the home is active in one of God's prime concerns. God made the family tho basic institution of society, but many of today's children are growing up in fractured homes. A person who encourages a child to obey his parents is building in the child a respect for the principle of authority in his life. The child who catches this principle in his home understands what it means to obey the Lord more realistically than a child who has not experienced the authority of his parents in his life.

Competition

Juniors like to compete. They like team games in which they learn to cooperate with others, while at the same time they enjoy competing with others. Competition is good when it encourages one to do better than he might do otherwise. It can be overdone if the person works to gain for himself at the harm of others. Bible drills and contests can be used to help juniors know how to find the books of the Bible and to know what the Bible says. However, a Bible drill leader needs to determine ways to keep a drill from becoming a contest between the fastest one on each side with all the others acting as a cheering team.

Here is how one teacher conducted a Bible drill that kept all the juniors "in the running" rather than sitting back and letting a few take part. The juniors had studied the Ten Commandments, one lesson on each, for ten weeks. For the eleventh week, the teacher printed the Ten Commandments (Ex 20:3-17) in short form on a large chart, which was placed at the front of the room.

Then she selected several New Testament verses to be used in the Bible drill. For each of the verses, a team was able to make three points. The first child who found the verse earned a point for his team. The team on which five children had found the verse before five on the other team had done so, earned another point. After that, the child who had found the verse first was given the opportunity to make another point for his team. To do so, he was to tell which of the Ten Commandments the New Testament verse was most like.

This drill was helpful in accomplishing several things:

1. It helped the children learn the location of the books of the New Testament.

2. It helped all the children get into the practice of finding the books. The slower ones did not give up because of a "Johnny always wins, so why try?" attitude.

3. It caused the juniors to think of what the verses used in the drill said. The child who found the verse the first time had time to read and think while the others were working on the "five first" part.

4. The juniors were seeing relationships between the Old and New Testaments. This helped keep the children from thinking that the Old Testament had no relevance today, or that the God of the Old Testament differs from the God of the New Testament.

5. The children were reviewing without having a "dry old review."

Justice

Juniors have a keen sense of justice, which helps them feel more responsible for their own wrongs. They are not so likely as younger children to blame someone else. At least if they do blame others, they do not easily rest with the idea that the incident is cared for. They still sense some responsibility for their own wrong. This makes it easier for them to understand that God must punish sin, that Jesus took that punishment, and that they need to give their lives to the Lord.

The junior age is a time when children are responsive to the gospel message. Teachers should not push juniors into a decision of accepting Christ as Saviour, but they should be alert to their growth in understanding of who Jesus Christ is and of the claims He makes on a person's life. Many persons who say they accepted Christ as Saviour when they were children also say that they did not really understand what it means to have a personal relationship with Him, to have Him as the manager of their lives, and to be free from doubts about their childhood decision. This is not to say that a child cannot make a meaningful response to the Lord, but rather that he needs more than a few stories to serve as a foundation for his response.

Because juniors have heard many stories in which the good side wins, some may interrupt the Bible storyteller with the words, "Oh, Stephen will win; the good guys always do." Then when he hears that Stephen was killed, he may say, "How come God let him die? Stephen was good." Juniors can grasp the concept that the "good" person is the one who stands for what is right even if it costs him something.

Though juniors have a sense of justice, many of them have been influenced by the lax attitude of our culture and have only a vague understanding of the significance or consequences of wrongdoing. In one class, the teacher was trying to point out that although David was forgiven for his sin against Bathsheba and Uriah, he did experience some consequences for his sin. She, in trying to explain *consequences* asked, "What happens if you don't study for your spelling test?" The group of juniors did not seem to think much would happen. They said they would have a chance to try again, and if they did not make it, it really would not matter much.

This shows how pupils bring all of themselves to the teaching-learning situation in the church. They interpret what they hear there in the context of their experiences at home and at school. One teacher, trying to explain the idea of judges at the city gates in Jerusalem in Old Testament times, said, "Where is it that decisions are made today in our town? When we have problems to be settled where are these settled?" The answer given was, "At the psychiatrist's." Children today are familiar with home friction, broken homes, and psychiatrists.

Juniors recognize sin as sin when they hear stories of people doing wrong, but to see sin in their own lives is not so easy. This is not just because they are children but because they are human. Juniors do not easily make applications into specific areas of their lives on the basis of a general application made at the end of a story. They need help in seeing how the principle applies. It is too general to aim to teach the juniors that they should be honest. They knew that before they came to the class. They consider themselves honest because they would not rob a bank, or steal a car, or take another person's coat. Juniors need to be confronted with specific illustrations showing what real honesty is. What about keeping five cents extra change? What about saying we are ten years old if we are really twelve in order to get half fare prices?

Parents need to see what they teach their children when they fail to practice honesty. At a plane ticket office, a mother was purchasing tickets for herself and two children. When she gave the ages of the children, the younger one's mouth dropped open. The other, being "wiser" and having caught onto the mother's reason for giving false ages, just looked at his sister with an air of disgust which said, "Keep your mouth shut." The next time, the daughter too will understand the "advantages" of lying. If teachers will use illustrations like this, children cannot accept a general notion of honesty without thinking of areas where they are being dishonest.

Parents too need illustrations that will cause them to realize that they are the most influential teachers of their children. One day, a pastor who taught a course once a week at a nearby school was driving to that school. En route, he was thinking about his class and did not notice a fifty-mile-an-hour speed limit sign. Soon a patrol car stopped him, and the officer began writing out a ticket. When he looked at the pastor's driver's license, he said, "Oh, I'm sorry; I didn't know you were a preacher. If I had, I wouldn't have given you a ticket, but now that I've started it, I have to finish it." The preacher responded with, "I'm just as guilty as if I weren't a preacher; go ahead and finish it." That patrolman had an unusual experience that day: he met a man who accepted responsibility for what he did and did not try to get himself out of it. That evening, the pastor said to his nine-year-old son, "Your dad's name is going to be in the paper tomorrow. I was driving too fast, and I got this ticket." That father gained much more respect with his son that day than if he had come home bragging about getting out of a fine.

Excellent Memory

Many teachers of juniors have realized that juniors have a good memory, when a child comes up with, "But last week you said *I* could do it this week." The teacher of juniors cannot brush a child aside by glibly saying, "You can do it next time." For the child will remember that "next time" and will claim his rights, even if it means taking it out some way on the child who was allowed to do what he thought he was to do.

Juniors can memorize Scripture, but they need help in understanding what the passages mean and how they apply to them. If they have been coaxed or paid for doing what they ought to do, they may have their price for scripture memorization too. If rewards are given, children should not receive them for haphazard jobs. Otherwise, when the pupils work harder and do a better job, they may want a greater reward than the one that came easy for less work. The reward should be within the reach of all. If a child knows he will receive an illustrated New Testament on completion of a certain number of verses memorized, he knows he can reach the goal, even if it takes him longer to do it than others. If only the first one to memorize that amount of Scripture receives the prize, the others will quit early, knowing that they cannot win anyway.

Humor

Jokes and tricks are favorites with juniors. They make funny remarks to get the attention of others in the class. If someone gives an answer that is wrong, others will repeat it several times just to make fun. If a teacher twists up some words, juniors are alert enough to catch it and make some comment about it.

One teacher asked a class of girls to sign their names on a paper she sent around the table. They were to include name, address, and birthday; thus it took some time for the children to do this, and the paper was still being sent around when the teacher was ready to tell the Bible story. She said, "Now I want you to pay attention to the story even if that paper is still going around. You'll have to listen with one ear, and write with the other." Quick as a flash, the juniors were saying, "Ha! You can't write with your ear." Some juniors might have even demonstrated what it looks like to write with one's ear! This kind of happening is not necessarily a fault of the teacher, but it shows what juniors consider funny. If the teacher understands this, he will not take this fun-making personally.

Juniors need to be taught that some things are not funny. It is not a funny thing to have a big scar on one's face, or to have the problem of stuttering, or to wear a brace on one's leg. They need to realize that to mimic and mock persons with these problems is hurting the person who needs acceptance rather than rejection. They can be taught to be grateful to God for the healthy bodies they have. They need to realize that often it is the person with physical limitations who develops inner qualities that make him more like Christ than the person who has it easy because of his good looks and his abilities.

Hobby-Loving

Advertisers recognize that juniors love hobbies. They offer pictures of baseball players and coupons toward the purchase of model autos along with the purchase of their products. Juniors are collectors—stamps, models, ribbons from fair entries, sports equipment, and charms for bracelets. As a teacher visits the home of his pupils, his interest in their hobbies will contribute to a mutual appreciation between teacher and pupil. It is wise to encourage juniors to relate their hobbies to church, if possible. For example, if a boy has some stamps depicting different aspects of the Christmas story, he may like to bring them to class. The teacher could ask the group to determine the order of the incidents in the pictures on the stamps. He could assign a stamp to each pupil, lettting the group retell the Christmas story, each contributing the part which his picture represents.

Relational Thinking

By studying history in school, juniors are learning to fit events of the past in sequential order. This helps juniors appreciate the historical sequence of Bible stories, which in their earlier years were isolated accounts. Juniors can now understand that Abraham was before Moses, and Moses before David. Maps and time charts help pupils place Bible acccounts in order.

One Christmas season, a teacher of juniors took old Christmas cards to class. The children were asked to sort them into two piles: one pile was to contain cards showing the real Christmas story, and the other pile was to contain other cards. Cards with pictures of Santa Claus, reindeer, fireplaces, and so on, went into one pile; cards showing shepherds, angels, and manger scenes went into the other pile. Next the teacher asked the children to sort cards with the real Christmas story into two piles—one depicting events recorded in Matthew and one depicting events mentioned in Luke. Bibles came out at this point, as the children needed help in separating the pictures into these two piles. Then the teacher divided the class into two groups and gave one group the set of Matthew pictures to put in order and the other group the Luke pictures. Now they were looking at the Scriptures more closely. For handwork that day, they each made a Christmas card with the real Christmas message. They were invited to use any of the pictures, greetings, or scripture passages printed on the cards they had been working with. Each left with a card to send to someone with whom he wanted to share the message of Jesus' coming to earth. After Christmas, one of the boys in that class said, "I looked at all our Christmas cards, and we didn't get many with the real Christmas message on them." This boy was not from a Christian home, and his parents may have heard more about Jesus Christ's coming to earth to give His life for them than that Sunday school teacher ever thought of when gathering old Christmas cards for that lesson. This was a good use of juniors' interest and ability in the chronology of events.

* * *

Readers will notice recurring references to parents in this chapter. This is because work with juniors means work with parents. It is difficult for a teacher who has a child in a class for an hour or less a week to build discipline into a child's life if he is undisciplined at home. If a child attends Sunday school every Sunday for a year, which is unlikely for most children, and if the actual teaching time each Sunday is forty minutes, he would receive less than thirty-five hours of instruction in the Bible in a year's time. The junior may also be in a worship service and in a club program, but even that hardly doubles those thirty-five hours for most children, as far as actual Bible teaching is concerned. If those few hours supplement and reinforce what the parents are taking responsibility for, they can be of great significance in the child's life. If not, one certainly cannot say it is useless, but it is much more difficult to have an effective ministry in the child's life.

Churches must place greater emphasis on the role of the father in the home. To have classes and clubs for children and missionary meetings for women is not enough to accomplish the work of the church in the lives of children. Fathers are the key. They are to be the spiritual heads of their homes. The junior-age child needs someone to give him direction, someone to guide his loyalty to Christ, someone whom he can admire, someone to provide security through discipline, someone to give him an example of serving the Lord and dependence on Him. The best "someone" to provide these things is the child's own dad.

Sunday school teachers, club leaders, and other adult leaders with juniors can supplement, but not supplant, the role of Christian dads in the home.

Churches that minister not only to juniors but also to the junior's family, will find that their ministry to the pupils themselves will be far more effective.

FOR FURTHER READING

Brubaker, J. Omar, and Clark, Robert E. *Understanding People.* Wheaton, Ill.: Evangelical Teacher Training Assn., 1972.

Dobson, James. *Dare to Discipline.* Wheaton, Ill.: Tyndale, 1970.

Gangel, Kenneth O. *The Family First.* Minneapolis: His International, 1972.

Getz, Gene A. "What Juniors Think About Honesty." *Teach* 12 (Fall, 1970): 4-5.

Jersild, Arthur. *Child Psychology.* Englewood Cliffs, N. J.: Prentice-Hall, 1968.

McDaniel, Elsiebeth. *How to Become God's Child.* Wheaton, Ill.: Scripture Press, 1970.

McDaniel, Elsiebeth, and Richards, Lawrence O. *You and Children.* Chicago: Moody, 1973.

Ramler, Phyllis, and Iverson, Gerry. "A Teacher's Case Book: Juniors." *Teach* 13 (Spring, 1972):39.

Smith, Charles T. *Ways to Plan and Organize Your Sunday School: Children, Grades 1 to 6.* Glendale, Calif.: Gospel Light, Regal Books, 1971.

Soderholm, Marjorie E. *Explaining Salvation to Children.* Minneapolis: His International, 1962.

———. *The Junior: A Handbook for the Sunday School Teacher.* Reprint. Grand Rapids: Baker, 1968.

———. *Salvation—Then What?* Minneapolis: Free Church, 1968.
———. "Teaching Junior Children." In *An Introduction to Evangelical Christian Education.* Ed. J. Edward Hakes. Chicago: Moody, 1964.
———. *Understanding the Pupil: Part II, The Primary and Junior Child.* Grand Rapids: Baker, 1956.

Part III

THEOLOGY FOR CHILDREN

9

Children and Their Theological Concepts

Norman Wakefield

DURING THE YEARS OF CHILDHOOD, the youngster is confronted with an awesome task. He must draw from bits and pieces of information and experiences and construct a world of reality. At birth, he is a tiny, responding creature, knowing little of the world. By the time he has completed high school, he will not only have amassed a remarkable fund of information, but this information will have been organized through cognitive processes into an unbelievably complex data bank.

An understanding of how the child forms concepts from images and percepts is vital to the Christian educator. He must appreciate how crucial it is that the growing child gain clear, accurate concepts related to God, Christ, the Holy Spirit, sin, death, and such. The educator should understand the process whereby concept formation occurs. He needs to ponder why theological misconceptions occur and what Christian parents and teachers can do to aid the child in accurate concept formation.

One might define a concept as "an image or representation whereby objects, events, or experiences may be classified and distinguished." Thus, when input from various sources and experiences is analyzed, one observes characteristics which tend to be common to all situations. These common attributes are incorporated to develop a concept.

Figure 1 illustrates the range of information that is used in concept building. Through the wide range of experiences with his own father, through visual representations of God the Father, and through stories and interpretations, a concept of God the Father gradually emerges. It may be grossly distorted or remarkably accurate, depending on a number of factors to be discussed later.

NORMAN WAKEFIELD, Ed.D., is Assistant Professor of Christian Education, Talbot Theological Seminary, La Mirada, California.

FIG. 1. *How a child's concept of God is formed*

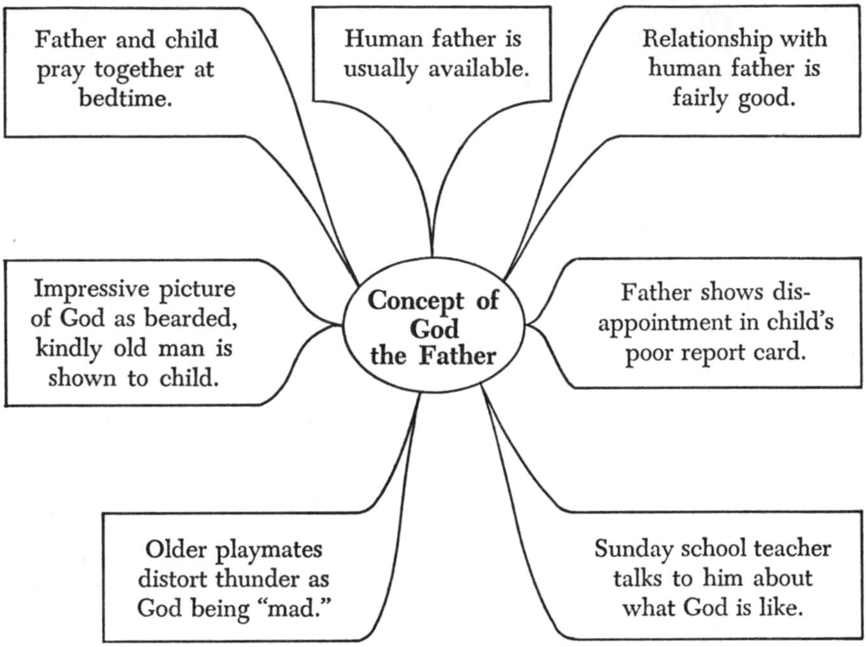

FACTORS INFLUENCING THEOLOGICAL CONCEPTS

Significant factors create a wide range of differences in the theological concepts of children. Two children in the same Sunday school class may have such a diverse background of personal experience and Christian training that one grasps the rudimentary elements of the Trinity, whereas the other has no concept in this area. Thus one might well ask, What influences the development of theological concepts?

1. Definite theological concepts do not appear to develop until in later childhood. However, *impressions* and *awarenesses* early in childhood are very influential in forming the foundation for theological concepts later on. Erikson has pointed out that the child develops his basic sense of trust and mistrust in the first eighteen months of life.[1] Before a child understands what it means to trust God, he has formulated feelings and attitudes about trust. The child who from infancy has experienced an emotionally warm, dependable home environment is better able to develop healthy attitudes toward life. He gains positive impressions of interpersonal relations, a sense of orderliness toward life, and an awareness of a harmonious world. These impressions are not rationally thought through, but felt within. As such, they are inner, unseen forces which shape future concepts toward God, the Bible, the universe, self, and others.

2. *Parents* possess great power to influence the roots of theological concepts. Erb notes, "The goodness of God can be learned by analogy from the goodness of father, the comfort of God from the comforting of a dear mother."[2] Christian parents have the privilege of conveying the reality of God as a living person who is vitally concerned about individuals. Parents interpret life events to the young in ways which reveal the many-faceted nature of God.

The parent's role is crucial for two reasons. First, he largely controls the quality of affective relationships in the early years. These relationships are the experiential structure on which the later concepts rest. Second, parents can most effectively stimulate the child intellectually as well as interpret the world to the child. Both mother and father can enrich the child's early precepts through conversation about God, reading well-chosen Bible stories, singing unto the Lord, praying with the child, and observing the wonders of God's world. Through these impressions, the young child builds up a valuable supply of positive, accurate images and precepts from which concepts will emerge.

"Though some parents would like to deny it, their children's concept of God is largely determined by what they as parents are."[3] An excellent example of the impact parents—and grandparents—can have upon their children's spiritual development is found in 2 Timothy 1:5. Paul indicates that the vital faith of both mother and grandmother had been communicated to son Timothy. Doctrine must be impregnated with a living experience of the reality of those truths.

Other significant persons also influence a child's understanding of spiritual concepts. His Sunday school teachers regularly confront him with Christian theological concepts embodied in songs and choruses, Bible stories, prayer, and related learning activities. Either through the communication process or in the actual content of the materials, children often pick up faulty ideas and images. For example, one young child is reported to have tearfully exclaimed, "Oh, Mommy, I am so frightened that the Lord Jesus will come out of my heart, it is beating so hard!"[4] Thus the quality of teaching within the children's agencies of the local church is a contributing factor to theological concept development.

3. Another factor influencing concept formation is the child's *intellectual development*. The Lord appears to have built a timetable within man whereby his intellectual development unfolds progressively. Studies by Jean Piaget and others have stressed that the young child does not have the mental structure to handle abstract concepts. The infant begins with a small number of impressions and gradually builds an ever enlarging network of experiences and impressions. Overstimulation to facilitate a more rapid intellectual development does not appear profitable. It amounts

to pouring in data more rapidly than the computer is programmed to assimilate. From the Christian perspective, overstimulation of the young child with too many Bible facts and "advanced" concepts will likely lead to confusion and distortion on the part of the child. One is reminded of the counsel of Garrison, "It should be emphasized that if the church is to be effective in character training, the teaching must follow the fundamental principles of learning set forth in educational psychology."[5]

4. A fourth factor that influences concept formation is the child's *level of language development and enrichment.* The ability to use words provides the youngster with symbols by which he can "handle" images and precepts. This is a necessary step before the child can generalize and comprehend objective concepts. In fact, Chomsky has noted that children often do not know the grammatical construction which is necessary to understand or interpret concepts.[6]

When the child's environment is void of conversation concerning spiritual topics, his development in this area is stunted. In many non-Christian homes, the child hears ideas and attitudes which are distortions of spiritual truth. It is unrealistic to expect a child coming to Sunday school from a non-Christian home to have an adequate and accurate vocabulary of biblical ideas related to God, Christ, and salvation.

The Process of Concept Development

"A person's relationship to God does not come within the bounds of human measurement. Nor can it be quantitatively known to what extent a faith has become vital enough to be shared with others. The inner core of Christian motivation is known only to God."[7]

The Christian educator must always respect the inner supernatural working of the Spirit of God in the life of the child. Christian educators should be careful not to limit what they think a child can do, because of research by behavioral scientists. At the same time, the discerning Christian educator may be aware of human behavior and child development.

The research of Jean Piaget has provided much insight into the process of concept development. Piaget has pointed out that the newborn enters the world with little more intellectual ability than mere reflex mechanisms. The infant's intellectual development consists of a progressive capacity to differentiate and integrate, utilizing the reflex mechanisms in his experience. Incoming external data is assimilated with existing internal data through an enlarging mental capacity. Until approximately eighteen to twenty-four months of age, the child is not able to produce a symbolic representation which makes possible a memory of past events as well as an anticipation of future events.

In these first eighteen to twenty-four months, the infant is gaining very influential awarenesses about the world he has entered. In the early months, he has no distinct sense of time, space, distance, or relationships. Through the slow process of experimenting with his environment and constantly assimilating new sensory data with existing impressions, the most basic structuring of his experiences begins.

The Christian educator should not minimize the seriousness of the infant's task. He is being forced to begin piecing together his design of reality. Taking bits and pieces of data from personal experimentations, parents, and other persons, he must come to understand his world. Too often adults hold a simplistic view of childhood ("he's just playing"), failing to realize the consequences of the early impressions and awarenesses. Each event in the child's life is an occasion for learning whereby the child's world of reality is enlarged and verified.

Following this foundational birth-to-two-year-old period, there appear to be three periods in the development of the child's maturity in forming concepts. Using age divisions suggested by Piaget, the following periods are identified: two to seven years, preconceptual period; seven to eleven years, period of concrete concepts; eleven to fifteen years, period of abstract concepts. The reader is encouraged not to view these as rigid divisions but helpful approximations. Concept development actually is a progressive development moving from disorganized to organized, formless to form, concrete to abstract, literal to symbolic.

PRECONCEPTUAL PERIOD

The preconceptual period ranges from ages two to seven. When the young child begins to talk, he gains a valuable tool for exploring his world. He is not restricted to action alone but can probably seek explanations. Language ability provides opportuntiy to explore ideas. Parents frequently are overwhelmed at the persistent questions that are voiced by the preschooler. "Where is Jesus?" "Who is God?" "Where does He live?" "Where is heaven?" One study of 6,000 children between the ages of three and twelve revealed that four- and five-year-olds asked more questions about God than any other age group.[8] The parent who can patiently respond to the youngster's inquiry both provides information and builds a relationship with the child.

Several characteristics of the child's thinking process at this age are important for parents and teachers to understand. First, he has little capacity to grasp concepts of *time, distance, numbers,* and *reversibility*. To speak of Jesus as having lived on earth 2,000 years ago is meaningless to the young child, for he has no concept of 2,000 years. Even though the five-year-old may say that he is five-years-old, he is repeating information that he has been given without grasping its meaning. Even brief periods of time, say thirty minutes, are not understood. The young child can better understand time in relationship to another event. "After Mother finishes the dishes, she will take you for a walk."

Concepts of distance and number have little meaning to the child unless they are transferred into measurement that he can see. For this reason, biblical data must be expressed in statements such as, "There were many, many, people listening to Jesus," rather than indicating a specific number.

FIG. 2. *The difference between preconceptual and conceptual thinking*

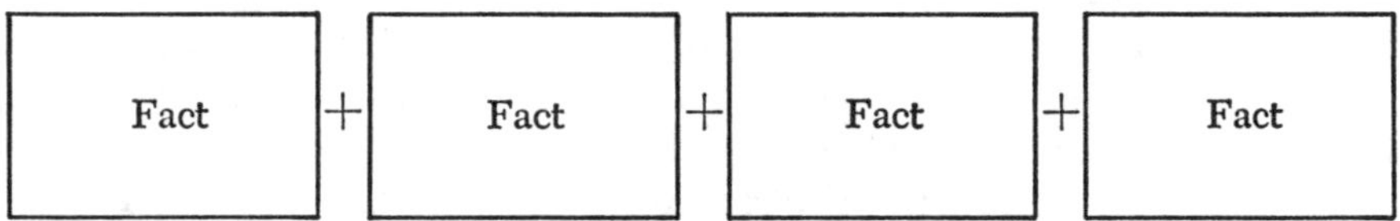

Preconceptual Thinking

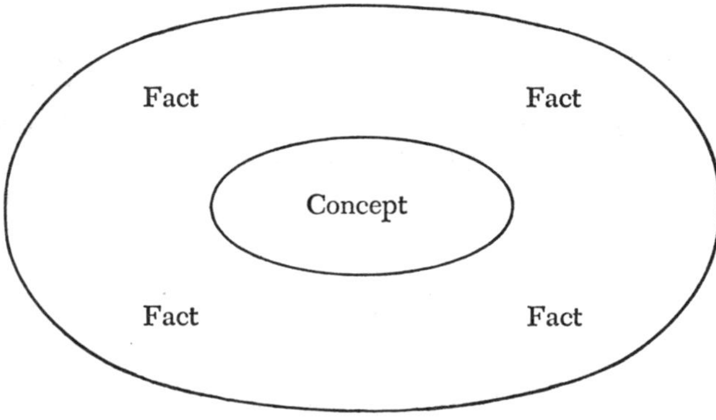

Conceptual Thinking

Second, the child's preconceptual thinking during this period is *transductive.* (See fig. 2.) The child tends to relate ideas on a one-to-one basis. He has difficulty making mental comparisons, but must build them up one at a time. He cannot group ideas together and draw a central principle. Each incident is taken separately because the child has such limited conceptual framework.

One important application of transductive thinking focuses on the child's response to what he learns from the Bible. Since he cannot generalize his learnings, application must be made specifically to a tangible situation. "Studies in honesty among children have shown that young children must learn moral behavior in specific situations; such learnings are later integrated into a unifying concept."[9]

The limitations of transductive thinking have implications for theological concepts. It is very difficult for the child to integrate information into an overall concept of Jesus Christ, sin, or death. As the child develops in the later part of this period (four to six years), he will have an increasing capacity to generalize his intellectual experience, to formulate the rudiments or relationships necessary for a conceptual hierarchy, and to assimilate ideas and preconcepts on a broader scale.

Parents and teachers often fail to grasp the importance of the child's inability to think conceptually. The youngster hears such statements as, "God made the world," "God is everywhere," "God lives in heaven," "God sent Jesus to earth," "God can see us." He lacks the ability, however, to focus this information into a meaningful, unified whole. Thus, the statements remain disjointed, even to the point that two statements, one immediately after the other, are in direct conflict.

Third, during the preconceptual period, the child's thought is characterized by *syncretism*. Syncretistic thinking links items and events or experiences that do not belong together. This may occur partly because the child cannot classify many relations. Susan may ask Mr. Jenkins, "Where is your mother?" Upon questioning, it is discovered that Susan was actually referring to Mr. Jenkins' wife, but she would not grasp the husband-wife concept. From a theological standpoint, the child may link ideas of God with ideas which are not related to God.

Fourth, preconceptual thought is dominated by *centering*. Centering refers to the tendency of the child to focus his attention on one characteristic or feature of an idea or experience and fail to see other important aspects. Thus, young children may listen to a Bible story and miss some aspects because their attention is focused on only one aspect. The young child has difficulty seeing the pattern or scope of an event. The same is true of visual experiences. A teacher, for example, may be visualizing the account of Jesus' triumphal entry, but little Johnny is so intrigued by the donkey that he misses other aspects of the account that the teacher considers more important.

Fifth, the thinking of the child during this period is *artificial* or *humanistic*. That is, he tends to assert that events in the natural world are caused by people. For example, he thinks of lightning or the movement of clouds as caused directly by people. Being highly imaginative, the child cannot distinguish clearly between the world of reality and the world of make-believe. Therefore, his preconcepts of God may not only be poorly related, but may also have dimensions which reflect the child's world of fantasy.

The following account reflects how much artificialism can influence a youngster's behavior: "A little boy hasn't eaten up his plums. It thunders that night. He comes downstairs in his pajamas to eat up his plums; he is afraid that God is angry with him."[10]

Sixth, the young child is *egocentric* in his thinking. *Egocentricism* should not be equated with selfishness. Rather it reflects the child's inability to see an idea, event, or experience from another person's perspective. For this reason, it is difficult to convey the concept of sharing, or help the child to understand how another child may feel.

One may well ask, "What are the implications of these limitations in the thinking ability of the two-to-seven-year-olds?" One obvious point is that parents and teachers must not expect too much of children at this age. Strictly speaking, the child may have difficulty developing and relating theological concepts during the preconceptual period. He has images and preconcepts, but his thinking is fragmentary and discrete. He is endeavoring to understand who God is, but his intellectual powers are not sufficiently developed to piece all the information together.

A second point is that the biblical information the child is given must be accurate and broken down to his level of comprehension. In spite of the limitations in the young child's thinking, parents and teachers must not neglect the opportunity to teach the Bible. According to Richards, "Whatever approach we take to preschool Christian education, it cannot neglect the Word and words of God, made understandable to tots on the threshold of learning."[11] It is an excellent time to create an awareness of God, as well as providing clear, accurate data concerning Bible events and truths. As parents endeavor to express the reality of Christ in the home, the young child can sense that God is a real person—though unseen—one who is powerful, compassionate, and concerned about the child, his family, and others.

A third implication is warranted. Young children gain a preconceptual awareness of the nature of God through observing others who express the love of God through their behavior. It is interesting to note that many of the young child's questions concerning God relate to his activity, which may be the child's way of investigating the nature of God as a *person*. For example, a five-year-old girl asks her mother, "God watches over us, doesn't he, Mother? He won't let anything hurt us?" This child is exploring the person of God in a most practical manner.[12]

CONCRETE CONCEPTS PERIOD

Between the ages of seven and eleven, the child begins to think in literal, or concrete, terms. The transition from the preconceptual period to the concrete concepts period is a movement from perceptions to intellectual operations. The level of development is significant because it represents a period when a form of conceptualization is possible. However, limitations accompany this advancement, and it is well to understand what they are.

During this period, the youngster is limited in his verbal reasoning. When children are asked to use verbal propositions rather than objects, they must consider one statement at a time in reasoning the proposition through. This would suggest that the ability to manipulate theological concepts becomes very difficult as the concept becomes more abstract.

Related to the above limitation, the seven-to-eleven-year-old is poor at generalizing beyond particular situations or examples. His intellectual abilities are restricted to physical actions which he can internalize. Thus, his understanding of theological concepts is limited to generalizations of specific incidents or information before him. Children within this age group wrestle with the concept of the Trinity, but find it difficult to grasp, because it is hard to conceive concretely. One must be careful to distinguish between a child's affirmation of belief in the Trinity and a conceptual understanding of the truth. Adults often mistakenly believe that because a child verbally acknowledges a theological concept, he genuinely understands what it means. A child's response, "Father, Son, and Holy Spirit" to the question, "What is the Trinity?" is not evidence that he has a concept of the Trinity. More likely, it demonstrates his ability to answer a question with facts he has previously acquired.

Probably the most significant advancement in the child's development during this period is his enlarging ability to classify data. This is a significant development toward forming theological concepts, for the youngster is formulating structures to categorize and identify common elements. As his skill at grouping common relationships becomes greater, the ability to form concepts grows.

Now that the child is gaining skill at grouping information, notable features become evident. At about nine years of age, children are becoming more competent at developing hierarchy of classes and relationships. For example, a child now begins to grasp divisions in the Bible, such as the minor prophets, the gospels, and the epistles. As he matures, he gains facility at working with multiplication of classes, such as the second of the Pauline epistles.

Grouping skills are invaluable for concept formation for two reasons. First, the child begins to comprehend what is included in that particular concept. When data can be classified according to certain relationships it is more easily categorized. Second, however of equal importance, the person has the power to determine what is to be excluded. He can ask, Is this information consistent with other facts I know about the topic?

At least six classifying operations are needed for concept building. The activities included are: (1) combining information; (2) distinguishing or separating; (3) dividing information into subgroupings; (4) organizing by placing in order; (5) substituting; and (6) repeating. Through these processes, the learner consolidates his expanding reservoir of learnings by discovering common associations, identifying elements and principles of identity. These skills are very important as a basis for developing sound concepts of God, Christ, salvation, and other doctrinal concepts.

At this point, the reader is cautioned to recall an important limitation in thinking at the seven-to-eleven-year-old period: Conceptual abilities are rooted in concrete situations. Grouping of relationships and classifying of information are limited to specific, concrete situations that the seven-to-eleven-year-old can manipulate. In forming an understanding of divisions in the Bible, the child could "see" the divisions because they could be outlined on paper and illustrated from the Bible. To comprehend a theological concept of sin would be more difficult, because it is more abstract and must draw from a less definitive, less concrete basis.

ABSTRACT CONCEPTS PERIOD

During the four-year period, between the ages of eleven and fourteen, the individual develops the mental ability for mature conceptual thinking. Especially important is the capacity to think in abstract terms, utilizing the world of propositions. Problems can be approached in a systematic manner and solved by using logical procedures which are expressed in abstract form. In addition, the classifying abilities which were emerging in the earlier period become more refined, better integrated, and more flexible. Whereas the seven-to-eleven-year-old is occupied with the immediate and the real, the eleven-to-fourteen-year-old is concerned with the theoretical, the remote, and the future.

This period is vitally important to the development of theological concepts. First, the older child is endeavoring to incorporate his earlier learnings into broader, more abstract principles and concepts. Parents and teachers should expect the eleven-to-fourteen-year-old to be reflective. Also, the individual in this period can range beyond the tangible, finite, and familiar, to conceive of hypothetical situations and infinite possibilities. From the perspective of Christian education, this period offers great opportunity for the formulation of a biblical foundation for Christian living.

How Adults Can Discover Children's Theological Concepts

Unfortunately, most adults have lost the precious memory of what it was like to be a child. They cannot recapture the intense feeling a child experiences of waiting two weeks for Christmas to arrive—while seeing those mysterious gifts under the tree. Adults fail to remember a world of words and ideas which were unclear, having to ask again and again, "What does that mean?" An essential task of parenthood and teaching children is to rediscover the world of childhood. Only then can the adult sense the meaning of what the youngster does, as well as act most wisely to guide the child toward insight.

In rediscovering the world of the child, the adult becomes aware of his concepts related to Christian truth. Teachers who neglect this task frequently demand more of the child than he is able to produce. The world is interpreted to him from an adult perspective on the assumption that he perceives and thinks as an adult. Thus, Jesus Christ is described as the light of the world, the bread of life, or the way, the truth, and the life—all concepts too difficult for the young child to grasp.

Parents and teachers of children can discover children's concepts by deepening their understanding of child development. Insight can be gained as one better understands what the mental, emotional, and spiritual characteristics are of a certain age. This insight can be enhanced by an alert observation of children in various settings. In this way, the information can be observed in actual life situations.

Also, the adult who desires to understand the child's world of thought must develop disciplined, perceptive skill in listening to children's conversations. One should note their choice of words. It is enlightening to observe how they sing songs, recite verses, and describe Bible stories. As one listens to the meanings the child gives to events, he realizes more fully the extent to which a child grasps a biblical truth. For example, the adult who asks the young child, Why? will probably be told, "Because," or "because he did." What one discovers is that the child does not have the intellectual maturity to reason out a cause. Thus, a simple "because" is used in reply.

In addition to perceptive listening, the adult should converse with and question children in informal, friendly situations. Asking an eight-year-old "What is sin?" will demonstrate where that individual is in his concept of sin. One who desires to discover the child's theological concepts can ask such questions as, "Tell me what you think of when you think of God"; "Who is Jesus?" "What does it mean to be born again?" One should purposely use commonly spoken terms to see if they really are understood: born again, gospel, heart, love, share, pray. Soon the adult will sense the range of understanding the individual child possesses. As more and more children are questioned, a more generalized awareness of the potential of age levels will emerge.

One, however, must be alert to two dangers. The first is the danger of generalizing from too small a group of children. Conversing with children in a primary class is not adequate to make definitive statements about the theological concepts of children in grades 1 through 3. For one thing, all the children might be from Christian homes where conscientious guidance had taken place. Or, a large number may have received little Christian education. The results would be noticeably different.

The other danger arises when the adult settles for pat answers as evidence of insight and understanding. Isolated biblical facts are not valid indicators of Christian concepts. The child must take objective facts, learn their meaning, and then realize for himself the implications of those facts.

Another way to discover children's theological concepts is to allow children to express their religious ideas through such means as art, music, and role play. By taking advantage of these forms, the child can often descriptively conceptualize his understandings. The results may sometimes be humorously revealing. A child, who was asked to draw a picture, produced a work depicting two adults in the back seat of an automobile and one person in the front. When asked what his picture was about, the youngster replied, "That's God driving Adam and Eve out of the garden." However humorous, the story vividly portrayed the child's understanding of the event.

Parents and children's workers should utilize as many means as possible to discover the concepts their children have of biblical ideas. Only as one perceives where the child is in his own development will he be able to guide the child to more mature concepts. Through personal investigation, the adult will realize the wide range of individual differences which exist among children.

How Misconceptions Occur

Many children formulate wrong precepts and concepts because of intellectual overstimulation. Two sources may be especially harmful. The first is the intense input of information from mass media. The child's mind may become cluttered with images and ideas which he cannot assimilate because he does not have the ability to organize them. Such data may be linked transductively with another idea so that two incompatible ideas exist side by side.

The other source of overstimulation is the eager parent or teacher who mistakes quantity for quality. Thus the child is prodded to memorize numerous Bible verses which he does not understand; is confronted with a volume of facts, incidents, and problems he can never master; and is taught hymns and choruses which contain concepts too advanced for him to comprehend. The child is given too much data and/or too advanced data. This results in confusion and misconceptions. A far better principle is to provide the child with smaller units of information and experience which he can digest healthily. It is wise not to push theological concepts on children before they can intellectually comprehend them.

Children also gain misconceptions because they have no accurate means to check their own observations and inferences. Russell notes that errors in concepts occur because of "overconfidence in the results of one's observations and conceptual thinking."[13] The child is also basically trusting of adults, feeling that whatever the adult says must be true. Thus, if the youngster processes his information incorrectly, or is given wrong ideas and attitudes by adults, he has little ability to correct the error without adult guidance.

Errors in concepts can also result when the preconcepts on which the concepts are built are faulty. This may also result when childhood experiences are in opposition to biblical concepts. The child who has experienced a very distorted father-son relationship may have difficulty building an adequate Father-son relationship.

Misconceptions result when misleading visual aids are used in teaching biblical concepts. One well-known Bible storybook portrayed Satan in a garb complete with horns, tail, and pitchfork. Such faulty images make lasting imprints in the child's mind. How many children conceive of angels with wings because of pictures visualizing them as such? Yet, is this biblically accurate?

By hearing words incorrectly, children gain inaccurate information for concept building. This often occurs in children's songs when the combined effects of poor adult pronunciation, group singing, and musical accompaniment distort or blur the words. One child wondered what "Jesus loves me, the sigh no," meant. In addition, children's songs are sometimes theologically confusing or heavily symbolic. For a very interesting learning experience—for the teacher—ask the students what such things as "He's the lily of the valley" mean.

Misconceptions also occur as a result of peer conversation. The child can easily gain incorrect impressions and information from playmates, especially those of different faiths. If other children are untaught in Christian truth, they may introduce the child to distortions or untruths which he readily integrates into his fund of data on the topic.

Since misconceptions can so readily occur, the following principles should be practiced:

1. Avoid teaching symbolic concepts before the child can understand them.
2. Clarify your own theological concepts before teaching children. What do I believe about the Holy Spirit? How can I state these truths in simple, nonmisleading terms?

3. Match words with experience and experience with words. Each reinforces and clarifies the other. Experience expresses the deeper meaning of words, and words clarify experience.
4. Teach nothing which shall later have to be unlearned.
5. Attempt to move theological concepts beyond "inert ideas" to principles of daily living. The youngster may accept that God is all powerful, yet he may not know how to apply the concept to his own life. Parents can help by demonstrating the reality of Christian truth.
6. Enrich rather than advance. Help the child gain an enriched meaning of basic truths rather than a cyclopedic understanding. For example, the concept of honesty could be built through many channels: life situations, life-related stories, Bible stories, songs, pictures, Bible verses.
7. Deal with one concept at a time.
8. Adjust information to the child's intellectual level.
9. Integrate information with the child's experience in a manner which allows him to test and comprehend its meaning.

NOTES

1. Erik H. Erikson, *Childhood and Society* (New York: Norton, 1963), p. 247.
2. Alta Mae Erb, *Christian Nurture of Children* (Scottdale, Pa.: Herald, 1955), p. 97.
3. Armin Grams, *Children and Their Parents* (Minneapolis: Denison, 1963), p. 77.
4. Johanna L. Klink, *Your Child and Religion* (Richmond, Va.: Knox, 1972), p. 116.
5. Karl C. Garrison, et al., *Educational Psychology* (New York: Appleton-Century-Crofts, 1964), p. 308.
6. Carol Chomsky, "Language Development After Age Six," in *Readings in Child Behavior and Development*, ed. Celia Lavatelli and Faith Stendler (New York: Harcourt, Brace, Jovanovich, 1972), p. 273.
7. Iris V. Cully, *Children in the Church* (Philadelphia: Westminster, 1960), p. 56.
8. Alice L. Goddard, "Children Ask About God," *International Journal of Religious Education*, 40 (Jan., 1964):20.
9. Garrison, p. 294.
10. Klink, p. 46.
11. Lawrence O. Richards, *Creative Bible Teaching* (Chicago: Moody, 1970), p. 150.
12. Mary E. Venable, "Little Children Ask Big Questions," *International Journal of Religious Education*, 40 (Oct., 1963):4-6.
13. David H. Russell, *Children's Thinking* (Boston: Ginn, 1956). p. 246.

FOR FURTHER READING

Almy, Millie C. *Young Children's Thinking: Studies of Some Aspects of Piaget Theory*. New York: Columbia U., Teachers College Press, 1966.

Beadle, Muriel. *A Child's Mind*. Garden City, N.Y.: Doubleday, Anchor Books, 1971.

Brearly, Molly, ed. *The Teaching of Young Children*. New York: Schocken, 1970.

Eastman, Frances M. "Was Jesus Born Like Me?" *International Journal of Religious Education* 40(Dec., 1963):16-17, 37.

———. "What Is the Bible?" *International Journal of Religious Education* 41(Oct., 1964):8-9, 38-39.

Elkind, David. *Children and Adolescents: Interpretive Essays on Jean Piaget.* Paperback ed. New York: Oxford U., 1971.

———. "The Development of Religious Understanding in Children and Adolescents." In *Research on Religious Development.* Ed. Merton P. Strommen. New York: Hawthorn, 1971.

Goldman, Ronald. *Readiness for Religion.* New York: Seabury, 1968.

———. *Religious Thinking from Childhood to Adolescence.* New York: Seabury, 1964.

Lichtenweiner, Muriel. "Children Ask About Death." *International Journal of Religious Education* 40(June, 1964):14-16.

McMichael, Anne. "As Children See the Church." *International Journal of Religious Education* 40(March, 1964):10-11, 40.

Phillips, John L., Jr. *Origins of Intellect: Piaget's Theory.* San Francisco: Freeman, 1969.

Piaget, Jean. *The Construction of Reality in the Child.* New York: Basic Books, 1954.

———. *The Origins of Intelligence in Children.* New York: International Universities, 1952.

Venable, Mary E. "Little Children Ask Big Questions." *International Journal of Religious Education* 40(Oct., 1963):4-6.

———. "Religious Concepts Affect Daily Living." *International Journal of Religious Education* 40(July-Aug., 1964):16-17, 37.

10

Teaching Theological Concepts to Children

V. Gilbert Beers

Here is a child. He is transparent, uncomplicated, understandable, and accessible. He is human, like the rest of us.

There is theology. To many, it seems opaque, complicated, difficult, and remote. It may seem philosophical, dealing with another world.

Are the two incompatible? "Theology" and "child" seem to be made of different stuff. Some are tempted to ask, Is theology really for a child? Isn't it more for a theologian?

Theology is complicated only when we make it so. It is as simple as the song nursery children sing, "Jesus loves me, this I know, for the Bible tells me so."

The Bible provides the truth about God and those subjects related to God. Men have organized that truth and called it theology. It usually encompasses the truth about God, Jesus, the Holy Spirit, the church, sin, salvation, man, angels, the Bible, heaven, hell, death, the last times, and Satan. These are topics that touch our eternal destinies, both here and in the hereafter.

Some theological concepts are admittedly beyond the thought and conversation level of the typical child. But most of the great truths of the Bible which we organize into theology can be stated in such a way that a child can understand them. It is a matter of putting the subject matter into the communications and learning level of the learner.

Peter and the author of Hebrews spoke of "milk" as the elementary truths and "meat" as the more advanced truths (1 Pe 2:2; Heb 5:14). Milk is for children and for those who are spiritually young. Meat is for those who are spiritually more mature.

In this chapter, we are concerned with milk, truth which can be assim-

---

V. Gilbert Beers, Th.D., Ph.D., is President of Creative Designs, Elgin, Illinois.

ilated into young lives. Whether we speak of theological concepts, doctrine for children, or biblical truth, we are speaking of the same—those concepts of God and related subjects which can be learned by a child.

Laying the Right Foundation

The basic foundation for this kind of teaching lies with you, the teacher. Whether you are a teacher or parent, you must first understand those truths yourself if you wish to communicate them to a child. It is vital also that you understand your child, at the level where he is learning and as an individual, and you must understand the processes which you will use in your teaching.

KNOW WHAT YOU ARE TO TEACH

We Evangelicals are often guilty of exchanging words without clarifying them. Do you find yourself using such words as *sin, salvation, repent, dedicated,* and *Saviour* with your child, but not really telling him what these words mean?

Have you ever tried to explain these words to yourself as if you were the four-year-old or six-year-old you teach? Try it. You may find that you are not sufficiently clear yourself as to the meaning of these terms.

Teaching is not merely the bartering of words. It is the clarification of ideas and the shaping of attitudes and lives. Clarify these truths in your own mind first; then help them become crystal clear to your child.

KNOW THE CHILD YOU WISH TO TEACH

Age-level characteristics are explained in chapters 4 through 8 in this book. Study those characteristics carefully for the age level you are teaching, for they are important keys to that learning level.

You will recognize that each individual child does not fit exactly into his expected learning level. There are some ten-year-olds who think like six-year-olds and some sixes who think like tens. But most children do fit into their proper learning level, and it is important for you to know what to expect at that level.

As you learn the characteristics of a certain age level or learning level, study also the individual characteristics of your child. "There is only one you" is a truth basic in good teaching. You must know your child as an individual as well as a representative of a certain learning level.

If you are the child's parent, or frequent teacher, you may be tempted to think that you do know that child because you see him often, or live under the same roof with him. However, that does not guarantee that you genuinely know him, any more than husbands and wives know each other because they live together.

Communication is the road to understanding. If you would know your child, you must communicate with him. Conversation will lead you into your child's mind and heart and help you to know him as he is. Then you will be ready to teach him.

KNOW HOW YOU PLAN TO TEACH

Why are you trying to teach that child? What do you hope to accomplish in him? Do you simply want him to know more about Bible truth? Or do you want his mind, heart, attitudes, and actions to change in response to that teaching?

True learning never ends with the head. It proceeds into the heart and hands also.

How do you hope to accomplish this change in your child? What processes will you use? These are all elementary considerations, but they do lay the proper foundation to the kind of learning you will want for your child as you share Bible truth with him.

God's Truth Is for Everyone

A child is a total person growing toward eternity. He is not a little adult. Nor is he a big infant, although there may be times when you may be tempted to think so. He is in a constantly changing pattern of development. Each day, week, month, and year sees him mature into a somewhat different person than he was before.

It is easier to see this change when we jump across the years. Today's adult was once yesterday's child. Each minister or criminal was once a child—growing through each age level. Each child today will become tomorrow's adult. What he does as an adult will depend much on what he learns as a child.

Growth is the road that leads through life toward the hereafter. It is God's provision for the gradual change of infants into children, children into youth, youth into adults, adults into old people, and old people into the inhabitants of another world. Each person passes through identical periods of life, although under very different circumstances.

How you teach God's truth to a child depends on where that child is in his growth, what kind of an individual he is, and a number of other factors. One important factor in teaching doctrine to children is the recognition of the changing needs in that child's life.

NEEDS CHANGE WITH GROWTH

Teachers and parents alike recognize that a child's personal needs change as he grows. Some of these basic personal needs include the need for love, the need to belong, the need for approval, the need for care or concern, the need for security, the need to succeed, and the need to serve others. The following chart, showing the growth in the need for love, represents the change in almost any of these basic needs.

THE GROWTH OF LOVE

AGE LEVEL	FOCAL POINT OF LOVE	ASPECT OF LOVE NEEDED
Infant	Parents, especially the mother	To be held in parent's arms, to be nursed
Preschool child	Parents, some close friends	To be secure in the family circle
Elementary school child	Parents, school friends, neighbor friends	To be a part of home, school, and friends
Junior high young person	Friends, parents, other sex	To be accepted by friends, parents, and other sex
High school young person	Friends, other sex, parents	To date, but also to be part of original family
Young adult	Other sex, friends, parents	To marry and/or to enjoy secure relationships with friends
Parents	Children, mate, friends	To enjoy a secure marriage and to give oneself in love to children
Older adults	Mate, children and grand-children, friends	To have a mature marriage, acceptance by children and grandchildren, and friends

It is important that you, the parent or teacher, recognize not only the learning level of your child, but also the need level. When you do, you will be able to bring God's truth to work on specific needs in that child's life. We must not be satisfied to teach subject matter without reference to daily living, and that includes daily, personal needs.

WHAT IT MEANS TO LEARN DOCTRINE

Too often parents and teachers associate learning with head knowledge. The child has "learned" something when he can repeat it. But that does not fulfill the child's needs for daily living. It is a start, but it is not enough.

There are four steps necessary for the effective learning of truth. Head knowledge is the first one. Knowing is a necessary step, for one must see clearly what Bible truth *is* or *says* before he can understand it.

The second step is understanding, or seeing clearly, what that Bible truth *means*. It is not possible to move on to the next steps in learning until the learner first understands what he is trying to put into his life.

The third step is applying. In applying Bible truth, the learner sees clearly what that truth means to *him*. He understands more than the meaning of that truth: he understands that meaning in relationship to his own life.

The fourth step is practicing. When a child learns what the truth is, then what it means, and then what it means to him, he is ready to put it into practice in his own life.

When someone says he is making Bible truth vital to a child, he is saying that he is helping the child incorporate that truth into his life. That reaches all the way through the four steps to good learning.

A GUIDE TO DOCTRINE FOR DIFFERENT LEARNING LEVELS

The charts on what children can learn suggest theological concepts which can be taught at each learning level.[1]

TABLE 10.1

WHAT A CHILD OF TWO AND THREE CAN LEARN

ABOUT GOD	God loves him. God takes care of him. God loves and cares for his family. God provides sun and rain. God does good for people. God is all about him. God wants him to talk with Him. God made the world. God made him. He can praise God by singing and praying. He can tell God he is sorry for the bad things he does. He should please and obey God.
ABOUT JESUS	Jesus loves him. Jesus once lived on earth, but now is in heaven. Jesus is God's Son. Jesus is a Friend. Jesus said good things which are in the Bible. Jesus was once a child like him.

About the Bible	The Bible tells about God. The Bible is a good Book. The Bible is a special Book. He should love the Bible.
About Home and Parents	God gave parents. He should obey parents.
About Church and Sunday School	Church is a place to learn about God. Church is a place to see friends. Church is God's house. He should like to go to church. He can give money to God's house to help buy things.
About Others	God gives grownups to care for him. Others may be good friends. Others may sometimes be unkind. Jesus wants him to be kind to others and share with them.
About Angels and Last Things	Angels came to tell people when Jesus was born. Angels love God and praise Him.

TABLE 10.2

What a Child of Four and Five Can Learn

About God	God loves him and others. God cares for all who love Him. God cares for and loves families. God made all things. God is to be trusted and depended on. God is everywhere. God will hear prayer any time. God sent Jesus to die for sin. God wants him to be thankful for all He has made. God wants him to obey Him by obeying his parents. God loves him.
About Jesus	Jesus loves him and is his best friend. Jesus came to be the Saviour. Jesus is now living in heaven. Jesus will help him obey and share. Jesus wants all children to love Him. Jesus is always with him. Jesus died for him. Jesus can help him do hard things.

About the Bible	The Bible tells about God. The Bible is God's Word. God tells us what He wants us to do in the Bible. The Bible helps him know what to do. The Bible is a Book of true stories.
About Home and Parents	God gave parents to care for him and teach him. God gave parents to pray for him. He should obey his parents. He should want to love and please his parents. He sins when he disobeys his parents or is unkind.
About Church and Sunday School	Church is a place to learn, sing, and worship God. Church is a place to meet with others who love the Lord. Church is a special place. Church is a place where we learn about God.
About Others	God made all people. God loves everyone and wants all to love Him. God wants him to tell others of Jesus. Others may not share as he does. Others may be loving and kind to him. He is to be kind, share, and pray for others. God wants him to share his money. God wants people to help others.
About Angels and Last Things	Some angels are good and some are bad. Satan (the devil) is a bad angel who did not want to please God. Satan and his angels want us to do bad things.

TABLE 10.3

What a Child of Six and Seven Can Learn

About God	God loves him and his family and his friends. God loves all the people of the world. God wants people to love Him too. God wants people to give their lives to Him. God provides food for men by letting plants grow. God takes care of the world He made. God is good, but He is also against evil. God wants us to pray and read our Bibles. God is holy and cannot fail. God has all power to help him.

About Jesus	Jesus is the Son of God. Jesus came to earth to die for sin. Jesus wants people to accept Him as their personal Saviour. Jesus wants to help people go to God. Jesus wants to take sin from our lives. Jesus never did anything wrong. Jesus rose from the dead and lives in heaven. Jesus loves us and wants to be our friend. Jesus did many wonderful miracles while on earth. Jesus can help him choose to do the right things.
About the Bible	The Bible is God's Book, for it tells about Him. The Bible tells us what God wants. The Bible tells how God worked with others. The Bible tells much about us. The Bible is a good Book to study, for it helps us. The Bible should be read and memorized. The Bible contains sixty-six books. The Bible has two major parts, called the Old and New Testaments.
About Home and Parents	Parents are God's leaders for us on earth. Parents want to help us, so we should obey them. Parents love us, so we should love them too. Parents provide food and clothing and home for us. God is an important guest in our home at all times.
About Church and Sunday School	Church is God's house. Church is a place where God's people go. Church is a happy place. Church is a place for songs and prayer and Bible study. Church needs our help to keep it clean and quiet. Church is not just a building but also the people in it. He can give to the Lord's work through the church.
About Others	Others may want the same thing he does; he must share. Others may not want to do the same thing he does; he must learn to give in halfway. Others may need something very much; he must learn to give. Others may be in trouble; he must learn to pray. Others may be unkind; he must learn to forgive. Others may not know Jesus; he must learn to tell them about Him.

About Angels and Last Things	Satan tempts us to sin and disobey God. Good angels worship and praise God. Good angels are God's servants. Jesus has gone to heaven to prepare a place there for all who love Him. Jesus is coming to take us to live with Him forever.

TABLE 10.4

What a Child of Eight and Nine Can Learn

About God	God is all powerful, all wise, and everywhere. God is present with him at all times. God wants to help him as he grows. God loves him and wants him to love God. God made the universe and all in it. God wants him to pray each day. God always answers prayers with "Yes," "No," or "Wait." God loves people all over the world. God the Holy Spirit is a person who is spirit. When he accepts Jesus as his Saviour, the Holy Spirit comes into his life.
About Jesus	Jesus is the Son of God, the Saviour. Jesus died on the cross for sin. Jesus can give salvation to those who ask. Jesus can forgive sin. Jesus loves him even when he sins. Jesus wants him to be a disciple and follow Him.
About the Bible	The Bible is an exciting Book to read. The Bible is a true Book, not fiction. The Bible is God's Word. The Bible should be read each day. The Bible has many important verses to be memorized. The Bible is God's truth. The Bible tells what God wants us to know.
About Home and Parents	Parents have rules for him to follow, but they also have God's rules to follow. Parents are to the child what God is to the parents. Parents want him to be a part of the family group. Home is a secure place where he can find his strength. Home is a happy place. Home is a place where he can talk over his problems with his parents. Home is a place where he can learn to follow rules.

About Church and Sunday School	Church is like a school, except that he learns about God and the Bible. Church is a place where he can worship God. Church is a place to sing about God. Church is a place for families. Church is a happy place where he wants to go. Church needs his help to be all that it should.
About Others	Others include a wider world, far beyond the community. Others include foreign boys and girls across the sea. Others need help, which he can give. Others need the gospel, which he can share. Others need his prayers. Others need his money, which he can give.
About Angels and Last Things	Satan is a beautiful angel who sinned against God. Satan is the most wicked of all created beings. Satan tempts Christians and leads them astray. Good angels protect God's people. Good angels are God's messengers to men and carry out God's judgments. Heaven is for those who have accepted Christ as their personal Saviour. People who do not accept Christ as their Saviour will be separated from God forever.

TABLE 10.5

What a Child of Ten and Eleven Can Learn

About God	God is Spirit, who is everywhere, but whose home is in heaven. God is all powerful, but He permits evil things to happen. God is all wise, but He permits men to choose between Him and sin, even though He knows what is best. God is one, but He is a triune being: Father, Son (Jesus Christ), and Holy Spirit. God is absolutely perfect, holy, and just. God hates all sin. God cares for and protects His children. God wants to show him His will for his life.

ABOUT JESUS	Jesus took on Himself the body of a man so He could do what God had planned. Jesus fulfilled part of God's great plan for the child, to bring him to God; the child must fulfill the other, to accept what Jesus did on the cross. Jesus shows him how to live for God, for His perfect life is a pattern for all. Jesus took the punishment for the sins of all people on Himself at Calvary. Jesus became alive again and lives in heaven. Jesus Christ was born of a virgin.
ABOUT THE BIBLE	The Bible has the answers to all his everyday problems. The Bible can help him live a happy life. The Bible tells the history of God's work among men. The Bible is God's Word, the authority for life. The Bible is set in the culture of another kind of people. He needs to understand that culture to understand the Bible. The Bible is without error. The Holy Spirit guided the writers of the Bible books. The Bible is a Book to honor and to memorize. It is God's truth to put into everyday practice. The Bible is God's truth for all men. He needs to share it with others. The Bible, which is God's Word, is to be obeyed.
ABOUT HOME AND PARENTS	The home and parents are part of God's plan for him. The home and parents function as part of God's plan, but he should do his part too. He should show loyalty to his home and parents. He should show honor to his home and parents. He should accept correction from his parents, for this will help him become a strong leader. He should begin to see what makes a Christian home, looking toward the day when he will start one.
ABOUT CHURCH AND SUNDAY SCHOOL	The church is a fellowship of believers in Christ. The church brings him in contact with Christian leaders. The church trains him in worship, study, prayer, witness, service, and fellowship. The church is a place where he can serve God. The church is a place where he can learn to practice Christian giving and outreach. He can learn about the ordinances.

About Others	Others need his respect for their thoughts, their possessions, their rights. Others need his understanding. Others need his help. He must show others honesty, loyalty, and fair play. Others need his forgiveness. Others need his prayers. Others fit into God's plans, just as he does.
About Angels and Last Things	Satan is the ruler of spiritual wickedness. Satan wants to keep people from coming to God. God has a plan for the future, which will come to pass. People who have trusted Christ as their Saviour and have died will be raised from the dead when Christ returns. Satan and his angels will be cast into the lake of fire for eternal punishment. People who have not trusted Christ as their Saviour will spend eternity in hell.

These are some of the many theological concepts, or Bible truths, which a child can learn. Some of these truths will need to be simplified for the very young child. Older children can understand more advanced concepts. These concepts are discussed more in *Leading Little Ones to God* and *Family Bible Library*.[2]

Know the Child You Want to Teach

YOUR CHILD IS AN INDIVIDUAL

Fingerprints, voiceprints, and other measuring devices show what we have known all along: there is nobody else exactly like your child. He is a unique creation. God made him to be different from all other children, even those of the same age.

While it is important for you to know the general characteristics of children of that same age or learning level, you cannot escape your responsibility to know your child as an individual. Talk with him in depth. Try to understand what he thinks and why. You will teach him doctrine more effectively as you understand who he is and how he functions.

YOUR CHILD IS NOT A LITTLE ADULT

Teaching a child is not merely downgrading adult concepts. It is "customizing" those concepts to the learning level of the child. The teacher who "talks down" to a child will lose his interest.

A teacher should not expect maturity beyond that which the child possesses. Too often we hear parents or teachers say, "I don't know why he doesn't show more interest in praying or in reading his Bible." Sometimes we simply expect that child or young person to have a maturity that comes with later years.

Remember that your child may have distractions from learning which are not apparent to you as an adult. His home atmosphere and the security generated in it, his relationship with his parents and other family members, the climate at school during the week, his health and sleeping habits—these all affect his interest in learning Bible truth. It may not be that he is disinterested in spiritual things. That child simply may have too many distractions to be interested. You cannot know this until you know that child as a person.

YOUR CHILD IS A TOTAL PERSON

He is a complex mixture of body, soul, mind, heritage, experiences, reactions, attitudes, thoughts, and associations with others. You are teaching a total person, not merely his mind or soul.

Some of these things are beyond the child's control. He did not choose his family or heritage. He did not select his own body, soul, or mind. Many of his experiences are planned for him by those with whom he lives.

A child who stays up too late on Saturday night to watch TV may not be too interested in your Bible teaching on Sunday morning. A child who has come to Sunday school from an unfortunate home situation may not be as quick to understand the delights of the family of God.

Doctrine is taught best in the context of daily living. You cannot isolate yourself from the child's experiences, heritage, homelife, and other determining factors, and expect to teach him successfully. Know your child, but know him as a total person. Then you can teach him doctrine that will change his life.

Some Methods to Use in Teaching Doctrine

Teaching a child is clarifying truth to him, not seeking to control his mind. If we seek to shape the child in our own image, we are trying to play God. Our task is to make truth so clear and so inviting that the child will become a happy student of the Word and, having given his life to Christ, will shape that life in the image of God.

This places on us, the parents and teachers, a responsibility which may sometimes seem frightening. But when we accept this responsibility as partners with God, it becomes a rich and rewarding experience.

Too often the word *teaching* forms in our minds the image of a direct transmission of knowledge to a learner. "Here are some truths for you to learn. Now learn them and practice them." This is a direct, or propositional, approach.

Some have found a degree of effectiveness in this approach, both in general education and in Christian education. But there is another very effective way of doing the job.

Some favor an indirect approach. In it, education is accomplished, not through propositions, but through motivation. A child will learn more when he wants to learn, when truths are presented in such a way that they are interesting and delightful to him.

Dr. Seuss, "Sesame Street," and Walt Disney have done much to show the effectiveness of this approach in general learning. Not much has been done with this approach in Christian literature for children. Some examples of books using this approach are *Cats and Bats and Things Like That; The ABQ Book; Coco's Candy Shop;* and other books in this series.[3] These books use fantasy, whimsical art, animal characters, and many other processes to capture the interest and imagination of the child before directing him toward the Bible truth to be learned.

Other methods to be used include the following:

1. *Example.* What you the parent or teacher do may speak louder than what you say. If you put the doctrine to work in your own life, it will show forth to the child as he observes you. You are really a living textbook.

2. *Reading.* Gladys Hunt has given an excellent book about the rewards of good reading with children and the learning values which come from that reading.[4] As she points out, we must not limit our reading to those books which are "biblical" or "religious." Many life-building values come from the great children's books of today and yesterday, often supporting some important doctrines which we teach.

3. *Shared experiences.* A hike in the woods, a trip in the family car, a walk around the block, or a dozen other experiences involving the learner and the teacher, can be rewarding. In the context of these experiences, much can be taught about God and His plans for us. Claudia Royal points out the values of associating nature with the God who made it all.[5]

Experiences are everywhere. They are waiting for the teacher and his child to participate in them and learn.

4. *Conversation.* Conversation is a pipeline between your mind and heart and the mind and heart of your child. To know your child thoroughly requires conversation. There is no other effective way to discover his innermost thoughts and attitudes. Ask the child questions that require more than just yes or no answers. Help him to reveal his own thoughts and ideas, to tell why he thinks as he does.

Conversation comes naturally through experiences which the teacher and child share. What is more natural than to talk about God the Creator as you walk through the autumn woods together or sit by a campfire and look up at the stars?

5. *Music and singing.* Christian songs are filled with important theological concepts for children. The songs for children, the great hymns, gospel songs—these are in themselves a course in doctrine.

There is something about singing doctrinal concepts that makes them stick in the mind and impress themselves upon the heart. Who does not remember the songs he learned as a child in Sunday school? They are theology. They touch the mind and heart of the child. But because they are sung, they are remembered better.

There is something wonderful about singing as a family. Singing together not only teaches, but helps to weld the family together.

6. *Picture reading.* Long before a child begins to read words, he learns to "read" pictures. The parent or teacher may point out many things in the pictures to focus the child's attention on the activity there. But the child will find more than the adult will. He will spontaneously find things the adult may miss.

Kenneth N. Taylor uses this method in *The Bible in Pictures for Little Eyes.*[6] By asking questions that focus attention on certain things, the parent or teacher helps the child learn many important Bible truths.

Many other methods can be used, but these more obvious ones will stimulate you to think of others. The creative teacher or parent will build quite a list of indirect methods which can help his child learn doctrine.

It is very important that you look for opportunities in everyday living which can help your child learn the great truths of the Bible. This was the kind of education that God told His people to practice in the time of Moses, "And these words, which I command thee this day, shall be in thine heart: And thou shalt teach them diligently unto thy children, and shalt talk of them when thou sittest in thine house, and when thou walkest by the way, and when thou liest down, and when thou risest up" (Deu 6:6-7).

NOTES

1. Adapted from V. Gilbert Beers, *Family Bible Library* (Nashville: Southwestern, 1971), 10:14-15, 18-19, 22-23, 26-27.
2. Marian M. Schoolland, *Leading Little Ones to God* (Grand Rapids: Eerdmans, 1962); Beers, 10:9-38.
3. Beers, *Cats and Bats and Things Like That; The ABQ Book; Coco's Candy Shop; The Magic Merry-Go-Round; Around the World with My Red Balloon; The House in the Hole in the Side of the Tree* (Chicago: Moody, 1972, 1973).
4. Gladys Hunt, *Honey for a Child's Heart* (Grand Rapids: Zondervan, 1969).
5. Claudia Royal, *Teaching Your Child About God* (Westwood, N.J.: Revell, 1960), pp. 144-46.
6. Kenneth N. Taylor, *The Bible in Pictures for Little Eyes* (Chicago: Moody, 1956).

For Further Reading

Baker, Dolores, and Rives, Elsie. *Teaching the Bible to Primaries.* Nashville: Convention, 1964.

Beers, V. Gilbert. *Family Bible Library.* Vol. 10. Nashville: Southwestern, 1971.

Bye, Beryl. *Teaching Our Children the Christian Faith.* London: Hodder & Stoughton, 1965.

Hargis, Pauline. *Teaching the Beginner Child.* Nashville: Baptist Sunday School Board, 1948.

Hunt, Gladys. *Honey for a Child's Heart.* Grand Rapids: Zondervan, 1969.

Ingle, Clifford, ed. *Children and Conversion.* Nashville: Broadman, 1970.

Klink, Johanna L. *Your Child and Religion.* Richmond, Va.: Knox, 1972.

Lapsley, Robert A., Jr. *Beside the Hearthstone.* Richmond, Va.: Knox, 1953.

LeBar, Lois. *Children in the Bible School.* Westwood, N.J.: Revell, 1952.

Moss, Sallie Rust. *Give Your Child a Chance.* Nashville: Broadman, 1938.

Mow, Anna B. *Your Child from Birth to Rebirth.* Grand Rapids: Zondervan, 1963.

Mumford, Edith Emily Read. *How We Can Help Children to Pray.* New York: Longmans, Green, 1933.

Royal, Claudia. *Teaching Your Child About God.* Westwood, N.J.: Revell, 1960.

Schoolland, Marian W. *Leading Little Ones to God.* Grand Rapids: Eerdmans, 1962.

Sweet, Herman J. *Opening the Door for God.* Philadelphia: Westminster, 1964.

Trent, Robbie. *Your Child and God.* Rev. ed. New York: Harper & Row, 1952.

Part IV

METHODOLOGY FOR CHILDREN

11

Evangelism of Children

Edward L. Hayes

Sparkling with controversy, the subject of child conversion prompts debate and discussion. The issue is one of theology as well as methodology. It is one of faith as well as feeling, dogma as well as response, crisis as well as process. It is at the core of our faith and is the root of true Christian education.

Jesus Himself said, "Except ye be converted, and become as little children, ye shall not enter into the kingdom of heaven" (Mt 18:3). To Him, the recovery of one lost child was top priority, and those who offended children were marked for judgment. Turning to Jesus was turning to God. And turning to God was and still is a fundamental need of all mankind.

Leading the young child to Christ has only within recent times become a specialized ministry in churches. This is due, in part at least, to particular viewpoints toward the concept of the soul, original sin, baptism, the nature of church membership, and the psychology of human maturation. For instance, the belief that infant baptism is not only legitimate but preferred over believers' baptism forestalls the necessity of evangelistic instruction to the young. Furthermore, concepts of grace in relationship to the depravity of human nature have led to at least two dominant positions on the nature of the soul and the necessity of early conversion. One view holds that a child's depravity demands an early conversion, as early as age three. Another holds that God's grace is operative in a child's innocence; until an age of accountability, no stress ought to be placed upon crisis conversion. Of course, the issue of church membership as it relates to baptism either fosters child evangelism or forbids it. Finally, since the rise of the religious education movement at the turn of our century, the

---

Edward L. Hayes, Ph.D., is Dean of the Conservative Baptist Theological Seminary, Denver, Colorado.

wedding of psychological insights with traditional or biblical truths has led to skepticism toward some evangelistic tactics with the very young. These and other issues combine to form a confusing mosaic. A theology of conversion, particularly as it relates to the child, is desperately needed.

The rise of child evangelism efforts can be traced to a vacuum which existed in Reformation theology. To be sure, the child was not ignored. Luther himself placed great value on the education of the young, but the matter of conversion was largely an adult concept. In the nineteenth century, revivalists stressed the necessity of a crisis conversion. Fired by the zeal of Sabbath school proponents, church leaders recaptured something of a primitive evangelistic fervor.

Augustus H. Strong, a leading theologian, was captive to an idea that the conversion of children was vital to Christian expansion. In a sermon preached in 1865 at the Baptist church in Haverhill, Massachusetts, Augustus H. Strong sanctioned the rise of the Sunday school, or Sabbath school as it was called. "Its beginning," he pronounced, "marks an era in the history of the church. It seems that God is fulfilling one of His last words of prophecy by turning the hearts of the fathers unto the children." He went on to recognize a renaissance in freedom. "At long last it is now believed that Christ died for the woman, the Negro, and the child. Only in recent centuries have men come to believe that any of these actually had a soul."[1] Strong, along with few others of his time, looked upon children as mortal, responsible spirits, capable of sin and just as capable of receiving salvation. With Augustus Strong, this teaching was tempered by a rising spirit of independence from either of the extremes of forced guilt by evangelistic excesses or evasion of the responsibility and validity of child conversion.

Today, child evangelism efforts are marked by increasing institutionalization and agency expansion. Specialization has entered the Christian marketplace, and organization efforts abound. Reaction and counteraction call for sound formulations and standards for proper assessment of their worth. This chapter attempts to answer at least five fundamental questions: Should the child be evangelized? What is the proper age for declaration of faith? Do children differ from adults in response? What is the relationship of evangelism to nurture? What implications does a theology of conversion have to church, home, and community evangelistic strategy?

The Child and the Church

There are comparatively few references to children in the New Testament. "This fact," says William B. Coble in *Children and Conversion,* "can easily lull us into the false assumption that children are to be treated in the same manner as adults."[2] But even so, children are of first-rate importance according to William Barclay in *Train up a Child.*[3]

It is clear that the New Testament builds on the Hebrew ideal of the father training the child. This assumption may explain, in part at least, the relative absence of instructional material in the New Testament regarding children. It is also clear that Jesus was never too busy for children. On the occasion when His disciples tried to hold back the children, Jesus allowed them to come to Him (Mt 19:13; Mk 10:13; Lk 18:15). On the way to Jerusalem, Jesus had time to hold the children. His reference in Matthew 18:10 to angels guarding children clearly refers to God's special place for children in the kingdom.

Fathers, in particular, were to care for the child in spiritual matters (Mt 7:11; Lk 11:13). This primary human duty was absolutely binding. To receive a child was to receive Jesus Himself (Mt 18:5; Mk 9:36; Lk 9:48). The fate of a man who provides the wrong example to a child is a more bitter fate than that which many other sins deserve. Jesus taught that it would be better for a man to have a great millstone hung around his neck and be drowned than to cause a child to stumble (Mt 18:6-14; Mk 9:42; Lk 17:2).

We must conclude from Jesus' teaching on the kingdom that children were important. The false sophistication of adults was placed in stark contrast to the simple faith of a child. "Whosoever shall not receive the kingdom of God as a little child, he shall not enter therein" (Mk 10:15). The child, according to Barclay, "is the very pattern of the citizen of the Kingdom."[4]

The child was a lesson on true greatness in Matthew 18:1-5; Mark 9:33-37; and Luke 9:46-48. When the disciples asked who is the greatest in the kingdom of heaven, Jesus called a little child unto Him. Conversion, or turning around, was the one essential requirement for entrance to heaven. Becoming as a little child was a natural way of saying two things: children are important in the kingdom, and adult faith must bear the marks of childlike simplicity. The child was not to imitate adult belief; instead the adult was to discover the simplicity of trust.

While the gospel passages do not indicate a methodology for child evangelism, they do emphasize the worth of the individual. We are reminded that every reference to children in the gospels adds to our understanding of the gospel message. It is for all mankind, rich or poor, great or small, adult or child. "Even so," said Jesus, "it is not the will of your Father which is in heaven, that one of these little ones should perish" (Mt 18:14).

The meager references in the Acts of the Apostles and the epistles lend little help in building a strong case for child evangelism as such, other than to build the case that the gospel is for all mankind. For instance, the promise in Acts 2:39 makes reference to "you and your children." The entire nation of Israel is in focus, not children. In the instance when Paul baptized the Philippian jailer, "he and all his" (Ac 16:33), apparently the whole family believed (v. 34). No support may be given for household faith, that is, an organic link between an adult believer and a child in a spiritual relationship. The children made their own decision.

The New Testament does lay down guidelines for nurture of children (Eph 6:4; Col 3:21). Barclay concludes:

> The New Testament lays down no kind of curriculum of training for the child; the New Testament knows nothing about religious education and nothing about schools; for the New Testament is certain that the only training which really matters is given within the home, and that there are no teachers so effective for good or evil as parents are.[5]

For at least two centuries, the early church apparently did not allow children to be baptized or enter the church. By A.D. 400, the doctrine of original sin had come to justify infant baptism. The issue of evangelizing children cannot be fully answered by direct references to the gospels or to the epistles. Certainly no methodology is implied. The tension between accepting a gospel for all and the scriptural teaching of universal sin transmitted from Adam to the present keeps Christians searching for a theology of child evangelism.

The Child and the Age of Accountability

The notion that a child is capable of sin and just as capable of receiving salvation leads to several questions. When should a child be held accountable for his sin? When should a child accept Jesus Christ as Saviour? When should he cope with divine grace?

An "age of accountability" is not taught in the Scriptures. In fact, there is no basis for it other than a logical inference. If we accept the biblical teaching of original sin as related to an Adamic nature, we infer that the infant is born in sin, needs divine grace, and is ultimately accountable for that sin. The observation that men are sinners by nature as well as by choice throws a burden upon an early concern for infants.

Advocates of infant baptism assume a covenant relationship between the child and the family of God. They argue from the silence of the New Testament on the issue, not from any direct teaching. The "unsafe" status of the child propounded by Augustine introduced the emergence of the concept of baptismal regeneration. Belief that the sacrament of baptism conveyed to the infant all the benefits of grace solved the logical problem, at least, of what to do with original sin. It remained for another rite, confirmation, to emerge. Confirmation conveyed the intent of personalization of faith and entrance to the church as an active member.

When children joined the catechumens during the time of Augustine (c. A.D. 400), the long tradition was begun which eventually led to complete sacramentalism in regard to child salvation. It was not until the Reformation that any dominant mood of dissent appeared, although "believers' baptism" was practiced from the earliest of Christian times.

Accountability had to be reckoned with by those who resisted infant baptism on grounds that personal faith was essential. How to account for this indispensable faith element in the New Testament led to the notion of an age of accountability. Denying the notion that the church is an hereditary body, in which fleshly birth rather than the new birth qualifies for membership, a personal act of faith and repentance would seem necessary. And if a personal act of faith would be necessary, then a rite with an infant would be insufficient.

What then is necessary for child conversion? The same thing that is essential in adult conversion: a conscious turning from sin and a turning toward God (Ac 9:35; 11:24; 26:20).

But when is a child accountable for his sin? We do not know for sure. A. H. Strong urged those who worked with children to heed several propositions: (1) the age of possible conversion begins with the first moment of moral consciousness; (2) the natural possibilities for good are greatest at the moment of that first unfolding and are less and less every moment thereafter; and (3) a character changed in early years is more promising of growth and power in the world than one dragged for years through the mire of sin.[6]

These propositions seem pertinent and reasonable. They imply a ground for both belief and action. However, they give no light on an exact age. From a central text such as Romans 14:12, "So then every one of us shall give account of himself to God," we conclude that accountability, not an exact age, is the issue. Harold Frazee declares,

> The age at which a declaration of faith is possible and to be expected is a relative matter. It is almost as difficult to assert that a given age is the proper one for a declaration of faith as it is to declare a particular age is the correct one at which to be married.[7]

The Child and Evangelistic Appeals

Accountability and a concept of age need not be linked together. Perhaps because we have attempted to tie the two together, excesses have been experienced in well-meaning attempts to convert the young. It is a mistake to set an arbitrary age for conversion. It is equally a mistake to set a certain day for "decisions." Somehow, God's sovereign Spirit does not evidence His regenerative work according to fixed days and years.

William Hendricks, writing in *Children and Conversion*, asserts, "It is highly doubtful that many children below the age of nine can express or have experienced despair for sin as radical separation from God." He continues with the emphatic declaration, "One cannot be 'saved' until he is aware he is 'lost.' "[8] His concern is that we not risk serious problems for the future by continuing to invade the preschool and children's departments for evangelistic prospects. As a Baptist theologian, his primary concern is that an adequate perspective be maintained regarding believers' baptism.

Indeed, he has a point, if baptism should follow conversion as closely as possible. The time lag between an early conversion and entrance into the church is a problem in many instances.

Those who hold that the evangelism of the child is to be as early as possible because of the damnation of the infant have not been altogether consistent. They would maintain that saving the child saves a life. But why the time lag from birth to, say, age five or six? Is not the child captive to his sin nature during that period as well? If an age of accountability occurs between ages three to five, or thereabouts, why not urge full obedience to our Lord and baptize at that early age of response? But most church leaders refuse to do this on pragmatic grounds. Few children, if any, know the demands of meaningful participation in the life of the church. One might also argue that few very young children know the demands of Christian discipleship as well.

Early conversions often lead to recommitments in later childhood or early adolescence. Also, they lead to outright defections from the faith. But that is true of individuals who were converted later in life as well. The outward response to an inner conviction is difficult to assess. Only God knows the human heart. We are limited to external assessment, which is faulty at best.

What happens between an early response to an appeal for salvation and a later "rededication," as many would call a recommitment? Often a child responds to a gospel appeal out of a deep desire to gain approval. It is part of the identity struggle within each of us to desire the approval of a parent or teacher. Winning the child according to this set of psychological principles, may be little more than instilling into the child the mysterious codes and mores of our society. Thus, willingly obedient, a child may gain his rightful place in the family or other adult institutions. Such a crass assessment, I recognize, must surely not be the case in every instance. For God even uses these faulty, inadequate steps of faith. Surrounded by love and continued teaching from the Scripture, the childish response may indeed lead to salvation. But to say that every child who indicated a desire to receive Christ was actually "saved" may be outright presumption.

Left to falter on his own with partial nurture, a child may drift into sin during his childhood or early adolescence. Without a concept of "lostness" at the time of his "conversion," the individual may thus be a candidate for delusion and some despair. Fortunately for some, the repeated proclamation of the gospel bears its fruit. Guilt, remorse, and finally repentance coupled again with faith, may lead the individual back into the fold. Adults often register some shock to see children repeatedly "walk the aisles" in evangelistic meetings. Have they not already been converted?

All of this discussion is meant to demonstrate the fact that when we seek to integrate a doctrine of salvation with a behavioral concept of evangelistic methodology, we encounter difficulty. Would it be better not to attempt an integration? Would it be better to leave unanswered the questions of when and how evangelistic appeals are to be made?

To do so is to evade a basic responsibility of integrating our faith with our actions. To do so is to admit to irrationality. What, then, are we to do in fulfillment of our Christian duty to proclaim the gospel to every creature? Here are my suggestions:

1. Incline the child to put his faith in Christ by sound Christian teaching surrounded by Christian love from birth onward. Such preevangelism, as it may be called, builds a proper foundation for intelligent faith and active discipleship. We find good support for this in the New Testament. Paul wrote to Timothy reminding him of his early heritage, "And that from childhood you have known the sacred writings which are able to give you the wisdom that leads to salvation through faith which is in Christ Jesus" (2 Ti 3:15, NASB).

2. Avoid anxiety-producing appeals to both parents and children. Here I speak of excesses and not the faithful teaching of the Scripture as it relates to both sin and salvation.

In any effort to evangelize children, youth, or adults, the Scriptures give us the clues. We are to balance our zeal with confidence in a sovereign God. Faith comes by hearing and hearing by the Word of God (Ro 10:17). Faith is the end, not the method, of providing the "hearing." Faith comes by the instrumentality of the Word. Excessive human motivation may work against the faith-prompting work of the Holy Spirit through the divine Scriptures.

3. Teach accountability as an action toward God, not toward men. Differentiating between the two is a primary point of maturity. Autonomy from the Christian perspective accounts for relationships between self, God, and others. When confronted with the claims of Jesus Christ upon the life, each individual must give an account for that which he knows.

In childhood, accountability is invariably toward parents, as commanded by God (Eph 6:1-2). Moving from childlike credulity to responsible autonomy involves transferring one's accountability to an authority higher than his parents. Of course, wise parents and leaders will instruct the young that all authority belongs to God and that any human authority is allowed by His permission. The power of the godly example in exercising authority prompts response toward God.

It is difficult to resolve the age-old problem of what happens when human authority—say, a parent's desire for a child not to go to church, make public profession of Christ, or be baptized—comes in conflict with divine authority. Do we appeal to the scriptural directive, "We ought to obey God rather than men" (Ac 5:29)? Does our duty to see the child converted, even against parental wishes, take precedence over the commandment of Ephesians 6:1? I believe it does not in most instances. Every reasonable effort should be made to enlist the parent in providing a climate for spiritual response. When that is impossible, no undue pressure should be placed on the young child to disobey. Older children are perhaps in a different category. Certainly, youth and young adults should have the freedom to believe, just as all men have freedom to reject Christ. But accountability is to be taught. Conflict between a desire to obey God rather than parents may find its resolution in time. God knows the heart, and its inward response is what counts.

4. Make appeals for young children to receive Christ that are prompted by pure motives and are given simply and in a nonpublic manner. The notable success of various child evangelism efforts cannot be denied. But the motive must never be numbers or outward response, nor should appeals be accompanied by offers of gifts, recognition, or special privileges. The abuses are not even worth mentioning, but they exist. Offers of free books, even a Bible, to children who accept Christ are questionable, if made in public. Any child would make a decision in order to receive a gift. The gift of salvation stands far above gimmickry. The offer of salvation is not an offer of silver and gold (Ac 3:6).

Public decision days, long popular among some Sunday schools, fail to account for the individuality of conversion. But at the same time, a wise attitude would be, "Forbid them not."

The key to successful evangelism for children is bringing truth to their own level, unmixed with argument. In presenting Christ to children, we must keep the message simple. Soderholm suggests several key principles to follow in presenting the gospel to children.[9]

1. The teacher should be clear in explaining what the child should know in order to appreciate the significance of Christ's death. God loves you,

you have sinned, Christ died to pay for your sin, you must admit to Him that you are a sinner and ask Him for forgiveness. Then you are in God's family and have everlasting life.

2. The teacher should be familiar with Scriptures that will help lead children to Christ. These include John 3:16; John 3:36; Romans 3:23; and Romans 5:6.
3. The teacher should be careful to explain the terms he uses.
4. The teacher should depend on the Holy Spirit. A decision prompted by the Spirit is the only genuine decision.
5. The teacher should use the Bible in sharing the gospel message.
6. The teacher should let the children ask questions. Questions open the windows of the mind and help prevent forcing the message on children.

The simplicity of salvation is evident in the following Bible stories, which can be used to help explain salvation to children: Nicodemus (Jn 3); the woman at the well (Jn 4); the lame man and Peter and John (Ac 3); Philip and the Ethiopian (Ac 8); the Philippian jailer (Ac 16).

Giving an invitation is a natural and normal part of the gospel presentation. How it is done is quite another thing. Teachers are wise not to force or push for decisions. The gospel, rightly presented, has it own appeal. The Saviour has His own drawing power. This is the divine work of the Holy Spirit in wedding human need and response to the winsomeness of Christ. Though there is no formula to follow in giving invitations, several ideas may prove helpful.

1. Ask children to respond "inside" before asking for outward response. A teacher might say, "If you want Jesus to be your Saviour, say to yourself, 'Yes, Jesus, I want You to be my Saviour.' "
2. Make the invitation clear. A child's mind wanders easily. Ask the child, "Can you tell me why you came to talk to me?"
3. Use natural situations to talk to children about receiving Christ. When a child asks, "Can I accept the Lord?" that is the time to stop and lead the child to Christ. Another simple and effective way is to invite children to remain after class if they desire to accept Christ.
4. Avoid making the invitation so easy that acceptance is not genuine. Some human response is necessary. Open "confession," or acknowledgment that they desire to accept Christ, often fixes the decision in the mind of a child.
5. Avoid group decisions with the young. Better results are obtained at the time of decision if the teacher deals with the child individually and personally.

A word of caution is necessary regarding the use of symbolism in explaining the gospel. While the Bible contains metaphors, analogies, and similes, these terms can be explained simply. Insights gained from child-learning research seem to indicate that the young learn symbolic terms and words if they are accompanied by meaningful adult actions, interpretive moods, and tones. Speaking the truth in love, according to the apostle Paul (Eph 4:15), enhances maturity. And love wins children to the Saviour.

Such terms as *heart, saved,* and even *sin* need to be explained. In fact, the New Testament often supplies alternative words such as the image of joining a family (Jn 1:12) or the analogy of birth (Jn 3:3) to explain "receiving Jesus into the heart." The concept of salvation is extremely rich in supportive concrete ideas, such as being set free from a prison, being bought like a gift, or receiving a prize or gift. Sin carries with it the notion of disobeying a law, wrongdoing, or not living up to what God expects.

Words alone will not win. Words—meaningful terms—combined with love, rich and deep feeling, make the gospel come alive in a child's experience. God stands ready to save the child on the exercise of the child's faith. If the child is a five-year-old, God will be pleased to accept a five-year-old response. If the child is ten, then God will accept a ten-year-old faith response.

Following Up a Child's Decision

The responsibility of leading the born-again child into normal, healthy, spiritual growth is primarily the task of parents. But if a child's parents do not possess spiritual life or know how to nurture spiritual growth, the whole community of the church needs to become involved. This is especially important for the child who comes from a non-Christian home. Several suggestions may help:

1. Explain to the child's parents what he has responded to and encourage them to provide a home environment that includes regular church attendance, prayer, and Bible reading.
2. Make sure the child has a Bible and knows how to find simple verses to read.
3. Provide a "This New Life of Yours" class for primaries and juniors to explain salvation more thoroughly. This may last several weeks and may be held during children's church, Sunday evening children's groups, or some time during the week.
4. Offer help and encouragement if you are a friend, but not the parent. Above all, pray and trust the Holy Spirit to continue the good work begun in the new child of God.

In the context of this chapter, words on follow-up may be too brief to give much more than a direction, a course, or a route to take. All that a church attempts to do, if it is following a biblical pattern, is designed to build up the child. Adequate provision for competent teachers, care by a loving pastor, and the surrounding concern of every church member will go a long way in assuring the child of normal spiritual growth.

W. O. Cushing's children's hymn, "When He Cometh," portrays the reward of children's work.

> Little children, little children, Who love their Redeemer,
> Are the jewels, precious jewels, His loved and His own.
>
> Like the stars of the morning,
> His bright crown adorning,
> They shall shine in their beauty,
> Bright gems for His crown.

The Child and Christian Nurture

Horace Bushnell's insistence "that the child is to grow up a Christian, and never know himself as being otherwise,"[10] has sparked controversy ever since it was written. Bushnell made that statement in opposition to the practice among the New England Calvinists at that time (1846) of expecting the child to grow up in sin and to be converted at maturity. His attitude toward revivalism was not as one-sided as it may appear. To quote from the man himself:

> I desire to speak with all caution of what are very unfortunately called revivals of religion; for, apart from the name, which is modern, and from certain crudities and excesses that go with it—which name, crudities, and excesses are wholly adventitious as regards the substantial merits of such scenes—apart from these, I say there is abundant reason to believe that God's spiritual economy includes varieties of exercise, answering, in all important respects, to these visitations of mercy, so much coveted in our churches. They are needed.[11]

Bushnell recognized that not all conversions would be by Christian nurture, so that other evangelistic efforts would be advisable and necessary. Nor was he opposed to a crisis experience as a matter of principle. Rather, he believed that they should be, in the case of children in the Christian home, prompted in the natural surroundings of Christian teaching.

Bushnell was vulnerable, it seems, in pushing for an organic link between parent and child. Presumptive grace, that is, the grace of God operating through the Christian parent, can be expected to bring the child to his own commitments. Infant baptism, he felt, was consistent with apostolic practice.

Regardless of a theology which had the effect of deemphasizing conversion, Bushnell pioneered children's work in churches. He was one of the first to insist on the importance of the first three years in formation of the child's basic outlook on life. He pointed out that learning takes place before the development of language. His emphasis on parental guidance was without parallel in his time. Only the home permeated by a Christian spirit, he contended, provides adequate Christian nurture. Mere outward and occasional observances of religion are self-defeating. If Bushnell's observations are correct, the home is the center of Christian education, whether the churches plan it that way or not.

Implications of a nurture approach are several. On the one hand, we cannot believe in any organic unity of the child with the parent by which the faith of the parent is the faith of the child. Latent faith is a contradiction in terms. Until a child knows the difference between sin and holiness, he cannot trust Christ who came to handle the sin question. On the other hand, let us guard against the opposite extreme of imagining that a course of doctrinal instruction is necessary before a child can apprehend the sufficiency of Christ. There are two simple demands of the gospel—renunciation of sin and trust in Jesus. A child can meet both of these demands.

The Child and Evangelistic Strategy

In this chapter, I desire to tread cautiously between extremes. I am convinced that churches have neglected family education and have tended to emphasize a highly individualistic approach to evangelism. A return to parental guidance in evangelism is needed. But churches must minister to fragments of society as well as whole families. In the history of Christian witness, the gospel has fallen on all kinds of soil. Any attempt to dogmatize away from early efforts to lead the young to the Saviour are fruitless. But the cautions are there. No exact strategy is to be found in the New Testament. Indeed the weight may well be on the side of adult evangelism over child and youth evangelism. But in regard to spiritual influence and training, the weight of effort is to be directed toward work with children. It is the duty of Christ's church, the faithful, to proclaim the gospel, to trust the power of Christ to preserve His own, to hold out all the help it can to aid the spiritual maturation of the young.

Theologian Augustus Strong wrote before the turn of the century what many firmly believe:

> Sometimes the conversion of an important worldly man in the community is thought of as a great proof of God's divine grace, but that worldly man, fettered by lifelong sinful habits, will probably do far less for Christ than a boy of twelve who is converted and consecrates his life

> to the Savior. . . . There is no good reason to doubt the fact of the importance of conversion in childhood.[12]

Maybe Martin Luther was correct when he wrote, "If Christendom is to be helped, one must begin with the children."[13]

NOTES

1. Augustus H. Strong, "The Conversion of Children," *The Watchman-Examiner,* 53(Sept. 23, 1965):583.
2. William B. Coble, "New Testament Passages About Children," in *Children and Conversion,* ed. Clifford Ingle (Nashville: Broadman, 1970), p. 36.
3. William Barclay, *Train Up a Child* (Philadelphia: Westminster, 1959), p. 234.
4. Ibid., p. 235.
5. Ibid., p. 236.
6. Strong, pp. 584-85.
7. Harold B. Frazee, "The Proper Age for a Declaration of Faith," *Religious Education,* 58(Sept.-Oct., 1963):439.
8. William Hendricks, "The Age of Accountability," in *Children and Conversion,* ed. Clifford Ingle (Nashville: Broadman, 1970), p. 95.
9. Marjorie E. Soderholm, *Explaining Salvation to Children* (Minneapolis: Free Church, 1962), pp. 10-14.
10. Horace Bushnell, *Christian Nurture* (New Haven, Conn.: Yale U., 1916), p. 4.
11. Ibid., p. 46.
12. Strong, p. 585.
13. *What Luther Says,* ed. Ewald M. Plass (St. Louis: Concordia, 1959), 1:141.

FOR FURTHER READING

Barclay, William. *Turning to God.* Philadelphia: Westminster, 1964.

Beabout, Florence. *This New Life of Yours for Boys and Girls.* Denver: Baptist Pubns., 1968.

Bye, Beryl. *Teaching Our Children the Christian Faith.* London: Hodder & Stoughton, 1965.

Dobbins, Gaines Stanley. *Winning Children.* Nashville: Broadman, 1953.

Jahsmann, Allan H. and Martin P. Simon. *Little Visits with God.* St. Louis: Concordia, 1957.

———. *More Little Visits with God.* St. Louis: Concordia, 1961.

LeBar, Lois E. *Children in the Bible School.* Westwood, N.J.: Revell, 1952.

LeBar, Mary E. *Living in God's Family.* Wheaton, Ill.: Scripture Press, 1957.

Orr, William. *How to Lead Young Children to Christ.* Wheaton, Ill.: Scripture Press, 1961.

Potts, Edwin C. *Evangelism in the Sunday School.* Chicago: National Sunday School Assn., 1960.

Soderholm, Marjorie E. *Explaining Salvation to Children.* Minneapolis: Free Church, 1962.

———. *Salvation—Then What?* Minneapolis: Free Church, 1968.

Swanson, Lawrence F. *Evangelism in Your Local Church.* Chicago: Harvest, 1959.

Trent, Robbie. *Your Child and God.* Rev. ed. New York: Harper & Row, 1952.

Waterink, Jan. *Leading Little Ones to Jesus.* Trans. Betty Vredevoogd. Grand Rapids: Zondervan, 1962.

Yoder, Gideon G. *The Nurture and Evangelism of Children.* Scottdale, Pa.: Herald, 1959.

12

How Children Learn

Julia Henkel Hobbs

Concepts of how children learn have changed dramatically in the past century. Current research is unveiling exciting possibilities about learning for even very young children.

Adults, and certainly parents, have generally recognized that children are learning something during their preschool years, but the extent of this learning has not been understood clearly. A young child learns how to feed himself; he hears parents and siblings use words in a certain language and then proceeds to imitate and learn that language too. Learnings such as these have commonly been called *natural learning* by educators.

A second kind of learning takes place when an adult, in an unorganized way, simply guides a child into certain behavior patterns which are desired by the adult. For example, the child is taught not to bite another child. He is taught to keep his room neat and clean. He is taught how to dress himself. This is usually called *informal learning*.

The third kind of learning for the child is *formal learning*. This is what most people talk about when they discuss the teaching-learning situation. Here, an adult specifically intends to teach a child something. For example, he wants him to learn to read, write, analyze a poem, or play the piano.

The first two kinds of learning are receiving more attention than in the past. It is much more commonly understood now how important these early experiences are in making the child ready to learn. Research is being conducted on why some home climates promote learning and others do not.[1] This relates to the whole area of motivation, which is now being explored. We are beginning to understand steps in the learning process, many false concepts of how children learn are being swept away, and we

---

Julia Henkel Hobbs, Ph.D., is former professor of Christian education at Grand Rapids Baptist College and Seminary, and Malone College.

are beginning to understand something about the educational technology of communicating with a child and helping him learn.

Readiness

Why is it that children just learning to talk are constantly curious? One of the characteristics of the preschool child is his inquiring mind. Common questions are "why, how, what, who?"

When a child asks a question, it is a clear signal that he is ready to learn something about the subject of that question. The adult who proceeds to give an elaborate treatise using his question as a springboard may confuse or bore a child. The wise adult knows how to answer the question in a simple, straightforward way and then encourage the child's curiosity so that more questions will follow. Somewhere along the way, many children stop asking questions and lose that priceless quality of curiosity. Why?

What series of circumstances, or what kinds of adult reaction, dull that early curiosity which is the fountainhead of all learning? If parents and educators had the complete answer to this question and then knew how to fan that spark of curiosity continually into a flaming desire to learn, they would solve one of the major problems in education.

Certainly we know some of the reasons. Adults who ridicule the child's questions or brush him aside with, "I'm too busy, go away," or, "Why are you always asking a million questions?" are squelching the child's spark of curiosity. Also an adult who expects too much of a child can dull the desire to learn.

Another reason for the child's curiosity to wane is that he must reach a certain maturation point for specific types of learning. No matter how clever the techniques or how persistently adults prod, children usually will not learn until they are ready to learn. The intriguing part of the concept of readiness is that it is not fixed and unchangeable. Adults can consciously produce a climate which may speed readiness in a child.

Climate Promotes Learning

Why is it that some homes, schools, and churches discourage learning and other climates promote learning? Some have few if any books, magazines, or newspapers, and the spirit of inquiry is almost completely lacking. Even television shows chosen are not the type to produce investigation. Unless a child encounters learning-promoting influences, it is quite possible that he will be as dull as his environment.

For example, the home that treasures and uses books, magazines, and newspapers, is a better place for learning. A home in which parents encourage questions, in which siblings and parents are constantly investigating with the young child, will greatly affect the continuation of his natural curiosity. If a brother, sister, or parent likes to look at picture books with the child or read to him, he will learn to treasure books. A wise parent may ask, "Isn't it wonderful that God gave you a mind so that you could learn new words?" If a young child is given a piece of paper on which a word is printed, it can become his own special property when he recognizes it and can point to a picture of that very object. Guessing games, like, "I see something blue," or "I see something hot; can you think what it is?" are fun for the whole family and a great way for a child to learn.

Children learn much more at an early age than was ever before imagined. Parents and teachers who understand this can do much to set the stage for learning when children are still in infancy. Now research indicates that the child in the crib is beginning to understand language long before he vocalizes it himself and learns to speak it. Emotions like fear, hate, anger and love are learned at the early stages. Angry words, loud noises, great emotional upheavals are indeed noticed by the young child and have a profound effect on his later development. All these aspects of learning have much to say about Christian education from birth through maturity. (See also chaps. 24, 28, and 29.)

Motivation

Good teachers have always tried to motivate pupils to learn. It is certain that a child will not learn unless he is motivated to learn in some way, accidental or casual though it may be.

Sometimes the motivation used by teachers is fear of punishment; sometimes the motivation is an extrinsic one, like learning for a tangible reward.

At times a child's motivation for learning is the expectation of his peers. He wants to do well because other children in the group expect him to do well, or perhaps he wants to be like them. At other times, a child is motivated to learn because he knows his parents expect him to learn and he wants to please them. Then there are also cases in which a child sees a negative example: he sees the results of someone who refuses to learn; he recognizes undesirable outcomes and determines that he will not be like that and he will in fact learn.

Steps in the Learning Process

When a child learns, there are many levels in the process. They have been variously described and explained, but perhaps the most simple and usable diagram could be illustrated like this:

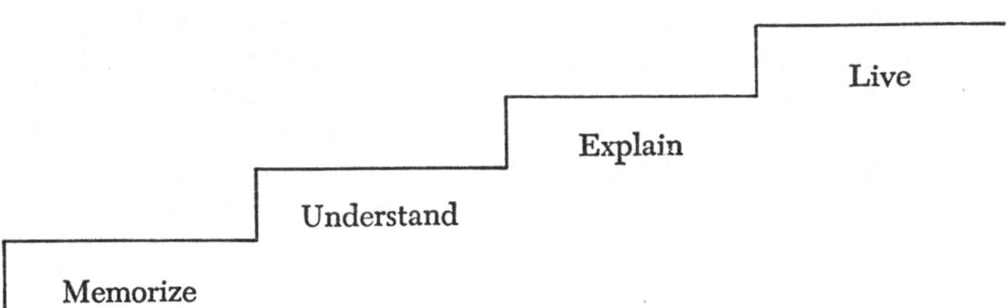

The first step, or level, in the learning process is memorization. Many have said memorization is not learning at all; it is simply imitating. This statement is not entirely true. Memorization is a very simple form of learning, though it is never the final desired outcome. However, rote memory work fell into disrepute some years ago when at last it was recognized that a pupil could memorize and recite volumes with no apparent change in behavior. Yet, in some cases, memorization is a first step, or first level, in the learning process. It is *not necessarily* a part of the learning process but it *may* be. If, for example, a child has learned, "Be ye kind," he at least knows that this is a biblical precept. He may not understand it; it may not be a part of his life at all, but it can be a beginning. If he moves from that step to the second level, understanding, he is making progress. The teacher's clue that he understands is the expression on his face, his smile, or other behavioral signals.

On the other hand, many pupils understand a basic concept without being able to verbalize it. Even adults have been known to say, "I understand what my church teaches on that subject, but I can't explain it. Won't you come with me to see my minister so that he can explain it?"

When a child expresses this, he sometimes says, "I remember what you said about it and I think I understand, but I don't know how to explain it."

When the teacher is able to assist the child to the third level of the learning process so that he can explain it in a way that someone else can understand, the child has indeed gone a long way in the learning process.

Yet no Christian educator ever dares to be content with achievements in the learning process unless he knows that the pupil has made that teaching a part of his life. When a child not only recites, understands, and explains "Be ye kind" but actually performs an act of kindness in his own life, then truly, he has travelled the steps in the learning process, and genuinely has learned.

It is in this connection that no teacher in any agency of the local church can be sure he has *fully* taught if there has been no interaction with his pupils. He cannot sit down smugly and say, "Well, I've taught my class today; I'm glad that's over."

Unless his pupils actually have learned, he has not taught. And this learning involves the fourth step, as well as steps one, two and three.

Relating the Bible to Life Needs

LeBar* presents a concept called Boy-Book-Boy which can be helpful in relating the Bible to the spiritual life needs of children. The concept involves three basic steps. In the first step, we begin teaching the child where he is intellectually and spiritually. We start with him as a person, and discover his questions, problems and needs. Then we take him to the content of the Written Word of God to show him how God can meet his needs through His Word. The final step is application of the Word to meet pupil needs and change behavior.

Richards† suggests a similar pattern of four steps. The first is *Hook*. The hook is used to bring the child in contact with the Word of life. It captures interest, sets a goal and leads naturally into the Bible study. The *Book* is the second step. This step involves the Bible study through which the teacher seeks to clarify the meaning of the passage by giving biblical information and helping in understanding. The *Look* enables the teacher to guide his class to insight in the relationship of the truth to life. The *Took* is the last step and requires a response in which the teacher helps his pupils respond by leading them to see God's will and by helping them decide and plan to do it.

Both of these concepts relate life needs of the child to the Word of God, and seek to bring about change in behavior through the work of the Spirit of God.

Theories of Learning

Children learn in many different ways and at individual rates of development. Vast amounts of material have been written about theories which affect children and how they learn.‡ No attempt is made in this section to treat all learning theories, but rather to present an overview of the major ones and how these theories affect children as they learn.

A knowledge of how persons learn is helpful for several reasons. Man needs to make sense out of the world in which he lives. Many anxieties and fears can be removed if we understand that occurrences around us are natural and normal. We need to operate on factual information rather

*For further treatment, see Lois E. LeBar, *Focus on People in Church Education*, pp. 48-54.

†Principles are illustrated in Lawrence O. Richards, *Creative Bible Teaching*, pp. 108-113.

‡A three-part film, *What Do You Think?*, on how children learn, is available from ACI Films, 35 West 45th Street, New York, New York 10036. The film is in color, thirty-two minutes long, and comes with a study guide.

than appearances. The laboratory has discovered facts on how people learn that can be applied in different situations. Many of our behavioral patterns cannot be explained simply. Learning is very complex and involves many variables, such as motivation, readiness, atmosphere, maturity, and a host of other factors.[1]

Learning occurs inside of the individual, though his environment affects how he responds and reacts. Learning has to do with developing for functioning. It affects the whole person and cannot be separated from human experience and behavior. Learning is an *aspect* of behavior, rather than a *kind* of behavior. The theories of learning are concerned with the *why* and the *how* of the learning process.

Lindgren has summarized the following theories of learning.[2]

REWARD AND PUNISHMENT

People will learn to do those things for which they are rewarded and avoid those things for which they are punished. "Johnny, if you will be a good boy, Mother will bring you a surprise from the store. If you don't behave, you'll get a spanking when I come home." Because Johnny wants a reward and desires to avoid punishment, he will display good behavior, if he feels the reward is worth the effort. The problem is, will children learn if they are not rewarded or punished? How are needs and individual differences related to this theory?

ADDITIVE THEORY

Learning is a process of acquiring, or absorbing, facts. Memorization is very important in this theory. The more facts a person masters, the more he learns. The learner's task is more passive. He is to be receptive, while the teacher or parent sees that he is "filled with learning." Are children's minds storehouses of information? How much factual material are they able to retain and recall meaningfully?

LEARNING IS PERMANENT

If materials are "properly learned," they cannot and will not be forgotten. Learning becomes a fixed and permanent status. The problem is that students tend to forget many things they have learned. Morgan and King suggest three variables which influence the amount retained in long-term memory: (1) meaningfulness of the material, (2) degree of learning of the material, and (3) interference with the material learned.[3]

"BEING TOLD"

Learning starts somewhere outside the learner and has to get inside him. The emphasis is on "what is said," and telling is the best way to communicate the message. The parent says emphatically, "How many times have I *told* you not to do that?" The child continues the behavior and acts as though he did not even hear the parent!

STEP-BY-STEP PROCESS

People learn according to predetermined patterns, or formulas. Theoretical principles are taught before practical aspects are emphasized. Sometimes the theory is forgotten because direct or personal experiences are essential for understanding and application.

AUTOMATIC TRANSFER OF TRAINING

Skills and concepts learned in one area or set of circumstances will be available for other quite different situations. Transfer can occur if the new situation resembles the learning situation. The problem is the way a child perceives and relates to make the transfer possible.

LEARNING IS PAINFUL

Learning is a mental discipline. The more difficult, frustrating, or unpleasant the subject, the greater the benefit. However, does a person necessarily learn more because the process has been painful?

LEARNING IS PLEASANT

This theory is a reaction to the theory that learning is painful. Learning can be enjoyable and pleasurable. We can have fun while we learn. Occasional frustrations, tensions, and anxieties may come in any learning experience and may be essential to help the child accomplish the desired goal.

Each of these theories of learning may have some element of truth but cannot be accepted completely on the basis that they are practiced by teachers and parents. Many of our traditional ideas about learning are derived from the way we have been taught. Some theories are unfounded, while others can be reinforced by laboratory experiments. We need to give careful analysis to the reasons *why* we do *what* we do to arrive at a sound educational basis in theory and in practice.

Major Families of Learning Theory

Learning theories may be divided into two major kinds: (1) the Gestalt Field theory, and (2) the Stimulus-Response theory. Both theories have many advocates who agree on basic premises but have different viewpoints as to definitions and functions. Each theory is based on experimental evidence in the laboratory. Animals have been used as the subjeccts because scientists can control the behavior of animals more easily than human beings. A limitation is that animals and human beings are not related in an evolutionary ladder, as some would have us believe. The behavior of an animal may not be identical with a human being. God created man in His own image, and man has the capacity to think, relate, and do far beyond any animal. We *can* learn from these theories, but we must recognize the limitations as these theories are applied to children and how they learn.

GESTALT SCHOOL

This theory is also referred to as the field theory, and the organismic approach. Leaders of this viewpoint were Max Wertheimer, Wolfgang Köhler, Kurt Koffka, and Kurt Lewin. All four of these leaders originated their ideas in Germany and migrated to the United States where they developed and refined their positions.

"*Gestalt* is a German noun for which there is no English word equivalent, so the term was carried over into English psychological literature. The nearest English translation of Gestalt is 'configuration,' "[4] meaning an organized whole or pattern in contrast to a collection of parts. The idea is that something cannot be totally understood by studying its parts, but rather by a study of the whole.

"The Gestaltist insists that the attributes or aspects of the component parts, insofar as they can be defined, are defined by their relations to the system as a whole in which they are functioning."[5]

According to this theory, we cannot understand a child unless we observe, study, and know him as a total personality. Each part of his personality contributes to the whole. We may consider the physical, mental, emotional, social, and spiritual areas, but unless we relate each of these areas to the whole, we cannot fully appreciate him as a *whole* individual.

> The key word of the Gestaltist-field psychologists in describing learning is *insight.* They regard learning as a process of developing new insights or modifying old ones. Insights occur when an individual, in pursuing his purposes, sees new ways of utilizing elements of his environment, including his own bodily structure. The noun *learning* connotes the new insights—or meanings—which are acquired.[6]

In order for teachers and parents to utilize the "insight" theory, they must be able to understand children totally, so that selected problems are appropriate to the maturity of the children and will meet their needs.

According to the Gestaltists, an important part of learning is to make discoveries and be able to organize and reorganize learning experiences. Learning should be purposive, explorative, imaginative, and creative.

Learning is more concerned with thoughts and concepts than with mechanical development in association.

The Gestaltist theory may be applied to studying the Bible. The purpose of teaching is *not* to tell the pupils everything, but to guide them through personal and group discovery to gain insight or new meanings. For example, if a teacher is leading a group of juniors to discover the qualities of a good neighbor, he could conduct a scripture search in which they would study Luke 10:30-36. After they have had opportunity to discover some of these qualities, and share their findings, new insights can be gained by making application of what they discovered.

Gestaltists think of a person's environment as psychological. The emphasis is on what he makes of his surroundings—his impressions, memories, and anticipations. The individual interprets his environment in ways that will be meaningful to him and that will assist him in designing his actions. Two individuals may be in the same room at the same time and perceive the environment quite differently. The individual is never able to recapture the old environment in the same way at another time because of the psychological differences. A teacher may ask a group of children what they saw in a particular incident which was a common experience to the group. The differences in reporting will vary greatly because each child interprets what he saw in view of his own personality, background, and perceptiveness.

The Gestalt theory of learning is helpful in analyzing the total personality development of children. We can accept the idea of wholeness of personality and the relationships of the parts to the whole. Children can gain insight to ideas and concepts through self-discovery. Perceptions are affected by background, purposes, and environment. Teachers and parents need to provide a stimulating, creative and explorative environment in order to assist children in organizing their learning experiences.

One tenet of Gestaltist psychology, which Christians reject, is that there are no absolutes. To Gestaltists, everything is relative and subject to change. Evangelicals, on the other hand, recognize that absolutes are revealed in the Word of God. It is the responsibility of parents and teachers to give the highest regard to the Bible, the written Word of God, which is our final authority, without error in all parts in the original writings. It is the responsibility of parents and teachers to make the eternal absolutes of the Bible applicable and meaningful to children.

STIMULUS-RESPONSE ASSOCIATIONISM

Another major family of psychological thought is referred to as the stimulus-response (S-R) theory. According to this theory, people learn because they are conditioned toward or away from various kinds of behavior. Behaviorism and connectionism are other names ascribed to this theory. Its early advocates were John Watson and Edward Thorndike.

Pavlov, a Russian physiologist, conducted animal experiments which have influenced the thinking of the S-R associationists. Thorndike built on Pavlov's ideas, and his famous "laws of learning" were derived mainly from his interpretation of how cats behave when placed in a cage from which they do not know how to escape—until they learn.[7]

The "trial and error" theory of learning is an example of the S-R theory and is based on Thorndike's experiments. He found that animals learn by

> blundering, trying something and then either succeeding or failing. Random, blind, accidental, chance-like behavior results, after many trials, in right response. Frequent practice gradually eliminated wrong responses and finally established the right response in direct line with the stimulus.[8]

Through trial and error, the individual is given several responses to reach a desired goal. He may select any of the alternatives presented. If the alternative fails, he may try another response until he succeeds. As he succeeds, he will be reinforced through the successful responses until he reaches the desired goal. Undesirable responses will be avoided and possibly eliminated in the process. This kind of learning may tend to be mechanical and leaves little room for thought, insight, or purpose.

Thorndike emphasized three laws of learning: the law of readiness, the law of exercise or repetition, and the law of effect. The law of readiness is in focus when a person feels he needs something. He will become self-active to discover ways to meet his need. Through the law of exercise or repetition, he is able to establish relationships between situation and response. Learning becomes more permanent as a person learns to use his knowledge in meaningful settings through practice. Acts of behavior can become habits through practice or be eliminated through avoidance. Pleasurable responses tend to be fixed as the individual feels the need for being satisfied and is reinforced through repetition.

Contemporary S-R associationists do not place so great an emphasis on the operation of the brain and the nervous systems. They consider conditioning of importance in changing response habits with a stimulus which strengthens or modifies.

S-R associationists are realists. They believe the physical world

> experienced by human beings is real and essentially what it appears to be when observed through the senses. . . . They also assume a basic principle of the universe is cause and effect; every event is determined by events that have gone before. Thus, the universe is a vast mechanism governed by laws which are essentially mechanical in nature.[9]

The assumption that the surrounding environment (including physical and social) should and will closely control learning and behavior is also supported by the S-R associationists. Qualified adults select and teach subject matter useful in contemporary society, with little emphasis on student goals, motives, and problem solving.

Programmed instruction is an outgrowth of the S-R learning theory. B. F. Skinner and others have developed programmed learning instruments which are based on the law of reinforcement. In this approach, a child (or other individual) is presented a stimulus (a question, for example) and he responds to this stimulus. If the answer he chooses is correct, he is rewarded by being allowed to proceed to the next question. If the answer is incorrect, he must review or study the material again. If he succeeds, he proceeds to the next question. Correct, positive responses are rewarded so he can move progressively toward the goal.

Teachers of children can glean several benefits from the stimulus-response theory.

1. Through a variety of responses, a child can be conditioned to change his behavior. Those elements which are desirable can be reinforced through positive responses. By omitting rewards, undesirable behavior can be avoided or eliminated.

2. The principle of cause and effect is important in understanding behavior. Some educators and psychologists claim that for every behavior there is a cause. Certainly we must be aware of real causes in behavior problems rather than treat only symptoms.

3. We learn through trial and error. As children are made aware of appropriate and positive responses, they can begin to relate to responses which will be more meaningful, and thus build strong, positive habits of behavior.

However, there are several problems with the stimulus-response theory. Lindgren mentions three difficulties which teachers and parents must be aware of in this theory: (1) laboratory research is based on the behavior of rats and other animals; (2) minute factors in behavior are isolated and measured precisely rather than complex behavior, which teachers and parents must work with, being analyzed; and (3) physical components of behavior are emphasized rather than the emotional and intellectual factors.[10]

Adult guidance is essential in selecting and teaching subject matter, as the S-R associationist emphasizes. However, more emphasis is needed on student goals, motives, and problem-solving. Children can be guided in analyzing their actions, defining goals, and solving problems.

Furthermore, present-day behaviorism, such as that advocated by B. F. Skinner, is based on a humanistic determinism. By teaching that man's actions are influenced by his environment, behaviorism rules out moral accountability.

Which learning theory is best and most acceptable in relating to children? All learning theories have basic ideas which can be applied by Christian teachers and parents. Each theory has its strong and weak points. Teachers and parents need to be aware of the main tenets of these theories and how they relate to children.

It must be recognized that such words as *intelligence, perception, motivation, role* and *practice,* and *transfer of learning* are defined differently by each major theory of learning. Even within the same theory, there is divergent thinking.

The eclectic approach to learning theory seems to be the most logical in developing a philosophy of how children learn—to glean from each theory the outstanding strengths which are not contrary to the laws of growth and scriptural principles. Many psychologists borrow from both schools of thought and do not align themselves with either. Perhaps this is the safest approach in studying learning theory.

Communication

Learning does not always take place when the teacher is the only one talking. Certainly a teacher cannot be sure if learning is taking place if he is using only the lecture technique. It has been said that learning is a two-way street: the pupil meeting the teacher. There must be some kind of visual or verbal response from the pupil in order to know what progress is being made.

This is why the teacher must be concerned with his technique. If he simply tells the pupils Bible stories and hopes to keep them quiet, or lectures endlessly, hoping to fill the time, he is generally not helping his pupils learn to the fullest.

Teachers can use many exciting ways to spark pupil learning. If pupils do not listen or are not interested, the teacher may safely conclude they are not learning much, if anything. What can a teacher do to get pupils interested in a study of the Word of God? If the teacher is a dedicated Christian, relies on the Holy Spirit, and reverences the Word of God, it is quite likely that the reason for the problem lies in the *way* the teacher handles the biblical content. The teacher who uses a variety of techniques which encourage communication and much interaction between the pupil and teacher is the one who is most likely to succeed in the teaching process.

There are many variations of the question-and-answer technique that can be used by teachers with children. If a teacher wants to tell a story, he can involve the pupils in the process by letting them help with the stick figures or the objects or the filmstrips.§

If the lesson lends itself to the drama technique, there are many variations, such as role playing, pantomime, and puppets which children enjoy.||

A teacher can assign a report and thus get a pupil involved in active research on a Bible topic. There are many projects that boys and girls enjoy which help them learn. They can be involved in "research teams." Juniors will work very seriously on a "case study" and search for a solution.

Interest centers can stimulate pupils to think, to enrich background, and to build and sustain interest. They are usually located on a surface or in a box or carton. Objects which are related to a particular idea or topic may be arranged attractively in a display for pupils to observe, examine, and discuss. For example, a group of juniors may visit an interest center which contains different kinds of lights: lanterns, flashlights, and electric lights. The source of power may be discussed, and lead naturally into a discussion on Christ, the light of the world. Interest centers can be constructed for almost any topic, and will appeal to any age group in the children's division, depending on the nature of the topic and purpose of the study.

A learning center is another exciting venture with children. It combines many different kinds of resources in a particular location designed for individualized learning. Pupils can come to the learning center to discover more information about specific topics in which they are interested. The pupils usually are guided by adults who begin in the learning process where the pupils are, and help them gain new understandings about the topics they are studying. The children discover for themselves by asking questions, doing research, observing and examining materials, and discussing and sharing ideas. The individual rate of development is significant in the process. Each child moves as rapidly or as slowly as required through various levels of learning to meet his individual needs.

Discovery learning can also open the doors of communication between the teacher and pupils. In its simplified form, the pupil discovers for himself ideas, facts, or concepts about a particular question, topic, or situation. Instead of *telling* the pupils the answers, the teacher encourages the pupils to discover on their own and then share their findings. In this way, the teacher acts as a guide, helps clarify, enrich, and correct inaccurate or wrong concepts. Pupils do not merely go on their own, but are guided by the teacher to discover truth for themselves. Also, the teacher

§Also see chap. 13, "Storytelling for Children."
||Also see chap. 14, "Storyplaying with Children."

helps pupils make personal application to their own lives. Discovery learning encourages self-involvement and emphasizes learning by doing. The teacher has responsibility in preparing for and guiding pupils in beneficial learning experiences. Discovery learning is appropriate for children from nursery through junior levels, with simplified procedures for younger children to more complex discoveries for older and more advanced pupils.

Guided conversation is a helpful way to reveal what pupils know about a particular topic and what they think, and to give them opportunities to express themselves through oral communication. In guided conversation, the teacher presents a basic idea or topic, and the pupils suggest related ideas which enable the group to expand its thinking. Also, in the process the pupils can be assisted in clarifying, evaluating, and applying their ideas. Guided conversation can build self-confidence and also encourage the shy pupils to participate. It is important that the teacher guides and gives purposeful direction to the discussion.

Team teaching is another exciting way of providing variety and in increasing learning possibilities. The concept usually involves two or more teachers and/or associates who plan, teach, and evaluate learning outcomes together. Large groups, small groups, and individualized learning experiences are integral parts of team teaching.#

These methods are just a few examples of ways in which teachers can encourage their pupils to participate actively in the learning process, to improve communication, to explore honestly the depth of Bible teacher together, and to discover implications for their own lives.

Teaching through these methods make individual differences more apparent. As the teacher becomes aware of these differences in pupil needs, interests, and abilities, he is much better able to deal with them and teach each child as an individual, precious in the sight of God.

Teaching Abstract Truths

Is it possible to teach abstract, doctrinal truths to children? This question has raised a great deal of controversy in the last several decades.

When some educational research indicated that children were not capable of understanding abstractions, many public school educators insisted that abstractions should be deleted from the curriculum. As a result, certain courses which had been taught in the first grade and up were postponed until much later. One example is the course on American history, which was postponed until at least late upper elementary grades.

#Also see chap. 22, "Leadership and Materials," for a more detailed study of team teaching.

This was justified by educators because of the many abstractions which are part of that study.

Religious educators became aware of what was happening and began to reconsider curricular planning in church schools. Some publishing houses, both independent and denominational, deleted doctrinal teachings in some children's departments on the premise that it was wasted time at least, and possibly even detrimental to the child. Certainly it could not be denied that doctrinal truth is abstract in nature. Some groups and publishers objected strenuously and declared that they would continue to teach the whole Bible and keep the curricular materials Bible-centered.

In all of this flurry of words, accusations, and counteraccusations, an important principle was often overlooked: if a teacher will begin with a concrete illustration or example, primaries and juniors can be led to a beginning or basic understanding of an abstract truth. This idea was tested with a number of groups. For example, Milford F. Henkel conducted a six-year research in the teaching of American history at Trump Road Elementary Schools in Canton, Ohio. His findings indicated that children can learn a great number of abstractions when teachers are careful to move from the concrete to the abstract in each instance. Older children, according to Piaget's theory of intellectual development, can be taught doctrinal truths if a teacher is careful to begin with a concrete "for instance" or example.

One of the surest techniques is the use of Bible examples. One of these illustrations used by our Lord Himself was His statement that He is the door. A teacher could use something like the following with a class of primaries or juniors:

"Boys and girls, today you recited John 10:9, 'I am the door: by me if any man enter in, he shall be saved.' Now, you know that Jesus isn't really a door. He's God, isn't He? Jesus didn't mean for us to think that He is a door made of wood or steel. He means that He is the door to heaven. He is giving us a 'for instance.' It's as if He said, 'Here is My beautiful home, heaven, but you can't get into heaven any way through Me.' He was referring to His death, which is the way He made for us to go into heaven. This doesn't mean that Jesus is a door, like the one coming into our classroom. Jesus means that He is *like* a door."

It is of vital importance that a teacher, attempting to explain doctrinal truths to children, work from the concrete to the abstract, as explained above. (For more on this subject, see chap. 9, "Children and Their Theological Concepts," and chap. 10, "Teaching Theological Concepts to Children.")

Another vital concern is that the teacher use a vocabulary that students understand. Teachers can learn much about vocabulary patterns by frequent conversations with children outside of class. A visit to a nearby nursery school or elementary school is also an excellent way for a teacher to improve his skill.

Children are also ready to learn new words. Once a teacher has communicated a new term, he may feel free to use that term with that group of children.

Sometimes, children do not learn because their teachers overestimate their attention span. An unruly or bored group of students sometimes has reached this stage because a well-meaning teacher has tried to "pour in" too much information too long. The wise teacher plans class time carefully. And, on the basis of the age of the pupils, he will interject breaks in the teaching process which will refresh the boys and girls and make them ready to go on in their learning. These breaks need not be recesses; they can simply be varied classroom activities that give a welcome change of pace.

The importance of the Christian teacher cannot be overestimated in the learning process with children. He teaches through his life, his precepts and his attitudes. Practically everything he does affects children in one way or another. The teacher may have a particular concept or body of knowledge to teach, but the concomitant, or by-product, learnings may be more significant to the children in changing their behavior than the lessons being taught.

Christian education is a supernatural process. The teacher is communicating a divine message through the Word of God. To effect change in others' lives, he is completely dependent on the ministry of the Holy Spirit.[11] As the Spirit of God works in the lives of the children, He may bring conviction of sin, remind of a truth or promise, or encourage the child to live for the Lord. A thrilling experience is in store for the Christian teacher who seeks to work both with the Holy Spirit and with children in order to produce eternal results.

NOTES

1. Henry Clay Lindgren, *Educational Psychology in the Classroom* (New York: Wiley, 1956), p. 204.
2. Ibid., pp. 175-95.
3. Clifford Morgan and Richard King, *Introduction to Psychology,* 3d ed. (New York: McGraw-Hill, 1966), p. 158.
4. Morris Bigge, *Learning Theories for Teachers* (New York: Harper & Row, 1964), p. 50.
5. Gardener Murphy, *Historical Introduction to Modern Psychology* (New York: Harcourt, Brace & World, 1949), p. 284.
6. Bigge, p. 102.
7. Ibid., p. 54.
8. Cornelius Jaarsma, *Human Development, Learning and Teaching* (Grand Rapids: Eerdmans, 1961), p. 190.
9. Bigge, p. 65.
10. Lindgren, pp. 206-207.
11. See Roy B. Zuck, *Spiritual Power in Your Teaching* (Chicago: Moody, 1972).

FOR FURTHER READING

Armstrong, Robert J.; Cornell, Terry D.; Kraner, Robert E.; and Robertson, E. Wayne. *The Development and Evaluation of Behavioral Objectives.* Worthington, Ohio: Jones, 1970.

Bernabei, Raymond, and Leles, Sam. *Behavioral Objectives in Curriculum and Evaluation.* Dubuque, Iowa: Kendall/Hunt, 1970.

Bolton, Barbara J., and Smith, Charles T. *Bible Learning Activities.* Glendale, Calif.: Gospel Light, Regal Books, 1973.

Borger, Robert, and Seaborne, A. E. M. *The Psychology of Learning.* Baltimore, Md.: Penguin, 1970.

Clark, Margaret L.; Erway, Ella; and Beltzer, Lee. *The Learning Encounter: The Classroom as a Communications Workshop.* New York: Random, 1971.

Deese, James, and Hulse, Stewart H. *The Psychology of Learning.* New York: McGraw-Hill, 1967.

Elkind, David. *Children and Adolescents: Interpretive Essays on Jean Piaget.* Paperback ed. New York: Oxford U., 1971.

Furth, Hans G., and Wachs, Harry. *Thinking Goes to School: Piaget's Theory in Practice.* New York: Oxford U., 1974.

Gagne, Robert M. *The Conditions of Learning.* New York: Holt, Rinehart, & Winston, 1967.

Gingell, Lesley P. *The ABC's of the Open Classroom.* Homewood, Ill.: ETC Publications, 1973.

———. *Learning and Individual Differences.* Columbus, Ohio: Merrill, 1967.

Goldstein, Henry; Krantz, David L.; and Rains, Jack D. *Controversial Issues in Learning.* New York: Appleton-Century-Crofts, 1965.

Holt, John. *How Children Learn.* New York: Pitman, 1967.

Kibler, Robert J.; Barker, Larry L.; and Miles, David T. *Behavioral Objectives and Instruction.* Boston: Allyn & Bacon, 1970.

Kintsch, Walter. *Learning, Memory, and Conceptual Processes.* New York: Wiley, 1970.

Learning Centers—Children on Their Own. Washington, D. C.: Association for Childhood Education Int., 1970.

LeBar, Lois E. *Children in the Bible School.* Westwood, N.J.: Revell, 1952.

———. *Focus on People in Church Education.* Westwood, N.J.: Revell, 1968.

Ligon, Ernest M. *Dimensions of Character.* New York: Macmillan, 1956.

Logan, Frank A. *Fundamentals of Learning and Motivation.* Dubuque, Iowa: Brown, 1970.

McDaniel, Elsiebeth, and Richards, Lawrence O. *You and Children.* Chicago: Moody, 1973.

Peck, Robert F., and Havighurst, Robert J. *The Psychology of Character Development.* New York: Wiley, 1961.

Richards, Lawrence O. *Creative Bible Teaching.* Chicago: Moody, 1970.

Smith, Leona J. *Guiding the Character Development of the Preschool Child.* New York: Association, 1968.

Staats, Arthur W. *Learning, Language, and Cognition.* New York: Holt, Rinehart, & Winston, 1968.

13

Storytelling for Children

Ruth Beam

Stories—Dynamic Vehicles

Throughout the Scriptures, God uses the story form to effect change.

The Pentateuch—a God-inspired, comprehensive, five-book recapitulation from Adam to Joshua—demonstrates the moving hand of God in history. A much shorter narrative, Nathan's carefully chosen parable of the rich man and the stolen ewe lamb, initiated a delicate, yet masterful confrontation between a little-known prophet and his multitalented king. Immediately, David is caught short. A dramatic, emotional, self-condemning response resulted in his conviction of sin.

Stories of Rebekah, Deborah, Ruth, and the Old Testament male contingent of heroes have motivated God's people through the ages to think and act sacrificially, yet triumphantly, amid adverse circumstances.

In New Testament times, Hebrews, Greeks, and Romans alike, were confronted with the paradoxical explosiveness of Jesus' philosophy of the turned cheek, the helping hand, and forgiving word. His parables, reinforced by His love, motivated the masses, the disciples, and apostles. These lives, born anew, were destined to transform the history of the next three centuries and provide all succeeding generations with a vivid account of the living and the written Word.

The world has profited from an impressive assemblage of God-motivated heroes ever since. However, as *Christianity Today* pointed out in "Who Is Our Pattern?" the modern Western world has largely rejected this traditional method of character training based on admiration for and emulation of great Bible figures.[1] Genuine villains and psychopathic criminals are

---

Ruth Beam, M.A., teaches oral interpretation and English at the Moody Bible Institute, Chicago.

being made into world celebrities, while present-day leaders are debunked and ridiculed. As the writer states, "Any reasonable man can see that if the earlier practices educated for virtues such as courage, altruism, and generosity of spirit, our present habits promote the opposing vices."[2]

In this age, children and adults are lured by preprogramed media which require the passive, relaxed attitude of a spectator. Unless a child is selective, sitting still with a television set for a companion can be stultifying.

Children are born creators and explorers of their here and now. They need the stimulation of Bible stories, classical stories, role play, and pantomimes to activate their imagination and cause their creativity to expand. They need to sense the pleasure and relaxation of tensions that stories radiate. In them is a power to enrich and soothe.

Through Bible stories, children can learn about the joys and faults bundled up in human relationships; they can develop kindness and right living which lead them to gain the favor of God, man, and even their enemies. Salvation, honesty, generosity, understanding, and the loving acceptance of others can become a part of all children, as the Holy Spirit, concerned parents, and teachers guide them—using stories as a vehicle.

> For leading the child to his God, there are no stories like the Bible stories. They are literally saturated with God, and the consciousness of His presence is as inevitably impressed upon the listener as the sunlight on his vision.[3]

The following chart illustrates some spiritual truths that Bible characters teach.

Bible Characters	What Their Stories Can Teach
NATHAN AND DAVID	The conviction of sin
JESUS AND THE SAMARITAN WOMAN	Salvation—the forgiveness, joy, and relief that can fill and change the round of life of the lonely, sinful, disappointed, misinformed, and discouraged
PRODIGAL SON	Repentance—the trip from wayward disobedience, suffering, to confession and reconciliation
DANIEL	Triumph—the refusal to trim godly conviction to fit the perimeter of a foreign, godless power
DAVID'S VALIANT MEN	Dedication—the performance of noble deeds; the purpose to avoid mistakes, excesses, and traps that all men can fall into

RUTH	Love—the gift of self to God and to others; guidance—the identification with the problems of others, serving selflessly, until God orders a multiple reward and destiny
DAVID AND SAUL	Growth—the desire and ability to love God more than revenge

Bulging Bookshelves

When a storyteller shops for tales, he will find no shortage. He may select any one of the following kinds from the bookshelves of the past and present. The following is a representative array of literary nuggets from the wealth of the Bible, Bible-related, and secular literature for children.

FROM THE BIBLE

Allegory: The trees look for a king, Judges 9:8-15
Animal: Creation; Noah, his ark and animals
Biography: Patriarchs, Samuel, Saul, David, Jesus, Paul
Character building: Joseph, Ruth, Daniel, Esther, Peter, Paul, and Timothy
Chronology, geography, history: Abraham's journeys; wilderness wanderings; Christ's birth, life, death, and resurrection; Paul's missionary journeys
Miracles: Creation; Elijah on Mount Carmel; Jonah and the big fish; birth of Jesus; water into wine; raising of Lazarus
Missionary: Jonah; Christ's earthly ministry to men; Paul's journeys
Parables: The sower; the prodigal son; the lost coin; the good Samaritan
Psalmists' songs: The shepherd, Psalm 23; the King of glory, Psalm 24; missionary song, Psalm 67; David's battle song, Psalm 144; David's hymn of praise, Psalm 145. (These are suitable for verse choirs, role playing, and pantomime.)
Salvation: Zacchaeus; woman at the well; Philippian jailer; Ethiopian eunuch
Symbolism: Tabernacle; Levitical offerings

FROM BIBLE-RELATED STORY COLLECTIONS

Allegory:
Pilgrim's Progress, John Bunyan
The Chronicles of Narnia, C. S. Lewis

Biography:
"Handel's Messiah"*
"Honest Abe"†
Doctrine:
"How Shall We Know Him?"†
"Thirty Pieces of Silver"*
Life choices:
"All This I Did for Thee"†
"The Seventeen Beggars"†
Missionary:
"A Live-the-Jesus-Book Girl"*
"Now's Your Chance, Lord"*
Salvation:
"All This I Did for Thee"†
"How Shall We Know Him?"†
"The Storm"†
"Tears of the Sea"†
Special Days:
"The Maid of Emmaus" (Easter)†
"Dopshun in Search of a Mother" (Mother's Day)†
"Thanksgivin' Ann" (Thanksgiving)†
"Be Thou Faithful" (Christmas)†
"The Browns' Christmas" (Christmas)‡
Steadfastness:
"Lions in the Way"*
Witnessing:
"Catarina's Ten Fingers"*

FROM SECULAR SOURCES

Animal:
Winnie-the-Pooh, A. A. Milne
Wind in the Willows, Kenneth Grahame
Lassie Come Home, Eric Knight
Misty of Chincoteague, Marguerite Henry
Rascal, Sterling North
Biography:
Abraham Lincoln, Ingri and Edgar Parin d'Aulaire
The Story of George Washington Carver, Arna Bontemps

*From *40 Stories for You to Tell,* compiled by Gladys Mary Talbot.
†From *Stories I Love to Tell,* compiled by Gladys Mary Talbot.
‡From *My Favorite Christmas Stories,* by Theresa Worman.

Character building:

The Adventures of Pinocchio, C. Collodi (pseudonym for Carlo Lorenzini)

The Plain Princess, Phyllis McGinley

The Door in the Wall, Marguerite de Angeli

Epic:

The Iliad and the Odyssey of Homer, retold, Alfred John Church

The Merry Adventures of Robin Hood, rewritten, Howard Pyle

Fable:

Aesop's Fables, selected and adapted, Louis Untermeyer

Fairy tale:

The Little Match Girl and *The Ugly Duckling,* Hans Christian Andersen

Fantasy:

The Secret Garden, Frances Hodgson Burnett

Tom's Midnight Garden, Philippa Pearce

Fiction:

Heidi, Johanna Spyri

Folk:

Uncle Remus Tales, Joel Chandler Harris

Historical fiction:

Caddie Woodlawn, Carol Ryrie Brink

The Courage of Sarah Noble, Alice Dalgliesh

The Long Winter, Laura Ingalls Wilder

Humor:

Madeline's Rescue, Ludwig Bemelmans

The Adventures of Tom Sawyer, Mark Twain

Mechanized Hero:

The Little Engine That Could, Wally Piper (retold from *The Pony Engine,* Mabel C. Bragg)

Mike Mulligan and His Steam Shovel, Virginia Burton

Nature:

Time of Wonder, Robert McCloskey

The Snowy Day, Ezra Jack Keats

Social:

Blue Willow, Doris Gates

The Hundred Dresses, Eleanor Estes

. . . And Now Miguel, Joseph Krumgold

Space:

Miss Pickerell Goes to Mars, Ellen MacGregor

Have Space Suit—Will Travel, Robert Heinlein

For additional titles, see *Honey for a Child's Heart* by Gladys Hunt and *Children's Reading in the Home* by May Hill Arbuthnot. Gladys Hunt's book is written from the evangelical Christian perspective and gives helpful insights concerning using classics with children.

Structuring Stories

Whether you are writing your own story, retelling a Bible story, preparing a story already written, or condensing a book-length story, construct it according to its four major parts, namely, the introduction, body, climax, and conclusion.

In the introduction, the teller should set the stage and plunge into the action immediately. He should tell who is there, establish where and when the action is taking place, and give a *hint* of what is about to happen. He should reveal a seed of the conflict or suspense to come. As Laura Emerson advises, "*Begin at the latest possible moment* as close to the conclusion as possible, rather than leisurely tuning up as an orchestra before a concert."[4] Arouse an emotion quickly. The two introductions which follow are contrasts in the extreme, but Emerson makes a point when she contrasts them side by side.

> Once we decided to have a picnic so Uncle Jack and Aunt Sue got out the old Ford. I like a Chevrolet much better. Then they found they had a flat tire. I wanted to tell you about the lunch. I like hamburgers, but they all wanted weiners. Well, after we were all ready to start, et cetera.
>
> I was eating a sandwich by the lake when I heard Jim call, "Help, help!"[5]

The body develops the "what" of the story; it relates the ups and downs of the hero. The hero generally starts out on top, but before long, an antagonist muddles the tempo of his life. Or in some cases, the conflict may be in the form of a disaster, a tedious trial, or temptation to violate right. The hero, or heroes, struggles against the conflict; suspense should build up and increase until the final clash or choice of action occurs. Mounting action forces opposition between good and evil. The dialogue, actions, and reactions of the characters should demonstrate the truths to be learned. The appeal and winsomeness of the love of God should operate powerfully in circumstances and lives.

The climax marks the pinnacle of action and suddenly reveals the "why" of the story, that is, its reason for existing. The plot generally turns in an unexpected manner; the true character of the hero and antagonist should emerge in the final outcome. To be of positive benefit in teaching biblical truth, the hero needs to *struggle* with right and wrong. His final choice should reveal what is exemplary. His life should be a challenge, not a truce.

The conclusion of the story should be short, account for all major characters, tie all ends together. No moralizing should need to be included. In children's stories, the ending should be satisfying; the truth should be palatable, understandable. Good should win out and evil be punished, and God should have His rightful place of glory.

The following list tells how to make each part add to the effectiveness of the story.

How to Structure Stories

INTRODUCTION

Introduce place, characters, time, mood, and pace.

Tell who, when, where, and give a hint of what or a promise of future action or problem.

Get attention and arouse emotion and suspense as soon as possible—e.g., love, compassion, dislike.

Get the story off the ground and moving.

Set the scene by introducing hero and antagonist with a *seed* of trouble to follow.

BODY

Develop the "what."

Hold attention with action and suspense.

Relate a series of incidents revealing project or difficulty, seeming fulfillment, touch of humor, the upset, near tragedy—clash on clash—leading to final clash between hero and problem (antagonist, adverse conditions in nature, conflict or handicap, error in judgment).

Weave in true teaching throughout body.

Include hazards to be overcome, choices to be made.

CLIMAX

Reach highest point of interest and suspense in story.

Require final choice to be made.

Show turn of plot.

Reveal characters' true selves by their actions and reactions.

Determine the way the story will go.

Explain mystery.

Reveal kernel of truth, purpose for which story was written.

CONCLUSION

Account for all major characters.

Tie up all ends.

Fulfill all promises.

Be brief, and for children, make it satisfying.
If possible, reiterate truth, but do not add a moral.
Depending on the story and audience, either fully answer question raised in the beginning or leave it open ended as a stimulus for discussion.

Choosing Stories

Apart from the intrinsic worth of a story, three factors affect the selection of a piece for telling. As Elbert R. Bowen, chairman of the department of speech and drama at Central Michigan University, observes:

> The reader chooses wisely when he selects literature which he has a strong desire to communicate and which he is confident will provide his audience with a satisfying experience. (If this is so obvious, tell me why so many readings are so dull.)[6]

Add to wise selection and strong desire to communicate, suitability for the occasion, and the dilemma of choice is largely resolved.

QUESTIONS TO ASK WHEN CHOOSING A STORY

Regarding the storyteller

Do you *like* the story and have a strong desire to communicate it?
Do you agree with its content?
Do you appreciate the style of writing?
Is it within your scope of ability to tell?

Regarding the audience

Will the story develop a companionship between you and your audience?
Will it interest the age group present?
Is it suitable for the sex or sexes present? (A rule of thumb: If the boys like it, the girls will also.)
Does it move with enough action, dialogue, and suspense to maintain interest?
Does it tell its own message?
Will it leave a lingering impact?

Regarding the occasion

Does the story fit the season of the year, or can it be adapted to do so?
Does it lend itself to the environment of the occasion?
Can the length be adjusted to meet your needs?
Does it fulfill your aim: to inform? to enrich? to stimulate emotions, imagination? to motivate? to comfort? to admonish? to entertain?
Can it be given to the glory of God?

A story chosen from a printed source indicates that a compiler, editor, and/or publication board will have already seen a measure of literary worth in it. Some stories emerge as unforgettable because the author interweaves layers of interest-catching material in an order and manner that has power to evoke an emotional response commonly felt by men—love or hate, hope or fear, joy or despair.

When the author applies personalized form to his arresting material by presenting it uniquely, as no man has, a literary gem can emerge.

If the attraction of the story lingers and suggests that the listener or reader bring something of his own background into his growing comprehension of the material—to fill in where the author purposely left space for thought—the piece gains a third dimension of worth.

To illustrate, consider the writings of Joseph Bayly. He takes a universal subject to which each man responds, then particularizes his treatment from a unique perspective. He did this with death in *The View from a Hearse,*[7] a book written after he had seen three of his sons die. The reader interacts with Bayly's assessment of death, then sifts his reactions together with Bayly's, thus producing an enriched perception concerning the loss of loved ones. He uses a similar technique in *Psalms of My Life.*[8] In-depth story literature, written in the same manner, is worthy of the time needed to prepare it for presentation.

Choosing Stories According to Age and Interests

As the storyteller becomes more adept at presenting stories, he becomes aware that certain subjects capture the attention and blend with the personalities of certain age groups.

The route to gaining this knowledge cannot come alone from words on a page. The chart that follows and the material in chapters 4-8 of this book will help, but the surer way of knowing what children like is to *know children.*

Talk with them. Learn what makes them laugh and cry. Invite them on fun outings; take them to museums, zoos, forest preserves, on bicycle trips—places that interest *them.* Invite the youngsters to eat at your house; find out what their favorite foods are. Help them to make crafts and gifts for others. Visit them in their homes. Listen to their joys and troubles—relationships at school, home, and church. Study Scripture together—verses that shed light on these interests, needs, and problems. Pray with them. Somewhere in the midst of knowing and loving them, there will be opportunities to tell these boys and girls stories that fit!

Adapting the Story

Oh, the disappointment of finding a story one likes, only to discover that certain elements within it will not fit the storyteller's purpose! Since most stories have been written to be read, many parts of a story frequently

TABLE 13.1 Stories for Each Age

Age Group	Story Characteristics	Suggested Bible Stories or Books	Suggested Secular Stories or Books
NURSERY 0-3 years	(Years) 0 (Story readiness) singing, finger plays, sentence-length conversational stories	Jesus blessing the children	Finger and toe plays
	1 Pictures of the familiar; "running" narratives by mother	Baby Jesus Baby Moses	Nursery rhymes
	2 Conversations about experiences: stars, thunder, dark, flowers	Infant Samuel	"Three Bears"
	3 Answering questions with verbal and written stories; some repetition in vocabulary	Little Lost Lamb	"Three Pigs" "Three Billy Goats Gruff"
KINDERGARTEN 4-5 years	Rhythm, rhyme, and repetition Familiar things and places: pets, toys, concrete objects; mechanized hero Concrete language; simple plot; few characters Animals—their names and calls	Creation Noah's ark Boy Samuel Boy Jesus Good Shepherd Jesus blessing the children Bible in Pictures for Little Eyes	"Gingerbread Boy" "Little Engine That Could" "Peter Rabbit" "Make Way for Ducklings"
PRIMARY 6-8 years	Fact, fairy tales, folk, and fantasy Bible miracles; "helping" situations One child in one foreign country Animals—their homes and habits	Crossing Red Sea Healing of Naaman Wedding at Cana Feeding of 5,000 Rescue of Peter	"Jack and the Beanstalk" "Rumpelstiltskin" "Sleeping Beauty" "Little Match Girl" *The Lion, the Witch and the Wardrobe* Winnie-the-Pooh stories
JUNIOR 9-11 years	Heroism: action, adventure, danger, daring Real people in physical conquest Chronology, biography, geography Animals—care and breeding	Wilderness wanderings Tabernacle Life of David, Daniel, Samson Paul's journeys	*Tom Sawyer* *Robinson Crusoe* *Heidi* *Little Women* *Misty of Chincoteague* *Rascal*

need adapting and can be changed without harming the original narrative. Numerous descriptive details, important to the silent reader, may be portrayed by the storyteller's tone of voice, facial expression, or gestures. Therefore the actual words may be eliminated.

Adaptation may also include some additions to the story as well as changes. Care should be taken to preserve the total effect desired by the author, and in no case should the adapted story be reproduced in printed form without permission in writing from the publisher or author, whichever holds the copyright.

PARTS OF A STORY THAT FREQUENTLY NEED ADAPTING

Title. If it conveys ambiguous meaning, such as "United Nation," then it may need to be revised as well as shifted from the past tense. Try "Uniting a Nation."

Length. Tales written to be read frequently need to be shortened.

Word choice. Obscure words such as *damsel, laconic,* and *atmospheric filament* should be changed and suitable synonyms put in their place.

Phrasing. If it is old-fashioned or involved, update and simplify it. "Lay this to his offence" should be changed to, "Blame him." Tedious sentences that run on for six lines need to be shortened.

Names. Some stories, especially the old folktales, include characters who have no names. If more than one character is involved and names would enliven the story as well as clarify who is speaking, add appropriate names.

Number of characters. In "The Gingerbread Boy," a farmer and a thresher appear. Since few children today understand the work of a thresher, this character can be eliminated without damaging the plot.

Number of events. In a retelling of *Pilgrim's Progress* some happenings in Interpreter's house would be beyond the knowledge of young children because they are highly symbolic. Rather than trying at great length to explain these, eliminate them.

Sequence of events. For young children, flashbacks should be eliminated and the story told in simple, chronological order.

Amount of narration. Usually there is too much in any given story. Eliminate lengthy descriptions, remove dialogue tags ("he said"), and delete references to minor incidents which do not advance the plot.

Amount of dialogue. In most cases, increase this. An author may write, "The woman screamed," but as Charles Dickens advised, "Don't say the woman screamed, bring her in and let her scream."

Person in which the story is told. If a long story is told in the first person, consider your ability to maintain the voice characterization of the speaker, since it is difficult to interpret paragraph after paragraph in a voice different from your own.

Placement of the moral. Weave in the truth being taught throughout the story. Make the truth come out of the characters' mouths.

Age level of the story. To raise it, remove the words such as *little, Daddy, Mommie,* and so on. To lower it, simplify the vocabulary and sentence structure, providing, of course, the subject matter is suitable.

Pace. Enliven the movement of the story by exchanging tired nouns, adjectives, and verbs which have little or no action in them, for kinetic words which *run* and *jump,* and *march* and *fight.* The moods are intensified by *kinesthetic* words which demonstrate reactions and attitudes. Add such words as *breathless, nervously, casually,* and *noisily.*

Spiritual truth. Often a secular book contains a gripping story of a character, such as Florence Nightingale or Madame Chiang Kai-shek. Since both of these women were called of God and used by Him, add specific information to portray this.

Season. When a long story, such as "Dopshun in Search of a Mother," is prepared, seek to change its seasonal emphasis by changing the Sunday school promotion program in the story to the type of program that fits the current event or season. Thereby the story may be used (with a new audience) more than once a year.

Preparing the Story for Telling

Storytelling, like any sport or art, requires utmost dedication if the spectators and participators are to be kept interested. However, as Gladys Mary Talbot once observed, "Unlike other arts, all of you may participate in this one, provided you are willing to pay the price—study, work and practice."[9]

Frequently, a student will remark that he or she has no special preaching or musical gift. As early in life as the college years, a feeling of hopelessness may develop over not having a "ministry." Great has been the astonishment of a student to find that he can speak and repeatedly hold the attention of an audience, not while preaching or making a speech but while sharing a story.

To become a storyteller, no expensive equipment is necessary. God has given us all a voice to speak with as narrator and to vary a little for the major characters. He has given us facial flexibility for imprinting our interpretation on words; and not the least, He has given us a body whereby we may gesture, assume various stances which depict a given mood, age, or state of health. We can bring a story to life without a thing in our hands. No construction paper, objects, or figures are needed, just ourselves as God made us, faithful preparation, and the Lord's love and help (cf. 1 Co 13:1-2).

Any performer will verify that much preparation goes into the presentation that looks so easy. The same is true of storytelling. To assist the one who must present a story or dramatic reading, the following guidelines are given.

1. Read the story to capture the central plot and to determine the main characters.
2. Reread, and, if necessary, adapt it as you go along. If it is possible, mark the copy you are using.
3. Read the story analytically; determine what paragraphs form the introduction, body, climax, and conclusion. Work toward giving each of these areas a differing mood and pace.
4. At least *two weeks before* telling the story in public, read the story through, aloud, each night before retiring. Use your own voice tone for the narration; for the characters, seek to give a hint of their personality, age, and sex by the manner in which you speak.
5. Practice telling the story aloud to an empty room, tape recorder, mirror, or to a friend. If you can include a number of gestures suitable to the characters and the action, they will put you and your audience at ease.

Presenting the Story

Present your story as a gift, to be given away with an outstretched arm of love. Do not be afraid. Love your audience, and they will love you. If discouragement and doubt come, as they surely will, remember what Lois LeBar said to this writer: "Remember, you are the authority on this material. No one to whom you will be speaking will have worked on it as thoroughly as you have."

Whether standing near a center of interest, such as a glistening Christmas tree, or in front of a story coordinated background before a large audience, or sitting in the midst of a discussion group, or while riding on a long trip, or sitting on a bed alongside a child when the lights are low, the well-chosen story will charm its way into the heart of a listener.

In an informal, impromptu, one-to-one situation, you will speak with ease if you visualize mentally the entire story movement as you present it. Make the language your own as each person, place, event, important conversation, and truth comes before your mental vision.

Stories for use in the church should be presented in a more structured manner. Prepare for Sunday school worship services, vacation Bible school, children's church, camp programs, missionary meetings and open-ended story discussions as outlined in Preparing the Story for Telling.

For little children, use short sentences and simple words; if they are sitting on a story rug, be seated among them so as to maintain eye contact with all. Whatever the setting or situation, the storyteller needs to be one level higher than his audience. Strong, resonant tones emerge with greater ease if the teller stands.

Use dramatic language. Speak loudly enough to be heard easily. Choose words and phrases to add atmosphere to the message. Observe light and shadow; make contrasts evident by raising and lowering your voice. Use the pause to create suspense and surprise, to show the passage of time, and, if need be, to gain or regain attention.

When you are invited to tell stories outside your home and church, seek to use material you have told elsewhere, some time before. You will be able to anticipate the outcome of your story if you give previously prepared and tested material. Also, your poise will be increased. Nothing is worse than fighting first-time fears in front of a large banquet, conference, rally, or retreat audience.

The larger the audience, the larger the gestures needed. Most important, though, the same earnest heart preparation before the Lord is required whether the story is given to one or many. Then when you walk into view, when you look into the faces of your audience, and open your mouth to speak, your inner self shines through; your whole person will speak.

Suggestions for Effective Storytelling

The storyteller succeeds best when the audience focuses its attention on the message, not on the messenger. The audience should not see the proverbial wheels go round; the mechanics should be hidden, but the vehicle should proceed smoothly.

Once the storyteller experiences the feeling of having presented a story as a carefully prepared gift, tied up with trimmings and given with love, no other approach to an audience will seem adequate. To glorify God and have an outward expression of ease that comes from within, consider the following suggestions:

1. Ask God to give you natural poise; be at one with Him.
2. *Know* your story; *live* your story.
3. Know and *love* your audience.
4. Stand erect before your audience in comfortable shoes. Avoid bending forward, leaning into the audience: it conveys a "talking down" impression.
5. *See* the scene you are setting. Do not allow your voice to say one thing and your body and face to say another.

6. Vary voice level, rate of speech, age level, personality, and sex of each character being interpreted.
7. Cultivate a pleasing, resonant voice.
8. Speak loudly enough to be heard by all, including the hard-of-hearing.
9. Avoid slang, grammatical errors, and mispronunciations.
10. Maintain gracious eye contact with all in your audience.
11. Use cultured, yet vivacious gestures.
12. Avoid nervous gestures, clasped hands, rocking backward and forward, and scraping feet.
13. Know how and when to vary narration speed, and introduce dialogue with a fast attack.
14. Know attention span of various age groups and audience types.
15. Know when to quit.
16. Take training in speech and gestures in an oral interpretation or storytelling class.
17. *Pray* over your stories. Let words live on your tongue for God's glory.

NOTES

1. "Who Is Our Pattern?" *Christianity Today*, 28 (July, 1972): 24-25.
2. Ibid.
3. Edna Dean Baker, *Kindergarten Method in the Church School* (Cincinnati: Abingdon, 1925), p. 161.
4. Laura S. Emerson, *Storytelling* (Grand Rapids: Zondervan, 1959), p. 47.
5. Ibid.
6. Elbert R. Bowen, "A Baker's Dozen for the Interpretative Reader," *The Speech Teacher*, 15 (Nov., 1966): 276.
7. Joseph Bayly, *The View from a Hearse* (Elgin, Ill.: David C. Cook, 1969).
8. ——. *Psalms of My Life* (Wheaton, Ill.: Tyndale, 1969).
9. Gladys Mary Talbot, ed., *Stories I Love to Tell* (Chicago: Moody, 1949), p. 9.

FOR FURTHER READING

Arbuthnot, May Hill. *Children and Books*. 3d ed. Rev. Glenview, Ill.: Scott, Foresman, 1964.

——. *Children's Reading in the Home*. Glenview, Ill.: Scott, Foresman, 1969.

Baker, Edna Dean. *Kindergarten Method in the Church School*. Cincinnati: Abingdon, 1925.

Barrett, Ethel. *Storytelling, It's Easy*. Los Angeles: Cowman, 1960.

Bayly, Joseph. *I Saw Gooley Fly*. Old Tappan, N.J.: Revell, 1968.

——. *Psalms of My Life*. Wheaton, Ill.: Tyndale, 1969.

——. *The View from a Hearse*. Elgin, Ill.: David C. Cook, 1969.

Bowen, Elbert R. "A Baker's Dozen for the Interpretative Reader." *The Speech Teacher*. 15, no. 4 (Nov., 1966).

Doyle, Brian, ed. *The Who's Who of Children's Literature*. New York: Schocken, 1971.

Duff, Annis. *Bequest of Wings*. New York: Viking, 1944.

Emerson, Laura S. *Storytelling*. Grand Rapids: Zondervan, 1959.

Hunt, Gladys. *Honey for a Child's Heart*. Grand Rapids: Zondervan, 1969.

Lee, Charlotte I. *Oral Interpretation.* 4th ed. Boston: Houghton Mifflin, 1971.
Sawyer, Ruth. *The Way of the Storyteller.* New York: Viking, 1957.
Talbot, Gladys Mary, ed. *Stories I Love to Tell.* Chicago: Moody, 1949.
Tooze, Ruth. *Storytelling.* Englewood Cliffs. N.J.: Prentice-Hall, 1959.
Trent, Robbie. *Your Child and God.* Rev. ed. New York: Harper & Row, 1952.
Ward, Winifred. *Stories to Dramatize.* Anchorage, Ky.: Children's Theater, 1952.
Worman, Theresa. *My Favorite Christmas Stories.* Chicago: Moody, 1965.

14

Story Playing with Children

Elsiebeth McDaniel

Story playing is a method of teaching frequently overlooked. There is little argument about the use of visuals, questions, discussion, and projects, but many teachers find it difficult to see values in relating "let's pretend" to Christian education. However, pretending is part of child growth. The young child pretends about many things: he is a policeman, daddy, mother, truck driver, nurse, doctor, astronaut, and many other roles.

Young children do not have to be taught to pretend. They engage in it spontaneously as a way to learn. If pretending, or "playing out," situations and relationships is a natural and effective way to learn, why eliminate this method is our teaching? "Let's pretend" can be refined and adapted to meet the needs of various age groups, including adults.

Why Story Play Is Effective

When has learning really taken place? "The process of learning, it is held, does not reach its consummation until reasoning has issued forth in creative expression."[1] Surely playing out the story may often be the creative expression necessary to complete the process of learning. This is especially true if the story play originates with the pupils' request. When children can dramatize a story in simple form, they more readily learn the story. If fifth graders can develop a skit to show application of Bible truth, they have understood the principles the teacher hoped to communicate.

Story playing may take one of several forms—skits, puppet plays, role playing, finger plays, or simple dramatization. In this chapter, we are not dealing with practiced dramatization. Practiced plays, even though they

---

Elsiebeth McDaniel, M.A., is Editor of Pre-Primary and Primary Lessons at Scripture Press Publications, Inc., Wheaton, Illinois.

may be written by pupils, are not a spontaneous form of "let's pretend." They are usually performed to entertain. Some students will enjoy being in a play, but the work of memorization, details of costuming, and the continuing rehearsals deprive children of the joy found in simple drama. This chapter is concerned with the story playing that is enjoyed as a more or less spontaneous response by the learners themselves—not a public production.

The main purpose of story play is to help a child "get inside the skin" of another person. Through taking a part—becoming another person—a child learns how a particular person felt in a specific situation and why he reacted in a certain way. Story playing is more valuable for its activation of emotion than its influence on factual recall.

Helping children empathize seems more important than ever before. Currently, there are desensitizing factors in every child's experience. Along with the advantages of TV come disadvantages. Television seems to provide an "instant mix" of emotions—violence, death, and individual accomplishment. Many scenes lack reality, but they are presented as reality. Constant exposure to this type of program can endanger the emotional health of a child: he learns not to feel.

A second factor dulling emotional reaction is the element of change. In the last few decades, change has occurred so frequently, rapidly, and universally that people seem to have learned to react unemotionally. Our present culture seems to play down emotional response.

However, the Bible makes it clear that man is an emotional creature. Any concordance lists many references for such emotions as anger, love, joy, covetousness, envy, fear, sadness, and jealousy. People respond emotionally in varying degrees. Educators recognize that affective learning occurs when emotions are stirred. The whole subject of story play is associated with emotions—feeling and responding.

Why do some teachers hesitate to use story play in any form? Some teachers think story play is entertainment only. Still others believe that telling is teaching and story play is a waste of time. And then there are some authoritarian teachers who feel insecure in a situation where children take the lead. This type of teacher finds it difficult to establish a free, open relationship with pupils to help them dramatize a story or event in a simple way. The authoritarian teacher is afraid of losing control of his class. At the bottom of his fear is a lack of trust in his pupils and in himself. A teacher who lives with and relates to children easily needs have no fear about introducing some form of story play. True, if pupils are not accustomed to this teaching method, it may take more than one attempt to provide a satisfactory learning experience. In time, however, the pupils will participate freely and prove to a doubting teacher that learning is taking place.

Books are available on creative dramatics, puppetry, role playing, finger plays, and action rhymes, but they will be useless unless a teacher understands the value of this teaching method. It is more important for a teacher to "want-to" than to know all details of the "how-to."

> Few teachers believe that creativity has no place in the Sunday school, but many teachers hesitate to put it to work for them. Some Christians think that creativity is a gift God has given only to the few. God has given some measure of creativity to very individual. However, if the gift is neglected, it withers and may disappear. Creativity is combining something old with something new to produce something different. It is thinking and learning in fresh, new ways.[2]

Story play may be a fresh, new way—an open door to many teachers.

The forms of story play discussed in this chapter will include finger plays and action rhymes, role playing, simple dramatizations, and puppetry. Successful use of these types of story play demands enthusiasm—belief in what you are doing, some know-how, and a respect and love for the pupils.

What Is Achieved Through Story Play?

There are several advantages to this method of teaching. Remember, a teacher must see the advantages of a method and have the "want-to" before he is interested in the "how-to."

1. Story play makes an event seem more real. Each involved pupil thinks and feels as someone in the story. He may become a person who formerly existed only as a name on a page.

2. Children may be more honest when they are not revealing themselves. When children are acting out endings to a problem situation, for example, they will probably suggest real action, not merely answers acceptable to a teacher.

3. Teachers benefit because they have an opportunity to know the children in a new way. They see the pupils' strengths and weaknesses as they show how they feel about situations. There are other factors, of course. A child may reveal selfishness and be insensitive to others. Perhaps another child, usually shy and self-conscious, will develop self-confidence through pretending to be someone else.

4. Ideas, feelings, and concepts of the story become a part of the child. It is good to talk about being kind, for example, but for a pupil to feel the part of a child who is excluded from the group helps him understand loneliness. Then he values being part of the group and may be interested in helping other children enjoy a sense of belonging.

5. Bible stories become real: they come alive. Children get a feel for characters of long ago.

6. Playing a story helps children think of others, reach out to other people, and turn away from their self-centeredness.

7. Story play, role play particularly, gives the learner an inside view of another person. This experience helps a child respect others and teaches him sensitivity in personal relationships. It helps pupils by providing insights few other methods can offer.

Perhaps this quotation best sums up the value of story play:

> The story the child plays, like the picture he paints, the figure he fashions from clay, the story he writes is a way of enjoying again and of sharing with another something that is important to him. In it he is forever adding more to himself, finding out more about himself, entering into new sets of relationships with others and learning from them. The story lived by acting stays long in his life. No one knows the limit of its teaching.[3]

Finger Plays and Action Rhymes

Finger plays and action rhymes are not a new method of teaching, but an old and effective technique. Often, parents use this type of teaching in "Pat-a-cake, pat-a-cake," or "How big is baby?" Even a young baby responds happily to these words and rhythms. Public school teachers and Christian educators can also utilize this successful method to help young children pretend both actions and characterizations through finger play.

Finger plays are used to relax children, to impress a story, to introduce a story, to teach rhythm, and are sometimes used to quiet children after an exciting activity. Both action rhymes and finger plays may be used with children from babyhood through the age of six or seven. Of course, the older children may be freer to suggest their own actions or even music for the words. Preschoolers, on the other hand, will enjoy doing the actions, but may not memorize the words. Some children, after hearing the rhyme a number of times, may enjoy repeating parts of it with the teacher.

The teacher is most concerned, however, with the children's participation in the actions. Even a shy or self-conscious child may lose himself in this type of group activity. And when a child is doing, he is learning! Finger plays and action rhymes become familiar friends as children act out the same one again and again.

Young children's muscles need action! Often the joy of moving head, arms, trunk, legs, and fingers is more important than the words. Because feeling the words and moving with them is important, it is not necessary for all children to make the same motions. Some children may demonstrate the round sun by holding their arms over their heads to make a circle. But other children will be happy making a small sun with fingers held in front of them. Encourage large muscle movements, but give each child an opportunity to gain satisfaction through participation.

Here is a typical action rhyme used with preschoolers.*

> The city wall was very high.
> (*Show great height by standing on tiptoe, arms reaching high.*)
> The gates were shut up tight.
> (*Interlace fingers of hands to form a tight gate.*)
> But God would take His people in.
> They would not need to fight.
> March, march, march, march,
> (*March around room or in place.*)
> Their feet went tramping round.
> The trumpets blew.
> (*Blow on pretend trumpet.*)
> The people marched.
> (*March around the room or in place.*)
> There was no other sound.
> Obeying God, they marched and marched.
> (*March around the room or in place.*)
> For seven days, around the wall.
> Then shouted loud.
> (*Pause and let children shout.*)
> Oh, what a shout!
> Crash! Bang!
> (*Clap hands.*)
> The walls did fall!
> (*Quickly stoop to floor.*)

To use finger plays, the teacher must tell the story, sing the song, or repeat the rhyme—whatever form the story play takes, demonstrating the appropriate gestures and facial expressions. The teacher should thoroughly learn the words and actions, because this teaching method cannot be effective if he is tied to a book. A teacher must make the finger play so much a part of him that he can use it spontaneously. Then finger play becomes a vehicle for new ideas, attitudes, and appreciations.

Some teachers may wish to use finger puppets to introduce or review a finger play, adding a new aspect. This is an interesting approach, but should be used sparingly. A teacher will soon discover that long finger plays are for him to recite or tell, but they are too long for the children to learn. He must also remember that young children cannot imitate him perfectly, and he must be willing to accept their performance.

In using finger plays, choose plays and rhythms for one unit of study.

A finger play may tell the story of a character in an individual lesson, but its use is limited. A finger play about a Bible character, for example, can best be used in teaching the lesson. Or it may be used for review. However, finger plays that fit the theme and purpose of the unit can be used again and again.

Many books of finger plays and action rhymes are available. However, do not overlook the opportunity to use recorded action rhymes—also available from some publishers. Records, along with homemade cassettes or tapes, add still another dimension to teaching—learning through music.

Role Play

In role playing, children assume the parts of other persons: they play a role. However, the play is not rehearsed, and it is not meant to entertain. Role play usually presents a problem situation before it has been developed to the point of solution. The children who assume the roles in the situation show what they would have done—how they would have reacted to an incident or situation. Because Christianity deals with personal relationships, role play serves effectively in teaching biblical principles about attitudes.

Unlike some teaching methods, a novice should not decide, "Today we'll try role play." The teacher using this method should understand the method and how to use it before trying it in a class situation. Role playing is used by some psychologists and psychiatrists, but no teacher should attempt to use role playing to solve psychological problems! Role playing in the classroom must be limited to typical everyday experiences of the boys and girls involved.

Before using role play, a teacher should try to learn as much about it as possible. He should read; observe role playing in a classroom; and, if possible, see a film about it and discuss the method with other teachers. Then he may be ready to try it. As a teacher works with role playing, he will develop insight into the possibilities of this method.

The teacher of second graders has decided to try role playing. She has also decided to use it to solve home problems. She says, "There is trouble in the Smith home. Bobby and Betty want different TV programs. What do you think happens?" Then after a few volunteers have suggested what might take place, the teacher may say, "Would you like to show us what you think happened?"

The teacher should choose children who have been quick to volunteer, because these children have sensed some identification with Bobby and Betty. The teacher repeats the situation so that all will understand.

"Now Ronnie and Janet, show us what you think took place. How did Bobby and Betty solve their problem?" After these children demonstrate their solution, the teacher may call on other volunteers. Perhaps some child will want to add a mother or father to the scene. The enactment may be repeated several times with different volunteers. The teacher will stop the action whenever players have developed a solution, have reached the end of their idea, or the teacher wants to add more information to the problem.

At the end of the role play, or after each enactment, the teacher should lead discussion about the solution. However, the teacher is always very careful never to suggest that there is only one solution he approves. If this happens, the children will slant any future role playing toward seeking the teacher's approval. The teacher must guide through evaluation toward the right solution. Or he may file various solutions for future reference, attempting to explain how they do or do not line up with Bible principles. If Ronnie suggests that Bobby gets his choice of TV because a parent intervenes after Betty hits him, this is not a Christian solution. However, the teacher must help the children reach this decision. He must not tell them what they should feel or think.

A beginning teacher may wish to use pantomime as an easy way to lead up to role play. Pantomime, acting out without words, can be introduced as a game. Play out situations that the children experience, asking, "What do you do before coming to Sunday school? before school? at bedtime? Sunday afternoon?" Even young children can enter into this type of role playing. However, problem solving or using several roles may be more effective with children in third grade and beyond. Role playing rewards the teacher with an opportunity to see problem-solving in action. As a result, children usually become more considerate of one another.

A teacher who wants to study this method can find a chapter on role play in many texts. The material in this chapter explains the method and lists some advantages. More information will be needed to use the method successfully. However, a sequence is given here to explain what may be necessary in a good role-playing of an unfinished story.[4]

1. Explain the purpose: to get ideas for endings to a story.
2. Read structured, open-end story, dramatically.
3. Define roles.
4. Choose "characters" from those who have identified with roles.
5. Set the stage: "This is the living room," etc.
6. Sensitize the audience and prepare them for intelligent and related observation.
7. Begin the enactment.
8. "Cut" at the proper time.

9. Repeat the enactments as interest and time permit.
10. Lead discussion and evaluation by the group.

Creative Drama

Dramatization may take several forms. Each form becomes more refined as the age of the group increases.

Pantomime is a demonstration, or acting, without words. All children enjoy it. They may pantomime an action, the end of a story, a Bible verse, or a song. Sometimes pantomime is used to show how a person feels as a reaction to music, Bible truth, or a story. Simple pantomiming can be done by fours and fives, but older children will want more involved pantomimes. Perhaps they will want more characters, a longer episode, or more practice before presenting the pantomime.

Posing pictures is a favorite activity with young children. The teacher may display a biblical or modern picture and then suggest that volunteers take the same positions as the pictured characters. This is an easy way to help young children feel the part of another person. When older children pose pictures, they will want costumes and suitable scenery. Picture-posing is a spontaneous activity with young children, and they will learn from it. Older children, too intent on details, may develop skills only and lose the learning value of acting out an event or situation. They will see the performance, not sense the feelings.

Tableaux are very similar to picture posing except that the teacher uses the children's original ideas of how to demonstrate a scene, event, or situation. The children are not trying to imitate or duplicate an illustration, they are showing how they think it might have been. Because a tableau is a "still" picture, older children may perform better than younger children. Children in grades three through six will want scenery, costumes, and possibly even music. When this form of dramatization concentrates on performance instead of feeling, some of the learning value may become secondary to development of skills and poise. The children may have learned how to perform without realizing how they felt.

Simple dramatization is a favorite activity with children of all ages because they are involved. The purpose of dramatizing, playing out, a story is not to present a finished play, but to help children feel the parts they take.

Very young children, under school age, enjoy dramatizing events in which all children can play the main character. A group of children may all be Jacob taking his long journey, lying down to sleep, seeing the angel vision, and awaking to set up a memorial stone. They will all enjoy placing the baby Moses in his basket and then being Miriam, standing guard. However, there are some stories that require more than the main character.

When playing crossing the Red Sea, one child may be Moses and the others the group of people following him. The story may be replayed with a new Moses. The crowning of Josiah is another story requiring a main character and a crowd of people. The teacher should follow the children's desires in deciding to assign parts or ask all children to be the main character.

No child should ever be allowed to play the part of the Lord Jesus. By asking an adult to read or speak Christ's words, we maintain the attitude that Jesus, the Son of God, was not a mere man. Since no one can adequately take His part, the teacher will say His words and be sure the children understand the teacher is not assuming His role.

Not all stories can or should be dramatized. Often the children are the best judges of the dramatic possibilities of a story. They seem to sense that good dramatization requires action and vivid dialogue. The characters must be real people. The story to be dramatized should have an emotional appeal and a climax. Children of school age can do good characterizations, and they will be interested in choosing parts. They may want to improvise scenery and costumes. However, the teacher must guide so that the spontaneity of original drama is not lost through a struggle to present a finished play. The important factor is the children's involvement in pretending to be another person. The children should have freedom in becoming those other persons; their speech and actions should be their own. A teacher may be tempted to write dialogue or define action, but this does not help children become the characters they have chosen to represent.

> Today's way—learning through informal dramatics—begins *not* when the teacher expresses preconceived notions about what the children are to do, but when the children themselves have an experience which so captures their attention, so sparks their imaginations, that they want, by means of words and actions, to relive the experience themselves.[5]

Children will not reproduce the event exactly as it happened. A teacher should not expect them to because the children are imagining, pretending, and feeling the event as they understand it. Perhaps no two groups of children would present the same enactment. However, the purpose of the acting is to give children the feeling of being another character and acting as they believe he would have acted.

What steps should be taken in dramatizing a story? First, the children should not enter into dramatization at the command of a teacher. They should follow the teacher's lead enthusiastically, if they are interested. If they have had previous good experiences with drama, the children may suggest dramatization after hearing a story. If the children seem ready to dramatize a story, the story should be reviewed. In reviewing the story, the children should notice the sequence of events, the people involved, what they did and said, and how they felt. Next, the group must decide who will play each part. If more than one child wants the same part, the teacher may suggest acting out the story more than once, allowing all interested pupils an opportunity to play the part.

The story should be played out without tedious rehearsals. And then the dramatization should be evaluated. Sometimes the evaluation will be on the performance itself, but at other times, depending on the teacher's reason for using the method, questions may center on how the characters felt, why they acted as they did, and the results of their actions. Questions to guide the evaluation are more helpful than a teacher's critique.

Puppetry

Children of all ages enjoy puppets! Puppets help children become familiar with the Bible stories and their application to modern life. Timid children are encouraged to participate because they may remain hidden behind a puppet screen, or they forget themselves in the fun of working a puppet. Aggressive children learn to share and participate as they join in presenting a puppet play. All puppeteers can release their feelings through the action of the puppets. Preschoolers are easily satisfied with finger or glove puppets, children in primary grades enjoy hand puppets, and older children will want to make their own puppets and write scripts.

There are several types of puppets. This chapter describes them briefly, but books on the subject, listed at the end of the chapter, give details of construction and manipulation. The size of puppet must be related to the size of the audience. Finger puppets, for example, should be used with no more than ten or twelve children—a small enough group so everyone can see the puppets. The type of puppet should usually be determined by the teacher. Certainly he is the one to decide whether making puppets is a justifiable activity to include in the curriculum. Making puppets, designing scenery, and writing scripts may need to be done outside of class.

Puppets need not always represent people. They may be talking animals or talking trees, articles of clothing or even furniture that speaks. The children's sense of "let's pretend" may lead to the creation of almost any character.

The puppet production may be done very simply. Finger, glove, hand puppets, paper bag, and sock puppets may all be used with or without a screen. Younger children will be satisfied with a simple production, merely holding the puppets in front of them. Older children will enjoy manipulating the puppets along a table edge, kneeling behind it to be out of sight. The top of an upright piano makes a good puppet stage. However, older children may be able to work with adults in designing a puppet stage from cardboard or plywood. This is a good project for junior high or high school woodworking students.

Finger puppets may be made of paper or cloth, or constructed from a short cardboard tube and a molded head made from a mixture of sawdust and wheat paste. The puppet or puppets are slipped over the tip of the fingers. This novel puppet has a limited use.

Paper bag puppets are, as the name implies, constructed from paper bags. Bags may be of various sizes and colors. However, children do best with a size 4 or 5 bag. A larger bag is too hard for them to control. The bag puppets may be made by using the flat surface of the folded bag for the head of the character. Then the mouth and bottom part of the face are placed under the bottom fold. The puppet can open its mouth to "speak." Another type of bag puppet is made by stuffing the bottom half of the bag with paper or cloth. Tie the bag in the center to form a head and use paint, crayon, or colored tape to make the face. Yarn may be added for hair. Bag puppets are worked by slipping the entire hand into the bag.

Molded puppets may be made from papier-mâché or Styrofoam balls. Puppet-making takes time! A teacher must consider how valuable this experience will be to his pupils. Because of the time involved, it is better to include this activity in weekday clubs or vacation Bible school. Puppet books give detailed directions on making papier-mâché from a commercial mix or by tearing newsprint and mixing it with a wheat paste or similar mixture. Styrofoam balls may be covered with masking tape, and decorated. However, the ball cannot be shaped as can the papier-mâché. A cardboard tube must be used for the base of the Styrofoam of papier-mâché head. The tube provides an opening to move the head or to attach a rod, as needed for some puppets.

Box puppets are similar to paper bag puppets. Boxes of various sizes can be used. The box must be covered with paper and two ends or sides left open to insert the fingers and work the puppet. Round boxes can also be used, but the bottom must be left open for the puppeteer to insert his hand.

Stick puppets are cutouts attached to a ruler, piece of cardboard, or other substitute for a stick. The characters, usually of paper, may be purchased, cut from magazines, or designed by the puppeteer. Stick puppets can be manipulated as other puppets or they may be used as shadow puppets. Anyone who knows how to make shadow pictures can use stick puppets in the same way. A sheet is suspended and a bright light placed behind it. The stick puppets must appear between the light and the sheet, thus casting a shadow on the sheet. However, only limited action can be shown, and the puppeteers must practice before presenting the play.

Glove puppets are made by gluing a puppet head to the fingers of a glove. The puppet heads may be made of paper or from matchboxes or small medicine bottles. Heads may be fastened to all fingers or only one finger, or the glove finger itself may be decorated to represent a head.

Hand puppets are available commercially. The audiovisual library of every church should have a collection of them. Hand puppets are available to represent Bible characters, modern people of many foreign lands, and a variety of animals. These puppets require no preparation on the part of the teacher or pupil and are simple to manipulate. The usual hand puppet consists of a head and a small garment which fits over the puppeteer's hand. The puppet is worked with two fingers and the thumb. The index finger is inserted into the hollow head.

Sock puppets are easily made and some are available commercially. The toe of the sock becomes the puppet's head. Buttons, yarn, or felt are attached to make the face. Animal puppets are often the sock type, because the foot of the sock lends itself to a variety of heads and the leg becomes the animal's neck.

Puppets must act! The action must have meaning, and the dialogue should relate to the action. Children will need practice to link action and conversation. It is easy for the puppeteer to become so engrossed with moving a puppet that he forgets to speak for the character. Here, as in any form of story play, if the teacher strives for perfection, the fun of "let's pretend" is lost. As children work with puppets, they will learn to "walk" the puppets or move them in other characteristic actions. Practically any story with action can be adapted to a puppet play. A teacher should follow the same steps in developing a puppet play as he does in creating a simple play.

Story play in any form requires some teacher preparation and much pupil participation. When used successfully, it helps pupils *feel* what is taught and helps a teacher evaluate what he thinks he has taught.

NOTES

1. Cornelius Jaarsma, *Human Development, Learning and Teaching* (Grand Rapids: Eerdmans, 1961), p. 212.
2. Elsiebeth McDaniel and Lawrence O. Richards, *You and Children* (Chicago: Moody, 1973), p. 88.
3. Elizabeth Allstrom, *You Can Teach Creatively* (Nashville: Abingdon, 1970), p. 63.
4. Hildred Nichols and Lois Williams, *Learning About Role-Playing for Children and Teachers* (Washington, D. C.: Association for Childhood Education, 1960), pp. 22-23.
5. Allstrom, p. 48.

Fig. 3. *Types of hand puppets*

FOR FURTHER READING

Allstrom, Elizabeth. *You Can Teach Creatively.* Nashville: Abingdon, 1970.

Autry, Ewart A., and Autry, Lola M. *Bible Puppet Plays.* Grand Rapids: Baker, 1972.

Beegle, Shirley. *Bible Story Finger Plays and Action Rhymes.* Cincinnati: Standard, 1964.

Bolton, Barbara J. *Ways to Help Them Learn: Children, Grades 1 to 6.* Glendale, Calif.: Gospel Light, Regal Books, 1972.

Colina, Tessa. *Finger Plays and How to Use Them.* Cincinnati: Standard, 1952.

Doan, Eleanor L. *Fascinating Finger Fun.* Grand Rapids: Zondervan, 1951.

Edwards, Mildred S., and Latham, Joy. *We Sing and Play.* Kansas City, Mo.: Lillenas, 1966.

Le Hays, Barbara. *Musical Bible Plays for Children.* Cincinnati: Standard, 1969.

London, Carolyn. *You Can Be a Puppeteer.* Chicago: Moody, 1972.

Morrison, Eleanor J., and Foster, Virgil E. *Creative Teaching in the Church.* Englewood Cliffs, N.J.: Prentice-Hall, 1963.

Nichols, Hildred, and Williams, Lois. *Learning About Role-Playing for Children and Teachers.* Washington, D. C.: Association for Childhood Education, 1960.

Rives, Elsie, and Sharp, Margaret. *Guiding Children.* Nashville: Convention, 1969.

Sapp, Phyllis Woodruff. *Creative Teaching in the Church School.* Nashville: Broadman, 1967.

Shaw, S. *Puppets for All Grades.* Danville, N.Y.: Owen, 1960.

15

Creative Activities for Children

Eleanor L. Doan

EVERY CHILD is a unique individual, a special creation of God. Everything about him is individual: development, personality, attitudes, abilities, needs, and responses. He learns at an individual rate, and progress is best when this is a one-to-one basis, particularly in early childhood.

God made each child to be creative in his own way and one of the most effective ways for him to learn is through creative activities. In this chapter, we will discuss creative activities for children ages two through eleven.

CHILDREN AND CREATIVITY

To be creative, according to Webster, is to be productive. And, an activity is an educational procedure designed to stimulate learning by firsthand experience. Therefore, a creative activity is a productive, firsthand, learning experience.

Creative activities have an important place in the total learning situation, bringing a new dimension into learning experiences. They enable a child to add doing to seeing and listening. They shift him from a passive to an active role where he can put himself totally into the learning experience. They help the child to discover for himself whether he can do what he thinks he can or what he wants to do. They present new opportunities to apply Bible truths to daily life.

Children enjoy creative activities. Their participation gives them opportunity for self-expression. When they are involved, they learn by doing—a firsthand learning experience which can be meaningful and lasting.

ELEANOR L. DOAN is Manager of Special Projects and Information Services, Gospel Light Publications, Glendale, California.

God has endowed children with a remarkable sensory system. We can use His gift of the five senses to help children experience learning through touching, smelling, tasting, seeing, and hearing. Through these experiences, children learn of the world and people about them with a growing awareness of God, His creation, and His Word.

God is creative. "All things were made by him" (Jn 1:3), and "All things were created by him" (Co 1:16). Man is the crowning achievement of His creation. God placed man in the midst of His creation and endowed him with creative abilities.

God established the basic growth pattern of man which was exemplified by the Lord Jesus Himself when He became God-man. "And Jesus increased in wisdom and stature, and in favour with God and man" (Lk 2:52). Jesus grew as a little child, went to school, played with other children, lived in a family, obeyed His parents, went to the synagogue, and learned about God. The fact that He lived and grew as other children is evidence that He experienced productive, firsthand learning experiences (creative activities).

As an adult, Jesus respected little children and suggested that His high regard for them should be heeded (Mt 18:5, 10). He was interested in their welfare and showed His love for them in a personal way, exhorting the people to do likewise (Mk 10:14-16). He accepted children as they were. He ministered to their needs (Mk 5:22-42; Lk 9:37-43; Jn 4:46-54). He paid attention to them individually (Mk 10:16).

With the involvement of various learning experiences comes the related teaching of such Bible truths as helping (2 Co 1:11), sharing (Heb 13:16, TCNT), consideration for others (Mt 7:12), and being doers of the Word and not hearers only (Ja 1:22).

The Purpose of Creative Activities

Creative activity is a method of teaching which can be used profitably to foster learning. These activities provide enjoyable ways for children to become more completely integrated personalities, opportunities to show loving concern and respect for others, and motivations to express their relationship to God and His Word in daily living.

Some of the purposes and values in the use of creative activities are as follows:

1. It makes learning more enjoyable, lasting, and meaningful.
2. It provides opportunity for self-expression and development of creativity.
3. It instills pride in accomplishment and builds self-confidence.
4. It contributes to the development of proper self-concepts.

5. It provides for participation in group situations and reaction to established group approval and behavior.

6. It deepens a child's sensitivity toward others and provides opportunity for him to demonstrate in words and action his loving concern.

7. It is therapeutic for the child's need for individual expression.

8. It relieves periods of physical restlessness with meaningful activity, coordinating mind and muscle.

9. It prompts respect for both adult and peer leadership.

10. It develops leadership abilities and a sensitivity to carrying out responsibilities.

11. It affords opportunity for the practice of the principles of Christian living.

12. It helps the child respect the property of others.

13. It teaches cooperation, sharing, and taking turns.

14. It can emphasize a Bible concept or illustrate a truth.

15. It provides opportunities for the child to express his relationship to God and his response to Bible teaching.

Keeping these purposes and values in mind, teachers and leaders will have opportunity to observe the children's developing theological concepts and behavioral responses. This will help guide the leaders in their teaching and in their relationships with the children and in the selection of creative activities to effect successful learning experiences.

How to Encourage Children to Be Creative

All children can be productive, or creative. But the extent to which they express their creativity depends, to a large degree, on the teacher. The following are some ways in which to encourage and foster creativity among children.

1. Discover each child's level of understanding—what he knows (or doesn't know)—about Bible teaching. This can come from observing him as he expresses himself through music, role playing, rhymes, games, verbalizing, and handcrafts, which are selected to retell and/or apply the Bible truths.

2. Be personally interested in each child. Commend him for work well done. Visit in the child's home and get acquainted with him and his parents. Take time with each child individually on Sunday. Comment on new clothing, birth of a sibling, and so on. Remember him with a card on his birthday. Listen to him; be sensitive to his feelings; encourage his efforts.

3. Choose purposeful activities which will meet children's needs. Evaluate the way(s) each activity considered will meet the needs of the children in your group: Will it help them relate to each other? cooperate?

develop physical skills by using excess energy? express creativity and originality? share? gain self-confidence? apply a Bible truth? communicate?

4. Provide a variety of activities and materials. Evaluate choices in view of children's ages, environment for activities, abilities and interests, physical needs, seasons, and learning goals. Consider activities for *listening* (records, cassette tapes); for *thinking* (writing stories and poems, riddles, rebuses, slogans, letters); for *doing* (games, role play, drama, arts and crafts, motion songs, finger plays).

Consider media: for *creating* (clay, newspapers and cardboard, seeds, household discards, string and yarn, shells, pictures); for *decorating* (paints, crayons, glitter, stickers); for *expressing a role* (costumes, yardage, wigs, paper sacks for puppets, hats, etc.).

5. Encourage children to do their best, to be original. Communicate your confidence in their ability to achieve by commending their efforts. Give suggestions to the less creative child and allow extra time for the child slower at manipulation. Stimulate originality through conversation. "Close your eyes and think about (name story or incident discussed or to be visualized). Now draw the picture you see." "What ideas do you have for a song? Can you think of a first line?" Also encourage originality by providing a variety of media and letting children choose what to use to illustrate a Bible verse, story, song, rebus, etc.

6. When children seem overly sure of their abilities, do not dispute their claims. Redirect their interests and guide them into activities compatible with their abilities. To redirect the child's interest, you might comment, "I'm sure you could (name the activity), but here's something which really requires the talent you have"; or, "Have you ever tried (name activity)? It just suits what you can do."

7. Guide the overactive child into activity which will hold his interest and work off his energy. Encourage his participation in games, music, field trips, and finger fun. Let him be your supply assistant, errand runner, prop man, and perform other energy-consuming jobs.

8. Provide challenging projects for the precocious child. Let him make patterns or prepare materials for the class, a second craft item to use as a gift, gather props for plays, write a TV play for using puppets children make, tape a story which the children can pantomime, do a research project.

9. Be firm and fair. Do not expect perfection. Do not do anything for a child that he can do for himself. Have some basic rules for all activities: completing one project before another is started, putting away materials and objects used, and sharing. Endeavor to keep a capable child from doing slipshod work. Do not let the less capable get discouraged from

seeming failure or by comparing his accomplishments with those of another.

10. Let the children select their activities occasionally. Periodically have "Choice Day" for activities. Encourage each child to tell why the activity he has chosen is his favorite. Have first, second, and third choices if a particular activity precludes many participants.

11. Display projects the children make. Provide bulletin boards and tables inside (at child's eye level) and outside the classroom for mounting and displaying projects. Occasionally let each child select what he feels is his best project for display. Sometimes have a committee (composed of children) choose the best projects from each child's contributions. Guide the children in arranging the display.

How to Lead Children in Various Kinds of Creative Activities

Here are some activities which children enjoy, with suggestions for leading them to participate.

CREATIVE WRITING

The learning tool of creative writing can help children crystallize their thoughts and reduce generalities to specifics. It can help them express random thoughts succinctly, and it can encourage originality.

Creative writing forms can include stories, poems, rebuses, riddles, songs, plays, finger plays, poster slogans, cartoon quips, and letters.

When encouraging children to write stories, motivate their thinking by asking questions. "What happened (this past week, during vacation, at school) that reminded you of something Jesus told us we should do?" Or prompt their thinking by starting a story and letting the children build on it (e.g., "On the way home from school, Steve saw a boy, much bigger than he was, breaking open a gum ball machine. And then, what happened?").

Ask children to choose subjects for a poem. Write these on the board. Ask the children to think of words which rhyme and write them on the board. If further help is needed, suggest a first line, such as "When I look around, I see—"

Have the children cut out magazine pictures and use them to write rebuses and riddles. (A rebus is a story which occasionally substitutes pictures for words.) Children can use the pictures literally for the words they want to use (e.g., the picture of a house to "read" *house*) or as the symbol of a word they want read (e.g., the picture of a tire plus the letter *D* for the word *tired*).

Songs (lyrics) can be written in somewhat the same way as poems, rebuses, and riddles. Select a familiar tune and let the children compose different verses. For younger children, "Mulberry Bush" is always a good tune. For older children, you might use "Brighten the Corner." Motion songs are fun for them to write. Discuss what they want to express and decide on words and motions that fit together.

Whereas it would be difficult for most children to write a play by themselves, they can enjoy composing a play together. Help the children think of a story they want to dramatize. "Shall we write a Bible-story play? a play that illustrates a Bible truth? a missionary story? an adventure story?" After the subject is selected, outline the story on the chalkboard as the children tell it. Questions, such as, "What happened first in the story play?" "What happened next?" might stimulate ideas. Follow the same procedure in listing the characters. Sometimes it helps to have the children stage the play impromptu before writing it.

Finger plays can be an individual or group activity. Explain that finger plays are messages or stories told by the hands. Ask some of the children to let their fingers "say something." Have others guess what they are "saying." Then reverse the procedure. Let the children then choose the most obvious "finger talk" and write words to go with it.

Writing poster slogans and cartoon quips is a fun activity for children. Mount magazine pictures on poster paper and let the children discuss "what the picture says." From the discussion, children come up with appropriate slogans and quips.

Letter writing is a good group activity for younger children and a good individual project for juniors. Guide the children in deciding who should receive the letter(s): a shut-in, class member who is sick, missionary friend, or pen-pal. Teachers will write the letter for preschoolers, incorporating their thoughts. The letter dictated by primaries can be written on the chalkboard by the teacher and then copied by the children. Juniors can compose or write their own letters. Sometimes rebus letters are fun for both juniors and primaries.

CONSTRUCTIVE CRAFTS AND ART

The possibilities of craft and art projects which can be made by children—and the materials from which they can be made—are almost endless. This is significant, in that the variety of opportunities afforded the child to express himself opens the door to new learning experiences.

The teacher-child relationship is an important key to the child becoming more self-confident and sure of his worth as an individual. This helps him more readily to accept and respond to God's love, and show love to others. The primary concern of the teacher should not be how well the child made the craft, but rather what he learned.

In the development of artistic expression, each child passes through various stages of development, and progresses at his own rate, just as he does in other areas of growth. His individuality is obvious: he makes a project "just the way I want it." His first experience in creative arts may not result in anything recognizable to anyone but himself. Ask him to tell you about his painting (picture, modeling, or whatever type of project he is working on). Never ask, "What is that?" An understanding, positive attitude encourages a child to respond with eagerness, confidence, and pride. His response communicates what he thinks and how he feels.

Usually a child's first creative art experience is manipulating materials such as clay, soft paint (finger paints or chocolate-pudding "paint"), and crayons. He squeezes and scribbles, making nothing specific. He discovers how these materials feel and smell and look (and sometimes how they taste!). As his muscle coordination improves, the child begins to control his materials. While his finished project is more readily identified, this is not as important as the teacher showing acceptance of the work. "You chose nice bright colors for your picture." "Your painting shows you worked hard." "Your animal is very good. I like the way you made the bear's ears."

As children grow, they become more adept in handling materials, and thus they put more effort into expressing what they think and feel. The teacher's role continues to be one of encouraging the child, making him feel important and needed, and accepting his efforts.

In leading children into art activities, keep in mind that you are teaching the children—not arts and crafts.

Involve the children as helpers. Ask them to help you gather and sort the supplies needed. After they have completed an activity, ask them to help you put the supplies away.

When you introduce a new project, demonstrate the use of materials, and show several made-up crafts as ideas. Ask the children, What else can be made from ________?"

Encourage individual creativity in thinking and doing. Do not give the impression that every child's project should be "just like teacher's."

Think of each art activity in relationship to Bible learning, directing the child's thoughts, conversation, and action to this end.

Allow the children freedom to experiment with materials. Be positive while observing their efforts and when making suggestions.

Be alert to the children's physical safety. Provide adequate supervision, especially when using tools.

With all this in mind, here are starter ideas for various materials to use in craft and art activities. Included are some "lead in" suggestions to use with the children.

Cardboard containers (all sizes and shapes). "Jerry, look at all these boxes. What do you think we could make out of them?" "Houses? Fine. How do you think we should go about making them?" "Nancy, what ideas do you have for using that box you are holding?" "Doll furniture is a good idea, and that box would make a nice table."

Here are some other ideas for cardboard containers. Cover graduated sizes of square boxes with bright, shelf paper for building blocks. Cut milk and cream cartons to appropriate height, cover with contact paper and use for planters or crayon holders. Use boxes to make dioramas. Small cereal boxes with perforation on one side make good puppet heads when folded on the side opposite the opened perforation. (To manipulate, place fingers in upper portion and thumb in lower portion).

Plastic containers (all sizes, shapes, colors, thoroughly washed and labels removed). "Do you know what we are going to do with these bottles, baskets, and plastic trays? Terri, you look eager to tell us." "You saw a sand scoop your cousin made from a big bottle? I think that's a good idea." "Lorrie, how do you think we could use this small bottle?" "Yes. You could paste a picture on it or wrap it with yarn, and it will be a beautiful vase."

Here are some other ideas for plastic containers. Make shadow pictures from meat trays by gluing on several plastic flowers. Trinket trays can be made by covering the container with contact paper. Surprise baskets can be made by attaching a long chenille wire to opposite sides of plastic berry or tomato baskets, lining them with a paper doily or napkin and filling with cookies. Cut off the bottom of a large bottle so that it will be about two inches deep, line it with felt, and use it for an offering plate in Sunday school or children's church. Make a food dish for pets by cutting off the bottom of a large plastic bottle, about four inches deep. Cut off the bottoms of small bottles (all colors), one-half inch deep, glue Christmas-card pictures in the bottom, attach a hanger by gluing string to the back or putting it through a hole punched in the tip, and you have attractive Christmas tree ornaments.

Cloth (assorted prints, colors, fabrics). "How do you think we can use this cloth to illustrate a Bible story?" "That green will make a nice tree, Steve. What story did you have in mind?" "The creation story in a collage picture is a very good idea." (A collage is a picture constructed out of commonplace scrap materials and glued to a flat surface.) The cloth can be cut in the shapes desired, to represent days of creation, then pasted on cardboard.

Seeds (assorted). "Yes, Susan, seeds can be used to make a collage picture. And a bird would be nice to make." Or, a child could make a show box of some of the seeds God made by gluing some of each kind of seed on a square of cardboard, gluing them in a box, and labeling the seed. Or, sprinkle some lettuce seeds on a damp sponge and place this in a shallow container, keeping the sponge moist so the seeds will sprout.

Paper sacks (assorted sizes and colors). "I am thinking of something we can all make from paper sacks and use to tell Bible stories. Who can guess what it is?" "Good, most of you said 'Puppets.' Think of the Bible character you want to make, and choose the materials you need." "Yes, I think a sheep would be a good 'character,' Ted. And I like your idea of covering the paper bag with bits of cotton too. With Tom's idea of using his David puppet, you and Tom can tell a story together."

There are many other uses for paper sacks. Choose a paper sack which will fit over the head, cut out one of the wide sides (one inch from all the creases) and use for a wig to represent a Bible character. From another paper bag the same size, cut a four-inch crown and glue it on to the "wig" to represent a king or queen. With paint, cloth, or crayons, draw a clown's face on the wide side of a large paper sack, then stuff it with shredded newspaper and tie it at the top with yarn to make a clown's head pillow. Cut an opening on one wide side of a paper sack, and cut a slit on each of the narrow sides (close to the crease) half-an-inch longer on each end, so you can use the sack as a TV "screen."

Magazine pictures. "How many things can you think of that we can make from these pictures, to tell of God's love?" Here are some ideas the children may think of. Murals can be made to illustrate Bible stories, such as "The Good Shepherd" or "God's Creation," by cutting out and pasting pictures on strips of shelf paper. Make a book from wrapping paper and have children find pictures to illustrate a favorite song. Find suitable pictures to paste onto construction paper to make greeting cards. Paste pictures on large cards to illustrate Bible verses. Make scrapbooks for children in hospitals. Magazine pictures can be pasted to cardboard, then cut in pieces as a puzzle, and placed in an envelope for a gift.

Straws (both plastic and paper). Cut straws in various lengths and glue them on construction paper to make pictures of flowers, birds, trees, or people. Cut several straws in varied lengths and string them on yarn to make necklaces. Squeeze little blobs of paint on construction paper, then point one end of a straw in the paint and blow to move the paint and "paint" a picture. Combine pieces of straws and gummed reinforcements to make figures of animals and people and illustrate the story of Noah and the ark.

Yarn and string. A yarn picture of Abraham's home can be made by arranging brown yarn in the shape of a tent and green and brown yarn to form trees on the sides of the "home." Talk about other Bible scenes that can be "drawn" with yarn. Suggest how children can make scenes on the flannelboard by using white yarn for clouds, brown and green for mountains and trees, blue for water, yellow for sun. (Flannelboard figures to represent Bible stories can be made from chenille wire.) Both yarn and string can be used on the flannelboard or glued on cardboard to make faces illustrating being happy, sad, mad, or whatever emotion you want.

There are many other ideas for making things of yarn and string. Paint with string by dipping the string in paint, arranging it inside a piece of folded paper, closing the paper, and pressing it under a book until dry. Glue a yarn or string border all around a piece of cardboard, and then "print" words, in yarn, from a Bible verse (e.g., "Be Ye Kind") to make a motto.

Cotton. Talk about where we get cotton. "Cotton represents which day of creation? How many things do we use every day that are made of cotton?" "Let us thank God for His gift of cotton." Have the class make a poster or mural showing all the things they named which are made from cotton.

Here are some other suggestions for ways to use cotton. Spread a thin layer of cotton on a plastic meat tray, saturate it with water, and sprinkle with a fast-growing seed (grass or radish) to observe how God makes seeds grow. Make a picture by gluing strips of brown yarn on a piece of construction paper, and then adding small, oblong cotton balls for pussy willows. Another use for cotton balls is to dip them in tempera paint and "paint" a design or picture on white construction paper.

Clay. Encourage the children to make something out of the clay that will help recall a Bible story or a Bible truth. They might make animals, waterpots, oil lamps, scrolls, or tablets of stone.

Spools (assorted sizes and colors). Use spools for design printing. Make designs by gluing to one end of a spool a piece of sponge, layer of cotton, piece of burlap, or strips of string. Dip designs in paint and stamp out pattern on construction paper or poster board. Fasten piece(s) of sponge (dipped in green paint) on tree twigs and stand up the twigs in spools. Cut out the front and back of animals, glue them on opposite ends of a spool, then cover the spool with cotton or material appropriate for the animal. Small children can string spools on long shoelaces. Make spool dolls by stringing spools on shoestrings for the arms, legs, body, and head.

Shells. Children never cease to be thrilled with God's wonders, and shells are one of His wonderful creations. Discuss what shells are, what lived in them, what day of creation they represent. Listen to the sounds inside big shells. If given an assortment of shells, children may glue them in a box and label them for a show box. Or a collage picture may be made of shells glued to posterboard.

Mosaics are ancient decorative art media (dating back as far as 4000 B.C.

in Mesopotamia) which have been used through the centuries to decorate, to communicate ideas, and to chronicle events. Today, mosaics offer scores of teaching-learning opportunities for children. Discuss with students various materials which can be used in making mosaics (list on a chalkboard for older children): seeds of all kinds; small, colored rocks; eggshells; seashells; fungi; leaves; pine cones; ceramic tiles; fruit stones; dried vegetables, such as, beans and peas; colored glass; beads; or pieces of colored paper.

Encourage discussion of how Bible stories or truths can be visualized in mosaics. "What story would mosaics of fish tell? ravens? doves? donkey? animals? basket? boat?" Yes, you could make a very interesting map from mosaics. And a Bible verse. And people—"

Mosaics can be made on boards, plywood, cardboard, dishes, paper plates, boxes, cork, plastic, or floor tiles.

While older children are making mosaics, tell about some of the mosaics which have been found and preserved in churches and buildings dating back to the time of Christ and the first century.

Decoupage (the art of decorating surfaces—usually wood—with paper cutouts) is an excellent activity for combining muscular dexterity, imagination, and learning recall. Children may cut pictures, Bible verses, mottoes, decorative designs from Sunday school papers, greeting cards, periodicals, calendars, or posters. The selection of materials and arrangement on the wood allow opportunity for discussion. Encourage the children to tell the meaning of their design, what the motto means to them, or the reason for the Bible verse or picture selected. Observe the originality shown in design and compliment the child's effort. The time spent distressing the wood and finishing the surface is enjoyable to children and provides muscle activity and dexterity. This activity also affords opportunity for cooperation and sharing.

Crayon techniques can open the door to a variety of meaningful, creative, craft projects. Since children feel at home using crayons, they can be challenged to new crayon techniques. For example, "Stained glass" can be made for classroom windows. Designs can be drawn with wax crayons on heavy paper, cut to fit the windows. The "window" design is completed when the entire surface has been colored. To add the stained-glass effect, children may dip cotton into baby oil (or cooking oil) and rub completely over the reverse side. Talk about the colors, the design, and why stained glass is used in churches.

Interesting wall hangings (e.g., a class motto or Bible verse) can be made by using wax crayons on muslin. Coloring is made easier if the cloth is stapled to a large piece of cardboard, held in embroidery hoops, or taped to the floor. Small children may use stencils. When completed, press the hangings on the "wrong" side with a warm iron.

Interesting crayon pictures can be drawn on sandpaper, cheesecloth glued over cardboard, or muslin glued to wood.

Relief printing (the application of ink to a raised surface) is a versatile art-craft project which can be used by children of almost all ages for making words or designs. It is an excellent medium to challenge students to explore new ideas and thus bring about new learning experiences.

Encourage children to talk about what they want to print—and *why*. Listening to the "what" and "why" of a project will prompt guidance in the conversation and activity for learning.

The most commonly used materials for carving raised designs are linoleum squares mounted on wood, balsa wood, potatoes, and spools. Raised surfaces can be made in numerous other ways. Toothpicks and string can be glued to a cork surface (or rough side of linoleum blocks), and rubber bands, paper clips, yarn, string, or spaghetti can be arranged at random and glued to bottles. A continuous design can be made on shelf paper by rolling the bottle over ink and pressing it on the paper. Words can be made from alphabet macaroni and glued (backwards and in reverse) on wood for printing Bible verses and mottoes.

A profitable project would be for the children to select and illustrate a favorite proverb or other Bible verse to illustrate and/or print.

Wire craft challenges the child's imagination and provides exercises in muscle coordination. Children in the middle grades can handle a wide range of wire—from chenille wire to coat hangers—while young children should be limited to using chenille wire.

What the child chooses to make will reflect past learning experiences and open vistas to new learning experiences. Asking the children to "Tell me about—" opens the door for the child to share his thinking. If the young child makes chenille wire figures, suggest that he place them on a flannelboard and tell the story he has in mind.

Older children may sculpture with copper wire, lightweight wire, or even coat hangers. Faces, butterflies, figures, and abstract forms can be fashioned from coat hangers. Dimensional forms are attractively shaped by winding string around the wire to fill out figures or designs, or to enclose a form.

Mobiles can tell a story, represent a season or illustrate a truth or scripture portion, and thus provide learning experiences. Chenille wire, buttons, paper objects, bits of plastic, and scores of other materials can be used in mobile making.

Macrame (creative knotting, braiding, and twisting) is a challenging and interesting craft for children. Suggest that they find twine, heavy cord, or rug yarn to make belts, necklaces, bookmarks, and wall hangings. Originality and imagination will be refreshing as each child expresses his ideas in knotting, braiding, and twisting the twine.

Psalm 139:14 (TLB) is a good Bible verse to discuss while children are engaged in this project: "Thank you for making me so wonderfully complex! It is amazing to think about. Your workmanship is marvelous—and how well I know it." Then the teacher could add this comment: "Our minds tell our hands what to do, and our eyes are guides to help our hands. God's workmanship is marvelous!" Or, "Everything God made is good. He made the plants from which we get cotton, jute, linen, and sisal, which is made into rope and twine."

Jewelry-making is an excellent craft to stimulate creativity and motivate children to think of others. Many of the materials for jewelry-making can be found in items usually considered junk. "Beads" can be made by rolling and gluing small triangles cut from colored magazine pictures, over a thin knitting needle. Remove from needle and spray with clear plastic. Children may roll small balls of patching plaster (tinted with vegetable coloring), then pierce with knitting needle for stringing. Colored plastic straws may be cut in varying lengths. Assorted sizes and colors of seeds may be gathered and pierced for stringing. Circles, triangles, and squares of cork and plastic (from bottles) can be cut out and punched.

Bracelets and necklaces may be made from stringing (use plastic thread for bracelets) seeds, magazine picture beads, cut-up plastic straws, assorted beads, buttons, small plastic foam shapes used for packing, and beads made from plaster. Pendants can be made by gluing seeds in a mosaic design on cork and fastening the design to a ribbon or shoelace. Cork covered with foil and "engraved" and wire fashioned in a design also make interesting pendants. Pins may be made from copper wire shaped to spell a name. Or use varied shapes of wood, cork, or plastic and make names from macaroni letters or designs from seeds, colored string, or buttons. Glue safety pins to back of pins. Headbands, wristbands, and belts can be made by sewing assorted buttons or beads on ribbon or burlap. Cut circles, squares, or triangles, from plastic bottles or cork, punch holes so that they can be fastened together with yarn, twine, ribbon, or shoelaces. Key chains can be made by fastening tumbled colored stones to copper wire, cutting various shapes from plastic, and attaching braided, plastic-coated wire.

Plastic foam comes in many shapes: sheets, balls, cones, cubes, circles, letters, and in assorted twists and macaroni shapes for packing. To cut plastic foam, use a sharp kitchen knife. If you wish to paint the foam, use a water-base paint.

"What shall we cut from the plastic foam to decorate our room? A fish? Good. What will a fish represent? Our class motto 'Fishers of Men.' That's a good idea, Gary." "A sword and shield for Ephesians 6 is a good idea too."

Guide children to think of things they can help make to visualize Bible stories, lesson applications, or mottoes. Puppet heads can be made from the balls, and figures can be made from cones and balls. Birds and animals can be cut from sheets for bulletin boards, murals, and posters. Small figures and letters can be used on the flannelboard. Houses can be made from pieces of thin sheet foam put together with toothpicks. The plastic foam used for packing can be tinted with vegetable coloring and glued on cardboard to make mosaics, or strung to make necklaces.

Other materials useful for crafts are chenille wire, crepe paper, egg cartons, felt, gimp, ice cream sticks, leather, and rope. Other ideas for crafts can be gained by visiting public schools, Christian day schools, Christian bookstores, craft and hobby shops, and by reading craft magazines. (See the list of craft magazines at the end of this chapter.)

Creative Activities in Various Church Agencies

SUNDAY SCHOOL

In all children's departments (except cradle roll and nursery), creative activities can be used during the presession moments (before Sunday school formally begins), during the class time (depending on available time), and during the extended sessions or children's church. For nursery-age children (twos and threes), creative activities are very desirable during church time.

SUNDAY EVENING

Sunday evening expressional programs for fours and fives, primaries, and juniors, offer excellent opportunities for creative activities.

CHURCH-RELATED PROGRAMS

Church-related programs may include nursery schools, day care programs, child care programs (in operation whenever parents of young children attend church activities), the home, and released time. Creative activities for preschoolers—and sometimes primaries—are desirable in all these programs, except the last, which should be for juniors.

WEEKDAY ACTIVITIES

Several weekday activities provide excellent opportunities for using creative activities: weekday clubs, weekly Bible classes (for primaries and juniors), recreational programs (for juniors), and missionary organizations (for primaries and juniors).

SUMMER AND VACATION MINISTRIES

Camping, vacation Bible school, and recreational activities are opportunities in summer when creative activities can be used for children ages two through eleven.

FOR FURTHER READING

Books

Allstrom, Elizabeth. *You Can Teach Creatively.* Nashville: Abingdon, 1970.

Arvois, Edmond. *Making Mosaics.* New York: Sterling, 1964.

Benson, Kenneth R. *Creative Crafts for Children.* Englewood Cliffs, N.J.: Prentice-Hall, 1958.

Bolton, Barbara J. *Ways to Help Them Learn: Children, Grades 1 to 6.* Glendale, Calif.: Gospel Light, Regal Books, 1972.

Crane, John, and Crane, Diane. *Scrap Craft.* Dansville, N.Y.: Owen, 1963.

Doan, Eleanor L. *Handcraft Encyclopedia.* Glendale, Calif.: Gospel Light, 1961.

———. *Creative Handcrafts for Early Childhood, Ages 3, 4, 5.* Glendale, Calif.: Gospel Light, 1973.

———. *Creative Handcrafts for Children, Grades 1, 2, 3.* Glendale, Calif.: Gospel Light, 1973.

———. *Creative Handcrafts for Children, Grades 4, 5, 6.* Glendale, Calif.: Gospel Light, 1973.

———. *Creative Handcrafts for Youth.* Glendale, Calif.: Gospel Light, 1973.

———. *261 Handcrafts and Fun for Little Ones.* Grand Rapids: Zondervan, 1963.

———. *145 Fun-to-Do Handcrafts.* Grand Rapids: Zondervan, 1972.

———. *157 More Fun-to-Do Handcrafts.* Grand Rapids: Zondervan, 1972.

Edge, Findley B. *Helping the Teacher.* Nashville: Broadman, 1959.

Gale, Elizabeth Wright. *Have You Tried This?* Valley Forge, Pa.: Judson, 1960.

Hammond, Phyllis E. *What to Do and Why.* Valley Forge, Pa.: Judson, 1963.

Hull, Opal. *Creative Crafts for Churches.* Anderson, Ind.: Warner, 1958.

Jackson, Sheila. *Simple Stage Costumes and How to Make Them.* New York: Watson-Guptill, 1969.

Morrison, Eleanor J., and Foster, Virgil E. *Creative Teaching in the Church.* Englewood Cliffs, N.J.: Prentice-Hall, 1963.

Pesch, Imelda Manalo. *Macramé.* New York: Sterling, 1970.

Pitcher, Evelyn, et al. *Helping Young Children Learn.* Columbus, Ohio: Merrill, 1966.

Richards, Lawrence O. *Creative Bible Teaching.* Chicago: Moody, 1970.

Rowen, Dolores. *Ways to Help Them Learn: Early Childhood, Birth to 5 Years.* Glendale, Calif.: Gospel Light, Regal Books, 1972.
Sapp, Phyllis. *Creative Teaching in the Church School.* Nashville: Broadman, 1967.
Self, Margaret M. *158 Things to Make.* Glendale, Calif.: Gospel Light, 1971.
———. *202 Things to Do.* Glendale, Calif.: Gospel Light, 1971.
Simms, Caryl, and Simms, Gordon. *Introducing Seed Collage.* New York: Watson-Guptill, 1971.
Smith, Charles T. *Ways to Plan and Organize Your Sunday School: Children, Grades 1 to 6.* Glendale, Calif.: Gospel Light, Regal Books, 1971.
Squires, John L. *Fun Crafts for Children.* Englewood Cliffs, N.J.: Prentice-Hall, 1964.
Sunderlin, Sylvia, ed. *Bits and Pieces,* Washington D. C.: Association for Childhood Education, 1967.
Taylor, Barbara. *When I Do, I Learn.* Provo, Utah: Brigham Young, n.d.
Turner, G. Alan. *Creative Crafts for Everyone.* New York: Viking, 1959.
Vermeer, Jackie, and Lariviere, Marian. *The Little Kids Craft Book.* New York: Taplinger, 1973.
Watson, Ernest W., and Kent, Norman. *The Relief Print.* New York: Watson-Guptill, 1955.
Weiss, Harvey. *Clay, Wood and Wire.* New York: Scott, 1956.
Wing, Frances S. *The Complete Book of Decoupage.* New York: Coward-McConn, 1965.
Wylie, Joanne, ed. *A Creative Guide for Preschool Teachers.* Racine, Wis.: Western, 1965.
Yates, Brock. *Plastic Foam for Arts and Crafts.* New York: Sterling, 1965.
Yoder, Glen. *Take It from Here.* Valley Forge, Pa.: Judson, 1973.

Magazines with Craft Ideas

Arts and Activities. 8150 North Central Park Ave., Skokie, Ill. 60076.
Church Recreation. 127 Ninth Ave. North, Nashville, Tenn. 37203.
Instructor. P. O. Box 6099, Duluth, Minn. 55806.
Pack-O-Fun. 14 Main St., Park Ridge, Ill. 60068.
School Arts. 50 Portland St., Worcester, Maine 01608.
Teacher. 22 West Putnam Ave., Greenwich, Conn. 06830.
Teachers' Arts and Crafts Workshops. Brookhill Dr., West Nyack, N.Y. 10994.

16

Using Visual and Audio Media with Children

Ruth C. Haycock

Storytelling, creative activities—and now, audio and visual media for teaching children: all of these are designed to produce meaningful involvement of children with the truth, which will enable them to learn and to change in the direction of conformity to the will of God. This is our objective as Christian educators.

The Necessity of Audiovisual Media

Several facts indicate forcibly and clearly that audio and visual materials must be a part of our teaching equipment.

First is the fact that in the years since World War II, their value has been proven over and over again. Hundreds of studies done in the armed services and in schools have pointed up the effectiveness of audiovisual media in speeding up learning, lengthening retention, clarifying concepts, and promoting action. There is overwhelming proof that the careful use of well-chosen materials improves learning.

Second, if we actually believe that God's Word is all important and that no occupation is more crucial than helping pupils to understand it, we are compelled to use every means for effective teaching. Failure to capitalize on available media indicates ignorance, laziness, or lack of concern.

Third, when we consider how much the life and future of each pupil depend on his understanding of God's plan, we sense also the brevity of time. Time is short in view of the prospect of the Lord's soon return. In addition, in the local church, we have only a short part of each week in which to teach eternal truth. We must, therefore, use every available means.

Ruth C. Haycock, Ed.D. is Chairman of the Department of Christian Education, Baptist Bible College of Pennsylvania, Clark's Summit, Pennsylvania.

Fourth, what about the other activities of our pupils each week? Consider television, with its realistic sight and sound, for several hours a day. Consider the public school room, with its well-trained teachers propagating, for the most part, a humanistic, nonbiblical viewpoint. Consider the children's secular organizations and their success in inculcating their philosophies. Consider the attractive literature for children, well illustrated and well written, each piece teaching some secular viewpoint. These competitors know that if they can mold the thinking of today's children, they will have tomorrow's adults.

Fifth, American boys and girls are 2000 years removed from the time of Christ and several thousand more years from the earlier events of the Bible. They are growing up in a modern culture, far from the rural and Middle Eastern setting of David or Abraham. Even rural children, through mass communication media, know the modern world, but not the Bible times world. This limited Bible background necessitates our being sure that children get the message we are giving them.

Sixth, believers, as those who trust the Bible both for its content and for the methods it reveals, have a reason beyond all of the above for using such instructional media. It has been said, "If we would teach scripturally, we must teach visually." On many occasions, God Himself used some visual object to emphasize a truth to Israel. Think of the burning bush, Moses' leprous hand, the rainbow, and Gideon's fleece. When Christ came and was known as the master Teacher, He too used things and events to portray truth. For example, He used a child to talk about the simplicity of faith and the folly of pride (Mt 18); and He used a coin to show man's responsibility to government as well as to God (Mk 12:17).

God knows the nature of man; God knows how we learn and understand. Jesus was an unusual teacher not only because He knew all the truth and was Himself the truth, but also because He knew people. He used visual teaching methods with adults; how much greater is our need, as we teach children, with their greater limitations of background and experience, to use audiovisuals?

The Selection of Audiovisual Media

The mere recognition of the values of supplementary materials, or even the use of an abundance of them in our teaching, does not guarantee that a child will understand the truth. Several criteria can help determine which materials to select: (1) our purpose in the particular lesson or part of the lesson; (2) our knowledge of our pupils; (3) the particular materials at our disposal including their quality, accuracy, legibility; (4) their possible relationship to other materials and experience.

For example, in the story of Zacchaeus, unless we are concerned with the geography of the situation, it is not necessary to use a map. Do we want youngsters to realize how urgently Zacchaeus wanted to see Jesus, even to the extent of putting aside his dignity? Perhaps, then, a picture or flannelboard presentation will help. These could also emphasize the crowd and the elegance of Zacchaeus' home, if desired; a filmstrip or standup figures could do likewise. If we wish to show the restitution which Zacchaeus made, we may use actual coins or dollar bills, or a chalkboard sketch of them. With a group of juniors who have heard the story before, we may merely write the name Zacchaeus on the chalkboard to fix the name and the spelling. Or a thought question may capture attention or relate the lesson to contemporary life.

We teachers must think carefully about our purposes as we choose materials, but we must think of our pupils too. Writers in earlier chapters have portrayed the pupil and his needs at each level. These stages of development must be kept in mind as we choose illustrative material.

The question is often asked, Which is a better visual medium for a particular lesson: a filmstrip, a flannelboard story, or something else? The answer depends, as we have just seen, on the purpose and the pupils, but the answer also depends on which *specific* filmstrip and other *specific* presentations we are comparing. How accurate is each? Is it biblical? How does the artwork affect the pupils? Are the words legible? Are the concepts simply and directly expressed or illustrated? A good teacher will consider these and other qualities when selecting a visual.

Another consideration in the selection of materials relates to other activities and experiences being provided within a lesson or unit. For example, it is often helpful to show a film or filmstrip in the departmental session; however, for this presentation to be valuable, teachers must plan together with their superintendent, so that they can relate other learning to it in the smaller groups. In a shepherd series, a filmstrip or picture series might be part of the preparation for a trip to a sheep farm, with other material as follow-up. Each separate item should fit into the total experience of the group.

The Variety of Audiovisual Media

In an attempt to present briefly some of the possibilities, materials will be considered under four major headings: visual, audio, manipulative, and real. These categories overlap, but no classification can be clear-cut since many materials combine more than one classification. Also, many may be used in several ways.

Visual Materials

Visual boards. Visual boards have been useful at all age levels for many years. Almost every classroom has had chalkboards and bulletin boards. More recently have come newer boards: flannel, pocket, magnetic, electric, plastic—and perhaps some others!

With all except electric boards, the basic idea is to devise some way to make pictures, words, or objects adhere to a board. Prepared figures can be of better quality than those produced on the spot; many are commercially produced.

Chalkboards suitable for personal or classroom use can be made by coating the smooth side of a sheet of Masonite with two coats of shellac and two coats of chalkboard paint. Most new chalkboards should be coated with chalk dust by rubbing the surface with the side of a stick of chalk, and then erasing it. This process prevents lines drawn on it from being so bold that they can never be erased.

The most popular flannelboards are twenty-four by thirty-six inches, since commercially made scenery and figures are usually designed for this size. Boards may be flat or hinged. If the flannelboard is made of double thickness, corrugated cardboard or lightweight wallboard, the hinging may be made with twenty-four-inch strips of adhesive tape two inches wide. For home Bible classes, chalkboard paint on the back is useful.

In recent years, pocketboards are no longer used exclusively by teachers of young children but are also being used with all age levels. Pocketboards are useful for getting words before a group—key words, Bible verses, an outline, a scrambled list. The word strips require no backing and easily go on the board straight. Children can arrange words for drills and reviews.

An electric board is a tool used in programmed learning. The child matches the correct answers to stated questions. When he connects the correct items he receives immediate reinforcement by the sound of a bell or the flashing of a light. The lists on the board may be Bible references and verses, places and people, people and events, writers and brief quotations, or cities and map locations.

Flat pictures and graphics. In this section are included pictures, murals, posters, charts, flash cards, and maps—that is, nonprojected materials produced by photography or by drawing and lettering in various combinations. They may vary in size from a single new word on a flash card to a wall-size mural.

We may divide pictures and graphics on the basis of their producers: those commercially produced, those prepared by the teacher or assistant, and those made by children as part of the learning experience.

Teachers of preschool and primary grade children have long used Bible pictures to accompany storytelling. Many are available with correlated story papers for children to take home. For use with children between the ages of two and five, these flat pictures are often preferred to flannelgraph, since they have no loose pieces to get lost. Young children need to see the same picture a number of times; flat pictures are easily stored and handled, even by children. A study of church supply catalogs shows also that an increasing number of pictures for background and application are being published. A teacher of juniors may, on occasion, use a print from a famous or contemporary artist in discussing a Bible event. Every church should develop a classified picture file in order to conserve purchased pictures and collect useful free ones.

Flash cards have grown in popularity and availability in the last fifteen years. Whereas they were once used only in day school for drilling children on words or arithmetic tables, now they are storytelling favorites as well. Usually a flash-card story is made up of several pictures showing consecutive scenes. The teacher displays them on an easel or holds them as he tells the story. They are convenient to handle and are especially valuable for outdoor work or situations where a teacher must move quickly from one class to another. Drill-type flash cards, usually made by the teacher, are as helpful in teaching Bible facts, verses, references, and books of the Bible as in fixing arithmetic combinations.

Fourth graders begin the serious study of maps in their geography class; so, in their Sunday school lessons, they should be introduced to maps of Bible lands. Particular care should be taken to relate the Bible history areas of the world to broader areas studied in school.

Many publishers today are providing correlated packets of teaching materials for church agencies and a host of supplementary materials from which a teacher may choose. In addition, most teachers will at times want to prepare their own illustrative material. It is helpful to remember that children do not expect perfection. They will accept stick figures for people, but this fact does not permit sloppiness; what we do should be done as unto the Lord.

Often when children are asked to review a unit of study and tell what they liked best, they will mention a project in which they themselves were involved, such as, "when we made the big mural of the life of Abraham," or "when we made the tabernacle model." These kinds of activities do not fit every agency because of their unusual demands in time and space, but in vacation Bible school or day camp, there can be opportunity for such pupil projects that visualize truth.

Projected materials. Projected materials include all those that require a projector: motion pictures, filmstrips, slides, overhead transparencies.

The term *film* is most often used for a 16-mm motion picture. The term distinguishes it from a series of still pictures printed on film known as a filmstrip and from a "movie" produced on 35-mm film and shown in the local theater. The term *movie* connotes the idea of entertainment and so is usually avoided by educators.

Sound films provide both visual and audio presentations for maximum impact. They are therefore particularly valuable in making a story live, in producing an emotional response which leads to action or discussion, and in providing the explanation of a process.

Partly because of the cost of film rental, they are most often used on special occasions and for large group assemblies. However, 8-mm and super-8 films, both silent and sound, are now becoming available for use in film loop projectors. Though few film loops in the religious field have been produced as yet, the future holds promise here.

In some schools, children have produced exciting 8-mm films to culminate study units in art, social studies, and science.[1] This kind of creative project might also be produced by a church group in situations where time and finances are sufficient. Simple movie cameras are on the market which require little knowledge of lighting or other photographic techniques.

Filmstrips, the most common of the projected materials, have several advantages: compactness, low-cost projectors, relatively low purchase price, availability in great variety. They are strips of still pictures, many with accompanying sound on phonograph records or cassettes. This means that a sound filmstrip does not require a sound filmstrip projector, but may use an easily available record player or cassette player for the narration.

Two adaptations of the standard filmstrip are phono-viewers and split-35 strips. A phono-viewer is a combination record player and projector. It uses a special kind of filmstrip and produces the picture on a television-like screen. Bible materials are available.[2]

Split-35 strips are small filmstrips made on half the width of 35-mm film. They may be projected by use of an inexpensive special projector or by a standard filmstrip projector, using an adapter; they are short and inexpensive. Bible and Bible-related strips are on the market, many with accompanying records.

Slides, usually in two-by-two inch mounts, are the simplest of the photographically produced media. Most cameras can use color film; many have automatic exposure control and simple focusing devices which enable even an amateur to get good slides. For children, some of the best uses of slides are for showing what has been done, presenting the work of "our missionary," promoting camp or VBS or other special program, leading into worship through a portrayal of God's handiwork.

Overhead projectors have become popular at all levels in schools and colleges. They project large transparencies which may be purchased,[3] hand-drawn on inexpensive film,[4] or reproduced from paper copy by use of a copy machine and special film. As with most other projectors, these can best be used in a department session. Here is an excellent way of getting before a group the words of a song, directions for a presession activity, a Bible verse to be discussed, or the contributions of pupils. During presession, each junior pupil can be given a sheet of film and a marker, along with instructions for preparing a chart, paragraph, or outline. Some of their work may then be projected and discussed.

Television and videotape. Closely related to projected materials are television and videotape, though these media operate electronically rather than photographically. By using a television camera and microphone in one room connected by cable to a monitor (or a home TV receiver plus an adapter) in another room, it is possible to show a class what is going on before the camera. This is known as closed-circuit television. The program is not broadcast but merely cabled to the monitor.

Closed-circuit television makes it possible for a teacher training class to observe a group of children unobtrusively, or to observe a teacher without the pupils' being conscious of visitors. It enables a group of children to role play without an obvious audience.

The next step beyond this use of television is recording on videotape in order to have playback later. The camera and microphone feed into the videotape recorder, which records both sound and picture signals. When playback is desired, the recorder is connected with the monitor and the program is produced on the TV screen.

The videotape program may be played again and again, or the tape may be reused. The initial cost of tape is likely to deter a church from saving many taped programs, but a church which telecasts its services can make many inexpensive uses of the same equipment and tape.

AUDIO MATERIALS

With listening materials becoming more plentiful each year, a Sunday school teacher has less excuse than ever for requiring children to listen to his rendition of the lesson fifty-two weeks of the year. Consider, for example, what can be done with phonograph records: they can set the mood as children enter the room, or as they rest in vacation Bible school or camp; they can introduce a new song, or provide accompaniment for singing; they can tell a story; they can give variety to scripture reading; they can provide activity music for preschoolers; they can be a source of short selections with which pupils may react.

Phonograph records are reasonably priced and do not require costly equipment. For use in children's work, a player for single records is often preferable to one with an automatic changer. The same player may be used for the narration of filmstrips.

A tape recorder may be used for all of the above purposes, though prerecorded material for children's departments is not abundant. Some publishers are providing either records or a cassette to accompany each quarter's Sunday school material. In most cases, these recordings, more available for older than for younger children, are made up of several sections, each for a different lesson.

A teacher may record material for use as a listening experience and for discussion. The recording may be a dramatization or telling of the Bible story or of a modern story similar to it, or a dialogue of children's voices applying the truth to be taught, or showing the need of such application. The taping may be done by adults, by primary or junior pupils, or as a special project by teenagers. Over a period of time, creative teachers can accumulate a small library of short recordings suitable for use in teaching situations.

In today's schoolrooms, many programs of individualized instruction depend heavily on the use of cassette recorders. Whole series of materials are prepared, using a combination of tapes, filmstrips, activity cards, and worksheets. Pupils progress at their own rate either within set limits or without limits.

The concept of individual study and progress is in keeping with the Bible's emphasis on the individual and his worth. Some vacation Bible schools have partially used this idea, with a number of activity centers in each department and each pupil making some choices. As Christian teachers give more attention to nonclass methods of instruction, they will undoubtedly use more recorded material, probably with cassettes and headphones.

Tape recorders are of several types: reel-to-reel and cassette, monaural and stereo, two-track and four- or eight-track, battery and AC operated. For many noncritical purposes, a monaural cassette recorder is practical and portable. Preferably, it should operate on either battery or alternating current. For most other church and school uses, a monaural, two-track, reel-to-reel recorder is adequate.

MANIPULATIVE MEDIA

In various ways throughout this book and in this chapter, the message has been reiterated: pupils must become involved with the truths of a lesson if they are to learn and change. When children use and react to media presentations, they are involved in learning; when, in some cases, they actually produce the materials, they are surely involved. Three-dimensional projects which children can manipulate give opportunity for further participation.

A fifth grade class, wanting to present the Christmas story to their parents, prepared a shadow box. They used a suit-box cover, cutting a large window and covering the window with blue tissue paper. They then stood the box on edge on a table, placed a light behind it and used silhouette figures, which they changed as a narrator read the story.

There is something secretive about a peep box. Perhaps it is the fact that only one person can see at a time and the rest must wait. Third graders can use a shoe box as a base, cut a viewing window on one end and a skylight in the top. They can use small, stand-up figures or pictures from take-home papers to portray their favorite story out of their current series.

Preschool children are often intrigued by stand-up figures or figurines, which they can move about in portraying a Bible story after they have seen their teacher do it. Primary children can prepare a sandbox or stand-up presentation themselves and then enjoy explaining their production. (Also see chap. 15.)

A model or replica of some real thing can solve several problems: the real thing may be too small or too large to see advantageously, such as a Palestinian village; it may not be available, or may no longer exist, such as the tabernacle in the wilderness or Noah's ark; it may be too fragile or too expensive to handle.

Models may be made of many materials: paper, papier-mâché, clay, soap, wood. Instructions for the use of a variety of materials may be found in craft books; also, project kits are listed in Sunday school supply catalogs. The production of a collection of models could be an exciting VBS project for a junior or older group.

A world globe is actually a model of the earth and should be used to help juniors visualize the location of Bible events, the placement of their missionaries, the time-zone differences where these missionaries serve, climate differences as shown by proximity to the equator.

A diorama is a model of a whole scene, rather than of one object. It may be small, made by children from a carton, or it may be life-size, in a museum. For pupils, the more valuable dioramas are usually those they make, depicting a Bible story, the camp of Israel, or a mission station.

Programmed learning is a form of teaching in which a learning task is divided into many small steps arranged so that the pupil must understand or complete one before going on to the next. Programmed learning may use only words and be prepared in book form, or it may involve the use of various audio, visual, or manipulative materials.

At present, little or no programmed material is available for church children's groups, though some experimentation is being done. Some public schools are using this method of instruction; as Christian educators envision more largely the possibilities of a nonclass approach in certain study areas, they will undoubtedly devise programs for use in churches.[5]

REAL OBJECTS

Almost all the visual and audio media which have been discussed thus far are in some way representations of real objects, but not real in themselves. Real things have been represented by words, lines, diagrams, maps, photographic reproductions, drawings, models, or combinations of these. Perhaps the infrequency with which we show children the real thing in church education grows out of the fact that we are teaching the Bible, theology, and interpersonal relationships. We are dealing with events of the past, with abstract matters, with applications to life that involve people with their viewpoints and emotional responses. These cannot be brought into the classroom for study as tangible objects can. The result is that the teacher of scriptural truth must look to the Lord for other ways to make the instruction clear and relevant.

Real objects, nevertheless, do have a place in Christian teaching. Missionaries have used curios to help people understand life in the countries where they work. One missionary, a children's worker in Africa, met the need of primary children by wearing an African dress and visiting with six children at a time at a children's party. The small groups permitted questions, explanations, and handling of items of special interest to the children.

A visit to certain museums can open the eyes of children to the high-quality workmanship exhibited by people who, in other ways, seem primitive. Such an experience can give children a respect for the people to whom their missionaries go. A trip to a children's home can lead juniors to a new appreciation of their own parents, as well as a desire to remember these needy children on special occasions.

Teachers have not only used objects for their own value, but have often used them to represent something else in object lessons. Such use can be valuable if the relationships are clear to the children. Teachers should ask these two questions regarding object lessons: First, does this object actually make the truth more clear, or are the relationships so symbolic that they make learning the real truth more difficult? Second, is the child so mystified by the object or action related to it that he remembers only the action and loses the meaning entirely, as is sometimes true of gospel magic? Real objects, like all other visual and audio materials, are of value whenever they *help* children to understand and learn.

Audio and visual media are valuable; their use is scriptural; and their variety is seemingly endless. However, visuals are effective only to the extent that they are used with purpose, discretion, preparation, and prayer.

NOTES

1. See, for example, Arden Rynew, *Filmmaking for Children* (Dayton, Ohio: Pflaum/Standard, 1971).
2. Canon Bible Program, Double Sixteen Company, 1028 College Ave., Wheaton, Ill. 60187.
3. Bible-teaching transparencies designed for use with children are still scarce. For life of Christ material and Bible maps, contact The 3M Company, 2501 Hudson Rd., St. Paul, Minn. 55119. For doctrinal lessons, write to United Transparencies, Faith Venture Visuals, P. O. Box 685, Lititz, Pa. 17543. For Bible maps and Bible lands series, contact Broadman Press, 129 Ninth Ave. North, Nashville, Tenn. 37234.
4. Reprocessed X-ray film on which colored markers may be used is available from Johnson Plastics, P. O. Box 523, Hazelton, Pa. 18201. This method is least expensive.
5. For more on this subject, see these articles: Alva I. Cox, Jr., "Programmed Instruction and Christian Education," *Children's Religion,* April 1964, pp. 18-19; Ralph W. Harris, "How Children Learn Through Programmed Instruction," *Eternity* 16 (Nov., 1965):26-27; Walter R. Hearn, "What? Sunday School Taught by Machines?" *Eternity* 16 (Nov., 1965):22-23, 27, 46-48; C. Ellis Nelson, "Machine-Taught Religion," *The Christian Century,* 80 (Jan. 2, 1963); Charles A. Pirolo, "A New Technique for an Old Lesson," *Christian Life,* 28 (June 1966):84-85.

FOR FURTHER READING

Barnhouse, Donald Grey. *Teaching the Word of Truth.* Grand Rapids: Eerdmans, 1958.

Brown, James W.; Lewis, Richard B.; and Harcleroad, Fred F. *AV Instruction: Media and Methods.* New York: McGraw-Hill, 1969.

Doan, Eleanor L. *Make-It-Yourself Visual Aid Encyclopedia.* Glendale, Calif.: Gospel Light, 1967.

Ellingboe, Betty. *Teaching Idea Kit.* Minneapolis: Augsburg, 1963.

Ford, LeRoy. *Tools for Teaching and Training.* Nashville: Broadman, 1961.

Getz, Gene A. *Audio-Visual Media in Christian Education.* Chicago: Moody, 1972.

Glander, James, and Thaemert, Ferol. "Tooling Up for Teaching with Cameras, Transparencies, and Slides." *Interaction* 13 (Jan., 1973):8-11.

How to Make Good Home Movies. Rochester, N. Y.: Eastman-Kodak, 1966.

Kemp, Jerrold E. *Planning and Producing Audiovisual Materials.* San Francisco: Chandler, 1968.

Minor, Ed, and Frye, Harvey R. *Techniques for Producing Visual Instructional Media.* Dubuque, Iowa: Kendall/Hunt, 1971.

Roper, David. *Teach with a Visual Punch.* Cincinnati: Standard, 1973.

Rynew, Arden. *Filmmaking for Children.* Dayton, Ohio: Pflaum/Standard, 1971.

Sloan, Robert, Jr. *The Tape Recorder.* Austin, Tex.: Visual Instruction Bureau, U. Texas, n.d.

Smith, Richard E. *The Overhead System: Production, Implementation and Utilization.* Austin, Tex.: Visual Instruction Bureau, U. Texas, n.d.
Wiman, Raymond V. *Instructional Materials.* Worthington, Ohio: Jones, 1972.

PROJECTED VISUALS

Broadman Films, 127 Ninth Ave. North, Nashville, Tenn. 37234
Cathedral Films, 2921 West Alameda Ave., Burbank, Calif. 91501
Concordia Films, 3558 South Jefferson Ave., St. Louis, Mo. 63118
Family Films, 5823 Santa Monica Blvd., Hollywood, Calif. 90038
Films For Christ, 1204 North Elmwood, Peoria, Ill. 61606
Gospel Films, P. O. Box 455, Muskegon, Mich. 49443
Ken Anderson Films, P. O. Box 618, Winona Lake, Ind. 46590
Moody Institute of Science Films, 12000 East Washington Blvd., Whittier, Calif. 90606

BULLETIN BOARD IDEAS

Caplan, Kate, and Rosenthal, Constance. *Guide to Better Bulletin Boards.* Dobbs Ferry, N.Y.: Oceana, 1970.
Robinson, James, and Robinson, Rowena. *Bulletin Board Ideas.* St. Louis: Concordia.
O'Brien, Bernard, and O'Brien, Carolyn. *Junior Bulletin Boards.* Wheaton, Ill.: Scripture Press, 1971.
LeBar, Mary E. *Preschool Bulletin Boards.* Wheaton, Ill.: Scripture Press, 1969.

FLANNELGRAPH AND/OR FLASH-CARD STORIES

Baker Book House, 1019 Wealthy Street, S.E., Grand Rapids, Mich. 49506
Bible Club Movement, Inc., 237 Fairfield Avenue, Upper Darby, Pa. 19082
Bible Games Company, 316 North Leeds, Eldon, Mo. 65026
Bible Visuals, Inc., P. O. Box 93, Londisville, Pa. 17538
Child Evangelism Fellowship Press, P. O. Box 1156, Grand Rapids, Mich. 49501
Christian Publications, Inc., 25 South Tenth Street, Harrisburg, Pa. 17101
David C. Cook Publishing Company, 850 N. Grove, Elgin, Ill. 60120
Gospel Folio Press, P. O. Box 2041, Grand Rapids, Mich. 49501
Gospel Light Publications, 110 West Broadway, Glendale, Calif. 91204
Higley Publishing Corporation, P. O. Box 2470, Jacksonville, Fla. 32203
Living Stories, Inc., P. O. Box 731, Milford, Ka. 66514
Message of Life, Inc., 58607 Road 600, Ahwahnee, Calif. 93601
Scripture Press Publications, Inc., 1825 College Ave., Wheaton, Ill. 60187
Standard Publishing Company, 8121 Hamilton Avenue, Cincinnati, Ohio 45231
Union Gospel Press, P. O. Box 6059, Cleveland, Ohio 44101

17

Using the Bible with Children

Elizabeth Gangel

Evangelical Christians are very quick to say that the Bible is the most important Book ever written. They believe it from "cover to cover," but in the reality of daily living, experience does not always support creed. The Bible is picked up on Sunday morning and carried to church and the returned to the shelf, not to be picked up again until the following Sunday. Many children are not seeing their parents reading and living God's Word. Martha Aycock suggests,

> Most educators and theologians agree that the most effective way for children to begin to know and understand the truths recorded in the Bible is to live with adults whose lives express these truths. When they do, children catch the spirit of Christ long before they can read or understand words about Him.[1]

Some objectives worth consideration while using the Bible with children are: (1) that the child may show a growing love for the Bible; (2) that the child may understand that the Bible is the basis of the Christian faith and the final authority on faith and conduct; (3) that the child may understand how Bible truth applies to daily living; (4) that the child may understand the origin of the Bible, including the preparing and preserving of it; (5) that the child may understand Bible content, customs, history, and geography; (6) that the child may commit Bible passages to memory.

The Importance and Place of the Bible in Teaching Children

When we say the Bible is a special Book, that it is very important and should have a prominent place of recognition, exactly what do we mean? Do we mean we should have a special location in which to put the Bible

---

Elizabeth Gangel, B.A., is a Christian education consultant, residing in Miami, Florida.

in our homes or Sunday school rooms? Do we mean one must be careful how he handles the Bible? Do we mean that a teacher should always be sure the children understand that the stories he is telling and the verses he is teaching are taken from the Bible?

All of these things may be important, but we must go beyond all of them and teach our children that the Bible is a "God-breathed," written message, which gives us the answers to questions about God, ourselves, and the Christian life. Children need to know that the Bible is our final authority—a Book without error in its original languages. It shows us the way to God through Jesus Christ, helps us to know how to live the Christian life, and gives us guidance for making everyday decisions.

The best reason that the Bible is important comes from the Bible itself. "The whole Bible was given to us by inspiration from God and is useful to teach us what is true and to make us realize what is wrong in our lives; it straightens us out and helps us do what is right. It is God's way of making us well prepared at every point, fully equipped to do good to everyone" (2 Ti 3:16-17, TLB).

The following passages of Scripture give just a few of the reasons that we teach the Bible. "How can a young man stay pure? By reading your Word and following its rules. . . . I have thought much about your words, and stored them in my heart so that they would hold me back from sin. . . . I am but a pilgrim here on earth: how I need a map—and your commands are my chart and guide. . . . Forever, O Lord, your Word stands firm in heaven" (Ps 119:9, 11, 19, 89, TLB). "These things that were written in the Scriptures so long ago are to teach us patience and to encourage us, so that we will look forward expectantly to the time when God will conquer sin and death" (Ro 15:4, TLB). "Jesus' disciples saw him do many other miracles besides the ones told about in this book, but these are recorded so that you will believe that he is the Messiah, the Son of God, and that believing in him you will have life" (Jn 20:30-31, TLB). "You know how, when you were a small child, you were taught the holy Scriptures; and it is these that make you wise to accept God's salvation by trusting in Christ Jesus" (2 Ti 3:15, TLB).

Second Timothy 3:15 is the key to our understanding of the task which we have while teaching the Bible to children. Even though the Bible was written by adults to adults, we, as adults, have the responsibility of training our children according to God's plan, and this must happen primarily in the home.

Principles in Using the Bible with Children

When using the Bible with children, we should keep in mind these three principles. The first principle is that children should be able to have and use their own Bibles. Many Sunday schools encourage this by counting the Bibles brought every Sunday morning and putting the number on the register. Other churches try to solve the problem by having extra Bibles in the pew racks and in each Sunday school class. Providing Bibles may be a step in the right direction, but the most important aspect of this principle is to teach the children how to *use* their *own* Bibles. In order to do this, we must have cooperation between parents and teachers.

The big family Bible is fine but will not lend itself to individual study and the feeling of ownership by each member of the family. Parents can be of great assistance to their children if, during family worship, they take the time to help each child find the scripture passages and generally to encourage him to become more familiar with his own Bible.

Teachers can help by doing the same things in the classroom. Many children become discouraged about taking their Bibles to Sunday school because they are not given the opportunity to use them and therefore, decided it is not worth the effort to carry their Bibles back and forth each week. Later in the chapter, we will come back to this subject with some specific suggestions.

The second principle to keep in mind is that we must teach the Bible as God's whole revelation and not build a doctrine or teaching from one passage of Scripture to the exclusion of others.

One guideline of hermeneutics, the science of interpretation, is that of progressive revelation. Our children must be taught to understand that God was constantly revealing more of Himself and His plan all through biblical history. Today we can understand more of God's plan of redemption than Moses was able to comprehend.

Another guideline is that of the proportion of the Bible which deals with certain themes. Because God chose to have four books with eighty-nine chapters given over to the life and ministry of Jesus Christ, we can be sure that it is a very important theme in God's total revelation.

Another guideline is that of context. We must teach our children that they cannot build a doctrine of prayer on one verse such as, "Yes, ask *anything,* using my name, and I will do it!" (Jn 14:14, TLB), without looking at the verses which precede or follow. All the passages in the Bible must be considered when we form our beliefs on a particular subject.

The third principle in using the Bible with children is that children should realize the Bible is their final authority. Children tend to follow much more readily and naturally the example of parents and teachers than the teachings of the Bible. They need to be guided away from this tendency.

Brubaker and Clark remind us, "It is important to be absolutely truthful in answering a child's spiritual questions and not take advantage of his trusting spirit."[2] They also suggest, "The primary child is God-inclined, with a tender conscience, a strong impulse to obey, and implicit faith. He still believes what he is told, but is already beginning to seek proof and certainty."[3]

Because of these facts about children, parents and teachers must be careful to live what they teach and to teach only biblical truths. Then at the proper time, children can begin to understand that the authority for all of spiritual truth has come directly from God through His Word.

By the time pupils reach their teens, they should not be claiming beliefs because a church teaches them or even because parents hold to those truths. Teens need to develop their own set of convictions and beliefs based on the teachings of Scripture. David put it well: "Your words are a flashlight to light the path ahead of me, and keep me from stumbling" (Ps 119:105, TLB).

Ways to Use the Bible with Children

Because it is important for children to begin to use their own Bibles, we might ask how parents and teachers can help to bring this about. The situation can be approached from two aspects, with some ideas and suggestions for each.

In the Classroom

Nursery and kindergarten children can grasp that the Bible is a special Book which tells us about God and Jesus. They can understand that from this Book come the stories that they love and the Bible words they have memorized.

The teacher should always have a Bible in hand as he tells the Bible story, referring often to the fact that the Bible is true. A Bible should always be kept at some important place in the classroom for quick use and reference as the source of authority.

If children at these ages begin to bring their own Bibles, the teacher should be sure to give them an opportunity to "pretend read" from them. The teacher could help the children to find the Bible story of the day, or he could underline the Bible verse lightly in pencil.

By the time a child has reached his primary years, he is beginning to read. Now many activities can help him begin to learn the joy of using and studying the Bible. Because primary children are eager to use their new skill, a teacher should have no difficulty in getting volunteers to read certain verses or passages during classroom teaching or discussion.

A modern paraphrase such as *The Living Bible* can help children read the Bible with more ease and understanding.

Children also enjoy group reading. This approach will help a shy child to get involved. Group reading can be done in several ways: reading in unison, taking turns, choral reading. Some teachers record a Bible passage on a tape recorder and then during classtime, allow the children to join in and read along with the teacher, or the teacher could lead the group in alternate reading.

Wise teachers encourage primary children to investigate the Bible individually. This can be done by utilizing the pupils' manuals printed by Sunday school publishing companies or by asking specific fact or thought questions to which the students must find answers in a certain passage.

Early elementary children will need help with the basic skill of locating an assigned Bible book, chapter, or verse. Teachers can facilitate this process by encouraging the children to memorize the books of the Bible in order and by giving plenty of opportunity to use this new information.

Juniors are ready for increased opportunities to use their Bibles. They are able to expand into areas such as problem-solving and research. Perhaps during class discussions, a question might come up which no one is able to answer. What a marvelous opportunity for personal Bible investigation! The students are sent home with an assignment to find the answer to the question in their Bibles.

A teacher may decide to spend some class time guiding students in solving a life-situation problem similar to experiences which they are facing at school or home. It could be a fictitious story with several possible endings. The students would investigate the Bible to decide on the right solution and then tell what passages of Scripture helped them solve the problem.

Juniors will also enjoy the competition of quizzes and sword drills. These activities will give them more opportunities to use and become familiar with their Bibles.

"Expressing" a Bible verse or passage has a lot of possibilities. Students may rewrite a verse in their own words, or verses may be expressed through art. The message in Romans 9:20-24 about the potter and the clay, for example, could be effectively taught with the use of clay modeling.

Rives and Sharp, in *Guiding Children,* say, "Today, a new emphasis is placed on providing the opportunities for children to experiment, research, think through, and to discover truths for themselves. Creative writing is one of these avenues."[4] Their chapter on "Learning Through Creative Writing" contains many helpful suggestions on how to write litanies, poems, stories, newspapers, and letters.

IN THE HOME

Recently, a group of fourth graders in a Christian school were asked some questions about the Bible. It was very interesting to evaluate their answers. When asked. "Do you ever read the Bible yourself?" 86% said "yes" or "I try," and only 14% said "not very much" or "not often."

When they were asked, "Does your mom and dad ever read the Bible to you?" 43% said "yes," and 57% said "no" or "sometimes."

In some homes, children may be more interested in reading and knowing about the Bible than are their parents. Some parents have the idea that the spiritual training of their children is the responsibility of the church or the Christian school. But God says, "You must think constantly about these commandments I am giving you today. You must teach them to your children and talk about them when you are at home or out for a walk; at bedtime and the first thing in the morning" (Deu 6:6-7, TLB).

Family worship, training, and sharing will not just happen, it must be planned and worked into the family schedule. During family worship, each member should feel an openness to ask questions about the Bible that he might never ask in Sunday school. It is a time to share prayer burdens and lean on the Lord as a family. As Shirley Rice says, "The family altar is the careful laying of the foundation of God's truth in the child's life. It will be done, little by little, line upon line."[5]

Allowing children to help in the planning of family devotional times will increase their interest. They may tire of always hearing the parents do the Bible reading and "preaching." Older children can help plan which subjects to discuss, which songs to sing, whether printed material should be used, and which Bible story to use. They can also help assign responsibilities to family members.*

Many books are available for use in family devotions. A list of Bible storybooks and devotional books that children can read in personal and family devotions is given at the end of this chapter.

Learning About the Bible

The same group of fourth-grade students referred to earlier were asked, "What is the Bible to you?" The answers varied from "It is a good Book," "It is love," "It is everything," to "It's the truth, the Word of God."

Most fourth graders are ready to explore such questions about the Bible as, How did we get our Bible? Who wrote it? How long ago was the Bible written? How was it protected all these years? In what languages was it originally written? What did those languages look like? How many people helped write the Bible? Is it one Book or many books?

In Idalee Vonk's book, *52 Primary Worship Programs,* she spends one month on the study of the Bible, answering such issues as, "Why God

*For more on children's personal devotions, see chap. 19, "Teaching Children to Worship and Pray."

Gave Us the Bible," "How God Gave Us the Bible," "What We Find in the Bible," and, "Using the Bible as Our Guide."

By the time children reach middle elementary years, they are beginning map study in school. We need to begin at the same time to acquaint them with maps in connection with certain Bible stories. How can they fully understand the story of the good Samaritan, the account of the woman at the well, the wanderings of the children of Israel, or Paul's missionary journeys without some map study? Yet Sunday school teachers are embarrassed at their lack of ability to draw a simple map of the land of Palestine.

Older children are also ready to learn how to use a Bible dictionary or concordance. Perhaps in the study of a certain passage of Scripture, a term is used which is unfamiliar to the children or which they find difficult to explain in their own words. Here is an opportunity to take time to help the children see how to consult a Bible dictionary to find the meanings of such terms.

A pictorial Bible dictionary can be a very interesting way to study proper names and a most helpful tool for pupils preparing a class report.

The concordance is basic to effective word study. Let's return to the word *prayer* for an example of a word study. Bring several concordances to class and pass them out among your students. The students may work in teams or individually, depending on the number of concordances available. Each team can be assigned to several books of the Bible. The team's responsibility would be to look up the verses in those books that talk about prayer and to write down what they teach. After reporting what they have found, the class will have a much better knowledge of what the Bible has to say about prayer.

Older children can also be taught how to use a commentary as an aid to understanding a Bible verse.

Using your imagination, make the study of God's Word an exciting adventure for your pupils in class and your children at home. May we never make the Bible seem boring.

Memorization of the Bible

Christ is our example in showing us the importance of memorizing Scripture. When Christ was tempted by Satan, He was able to defeat him by the authority of God's Word. This victory was possible because He knew the Scriptures from memory. To the extent children know the Scriptures they can overcome Satan's temptations against their young lives. "I have thought much about your words, and stored them in my heart so that they would hold me back from sin" (Ps 119:11, TLB).

Clark suggests several reasons for children memorizing Bible verses:

> God uses His Word not only to convict of sin but to guide in right and holy living. Memorized Scripture can help children obey authority, find encouragement, resist temptation, witness, make decisions to glorify the Lord, express their thoughts to God, claim God's promises and prepare for the future.[6]

Children can also be encouraged to memorize Bible portions as a means of being able to answer their friends' questions about God and the Bible. "Quietly trust yourself to Christ your Lord and if anybody asks why you believe as you do, be ready to tell him, and do it in a gentle and respectful way" (1 Pe 3:15, TLB).

Many Christian young people and adults, while hospitalized or undergoing other troubles, have been blessed by recalling many Bible verses which they had committed to memory when they were children.

PRINCIPLES OF MEMORIZATION

For many people, memorizing is only a repetition of words which are soon forgotten. Some ways to make Bible memory work more meaningful and lasting are suggested in the following paragraphs.

1. Help the children understand the meaning of the verse(s) to be memorized. After a verse is understood, it is easier to memorize. Comprehension aids memorization.

2. Review the verses memorized. Most people have experienced the type of rote learning which was done exclusively in order to pass a test or receive a certain recognition. Without periodic review, such "learning" fades rapidly. Referring to the memory verse several times throughout the lesson helps the children retain it.

3. Use visual aids when teaching memory verses. Flash cards, overhead projection, tape recorders, puppets, pictures, posters, puzzles, secret codes, and songs are tools that can help children remember Bible verses. (One such visual is the Salvation Verses Memory Word Cards, comprising suede-backed cards with words from seventeen verses, published by Scripture Press.)

4. Consider having the children memorize occasionally from a modern Bible version or paraphrase. Suppose a memory verse for juniors is 2 Timothy 2:15. Which one of these translations would be most meaningful for a junior?

"Study to shew thyself approved unto God, a workman that needeth not be ashamed, rightly dividing the word of truth" (KJV).

"Be diligent to present yourself approved to God as a workman who does not need to be ashamed, handling accurately the word of truth" (NASB).

"Do your utmost to present yourself to God approved, a workman who has no cause to be ashamed, correctly interpreting the message of the truth" (Berkeley).

"Work hard so God can say to you, 'Well done.' Be a good workman, one who does not need to be ashamed when God examines your work. Know what his word says and means" (TLB).

Should all memorization center on the King James Version? This is a debated question. If a child can understand and apply the verse more easily from a modern version, perhaps we should not allow tradition to stand in the way. On the other hand, if all of the children in the class have the King James Version, it may be less confusing to teach from it than to teach from a version or paraphrase owned by only a few pupils in the class.

5. Enlist the cooperation of parents in memory work. Parents can be a great help in encouraging the memorization of Scripture. They have the entire week to review the verse and to help their children become aware of situations in which the verse applies.

6. Weave the memory verse into the lesson. Clark suggests,

> One of the best ways to teach a memory verse is to weave it into the lesson where it fits naturally. The verse may be repeated several times throughout the session and by the end of the period the pupils will be acquainted with the basic content and meaning of the verse.[7]

7. Help the children comprehend how the verse applies to their lives. It is important to memorize Bible verses and entire passages, but if the memorized verses have no meaning or bring about no change in the lives of the children we teach, then they are of little value.

If a preschooler is able to recite "Be ye kind one to another," and is constantly found hitting, biting, kicking, and grabbing toys, he has not really learned that verse. If a seven-year-old is able to say, "Children, obey your parents in the Lord; for this is right," but continues to ignore his parents' commands to turn off the television or get ready for bed, he has not truly learned that verse.

Are these children just very difficult and incorrigible? Not necessarily. Perhaps the problem lies with the teacher or parent. All too often, memory verses are handled like this:

Teacher: How many of you boys and girls know your memory verse this week? (Several hands go up.) OK, Billy, you say it first.

Billy: "It is a good thing to give thanks unto the Lord," Psalm 92:1.

Teacher: Very good, Billy, you may put a star on the chart. Susan, you are next.

By the time the three or four children who know the verse have said it, there are probably three or four more children who are ready to say it just from listening to the others repeat it. The children are very pleased that they are able to perform and to put a star on the chart. The teacher moves on to another activity, but when it comes time to have prayer, there is no connection made between the verse and giving thanks to God. Even helping the children grasp the meaning of the verse is not enough; they must understand how that verse applies to their lives. Verses can be used that illustrate different aspects of a child's life at home, school, playground, church, and his relationships with his parents, brothers and sisters, and friends.

STEPS IN MEMORIZATION

In teaching children to memorize Scripture, it is helpful to follow these steps:

1. Be sure to select Scripture according to the characteristics and needs of the pupils being taught.
2. Learn the material well yourself.
3. Present the material in a setting. Weave the verse or passage naturally into the lesson, teach with a melody or song, tell a story in which the Scripture is repeated with variety, use pictures to illustrate the Scripture, or relate the verse or passage to a natural setting, such as the creation.
4. Introduce the whole passage before analyzing its parts.
5. Break the selection into parts and analyze each part carefully: vocabulary, concepts, relationships, illustrations for clarification.
6. Repeat the whole verse or passage.
7. Show specifically how the selection can relate to daily life.
8. Drill for fun, and in a variety of ways.
9. Use the verse or passage in department or class activities. Review often and meaningfully.
10. Encourage practice in real life with follow-up as to how God has used His Word.

It is far better to help children learn a few verses or passages well than many poorly.

PROGRAMS FOR MEMORIZATION

Most evangelical publishers of curriculum materials include a memory verse correlated with each lesson. When used properly, these passages are excellent teaching tools. The Bible verse helps reinforce the truth of the lesson.

Memory work is an important part of the programs of the Awana Youth Association, Christian Service Brigade, Pioneer Girls, and denominational club programs. In these programs, awards encourage the children to memorize Scripture.

In some churches, children are required to memorize verses in each of several educational ministries, including Sunday school, children's church, Sunday evening children's group. This demands careful supervision in order to avoid overloading the children with more than they can retain, and to avoid needless repetition of the same verses.

The Bible Memory Association† produces age-graded materials that encourage Bible memorization on a regular basis. Children ages three through six may participate in the "ABC plan," which includes three stages, one stage per year for the three years. The plan includes twenty-four verses altogether. Stage 1 is for ages three or four, in which the child learns a short verse each week for twelve weeks. Stage 2 is for ages four or five, in which the child learns two short verses a week for twelve weeks. And stage 3 is for ages five or six, in which the child learns two short verses with references each week for twelve weeks. Each year, the child builds on what was learned the previous year, reviewing the twenty-four short verses.

The "Beginner plan," for children in grades 1 through 5, includes memorizing four or five verses each week during January, February, and March.

Success with Youth, Inc.,‡ publishes "Power Flight 52," a memorization program for juniors. It is designed to be completed in fifty-two weeks or less.

Of course, it is always possible for teachers or parents to work out their own particular memorization programs. The following section contains suggested verses or passages for each age level.

PORTIONS FOR MEMORIZATION

For preschoolers. Generally a portion of a verse is best to use in teaching memory work to preschoolers. The following are some verses suitable for young children, given here to illustrate that portions of verses are sufficient.

THEME	BIBLE WORDS	REFERENCE
Child's behavior	"Love one another"	1 Jn 4:7
	"Be kind to each other"	Eph 4:7 (TLB)
	"Don't forget to do good"	Heb 13:16 (TLB)
	"Children, obey your parents"	Eph 6:1

†Write to: Bible Memory Association, Box 12000, St. Louis, Mo. 63112.
‡Write to: Success with Youth, Inc., Box 27028, Tempe, Ariz. 85202.

Creation	"He hath made everything beautiful"	Ec 3:11
	"God created the heaven and the earth."	Gen 1:1
Lord's attitude to us	"The Lord is my Helper"	Heb 13:6 (TLB)
	"He careth for you"	1 Pe 5:7
	"He loved us, and sent his Son"	1 Jn 4:10
Our attitude to the Lord	"We love him, because he first loved us"	1 Jn 4:19
	"I will love thee, O LORD	Psalm 18:1
	"I will sing unto the LORD"	Psalm 13:6

For primaries. Because many of the passages used for preschoolers are parts of verses, the primary years are a good time for children to learn the complete verses. For example, all of Ephesians 6:1 is as follows: "Children, obey your parents in the Lord: for this is right." The words for preschoolers from Psalm 13:6 can be expanded as follows for primaries: "I will sing unto the Lord, because he hath dealt bountifully with me."

Some older primaries are able to learn passages that are fairly short and easy to understand. Several examples are Psalms 23; 100; 136:1-9; and John 14:1-6.

For juniors. Juniors are capable of tackling large sections of Scripture (in addition to the weekly verse with the Bible lesson.) Some passages on selected themes are these: love, 1 Corinthians 13; faith, Hebrews 11; salvation, John 3; Ten Commandments, Exodus 20; Beatitudes, Matthew 5:1-12; Christ's return, 1 Thessalonians 4:13-18.

CRITERIA FOR SELECTING MEMORY PASSAGES

The following questions can be kept in mind when selecting Bible passages for memorization:

1. Is the content of the passage or verse within the range of ability for comprehension?
2. Is the meaning of the passage or verse given in literal and concrete terms which children can grasp?
3. Can the vocabulary be explained for understanding?
4. Is the passage or verse appropriate in length for the attention span?
5. Can the passage or verse be applied specifically to their everyday experiences?

RELATING THE BIBLE TO LIFE

A fine Sunday school teacher I know is always trying something new and creative with her fifth-grade students. Her students could recite several verses on prayer, including these: "Pray always with all prayer and supplication"; "Men ought always to pray"; "Pray for one another." But she could not get any of her students to lead in prayer.

She decided on a behavioral objective for her class: each student will learn to pray orally during this quarter. Then she set about to accomplish that objective. The next Sunday, when they came into class, she brought in an extra chair and placed it in the circle. She told the students that Jesus was sitting in that chair, even though He could not be seen with human eyes, and she wanted each of them to say something to Him as if He were really there. Slowly, awkwardly, each child began to say something. One boy, who had tried very hard not to get involved, said, "I love You, Jesus." What a breakthrough! Over a period of time, this teacher saw her objective accomplished, and the students were beginning to see how the Bible related to their individual lives. They began to understand that the Lord was right there with them and that they could talk to Him about anything just as easily as they could talk to their teacher or their friends.

One night, our nine-year-old daughter was hesitant to go to bed and said she was afraid to fall asleep. A couple days later, we were reading from the book of Psalms, "I will lie down in peace and sleep, for though I am alone, O Lord, you will keep me safe" (Ps 4:8, TLB). Julie looked up at me, smiled, and said, "I didn't know the Bible said that." She had discovered that the Bible had something to say about the problem she was facing.

When we begin to see changes in the lives of our students as a result of Bible stories, Bible study, and memorization, we have begun to accomplish our goal.

NOTES

1. Martha B. Aycock, ed., *Understand* (Richmond, Va.: Knox, 1972), p. 115.
2. J. Omar Brubaker and Robert E. Clark, *Understanding People* (Wheaton, Ill.: Evangelical Teacher Training Assn., 1972), p. 38.
3. Ibid., p. 46.
4. Elsie Rives and Margaret Sharp, *Guiding Children* (Nashville: Convention, 1969), p. 100.
5. Shirley Rice, *The Christian Home* (Norfolk, Va.: Norfolk Christian Schools, 1967), p. 72.
6. Robert E. Clark, "Helping Children Memorize Scripture," *Moody Monthly* 72 (July-Aug., 1972):66.
7. Ibid.

FOR FURTHER READING

Aycock, Martha B., ed. *Understand.* Richmond, Va.: Knox, 1972.

Baker, Dolores, and Rives, Elsie. *Teaching the Bible to Primaries.* Nashville: Convention, 1964.

Bolton, Barbara J. *Ways to Help Them Learn: Children, Grades 1 to 6.* Glendale, Calif.: Gospel Light, Regal Books, 1972.
Brubaker, J. Omar, and Clark, Robert E., *Understanding People.* Wheaton, Ill.: Evangelical Teacher Training Assn., 1972.
Caldwell, Irene Smith. *Our Concern Is Children.* Anderson, Ind.: Warner, 1954.
Chamberlain, Eugene, and Fulbright, Robert. *Children's Sunday School Work.* Nashville: Convention, 1969.
Edge, Findley B. *Helping the Teacher.* Nashville: Broadman, 1959.
———. *Teaching for Results.* Nashville: Broadman, 1956.
Gangel, Kenneth O. "Teaching for Memorization." *The Sunday School Times and Gospel Herald* 70 (July 15, 1972):28-29.
Harty, Robert A. *Children and Church Training.* Nashville: Convention, 1969.
Jahsmann, Allan Hart, ed. *Leading Children into the Bible.* St. Louis: Concordia, 1959.
Klink, Johanna L. *Your Child and Religion.* Richmond, Va.: Knox, 1971.
LeBar, Lois E. *Children in the Bible School.* Westwood, N.J.: Revell, 1952.
McDaniel, Elsiebeth, and Richards, Lawrence O. *You and Children.* Chicago: Moody, 1973.
Morningstar, Mildred. *Reaching Children.* Chicago: Moody, 1944.
Rice, Lillian Moore. *How to Work with Juniors in the Sunday School.* Nashville: Convention, 1956.
Rice, Shirley. *The Christian Home.* Norfolk, Va.: Norfolk Christian Schools, 1967.
Rives, Elsie, and Sharp, Margaret. *Guiding Children.* Nashville: Convention, 1969.
Rood, Wayne R. *On Nurturing Christians.* Nashville: Abingdon, 1972.
Rowen, Dolores. *Ways to Help Them Learn: Early Childhood, Birth to 5 Years.* Glendale, Calif.: Gospel Light, Regal Books, 1972.
Sholund, Milford. "Uses of Memory in the Sunday School." *The Christlife Magazine* (July, 1961), pp. 11-16.
Stickland, Hazel N., and Leatherwood, Mattie C. *Beginner Sunday School Work.* Nashville: Convention, 1955.
Trent, Robbie. *How the Bible Came to Us.* Nashville: Broadman, 1964.
Vonk, Idalee Wolf. *52 Primary Worship Programs.* Cincinnati: Standard, 1953.
Weatherly, G. "The Bible and Your Children." *The Sunday School Times and Gospel Herald.* 70(Nov. 15, 1972):22-23.

Books for Children's Devotions

Daily Bread. Grand Rapids: Child Evangelism Fellowship.
Hook, Martha, and Boren, Tinka. *Little Ones Listen to God.* Grand Rapids: Zondervan, 1971.
Jahsmann, Allan Hart, and Simon, Martin P. *Little Visits with God.* St. Louis: Concordia, 1957.
———. *More Little Visits with God.* St. Louis: Concordia, 1961.

Johnson, Ruth I. *Daily Devotions for Juniors.* Vol 1. Chicago: Moody, 1964.
———. *Daily Devotions for Juniors.* Vol. 2. Chicago: Moody, 1965.
———. *Daily Devotions for Juniors.* Vol. 3. Chicago: Moody, 1967.
Johnston, Dorothy Grunbock. *Pete and Penny Know and Grow.* Chicago: Moody, 1973.
———. *Pete and Penny Plan and Pray.* Chicago: Moody, 1973.
———. *Pete and Penny Think and Thank.* Chicago: Moody, 1973.
Korfker, Dena. *Can You Tell Me?* Grand Rapids: Zondervan, 1970.
LeBar, Lois E. *Family Devotions with School-age Children.* Westwood, N.J.: Revell, 1973.
LeBar, Mary E. *Living in God's Family.* Wheaton, Ill.: Scripture Press, 1957.
Peterson, Gladys J. *Devotional Prayer Fellowship for Juniors.* Elgin, Ill.: David C. Cook.
Prime, Derek. *Tell Me About Becoming a Christian.* Chicago: Moody, 1969.
———. *Tell Me About the Bible, About God.* Chicago: Moody, 1967.
———. *Tell Me About the Holy Spirit, About the Church.* Chicago: Moody, 1967.
———. *Tell Me About the Lord Jesus.* Chicago: Moody, 1967.
———. *Tell Me About the Lord's Prayer.* Chicago: Moody, 1967.
———. *Tell Me About the Ten Commandments.* Chicago: Moody, 1969.
Taylor, Kenneth N. *Stories for the Children's Hour.* Rev. ed. Chicago: Moody, 1968.

Bible Storybooks for Children

Adcock, Roger. *God's Early Heroes.* Wheaton, Ill.: Scripture Press, 1971.
———. *Stories of Jesus.* Wheaton, Ill.: Scripture Press, 1971.
Barrett, Ethel. *It Didn't Just Happen.* Glendale, Calif.: Gospel Light, Regal Books, 1967.

Basic Bible Readers series. Cincinnati: Standard, 1962.

Grade: 1 Runyon, Leilah E. *I Learn to Read About Jesus.*
Grade 2: Ferntheil, Carol. *I Read About God's Gifts.*
———. *I Read About God's Love.*
Grade 3: ———. *Bible Adventures.*
Odor, Ruth Shannon. *Bible Heroes.*

Beers, V. Gilbert. *A Child's Treasury of Bible Stories.* New York: World, 1971.
———. *Family Bible Library.* 10 vols. Nashville: Southwestern, 1971.
The Children's New Testament. Waco, Tex.: Word, 1969.
Egermeier, Elsie E. *Egermeier's Bible Story Book.* Rev. ed. Anderson, Ind.: Warner, 1969.
Gross, Arthur W. *Concordia Bible Story Book.* St. Louis: Concordia, 1971.
Haan, Sheri Dunham. *A Child's Storybook of Bible People.* Grand Rapids: Baker, 1973.
———. *Good News for Children.* Grand Rapids: Baker, 1969.
Korfker, Dena. *The Bible in Stories for Young Folks.* Nashville: Royal, 1960.

———. *My Picture Story Bible.* Grand Rapids: Zondervan, 1960.
The Moody Bible Story Book. Chicago: Moody, 1960.
Richards, Jean Hosking. *The Richards Bible Story Book.* Grand Rapids: Zondervan, 1968.
Taylor, Kenneth N. *Taylor's Bible Story Book.* Wheaton, Ill.: Tyndale, 1970.
———. *The Bible in Pictures for Little Eyes.* Chicago: Moody, 1956.
Van Ness, Bethann. *The Bible Story Book.* Nashville: Broadman, 1963.
Vos, Catherine F. *Child Story Bible.* Grand Rapids: Eerdmans, 1969.

18

Using Music with Children

John F. Wilson

MUSIC IS OFTEN CONSIDERED a combination of art and science, which makes it both structured and unstructured, definable and indefinable. The structured, definable aspects of song (words, melody, rhythm, and harmony) make it possible for it to be formed into logical phrases which communicate ideas and thoughts. However, music is meaningless until it is heard. Prior to being heard, it is merely a scientific formula. The unstructured and indefinable aspect is what permits the performer to feel emotions (love, joy, sadness) and to superimpose his own interpretation of the message in the words and music.

In this chapter, our primary consideration is on the vocal rather than the instrumental. Instrumental music can also be used in children's work in the church, but the concern of this chapter is more with songs that are selected and used with children because of message content and teaching value.

HISTORICAL BACKGROUND

The use of music to teach children the Word of God has been successfully practiced throughout history, dating at least as far back as the time of David and Solomon. At the time of the establishing of temple worship, David commanded the chief Levites to appoint "singers, with instruments of music . . . to raise sounds of joy" (1 Ch 15:16, NASB). Later he set aside three of the chief musicians, Heman, Asaph, and Jeduthun, to instruct the children in song (1 Ch 25). The educational activities during that period included "the reciting of Scriptures, praying, various types of singing, and discussion and explanation of the Scriptures that had great

---

JOHN F. WILSON, M.Mus., is Editor, Hope Publishing Company, Carol Stream, Illinois.

value in helping the people understand the way of the Lord more perfectly."[1]

In New Testament days, the apostle Paul recognized the teaching potential of music when he charged the Colossian Christians, "Let the word of Christ richly dwell within you; with all wisdom teaching and admonishing one another with psalms and hymns and spiritual songs, singing with thankfulness in your hearts to God" (Col 3:16, NASB).

In the early Christian church, choir schools were established to teach music and to train children in the worship and doctrines of the church. In some parts of the world and among some denominational groups in America, similar schools are still in existence.

During the Protestant Reformation, music again played an important part in the teaching of God's Word. Congregational singing was restored to the possession of the people for the first time since the early years of the Christian church, so that, in the words of Martin Luther, "God might speak directly to them in His Word and . . . they might directly answer Him in their songs."[2]

In the Sunday school movement of the nineteenth century, new gospel songs were composed to teach the Word of God to children in simplicity and directness. Today, music not only continues to be effective in the Sunday school but also in many of the newer Christian education agencies, such as children's churches, Bible clubs, vacation Bible schools, and camps.

Values of Music

Music is valuable to children for at least the following reasons.

JOY IN EXPRESSION

Early in life, children learn to respond to singing and to express themselves through music. In our day, radio and television commercials and popular songs are invading their ears and reaching their minds with questionable philosophies, low moral standards, and non-Christian values. We must make equal use of this media of expression to fill their hearts and lives with the truth and to teach them to verbalize their love for God and concern for others. The fact that music brings pleasurable experience makes it an even more effective teaching tool. When something is fun to do, the learning comes more easily and the powers of retention are greater.

EVANGELISTIC WITNESS

Music enhances the ministry of outreach. Children are often drawn to a church because of a special interest in an activity, whether it be recreation, handcraft, or music. Any of these can be valuable initial contacts toward winning children to Christ. When a child is attracted through music, opportunities are provided for personal contact with the leaders and for confrontation with the message of salvation. This evangelistic potential may best be illustrated by the following set of steps.

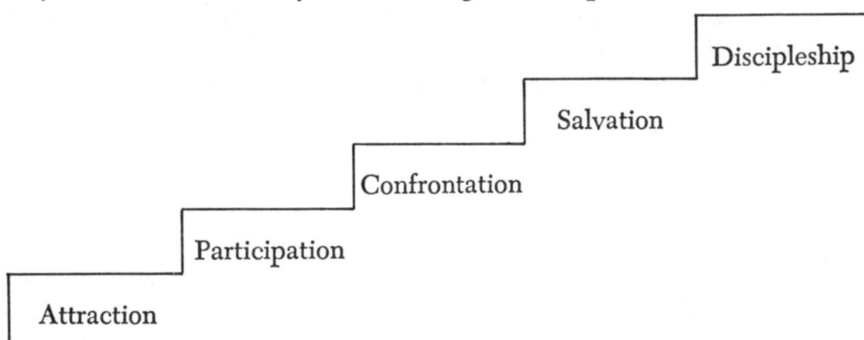

VARIETY IN PROGRAM

The attention span of the average child is short. Though it usually increases with age, young children have difficulty concentrating on one thing for more than a few minutes. An effective use of well-chosen songs will not only add variety but will greatly reinforce the subject matter being taught.

PERSONAL INVOLVEMENT

Participation leads to a more direct confrontation with the message. Statistically, one is assured of learning far more through involvement than by mere listening. Since music serves as a means of personal involvement in worship and self-expression, it increases the potential of grasping the truth and being changed by it. Involvement also makes one feel more a part of a group.

Music in the Church Program

Music can be integrated into each of the church's agencies and activities for children. Ways in which music can be used in each agency are indicated below.

SUNDAY SCHOOL

This organization is the main Bible teaching ministry of the church and has great potential for outreach. Ideally, each department of the Sunday school will devote some time each week to music activities. Someone must be responsible for planning, conducting, and accompanying the music, though he may enlist others to share this responsibility. Regular workers in the department, members of the church choir, or other talented youth or adults can be enlisted to fulfill this need.

Many smaller churches may find it difficult to maintain a consistent music program in all departments. The groups may be small, or the churches may lack capable musicians or suitable facilities. Sometimes these problems can be solved by combining two or more departments for a brief period, or by scheduling music so that departments can share the services of musicians at different times. If necessary, music activities can be conducted in alternate sessions, or even once a month, with an extended time for music.

The primary purpose of the Sunday school is to teach the Word of God and to help each child come to know Christ as Saviour and develop a growing relationship with Jesus Christ. A carefully planned program of music, under enthusiastic and competent leadership, can contribute greatly to the fulfillment of this purpose.

CHILDREN'S CHURCHES

The purposes of children's churches are to train children in worship, to provide opportunity for worship experience on the level of the children, and to prepare them to enter the regular church services later on. Music in children's churches should include both standard hymnody and contemporary expressions of praise and adoration. Primary and junior children should also learn to sing the Doxology and the Gloria Patri, plus any other traditional parts of the service, and should be taught the true function of each of these and other aspects of public worship.*

Another distinctive feature of children's churches is the opportunity children are given to participate in leadership roles, such as reading the Scriptures, leading in prayer, and ushering. They should also be taught to lead the singing, and others can render special musical numbers or perhaps sing in a choir or small ensemble. Children who are studying musical instruments should be given opportunity to play in children's churches, perhaps for the prelude or offertory.

Active involvement ought to be encouraged, even if abilities have not been developed fully or the choice of material is not along the usual lines of acceptable church music. This first step may ultimately lead to a lifetime dedication of a child's talents to the Lord.

CHILDREN'S CHOIRS

The choir activities of any church should be structured to meet the needs of children. Some larger churches are able to maintain successfully a choir for every age group including younger children. Because of size, lack of leadership, or overscheduling of other activities, other churches

*For more on children's churches and worship, see chap. 19, "Teaching Children to Worship and Pray."

would find this impractical. Perhaps the most commonly used plans consist of either two or three choirs (in addition to the adult choir).

Two choirs.
Junior—grades 3 through 5
Youth—grades 6 through 8

Three choirs.
Primary—grades 2 and 3 (possibly grade 1 also)
Junior—grades 4 through 6
Youth—grades 7 and 8 (occasionally grade 9 also)

A more expanded system gives opportunity for adjusting the activities to meet varied interests and learning abilities of children. However, it would be better to use two choirs, or even begin with only one choir (grades 4 through 8 is a suggested starter), if there are not enough children available to make the experience a satisfactory one. It is generally agreed that a larger group will result in a better choral sound, especially with very young voices.

Rehearsal times should be planned around local school schedules, scouting, athletics, and other community activities. Also they need to be coordinated with church activities to avoid transportation problems and conflicts involving the same age groups. If several children's activities are scheduled, have them on the same day or evening, if possible. Many churches find it best to have the primary and junior choirs practice on Saturday mornings. In some churches, the junior choir practices during a portion of the children's church hour or on Sunday evenings before the church service.

Under proper leadership, children's choirs can become effective singing groups that can perform in church services and in special musical programs. Another significant contribution is the effect on the lives of those who participate. The following are the basic functions of the ministry of children's choirs with particular values to the children themselves.

To evangelize. Choirs attract unchurched children who are interested in music. This participation can reach not only the children but also entire unchurched families.

To teach worship. Because of their involvement in the services of the church, children learn to conduct themselves properly in worship, take part in singing, praying, sitting, and standing reverently. In addition, they can realize the value of a true worship experience.

To develop spiritual growth. A carefully chosen choir repertoire includes hymns and anthems based on truths from the Word of God. The constant repetition in rehearsal and the encouragement of the leader to interpret the meaning of the texts open up new areas of understanding and knowledge, whereby children may grow.

To give opportunity for Christian service. Through participation in the church services, children learn to discover the way God uses people to minister His Word to others. They soon realize that they are ministers of the gospel when they sing. Often this helps them develop a lifelong positive attitude toward Christian service.

Music in Other Activities

Unlimited possibilities exist for use of children's musical interests and abilities outside the regular services and department activities. Leaders must seek ways of discovering interests and then provide ways in which they can be stimulated and encouraged. This can be done by having talent programs and musical concerts in which children are encouraged to perform, or by awarding scholarships or financial assistance for music camps or schools. Attendance at a local children's symphony concert or a choir program by some visiting children's group (such as the Vienna Boys' Choir or the Korean Orphans' Choir) may be helpful. These activities can generate new interests in musical activities and stimulate the desire to develop talents God has given.

Choosing Music for Children

Hymns for children have not always been appropriate theologically or pedagogically. One of the first published books of children's songs in the United States was *Divine and Moral Songs,* published by Isaac Watts in 1720. While it included some good hymns, it also included many which were moralistic in nature, bad actions a child must avoid if he wishes to please God. Later writers in the eighteenth and nineteenth centuries did not greatly improve the quality of content. Some tended to "talk down" to the children, referring to them as "little lambs." Still others "sugar-coated" the gospel message until it was fairly obscure. Unfortunately the problem still exists today.

In evaluating the words of a song for children, the following questions may be asked:

1. Are the words consistent with the Scriptures?
2. Do the words emphasize important truths?
3. Are the words interesting and clear?
4. Are they on the level of the age group?
5. Do they encourage a spirit of reverence?

Criteria for evaluating the melody of children's hymns and songs may include the following:

1. The younger the age group, the shorter the phrases should be.
2. The pitch should range in the octave above middle C, preferably from about D to D.
3. The rhythm should have a moderate tempo.
4. The melody and harmony should have variety with distinctives that make the song easier to learn and remember.
5. The music should bring out the best interpretation of the text.

Criteria for Selecting Music

FOR TWOS AND THREES

1. *Rhythm.* This should not be jerky or "catchy" (characterized by dotted notes), but instead, a series of one type of note with little change in rhythm (as in "America"). Choose songs in 2/4 or 4/4 time, because this is easiest to gear to the natural pulsation of their bodies and activities (walking, marching, clapping hands, etc.).

2. *Melody.* This should be simple, pretty, easy to listen to, smooth (no wide leaps), and repetitious.

3. *Harmony.* This should include only basic chords (no discord or close harmony), smooth chord progressions characterized by very few moves of the parts from chord to chord. Should be in major mood (not minor).

4. *Volume.* This should be characterized by one general level, in contrast to use of crescendos or any other startling changes.

5. *Tempo.* This should be a medium pace, but not so slow that they cannot sustain notes if singing or lose interest if listening, nor so fast that they are unable to follow either singing or listening. It should also fit in with the tempo of their activity.

6. *Tone Quality.* This should be pleasant and free from harshness, with no wide vibrato, nor such a lack of vibrato that the tone seems thin or sounds almost flat.

7. *Words.* The songs should contain words that will communicate in the realm of their experience. These words should be easy to pronounce, built on vowels, simple, and repetitious.

FOR FOURS AND FIVES

1. *Rhythm.* The teacher may begin to use songs with slightly syncopated rhythm, if it is such that they are able to synchronize their developing rhythmic sensitivity with it.

2. *Melody.* The same rule as for twos and threes applies here.

3. *Harmony.* The teacher may begin to employ music that contains a greater variety of types of chords but still in the major mood.

4. *Volume.* The teacher may begin to use dynamics if they are smooth and used meaningfully for emphasis.

5. *Tempo.* The teacher may begin to brighten the tempo (make it more lively) to fit increased activity, but he should vary it from song to song.
6. *Tone quality.* The same rule for twos and threes applies here.
7. *Words.* The teacher may begin to use songs with new words if they are in a context of known words which will bring out the meaning of the new word.
8. *Mediums.* Songs should still be sung in unison. Let the children listen to choral music, if it is simple, well done, and of high quality (hymns, but not gospel songs or choruses). Begin a rhythm band. Use recorded music related to activities. The children may want to dramatize the songs.
9. *Style.* It is best to use songs with short, repetitious phrases. Keep songs in their range. Associate music with worship by attitudes, using simple but high-quality music (not necessarily choral) to do this. The children may enjoy a special organ concert, or listen to records and the church choir.

FOR PRIMARIES

1. *Rhythm.* The teacher can introduce songs of 3/4 and 6/8 time, and may employ more variety in rhythm.
2. *Melody.* This can have wider leaps if intervals are thirds or fourths.
3. *Harmony.* The same rule for fours and fives applies here.
4. *Volume.* The teacher may emphasize dynamics to increase expression. He may also use more shading of overall level.
5. *Tempo.* The teacher may vary it more from song to song, but still the tempo should not be extreme.
6. *Tone quality.* The teacher may introduce the children to new sounds through instrumental music.
7. *Mediums.* The teacher may introduce two-part harmony in singing. Have them listen to junior choir and instrumental music. Acquaint primaries with names and sounds of instruments.
8. *Style.* The teacher may begin to expand to new areas and types of musical expression. He should continue to associate worship with fine music.

FOR JUNIORS

1. *Rhythm.* Juniors can increase their accuracy of reproduction of syncopation. Use stirring rhythmic patterns, such as 2/4 or 4/4 march time, strongly accented on first beat and third beat of the measure.
2. *Melody.* The teacher may use melodies that stir and awaken new religious experiences, even if they are difficult to reproduce.

3. *Harmony.* The teacher may introduce minor mood, if song meets other standards (such as "The God of Abraham Praise").

4. *Volume.* The teacher may make full use of dynamics for expression.

5. *Tempo.* The teacher may use wide variety in tempo.

6. *Tone quality.* The teacher should strive for good quality and a blend between voices. He should encourage expression, even if quality is not good.

7. *Mediums.* The teacher may organize musical groups, such as a junior choir or orchestra. The children may enjoy listening to sacred masterpieces.

8. *Style.* The children can expand to four-part harmonies in singing. *Variety* should be a byword. Reach out to new areas, while improving quality.

In our day, more variety in styles of church music is evident than perhaps ever before. Our wonderful heritage of hymnody and our more recent background of gospel songs of personal testimony are now greatly enhanced by the new type of folk songs, with which many children can immediately identify.

The following are a few examples of songs and hymns suitable for children of various age groups. These are included in one or more of the songbooks listed at the end of this chapter.

TODDLERS (12-24 months)

"Dear Little Baby Jesus"
"Flowers"
"God Made Fish"
"God Made Sheep to Baa"
"Moon and Stars"
"Snow Is Falling"

TWOS AND THREES

"I Clap, Clap, Clap My Hands"
"I Open God's Book"
"Jesus Is Wonderful"
"Jesus Loves Me"
"My Best Friend"
"Thank You, God"

FOURS AND FIVES

"All the Children Praise Him"
"Be Ye Kind"
"He Cares for Me"

"I Love Jesus"
"Jesus Loves the Little Children"
"Praise Him, Praise Him"

PRIMARIES

"The Bible Is the Best Book"
"A Child of the King"
"Clap Your Hands"
"Every Day Jesus Loves Me"
"Go Tell He Is Risen"
"Saviour, Like a Shepherd Lead Us"

JUNIORS

"Dare to Be a Daniel"
"Fairest Lord Jesus"
"Great Is Thy Faithfulness"
"Heaven Came Down and Glory Filled My Soul"
"In My Heart There Rings a Melody"
"Onward, Christian Soldiers"
"This Is My Father's World"

Developing a Hymn Curriculum

Clarence H. Benson has suggested, "A graded course in sacred song may be covered just as effectively as a graded curriculum of the Bible."[3] It is important that a carefully planned curriculum of hymns and songs be outlined for each children's department. This kind of planning not only assures a better correlation of songs with study material, but also helps prevent an overbalance of any one style of music which may be favored by either the leaders or the children. Besides standard songs from the hymnal, a new song should be used occasionally. They must be chosen according to meaning of the words and the appropriateness of the music.

After the hymns have been chosen, there are at least two ways in which they can be implemented. One of the most popular ways is through a "hymn-of-the-month" program, in which one new hymn is learned every month. The hymn is taught each week during the month in as many different ways as possible (sung, played, discussed, and memorized). This plan assures the learning of ten to twelve new hymns every year. It can either be carried on departmentally, with each age group learning a different set of hymns, or on a churchwide basis, with all departments learning the same hymns. Another way is to schedule a monthly music class devoted to learning new hymns. If possible, this time should be separate from the Sunday school or church services, and may be part of a social hour or other time during the week.

Ways of Teaching Music to Children

Specific approaches in teaching music to different age groups should be considered in the use of music with children. These are general guidelines, and it must be emphasized that specific levels vary considerably within each age group.

TWOS THROUGH FIVES

With children ages two through five, it is not necessary to have a piano for accompaniment of songs. If a piano is used, it should be played softly in an easy, flowing manner rather than with heavy, block chords. The primary purpose in piano playing for young children is to create moods and atmosphere. A record player accomplishes the same purpose and takes far less space.

The tempo should never be fast, the phrases should be short, and the range should be between E and C above middle C.

Before teaching a new song, the teacher should first learn the song himself. He should place it in a setting and sing it several times before the children sing with him. Also the melody and tempo should be clear. The children should not be encouraged to sing loud or forced tones which may be damaging to their undeveloped voices.

Using illustrated slides, pictures, or flannelgraph figures can help children understand the message of the songs. Since younger children usually have very short interest spans, it is better to sing a few songs frequently than to try to teach too many songs at once.

Bernice T. Cory gives several suggestions for teaching a new song to two- and three-year olds:

> The "play sing" method, in which you sing a song while the children watch your lips and try to say the words silently, helps older Nursery children to learn a song. Letting them supply a simple phrase while you sing most of a song is another effective method to teach new songs. Don't sing too fast. It takes time for a child to say the words, let alone to associate the words with a melody. Be sure to pitch the songs within his range, not too high or too low.
>
> Finger plays, like action songs, invite the children to imitate, and further the teaching process to the extent that the children participate.[4]

Music with four- and five-year-olds should be short and simple, not loud, jazzy tunes that cause confusion. With fours and fives, music can "tell" the children when to put away materials, when to tiptoe to their places, or when to bring an offering. A record player or autoharp is as effective as a piano.

A rhythm band, using a few simple instruments, is a good means of musical expression for fours and fives.

Songs for young children should not include words with symbolism such as "Climb, Climb up Sunshine Mountain" or "This Little Light of Mine."

PRIMARIES

Primary children learn very quickly but also forget easily; therefore, it is important to repeat the same song several weeks in a row until it is remembered. Song phrases should be short and the pitch ranges moderate, but the tempo should be faster than with younger children. The songs should be more rhythmic and bright. Hymns and songs with symbolism, such as "O For a Thousand Tongues," are difficult for primaries to sing with meaning. Published "song charts" are helpful visual aids in teaching songs to primaries.

JUNIORS

Juniors have developed their skills in reading and their ability to memorize. It is important to capitalize on this ability to challenge them to memorize song texts as well as scripture verses and passages. Since juniors thrive on competition, contests and awards may be used. One procedure for teaching songs is to write the verses on a chalkboard, and as the children sing them aloud, erase several of the words, perhaps the verbs first, then the nouns, and other parts of speech, until the board is empty. To help children understand the meaning of songs, ask them to rephrase the verses in their own nonpoetic way, or ask them to explain in their own words what the text says. This will not only help them increase their understanding, but will also help them discern between good and bad texts and ultimately will influence their musical tastes and listening habits outside the church.

At the junior level, pitch ranges and lengths of phrases can be more challenging. Styles of music can vary greatly, and should include wholesome entertainment and hymns with great depth and dignity. It is important for the music session to be exciting and enjoyable without cheapening the quality of the literature used or neglecting the worthy hymns.

Songs for juniors should emphasize salvation, service, prayer commitment, stewardship, and missions.

To help juniors learn to choose music on their own, teachers can explain the topical index in the hymnal and ask them to choose songs based on "God's love," "faith" or other subjects. Juniors also need to be encouraged to write their own songs, or at least attempt to express their own thoughts poetically. Self-expression, rather than academic perfection, is the goal.

The influence of popular music is greatly felt by all children, especially as they grow older and come closer to the teen years. It is recommended that leaders of these children become aware of the style and messages of the songs they are listening to. While many of these songs may undermine morals and values, others are quite acceptable. A knowledge of this background could lead to some very important and meaningful discussions with juniors. Some of the better songs could be analyzed in light of the Scriptures, discussing both acceptable and conflicting philosophies found in them. The students may gain a new appreciation for the teacher's interest and concern with their generation.

On the other hand, it is erroneous to assume that the only kind of music a child is attracted to is what is on the radio's top ten list. Other aspects of his musical interests, such as his participation in school band, choir, or private lessons, should also be recognized, and the leaders should show and express interest in these aspects as well.

Summary

Since the basic goal of Christian education is to develop the whole person, the concern of each worker with children in the church must go beyond the music that he teaches in the class, club, or rehearsal group. This concern should challenge him to seek to improve the quality of the music he permits them to carry out into the world week after week. He must do everything within his power to help children benefit spiritually from music. The effectiveness of music as a tool in Christian education is measured by the results seen in the lives of the children.

Our goal in this chapter has been to lay the groundwork upon which one may develop a functional and meaningful church music program with children. It is hoped that each leader will discover his department's strengths and needs for improvement and will build a program that will meet the needs of the children for whom he is responsible.

NOTES

1. J. M. Price; James H. Chapman; L. L. Carpenter; and W. Forbes Yarborough, *A Survey of Religious Education* (New York: Ronald, 1940), p. 31.
2. E. S. Lorenz, *Practical Church Music* (Westwood, N.J.: Revell, 1909), p. 191.
3. Clarence C. Benson, *The Sunday School in Action* (Chicago: Moody, 1948), p. 81.
4. Bernice T. Cory, *Debby and Dan Go to the Nursery Class* (Wheaton, Ill.: Scripture Press, 1954), p. 18.

FOR FURTHER READING

Baker, Susan; Key, Glennella; and Butler, Talmadge. *Guiding Fours and Fives in Musical Expression.* Nashville: Convention, 1972.

Kettring, D. D. *Steps Toward a Singing Church.* Philadelphia: Westminster, 1948.

Lovelore, Austin C., and Rice, William C. *Music and Worship in the Church.* Nashville: Abingdon, 1960.

Morsch, Vivian. *The Use of Music in Christian Education.* Philadelphia: Westminster, 1956.

Nininger, R. *Church Music Comes of Age.* New York: Fischer, 1957.

Osbeck, Kenneth W. *The Ministry of Music.* Grand Rapids: Zondervan, 1961.

Sample, Mabel Warkentin. *Leading Children's Choirs.* Nashville: Broadman, 1966.

———. *Music Making with Older Children.* Nashville: Convention, 1972.

Stillwell, Martha; Scroggins, Roy, Jr.; Williams, Ruth; and Robinson, V. Kenneth. *Music Making with Younger Children.* Nashville: Convention, 1970.

Thayer, Lynn W. *The Church Music Handbook.* Grand Rapids: Zondervan, 1971.

Thomas, Edith L. *Music in Christian Education.* Nashville: Abingdon, 1953.

———. *Singing Worship with Boys and Girls.* Nashville: Abingdon, 1953.

Whittlesey, F. L. *A Comprehensive Program of Church Music.* Philadelphia: Westminster, 1957.

Wilson, John F. *An Introduction to Church Music.* Chicago: Moody, 1965.

SELECTED COLLECTIONS OF MUSIC FOR CHILDREN AND CHILDREN'S CHOIRS

Augsburg, Minneapolis
Junior Choir Anthems for the Church Year, 4 vols.†
Young Children Sing

Broadman, Nashville, Tenn.
Easy Anthems for Children's Voices†
Hymn Anthems for the Junior Choir†
Junior Hymnal
Now Let Us Praise
Sing-A-Long Songs for Children
Sing for Joy
Songs for 4's and 5's
Songs for Primaries
Songs for the Young Child
The Carol Choir Sings†
The Junior Choir Sings†
When Children Sing

†Music books for children's choirs

Child Evangelism, Grand Rapids
Salvation Songs for Children, 4 vols.

David C. Cook, Elgin, Ill.
Preschoolers Sing

Hope, Carol Stream, Ill.
Music for Young Voices and Instruments
Youth Worship and Sing

Kregel, Grand Rapids
A Junior's Praise

Lillenas, Kansas City, Mo.
Autoharp Songs for Sunday School
Sing, Boys and Girls
Sing Together
Tell the Good News
The Younger Choir, 3 vols.†
We Sing and Play

Lutheran Church, New York
Music Resource Book
Youth Worship and Sing

Praise Book, Mound, Minn.
Little Ones Sing
Primary Children Sing

Rodeheaver, Fort Wayne, Ind.
Sing and Be Happy Songs for Children

Scripture Press, Wheaton, Ill.
Nursery Children Sing
Primaries Sing
Young Children Sing

Singspiration, Inc., Grand Rapids
Action Songs for Boys and Girls, 7 vols.
Cherub Choir, 4 vols†.
Children's Unison Choir, 3 vols.†
Happy Time Songs
Junior Choir, 6 vols.†
Simple Songs for Toddlers
Sing Along Songs
Sunshine Choir, 2 vols.†

Word, Waco, Tex.
A Singing Faith for Junior Choir†
Music for the Young Choir†

†Music books for children's choirs

Selected Sources of Recordings for Children

Broadman Films, 172 Ninth Ave., North, Nashville, Tenn. 37234
Concordia Publishing House, 3558 South Jefferson, St. Louis, Mo. 63118
Praise Book Publications, 110 West Broadway, Glendale, Calif. 91204
Radiant Productions, 908 South Tower Lane, Mt. Prospect, Ill. 60056
Scripture Press Publications, Inc., 1825 College Ave., Wheaton, Ill. 60187
Word, Inc., Box 1790, Waco, Tex. 76703
Zondervan Recordings, 1415 Lake Dr., S.E., Grand Rapids, Mich. 49506

Selected Sources of Song Charts and Visualized Songs for Children

Bible Visuals, Box 93, Landisville, Pa. 17538
Child Evangelism Fellowship, Box 1156, Grand Rapids, Mich. 49501
Christian Publications, Inc., 25 South Tenth Street, Harrisburg, Pa. 17101
Praise Book Publications, 110 West Broadway, Glendale, Calif. 91204
Scripture Press Publications, Inc., 1825 College Ave., Wheaton, Ill. 60187
Standard Publishing Company, 8121 Hamilton Ave., Cincinnati, Ohio 45231

Filmstrips

Building Graded Choirs. Broadman Films.
Using Music Creatively. Broadman Films.

19

Teaching Children to Worship and Pray

Eleanor Hance

What Is Worship?

Do the following phrases produce mental images of any children's "worship" you have observed? Chairs askew, crumpled papers, tattered songbooks, chalkboard scribblings, outdated posters, children scuffing, poking, squeaking chairs, teachers chatting, thumbing materials, pianist asking pages, shuffling music, leader calling for order, raising voice, loud singing, mumbled prayer, ho-hum announcements, noisy offering, Bible teaching, dismissal scramble.

Worship is the highest calling of Christians, and yet, judging by the atmosphere of the average worship experience, the least understood. Perhaps it is because some Christian adults have not examined the meaning of worship themselves that they do not value it more for children.

What is worship? It is easier to discuss than define. In the broad sense, it is the whole reason God redeemed us through the sacrifice of His own Son—for communion with Him. It involves a person-to-Person relationship. When we realize that God is vitally alive, present, loving and seeking us, we respond with an outpouring of love and honor for Him. We do not seek this fellowship with the Lord for what we can get out of Him in benefits to ourselves—although there are residual benefits—but we seek Him because of who He is, because we are impelled to tell Him how wonderful He is. Worship is not primarily self-getting (subjective) but self-giving (objective).

In the narrow sense, worship is the specific act of adoring contemplation of God. R. A. Torrey believed this is indeed the biblical use of the word.[1] So conceived, hearing the Scripture, singing, praying, listening to the

---

Eleanor Hance, M.A., is a curriculum writer for juniors, residing in Sarasota, Florida.

sermon, are not worship in themselves, although they may lead to worship.

In this chapter, the term *worship* is extended to the whole communion experience, with adoration the climax. God reveals Himself and thus extends an invitation. Those made holy by the redemption of Jesus Christ fulfill the joy of their personal relationship by entering into close communion. Such awesome encounter produces a response of adoration, which is surely the heart of worship and, as stated previously, often used as the limited definition of worship. But this response may be accompanied by other responses, and often is in God's Word:

> Praise to God for His goodness and love; confession of sin and unworthiness in the presence of God's holiness; thanksgiving to God for his blessings of forgiveness and new life; petition to God with prayer for ourselves and intercession for others; dedication of self, personal commitment, the offering of one's whole self to God.[2]

It is difficult to express sublime experience in words, but the following statements show something of the different aspects of this experience:

> (Worship is) man's response to the greatness and goodness of God, his personal act of communion, in which God is addressed and heard. It engages man's whole being, informing and ennobling the mind, exalting the heart, and moving the will to action.[3]

> Worship is an activity that includes, when complete, six components: an outreach of the self toward God; a felt inreach of God toward the self; resultant communion; some thought about things of God and godliness; an emotional reaction to the same; and, above all, some response in peace, purpose, or action.[4]

> To worship is man's highest prerogative, because in it God is all. It is submissive adoration of the King of kings and the Lord of lords. The other exercises of the spiritual life all tend toward worship—reading the Word, prayer, love, faith, surrender, and obedience. In an attitude of worship the spiritual life is in control over the mental and physical, as God intended it to be.[5]

Scriptural Basis of Worship

There is only one authoritative source for an understanding of worship and that is the Word of the Person whom we worship. God has given us a spiritual banquet of information which we can only sample here.

John's exalted vision underscores the highest goal of worship. "The twenty-four Elders fell down before him and worshiped him, the Eternal Living One, and cast their crowns before the throne, singing, 'O Lord, you are worthy to receive the glory and the honor and the power, for you have created all things. They were created and called into being by your act of will'" (Rev 4:10-11, TLB). The created ones worship their eternal living Creator because He alone is worthy. Indeed, the word *worship* derives from the earlier word *worthship*, giving reverence and honor to that which is worthy.

Scripture after Scripture, from the beginning of God's Word to the end, exhorts us to give the Lord the glory due His name (Ps 96:8-9) and simply because He is worthy. Not to worship is to disobey God. It follows that not to teach children to worship is also to disobey God.

Not all worship is acceptable. God lays down certain principles. Only those whose sins have been purged by the blood of Christ may be bold to enter the presence of the holiest (Heb 9:7, 14; 10:19). In Exodus 34:14, God commands that our worship be singlehearted, because God claims absolute loyalty and exclusive devotion. And in John 4:23-24, Jesus explains to the Samaritan woman that although the place of worship is not important—nor the manner—the quality of worship is. It must be "in spirit"—not in man's own strength and to his credit, but Spirit-inspired with no confidence in the flesh. It must also be "in truth"—real and sincere, without pretense of form or mere profession.

When our worship is pleasing to the Lord, something happens. In Exodus 34:5-8, we find God revealing who He is to Moses on Mt. Sinai. Moses worships. When Moses finally comes down from the mountain with the tablets of the Ten Commandments, his face glows from being in the presence of God (v. 35). Although God's Shekinah glory does not manifest itself in the physical body of the worshiper, something of God's glory does shine through in the worshiper's radiant spiritual life.

Worship and the Spiritual Growth of Children

Although worship experience is an objective end in itself (glorification of God), it has a subjective result (change in the worshiper). We cannot have true communion with the high and holy One, the Lord of lords, without some personal reaction. The change starts inwardly and manifests itself outwardly. Change in the direction of growth toward Christian maturity is the central concern of Christian education. Paul says, "We all, with open face beholding as in a glass the glory of the Lord, are changed into the same image from glory to glory, even as by the Spirit of the Lord" (2 Co 3:18). So, although spiritual changes are not the purpose of worship, they can be expected as results of worship in the lives of children as well as adults.

Worship produces awareness of personal need. When we are confronted with God's perfection, then our own weaknesses, failures, omissions, and sins become more evident. In contrition, we submit our needs, enjoy His loving forgiveness, and receive His assurance of help. Both

Isaiah 6:5 and Job 42:5-6 describe the impact of personal encounter with the Lord. A child can sense his own need if he is given opportunity to have personal fellowship with the Lord through worship.

Worship strengthens faith. It would be impossible to have contact with the real, living God without believing more firmly who He is and what He is like. (Witness again the experience of Moses in Exodus 34.) Children have simple faith and can express that faith through worship.

Worship results in commitment. Worship is indeed adoration of God, but adoration is expressed through more than the lips: it involves the whole being. Such adoration would be hollow mockery without total commitment of self. Thus, a worshiper's intellect, emotions, and actions all reflect this identification of his own will with the Lord's. Romans 12:1 instructs the believer to give himself in total commitment. The concept of commitment may be very simply presented to a child by saying, "Jesus wants me to love Him more than anyone or anything else and to tell Him that I do."

Worship brings personal fulfillment. Since the creature was created for relationship with His creator, as so well expressed in Revelation 4:11, there is inner satisfaction in communion experience. Fulfillment of that for which we were created results in the only true inner peace and joy we experience. The child can be led to worship and to experience this peace and joy by singing, listening to and reading God's Word, and by talking to God.

Worship provides power. Isaiah 40:29-31 attests to the spiritual power which results from waiting on the Lord. We can soar in our Christian life with wings like eagles. Even children get tired and discouraged with their spiritual failures, but worship impels and encourages the new life of Christ through the power of the Holy Spirit.

Contribution of Worship to the Total Program

The total Christian education program is all the learning activities under guidance of mature Christians which maximize Christian growth. Those activities have been variously classified, but traditionally they include instruction, worship, fellowship, and service. Sometimes these are all understood to include the element of evangelism; sometimes evangelism is listed separately to heighten its importance.

Instruction in the Word is usually limited to formal teaching-learning activities. By instruction, we communicate God's standard of perfection through the precept and example of His Word, and we indoctrinate, convince, convict, and guide. *Fellowship* includes all informal activities which lend themselves to interaction with others. Fellowship is the practical laboratory of example and relationship through which Christians gain insight, shape attitudes, test actions. *Expression-service* opportunities are outlets for fulfilling God's command to love one another. They serve as an athletic field for the exercise which strengthens, and provide the God-given reward of joy.

Worship fits in most appropriately after instruction. The Godward relationship comes before the manward relationship and provides the impetus of love and concern demonstrated in practical living. To adore God is to submit wholly to His will. To submit to His will is to carry it out—inwardly and outwardly. As its contribution to Christian growth, worship provides incentive for spiritual change and energizes for that change. "With eyes wide open to the mercies of God, I beg you, my brothers, as an act of intelligent worship, to give him your bodies, as a living sacrifice, consecrated to him and acceptable by him" (Ro 12:1, Phillips). Notice that the practical admonitions set forth in the rest of Romans 12 flow from this submission to the Lord which is designated an act of worship.

Types of Worship for Children

Worship experiences are often classified by contrasting private and public worship, formal and informal, planned and spontaneous. For children, each of these must be considered by more than definition. The factor of maturity level figures to a large degree.

Chapters 4-8 of this book deal with developmental characteristics of children with their many implications for worship. Vieth[6] and McGavran[7] have much helpful material on worship needs of children of various ages.

Worship for twos and threes is best characterized as spontaneous. One of the mistakes of well-meaning adults is to plan worship for younger children patterned after that of older children. But twos and threes have attention spans of only a couple of minutes for a listening activity. Because they are limited in vocabulary and concept, they respond better to experience than to verbal content. Their activity is incessant, directed by the inner urge to move, explore, manipulate, question. And they are better oriented to individual or parallel activity than cooperative activity. It is clear, then, that group worship with a set program may not be fruitful. This does not mean that nursery worship is not planned at all. It is planned to the degree that the leader provides materials and experiences which may lead to moments of informal worship—a conch shell to help the youngster who shares its wonder say thank You to God; recorded songs about the Lord's love for those who care to listen a moment and praise God for His Son; animal crackers to munch and give occasion to express happiness for God's care. But the worship is spontaneous, for who can predict which child will be ready and when?

Worship for fours and fives might be characterized as informal. More able now to engage in cooperative activity, fours and fives can experience simple group worship of short duration. But although much planning goes into the worship, and it may have form, it is still more informal than formal. The leader must be flexible, adept at guiding conversation and sensitive to immediate needs—wonder, perplexity, decision, joy, achievement—turning them into worship experience. The worship attitudes and actions of adults—so easily imitated—and the feeling tone of the group—so easily caught—are especially important. One brief illustration of a worship moment for preschoolers may serve us here:

> "But no one cares," sobbed five-year-old Jane, "and Mittens is gone." "I do," responded Joey. "And I do," said Mary. "And God does, too," added David. There was a hush in the kindergarten room. "Dear God, we are sorry about Mittens. Help grownups to drive more carefully so that we and our pets can cross streets safely. Help Jane to feel better."[8]

Primary and junior worship moves from informal to formal worship. There is more separation now between worship experience and learning experience. Planned group worship increases as pupils become more capable of attending, participating, and deriving meaning from form. But let us never forget, "Form may express experience and it may induce and intensify experience, but form alone cannot be depended on."[9] Primary worship must be vital to primaries, and junior worship to juniors. The material must be graded to their comprehension; the content related to their experiences; the timing paced to their attentiveness. Leaders must be especially aware of the characteristics, capabilities, and interests of the children. For example, juniors, for all their professed scorn of emotion and clamor for action, are capable of worshiping in considerable depth. Their growing insights, increased vocabulary, favorable response to beauty, order, and a little symbolism make for more fruitful worship in a more formal setting and structure. Nor should we overlook the abilities of elementary school children in planning and leading their own worship under capable adults. The more they are involved actively, the more valuable the worship experience becomes.

Time for Children's Worship

When can children best worship? An aware leader or teacher is prepared to use any time of special "God-consciousness" to guide children in approaching God. Since spiritual insight is not likely to occur if children are bored, restless, overexcited, or tired, we do not expect to induce worship during or after periods of dulling inactivity or overstimulating activity. But when learning experiences are structured to lead pupils into amazing new discoveries about the Lord, it is natural for them to respond by expressing wonder, awe, and joy. We encourage children to worship at any moment they are ready for it.

Should a part of the Sunday school period be set aside for planned graded worship? If children are not worshiping on their own level anywhere else, by all means. If they are worshiping in graded children's churches, then use a larger portion of the Sunday school period for Bible instruction. For the sake of economy in Christian education, avoid duplication of worship experience as well as omission.

If a planned worship program is included in the Sunday school period, should it occur at the beginning of the hour or the end? Those who advocate the latter, do so on the grounds that Bible instruction prepares the heart for worship. Response to God grows out of His revelation and is its consummation. Lois LeBar's suggestions along this line are particularly helpful.[10] Those who would put worship first, do so on practical grounds. Pupils are more alert and attentive at the beginning of the period. They are physically, mentally, and emotionally prepared to enter into a large group program. When the worship service is properly structured to reveal God, they readily respond in worship. Either way, the theme of worship should be closely tied in with the lesson to provide wholeness of experience. Children are easily confused by too many truths in a short span.

Many churches provide time for correlated worship and expression by extending the Sunday school hour or establishing separate church times, departmentally graded, concurrent with adult worship.* Larry Richards strongly favors departmentally graded children's churches, warning that grouping children ages four to eleven into a single worship group produces the same problems as placing them in adult services—too wide a diversity of attention spans, abilities, and comprehension.[11] He suggests that the same grouping used for Sunday school provide the basis for children's church divisions.

A word is in order about children in adult worship services. There are those who contend that children absorb the worship atmosphere from the beauty of adult worship, even though they do not understand the worship language and materials. The quiet atmosphere and reverence of adults produce in children a sense of awe and wonder which is beneficial. It is also suggested that they learn by imitation and thus become proficient in worship skills. But we need to balance this optimistic view by remembering that restless, bored children may become immune to the beauty and may actually be learning habits of inattention—the very thing we deplore. Would it not be wiser to provide each age with its own meaningful train-

*For a discussion on children's church, see chap. 21.

ing and experience in worship? Periodically, children may join in adult worship in the sanctuary, but they should be prepared for the experience and then discuss it afterward in order to heighten understanding and appreciation.

Planning a Worship Service

In preparing a worship service, we determine the needs of the pupils, define the aim, select the content and materials, decide on the form they will take, and arrange them in sequence to be used.

PRINCIPLES FOR BUILDING THE SERVICE

There are a number of fundamental rules for structuring meaningful worship experience. These three capsule the major considerations.

The first is the principle of centrality. A service should center on only one truth or theme. All elements in the service then support this central theme. If there is no unity in the service, thought and feeling are fragmented and dispersed, rather than culminating in worship.

The second is the principle of creativity. This is the opposite of anything stereotyped—fixed or routine. Creativity is meaningful, fresh, stimulating. Worship which is creative has three characteristics: (1) It grows out of the needs, interests, and abilities of the group and thus has personal meaning; (2) it is flexible, moving forward on genuine awareness of God's reality and presence; but when these are lacking, it quickly gives place to other spiritual activity; it is not forced; (3) it is varied, recognizing that monotony destroys sensitivity and attention. This does not mean that to be creative each service must have a different format and brand new material. On the contrary, structure must be consistent enough to be comfortable, and the material must be familiar enough to use with ease. There should be just enough newness and variety to promote awareness.

The third is the principle of climax. Worship leads from revelation—insight into our great God—to response of adoration and accompanying praise, confession, thanksgiving, petition, intercession, or dedication. This climax must always be characterized by adoration, but usually is affirmed in some expression of personal commitment.

FORM FOR GROUP WORSHIP

To consummate worship in adoration, submission, and commitment, we must provide a crescendo of experience. The basic structure usually consists of four main divisions.

1. *Preparation.* This may include a quiet prelude to prepare hearts by

turning thoughts to the Lord, an opening song which emphasizes the theme, a call to worship to remind us of the need and privilege of worship, and an opening prayer for readiness to worship.

2. *Presentation.* This is the body of the service and may include a variety of content: Scripture, songs, poetry, picture appreciation, devotional talk, or other inspirational presentation.
3. *Response.* This is the climax or consummation to which the other two divisions lead, and therefore is of utmost importance. Unfortunately, many worship services actually skip the very purpose for which they were created. Children may express this heart of worship in song, prayer, affirmations of submission or dedication or aspiration, poetry, gifts to the Lord, or silent adoration.
4. *Closing.* Usually this is a benediction in song, prayer, or poem which invokes the Lord's blessing. It can be any response which signals the end of worship and provides a satisfying conclusion.

ELEMENTS OF WORSHIP

Scripture. God's Word provides profound, beautiful, and authoritative utterances not found elsewhere. Through His Word, God reveals Himself to man and man responds to God in expressions of faith, wonder, love, adoration, praise, repentance, thanksgiving, petition, and commitment. To serve children's worship, both scriptural revelation and response must be chosen and used wisely. The passage should be appropriate to the purpose of the worship and the age group, understandable, and generally just familiar enough for comfort. It can then be used in a variety of ways. Since newness heightens awareness, and awareness of God is a prerequisite for worship, we need to be open to new ways to use the Word of God. LeBar gives a helpful list of sixteen of these.[12] But creative use of Scripture must not preclude ease of use if worship is to be achieved.

McGavran suggests two common misuses of Scripture: (1) group reading of selections responsively when it breaks up the meaning and focuses too much on when to stop and start, and (2) individual reading of difficult passages aloud when it causes embarrassment over mistakes and stumbling, which hinders worship.[13]

Music. Music sets the tone for worship, communicates God's Word, and in particular, provides a special avenue for worship response. The beauty of melody and words permits expression of feeling not always possible otherwise. Some important criteria for worship songs are: (1) do the words have valid spiritual content as well as beauty, and do they communicate this well? (2) do children understand what they are singing so they can truly worship the Lord? (3) do the words and music fit together to achieve the same message, emphasizing important thoughts?

(4) is the music within the children's range, easy to sing, and of good quality?

Offering. It is the attitude of heart in the act of giving which makes this such a fine means of expressing worship. Too often, leaders emphasize collecting from children rather than children joyously giving to the Lord whatever they have, whether tangible possessions or intangible abilities and will. We need to teach children that the offering is an act of commitment (Macedonian Christians first gave themselves to the Lord, 2 Co 8:5) as well as thanksgiving. The offering will be heightened as a worship experience if it (1) proceeds in a spirit of worship; (2) is tied in to the purpose of the service; (3) is personal, in that the child gives of his own, not someone else's possessions; (4) is sacrificial, in that the child gives what is valuable to him; and (5) is specific, in that the child knows that his offering meets a definite need.

Prayer. Prayer is an absolutely essential part of worship. It may be voiced by the leader in words and ideas of children; it may be the spontaneous and creative expression of children themselves; it may be in the words of Scripture, song, or poem; it may be silent, guided only by music or the leader's comment. Whatever the form, it must be meaningful, vital, direct, and brief.

Devotional features. It is hard to classify the many ways we proclaim God's message to children—roughly equating to the sermon in adult worship. But whether we use stories or materials which are visualized, dramatized, or projected, we must always go beyond instruction. The proclamation must not only clarify God's revelation, but have an inspirational, uplifting quality which touches the heart as well as the mind and stirs up worship response. This is one of the reasons the story form is particularly useful in worship: it allows for an emotional element.

STEPS IN PLANNING WORSHIP

In developing a worship program, the first step is to discover the particular spiritual needs of the children with whom you are concerned. Do they need increased assurance of the faithfulness of the Lord, or a sense of His holiness, or recognition of His power to overcome temptation? If you are planning your own services, be sure to build them to meet these needs. If you are using preplanned programs, check to see that they include the particular needs of your pupils.

Plan the themes of the programs for a whole year, if at all possible, particularly noting special days and emphases, such as missions and evangelism. Check your themes to be sure that they will meet those particular needs mentioned above. By grouping a number of related services into one unit with an "umbrella" theme, it is possible to meet a more expansive need, each service developing one facet. If possible correlate the worship themes with the lesson themes.

Detailed planning should be done for at least a month's programs at a time. This allows time to gather and prepare materials and to choose and prepare participants. Children need to practice beforehand so that they take part effortlessly, contributing to the smoothness of the service, rather than causing distraction.

Before the service itself, use the following checklist to be sure everything is ready:

_______Room orderly and arranged for worship, with proper temperature, ventilation, lighting.

_______All materials and equipment prepared and in place, such as worship center, offering plates, music, and any visuals to be used.

_______Copies of order of service to pianist and others assisting.

_______Participants ready and instructed in responsibilities.

_______Worshipers prepared in attitude and in materials to be used.

The Leader's Part in Worship

The purpose of the leader is to facilitate worship. To do this adequately, he must know the Lord personally and be in close communion with Him, enjoying a genuine deep and growing spiritual life which expresses itself in radiant Christian personality.

In his role of facilitator, a worship leader has a number of responsibilities. He needs to understand and value worship experience and know how to develop it. He prepares the service, chooses and prepares the participants, provides the setting and atmosphere, and then speaks, declaring God's Word and will to the children and often voicing the worship thoughts of the children to God, or guiding them in expressing this twofold communication. Thus for his role before the group, he must have an attractive, warm personality, easy manner, reassuring confidence, good rapport, ability to speak naturally and clearly. Vieth gives excellent additional helps for the worship leader.[14]

Aids to Effective Worship

The best laid plans and training cannot *make* children worship. We cannot command children to commune with the Lord, but we can provide a setting, materials, and form that are conducive to worship, eliminating anything which would hinder worship. We attempt to stimulate and encourage worship.

PREPARATION FOR WORSHIP

Whereas adults may need only the opening of the worship service itself to prepare them, children need more extensive preparation. Locating and understanding Scripture, finding and learning songs, choosing and preparing participants—all take time and effort. If these preparatory activities are not cared for before the worship time, they interrupt the act of worship. In addition, this period can be used to learn about worship. Vieth suggests that ten to fifteen minutes be used for training, and that the transition from preparation to experience be made by a quiet musical prelude.[15]

ORDER AND BEAUTY

Environment affects our emotions, and emotions play a large part in worship. How can we contemplate a God of beauty and order when our eyes are offended by peeling paint, dirty floors, scarred furniture, glaring lights, or clutter? Do we produce a visual for children and then ask them to ignore it? The environment for worship needs to reflect God in cleanliness, orderliness, pleasing color and tasteful accessories in good repair. Beauty is not necessarily found in the ornate or expensive, but in pleasing structure, line, form, and even simplicity. Yet, response must not be only to environment. "For response to become worship, it must be response to God, not just response to beauty, to nature, or anything beside God Himself."[16]

COMFORT

We cannot expect children to contemplate God when they are distracted by bodily discomfort or inability to see and hear. So we try to eliminate overcrowding, keep the temperature comfortable, see that the room is ventilated, use soft but adequate lighting, and make sure that chairs are the right size for the age group.

FOCUS OF ATTENTION

Did you ever try to concentrate in a group when there was nothing to fix your eyes on? You glanced left and right, up and down, and your thoughts roamed with your eyes. In worship, we would rather not fix attention solely on a leader, but our eyes must focus on something. Many leaders plan a visual which directs children's thoughts to God as the center of attention: a Bible, meaningful picture, symbol, or object of God's handiwork. Whatever is displayed should be large enough to make an impression and should be placed in a simple, harmonious, beautiful setting. Drapes of pleasing texture and color may cover the functional chalkboard and hide the common desk. Sometimes a few words in large letters on the backdrop silently guide the children's thoughts (e.g., "Worship the Lord in the beauty of holiness"). Periodically changing the center will heighten awareness.

ATMOSPHERE

Meaningful worship demands an atmosphere of reverence, quietness, orderliness, happiness, and expectancy. Physical environment aids immeasurably, but atmosphere is also produced by participants and activities. The following suggestions will help preserve and enhance the worship atmosphere: (1) encourage adults to exhibit attitudes conducive to worship, bowing hearts as well as heads; (2) have worship leaders prepared, confident, reverent, expectant, pleasant, sensitive to mood; (3) eliminate disturbances and interruptions of latecomers, secretaries, and trespassers; (4) assign activities, such as memorizing, drilling, and explaining, to times other than worship.

APPRECIATION

To appreciate something is to realize the value of it and to be thankful for it. We usually attach value to what we understand, what meets our needs, what we ourselves are personally involved in, what we feel comfortable with, and what is valued by people we esteem.

We can readily transfer these ideas to worship. Children appreciate worship when they understand the form and content of the service; when it taps their interests and is linked to their experiences; when they help prepare and participate; when they know the songs, can handle the Scripture with ease, and are confident of what comes next; and when adults they esteem worship and attach importance to it.

SOLITUDE

Children are not loners, but worship by its very nature is an individual matter and needs a feeling of "aloneness with the Lord" and a "coming apart" from ordinary preoccupations. Simplicity, quietness, beauty, reverence, and quiet music all help promote this deeply personal element in worship. Eliminating any sense of crowding helps children feel alone with God. We can even guide children to planned moments of silence for individual expression of communion with the Lord.

QUIET MUSIC

We have all experienced the power of music to guide wordlessly, to calm anxious or angry hearts, to lift thoughts from mundane matters to delights of the Lord, to turn failure to faith. Music chosen for the purposes of quieting, of producing desire for worship, of bringing to mind spiritual content, and of providing support for moments of communion with God can be one of the most valuable aids to worship.

VISUAL AIDS

Aesthetic beauty expressed in visual form is of special value in worship. The beauty of a picture not only catches attention, it draws forth positive feeling, subduing negative emotion, and opening up the heart for the entrance of God's Word. For example, a picture of a sparrow feeding in the snow helps make God's promise of loving care in Matthew 10:31 come alive. The clarity, vividness, and emotional impact which a picture brings to new spiritual truth, prompts a natural response of worship.

Criteria for Evaluating Worship

In order to improve the effectiveness of our worship services, we need to evaluate progress periodically. Some questions we can use as criteria in evaluation are these:

Was the room in readiness for worship?
Were the people responsible for the worship service on time and prepared?
Was the atmosphere conducive to the worship service?
Did the worship service begin on time?
Was the worship service appropriate for the age level?
Were the needs of the pupils considered?
Was the objective of the worship service accomplished?
Was the worship service developed and correlated with a theme in mind?
Was there quality in the selection of content?
Did the order of the service build to a climax?
Was there variety in presentation?
Were the elements of worship effectively used (analyze each separately)?
Were transitions smooth from one part of the service to the other?
Did each person participating do his part satisfactorily?
Was there a spirit of expectancy?
Did each individual take an active part in the worship service?

Teaching Children to Pray

Prayer is an experience not only akin to worship, but involved in the very heart of worship. What a privilege—God planned, even yearns, for the humans He created to converse with Him! Meditate on such a marvel, and then dare to neglect teaching children to fulfill the desire of God's heart—and theirs.

It is often said of children's learning that as much occurs when "caught" unconsciously, or when "sought" through sense of need, as occurs when "taught" directly. And this is certainly true of prayer. Fortunate is the child who from his earliest years hears sincere prayer in understandable words about meaningful concerns. Prayer is "caught."

Prayer is also "sought," for children need to want to pray before they will express themselves to God. We encourage readiness by talking earnestly about the wonder of prayer, the way to pray, situations which need prayer, and answers to prayer. Appropriate pictures and other visuals can heighten the desire to pray. Pictures of everyday things for which to be thankful, or pictures of people praying, especially help young children. Music and prayer poems can also promote heart attitude for prayer. For example, children may sing these words before prayer time to the hymn tune "Serenity" ("We May Not Climb the Heavenly Steeps"):

With folded hands and heads that bow
We come, dear Lord, today;
Help us to worship only Thee,
And teach us all to pray.

But prayer, especially group prayer, is also "taught" in a step-by-step process.

The simplest place to begin teaching group prayer is with "thank you" prayer. One teacher found that a prayer picture such as "The Angelus" by Jean Francois Millet stimulated conversation which easily led into individual thank You's to God. She asked what the children saw in the picture and let them enumerate items. Then she asked them to decide what was happening. They composed a story about the picture: "The church bell, called the Angelus, has rung for evening prayer. The farmer and his wife have been working hard digging up potatoes all day. They cannot get to the church to pray, so they bow right in the field and say thank you to God for the Lord Jesus Christ." Then she continued, "What else do you think these farmers are thankful for?"

The children readily responded, "Potatoes."

This provided a good opportunity to encourage each child to name just one thing he was sincerely thankful for, going around the class in order.

Then the teacher proceeded, "To whom are you thankful for these things?"

"God."

"You have told me that you are thankful, but since God is the One who has given us all good things, He would surely be pleased to have you say thank You to Him. Those who are really thankful may say so to God right now by telling Him what you have just told me."

Children who have never expressed their prayers aloud in a group will need special instruction on how to begin their prayer (by speaking God's name, "Dear God"), what to say ("Dear God, I am thankful for—"), and how to end the prayer ("In Jesus' name, Amen"). You may want to save a full explanation of the closing until you have time to develop the idea of coming to God through Jesus. It is sufficient to say that *Amen* means something like "May it be so." If several pupils are praying for the first time, name the pupil who should begin first and the order in which the rest should follow. During the prayer time, you may need to nod to or name each pupil as his turn arrives. Later, help pupils to understand that in group prayer, a person prays after the "Amen" of the person praying before him without waiting to be called on by name.

After a number of occasions for "thank you" group prayers, introduce children to the "please help me" petition prayer. You may talk about how King David prayed "Help me, O Lord my God" in Psalm 109:26. Encourage pupils to talk about situations in which they need God's help—when they are angry, sad, troubled, hurt, in need. Remind them that they have told you and each other, but God is the One who can help them. Then let each one voice his petition to God.

As the group prayer participation becomes more natural, combine "thank you" prayers and "please help me" prayers. Broaden the prayers to "please help someone else" (intercession), possibly illustrating with a prayer of Moses as in Numbers 14:19 or Jesus' prayer for His disciples in John 17. Later, instruct in "forgive me" prayer and add the element of confession. Teach pupils to include "I love You" (adoration and praise) in all their prayers.

Answering Questions About Prayer

Children need to feel comfortable and secure in participating in the group. Clearing up their questions will help. "Should we say 'Thee' and 'Thou' when we pray?" "Should we close our eyes?" "Can we pray for anything at all and get it?"

Keeping in mind that effective prayer calls for genuineness as opposed to artificiality, it would follow that verbal expression, posture, and content should be natural. Unfamiliar concepts need to be explained carefully. Children who have been exposed to "Thee" and "Thou" all their lives may use them naturally. Children who have not may begin with "You" and "Your." Posture should also reflect honor to God. Pupils should decide for themselves how they can outwardly show inward attitude. One eight-year-old concluded, "We should close our eyes to shut out the world and shut in God."

Concerning praying for what we want, it is indeed natural for the child to express "wants" to adults and thus to God. And God admonishes us that we have not because we ask not (Ja 4:2) and promises to give us the desires of our hearts (Ps 37:4). Then surely we cannot criticize a child's natural impulse to ask. What we can do is explain that God, like parents, does what is best because He loves us. For this reason, He sometimes does not give us what we want immediately. We can compare our wants to our needs and thus help discourage greed. We can expand answers to include the idea of "wait" and "no" as well as "yes." (McGavran[17] and Lebar[18] both provide fuller treatments on children's expressions of prayer.)

Two further questions often trouble teachers: Should pupils repeat memorized prayers? Should pupils who have not made a profession of faith in Christ be called on to pray? Mary LeBar has given excellent answers to both:

> A memorized prayer poem (such as those frequently used for table graces, or with older children, the Lord's Prayer) has a place—*after* spontaneous prayer has first established prayer as vital communion with God. Memorized prayers have both advantages and dangers. Four and five year olds enjoy the unifying effect of praying together. Such a prayer gives them the form, the vocabulary, and the expression which they need help in learning. A timid child gains security in thus hearing his voice aloud. The unchurched child may be helped to remember a rhymed grace or prayer at home. But it is not easy to find rhymed prayers that are simple enough for young children to understand and that also fit their needs. And once the prayer is learned, it all too quickly becomes mechanical. Unlike the spontaneous prayer, the memorized prayer is very limited in application.[19]
>
> The question as to whether to have unsaved children pray, is a touchier problem. Here the teacher's theology must enter the picture. If he feels a child is definitely not saved because he is sinning against the Light, he should not ask the child to pray—except a prayer for salvation. With young children who love Jesus and wish to please Him, most workers with children will not hesitate to have them pray. Scripture does not say much to guide us at this point.[20]

The practical reasons for this emphasis are to lay a foundation and to build positive attitudes when children are pliable and easily molded. This preparation can pave the way for the child to accept Christ as Saviour when he is ready.

Private Worship

Christian parents and teachers have the added responsibility of teaching children to worship and pray as individuals apart from the group. Such worship includes both immediate, spontaneous response to God in life's moments, and a regularly scheduled, brief period of private devotions. Private worship is one of the most neglected areas in Christian education of children. One reason may be that children need continual and close adult guidance and supervision to begin and sustain a practice which they must carry on as individuals. They are rarely sufficiently self-motivated or skilled or persevering by themselves. Nor is casual suggestion or a list of Bible references in Sunday school lesson quarterlies sufficient incentive. From inadequate guidance springs unfruitful practice which can soon lead to discouragement. It takes much effort and know-how to teach private worship. It is time that the church woke up to its responsibility and embarked on an energetic program to communicate the value of private worship, when, where, and how to carry it on, and the materials to use.

Not much research has been done on how to communicate values. However, there is some evidence that the family is the vital factor. Donald M. Joy cites recent Stanford University studies on conscience, Merton Strommen's studies of Lutheran young people's beliefs, and his own nationwide survey of Free Methodist youth activity. Findings point to strong parental identification as basic to strong conscience, Christian belief, and Christian activity.[21] We would expect then that the family which exemplifies Christian devotional practices and trains its children to set aside time for individual worship can be the most effective Christian education agency for the job.

Although the family is the crucial agency, the church must support and augment its efforts. Parents, teachers, and leaders need training in the where, when, what, and how of private worship. How adequate is the guidance provided by your church?

In several chapters, McGavran gives particularly helpful illustrations of how to stimulate individual worship.[22] Our purpose here is to summarize and suggest a few additional pointers for parents, church leaders, and teachers.

FOR PARENTS

1. Make worship a part of the family living pattern through sharing both spontaneous worship moments and scheduled family worship.
2. Set aside time for your own private devotions and help children become aware of the joy and strength they supply.
3. Help children establish a time for daily prayer from their earliest years. Bedtime is most common. It is particularly valuable for a father to take a few quiet moments with his children to talk over the day's experiences and then encourage them to talk to the Lord personally.
4. Guide the child in reading devotional literature on his own level as soon as he develops his reading skill to the point of ease and enjoyment.

A modern language Bible may encourage a systematic program of Bible reading. There are an increasing number of devotional reading materials available from Christian bookstores. One of the best-written, best-illustrated Bible storybooks is V. Gilbert Beers' ten-volume *Family Bible Library*. The questions at the end of each story guide young hearts to think reflectively about God and often lead to worship. Some Sunday school pupil's manuals are structured for daily Bible study.

5. Try to start the evening bedtime rituals soon enough to allow for warm, intimate, companionable guidance in devotions without nagging the child to hurry.

FOR CHURCH LEADERS AND TEACHERS

1. Let children in on some of your personal joys of private worship.
2. Check through opportunities to provide experience in private worship. For example, Christian camping contributes much through its Christian leadership example and coaching, age-mate influence, the setting and stimulus of God's revelation in nature, adequate time in a relaxed, extended, and consecutive live-in program. Weekday clubs, such as Pioneer Girls and Christian Service Brigade, also especially emphasize training in daily devotions.
3. Talk frequently with children about their time, place, and means of personal devotions.
4. See that the church library has a good supply of daily devotional readings for children and helps for parents in child training. Show juniors how to use concordances, hymnbooks, and other resources.
5. Include the subject of children's private devotions in parent-teacher meetings and teacher-training sessions.
6. Visit parents to talk about coaching children in private worship. Supply parents with helpful literature.

Summary

Worship then, whether private or public, individual or group, spontaneous or planned, informal or formal, is the apex of the whole Christian education program. Evangelism and instruction move toward it; fellowship and service flow from it. It is the crowning experience of a Christian, this bowing down of the heart in submission, awe, reverence, honor, and commitment. The more we as leaders become aware of and experience the reality of God in our own lives, the more we will be challenged for the sensitive task of leading children into the presence of the Lord.

NOTES

1. R. A. Torrey, *What the Bible Teaches* (Westwood, N.J.: Revell, 1898), p. 472.
2. R. Harold Terry, "A New Look at Worship," *Church School Worker* 13 (June, 1963):11.
3. Paul H. Vieth, *Worship in Christian Education* (Philadelphia: United Church, 1965), pp. 24-25.
4. Ralph D. Heim, *Leading a Church School* (Philadelphia: Fortress, 1968), p. 187.
5. Lois E. LeBar, *Children in the Bible School* (Westwood, N.J.: Revell, 1952), p. 295.
6. Vieth, chaps. 8 and 9.
7. Grace W. McGavran, *Learning How Children Worship* (St. Louis: Bethany, 1964), chap. 7.
8. Christine P. Stockley, "Do We Only 'Sit and Wait'?" *Children's Religion* 23 (Aug., 1962):6.
9. LeBar, p. 298.
10. Lois E. LeBar, *Focus on People in Church Education* (Westwood, N.J.: Revell, 1968), pp. 39-42, 175-79.
11. Lawrence O. Richards, "The Pastor and Children's Church," Christian Education Monographs, Pastors' Series, No. 2 (Glen Ellyn, Ill.: Scripture Press Foundation, 1966).
12. LeBar, *Children in the Bible School,* pp. 311-14.
13. McGavran, pp. 55-56.
14. Vieth, chap. 5.
15. Ibid., pp. 84-85.
16. McGavran, p. 11.
17. Ibid., pp. 72-74.
18. LeBar, *Children in the Bible School,* pp. 355-58.
19. Mary E. LeBar, "Teaching Children to Pray," *Link* 8(May, 1960):6.
20. Ibid., p. 7.
21. Donald M. Joy, *Meaningful Learning in the Church* (Winona Lake, Ind.: Light & Life, 1969), pp. 114-15.
22. McGavran, chaps. 5, 6, and 8.

FOR FURTHER READING

Baxter, Edna M. *Learning to Worship.* Valley Forge, Pa.: Judson, 1965.

Bolton, Barbara J. "When Children Worship." *Teach* 15(Winter, 1974):43-46, 48.

Bowman, Clarice M. *Resources for Worship.* New York: Association, 1961.

———. *Restoring Worship.* New York: Abingdon, 1951.

Brown, Jeannette. *Children's Worship in the Church School.* New York: Harper, 1939.

Cully, Iris V. *Christian Worship and Church Education.* Philadelphia: Westminster, 1967.

Fahs, Sophia L. *Worshipping Together with Questioning Minds.* Boston: Beacon, 1965.

Herzel, Catherine. *Helping Children Worship.* Philadelphia: Fortress, 1963.

LeBar, Lois E. *Children in the Bible School.* Westwood, N.J.: Revell, 1952.

———. *Focus on People in Church Education.* Westwood, N.J.: Revell, 1968.

Lee, Florence B., et al. *When Children Worship.* Philadelphia: Judson, 1962.

Martin, Mary G. *We Worship Together: A Worship Guide for Leaders of Children's Groups of Mixed Ages.* Philadelphia: Judson, 1948.

McDormand, Thomas B. *The Art of Building Worship Services.* Nashville: Broadman, 1958.
McGavran, Grace W. *Learning How Children Worship.* St. Louis: Bethany, 1964.
Paulsen, Irwin G. *The Church School and Worship.* Rev. ed. New York: Abingdon, 1960.
Powell, Marie C. *Guiding the Experience of Worship.* New York: Methodist Book, 1935.
Sullivan, Jessie D. *Children's Church Handbook.* Grand Rapids: Baker, 1970.
Towner, Vesta. *Guiding Children in Worship.* New York: Abingdon, 1946.
Vieth, Paul H. *Worship in Christian Education.* Philadelphia: United Church, 1965.
Williams, John G. *Worship and the Modern Child.* New York: Seabury, 1957.

20

Missionary, Stewardship, and Vocational Education of Children

Joyce L. Gibson

"NEXT WEEK is missionary Sunday, boys and girls. Be sure to ask your parents for extra offering," urged the primary department superintendent. "Now who can remember the names of our missionaries?"

The superintendent pointed to a battered world map with sagging name flags and curled-up photos of missionaries. The primaries wiggled impatiently with a bored "we go through this every month" look on their faces.

Later the superintendent complained to the mother of one of the primary boys. "I can't understand why the children take so little interest in bringing offering money to Sunday school. You'd think they would at least care about our missionaries!"

"What missionaries?" the mother asked blankly.

Contrast this true incident with others, like Lynn, who became delighted when her aunt gave her some money. "God answered my prayer!" she confided with a smile. "Now I have something to give Him to say thank You." Lynn's conversion just a few weeks before seemed to call for this tangible expression of love. Though her sisters quickly spent their money at the store, Lynn saved hers till Sunday, eagerly anticipating the joy of giving all so that others could be reached.

Consider also the experience of a nine-year-old boy who felt so concerned for missionary Lynn Holm in Africa that he woke up his mother at three in the morning, saying urgently, "Mother, I feel we must pray for Mr. Holm right now." Later, when the missionary was home on furlough

---

JOYCE L. GIBSON is Junior Department Editor at Scripture Press Publications, Inc., Wheaton, Illinois.

and the boy's mother checked with him, they learned that at the very time the boy felt his real concern, Mr. Holm had been faced unarmed with a charging elephant![1] Somewhere, missionary education had made a significant impact on that boy.

Giving of life and service, time and talents is woven throughout Scripture, never as a dreary treadmill duty, but as a glad, reasonable response to the one who has shown us mercy (Ro 12:1). It is well, then, to study carefully the place in Christian education of missionary and stewardship training of children.

Missionary Education

IMPORTANCE OF INCLUDING MISSIONS IN CHILDREN'S PROGRAM

Why are some churches deeply involved in missions? The members give generously, even sacrificially. A significant number of young people volunteer for service at home and overseas. How do we account for this, when many churches of the same denomination give only a token nod to missionary work? One answer is the difference in missionary education. Instead of making missions an incidental part of the education program, it forms the heartbeat of the church.

Basic to missionary education is the need to recognize that missionary outreach is not optional to the church. It is not a special treat in the form of a film or a guest speaker to be squeezed into the Sunday school hour on the fifth Sunday of a month. Missions is God's imperative. Missions is Christ Himself reaching out in the power of the Holy Spirit through His body, the church, with God's Word to the world.

Missionary education, then, is a program of learning through which children discover God's view of the world and are thereby led to respond to Him by doing their part in taking the gospel to that world, whether nearby or far away. Missionary education, to be effective, must be saturated with prayer (Mt 9:37-38), woven throughout by thoughtful planning, and sustained by the love of Christ, which compels true believers to consider themselves debtors to all mankind.

INGREDIENTS OF EFFECTIVE MISSIONS EDUCATION

Inspiration. Some would name as motives for missions the plight of the unfortunate, the strangeness of foreign cultures, or the prospective missionary's appetite for adventure. The biblical motive for missions, however, is not pity, or duty, or even desire for heavenly reward. The inspiration of missions is glad obedience prompted by the love of Christ. A lesser motive is unworthy of the one who died in our place. The church that is faithful in missionary education will teach clearly and compellingly Christ's command, "Go ye."

Information. Children should be given the facts of missions and not a vague stereotype of missionary work.

Missions, according to the New Testament pattern, grows out of a local body of believers who represent Christ and is seeking to win the lost in its community. From this body, the Holy Spirit calls some believers to represent Christ away from the local church. These witnesses-away-from-home are called missionaries. They may serve only a few miles from the home church, involved in what we call home missions; or they may be halfway around the world in what we call foreign missions. They usually work under the direction of a mission or a sending agency. Wherever they are and in whatever capacity they serve, these sent ones cooperate with the local body of believers in their new area.

Michael Griffiths, general director of the Overseas Missionary Fellowship, wrote, "Today missionaries are comrades in arms, international reinforcements to work alongside national brethren in small, struggling emerging churches. We need a truly international and interracial missionary force. The modern missionary may be an Asian, an African, or a South American just as much as a North American or a European."[2]

In informing children of missionary work today, we can no longer leave the impression that a missionary will necessarily sign up with one mission board for a lifetime of service in one country, doing one kind of work. Christians are needed who are available for specialized service for a specific period of time.

For example, the 1973 directory compiled by Short Terms Abroad, a service agency informing personnel of short-term assignments abroad and in the United States, listed some 5,600 full- or part-time job openings. Some workers give a one-year term for a specific assignment. Others stay for only a few weeks, or may stay on for two years and more.[3]

In giving children factual information about missions, church workers should avoid undue emphasis on strange customs, costumes, culture, or language. They should not expose children only to the scenic tourist attractions of the country. Neither should they picture only the rural areas, ignoring the modern cities teeming with well-educated people.

Involvement. At each level, the church will seek to involve children in appropriate learning activities and practical projects that are within the understanding of the age group. These activities will include remembering specific prayer requests, giving personal spending money for both home and foreign needs, and personal experience in reaching out to the world near at hand.

Since outreach is basic to the local church program, it will be perfectly natural to integrate a planned curriculum of missionary education in many different situations within the varied church educational agencies.

Each department should have a specifically designed program with goals, content, and methods fitted to its age group.

Illustration. Elton Trueblood defines a missionary as "anyone who serves as a consequence of being profoundly touched by the love of Christ. The validity of the conception has little to do with geography."[4]

For missionary education to do its job, the local church at home must embody the same compassion for the lost here that it expects its missionaries to have overseas.

Ralph R. Covell wrote about this desperate need:

> Many churches continue to operate on a "come-to-me" philosophy which is the very opposite of missions. We profess a great concern for people if only they will come to us and receive from our generosity. Missions by proxy is easy because we need not be involved. And where we might become involved, we have quickly tucked our robes about us and gone by on the other side as we seek a comfortable haven in the safe suburbs.
>
> In doing this, we have forsaken multitudes who need the Saviour whom we proclaim. Some are black; some are white; some are rich; some are poor. Are we as concerned about these at home as we are about those abroad? Only as we are, will there be integrity and authenticity to our work overseas. Only then will we continue to attract committed young people. Only then will we be willing to give in the increasing measure that is necessary. Only then will our missionaries have that deeply-rooted concern—rooted in the community of concern at home—to convey Christ's love adequately to the distant lost sheep.[5]

Since missions is Christ reaching out through a believer, all Christian education workers in the local church at home should be vitally concerned with missions. They should be working out in their daily lives the same quality of concern that they picture in foreign missionaries. We cannot allow our children to think of missionaries as the only Christians who live sacrificial lives, giving themselves in tireless service for the lost. Hudson Taylor, founder of the China Inland Mission (now Overseas Missionary Fellowship), wrote, "There are not two Christs—an easy-going one for easy-going Christians, and a suffering, toiling one for exceptional believers. There is only one Christ. Are you willing to abide in Him, and thus to bear much fruit?"[6] This searching question should be in the forefront of each teacher's thinking.

Findley B. Edge said this about the Christians' attitude:

> The desperate need of the world is for people who care. This is what the Gospel is all about. God cares and cares deeply. He calls us to be a people who care and care deeply. No greater opportunity for evangelism is open to us. The world can be won by a people who are willing to care

> and to care deeply—who are willing to love and to love unconditionally. To be an expression of this caring love in the general mission to which all Christians are called *all of the time.* It must be repeated here . . . we do not have the motivation to give ourselves in this type of unconditional caring unless we are so committed to God that to give a witness of Him is the deepest desire and basic purpose of our existence. This kind of caring goes back to the depth and quality of a person's experience with God.[7]

This kind of caring and willingness to become personally involved must be illustrated to our children. We will show it as we welcome newcomers, follow up absentees, or reach out into the community through weekday clubs or vacation Bible school. We will show it as we maintain discipline in a classroom and as we pay the price of opening clear channels of communication with even the most difficult pupils.

HOW TO TEACH MISSIONS

Like other aspects of Christian instruction, the content and method of missionary education should be regulated by the needs and capacities of the pupils. A total church program should be drawn up, correlating the scope of missionary education for each age group and for each agency working with that age group. A committee should review this periodically to be sure there is no overlapping or overlooking in the program. If copies of the program are distributed to all Christian education workers and parents of the children, the whole church can cooperate in making missionary education balanced and effective.

Lois LeBar wrote,

> In a worthy attempt to give missions the place it should have in Sunday School, some schools set aside their regular lessons once each month or quarter in favor of a missions emphasis. This seriously disrupts the continuity of a curriculum unit that is progressively developed. Another idea is to feature one country in each year of the school, such as Japan in first grade, Guatemala in second grade, Germany in third, etc. Each room or department then keeps its own mission museum of pictures, curios, and costumes. These collections are valuable, but this system is not adaptable to the special interests of local churches. If a church is especially interested in missionaries who have recently gone from their midst to Taiwan, Peru and France, pupils in three grades would be concentrating on these countries, but all the other grades would be studying other countries. Because mission emphasis is woven into the warp and woof of Scripture, it becomes an integral part of all Bible study. If each teacher stresses missions whenever Scripture stresses it, it will have a constant emphasis. Once or twice a year the whole church can have a special missions week

in which missionaries speak, classes make exhibits, current needs are presented, and calls to prayer, giving and enlistment are given.[8]

When should missionary education begin? In the nursery! If we lay a firm foundation in the preschool years, we will not have to tear down faulty concepts later and rebuild according to God's Word.

NURSERY

Biblical concepts. God loves everyone. God wants everyone to love Him.

Methods and materials. Two- and three-year-olds are naturally curious. They enjoy handling a new object—looking at it, feeling it, even smelling it! Take advantage of this natural curiosity when giving a missions presentation, and have several objects available that they can see and touch. Such items as eating utensils, models of homes, and articles of clothing will help nursery-age children realize that life is different for the missionaries who live "far away."

A discussion of pictures depicting foreign families eating, playing, and working, can also be used to help the children become aware that there are people in the world whose skin color and way of life is different from theirs.

Two- and three-year-olds enjoy playacting. Let them act out situations that demonstrate giving and expressing love to others, such as the following: lending toys to a friend, helping Mother with a simple task, and giving a small gift to an elderly neighbor or relative.

Other possible approaches include telling true missionary stories, visualizing stories with puppets, inviting a missionary to visit the department, and providing handwork for the children to do which emphasizes God's love in action.

FOURS AND FIVES

Biblical concepts. Sin is disobeying God. Jesus died for everyone's sin. Jesus is our Saviour. Jesus will save everyone who comes to Him.

Methods and materials. Emphasize needs nearby (home missions), being sure that we do not talk simply about physical needs and arouse only sympathy. Stress that these boys and girls have not heard about Jesus.

However, do not ignore foreign missions. Recognize the fact that four- and five-year-olds have a broadening world awareness because of television, books, magazines, and travel.

Introduce missionary families of the church who have small children. Point out, "These children are going to help their parents tell boys and girls in the land of ________ about Jesus."

Work with missionary speakers to help them present information on a level that preschoolers can understand.

What four- and five-year-olds can do. They can understand simple, concrete needs of a particular missionary and his children and pray for them; give money; share what they are learning with visitors and newcomers; listen to and act out missionary stories,* enjoy missionary visits; view slides and handle curios; view missionary pictures and picture books;† learn missionary songs that have been carefully visualized; play games of the country being studied;‡ color missionary coloring books (available in Christian bookstores); and play with missionary paper dolls and stand-up figures.§

These children can understand the need for giving money for missions if they are presented with a specific missionary project to which their money will go. In selecting a project, choose one that will be meaningful to their age, a project that fits into the overall church program, and one that reminds children of a missionary's ministry.

In one church, the children in the fours and fives department were asked over a period of several weeks to bring boxes of Jello for their missionary to take back to the field with her. (She served in Korea where Jello was not available.) On the last Sunday, the missionary visited the department to receive the supply of the product. In introducing the missionary, the superintendent asked the boys and girls what the missionary did in the country far across the ocean. It is not surprising that one bright boy answered, "Eat Jello!" How unfortunate that these youngsters had not heard anything about their missionary's work in Christian radio through which she was reaching many children with the love of Christ!

PRIMARY

Biblical concepts. Everyone has sinned. Sinners need the Saviour. Jesus died to take the punishment for everyone's sins. Jesus wants me to tell others about Him. Jesus wants me to give money and pray for missionaries and nationals.

Methods and materials. Expand missionary information as the group is ready for it. Use books, prayer reminders, letters from missionaries, pic-

*See the list of books with missionary stories for children at the end of this chapter. Also see chap. 14, "Story Playing with Children."

†For example, see Dana Eynon, *World Full of Children* (Cincinnati: Standard); *'Round the World Storybook* (Cincinnati: Standard); and Margaret C. Hayes, *Children in God's World* (Cincinnati: Standard). See also the list of picture sets at the end of this chapter.

‡See the list of books with missionary games, programs, and activities at the end of this chapter.

§See for example, *Children of God's World Paper Dolls* (Cincinnati: Standard); *World Children Stand-Up Figures* (Wheaton, Ill.: Scripture Press); and *World's Children Cutouts* (Grand Rapids: Child Evangelism Fellowship.)

tures, filmstrips; slides; murals; posters; missionary stories on flannelgraph or flash cards. Teach the children missionary songs, explaining the meaning of the words to them. Primaries enjoy playing games from foreign countries, dressing in the costumes of foreign lands, eating foods and singing songs from other nations.

What children this age can do. Primaries can assume personal responsibility for inviting friends to Sunday school and can understand that this is an important part of the church's missionary program. They can tell others about Jesus, and they can show unselfish love to their families and friends. They can give their money, and they can remember prayer requests both at church and at home. Primaries can write letters or tape-record messages to missionary children and/or national children, collect clothing or food for missionaries, take handmade gifts to shut-ins, collect and send used Christmas cards to missionaries, and do many other things. They can also make murals or tabletop scenes of missionary villages.

JUNIOR

Biblical concepts. Juniors can comprehend deeper understanding of Bible truths already taught. Children are lost not because they live in a different country and have different customs, but because they have not received Christ as Saviour. We must choose daily what is important to us—the self-centered values of society around us or the values of following Christ and expanding His work here on earth.

Methods and materials. Many of the ideas suggested for primaries can also be used with juniors. Teach juniors the plan of salvation. Encourage them to share Christ with others. Juniors enjoy relating current events to missionary work. Relate geographical knowledge gained in school to missions. Use maps, population charts, factual studies of people, and photos. Acquaint pupils with basic facts about mission fields and mission boards. Present the lives of well-known missionaries, from the past as well as the present. Encourage individual and group study about national Christians and the church overseas. Stimulate personal research and reading of missionary stories and biographies. Field trips can be profitable if juniors see firsthand how Christians are reaching out to the lost with Christ's love.

An occasional social can have the flair and flavor of a foreign country—with food, games, songs, or visit in a home or church of another nation.||

One group of junior boys consulted a file of correspondence from a mission school in India to make puppets, write a factual script, and present

||See the list of books with missionary games, programs, and activities at the end of this chapter. Decorations, place mats, party favors, and visuals on missionary themes are available from Wright Studios, 5264 Brookville Road, Indianapolis, Ind. 46219.

a puppet playlet for the whole church, making the work of the mission school come alive for children and parents. With a little encouragement, juniors can illustrate missionary passages from Scripture and missionary songs, make posters for a missionary conference, and provide tours through a curio display.

What this age can do. Juniors can express genuine concern for people they know who have not received the Saviour. They can pray with a deeper understanding regarding their personal contribution to the Lord's work in another country.

Most juniors have more spending money to give than primary children. They want practical projects for both foreign and home missions. They prefer giving money for a specific piece of equipment rather than for a general fund. They may wish to support an orphan out of their missions fund. Juniors like a slice of the action at home too, and enjoy distributing flyers for the church, going with adults to call on prospect families, and planning picnics and socials that are aimed at an evangelistic thrust for their unchurched peers.

Juniors can plan and produce missions-oriented bulletin boards, posters, and charts. They can build model villages, representing the "fields" of specific missionaries. Girls enjoy dressing dolls in national costumes. Some juniors may be interested in starting a pen-pal club, each writing regularly to a missionary child.

Today, many teens are involved in outreach through service and musical groups working in their own communities and through summer programs in which they teach Bible school in urban or rural areas or go abroad to serve on a mission station. Many of these teens can have a dynamic influence on hero-worshiping preteens. Since today's juniors are tuned in to the teen world, church young people returning with glowing testimonies can communicate with an authenticity that a secondhand missionary story can never do! Let juniors become as deeply involved in this type of ministry as possible.

WHERE TO TEACH MISSIONS

Each church agency offers a unique opportunity for missionary education.

Sunday school. Wherever natural, missionary emphasis should be woven into the Bible instruction. For example, a lesson on prayer could include references to answered prayer for missionaries; a lesson on God's will could include, perhaps, the testimony of a missionary supported by the church. In addition, each department should have a bulletin board which should feature up-to-date information on various aspects of the church's missionary outreach. Most Sunday schools encourage missionary giving on a weekly or monthly basis.

Children's church. In worship, where the focus is on God and the service is designed for response to Him, leaders have a prime privilege of opening lives to missionary commitment. Through careful choice of Scripture, music, and Bible talks, boys and girls can be challenged to set their lives according to God's values.

Training hour, Sunday evening youth groups, or family-night groups. These agencies, with their more informal programming, are ideal for in-depth studies of missions. Here, youngsters can listen to true accounts, become involved in research, and express creatively what they are learning of needs around the world, as well as in their own community.

Weekday clubs. Here, missionary education has practical application as children work for badges and seek to bring in their nonchurched friends. Counselors, when working on an individual basis with the children, can keep children alert to God's call to service.

Choir. In selecting choir numbers, a director asks, Does this music glorify God and bring us to a clearer understanding of Him and His purposes for man? Much of our fine Christian music is on the theme of God reaching out to man. If the director is sensitive to the message of the song, he can enrich the choir's appreciation of it. Where music is linked with meaning, children's attitudes can be deeply influenced.

Vacation Bible school. This agency offers tremendous opportunity for children to reach out into the community, thus giving them practical experience in missions at home. In addition, through the concentrated instruction, especially in ten-day schools, greater concern for missions is generated. Many vacation Bible schools have a missionary offering project, and through brief talks each day, teachers draw a clear picture of at least one aspect of missionary work.

Stewardship Education

WHAT STEWARDSHIP EDUCATION INCLUDES

Missionary education touches on another aspect of Christian training—stewardship, or total life commitment. It is natural to think of money when we consider stewardship, but the Bible reflects no such narrow view. It teaches, rather, that every area of a Christian's life is a trust from God. It involves holding time, talents, and treasures in an open hand to be invested for eternity, under God's direction.

Giving of life or money, time or talents is woven throughout Scripture, never as a dreary duty, but as an aspect of Christian life that is joyous, victorious, freely expressed. This wholehearted investment of self is contrary to the attitudes of children who are growing up in a pleasure-oriented society. "Boredom, underachievement (failure), hostility, negative work values are common circumstances prevalent among too many youths in our schools today,"[9] wrote a public school educator. But this is not so for the Christian child who views all of life's opportunities as possible calls to stewardship under God's direction. Children find purpose as they make the most of opportunities to invest in heaven's treasuries.

Stewardship education is a program of learning through which children are led to discover God's claim on all resources, including time, talents, and money.

CONTRIBUTION OF STEWARDSHIP EDUCATION TO THE TOTAL PROGRAM

Education for total life commitment gives a perspective and relevance to Bible instruction for which there is no substitute. Imagine the congregation in which each believer is actively offering time, talents, and treasures to his Lord. The local church program would flourish as Christians invest their time, creativity, and skills in the Lord's work, both in the local church and the community and beyond to the ends of the earth.

A group of Sunday school teachers were sharing insights in a teacher training class. As the discussion progressed, enthusiasm mounted. How much they could do if only the budget were not so limited, if the supply cupboard were not so bare, if the facilities and furnishings were not so inadequate!

Then the teachers had an idea. Going over the church directory, they listed each person high school age and older, jotting down the known interests, hobbies, and profession of each. Within a few minutes, an amazing picture began to form. If each person on the list gave the Lord only a few hours doing what he enjoyed most, the learning resources would be stockpiled!

Attractive furnishings for the nursery department, for example, could be made by teen boys, led by a young father who had recently designed creative items for his child's room. In the primary department, photos to illustrate hymns and Scripture could be flashed on a screen. God-honoring nature and science displays would decorate the junior department. Walls in the teen area would be covered with meaningful banners and posters. For problem readers, the library would offer true stories from missionary literature and take-home papers recorded on cassettes. The supply closet would bulge with Bibletime and foreign costumes, models, and curios. Talented church members could write missionary and seasonal worship programs, geared to the needs of the congregation. Creative forms of outreach into the community would capture interest through art, puppets, music, and testimony. These and many other resources could be made available if only people would tithe their *time* for a month or two. Surrounded by such evidences of the joy of giving, children would clearly see the benefits of stewardship.

But who would start the ball rolling? Where does this type of stewardship begin? Again, in the Christian education program in the children's division.

HOW TO TEACH STEWARDSHIP EDUCATION

By God's Word. Almost any Bible lesson leads to a practical discussion of giving God first place. Whenever teachers take time to probe behind the factual content of the Bible stories, they find concepts which enable them to view some aspect of life and its values from God's point of view. *My Utmost for His Highest*, wrote Oswald Chambers to adults. We translate this for your youngsters as "My best for Jesus," whether it is memorizing songs or Scripture for a special program, working on a poster or bulletin board display, giving part of their spending money, or developing skills of reading and writing.

By personal example. Children quickly sense the value system of their instructors. Though they are not able to articulate their discoveries, children discern the difference in Christians whose choices are governed by time and whose choices are governed by eternity. Do they sense in us a glad abandonment to Christ's claims in the everyday decisions we make?

By personal testimonies. Christians who are being good stewards can give brief testimonies to boys and girls. The church library can make available the stories of Christians who are gladly investing time and talents for Christ and His church. We will not limit these testimonies to those who have spectacular stories, but will include the housewife who decorates the church so tastefully for special days, the high school student who leads singing in vacation Bible school, the mechanic who keeps things in order around the church, or the businessman who is letting God run his factory.

By personal experience. Many teachers who are faithful with exhortation, personal example, and true life stories, hope that instruction will automatically become a part of life. However, in stewardship education, the old adage holds true: experience is the best teacher. Lois LeBar described the way to teach one principle through experience.

> Although children in the Bible school often repeat the Scripture verse, "It is more blessed to give than to receive," they seldom really believe those words until they have personally enjoyed a practical experience in giving. If we are to change the natural tendency of *getting* to the transcendent attitude of *giving*, we must so arrange circumstances that the child receives more satisfaction from giving than from getting. During the early formative years most children have never been privileged to have this experience, they see very few examples of sacrificial giving in

> the people they know, and thus they grow up secretly questioning God's high standards of stewardship.[10]

In the nursery department, children can enjoy a book with colorful pictures that show specific ways their money is used when they give because they love Jesus.

Four- and five-year-olds respond to specific needs. They can learn to give so that someone else can hear about Jesus and so that the home base can meet its practical needs for Sunday school supplies, heat, electricity, and so forth.

Primaries and juniors usually have a little money of their own. They can give because they want to offer a part of themselves in this way. The act of giving can be made especially significant when the leader uses Scripture, a brief responsive reading, poem, prayer, or song to involve the children in genuine worship.

Primaries and juniors should understand that giving is broader than the definition of "Contributions" provided by the Internal Revenue Service!

> There are the intangible gifts of love and trust and devotion and prayer which we can give personally to Christ, but material things go to others in His name, for He said, "Inasmuch as ye have done it unto one of the least of these My brethren, ye have done it unto Me.[11]

Children who are taught the joy of full life commitment can grow up forming the habits of simple living and regular, liberal giving. They will not speak of making great sacrifices, for they will be investing time and talents in what their hearts love best.

Vocational Guidance

WHAT VOCATIONAL GUIDANCE IS

Several years ago, when an adult asked a child, "What do you want to be when you grow up?" he would have received a specific reply, such as "Airplane pilot," "Nurse," or, "Mechanic."

Today's child is apt to answer such a question with a shrug, "How do I know what jobs will be needed when I'm grown up?"

And he's right! Some of today's current fields of work—ecology and lunar geology, for example— were almost unheard of a few years ago. In the technological explosion, vocational guidance is even more necessary for young people than previously. They need assistance in discovering their aptitudes and developing skills needed for general categories of work.

Though the public schools have made an effort to educate young people to go out and fill jobs, more than 1.5 million youngsters left school in 1971 with no marketable skills in the working world. Nearly half of these young people were graduates who had received twelve years of schooling.

WHY VOCATIONAL GUIDANCE AT EARLIER LEVELS

Today's schools are working on the elementary level to gear their goals to career education. The US Office of Education has suggested fifteen types of job clusters: agri-business and natural resources, business and office, communications and media, construction, consumer and home-making occupations, environment, fine arts and humanities, health, hospitality and recreation, manufacturing, marine science, marketing and distribution, personal service, public service, transportation.[12]

The goal in public school education is to see all children starting at an early age to study job clusters, gradually narrowing career choices with guidance and counseling, and then developing a skill in the chosen job cluster.

Even in primary grades, children are having some firsthand experience with jobs. They are studying the skills required in various occupations and are beginning to get the big picture of job choices. Today's vocational guidance at school is eliminating the emphasis on sex-based work. For example, equal opportunity will expose girls to such training as welding.

Research reveals that career decisions are rooted back in early childhood when the "career image" starts to form. By sixth grade, most children have at least tentatively outlined the courses of study they will select in junior high school, based on vocational potential.

HOW TO TEACH VOCATIONAL GUIDANCE

The church, keeping in mind its goal of life commitment, can make career exploration a valid part of Christian education. Future work should be considered from the viewpoint of God's will, opportunities it presents for Christian witness, and opportunities for investing talents and skills in serving Christ, whether in so-called secular work or full-time Christian service. Whatever career a person chooses, he needs to be a full-time Christian. God has given special abilities and gifts to do specialized work. The child needs to be aware of this.

Christian educators need to recognize that they do not know now what is best for children when they grow up. The future is in God's hands. Adults' ignorance of future opportunities, plus their tendency to impose their own hopes on young people may account for some of the restlessness and defeats experienced by youth. How much stability and assurance young people have when they sense they are being directed by the Lord in their career preparation!

In counseling children, we will want to stimulate them to think big, to anticipate new ways of serving the Lord, new mediums for communicating the gospel, and new God-honoring channels to express creativity and learning. The possibilities are almost endless! The minds of children should be closed only to those career possibilities that are not in harmony with the Word of God.

Lois LeBar wrote,

> Should Christians be more or less colorful and productive than other people? Does the dull, drab personality reflect the Christian life? Where are the Christian scholars who are forging new frontiers of knowledge based on scriptural foundations? Where are the writers who give vision of the Christian pathway from the realistic existential situation to exalted heights in Christ? Who will conduct the scientific experiments? Where are the educators who are working out on the growing edge of the field?[13]

While stimulating children to explore vocational possibilities, we will also stress that building Christian character and developing spiritual gifts are key ways to prepare for any vocation. Such biblical virtues as diligence, cooperation, and self-control are desirable in all professions.

RESOURCES AND ACTIVITIES IN VOCATIONAL GUIDANCE

Personal testimonies, library materials, and field trips all provide learning opportunities for children. Adults who are alive to the potential in their chosen vocation can share insights with children and arouse appreciation for the avenues of serving God in various kinds of work.

Although not *every* Christian can be employed as a pastor, Christian education director, missionary, or teacher in a Bible college, it is important that all young people in the church be made aware of all the possibilities in "specialized Christian ministries." Preparing youth to consider such careers can be provided in the church, using methods similar to these: provide instruction for the various kinds of ministry as part of the total curriculum in the church and the home; encourage children to serve the Lord *now* in specific ways, telling others about Christ, passing out tracts and other Christian literature, visiting the sick and aged, going to rest homes, and doing projects in the church and at home; invite resource people into the department to present their ministry; conduct field trips of Christian organizations, publishing houses, mission board offices, other churches; have personal or taped interviews with people working in a variety of ministries, encouraging the children to ask their own questions, and possibly do part of the interviewing themselves, reporting their findings; encourage parents to invite guests home for dinner or overnight to get acquainted on a more informal basis; show slides or filmstrips; provide literature about different kinds of ministries; have children write for materials, study what they receive, and make a scrapbook of the materials; provide books, magazines, and pamphlets which relate to Christian ministries; train parents in specialized ministries so they can teach their children at home.

NOTES

1. "Nine-Year-Old Boy Stops Elephant," *Conservative Baptist Impact* 26 (Feb., 1969): 10.
2. Michael Griffiths, "The Lord's Guerilleros," *East Asia Millions* 81 (Feb.-Mar., 1973): 9.
3. *Opportunities 1973*, Short Terms Abroad, Downers Grove, Ill.
4. Elton Trueblood, *Validity of the Christian Mission* (New York: Harper, 1972), p. x.
5. Ralph R. Covell, "Urban Crisis: Test of Our Missionary Concern," *World Vision Magazine* 13 (Oct., 1969): 12.
6. Dr. and Mrs. Howard Taylor, *Hudson Taylor and the China Inland Mission* (London: CIM, 1918), p. 626.
7. Findley B. Edge, *The Greening of the Church* (Waco, Tex.: Word, 1971), p. 148.
8. Lois E. LeBar, *Focus on People in Church Education* (Westwood, N.J.: Revell, 1968), p. 173.
9. Joyce Fern Glasser, *The Elementary School Learning Center for Independent Study* (West Nyack, N.Y.: Parker, 1971), p. 189.
10. Lois E. LeBar, *Children in the Bible School* (Westwood, N.J.: Revell, 1952), p. 315.
11. Ibid., p. 318.
12. Sidney P. Marland, Jr., US Commissioner of Education, "Career Education–What Is It?" *My Weekly Reader*, Teachers' ed., 53 (Mar. 1, 1972): 1.
13. Lois E. LeBar, *Education That Is Christian* (Westwood, N.J.: Revell, 1958), p. 174.

FOR FURTHER READING

Anderson, Virginia. *Making Missions Meaningful.* Wheaton, Ill.: Pioneer Girls, 1966.

Bartlett, Margaret. "Teaching Missions to Primaries." *Key* 9 (Fall, 1969): 29-32.

Chambers, Oswald. *So Send I You.* Fort Washington, Pa.: Christian Literature Crusade, 1930.

Cook, Harold R. *Highlights of Christian Missions.* Chicago: Moody, 1967.

———. *Introduction to Christian Missions.* Chicago: Moody, 1971.

———. *Missionary Life and Work.* Chicago: Moody, 1959.

———. *Next Steps for the Missionary Volunteer.* Chicago: Moody, 1949.

Elsdon, Wilma. "Begin Early to Teach About Missions." *Key* 5 (April-June, 1965): 37-38.

Gerber, Vergil, ed. *Missions in Creative Tension.* South Pasadena, Calif.: William Carey Library, 1971.

Gilleo, Alma. *How to Teach Missions.* Elgin, Ill.: David C. Cook, 1964.

Griffiths, Michael C. *Give Up Your Small Ambitions.* Chicago: Moody, 1971.

Haskin, Dorothy C. "How You Can Teach Missions to Children." *World Vision* 16 (Feb., 1972): 12-13.

Howard, David M. *Student Power in World Evangelism.* Downers Grove, Ill.: Inter-Varsity, 1970.

———. *Why World Evangelism?* Downers Grove, Ill.: Inter-Varsity, 1971.

Lovering, Kerry. *Missions Idea Notebook.* New York: SIM, 1967.

McGavran, Donald, ed. *Crucial Issues in Missions Tomorrow.* Chicago: Moody, 1972.

Meyer, Frederick A. "Helping Children Develop a World View." *Interaction* 2 (March, 1962): 11-13.

Morningstar, Mildred. *Teaching Johnny to Give.* Chicago: Moody, 1972.

Pearson, Dick. *Missionary Education Helps for the Local Church.* Palo Alto, Calif.: Overseas Crusades, 1966.

Peters, George W. *A Biblical Theology of Missions.* Chicago: Moody, 1972.

Olford, Stephen. *The Grace of Giving.* Grand Rapids: Zondervan, 1972.

Summers, Sandra Kay. *Teaching Missions–A Plan and a Program.* Cincinnati: Standard, 1967.

Vinkemulder, Yvonne. *Enrich Your Life.* Downers Grove, Ill.: Inter-Varsity, 1972.

Wagner, C. Peter, ed. *Church/Mission Tensions Today.* Chicago: Moody, 1972.

Zuck, Roy B. *The Pastor and Missionary Education.* Christian Education Monographs, Pastors' Series, No. 22. Glen Ellyn, Ill.: Scripture Press Foundation, 1967.

———. "Teach Them to Give." *Link* 7 (July, 1959):1, 2, 4-6.

OTHER SOURCES

Materials with Missionary Games, Programs, and Activities

Asks 'n Answers. Overseas Missionary Fellowship, 237 West School House Lane, Philadelphia, Pa., 19144.

Carlos Requests. Central American Theological Seminary, Apartado 213, Guatemala, Central America.

"Fun and Festival" Series. New York: Friendship Press.

Eisenberg, Larry. *Fun and Festival from the United States and Canada,* 1966.

Gwinn, Alice E. and Hibbard, Esther L. *Fun and Festival from Japan,* 1966.

Hallock, Constance M. *Fun and Festival from Southeast Asia,* 1956.

Rohrbough, Katherine Ferris. *Fun and Festival Among America's Peoples,* 1970.

Rowland, Joan. *Fun and Festival from the Middle East,* 1970.

Wells, Irene, and Bothwell, Jean. *Fun and Festival from India, Pakistan, and Ceylon,* 1972.

Wright, Rose H. *Fun and Festival from Africa,* 1970.

———. *Fun and Festival from China,* n.d.

———. *Fun and Festival from the Other Americas,* n.d.

Keiser, Armilda B. *Here's How and When.* New York: Friendship, 1952.

Millen, Nina. *Children's Games from Many Lands.* New York: Friendship, 1964.

Books with Missionary Stories for Children

Arnold, Charlotte E. *Missionary Stories and Illustrations.* Grand Rapids: Baker, 1970.

Doan, Eleanor L., and McElroy, Gladys. *Missionary Stories for Preschoolers.* Glendale, Calif.: Gospel Light, 1963.
———. *Missionary Stories for Primaries.* Glendale, Calif.: Gospel Light, 1963.
———. *Missionary Stories for Juniors.* Glendale, Calif.: Gospel Light, 1963.
Haskin, Dorothy C. *Tell Every Man.* Grand Rapids: Baker, 1968.
Millen, Nina. *Missionary Stories to Play and Tell.* New York: Fellowship, 1958.
Worman, Theresa. *Missionary Stories and More Missionary Stories.* Chicago: Moody, 1974.
———. *More Missionary Stories.* Chicago: Moody, 1951.

Missionary Picture Sets

American Indians. Cincinnati: Standard.
Children Around the World. Cincinnati: Standard.
Felipe of the Philippine Islands. Wheaton, Ill.: Scripture Press.
Haruko of Japan. Wheaton, Ill.: Scripture Press.
Kittebah, Navajo Indian Girl. Wheaton, Ill.: Scripture Press.
Maku of Africa. Wheaton, Ill.: Scripture Press.
Myyuca from South America. Wheaton, Ill.: Scripture Press.
Preeta of India. Wheaton, Ill.: Scripture Press.

Missionary Songbooks for Children

Holcomb, Louanah. *Missionary Melodies.* Nashville: Broadman, n.d.
Thomas, Edith. *The Whole World Singing.* New York: Friendship, 1950.

Sources of Missionary Flannelgraph and/or Flash Card Stories

Bible Visuals, Inc., Box 93, Landisville, Pa. 17538.
Child Evangelism Fellowship, P.O. Box 1156, Grand Rapids, Mich. 49501.
Scripture Press Publications, Inc., 1825 College Ave., Wheaton, Ill. 60187.
Standard Publishing Company, 8121 Hamilton Ave., Cincinnati, Ohio 45231.

Part V

ADMINISTRATION OF CHILDREN'S WORK

21

Church Agencies for Children

Ruth C. Haycock

The Beginnings of Church Agencies

Through seventeen centuries of church history, we read of no agencies designed especially to meet the spiritual needs of children. Then in 1780 came Sunday schools, first in England, and then in the Christian world at large. Here was an organized effort to teach the Bible to children. Sunday schools arose in response to a need for general and Bible instruction. They began independently of churches and were opposed by them on the bases of misuse of the Lord's Day and the futility of teaching poor children.

Sunday schools multiplied. The Wesleys urged every new Methodist church to institute a Sunday school. Other denominations were slower to respond, and it was about 1900 before Sunday schools had general denominational acceptance.

This pattern was repeated again and again in the history of Christian education: a need became evident; churches were unresponsive; outside groups organized; a coordinating agency arose to provide direction and materials; the organization fought for acceptance by churches; gradually acceptance came. Sometimes churches ignored the outside group; in other cases, they recognized it as an ally.

This tendency for agencies to originate as extrachurch groups provides a partial explanation for the spirit of independence in some church agencies. It stresses also the need for churches to adapt their own programs to prevailing needs, rather than waiting for those outside the church to meet those needs.

Ruth C. Haycock, Ed.D., is Chairman of the Department of Christian Education, Baptist Bible College of Pennsylvania, Clarks Summit, Pennsylvania.

In the following sections, the distinctives of the Sunday school and other agencies with a primary interest in children will be discussed; then, how to coordinate those agencies within a church will be considered.

Distinctives of Specific Agencies

THE SUNDAY SCHOOL

The Sunday school, in addition to having the longest history of any church educational agency, is also the most comprehensive. In Bible-believing churches, it has the largest attendance, covers the widest span of years, has available the richest curriculum resources, is graded most carefully, and has the most influence on the church's decisions about facilities.

The choice of a Sunday school curriculum is of utmost concern. Both teachers and pupils learn Bible content and doctrine largely through this curriculum. A good curriculum should, therefore, be thoroughly biblical, agree with the church's doctrine, be carefully graded, and furnish the teacher with helps adequate for a well-conducted class.

The major purpose of the Sunday school is to teach the Word of God in order that lives may be changed. Thorough Bible instruction will result in worship, expression, and service. If instruction does not lead to such response, it is incomplete.

The children's division of a Sunday school is generally divided into departments and classes. In most churches, preschool children are divided into three departments: infants and toddlers, birth to age two; nursery, ages two and three; and beginners, ages four and five. In some churches, this latter department is referred to as the "fours and fives"; in others, it is called the kindergarten department, the beginner department, or the preprimary department. In larger churches, there are six preschool departments, one for each year.

School-age departments often include three years for primaries (grades 1 to 3) and three for juniors (grades 4 to 6); however, some churches use two-year departments (grades 1 and 2; 3 and 4; 5 and 6); and large churches provide a separate department for each school grade.

Within each department, pupils are classified into groups of four to eight children for at least part of the period. These small classes allow for discussion, memory time, and expressional work. The departmental sessions stress worship and promotional activities, and in the primary and junior departments, scripture memorization and missionary education are often included. Whether the Bible lesson is taught in the assembly or in classes depends largely on the teaching methods considered desirable.

A departmental staff consists of a superintendent, secretary, pianist-helper, and several teachers.* This group meets for prayer, planning, and specialized training.

Though there have been critics of the Sunday school, God has honored and used it to the salvation and spiritual growth of multitudes.

CHILDREN'S CHURCH AND EXTENDED SESSION

When a church makes no special provision for children during the morning service, the youngsters develop the habit of turning off the service and thinking about more interesting things. Once this habit develops, it often lingers into youth and adult years and accounts for the slowness of adults to learn from regular worship services.

"Junior church" was the first effort to provide meaningful worship for children, but the term *junior* included those of junior age and below. More recently, churches have graded their children's churches, following the Sunday school terminology, nursery through junior.

A children's church usually meets simultaneously with the adult service. Some children's churches meet separately during the entire hour; whereas, in some churches, children meet with the adults for part of the service and are then dismissed for their own program. Children may plan and participate in graded worship. Primaries and juniors may gain understanding of the church and its services, government, missionary program, and distinctives; they, as well as preschoolers can profit from added Bible teaching.

When this second hour elaborates in various ways on the Bible teaching of the Sunday school, it is called "extended session." Several publishers provide church-time materials which build on their Sunday school curriculum. This feature can be helpful, since, in order to handle an extended session otherwise, a local worker must plan supplementary materials to add depth and breadth to the Sunday school topic each week.

A children's church program needs at least two workers, with one additional person for every eight or ten children. Also a pianist and secretary are needed. Men should be included on the staff to help emphasize the relevance of God and church to men and boys.

Children's church can teach saved children to worship the Lord and to appreciate what He has done, and it can help unsaved ones to see their need of Christ. Graded sessions can provide instruction on subjects that might otherwise be omitted, while at the same time removing distractions from adult services.

*The general qualifications and specific responsibilities of each department worker are discussed in chap. 22, "Leadership and Materials."

TRAINING HOUR

When Francis Clark organized his first Society of Christian Endeavor in 1881, he did not know that one day there would be youth groups in most churches. Neither could he foresee training hour sessions on Sunday nights for *every* age level.

Training hour is a regular Sunday night function for many Christian families. For adult attendance to be possible, there must be sessions for children.

There are certain advantages in an all-family training hour: it promotes attendance at Sunday evening services; it gives additional time for the instruction of believers; it permits a high degree of pupil involvement; it allows participation in leadership to some who attend their own Sunday school classes.

Historically, training hour has emphasized learning how to live the Christian life and gaining experience in carrying responsibility. Participants learn to speak, preside, lead singing, share their faith, and discuss contemporary problems in the light of Bible teaching. Training hour should not be another preaching service or Sunday school class, but a situation in which children are guided to think through problems and to express themselves. Application receives more stress here than learning Bible stories.

Each age-group for which a church sets up a training hour program needs a staff of two to four persons, depending on the size of the group, preferably including at least one married couple. When departmental groups exceed twenty-five children, they should be divided by school grade. The suggested minimum of four staff members permits the children to be grouped, each group with a leader, for planning, preparing programs, or for Bible study.

In choosing curriculum materials for children's training hour, a committee must make several decisions: (1) do we want a theme which continues through the total program? Several publishers produce such materials, capitalizing on children's interest in space travel or animals; (2) do we desire an individual achievement program with awards or ranks? (3) what emphasis do we want on scripture memorization? (4) do we prefer the same routine from week to week? Children sense security in familiar routines, yet routines can be deadening; (5) to what extent should we use or try to develop the children's creativity?†

For many children, a well-executed training hour provides an extra experience, enabling them to meet the problems of everyday life and use the Bible in solving them.

†Choosing curriculum materials is also discussed in chap. 22, "Leadership and Materials."

RELEASED TIME CLASSES

As American public education has become increasingly secular, church leaders and many educators have recognized that in some way, the public school must show its pupils the contribution of religion to life. If schools ignore religion completely, they tell children, in effect, that it is unimportant.

In an effort to highlight the significant nature of religion, many states have authorized schools to release pupils each week to go to their churches for instruction. Parents give permission for their children's attendance. In some cases, the church is responsible to the school for attendance records, since the instruction is considered part of the school day. In other situations, pupils are dismissed early, either to attend the special classes or to go home.

Released-time programs have certain advantages: attendance is regular because, once parents have given permission, the pupils must attend; many children from unsaved homes will participate; pupils and parents tend to be serious about the classes, as an extension of the school.

In spite of these plusses, however, a church should consider carefully before starting a released-time program. Success depends on a staff adequate to teach classes simultaneously, to escort children to and from the church, to keep records, and to handle the program on a regular basis. Sufficient classroom space is also crucial. Good discipline is important too, because a church's reputation is not improved when children go from an orderly school to a disorderly church.

The curriculum should be grouped by school grades, if possible, so that learning activities may be suitable and each year may build on the preceding ones. Many churches, however, have satisfactorily grouped children over a two- or three-grade range and have used a rotating curriculum. Because many children receive no other solid Bible instruction and others have learned much in church and home, the curriculum decision is often a difficult one. Long-range planning should, therefore, precede the initial classes.

Released time is meant primarily for instruction; learning experiences should be planned using large and small groups, individual work, testing, and evaluation. Expressional work and worship should relate to the content studied and should be included in the classes.

Staff needs of such a program vary according to the number of children expected and the grades included. This in turn depends on the proximity of the public school, the reputation of the church, and the number and strength of competing groups. In addition to a teacher and assistant for each class, a director and secretary are needed. Their responsibility includes counseling children and leading them to the Lord. In many situations, children may not remain after class for counsel and must return to school for dismissal and bus transportation.

Released-time classes are not for every church, but where they are permitted and where other factors indicate the Lord's leading, they can provide many new contacts for church follow-up.

WEEKDAY BIBLE CLUBS (OR CLASSES)

Home Bible classes for children go by several names: Good News Clubs, Bible Clubs, and Joy Clubs, among others. Certain characteristics are true of all: (1) they gather neighborhood children into a Christian home for a one-hour club; (2) they serve kindergarten and elementary school children, often without grading, sometimes with two separate groups for the Bible lesson; (3) they stress chronological, visualized Bible study; (4) they emphasize evangelism and encourage children to bring friends.

Because such classes meet after school, children are already dressed suitably. Because they are neighborhood groups, the economic and social level of the host home is comparable with that of the attending children. Because the classes are informal, they are a welcome change from the school day.

Weekday classes are usually staffed by a teacher, a helper, and a hostess (or the hostess may also be the helper).

An effective ministry in children's Bible classes depends on careful preparation and workers showing love for the children in club, casual contacts, and home calls. Clubs with a church's prayer backing reach many children and homes for the Lord. Any affiliation with an outside organization must not overshadow the fact that God has given the local church responsibility to reach out into the community.

ACTIVITY CLUBS

Psychologists often point out that we need new experiences if we are not to go stale. Doing something different is a thrill and a challenge at any age. In all preparation for children's sessions, we strive for variety and freshness, but most youngsters need more than we give them in the classroom. They need cookouts and field days; they respond to learning to build campfires and to tie knots; they enjoy crafts and projects. Here they can learn lessons which relate Bible truths to life; they can see their leaders informally; they can learn to express themselves and to discipline themselves; they can learn Christian sportsmanship.

Earlier generations engaged in some of these experiences at home with older family members; some were members of scouts or Camp Fire Girls. It was to young adults who had known the enthusiasm and thrill of these secular organizations that God gave a vision for Christ-centered clubs sponsored by Bible-believing churches. Christian Service Brigade began for boys, with Pioneer Girls following. Then came the Awana Youth Association, Sky Pilots, and others.

All activity clubs are somewhat similar: they meet weekly for two hours; they include games and crafts as well as Bible study; their members work for badges and ranks; they exist as an integral part of a church program, with emphasis on evangelism and Christian growth; they require leadership training before a group is formed; they have divisions for several age-groups.

The specific leadership needed depends on which program a church chooses. Each organization publishes an array of guidebooks for leaders and manuals for members. Careful study should precede the adoption of a club program. Persons likely to be involved should visit other clubs and discuss their effectiveness with the clubs' leaders. They should send for materials and examine them prayerfully. If possible, they should invite a field representative from the organization to present the program and answer questions. Conviction based on thorough preparation can lead to a wise decision and a fruitful ministry.

VACATION BIBLE SCHOOL

Vacation Bible school provides time for concentrated Bible study and varied activities. The maintenance of a high degree of enthusiasm and continuity is difficult in sessions which are spaced a week apart, but here is an agency meeting several hours a day for five to ten consecutive days.

The results can be fantastic in spirit, achievement, and depth of study. Children can become involved in projects for which there is little time in shorter sessions. They can play together under the direction of adults and teenagers who exemplify Christian virtues and teach biblical attitudes.

Most schools are organized into departments and classes, following the grading of the Sunday school. Classification should be by school grade just completed to avoid mixing children who do not read and write with those who have had school training. In schools with limited space for departmental activities, all school children can meet for an assembly, which helps build school spirit and center attention on the Lord Jesus Christ.

Since the day's session is divided into a number of periods, team teaching is preferable.‡ When a teacher is responsible for only the Bible lesson, or only the scripture memory work, or the handwork, that teacher can prepare adequately; as a result, more workers are willing to serve. An experienced teacher should present the Bible lesson, the basis for the

‡For more on team teaching, also see chap. 22, "Leadership and Materials."

day's work. As inexperienced workers observe others teach and lead, they too learn and grow.

In order for children to use workbooks comfortably and do creative projects, they need table space and tools. While boys and girls must learn to share, it is unreasonable that they should spend half of their work period waiting for scissors or paste.

The most familiar curriculum materials are probably the departmentally graded lessons available from major Sunday school publishers. Each publisher chooses an overall theme for the year and rotates several lesson series within each department. Correlated with the Bible lessons are worship plans, games, songs, handwork, and special features. Workbooks and visual materials enable a staff with limited training to work effectively.

In addition, uniform series, with all grades studying the same Bible content, are available from some Sunday school publishers, from some missionary agencies which do children's work, and from individual churches. Some series are planned well and provide excellent graded material for pupils and teachers. Others provide little supplementary helps but have been used effectively by trained workers in low-budget situations.

Closely graded lessons, with a separate series for each school grade, are produced by a few publishers and may be used year after year.

Organization of the Children's Division

THE NEED FOR COORDINATION

Mrs. James needed help! She was teaching a released-time class of fifth-graders and getting nowhere. What was she doing wrong? In desperation she came, seeking a solution. The lesson series she used was a good choice. Her plan for the teaching period was one others had used successfully. She was known as an effective teacher.

Investigation showed these facts: the children attended Sunday school, junior youth group, church-sponsored home clubs, an after-school junior missionary meeting, as well as her released-time classes. In most sessions, the teacher used a flannelgraph Bible story; in Sunday school, home clubs, and released time, lessons were from the Pentateuch; in the junior youth group, the lessons were based on the Pentateuch, though they were not direct Bible study; the home clubs taught the identical series used in released time and were two weeks ahead! Every agency taught a weekly memory verse. Except for the missionary group, no children could bemember learning any new song.

It was evident that these juniors were learning. They were learning to occupy themselves otherwise when the Word of God was taught. They were convinced that no teacher expected them to learn very much because of the constant repetition. They were also learning that only the Pentateuch is important.

Whatever the combination of agencies a church uses in its efforts to reach and teach children, coordination is necessary for meaningful accomplishment.

SUGGESTED ORGANIZATIONAL STRUCTURE

When a new church begins, coordinating church functions is relatively easy. The same few people are involved; the number of agencies is limited; the pastor is in close touch with what goes on. It is often he and his wife who train workers for their responsibilities.

As a church grows, these factors change. Agencies multiply; leadership expands; the pastor cannot supervise all that goes on. As he works with his board, it soon becomes apparent that their responsibilites cover too many other areas to include coordinating all the areas of the church's ministry.

The next step in organizational structure is a board (or committee) of Christian education. Such a board usually includes the head of each educational agency, the pastor or director of Christian education, a representative from the church board, and sometimes a member elected from the church at large. It often meets monthly to recommend or set policy, approve personnel and curriculum, and coordinate the educational program in general.

Growing out of this board, several committees prove helpful: children's work, youth work, adult work, and leadership development.

The children's-work committee, for instance, may consist of the leader of or an elected representative from each agency (Sunday school, children's church, vacation Bible school, training hour, weekday clubs). Another way to organize the children's-work committee is to have a representative from each of the age groups in the children's division (cradle roll, twos and threes, fours and fives, primaries, and juniors). These representatives meet together to organize, administer, and supervise the work of the children's division.

At times, the committee may call all workers in the children's division together for the consideration of needs or for inservice training. The amount of responsibility given to the committee will determine how often it should meet. The chairman of the committee may be appointed by the board of Christian education or elected by the committee to serve a designated length of time.

The responsibilities of the committee should be delineated in the church constitution or by-laws, so that as members change, a functional committee

TABLE 21.1.

Children's Agencies

Level	Sunday School	Children's Church	Training Hour	Vacation Bible School	Weekday Bible Classes	Released-Time Classes	Activity Clubs
Birth to age 2	Cradle roll	Nursery (baby care)	Church nursery if adult training hour meets	Nursery for children of workers			
Ages 2 and 3	Nursery or twos and threes	Nursery church	Church nursery if adult training hour meets	Nursery			
Ages 4 and 5	Four and fives	Kindergarten church	Kindergarten training hour	Kindergarten	Preschool classes	Kindergarten	
Grades 1, 2, 3	Primary	Primary church	Primary training hour	Primary	Grades 1 to 6 often together in one club in each neighborhood	Grade 1 Grade 2 Grade 3	Primary
Grades 4, 5, 6	Junior	Junior church	Junior training hour	Junior		Grade 4 Grade 5 Grade 6	Junior

continues. Some of the specific responsibilities of the committee are as follows:

Prepare a list of needs in the children's division.
Write realistic goals which can be accomplished within specified times.
Give guidance in organizing, administering, and supervising the departments.
Correlate the work of the departments and agencies.
Provide a balanced program in instruction, worship, fellowship, and expression-service.
Seek to improve specific activities in music, worship, memorization, recreation, and teaching-learning.
Publicize and promote the work of the children's division.
Discover, enlist, and provide training for workers with children.
Suggest and recommend curriculum for use in the children's division.
Develop wholesome human relations and build a cooperative team spirit among the workers.
Evaluate the work of the children's division periodically.

Table 21.1 shows children's agencies and the age groups which they most often serve. Though a particular church seldom includes every agency, careful planning is needed to provide adequate staff and curriculum for each age level and effective progress from one level to the next.

SUCCESS FACTORS

The effectiveness of a church program is not measured by the number of agencies; neither is it judged by quantity of scripture verses memorized or the number of times the children go through the Bible. Factors which really count relate to objectives the church seeks to achieve.

Clear objectives. In chapters 4 through 8, the needs of each age group were discussed. Those chapters pointed out that because certain things are happening in the lives of primaries, for example, these boys and girls have particular needs. Some are common to people of all ages; others are specific developmental tasks of the primary years. If each agency ministering to primary children takes responsibility for all those needs, leaders will have more goals than they can achieve, with resultant discouragement and frustration.

One task of the children's work committee is to study pupils' needs and then determine which agency should accept specific responsibility for which needs. Some overlapping is unavoidable and probably desirable, but a clear understanding of agency objectives provides for leaders a basis for selecting materials and activities and makes evaluation and progress possible.

TABLE 21.2

COORDINATING CURRICULUM

		SUNDAY SCHOOL	CHILDREN'S CHURCH	WEEKDAY CLUB	TRAINING HOUR	MISCELLANEOUS
Objectives						
Curriculum, Year 1	1 2 3 4					
Year 2	1 2 3 4					
Year 3	1 2 3 4					
Memory work						
Songs or bases for selection.						
Special activities						

Coordination of curriculum. A departmental curriculum chart, such as Table 21.2 illustrates, can help children's workers coordinate their activities. The table shown is only a possible skeleton. The actual chart should be on a large sheet of paper.

Some church publishers have available a prospectus, outlining their long-range curriculum. To find the three-year cycle of memory work, one must often study the manuals for the three-year span.

If for some agency the materials used are not satisfactory, the chart for that agency should be prepared last. Out of a study of the total curriculum, the lack of need for the agency may become evident. On the other hand, gaps may appear which indicate the necessity for a program different from what has been used. To leave the selection of lesson content to each leader is to invite chaos.

Before any new agency is introduced, the need for it should be established. Somehow it is easier to start something else than to make what we have function at the top level. The result of adding agencies is competition for children, attention, workers, curriculum, time—an ineffective but busy program.

Growing leadership. Ministries to children grow when their leaders grow. This statement is true whether we are concerned with children's development in spiritual dimensions or in enthusiasm and attendance. Youngsters are quick to detect hypocrisy; they sense boredom even when leaders refuse to admit they are bored. When a leader has prepared only superficially, children are quick to take advantage of the situation.

Growth in leaders must begin in their personal lives with the Lord and then in their relationships with others. It must include responsibility to their church in capacities other than teacher or leader. Growth should result in wholesome influence in the neighborhood and at work.

All those who work in one agency must understand their objectives and the way in which their program relates to others. This understanding comes through group study of agency materials, attendance at area rallies, training sessions, and local staff meetings, and time for united prayer and planning. Lack of this knowledge leads to branching out at the whims of leaders until everyone does "that which is right in his own eyes."

Prospective workers for all agencies should be approved by the board of Christian education. New workers should visit sessions before they take responsibility; they should serve as apprentices before they become leaders.

Profitable presessions. It has been repeatedly said that a Sunday school teacher is late if he is not present fifteen minutes early. Teachers should be ready for pupils in order to capitalize on those precious minutes with the early birds before the session officially begins. In addition to providing a get-acquainted and counseling time, many departments plan specific projects which involve one or several youngsters and which relate to the Bible lesson. The use of presession adds to the teaching time, but it also prevents the discipline problems that develop when children are unsupervised.

The same principle may be applied to other agencies. The shy child may open up in this period; any child may reveal his understanding or lack of it; the teacher may behave less formally; special interests may reveal themselves. In longer sessions, as in vacation Bible school, when the weather is favorable, outdoor activities will work better than indoor ones.

In their teacher's manuals, many curriculum writers suggest pre-session activities related to the lessons. Activities should be simple enough to be completed in a short time or suitable for continuation from session to session without too much handling of materials.

Two- to five-year-olds can look at picture books, draw pictures, listen to records or tapes, explore a nature center, play a story, participate in finger plays, present their offering, help with a bulletin board, listen to a story or review information in a variety of ways.

Primaries and juniors are less limited because they can read and write. In addition to the above activities, they can sing around the piano; learn new songs; review memory verses; prepare scrapbooks or posters; look at Bible stories using View-Masters, filmstrips, or a phonoviewer; play Bible games; write letters to missionaries, absentees, or shut-ins; drill on vocabulary; prepare something special for the opening assembly; read books; prepare a diorama or a box movie; examine a missionary display, or make a tape recording.

The uses of presession time are limited only by the imagination of the adult leaders. The informality of smaller groups makes possible unusual supplementary activity.

Communication with the church. The success of church agencies is never merely a matter of a top-notch program, excellent leadership, and superior organization. Our ministry is a spiritual matter; we are interested in seeing boys and girls trust the Saviour and grow in Him. These results come only as the Holy Spirit is active both in the leadership and in the hearts and minds of children. If we see no results, perhaps we have not asked God to change our lives and those we teach. He delights to respond as we look to Him.

Not only does God respond to individual prayer, but in a special way, He honors group prayer and agreement in prayer. Because this is true, a church must be kept up to date about its children's work. When there are victories, church members should join in praise to God; when there are needs wisely shared, they should join in petition. Prayer partners are always an asset but especially so when problems should not be publicly reported.

Communication with the church has other values. When people know what goes on, they are more sympathetic; they supply needs rather than wonder what costs so much; they consider helping instead of relegating responsibility to others; they promote the *whole* church program.

Innovations and Trends

Church agencies are constantly, though slowly, changing in response to developments in the school system, new community conditions, and further insights into scriptural teaching.

INCREASING CHURCH-CENTEREDNESS

With an increasing emphasis on the establishment of indigenous national churches on the foreign field and new churches at home, has come a general acceptance of the importance of the local church in New Testament teaching. Churches which once operated no weekday children's work but often encouraged their members to work with extrachurch groups now provide a church-related program.

The result is improved coordination with other church agencies, better opportunity for follow-up, and a more solid status for the weekday classes because of the church's reputation. Children are learning that their church is concerned about them. As they outgrow a particular agency, the church still has a place for them.

LESSENED DISTINCTIVENESS AMONG AGENCIES

When each church agency began, it was out of a conviction that children had particular needs that it could meet. Therefore, each group within a church was distinctive. As time went on and each agency sought to improve its program and materials, it dipped into other areas where it had not previously worked. As a result, each program has increased in breadth, and some of the earlier distinctives have been lost. A problem arises when we seek to make each agency complete in itself for the benefit of those who attend only one and when we also want each program to be part of a coordinated whole.

SPECIAL CLASSES OR GROUPS

Contemporary churches are probably doing more than at any time in history to consider the needs of special groups: the mentally retarded, the physically handicapped, the deaf, and others (see chaps. 25 to 27). A church's provision for such children recognizes the fact that God loves them and that they need the Saviour. It proves to the community that a church cares.

VARIETY OF ORGANIZATIONAL PATTERNS

No longer must vacation Bible school be two weeks long and two-and-a-half hours each forenoon. VBS may operate for five days or eight; it may meet in the evening or both morning and evening; it may meet in backyards all around the community; it may run one evening a week for ten weeks. Day camp or Indian village Bible camp may be substituted for the more formal VBS.

Some Sunday schools meet longer than one hour; some combine with children's church for a longer session. Some have no opening assembly but meet for a closing session instead.

NEW GROUPINGS OF PUPILS

Whereas controlled class sizes have been rather consistently recommended for each age group, now it seems there are no rules. With an increase in team teaching, the trend is to meet in larger groups for parts of each period, breaking into small groups for specific activities. As individualized instruction and small group projects have become common in public schools, adaptations are being made in church classes. There seems to be a widespread recognition that the use of various sized groups provides variety for the children and more effective use of leaders and that children should not be grouped in the same way for all activities.

Church agencies for children are, first, *church* agencies. They are part of a church's ministry to people. Second, they are *for children,* and must therefore provide for the needs of youngsters, both saved and unsaved. Together they must offer understanding and experience to enable a believing child to grow into a mature follower of the Lord Jesus Christ.

FOR FURTHER READING

Activity Clubs

Awana Clubs Leadership Training: Instructor's Manual. Chicago: Awana Youth Assn., 1966.

Blueprint for Christian Boys' Work: A Guide to Committee Action in Christian Service Brigade. Wheaton, Ill.: Christian Service Brigade, 1964.

Boys for Christ: Official Manual for Leaders in Christian Service Brigade. Wheaton, Ill.: Christian Service Brigade, 1962.

Bubar, Joseph B. *The Pastor and His Weekday Clubs.* Christian Educ. Monographs, Pastors' Series, No. 11. Glen Ellyn, Ill.: Scripture Press Foundation, 1966.

Developing Leaders for Girls Clubs. Evanston, Ill.: Baptist General Conference, 1973.

The Leader's Handbook for Awana Boys' Clubs. Chicago: Awana Youth Assn., 1968.

The Leader's Handbook for Awana Girls' Clubs. Chicago: Awana Youth Assn., 1967.

Ministry Through Girls' Clubs. Evanston, Ill.: Baptist General Conference, 1973.

The Pioneer Girls Committee. Wheaton, Ill.: Pioneer Girls, 1965.

The Pioneer Girls Guide: Basic Manual for Leaders. Wheaton, Ill.: Pioneer Girls, 1963.

Your Church and the Pioneer Girls Program. Wheaton, Ill.: Pioneer Girls, n.d.

Children's Agencies and Their Administration

Church Educational Agencies. Wheaton, Ill.: Evangelical Teacher Training Assn., 1968.

Correlated Christian Education in the Local Church: Curriculum Guidebook. Chicago: Harvest, 1962.

Eavey, Charles B. *History of Christian Education.* Chicago: Moody, 1964.

Nursery. Beginner. Primary. Junior. (Four age-group pamphlets, each dealing with agencies for that level.) New York: Christian & Missionary Alliance, n.d.

Research Report on Church Educational Ministries. Wheaton, Ill.: Scripture Press, 1970.

Weidman, Mavis. *Christian Education Guide.* New York: Christian & Missionary Alliance, n.d.

Children's Church

Doan, Eleanor L. *How to Plan and Conduct a Junior Church.* Grand Rapids: Zondervan, 1954.

Frost, Marie. *Kindergarten Children's Church Guide.* Elgin, Ill.: David C. Cook, 1967.

Gorman, Julia A. *Church-Time for Juniors.* Wheaton, Ill.: Scripture Press, 1960.

Huttar, Leora W. *Jack and Jill Stay for Church: How to Lead a Churchtime Nursery.* Chicago: Moody, 1965.

LeBar, Mary E. *Wonder Programs for 4s and 5s. Yearbook 1.* Wheaton, Ill.: Scripture Press, 1973.

———. *Wonder Programs for 4s and 5s. Yearbook 2.* Wheaton, Ill.: Scripture Press, 1973.

Richards, Lawrence O. *The Pastor and Children's Church.* Christian Educ. Monographs, Pastors' Series, No. 2. Glen Ellyn, Ill.: Scripture Press Foundation, 1966.

Sullivan, Jessie P. *Children's Church Handbook.* Grand Rapids: Baker, 1970.

Home Bible Clubs

Coleman, Frank. *The Romance of Winning Children.* Cleveland: Union Gospel, 1967.

Good News Club Manual. Grand Rapids: Child Evangelism, 1972.

Jordan, Bernice C. *Guidebook to Better Teaching.* Philadelphia: Bible Club Movement, 1962.

King, Virginia, and Beliasov, Jann. *Guidebook for Establishing Joy Clubs.* Elyria, Ohio: Fellowship of Baptists for Home Missions, 1965.

Released Time

Shaver, Erwin. *The Weekday Church School: How to Organize and Conduct a Program of Weekday Religious Education on Released Time.* Boston: Pilgrim, 1956.

Weekday Church School: What It Is; How to Run It. Joshua Tree, Calif.: Radiant Life Pubns., n.d.

Sunday School

Guide for Junior Department Superintendent. Wheaton, Ill.: Scripture Press. n.d.

Guide for Nursery Department Superintendent. Wheaton, Ill.: Scripture Press, n.d.

Guide for Pre-Primary Department Superintendent. Wheaton, Ill.: Scripture Press, n.d.

Guide for Primary Department Superintendent. Wheaton, Ill.: Scripture Press, n.d.

Haystead, Wesley. *Ways to Plan and Organize Your Sunday School: Early Childhood, Birth to Five Years.* Glendale, Calif.: Gospel Light, Regal Books, 1971.

LeBar, Lois E. *Children in the Bible School.* Westwood, N.J.: Revell, 1952.

Smith, Charles T. *Ways to Plan and Organize Your Sunday School: Children, Grades 1 to 6.* Glendale, Calif.: Gospel Light, Regal Books, 1971.

Training Hour

Clark, F. E. *Young People's Prayer Meetings.* New York: Funk & Wagnalls, 1887.

Director's Guidebook: Ways for Juniors and Junior and Senior High. Des Plaines, Ill.: Regular Baptist, 1972.

Eager Beavers for Primary Training Time: Leader's Manual. Denver: Baptist Pubns., 1972.

How to Build an Exciting Junior Program in Your Church: Jet Cadets. Chicago: Success With Youth, 1969.

How to Build a Workable Primary Program in Your Church: Whirlybirds. Chicago: Success With Youth, 1969.

Jet Cadet Leader's Manual. Chicago: Success With Youth, 1968.

Junior Action, Youth Programs and Sponsor's Kit. Wheaton, Ill.: Scripture Press, 1971.

Junior Astronauts: Leader's Manual. Denver: Baptist Pubns., 1972.

LeBar, Mary E. *Wonder Programs for 4s and 5s: Yearbooks 1 and 2.* Wheaton, Ill.: Scripture Press, 1972, 1973.

Peterson, Gladys I. *The I.A.H. Club: What It Is; How to Use It.* Elgin, Ill.: David C. Cook, 1970.

———. *The Leader's Guide, I.A.H. Club: Devotional Prayer Fellowship for Juniors.* Elgin, Ill.: David C. Cook, 1970.

Primary Adventure Programs, Leader's Guide. Yearbooks 1, 2, 3. Wheaton, Ill.: Scripture Press, 1971, 1972, 1973.

Sharp, Margaret. *A Church Training Juniors.* Nashville: Convention, 1966.

Swanson, Ruth. *Whirlybird Sponsor's Manual.* Chicago: Success With Youth, 1969.

Tot-Time. Denver: Baptist Pubns., 1972.

Vacation Bible School

Burnett, Sibley. *Better Vacation Bible Schools.* Nashville: Convention, 1957.

Getz, Gene A. *The Vacation Bible School in the Local Church.* Chicago: Moody, 1962.

Richards, Lawrence O. *The Pastor and His Vacation Bible School.* Christian Educ. Monographs, Pastors' Series, No. 4. Glen Ellyn, Ill.: Scripture Press Foundation, 1966.

VBS—New Patterns for Growth: Nineteen Ways to Teach More Bible and Reach More People This Summer. Glendale, Calif.: Gospel Light, 1967.

22

Leadership and Materials

Robert E. Clark

THE GREATEST NEED in the local church today is for dedicated Christian leadership. Why? Because success in each area of the church depends largely on the quality of its leadership.

If leadership is the key need in the local church, why is it that so little is done in preparing leaders to be effective? Why are many staff members in the church placed in positions without adequate preparation? A willingness to serve or an obligation to fulfill a responsibility sometimes appears to be the outstanding reason for involvement. Take Harry Dixon for example:

Harry Dixon is a dedicated layman at First Avenue Church who sincerely desires to serve the Lord. Last month he was asked to superintend the junior department of the Sunday school. Harry reluctantly accepted, because Jim Hatch, the general superintendent, was desperate for someone to take the position. The woman who had been in charge resigned because, she said, juniors are unruly, disrespectful, and uninterested in studying God's Word, and she was tired of trying to keep them quiet.

Harry loves children and appreciates the enthusiasm of vivacious juniors. He is challenged with the potential of these energy-filled, abounding, adventurous and fun-loving youngsters. Harry readily admits that he was not selected on the basis of training or his knowledge of the position.

In fact, Harry felt quite the opposite! He had not even had one hour of formal training or experience in working with juniors. His "exposure" was his experience with his own two junior-age children. At the time he was approached, he was not involved in any other responsibility in the

---

ROBERT E. CLARK, Ed.D., is a faculty member in the Christian Education Department, Moody Bible Institute, Chicago, Illinois.

church, and he thought he should at least be doing something to help out in an emergency.

Jim assured Harry that the position was only temporary and that he would assist him in whatever way he could. Jim was new at his responsibility, and he said that Harry and he could learn together. Little did Harry realize the great challenge in store for him! Perhaps it was best he did not know, for, otherwise, he may never have accepted the position. What an introduction to such an important ministry! With circumstances like these, is it any wonder that there is such a high attrition rate among church leaders? What kind of training or experience was needful to prepare Harry for his new position? What are some of the basics he should know to function efficiently as a department superintendent? How can Harry succeed in his leadership role without becoming discouraged and disillusioned?

Many a worker has found himself in a predicament similar to Harry's. If staff members are to perform effectively, they need careful preparation, training, and guidance. It is essential that a staff member know his qualifications and responsibilities. He needs to view himself in relation to other people and their responsibilities. He must be sensitive to human relations and be a diplomatic problem-solver. He needs to recognize himself as the leader of a team. All the available training and experience he can gain will profit in guiding others toward desired goals. Leadership at any level demands our best, especially in the children's division, where exemplary leadership is of prime importance.

What Leadership Is

Webster indicates that a leader is a person who guides, conducts, or directs, he is a person who holds first place or is fitted to do so.

Dwight Eisenhower is credited with saying, "Leadership is the ability to get a person to do what you want him to do, when you want it done, in a way you want it done, because he wants to do it."[1]

Effective leadership requires a willingness to follow directions and a cooperative spirit on the part of group members. The effective leader spends much of his time motivating his staff to do what needs to be done. One of his greatest challenges is to encourage his workers to *want* to do their tasks. Carefully laid plans based on needs, clear-cut and realistic objectives, and efficient organization to put plans into operation are required for effective leadership. The leader must be in control of the situation so that efforts are directed toward desired goals.

Rationale for Leadership

Leadership is essential for progress. Someone must be responsible for planning, organizing, directing, and making decisions. Some groups operate in a leaderless structure with group members sharing in the responsibility. However, unless individuals are skillfully trained and experienced, they need leadership to motivate them toward goals to be accomplished. The leader must be a guide to show the way.

Many people are eager to study and to serve, but they need guidance in what to do and how to do it. The effective leader will want the group to accept the challenge of dependability, responsibility, and decision making, but it will be his role to give the direction needed. Leadership which focuses on people provides security, encouragement, and progress.

Types of Leadership

Leadership will vary in every situation, depending on one's definition and philosophy of it. Basically, leaders fall into one of the following types:

AUTOCRATIC

Autocratic leadership is dictatorial. The leader makes most of the decisions, policies, and plans. He may be aggressive and even hostile. Initiative and independence from group members may be stifled. One-way communication is preferred.

LAISSEZ-FAIRE

The leader with a laissez-faire policy assumes a passive or permissive role. He refuses to make decisions for the group and may refrain from giving counsel or even stating his opinion. The group may become frustrated and insecure because positive, active leadership is lacking.

BUREAUCRATIC

The problem with bureaucratic leadership is that is requires too much "red tape." Rules and regulations are handed down through lines of authority. The leader refers to what "they" want, without clearly defining who "they" are. The organizational structure is formal with much routine and mechanics involved. Decisions may be postponed indefinitely, and progress is likely to be slow.

DEMOCRATIC

Democratic leadership is invested in the group. In the church democratic leadership must be under God's authority and follow scriptural principles. In this type of leadership, the leader acts as a guide and offers suggestions when they are needed. He provides positive direction and encourages each member of the group to participate. Decisions are made by the group and the vote of the majority rules. Teamwork is evident, and a feeling of interdependence of group members and togetherness is stressed.

In children's work in the local church, each of these kinds of leadership may need to be exerted at times by leaders. Autocratic leadership may be needed when the group lacks ability to make decisions, is not united, or is insecure, or when immediate decisions must be made by the leader. Laissez-faire leadership may be helpful when the leader is eager for the group members to think for themselves and assume the responsibility of decision making. Proper lines of authority, as suggested by bureaucratic leadership, must be followed so that decisions can be made at the proper levels. Various kinds of decisions need to be made by the group, and democratic leadership will encourage team spirit, unity, and loyalty. A combination of different types of leadership provides healthy balance in planning and decision making.

Theories of Leadership

Kraus has suggested three basic theories of leadership: trait leadership, situational leadership, and functional leadership.[2]

TRAIT

Trait leadership consists of certain personal qualities which are essential to successful performance of a leadership task. Traits such as intelligence, courage, enthusiasm, sensitivity, energy, and responsibility may be inborn or learned. The emphasis in this type of leadership is on what sort of person the leader *is*.

SITUATIONAL

The person who becomes a situational leader is chosen because of the requirements for the task at hand. There seems to be a great divergence of leadership behavior in different situations. This type of leadership emphasizes superior competence or knowledge. What the leader *knows* in the situtation is significant.

FUNCTIONAL

The emphasis in functional leadership is more on what a person *does* than on what he is or knows. Leadership is not exclusively invested in an individual leader but is viewed as a function of group structure. The effectiveness of leadership acts is judged in terms of meeting functional group needs.

Perhaps the most logical position to take in the children's division is that a composite of these three types of leadership is most effective. In any situation, varying qualities and abilities are needed. Leaders must know their responsibilities in order to function effectively. Leadership is also a shared process and, at times, will be in the hands of individuals other than the appointed leader. General personality characteristics, proper attitudes toward people and ability to work with them, and the qualities of functional importance are all essential aspects of effective leadership.

Christian Leadership

Christian leadership is a distinctive type of leadership. The basic definition of leadership does not change, but a dimension is added. Christian leadership requires that a leader know Jesus Christ as his personal Saviour. The individual depends not on his own abilities and talents in leadership but on Jesus Christ who can strengthen him for any kind of responsibility (Phil 4:13). Jesus Christ said, "Without me ye can do nothing" (Jn 15:5). It is not by personal might, nor by human power, but by the Spirit of God that spiritual results are attained (Zec 4:6*b*). Leadership is a spiritual gift—one of administration, supervision, or management (Ro 12:8). Christ gives this gift to individuals whom He chooses in His body, the church.

Henrietta Mears, founder of Gospel Light Publications, said that we are all leaders. Either we lead people *to* the Lord or *away* from Him by the way we live. Our personal example is extremely important as we relate to people in leadership. Everyone has the responsibility to lead an exemplary life, but some individuals are given greater responsibility in leading and guiding others so that the work of God may flourish and bring eternal results. Any leader is only an instrument in the hand of God. It is God who does the work and brings the results.

The effective Christian leader possesses several important attributes. Though these may vary, the following general qualifications should be expected of those in leadership roles in children's work.

PHYSICAL HEALTH

Is in good health to attend to his responsibilities
Is alert and active; exercises in order to keep his body in good condition
Is neat and attractive in appearance and dress
Is seeking to get physical rest and to have a proper diet in order to function effectively

MENTAL ABILITY

Is well organized, can plan, and give directions to his staff
Is eager to learn and keeps alert mentally
Is keeping current in his thinking, ideas, and practices

Is resourceful, creative, and flexible
Is able to adjust to the level of children
Has an awareness of characteristics, needs, and potential of children

EMOTIONAL STABILITY

Is able to express his emotions in constructive ways
Is able to empathize with those he is leading and seeks to understand them as people
Is able to find constructive ways to release emotional energy
Is relaxed and secure in his position

SOCIAL ADJUSTMENT

Is friendly, cheerful, sociable, and relates well to others
Is concerned about others and their needs
Practices acceptable social habits and courtesies in his own life
Is a friend of children

SPIRITUAL MATURITY

Is a growing Christian, exemplifying a close spiritual fellowship with Christ
Is obedient to the Word of God in his daily life
Is pursuing defined spiritual goals
Is enthusiastic about the Lord's work and his own position
Is dependable, punctual, and regular in attendance
Is dedicated to the work of God through the local church
Is a good Christian example for others to follow
Is dependent on the Lord Jesus Christ for strength to do his work

No one individual possesses all these qualifications to the same degree. Though some traits may be more difficult to attain than others, the list can serve as a standard by which to encourage leaders to improve in their service for Jesus Christ. The Christian life is a continuous growing process.

Quality leadership in the children's division does not just happen. Because of the importance of child life and the tremendous responsibility we have in ministering to children, we must provide enthusiastic, well-trained, and dedicated leadership. It is essential that workers love children. That is basic. In addition, however, effective organization, administration, and supervision are necessary in guiding children step by step in developing the potential God has given them! We are not babysitting children but assisting them to become all that God has planned for them!

Organization, Administration, and Supervision

Most leaders in the local church find that effective functioning of their work involves them in organizing, administering, and supervising.

ORGANIZATION

Organization refers to the framework, structure, or plan to be followed. It involves the order or arrangement of people or activities and the relationships which exist between people or things. It may be an outline of what the leader plans to do. Organization is what one sees as he draws a diagram or writes an outline. Organization is the first step toward progress in any situation. The individual must visualize how people and things fit together in a total pattern. Organization involves deciding *who* will do *what*. It may include a list of general and specific duties staff members are to perform, or it may include steps involved to get a particular job done. One of the problems in organization is that flowery or ivory-tower plans can be drawn theoretically, but implementation must become a reality in order for the plan to be effective.

Lois LeBar suggests that organization should be *simple*, with every nonessential eliminated; *flexible*; and *democratic*, under God's authority.[3] If too much red tape is required to arrive at a decision or to complete a job, little progress will be evident and staff members may become discouraged and stop trying. It is also important that adults be flexible and be willing to change their plans if necessary in order to meet children's needs.

In effective organization, workers with children must function as a team. Staff members should be consulted for their ideas. Changes should be discussed and decisions made by the group. An atmosphere of acceptance and rapport encourages staff members to feel at ease in expressing themselves. It is important for leaders to keep in mind the following principles of organization:

1. Organization is a means to an end and not an end in itself.
2. Organizational structure must be based on the characteristics and needs of children.
3. Changes in organization should be thought through carefully and carried out systematically.
4. Individuals involved in the situation should be consulted before organizational changes are made.
5. Organizational plans will vary according to the needs and size of the church.

ADMINISTRATION

Administration is organization in action. It means carrying out plans and decisions made in organization by managing or directing in order to accomplish stated goals. Administration is the process of putting people to work in service.

Gulick and Urwick indicate that effective administration includes planning, organizing, staffing, directing, coordinating, reporting, and budgeting.[4] Each of these functions, properly carried out, encourages efficiency and more effective results. The ministry of the church deserves to be carried on by competent and trained personnel who know what they are doing and have a vision to carry the program to desired goals. Adequate directions enable workers to know their responsibilities and how to follow through efficiently. Efforts to coordinate the work are necessary in order to avoid omitting, overlapping, or duplicating responsibilities.

The following are some basic principles in administration:

1. Every worker needs a clear, written description of his position.
2. Lines of authority must be clearly established.
3. Responsibilities must be delegated and accountability should be expected.
4. Significant policies and procedures need to be written out.
5. Every problem must be solved at the level where it ought to be solved.
6. The plans of the workers and of the leaders must be integrated.
7. Lines of communication must be kept open in effective administration.

Many administrative problems are due to the failure to define responsibilities or lines of authority, unwritten plans, poorly stated policies and procedures, resistance to change, negative attitudes, lack of purpose, lack of communication, lack of vision and initiative, or lack of dedicated personnel.

SUPERVISION

Supervision refers to the improvement of the quality of personnel and program. Supervision focuses on people and their effectiveness in carrying the program toward its goals. Staff members can be caught up in the busyness of activity in the church, and in the final result see little progress in the lives of individuals. Quality is more important than quantity. The number of activities or personal involvements does not determine success. What occurs in the lives of people as a result of careful planning, instruction, and follow through is far more significant.

LeBar wisely suggests that the personality of the supervisor is very important in supervision:

> As the supervisor helps workers improve their work, he himself must of course be proficient in both principles and practice. In all his contacts

> he must demonstrate Scriptural methods, be a good administrator, a good communicator, provide recognition for work well done, and help teachers continually evaluate. . . . More difficult than these skills, and more important, are his personal relations—with God, with himself, and with others.[5]

Supervision includes *discovering, enlisting, developing, training, guiding,* and *evaluating* others.

Discovering and enlisting personnel. By the time a child is six, his personality structure is largely formed. In childhood, spiritual concepts are acquired and attitudes taught which may affect the person the remainder of his life. In addition, children are eager to learn and can learn rapidly if sound educational principles and methods are applied. By the time a child starts school, he may have learned as much as he will learn the rest of his life.

This means that children's workers should be carefully and prayerfully enlisted. Not everyone can nor should teach children.

Enlisting men to work with children cannot be overemphasized. Boys, early in their educational experiences, need to identify with men. Many boys in our society come from fatherless or broken homes and need to relate to the male image. Men can understand and communicate with children better than women in some situations, especially as children grow older. Many times, potential discipline problems can be solved through responsible men. Even in the cradle roll department, men can exemplify a father image and begin to build positive attitudes that church is for men and boys as well as women and girls.

What staff members are needed in the children's division of the church? The following list shows the wide variety of personnel, though not every church will need all these workers.

- Department superintendents for Sunday school and vacation Bible school
- Teachers for Sunday school
- Teachers for Sunday school, vacation Bible school, and weekday classes
- Leaders for children's churches
- Helpers and assistants
- Pianists
- Training hour leaders (sponsors)
- Club workers for weekday clubs
- Recreational leaders
- Visitation workers
- Camp counselors and teachers
- Committee members
- Prayer partners
- Secretaries

How can a church discover workers who can serve effectively with children? These are some suggestions:

1. Pray earnestly for the Lord's guidance in discovering workers (Mt 9:38). So often we try everything but prayer and consequently see few results.

2. Use talent surveys or interest finders.
3. Interview individuals to discover their gifts, abilities, and interests.
4. Check membership applications for areas of interest, abilities, past training, and experience.
5. Be a good listener; be on the lookout for key ideas or clues in talent discoveries.
6. Set up a card file on all the people in the church who are potentials for service. Each card could include personal data, qualifications, training, experience, types of service for which the individual is best suited, age-group interests, and records of interviews or contacts.
7. Keep a current list of personnel needs. The children's division of the board of Christian education or other responsible committee can compile a list of persons needed, the qualifications and responsibilities required, and the date the position is to be filled.
8. Encourage the pastor to challenge individuals for service through his sermons.
9. Ask other staff members for names of potential workers.

As workers are discovered, they need to be enlisted for specific ministries.

Here are some basic principles to consider in enlisting people:

1. Have a personnel committee who will contact and follow up prospective workers.
2. Keep the church informed as to personnel needs through bulletins, newsletters, sermons, and personal contact.
3. Make contacts in a businesslike manner. Do not make the person feel he is a last resort or the only one left. Stress also the importance of the position.
4. Stress spiritual service rather than a job to be filled, a duty to perform, or an obligation to fulfill.
5. Explain carefully the position and provide materials necessary for efficient operation.
6. After the person has been interviewed, write him a letter of invitation.
7. Conduct impressive installation services, stressing the importance of spiritual service.
8. Have a standard for each enlisted leader to sign as he joins the staff. Be sure to explain the standard as a goal. Emphasize important responsibilities, such as thorough preparation and attendance at workers' conferences.
9. Set a good example in leadership that is worth emulating.
10. Have an "Opportunities for Service" night in the church. Give a brief

survey of positions available, qualifications, types of training needed, and the contribution the positions make to the total program.

11. After workers take positions, encourage them, answer their questions, and seek to assist in whatever way you can.
12. Encourage workers to attend conferences, leadership seminars, and other in-service activities for personal and professional growth.

The strength of any educational enterprise lies in the kind of leadership enlisted. One of the greatest challenges of the church is to enlist staff members who are dedicated, willing to learn, and eager to grow. A careful and well-planned program of enlistment will pay great dividends in building a quality staff.

Training personnel. As individuals are discovered and enlisted, they need to be trained.[6] Preservice and in-service programs will help meet the varied needs of personnel. Training can be provided in many different forms. The following outlines suggest kinds of training that can be made available to children's workers in most churches.

Training Class

What it is: A class conducted on a regular basis in which various topics are discussed, information is shared, and individuals are taught how to make application to specific situations

For whom: All workers in the church (depending on the content of the course)

When: During Sunday school, training hour, a weekday, or week night

Study:

Bible survey	Bible-related courses	Psychology
Bible analysis	Doctrine	Christian living
Christian education	Missions	Leadership development
Music	Apologetics	

Procedure:

Plan a continuous, systematic program based on needs of people.

Consider both prospective and experienced workers in planning courses to be offered.

Offer the program at the most convenient time for the majority of people.

Begin with a limited program and expand as interests and needs emerge.

Encourage (or require) teachers to enroll in a minimum number of classes each year.

Grant a leave of absence from teaching and other responsibilities for three months or longer so that workers can take refresher courses.

Provide qualified teachers who can give quality instruction related to practical situations.
Set attainable standards for courses.

Workers' Seminar

What it is: Regularly scheduled meetings to instruct and inspire, and to help workers find practical solutions to problems they encounter in their work
For whom: Workers of a particular agency, department, or group in the church
When: Depends on type of meeting and people involved; should be scheduled regularly at the same time each month or quarter
Topics: Topics chosen according to the needs and interests of the group
How to lead it:
Schedule them at times most of the workers can be present.
Keep business to a minimum.
Discuss topics of interest to workers.
Vary the methods used.
Plan the meetings well and keep within time limits.
Plan the topics six months or a year in advance.
Expect workers to be present at meetings.
Involve workers in presentation of topics.
Carry out decisions made by workers.

Apprenticeship

What it is: On-the-job training in which an inexperienced worker works closely with an experienced leader
For whom: For the inexperienced and prospective worker who needs to learn a particular task
When: Any time; any agency or department in the church; any position
Types: Assistant teachers, team teachers, helpers, leaders
How to lead it:
Use personnel who themselves are adequately prepared to guide others in quality experiences.
Encourage those who supervise others to try new ideas and to become resource people.
Provide brief human relations courses for supervisors.
Encourage supervisors to develop "team relationships" rather than being "snoopervisors."
Help the in-training worker to develop the skill of evaluating his own work.

Have periodic conferences in which the supervisor and his trainee can evaluate progress and be able to set new goals and plans for improvement.

Encourage the apprentice to become increasingly less dependent on the supervisor until he can function without the help of the supervisor.

Take a positive attitude in helping others develop; try to see the apprentice's potential.

Convention

What it is: A planned program of general meetings and workshops in which workers from several local churches meet for inspiration, instruction, and fellowship

For whom: Active and prospective workers of a particular denomination or association or group of churches

When: Usually during fall or spring; may range from one to several days; may be a Sunday school convention or a Christian education convention

How to use it:

Plan to take workers to conventions at least once a year.

Help workers select workshops that will be most beneficial to them.

Encourage workers to visit displays, to get acquainted with workshop leaders, and to ask questions.

Encourage workers to take notes on workshops they attend and to share ideas with others as they return home.

Arrange a time for workers to share ideas with those who could not attend the convention.

Follow up suggestions with practical implementation in the church.

Conference

What it is: Key Christian education leaders invited to a local church or churches to encourage, stimulate, instruct, and challenge the workers

For whom: Workers and prospective workers in the local church

When: Usually an all day or weekend conference; fall and spring usually the best times of the year

Types: Program geared either to a specific agency, such as the Sunday school, or to the total church program

How to lead it:

Contact key speakers and leaders who can minister to the specific needs of workers.

Be sure to confirm dates and schedules with leaders in advance.

Plan general sessions and workshops.

Build enthusiasm for the conference through prayer, long-range planning and varied publicity.

Plan programs which will meet needs of workers and give solutions to some of the problems which they are trying to solve.
Expect workers to attend as many of the sessions as possible.
Schedule sessions when most of the workers can attend.
Do not plan too full a schedule.
Follow up suggestions for improvement which leaders have presented.

Church Library

What it is: A resource center in the church, which contains a variety of resource materials
For whom: All workers in the church
When: Open at times convenient for most workers

How to use it:
Appoint a library committee for supervising the library.
Choose a librarian who has vision and potential to develop the library.
Discover ways to make the library functional.
Locate the library in a central area easily accessible from the sanctuary.
Provide suitable equipment in the library so that materials can be stored orderly and neatly.
Organize all materials efficiently in the library so that they can be located readily and checked out properly.
Have the library open at times convenient for most of the workers.
Continue to add materials to meet contemporary needs.
Publicize and enthusiastically promote the library.

Guiding personnel. Though most lay workers need and appreciate guidance, they may seldom let this be known. Some reasons for this are that they may not be aware of what they need, they may feel stupid asking for help, or they may desire to leave things as they are because of a lack of time or concern. The supervisor must be alert to determine the real needs of the individual and to begin where he is.

One profitable way to guide workers is through a combination conference-observation plan, in which the supervisor observes the teacher or leader "in action" and then confers with him about the session observed. Before the observation, the supervisor should discuss with the teacher the purpose of the observation, agree on a definite date and time for the observation, and briefly talk over what the teacher plans to do. He should then discuss any matters that will help the teacher become more at ease during the observation. Then have prayer together and commit the session to the Lord for His blessing.

During the observation of the class or group, the supervisor should follow these steps:

Arrive *before* the session begins.
Sit where the teacher feels most comfortable.
Ask the teacher to introduce him as a visitor.
Take part in the session as the teacher suggests.
Stay for the entire session if possible.
Take notes inconspicuously or wait until later to record observations.

Immediately after the session, he should thank the teacher for the privilege of observing. Mentioning some positive things noted about the session will help put the teacher at ease. Then the supervisor should schedule a conference to discuss the session in more detail. At this conference, he should do the following:

Establish rapport through a comfortable atmosphere and informal greetings.
Have prayer together and seek the Lord's direction in the discussion.
Ask the teacher to express himself about the situation.
Commend him for evident strengths.
Discuss areas which may need improvement, without dwelling on the insignificant.
Discuss practical ways the problems or weaknesses can be overcome.
Suggest some possible resources the teacher can use for follow-up.
Leave the situation in a positive manner, mentioning that he is available for help.
Follow up with future opportunities to encourage growth and enrichment.

The same procedure can be used with other staff members as well as teachers. The principles can be adapted to the type of situation. In successful counseling, we need to help staff members become more independent in solving their own problems.

Evaluating personnel. An important aspect of supervision is regular and systematic evaluation of the staff. The purpose of evaluation is to discover and analyze the strengths and needs for improvement. Staff members can evaluate themselves or they can be evaluated by their supervisors. Self-evaluation may be most effective when the staff members objectively evaluate their own work and look for ways of improvement.

Encourage workers to discover specific ways to improve and follow through with implementing their discoveries. Merely listing needs for improvement can discourage workers, since human weaknesses tend to be more glaring than strengths. Positive attitudes must exist in evaluation, with the desire to see progress and the determination to accomplish anticipated goals.

The following steps in evaluation and follow up are positive and constructive:

List strengths and needs for improvement.
Determine specific ways to strengthen each need discovered.
Implement suggested ideas.
Evaluate progress and, if necessary, make new recommendations.

Here are questions that can be used in evaluating a leader in any area of church education.

Is he organized in his work?
Is he prepared?
Does he have clearly defined goals?
Is he enthusiastic about his work?
Does he give clear directions and assignments?
Does he relate well to those under him?
Does he welcome suggestions from the group?
Does he provide training for his workers?
Does he set a good example for others to follow?

Workers may ask the following questions in evaluating themselves:

Am I prepared for my task?
Do I have a clear concept of my responsibilities?
Am I organized in my work?
Do I have vision and enthusiasm for my work?
Do I have initiative?
Am I dependable and faithful in my work?
Am I a good listener?
Do I take advantage of in-service opportunities?
Do I get along well with others?
Am I developing my creativity?
Am I growing as a whole person?
Am I genuinely interested in each child in my class or group?
Am I growing in my relationship with the Lord?

General Responsibilities of Personnel

The position of the worker determines his specific responsibilities. However, in any agency or activity in the children's division, all staff members have some of the following general responsibilities:

Be regular in attendance and on time for presession activities.
Be well prepared and flexible to change plans if necessary.

Take care of routine matters efficiently.
Supervise and have control of their own area of responsibility.
Enroll in training opportunities provided by the church and other sources.
Follow up present and absent pupils.
Attend all workers' conferences and other meetings scheduled for workers.
Know how to lead pupils to Christ and guide them in Christian growth.
Provide social activities.
Participate actively in the program whether it is the opening worship, lesson, presession, or other activity.
Be alert for new ideas, be creative, and use variety.
Use teaching tools provided.
Correlate activities with other workers, agencies, and departments.

Specific Responsibilities of Personnel

Every agency may not utilize all the positions listed below, but the specific responsibilities listed can serve as a brief description of each position.

LEADER (superintendent, sponsor, director of a particular agency)

Is responsible for activities of the department or agency
Is responsible for recruiting personnel with approval from the children's division committee or board of Christian education
Does long-range planning with his staff
Delegates responsibility to each worker
Prepares each activity for which he is responsible
Is responsible for arrangement and provision of rooms and equipment
Sees that materials and supplies are ordered and available when needed
Gives guidance, assists in problem solving, and counsels
Provides training and supervision of workers
Conducts conferences with his workers
Evaluates the situation and the workers periodically

TEACHER

Is responsible for the group assigned him and prays regularly for his pupils
Is well prepared in his responsibilities
Acquaints himself with his pupils through personal contact, home visitation, and social activities
Keeps his room and equipment in good order and reports needed repairs

Attends meetings for which he is responsible and reports on progress made

ASSOCIATE, ASSISTANT, OR HELPER

Assists in specific responsibilities assigned by the leader
Prepares for specific responsibilities assigned
Is cooperative and helpful in every way possible

PIANIST

Is responsible to be proficient in the music used in the agency or department
Spends time in practice to improve his skill
Finds music selected by the leader and builds a loose-leaf book of selections
Arrives early and sees that everything is in readiness

SECRETARY

Becomes acquainted with types of records and procedures used
Is responsible for maintaining the records in his area of responsibility
Keeps cupboards clean and neat
Orders supplies for the agency or department
Helps in whatever ways he can to make the work of the department more pleasant

Every staff member needs a written job description. The job description should include a definition of the position, its qualifications, his specific responsibilities, and how the position relates to other parts of the children's division and total church program. Written job descriptions are effective only as they are implemented.

To keep job descriptions current, ask staff members to evaluate their position in view of their job descriptions and to submit an evaluation in writing. Then compare those suggestions from the staff member with the job description, discuss the job description with him, and determine what revisions need to be made.

Team Teaching

A concept currently gaining momentum in Christian education is team teaching. Many children are exposed to team teaching in elementary school. Because of the interest in and apparent success of team teaching, church leaders will profit from knowing how team teaching functions. Not every church should have team teaching. The fact that this approach to teaching is popular in public education is not sufficient reason for introducing it in the church. However, when many pupils experience team teaching during the week, they may become bored by the traditional patterns of education in the church.

WHAT TEAM TEACHING IS

Several variations of team teaching are currently practiced.

1. *The master-associate-helper arrangement.* A lead teacher is usually a more experienced person who is responsible for the leadership of the group. The associates and helpers work with the supervisor in a team effort. Responsibility is shared under the guidance of the lead teacher. This plan is especially helpful in apprenticeship programs to train inexperienced teachers.

2. *Coteaching.* The time is divided between two teachers with equal responsibility. Each teacher conducts his own activities and teaches his specialty in the time allotted.

3. *Equal sharing.* This type is a daring enterprise in which two or more teachers equally plan, conduct, and evaluate a specific learning situation. A coordinator is usually designated to give directions to the group and to correlate activities. The teachers volunteer or are assigned activities according to their abilities and interests. A team spirit is developed in which each teacher contributes to the whole.

Adaptations or combinations may be made in the these three types, but the kind and quality of staff members available will determine the program best suited for a local setting.

ADVANTAGES AND LIMITATIONS OF TEAM TEACHING

Advantages	*Limitations*
Brings life and vitality to teaching and learning	May lack clear and well-defined goals
Provides variety in the use of methods and materials	May not have roles and responsibilities clearly established
Allows for more flexible scheduling	May cause some team members to be too dependent on others
Utilizes teaching strengths and specialties	May be difficult to find a time to meet or allow sufficient time for preparation
Builds enthusiasm and morale	May have unresolved conflicts in personalities and teaching philosophies
Provides variety in teacher personalities	May have inadequate facilities and equipment to do the job well
Encourages effective teamwork	May not have sufficient leadership to function effectively
Encourages more pupil involvement	
Allows for large groups, small groups, and independent study	
Is excellent training for new teachers	

Teaching teams can capitalize on their strengths and continue to improve apparent weaknesses. For those weaknesses which are outstanding, specific and practical ways of overcoming the need should be suggested and implemented by the team members. Each of the above limitations *can* become strengths if positive steps are taken to improve the situation.

SUGGESTIONS FOR EFFECTIVE TEAM TEACHING

Careful, long-range planning and detailed preparation are essential in successful team teaching. A basic philosophy of team teaching must be developed by those involved in the process. A teaching team cannot work effectively if there is lack of definition, rationale, or knowledge of how the team is to function.

Here are some steps the leader may follow, which may create a positive climate and aid in preparing for this teamed instructional experience.

1. Determine what kind of team teaching is to be done.
2. Decide who will be involved: coordinator, teachers, assistants, resource people.
3. Organize several training sessions (as many as are needed to be thoroughly prepared) which are conveniently arranged in time and length. Cover the following aspects of team teaching:
   - Develop a clear understanding of what is to be done.
   - Identify and discuss the roles and responsibilities of each team member and how each one relates to the others on the team.
   - Select and study the curriculum materials to be used.
   - Determine the characteristics and needs of pupils to be taught.
   - Write out aims to be accomplished based on pupil needs and content.
   - Develop a functional schedule which includes activities, methods, and materials, time to be allotted for each activity, and individuals responsible. The same kind of planning needs to be done for each session.
   - Work out detailed plans for each activity. (This may be done on an individual basis rather than in group work.)
   - Evaluate progress; check all details to be sure everyone is prepared.
   - Carry out plans in actual teaching.
4. Meet weekly as a team to evaluate the session, to plan for the coming session, and to plan long range goals.
5. Evaluate the complete process periodically to determine whether goals are being accomplished and are meeting emerging needs.

Team teaching can be exciting if team members meet together to plan, if someone is responsible to coordinate the process and encourage progress, if resources are available, and if pupil needs are being met through the experience.

Rooms and Equipment

Do the facilities in which children meet affect their learning? Rooms may not be as important as people who teach or what is being taught, but if maximum learning is to be attained, the environment is one of the most important factors to consider.

Children are sensitive to atmosphere, color, and beauty. Much of their learning is through the five senses, and attitudes are developed through what is "caught" as well as what is taught. The personalities of children are easily molded, pliable, and affected by their environment. They respond to a reverent, quiet atmosphere and are eager for happy learning experiences in the church.

Children need a comfortable, secure atmosphere which is very clean and attractive. A good rule to keep in mind is that the younger the child, the more space he needs. First floor arrangements are best for younger children, but basement rooms can be decorated with delightful color schemes and furnished with suitable equipment to provide the kind of atmosphere needed. Churches must work with what they have; but with little cost, ingenuity, soap and water, and a willingness to work, rooms can be transformed into beautiful and acceptable environments for children.

Facilities and furnishings must be planned for children, not for the adults who work with children. Heim has suggested five standards for church buildings which can be applied to children's rooms.[7]

BEAUTY

Order, symmetry, strength, grace, and color should impart their ministry to each pupil's spiritual growth.

UTILITY

Facilities should be useful and functional. The purpose of the room determines how it should be planned.

COMFORT

Proper heating, cooling, lighting, ventilation, acoustics, safety—all are important for children. Sunday school should be a temple, a schoolroom, and an inviting haven.

ECONOMY

True economy—accomplishing the maximum service with minimum space—comes from careful planning. Christian stewardship requires making every dollar buy the most in permanent values while avoiding elaborateness.

ADAPTABILITY

A building or room which can be enlarged or modified would be the ideal.

The following suggestions are given to help insure more productive use of facilities and furnishings.

1. Use the same facilities for various activities of each department of the church.
2. Be aware of age-group characteristics and needs when planning buildings and purchasing equipment.
3. Buy durable equipment that will stand up with normal wear and tear.
4. Buy adjustable folding tables to serve multiple purposes.
5. Provide cupboard and closet space for each department. Encourage workers to keep cupboards and closets in good order.
6. Redecorate periodically to keep the appearance of the building fresh and clean. Departments can do redecorating with approval from the supervisory board or committee in charge of facilities and furnishings.
7. Keep an accurate and current inventory of the equipment and supplies.
8. Remove unnecessary items from the premises. Store items which are used only periodically to keep the building neat, attractive, and free from fire hazards.
9. Replace worn-out equipment and repair equipment which is broken or damaged.
10. Install good lighting, heating, and ventilation systems.
11. Set up a fire alarm plan in the building so that people know how to evacuate in case of fire.
12. Evaluate the use of the total facilities of the church periodically to determine if the best use of building space is being made. Discourage departments from claiming "lifetime leases" on any particular room or furnishing in the church. Educate people that departments, rooms, and facilities may have to be changed to make better use of the available space.

In each department of the children's division, the following guidelines will prove helpful to those responsible for facilities and furnishings.

CRADLE ROLL

The cradle roll department needs facilities at the church for parents who bring their children to be cared for during Sunday school, church services, and other special activities. The room should be located on the first floor near the sanctuary and the parents' classroom(s). The facilities should be spacious and attractively decorated and carpeted. They must be very clean and neat, with equipment suitable for meeting needs of very young children. It is best to have separate rooms for crib babies and for toddlers and walkers.

Desirable furnishings include a built-in sink, toilet facilities, cupboards for storage, secretary's desk, platform rockers, adult-size chairs, playpen, cribs, baby-size chairs and tables, refrigerator, washable and unbreakable toys, toy box, bottle warmer, basket for babies' belongings, and wastebasket. Also, clean sheets, towels, diapers, and first-aid supplies are necessary. A dutch-door and built-in diaper changing table is also desirable. Cradle roll staff workers should be the only personnel allowed in the cradle roll facilities for sanitary and safety reasons.

TWOS AND THREES

The room for twos and threes needs to be located on the first floor (preferably in the southeast corner of the building) near the parents. It should be accessible by an outside entrance with a door at the rear of the room. The room should be large with space for fifteen to twenty pupils. The ideal space per child is twenty-five to thirty square feet. Small classrooms should be eliminated to provide a more flexible room arrangement and to make better use of the space. The walls should be soundproof and decorated with bright, cheerful, and warm colors with light woodwork. Low windows with clear glass, equal to one-fourth of the wall space and on the children's eye level, are desirable. Attractive drapes and carpets aid in absorbing sound in the room and provide a warm, homelike atmosphere. Chairs should be eight to ten inches in height and made of solid oak or fiber glass. Tables may be rectangular or round with adjustable legs and ten inches higher than the seat of the chairs. Coat racks and toilet facilities should be on the level of the children. Story rugs and individual resting mats, secretary's desk, a department Bible, offering receptacles, record players, toy center, interest centers, supply cupboards, and closets are some of the essential items of equipment.

FOURS AND FIVES

The items mentioned for twos and threes should also be provided for fours and fives. However, the height of chair seats should be ten to twelve inches from the floor. The room should be large enough to provide space for twenty to twenty-five pupils. A chalkboard, bulletin and flannelboard, a piano, portable library with round book table, visual files with flat pictures, and permanent pictures hung at the children's eye level are also needed to furnish the room.[8]

PRIMARY

Primary children can occupy a basement, first, or second floor room, with a door in the rear. Soundproofing should be included in order to reduce noise. At least fifteen to twenty square feet of space are needed for each child. The equipment should be primary size, with the chair seats twelve to fourteen inches in height and the tables ten inches higher than the chairs. A large, flexible room is necessary with movable partitions so that it can be used for multiple purposes. The maximum number of children for one room is forty in the department plan and twenty-five in the closely graded set up (where there is a separate room for each grade). A toy center is not essential, but objects, curios, and the American and Christian flags should be part of the equipment.

JUNIOR

The junior department room should have space for a maximum of fifty pupils in the department plan and twenty-five pupils per grade in the closely graded plan. Facilities and equipment mentioned in the previous paragraphs for younger age levels are needed in the junior department and geared to the junior level. Chair seat height should be fourteen to sixteen inches. Hymnbooks are appropriate for this department. Since juniors love adventure and the outdoors, and have exuberant energy, they need plenty of playground space for play activities and release of excess energy.

Interest Centers

Each department of the children's division should have interest centers for the children. These interest centers may be located in a corner of the room or on a table. Interest centers arouse curiosity in objects, acquaint children with new ideas or materials, or provide activities which children enjoy doing or in which they have special interest. A display of sea shells, missionary curios, dioramas, book tables, grocery store, games to play, pretend activity, or a table depicting the theme of a learning unit, a worship service, or season of the year are some suggestions for interest centers. Kinds of interest centers will vary according to the interests and needs of the group.

Since children depend on the five senses for much of their learning, they need to be able to touch and handle objects. Unbreakable and durable materials should be used, especially with younger ages. Pictures can be sprayed with clear plastic so that the children can handle, touch, and feel them without damaging them. Cloth objects and three-dimensional material with varied kinds of surfaces can be used in displays. Personal involvement in activities will provide opportunities for self-discovery, securing attention, creating interest, emotional release, self-expression, and manipulation of objects.

Interest centers can be used during presession, group participation, show-and-tell, teaching of new and unfamiliar ideas, free play, and guided activities. They can also be used as springboards for informal discussion with younger children and in lesson approaches and applications. Pupils can help in constructing interest centers, depending on the age and type. Perhaps the greatest asset to effective use of interest centers is the creativity and ingenuity of the teaching staff!

Curriculum in the Children's Division

Planning the curriculum is one of the most important responsibilities of the workers in the children's departments. Traditionally, curriculum has been thought of as a course of study, a prescribed program to follow, or a lesson to be taught. The teacher or department superintendent studied his quarterly and followed it meticulously. Many teachers became frustrated because they could not do everything the lesson plan suggested. Some resorted to the reading of the manual because they felt they could not tell it as well as the writer said it. Others spent so little time in preparation that they could not present the ideas without reading them. Curriculum materials have often become crutches or hindrances because of misuse.

In contemporary usage, curriculum has become broader in meaning. In public education, Doll indicates the trend toward a more inclusive definition: "The commonly accepted definition of the curriculum has changed from content of courses of study and list of subjects to all the experiences which are offered to learners under the auspices or direction of the school."[9]

Paul Vieth has suggested, "in the broadest sense of the term that all life is the curriculum. There is no experience which does not have an influence on what people become."[10] However, curriculum can be so broad in its meaning that it becomes vague and difficult to define. Boundaries must be determined in order for the workers to use the term intelligently and develop a functional curriculum.

Curriculum for the children's division may be defined as the total program for children, including integration of content (subject matter) and experiences utilized by Christian leadership, in accord with biblical principles in the written Word and centered in Jesus Christ, the living Word, under the guidance of the Holy Spirit.

The curriculum in the Christian education of children should accomplish three basic purposes: (1) lead children to Jesus Christ as Saviour from sin; (2) guide children in continued growth toward Christlikeness; (3) equip children for effective service in the will of God.

In evangelical Christian education, we have a body of content or subject matter which we believe is of utmost importance to teach our children. The Bible is our textbook and main source for what we teach. Other relevant subject matter may be taught, or secondary sources may be used, but the Bible is the foundation and the final authority. We want our children to know facts and principles from the Word of God and to have a thorough understanding of what the Bible teaches. We also want our children to apply the Bible to their lives and to obey it. Experience is an essential part of growth and is provided through activities in the classroom and carry-over outside the classroom. It is our responsibility to arrange significant experiences for the children so that the Bible can be meaningful in everyday life and applied to encourage change in behavior.

Those who are in places of responsibility in the children's division (superintendents, teachers, secretaries, assistants, pianists) have tremendous responsibility in leading children to the Saviour and in guiding them in continued growth after they accept Christ. Only dedicated Christian leaders can provide the example necessary to guide children in the church, for God has chosen human vessels to communicate His message of a living Saviour and Guide for life.

The curriculum for children must be Bible based and Christ centered. In laying the foundation, we must be careful that what we teach is accurate and true to the Scriptures and glorifying to Jesus Christ. We must be enabled and led by the Holy Spirit to do our work in His strength and wisdom. Competent, well-trained leaders who are yielded to the Holy Spirit are essential in producing life-changing curriculum.

To accomplish what God has intended, our purposes must be clear. Every child needs Jesus Christ as his personal Saviour from sin. Those who accept Him as Saviour need to become more like Him in daily living and to grow up in Him (Eph 4:15). Children who are living for Christ need to be challenged to equip themselves to do what God wants in their everyday experiences. A child does not have to wait until he is grown up to serve Jesus Christ effectively.

Curriculum includes more than lesson materials. It involves the total ministry with children in the church. It includes what, when, where, and how subject matter is to be taught. Curriculum is determined by the characteristics, needs, interests, capacities, backgrounds, and goals of the learners. Objectives (aims, purposes, goals) must be determined by needs so that we know what we want to accomplish. The schedule to follow, staff members who teach or have other responsibilities, grouping of students, facilities and furnishings, methods (ways of doing) and materials (tools in doing), and the administration and supervision of the program, are all parts of the curriculum of Christian education for children.

The need for correlation of curriculum from one agency or department to another is a perennial problem in the church. Sunday school teachers should be concerned not only with what *they* are teaching but also with what is being taught their pupils in church time, club work, and vacation Bible school. It would be well for leaders to meet together and share what they are using in order to avoid duplication and omissions. A curriculum chart indicating what is being studied in each agency and department of the church may be helpful in beginning to correlate curriculum.

Long-range planning in curriculum is also essential. Those working with children need to be concerned about articulation, that is, building progressively from one level to another. As children progress through the foundation years, Bible content and theological concepts need to be taught when they are most meaningful. As a child grows in experience, his knowledge needs to be expanded and enriched, and he should begin to find answers to his life problems in the Word of God. He must begin to obey the truth as well as know it.

Units of Learning

Some kind of organization is necessary in order to accomplish desired objectives in curriculum. A unit of learning is one way to organize and integrate content and experience to bring about changes in behavior. A unit may be defined as a series of two or more lessons which are related to the same topic, and which integrate content and experience to bring about a change in behavior. In effective unit planning, both subject matter and experience are essential. Emphasis is given to three kinds of objectives—knowing, feeling, and doing—with the ultimate goal being a change of behavior.

A unit of learning has many advantages. It encourages long-range planning, emphasizes a central theme or focal problem, focuses on the learner and his needs, allows time for accomplishment of objectives and meeting of needs, provides variety in use of methods and materials, and gives opportunities for review and application. A unit provides opportunity for better introduction to a new study and culmination at the conclusion of a study with possible carry-over into life. LeBar suggests four steps in effective unit planning: the teacher's preplanning, planning with the pupils, finding and sharing the answers, and planning a culminating activity to consummate the unit.[11]

Curriculum materials play a vital role in curriculum planning because they provide ideas that can stimulate lay workers' thinking and doing and can assist in organizing units for teaching and learning. Selection of materials is, therefore, very important. A wide variety of materials is available currently. The frustration comes in selecting the *best* materials for a particular local church. No publisher can produce exactly what every church needs, since publishers serve such a wide constituency. Some churches have ventured to write their own curriculum materials, but the task is tremendous, and unless one has much training in writing and editing and much time and resources, the process can be very discouraging. Adapting already published materials is a more feasible plan for most churches.

Several types of curriculum materials are published: closely graded—a separate lesson for each age or grade; group (or departmentally) graded—the same lesson for two or more ages or grades; uniform—a lesson based on the same Scripture for all departments; unified—all departments study the same basic theme; elective—the department or group chooses what it wants to study. Some of these types may be combined in materials from the same publisher. Most agencies beyond the Sunday school use some type of group-graded materials. It is important for a church to know the type of curriculum materials a publisher produces, since correlation and articulation are important factors in curriculum development.

In selecting materials, it is necessary to develop criteria for evaluating what is best for a local situation. Naturally, the size of the church and department or agency; the staff members' background, experience, and training; the type of community in which the church is located; the philosophy of the church in selecting and using materials; and financial resources will affect curriculum selection. Doll has developed a list of twenty questions which teachers should ask themselves as they decide which materials to use.[12] These questions must be interpreted in view of the age, grade or department to be taught.

Criteria for Evaluating Curriculum Materials

THEOLOGICAL CONSIDERATIONS

1. Are the materials based on the Scriptures as the major instructional source for Christian education?
2. Do they provide a faithful record of and a friendly commentary on biblical events and teachings, rather than an interpretation of events and teachings that is actually or potentially negative?
3. Do the materials speak with assurance of God's power and goodness

in performing miracles, including the great miracles of Christ's virgin birth and His resurrection?

4. Do they uphold the Bible's validity in helping people solve problems today?
5. Do they emphasize the stable, dependable values that the Scriptures teach?
6. Do the materials encourage the learner to commit himself to Jesus Christ as his personal Saviour?
7. Do they make it clear that the learner's right relationship with God is a necessary precondition to his having right relationships with his fellowmen?
8. Do they help those learners who have given themselves to Christ to increase their faith and trust in Him?

SUBSTANCE AND ORGANIZATION

9. Do the materials state understandable and acceptable objectives?
10. Do they contain specific data, main ideas, and key concepts in balanced proportion and arrangement?
11. Do they achieve a focus on main ideas and key concepts to which all other content clearly contributes?
12. Are the materials appropriate to learners' abilities, needs and interests?
13. Do they cause learners to repeat important experiences and review important ideas?
14. Do the materials increase in difficulty throughout the span of years they cover?

FEATURES HELPFUL IN LEARNING

15. Do the materials provide a variety of ways to stimulate learning?
16. Do they contain and suggest supplementary aids to learning?
17. Do they make thrifty use of the time available for learning?

FEATURES HELPFUL IN TEACHING

18. Are inexperienced teachers able to use the materials without difficulty or confusion?
19. Are teachers' guides or teachers' editions of the materials genuinely helpful, suggesting procedures that make teaching easier and more effective?
20. Do they contain suggestions for teacher planning and growth and for ways of evaluating teaching and learning?

After selecting curriculum materials, the work has just begun. The staff members need to become thoroughly familiar with the layout, content, aims, and helps provided and suggested, and to adapt the ideas to their own situation. Teachers must remember they are teaching pupils, not lessons. They need to ask themselves, "What can we do to derive maximum benefit from these materials in making them relevant to our situation and to bring about change in the behavior of our pupils?" Several questions may be asked by children's workers as they seek to adapt materials:

What changes, if any, must be made in doctrinal emphases in order to be able to use the materials according to our doctrinal position?
What adaptations are necessary to use the materials in the community setting?
What are the current practices of the church in the use of curriculum?
What are the present needs of our pupils?
What objectives do we need to accomplish in our church?
How can we adapt the materials to meet the needs of the less advanced and more advanced pupils?
What facilities do we need to change in order to derive maximum benefit from the materials?
What additional resources should we purchase?
What, if any, changes in our schedule are necessary in order to use the materials most effectively?
What kind of training do our leaders or teachers need?
Should we meet with the leaders and teachers in order to plan our use of the materials?
What suggestions made in the teachers' or leaders' manuals must we implement?
Which visuals and other aids suggested by the publisher should we use?
How can we effectively use pupils' manuals and activities suggested?
How can we correlate the activities suggested in the materials with the activities of other agencies?

Records

Enrollment, attendance, visitation, follow-up, personnel, and progress reports are some of the kinds of records a church may find helpful. Record systems are available for purchase from several of the Christian education publishers listed at the end of this chapter.

Keeping an accurate record of attendance for regular pupils, visitors, and staff members will enable workers to know attendance trends and to know what follow-up contacts need to be made. The system should be simple and require little time. Also, follow-up records for absentees and regular visitation on all regular attenders and visitors will help systematize the follow-up procedures. Prospect and survey records will enable visitation workers to make new contacts for the church. A permanent enrollment file, with basic information about each individual who attends the church, is of tremendous help to new workers. Records on the personnel working in the children's division may be a part of the records developed by the board of Christian education or the children's division committee.

Some tips to follow in developing and using a record system are as follows.

1. Provide sufficient secretarial help.
2. Have a convenient place for the secretarial staff to work.
3. Provide storage for records in a file or cupboard.
4. Have sufficient forms for maintaining records.
5. Keep the record system simple in procedures and policies.
6. Maintain the records neatly and efficiently according to approved procedures.
7. Keep records current and well organized in the filing system.
8. Use information from records in various ways.
9. Evaluate the record system often to see how it may be improved.

Finances

The agencies and departments in the children's division, as part of the total program of the church, merit adequate financing to enable them to accomplish their goals.

Usually it is best to finance the children's work through the Christian education budget. The budget is planned by the board of Christian education in conjunction with the agencies and departments involved. Each year at the appropriate time, the board of Christian education asks each agency and department to submit a budget for approval for the next year. All items, including redecorating or remodeling, equipment, materials, and supplies, are considered in the budget. One advantage of this kind of budgeting is that it necessitates advance planning. Funds need to be allocated wisely and used efficiently, but workers should be trusted to use funds with discretion in order to meet the needs of children without having to pinch pennies.

It is helpful to require workers to secure permission from the proper authority for purchasing equipment, materials, and supplies. By having one person in a department or agency responsible for ordering equipment and supplies, proper control can be exercised. Any changes needed in the physical plant should be submitted in writing to the appropriate board for approval before work is done. Also, projects which are undertaken should be completed to conserve finances and keep the building in good condition.

It is important that children be taught Christian stewardship in the use of time, talents, and treasures. (Practical suggestions as to how to do this are given in chap. 20, "Missionary and Stewardship Education of Children.") Adults can set a good example for children by the way funds are handled and used. Many churches operate on limited budgets and cannot afford elaborate furnishings. However, if proper care of facilities and equipment is encouraged, children can be taught to respect and care for personal and church property. Involvement in caring for the building and equipment will teach children far more than verbalizing negatively when they do not care for things as they should.

Special financial projects can be sponsored by departments and agencies in the children's division. One caution must be kept in mind, however: special projects ought to be approved by a central committee, whether it be the board of Christian education, the children's division committee, or the Sunday school board or council. Otherwise, some projects may overlap others or may not be within reach of the goal.

When children see how their money is spent in practical ways—such as replacing burned-out lightbulbs, redecorating a room, buying a new filmstrip projector or chairs for the department, or giving a file cabinet to a missionary—their sense of responsibility is increased and they enjoy the blessing of giving. We must always remember that the foundations for teaching Christian stewardship are laid during childhood years!

NOTES

1. Eisenhower, in Bradford B. Boyd, *Management-Minded Supervision* (New York: McGraw-Hill, 1968), p. 113.
2. Richard Kraus, *Recreation Today Program Planning and Leadership* (New York: Appleton-Century-Crofts, 1966), pp. 54-57.
3. Lois E. LeBar, *Focus on People in Church Education* (Westwood, N.J.: Revell, 1968), pp. 70-72.
4. Luther Gulick and L. Urwick, "POSDCORB," in *An Introduction to School Administration Selected Readings*, ed. M. Chester Nolte (New York: Macmillan, 1966), pp. 223-24.
5. LeBar, pp. 208-209.
6. For additional suggestions on training personnel, see Paul Loth "Recruiting and Training Leaders," in *Adult Education in the Church*, ed. Roy B. Zuck and Gene A. Getz (Chicago: Moody, 1970).
7. Ralph Heim, *Leading a Sunday Church School* (Philadelphia: Muhlenberg, 1950), pp. 259-62.
8. Additional suggestions are given in "Beginner Department Equipment and Furnishings," *Baptist Training Union Magazine* 35 (Feb., 1960): 52-53.
9. Ronald C. Doll, *Curriculum Improvement: Decision-Making and Process* (Boston: Allyn & Bacon, 1970), p. 21.
10. Paul Vieth, *The Church and Christian Education* (St. Louis: Bethany, 1947), p. 134.
11. Lois LeBar, *Education That Is Christian* (Westwood, N.J.: Revell, 1958), pp. 207-219.
12. Ronald C. Doll, "Twenty Questions to Ask About Sunday-School Materials," *Christianity Today* 16 (Mar. 3, 1972): 7-8.

FOR FURTHER READING

Byrne, H. W. *Christian Education for the Local Church.* Grand Rapids: Zondervan, 1963.

Chamberlain, Eugene, and Fullbright, Robert G. *Children's Sunday School Work.* Nashville: Convention, 1969.

Fullbright, Robert. *New Dimensions in Teaching Children.* Nashville: Broadman, 1971.

Gangel, Kenneth O. *Leadership for Church Education.* Chicago: Moody, 1970.

Griffin, Dale E. "Interest Centers That Attract." *Interaction* 10 (Sept., 1970): 15-17.

Gwynn, Price H. *Leadership Education in the Local Church.* Philadelphia: Westminster, 1952.

Hammack, Mary. "Organize an Instructional Materials Center." *Success* 23 (Fall, 1971): 6-7.

LeBar, Lois E. *Children in the Bible School.* Westwood, N.J.: Revell, 1952.

McDaniel, Elsiebeth, and Richards, Lawrence O. *You and Children.* Chicago: Moody, 1973.

Richards, Lawrence O. *The Pastor and His Christian Education Facilities.* Christian Education Monographs, Pastors' Series, No. 20. Glen Ellyn, Ill.: Scripture Press Foundation, 1967.

Rives, Elsie, and Sharp, Margaret. *Guiding Children.* Nashville: Convention, 1969.

"Seven Ways Unit Planning Can Make You a Better Teacher," *Teach* 14 (Winter, 1973): 52-53.

Sisemore, John T., ed. *Vital Principles in Religious Education.* Nashville: Broadman, 1966.

Tobey, Kathrene. *Learning and Teaching through the Senses.* Philadelphia: Westminster, 1970.

Towns, Elmer L. *Team Teaching with Success.* Cincinnati: Standard, 1971.

Widber, Mildred, and Ritenour, Scott. *Focus: Building to Christian Education.* Boston: Pilgrim, 1969.

Wiedman, Mavis. *The Superintendent and Sunday School Records.* Christian Education Monographs, Superintendents' Series, No. 4. Glen Ellyn, Ill.: Scripture Press Foundation, 1968.

Zuck, Roy B. *The Superintendent and Teacher Enlistment.* Christian Education Monographs, Superintendents' Series, No. 3. Glen Ellyn, Ill.: Scripture Press Foundation, 1968.

Zuck, Roy B., and Getz, Gene A., eds. *Adult Education in the Church.* Chicago: Moody, 1970.

Selected Publishers and Service Organizations

Awana Youth Association, 3215 Algonquin Rd., Rolling Meadows, Ill. 60008

Bible Club Movement, 237 Fairfield Avenue, Upper Darby, Pa. 19082

Child Evangelism Fellowship, Box 1156, Grand Rapids, Mich. 49501

Christian Service Brigade, Box 150, Wheaton, Ill. 60187
David C. Cook Publishing House, 850 North Grove, Elgin, Ill. 60120
Evangelical Teacher Training Association, Box 327, Wheaton, Ill. 60187
Gospel Light Publications, 110 West Broadway, Glendale, Calif. 91204
Pioneer Girls, Box 788, Wheaton, Ill. 60187
Scripture Press Publications, Inc., 1825 College Ave., Wheaton, Ill. 60187
Success With Youth, Inc., Box 27028, Tempe, Ariz. 85282
Union Gospel Press, Cleveland, Ohio 44101

23

Recreation and Camps

Richard E. Troup

Recreation

Children have a great amount of free time. Even after they enter first grade, school involves only about thirty hours a week. A child's afternoons, early evenings, Saturdays, and Sundays are normally his to use as he wants.

Much of his free time, however, may be under the secularizing influence of non-Christian friends or adults, television, clubs, or other groups. One way in which churches can counteract those influences is by a program of meaningful leisure and recreational activities.

WHAT RECREATION IS

Recreation usually occurs during one's leisure time when he is free from his occupation or work, after the practical necessities have been met. Webster defines recreation as "a means of refreshment or diversion." Recreation is enjoyable, pleasureful, and can be free from financial involvement. It restores the body or mind, recreates, and refreshes.

A functional definition of recreation is, "a voluntary activity or experience which one pursues in his leisure time and which brings personal satisfaction and enjoyment." Meyer, Brightbill, and Sessoms indicate nine basic characteristics of recreation: (1) it involves activity; (2) it has no single form; (3) it is determined by motivation; (4) it occurs in unobligated time; (5) it is entirely voluntary; (6) it is universally practiced and sought; (7) it is serious and purposeful; (8) it is flexible; (9) it has by-products.[1] One little boy said recreation is "what you do when you don't have to."

Recreation for children will vary according to individual interests,

---

Richard E. Troup, M.R.E., is on the staff of Success with Youth, Inc., Tempe, Arizona.

needs, and capacities. Those who conduct recreation activities with children must recognize these variations and not force every child into the same program. For recreation to refresh, build up, and encourage happy and worthwhile experiences, it must be individualized.

HISTORY OF RECREATION

The outlook on recreation has changed considerably over the years. From the earliest times, man has had leisure moments in which he has engaged in pottery making, sculpture, painting, music, drama, and athletics. During the Middle Ages, contests and tournaments were held by the knights. The Renaissance created new interests in the great works of art and literature from the Roman and Grecian empires. In Colonial America, recreation was not held in high esteem. In fact, idleness was associated with evil, loose morals, and personal degeneration. In spite of the general feeling in that era, individuals praticipated in sleigh rides, skating, outings in parks, circuses, taffy pulls, and the like.

The twentieth century has brought about drastic changes in recreation. The industrial revolution, affluence, urbanization, and travel have allowed more time and opportunity for leisure and recreation. Tourist trade has become a major economic pursuit. A return to the artistic and cultural values, the linkage of recreation with education and spiritual goals and programs have been some of the underlying elements in the growing concern for recreation.[2]

The National Recreation and Park Association (formerly known as the National Recreation Association) was established in 1906. The scouting movement, Campfire Girls, YMCA and YWCA, and other service organizations have all contributed to recreation.

For today's children, recreation has become an integral part of life. As we view the future, the problems in providing worthwhile recreation may increase in volume and depth. Parents and leaders in churches have the responsibility to meet the needs of children in recreation and to guide them in the wise use of leisure time.

VALUES OF RECREATION

Many values can be derived from recreation, with fellowship being basic. Tensions can be released and excess energies used in worthwhile ways. Children can be taught how to be good sports in various activities, and individual skills may be developed and improved through recreation. Children need to learn to relate to others on the playground as well as in the classroom or home. Creativity can be encouraged and developed, and new ways of doing can be introduced. One of the outstanding benefits of recreation is to develop character. Through a constructive and well-planned recreational program, children can learn to enjoy making the best use of time. The challenges for effective teaching in natural settings are unlimited for leaders and teachers of children.

SCRIPTURAL BASIS OF RECREATION

Sometimes Christians develop a list of dos and don'ts, but fail to apply Scripture in considering recreation as part of the development of the total personality. Proverbs 17:22 tells us, "A merry heart doeth good like a medicine." In Eclessiastes 3:1-8, we note there is a time for everything. Christ developed as a total person "in favour with . . . man" (Lk 2:52). Paul uses the athletic contest as an analogy to the Christian life (1 Co 9:24-27). Timothy was instructed, "Bodily exercise is all right" (1 Ti 4:8, TLB).

Though no specific Scripture states, "Thou shalt have recreation," we must be aware that man is a total personality and a social as well as a spiritual being. Children need to develop wholesome attitudes toward life and a broad perspective on the whole of life.

MEETING AGE-GROUP NEEDS

Many of the needs of children can be met in recreation if we select activities according to several principles:

1. Provide opportunity to develop the physical life normally and naturally.
2. Emphasize balance betwen active and quiet activities and between indoor and outdoor activities.
3. Use variety in activities with short duration according to the attention span.
4. Provide activities that are purposeful and lead to a learning experience.
5. Select activities that meet the needs of particular age levels.
6. Give adequate adult supervision in *all* activities.
7. Set a good example to follow.
8. Give careful, clear directions; if necessary, demonstrate what to do.
9. Provide opportunities for use of imagination and creative expression.
10. Enlist youthful and fun-loving leaders who are able to relate to children.

A thorough understanding of the characteristics and needs of children is basic to a successful recreation program.* Only as the nature and needs of children are understood can the best kinds of recreational activities be selected in developing well-rounded personalities.

*Chapters 4-8 present the characteristics and needs of children.

KINDS OF RECREATION

Recreation is as diversified as the individuals who participate. Below are some of the general categories with specific activities which may be used in recreation with children.

Social Recreation

- Parties
- Games—indoor
  - icebreakers
  - musical chairs
  - table games
  - writing games
  - musical
- Games—outdoor
  - relays
  - races
  - tag
- Eating together
  - banquets
  - desserts
  - picnics
  - potlucks
  - progressive dinners

Outdoor Recreation

- Nature activities
  - bird walks
  - field trips
  - scavenger hunts
- Camping
  - day
  - resident
  - trip
  - weekend
- Sports
  - badminton
  - baseball
  - basketball
  - bicycling
  - boating
  - climbing
  - croquet
  - fishing
  - horseback riding
  - hunting
  - skating
  - snow activities
  - swimming
  - volleyball

Cultural and Creative Recreation

- Drama
  - charades
  - pageants
  - pantomimes
  - play readings
  - plays
  - role plays
  - shadow plays
  - story plays
  - tableaux
- Literature
  - choral speaking
  - poems
  - scripture reading
  - story hour
  - story reading
- Storytelling
  - humorous
  - sacred
  - seasonal
  - secular
- Arts and Crafts
  - cartooning
  - ceramics
  - drawing
  - jewelry craft
  - junk crafts
  - metal craft
  - mounting
  - painting
  - papercraft
  - printing and lettering
  - woodcraft

Hobbies

collecting	creating	doing	learning
by age	creative writing	games	field trips
by composition	drama	photography	museums
by colors	music	sports	reading
by design		taking trips	specialists
by shapes			

The interests, abilities, and needs of children are significant factors to be considered in selecting recreational activities. Focus must be on the children as individuals. Activities that are above the children's level of comprehension or are too difficult for them to perform should be avoided due to frustration, discouragement, and failure.

PLANNING FOR RECREATION

In planning recreational activities, six basic questions need to be answered:

Who: the people involved in the activity, their characteristics, needs, interests, and capacities

What: the type of activity, the theme, or main emphasis of the activity

Why: the specific, clearly stated purpose or aim for the activity

When: the month, day, year, hours for the activity

Where: the location and directions on finding the location

How: the outline, plan, and arrangement of the program; what is to be done, the activities, methods, materials, time schedule, and leadership needed

KINDS OF PARTIES AND PICNICS

A well-developed program of recreation for children may include the following kinds of parties and picnics:

Seasonal. Children enjoy attending parties at Halloween, Christmas, Easter. This gives opportunities to reach unchurched neighborhood children and to teach children of believers the true meaning of special days.

Birthday. A large children's department could have a monthly party for those with birthdays that month. Some churches have a once-a-year birthday to celebrate all the children's birthdays for that year. For such an annual event, it is best to choose a month when no regular holiday exists, such as January.

Special emphases. If many children are gone for the summer, plan a "before-you-leave" party in the spring or a "welcome back" September party.

PLANNING CHILDREN'S PARTIES

Successful parties can be planned by applying these ideas:

1. Plan each social around an interesting theme, with each phase of the party coordinated into this theme.
2. Vary the time and place of the activity from month to month, according to the season of the year and the theme selected.
3. Rotate the responsibility of social chairman. This will help assure new and fresh ideas.
4. Use a variety of promotional media, such as postcards, brochures, bulletin boards, and skits.
5. Plan decorations that are not expensive but which relate creatively to the theme.
6. Use a variety of games, including opening ice-breaking games, more active games (perhaps of a partner or team variety), and transitional games of a quieter nature (perhaps while seated in a circle).
7. Have a brief devotional period, if appropriate, while the group is still seated in the circle for the last game or while the children are seated at tables.
8. Relate refreshments to the theme. Also, at each social, have a different committee or person plan the refreshments in order to avoid having the same things repeatedly.
9. Be sure that clean-up responsibilities are delegated.
10. Send invitations to the visitors who were present, encouraging them to attend other activities of the church.[3]

To avoid duplication and to coordinate activities, it is helpful for the children's leaders to plan a year's social activities together. A typical once-a-month program schedule might look like this:

September:	Welcome-back party
October:	Halloween party
November:	Trip to museum, zoo; special event
December:	Christmas party
January:	All-church, all-age social (birthdays)
February:	Valentine party
March:	Teacher's convention picnic
April:	Easter (vacation) party
May:	Before-you-leave party
June:	Sunday school picnic
July:	Family Independence Day camp
August:	Beach party

PICNICS

1. *Annual picnic.* Most churches have an all-church picnic with separate activities for each department. Larger churches may have several picnics, each for a separate department.

2. *Holidays.* Obtain a public school calendar and plan an outing on the date of the teachers' institute or convention. A long holiday weekend makes an ideal time for a children's all-day field trip with a picnic. Other long weekends from which to choose are Labor Day, Lincoln's birthday, Washington's birthday, Memorial Day, Independence Day.

3. *Regular day, plus.* A teacher may wish to have a picnic breakfast on a Sunday morning with his class at a picnic site, returning to the church in time for Sunday school or the morning service. Others may prefer a Sunday afternoon picnic right after church. Or a picnic could be held on a weekday immediately before the regularly scheduled, weekday club activities, with the meeting being held outdoors. The picnic may replace the club activities for that one week.

GAME LEADERSHIP

Every leader in recreation will have opportunity to lead games. For each game, he needs to be familiar with the basic rules and how to explain the game to children. Thorough preparation for the game enables him to lead it smoothly, efficiently, and flexibly. Also, better control of the group is possible, and discipline problems may be avoided or kept to a minimum. The leader should be so familiar with the game that he can absorb himself in leading and enjoying it without undue concern for technique. Many leaders find it helpful to write the steps of the game on a three-by-five-inch card.

The following questions will assist the leader in evaluating himself regarding his game leadership:

Did I know my group in selecting the game?
Was I familiar with the basic rules and regulations?
Did I prepare the best room arrangement?
Were necessary equipment and materials available?
Did I secure the attention of the entire group before trying to explain the game?
Did I name the game?
Were my explanations clear and concise?
Did I demonstrate the steps in logical order?
Did I answer questions to clarify and correct mistakes?
Was the game concluded while interest was high?
Did the group enjoy the game?
What changes would I make if I were to lead the game again?

RESOURCES FOR CHILDREN'S RECREATION

Church libraries are expanding to include more than books and periodicals. Projected materials, catalogs of sources, packets and notebooks or file cabinets of visual nonprojected aids, mimeographed items, and pamphlets are changing many church libraries into full Instructional Materials Centers (IMC).

The recreation section of an IMC could include materials under the groups suggested earlier in this chapter under "Kinds of Recreation." At the end of each quarter, any new materials purchased by the children's agencies should be turned in to the IMC, filed by topic, to be used as often as needed.

ORGANIZATION, ADMINISTRATION, AND SUPERVISION OF RECREATION

Successful recreation programs do not just happen! Careful planning, prayer, and work are essential. *Organization* is the first step—planning the program, schedules, and activities. *Administration* is related to carrying out the plans the leaders have made. Administration is organization in action. In organization, we plan the work, and, in administration, we work the plan. Personnel, buildings and equipment, finances, and publicity are vital areas to consider in administration. *Supervision* has to do with building a quality staff and program. In supervision, we are concerned with training, guiding, counseling, developing effective human relations, and evaluating.

Here are some general principles in organizing, administering, and supervising recreation for children:

1. Plan the program with the children's needs in focus.
2. Set realistic goals which can be accomplished.
3. Begin with fewer activities and expand as needs emerge.
4. Make long-range plans. Schedule activities on a calendar and correlate them with activities in the total church program.
5. Discover and enlist those who have potential in leadership.
6. Provide training for workers to assist them in developing leadership ability.
7. Provide sufficient housing, equipment, and materials to do the work.
8. Make funds available through the church budget or other means.
9. Publicize recreation activities well in advance and in various ways.
10. Evaluate the program periodically to determine strengths and needs for improvement.

The above principles can be stated in question form to serve as criteria for evaluating recreation for children.

Recreation programs can be carried on through Sunday school classes or departments, clubs, vacation Bible school, or camp. The board of Christian education or children's division committee may supervise and guide recreation, but specific activities will be conducted by those who work with children.

If a local church has no recreation program for children, it may begin small, but it should begin. Even a biweekly hobby club led by the pastor or a Sunday school teacher is a step in the right direction.

A church may evaluate its situation by asking these questions: How many children are now attending our church activities? How many are within walking distance of our church building? How do these children spend their after-school hours? What are their interests and desires?

If a church does not have a ball field, gymnasium, or game area, it may consider using a nearby field, hall, or public park.[4]

Persons who are not Bible teachers or public speakers could possibly function as leaders or helpers for games, sports, or crafts. Many high schoolers and college-age youth can be trained, supervised, and utilized with great effectiveness.

After school is often a good time for a recreational program. Having activities then will not pressure the child or invade the evening hours when family, school, and usual church activities already function.

Few churches have a consistent program of recreation for boys and girls. Only a few of these programs are developed with distinctively Christian purposes in mind.

Too many of the adults involved with children in recreational activities have a guilty conscience. They feel they are not engaged in a legitimately "spiritual" activity. However, as those adults recall their childhood, they must admit that many of their warmest recollections are of recreational activities Often the adults who made the deepest impression on them are those who were involved with them in fun times. This underscores the fact that Christ-centered recreation is one of the most productive areas of the church's ministry.

The Christian Camp

Camping is one of the church's most effective programs for accomplishing its biblically developed objectives.

Why camp?

Evangelism, Christian commitment, Christ-centered character development, vocational direction from the Christian perspective, Spirit-led person-to-person relationships, skills for practical Christian living—all these are developed in children through the Christian camp to an extent that exceeds many, if not all, other ministries of the local church.

Evangelism. The pastor of the largest church of his denomination reported that every one of the teenagers who had joined the church during that year had trusted Christ as Saviour at their camp.

A large Arizona conference grounds, with a highly developed evangelistic program featuring several directly evangelistic services in its chapel each day, reported that one out of ten campers received Christ as Saviour. Later, this conference developed a pioneer satellite camp, featuring trained counselors who directed a smaller number of campers in a decentralized activity program. An average of one salvation response was reported by each counselor for every six campers. This program included no chapel services, no professional Bible teacher, and no overtly evangelistic outreach. Instead, the emphasis was on personal influence and guidance, with open Bible discussions, led by the counselor, with his handful of junior or junior high campers drawn from churched homes.

Challenge to Christian service. An evangelical denomination of more than one thousand churches has reported that more of its pastors responded to God's will to enter the ministry in a summer camp than in any other setting. An independent mission society serving in the Orient discovered that more of its personnel felt called to missionary service in a camp than through any other means.

Christian growth. Few camps make an attempt to determine how Christian attitudes and habits are developed within their programs. A survey in one liberal denomination disclosed that, of those persons who had attended camp, 87 percent felt that they had had a "rich and lasting experience," the best proportionate response to any activity except "ecumenical" meetings, and double or triple the response to its traditional agencies of Christian education.

Richard Doty did extensive evaluation of character development in a camp and reported exceptional levels of growth when specific goals are aimed for with measurable techniques.[5] Christ-centered camping has yet to develop such tools, but, even so, increasingly greater results are evident.

Some of the changes experienced in campers' lives include dishonesty being replaced with honesty, reliance on parents' directions for religious habits giving place to a direct response to God, mechanistic conformity to church rules yielding to a Spirit-produced morality.

WHY THE CHILDREN'S CAMP?

Families, senior adults, as well as teens can benefit tremendously from Christ-centered camping. But camps for children have their own distinctive values in addition to those values mentioned earlier for all camps.

Christian peer relationships. Many children ages six through eleven unconsciously pass judgment on their peers, thereby excluding those whom they dislike and even hate.

Proper relationships with peers can be encouraged and developed in a Christian camp. To help accomplish this, the camping program for elementary children should be built around the cabin group of four to seven campers. As the counselor and his cabin or tent group spend time together, the campers can learn to function in a Christ-centered way. This kind of opportunity for building Christ-honoring attitudes toward peers is unique to camping.

Christian intergenerational relationships. Few children have a relationship with an adult in which each has the opportunity to discover the personality and ability of the other and to relate to the other within a mutually accepting and supporting Christ-centered spirit. Even Christian parents often find it difficult to develop such a relationship with their children.

Most elementary teachers in secular schools are not Christians, and those who are believers are prohibited by law from functioning in the classroom as Christian leaders. This makes it difficult—if not impossible—for the public school to develop Christian adult-child relationships. This is frequently a problem also in the typical Sunday school class because of time limitations.

Many elementary education classes are taught by women. A boy can go from kindergarten through grade six without ever having a male teacher, much less a Christian father-hero-model figure. Whenever dedicated Christian men are used in junior boys' camps, they can have an unusual impact on young boys' lives.

Christian skill development. "What did you do to our son?" This question stopped the camp director in his tracks. Then he breathed with relief and thanksgiving as the parents continued, "We sent you a boy and you returned to us a man."

After camp, a boy spent a Saturday afternoon chopping up a fallen tree into fireplace-size pieces and stacking them in a neat pile—without even being asked. Before camp, however, he had detested his parents' requests to help with the woodchopping. When another junior returned from a wilderness camp, he proudly told his mother, "Mom, at camp I learned to pray on my own."

How to enjoy the Bible, how to share with others what Christ means to them, how to trust the Lord in difficult times—these are some of the many Christian skills children can learn at camp.

At least six kinds of camps are possible with children.

KINDS OF CAMPS

1. *Trip camping.* Campers travel by bus or van from site to site. (It is usually best not to travel by car because of the cost, insurance problems, not enough drivers, etc.) Because of the tedium of travel for children, this type of camp is normally not used extensively with boys and girls.

One camp in Arizona has a modified trip camp which includes juniors. The week is divided between two sites, with the camp moving in the middle of the week to the second location by bus. When state and national parks and forests are used for trip camping, tents are needed for sleeping, and a mobile kitchen and supply trailers complete the facilities.

2. *Trail camping.* On foot, bike, minibike, horse, or canoe, the trail moves as a trip camp does, except that it goes by "camper power." An advantage of both trail and trip camping is that expensive facilities are not needed.

Public lands contain thousands of miles of developed trails. A topographical or "quad" map, such as those published by the US Geological Survey (normally available at office supply stores or blueprint stores), indicates foot trails by single dotted lines or jeep trails by double dotted lines. These maps are ready-made for rough trail hikes.

Children enjoy backpack camping as a family, with mother and father doing most of the detailed planning, carrying, cooking, and shelter construction.

Though most camps do not provide this type of program for children, some trail camps are conducted for older juniors who are involved in outdoor skill achievement through an organized boys' or girls' weekday club program.

3. *Weekend camping.* Campsites are increasing rapidly, with facilities for year-round camping. By including winter and spring school vacations plus long weekends, a camp can add up to one hundred days to its ninety-day summer season.

Family weekends, couples' conferences, and leadership workshops are naturals for this off-season thrust. Children can participate as they come with adults to the above kinds of camps. The camp can provide separate activities for children, and they sleep in the same cabin with their parents at night.

Church organizations for older children can include a carefully structured twenty-four-hour weekend camp as a highlight of its activities. The time of year should be chosen carefully so that weather and activities will not to be overly strange to the campers. If the church is located in a city where January weather is sunny and gets up to eighty degrees, and the desired campsite usually has snow and below-zero temperatures in January, then the weekend "campspiration" should be scheduled two or three months later. A church with an evangelistic children's club outreach may offer such a twenty-four-hour outing as a reward for children who have earned points by attending regularly, bringing visitors, and memorizing scripture verses and songs.

4. *Family camping.* In a family camp, children attend with their parents as family groups. Long weekends are desirable for family camps. All (or most) activities are conducted by families. At mealtimes, one or two families are seated at each table; table devotions are led by the parents; family Bible studies are conducted using special resources provided. Depending on the ages and number of children, activities may include swimming, with parents responsible for their children; crafts; table games; hikes by families; and even tournaments, with family units or with representatives competing, such as father-son Ping-Pong doubles and four-member-family volleyball. Separate game sessions may be conducted for children, while other camp sessions are held for youth and adults.

A growing number of campgrounds are providing this kind of camping for families who are not attending the traditional summer Bible conference with its age-segregated meeting-oriented program. A church can rent facilities and operate its own program with a full family emphasis or an age-level conference or an adaptation of the two.

A church in Phoenix had enthusiastic response to such a ministry during the week, including Independence Day, so much so that the Sunday services at the church were cancelled and the services were held at the campgrounds.

5. *Day camping.* This is one of the most rapidly expanding outreaches of today's aggressive church. Day camping is ideal for primaries and juniors and can also be used occasionally for four- and five-year-olds.

In contrast to traditional resident camps, a day camp operates only during daylight hours, with the exception of youth day camps held in the evenings or an overnight special event toward the end of a day-camp period for older children.

Children usually bring their own bag lunch, and the camp provides the drink for lunch and treats for midmorning and/or midafternoon. With no sleeping or eating facilities needed, the costs are held down, so that this type of camp can be not only financially self-supporting but in some cases can even provide a source of income to the director or sponsoring agency.

Some churches hold day camp at their church site. Other day camps are held at city parks or on lawns of large residences (be sure to check with neighbors and to check on insurance, rest-room facilities, etc.) or county or state forests, meeting each day at the same location or rotating between several locations.

Some resident camp properties were originally located too close to towns, but what has handicapped outdoor camping now becomes an open door to converting all or part of the grounds to a day camp.

In some areas special day camp facilities are being developed where farmland or county park areas are available. If children meet at a city location (such as the church building) the day-camp site should be no more than a thirty- to forty-five-minute bus ride away. A church that meets near an expressway may find within twenty-five miles a highly usable site or a variety of sites.

Vacation Bible school materials may often be easily adaptable to day camp for Bible study, crafts, and game times. Curricular materials for day-camp use are being published by the Southern Baptist Sunday School Board.

What are the values of day camping? Two pastors, Dale Cowling, of Little Rock, Arkansas, and W. A. Criswell, of Dallas, Texas, cite advantages of their day camping:

> Our day camping program gives our church a two-fold opportunity: (1) it enables us to do an intensive job of character building in lives of boys and girls, relating them to God through normal experiences in the out-of-doors; (2) it provides an opportunity for graduating high school students and college students to minister through small group involvement to boys and girls of unstable background.
>
> Our church uses day camping to share Christ and develop Christian character in campers and counselors. This year we had forty decisions for Christ the first eight days of camp. Day camping has become an indispensable part of our church program.[6]

6. *Resident camping.* Overnight camps, lasting from five full twenty-four-hour periods to as long as a full summer-long session of ten weeks (with the summer's first weeks for staff training), have been a part of the church's ministry for a century. Usually age-graded, separate sessions are held for juniors, children who have completed school grades four to six.

Often separate sessions are conducted for boys and girls, but successful coed junior camps are common. Segregation by sex is determined by whether the other church agencies provide adequate association in coed or boy-girl groupings.

Some camps do not accept campers until they have completed grade five, unless they have been active in church weekday clubs during grade four. Some camps combine third and fourth graders into one camping program and fifth and sixth graders into another.

Rather than one large, junior boys' camp one week of the summer (along with other one-week single age-group sessions), some camps are developing summer-long programs (or at least several weeks) for one age or several ages.

Instead of two hundred junior boys in one mass program, utilizing all facilities for one week, and two hundred girls the next, a camp could take fifty juniors a week for eight weeks. Some campers would want to come for two-week periods and would be housed and led in separate subunits. Thus the same two hundred campers might involve two hundred and fifty camper weeks.

Living facilities would need to be separated from those of other older ages because of the difference in rising hours (juniors later) and lights out (juniors earlier), rest hour after lunch (longer and quieter for juniors), and activity period lengths (shorter for juniors with less free time between).

Meeting rooms, dining rooms (or subdivisions of a room by planters, screens, folding walls, etc.), outdoor activity areas (softball; volleyball; individual games, such as tetherball; swimming; crafts; archery; riflery; etc.) can be assigned to various groups or ages sharing the grounds. Otherwise the facilities can be used on a rotating basis: for example, juniors may eat at 11:15, teens at 12:00 noon, and families at 12:45; juniors may be in chapel at 10:00, while teens are in cabin Bible study and family camp is using the activity area.

Principles of camp programming[7] true for all ages need to be adjusted to the needs of younger campers. Growing bodies need longer periods of rest at night and after lunch. The menu in a junior camp will contain different vegetables, desserts, and hot drinks, more milk, and less salads than a teen or adult camp. The intensity of the spiritual thrust will be geared to the emotional level of children as well as to their less developed spiritual concepts.

It is generally best to have one counselor for every four children in an activity camp and one for every seven in a conference camp. Counselors need to be especially aware of the needs of the children nearing adolescence, some of whom are already involved in adolescent-level questions.

Sixteen- and seventeen-year-olds make effective children's camp counselors if they (1) are experienced campers; (2) are proven leaders in church club programs or youth groups; (3) possess unquestionable references from pastor, teacher, and parent; (4) have received a week of on-site camp leadership training; (5) are in a camp with continuing in-service training and counselor supervision; and (6) can be given a two-hour duty-free rest period each day completely apart from camper observation.

A number of experimental camps are being conducted for children.

Under adequate controls, where there is a reasonable hope for success and almost no possibility for any harm, a church or camp could try some "growing edge" camping. A Rhinebeck, New York, secular camp conducted a two-week trial session for ten metropolitan New York children under the age of six from deprived homes. The director was assisted in the specialized program by fourteen counselors.

Each Monday of July and August, five boys of elementary age were driven from the Phoenix inner city to the high mountains two hours away. Here a second counselor waited at their tent site to lead them in a five-day unstructured camp of their own planning, scheduling, cooking, and woodsland-mountains-oriented pioneer camp.

PLANNING A CHILDREN'S CAMP

A successful camp begins with a well-worked-out plan of activities. This schedule should be posted in the leadership room for the camp staff to know what is projected. As the week progresses, however, and the weather changes or the spiritual tempo accelerates or slows, the reason for the schedule being written in *pencil* becomes apparent. Planned flexibility is a basic programming principle.

The following are *possible* schedules for three kinds of camps, to be *modified* by the individual camp within legitimate limits.

WEEKEND

FRIDAY P.M.

4:30	buses leave church building
6:30	arrive at camp bunks assigned
7:00	supper
7:30	orientation hike
8:00	game time
8:45	campfire
9:30	fireside devotions
9:45	clean up for bed
10:15	cabin sharing
10:30	lights out (unusually late for children, but acceptable on Friday in a one-night camp)

SATURDAY A.M.

7:30	rise and clean up
8:00	breakfast
8:30	cabin devotions
9:00	choice of outdoor activities
10:00	chapel
10:30	team activities (or by cabin)
11:30	leisure

SATURDAY P.M.

12:00 lunch
12:30 cabin sharing (rest hour)
1:30 activities
2:30 all-camp sharing time
3:00 cabin cleanup, snack
3:30 bus departs

Day

9:00 buses leave church building (if buses pick up children at their homes, begin pickups as early as necessary)
9:30 arrive at site
orientation
9:45 activity 1 (crafts, games, missions project, Bible study)
10:15 activity 2 (same as above or chapel)
10:45 snack time
11:15 activity 3 (same as above or special event)
11:45 cleanup, leisure
12:00 lunch
12:30 planned rest
1:00 activity 4 (slower paced)
1:45 activity 5 and group meeting
2:30 leave site by bus
3:00 return to church building
staff meeting

Resident

7:00 rise, cleanup
8:00 breakfast
8:30 personal devotions
cabin cleanup
9:15 activity 1†
10:30 activity 2
(If a chapel is desired, the first activity period may be from 9:15 to 10:15, chapel from 10:15 to 10:45, and activity 2 from 10:45 to 11:45.)
11:45 cleanup
12:00 lunch, and table fun time
1:00 rest hour
2:00 cabin activities
3:30 choice of unstructured activities
5:30 supper

†A staff meeting for half the counselors may be held at each of the first two activity periods.

6:30 all-camp special activity‡
7:30 cabin time—sharing, planning, devotions
8:30 lights out

LEADERSHIP FOR CHILDREN'S CAMPS

The single most important element in a successful camp is leadership. *Every* leader must meet basic qualifications, have the special skills required by his position, be trained in camp leadership, have proper orientation to this camp and its distinctives, and be adequately helped throughout the camp.

Table 23:1 shows the basic staff requirements for an ideal-size camp of fifty-six to eighty campers (four pairs of cabins with seven campers each, or eight pairs of five cabins with five campers each).

TABLE 23:1
BASIC STAFF REQUIREMENTS

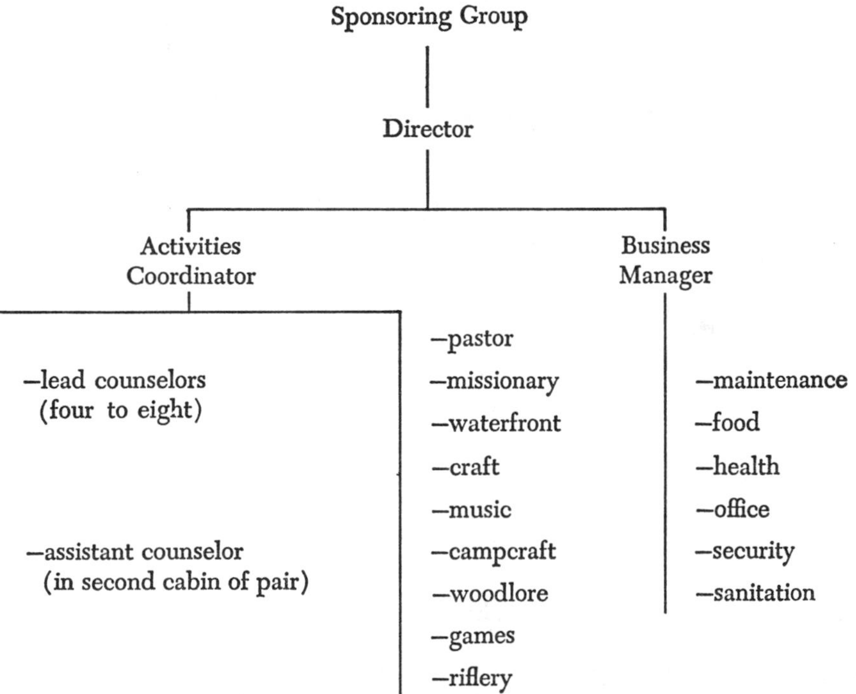

‡The final activity should be varied each day. Normally, each day, provide an all-camp and a cabin (or two-cabin) activity, one of which is spiritual in nature (campfire, testimony meeting, musical program, missions seminar, dedication service) and the other recreational (watermelon hunt, scavenger hunt, treasure hike, moonlight hike without flashlights, wiener and marshmallow roast, skit night, film).

Some staff members may hold more than one position, so long as the total staff is at least on a one-to-five ratio with campers.

In order to reach the unsaved, the church must depart from its "Come to our meetings in our buildings at our times and hear the message as we know it and want to define it" format. We need to communicate to our potential "customer" where he is and in the setting he prefers. Outdoor leisure-time settings, involving activities that are fun, offer ideal evangelistic opportunities.

Small groups, unhurried pace, and close relationships with skilled and dedicated leaders all add up to an ideal educational camp setting.

Camping resembles the work of an Evangelist-Educator who taught on a mountainside, who counseled in a boat, who admonished by a campfire, who preached as He led a day's hike to Emmaus. In the name and spirit of Christ, using a setting He loved and mastered, let us adventure outdoors for Christ.

NOTES

1. Harold Meyer, Charles Brightbill, and Douglas Sessoms, *Community Recreation: A Guide to Its Organization,* 4th ed. (Englewood Cliffs, N.J.: Prentice-Hall, 1969), pp. 34-38.
2. Richard Kraus, *Recreation Today: Program Planning and Leadership* (New York: Appleton-Century-Crofts, 1966), pp. 3-27.
3. Richard E. Troup, "Church Recreation for Adults," in *Adult Education in the Church,* ed. Roy B. Zuck and Gene A. Getz (Chicago: Moody, 1970), p. 207.
4. For excellent suggestions on ways to utilize limited facilities, see Edward L. Hayes, "Recreational Activities," in *Youth and the Church,* ed. Roy G. Irving and Roy B. Zuck (Chicago: Moody, 1968), p. 250.
5. Richard S. Doty, *The Character Dimension of Camping* (New York: Association, 1960), p. 15.
6. *Day Camping,* brochure, Baptist Sunday School Board, Nashville, Tenn., p. 4.
7. See, for example, Joy Mackay, *Creative Counseling for Christian Camps,* chaps. 5-7; Lloyd D. Mattson, *Camping Guideposts,* chaps. 1-4, 8; Floyd and Pauline Todd, *Camping for Christian Youth,* chaps. 16-17.

FOR FURTHER READING

Recreation

BOOKS AND ARTICLES

Beeker, Mabel. *Banquets Plus.* Nashville: Broadman, 1958.

Bergman, Bernice. "Planning the Picnic." *Christian Herald* 86 (June, 1963: 67-68.

Books on Parks, Recreation and Leisure 1973, 16th ed. Arlington, Va.: National Recreation and Park Assoc., 1973.

Boyd, Bob. *Recreation for Churches.* Nashville: Convention, 1962.

Butler, George D., ed. *Recreation Activities for Adults.* New York: Association, 1950.

Cathcart, Mildred Dooley. *Let's Have a Party.* Chicago: Moody, 1958.

Cleaver, Nancy. *Fell's Guide to Camping and Family Fun Outdoors.* New York: Fell, Frederick, 1965.

Cox, Claire. *Rainy Day Fun for Kids.* New York: Association, 1962.

Eisenberg, Helen, and Eisenberg, Larry. *The Handbook of Skits and Stunts.* New York: Association, 1953.

———. *Omnibus of Fun.* New York: Association, 1953.

Epp, Margaret. *Come to My Party.* Grand Rapids: Zondervan, 1964.

Games and Self-Testing Activities for the Classroom. Washington, D.C.: US Government Printing Office, 1961.

Handbook for Recreation. Washington, D.C.: US Government Printing Office, 1960.

Harbin, E. O. *Games of Many Nations.* Nashville: Abingdon, 1954.

———. *The Fun Encyclopedia.* Nashville: Abingdon, 1940.

———. *The Recreation Leader.* New York: Abingdon-Cokesbury, 1952.

———. *Recreational Materials and Methods.* Nashville: Abingdon, 1931.

Harris, Kate. *Party Plans for Tots.* Chicago: Follett, 1967.

Jacobsen, Marion. *Good Times for God's People.* Grand Rapids: Zondervan, 1952.

Kraus, Richard. *Recreation Leader's Handbook.* New York: McGraw-Hill, 1955.

———. *Recreation Today: Program Planning and Leadership.* New York: Appleton-Century-Crofts, 1966.

Latchaw, Marjorie. *A Pocket Guide of Games and Rhythms for the Elementary School.* Englewood Cliffs, N.J.: Prentice-Hall, 1956.

Meyer, Harold; Brightbill, Charles; and Sessoms, Douglas. *Community Recreation: A Guide to Its Organization.* 4th ed. Englewood Cliffs, N.J.: Prentice-Hall, 1969.

Mulac, Margaret. *Fun and Games.* New York: Harper, 1956.

———. *Games and Stunts for Schools, Camp, and Playgrounds.* New York: Harper & Row, 1964.

———. *Party Fun for Holidays and Special Occasions.* New York: Harper & Row, 1960.

Mulac, Margaret, and Holmes, Marian. *The Party Game Book.* New York: Harper & Row, 1951.

Opie, Iona, and Opie, Peter. *Children's Games in Street and Playground.* London: Clarendon, 1969.

Pylant, Agnes. *Fun Plans for Church Recreation.* Nashville: Broadman, 1958.

Richart, Genevieve. *The Master Game and Party Book.* Grand Rapids: Baker, 1973.

Schwartz, Alvin. *The Rainy Day Book.* New York: Trident, 1968.

Shipley, Joseph T. *Playing with Words.* Englewood Cliffs, N.J.: Prentice-Hall, 1960.

Teaching Lifetime Sport Skills. Washington, D.C.: US Government Printing Office, 1966.

Wackerbarth, Marjorie, and Graham, Lillian S. *Games for All Ages and How to Use Them.* Grand Rapids: Baker, 1973.

———. *Successful Parties and How to Give Them.* Minneapolis: Denison, 1961.

Yukic, Thomas. *Fundamentals of Recreation.* New York: Harper & Row, 1970.

MAGAZINES

Child Life. 1100 Waterway Blvd., Indianapolis, Ind. 46202.
Church Recreation. Department of Church Recreation, Southern Baptist Convention, 127 Ninth Ave. North, Nashville, Tenn. 37203.
Highlights for Children. Highlights for Children, Inc., P. O. Box 269, Columbus, Ohio 43216.
Pack-O-Fun. 14 Main St., Park Ridge, Ill. 60068.
Recreation. National Recreation and Park Association, 1601 North Kent St., Arlington, Va. 22209.

SOURCES OF GAMES AND INFORMATION

American Art Clay Co., Indianapolis, Ind. 46222.
American Association for Health, Physical Education and Recreation, 1201 Sixteenth St., N.W., Washington, D.C. 20036.
American Crayon Co., Sandusky, Ohio 44870.
Berea College, Berea, Kentucky 40403.
Burgess Publishing Co., 426 South Sixth St., Minneapolis, Minn. 55415.
Church Recreation Service, Baptist Sunday School Board, 127 Ninth Ave. North, Nashville, Tenn. 37203.
Cooperative Recreation Service, Inc., Delaware, Ohio 43015.
Color-Graphics Division, D. C. Harris Company, Wooster, Ohio 44691.
Dennison Manufacturing Co., Framingham, Mass. 01701.
Fun Books, 5847 Gregory, Hollywood, Calif. 90028.
League of Federal Recreation Association, 927 Fifteenth Street, N.W., Washington, D.C. 20005.
National Association of County Park and Recreation Officials, 1001 Connecticut Avenue, N.W., Washington, D.C. 20036.
National Recreation and Park Association, 1601 North Kent St., Arlington, Va.: 22209.
Rainbow Crafts, Inc., Cincinnati, Ohio 45212.
World Wide Games, Inc., Box 450, Delaware, Ohio 43015.

Camping

BOOKS AND ARTICLES

Block, Frank. *Royal Ambassador Campcraft.* Memphis, Tenn.: Brotherhood Commission, Southern Baptist Convention, 1972.
Cowle, Irving M. *Day Camping.* Minneapolis: Burgess, 1964.
Doty, Richard S. *The Character Dimension of Camping.* New York: Association, 1960.
Johnson, L. Ted. "Day Camping." *The Standard,* April 3, 1972, pp. 25-26.
Leypoldt, Martha M., and Binder, Barbara Weisser. *Dynamic Junior Camping.* Forest Park, Ill.: Williams, n.d.
Mackay, Joy. *Creative Counseling for Christian Camps.* Wheaton, Ill.: Scripture Press, 1966.

———. *Raindrops Keep Falling on My Tent.* Wheaton, Ill.: Scripture Press, 1972.

Mattson, Lloyd D. *Camping Guideposts.* Chicago: Moody, 1972.

———. *Family Camping.* Chicago: Moody, 1973.

———. *Way to Grow!* Wheaton, Ill.: Scripture Press, 1973.

Mitchell, Grace L. *Fundamentals of Day Camping.* New York: Association, 1961.

The Day Camp Director's Package. Nashville: Baptist Sunday School Board, 1973. Contains one each of these books: *The Day Camp Director's Guide; The Counselor's Guide for Day Camping. The Unit 1 Camper's Book for Day Camping; The Unit 2 Camper's Book for Day Camping.*

To the Activity Specialist. Wheaton, Ill.: Pioneer Girls, 1964.

Todd, Floyd, and Todd, Pauline. *Camping for Christian Youth.* New York: Harper & Row, 1963.

Troup, Richard E. *Marks of Quality for Christ-centered Camping.* Somonauk, Ill.: Christian Camping Int., n.d.

MAGAZINES

Journal of Christian Camping. Christian Camping Int., Box 400, Somonauk, Ill. 60552.

24

Child Care Programs in the Church

Elsiebeth McDaniel

IN THE LAST TEN YEARS, at least three factors have contributed to the rapid development of child-care programs in the United States. First, Head Start, a government-sponsored program of early childhood education for children in poverty areas, has focused attention on the needs of young children. Second, the growing number of working mothers has emphasized the need for child care. And third, research in human development has revealed that the first four or five years of life are the period of most rapid physical and intellectual growth and that quality care during these years is therefore very important.

The number of working mothers in the United States has more than doubled in the last twenty years. In 1970, there were 4.2 million mothers working outside their homes; and current projections say their ranks will swell to more than six million by the early 1980s. While mothers are solving financial problems and perhaps fulfilling their own need to make contributions to society beyond that of a homemaker, they are creating other problems. The most common problem is that of finding adequate day care for their children.

However, day-care centers and nursery schools do far more than solve the working mother's problem. Good day-care centers and nursery schools provide a child with many learning experiences during his most impressionable years. A good day-care facility provides a child with more than custodial care. It is also dedicated to the development of vigorous minds and bodies.

Currently there are more than six million children needing some form of day care. It is estimated that of this total, about one million are "latch-

---

ELSIEBETH MCDANIEL, M.A., is Editor of Pre-Primary and Primary Lessons, Scripture Press Publications, Inc., Wheaton, Illinois.

key children" who must fend for themselves. Perhaps most of the children needing day care are from the inner city, but many small town and suburban communities are also interested in day care. It should be understood that a day-care center is not a substitute for a strong family life. The vast majority of children are better off in the care of their own parents twenty-four hours a day whenever possible.

However, a day-care program can provide these advantages: (1) intellectual stimulation at the child's level and suited to his capacity; (2) activities that promote healthy physical growth; (3) opportunities for maximum social growth in relationship to adults and other children; (4) assistance in sound emotional development; and (5) help for each child in building self-confidence and awareness of his unique, creative potential.

Types of Child Care Programs

What types of church child care are available? In the last few years, many churches have begun child-care programs, called either nursery schools, church kindergartens, or church day-care centers. According to one study, one in every eight churches (of the 3,100 surveyed) had some kind of during-the-week early childhood educational program.[1] This is a significant trend among churches, reflecting the national concern for young children. Most churches, of course, are challenged by the opportunity to add a spiritual dimension to child care.

Nursery schools, in contrast to day-care centers, are designed for a portion of the day—either five, three, or two mornings or afternoons a week. Nursery schools are designed to promote experiences manageable by young children. Because it is a structured program with planned activities, a shorter time—two or three hours—is advisable. Young children cannot function well in a structured program for a full school day. That is why the day-care center program, often lasting eight or ten hours each day, emphasizes free play and rest.

Nursery school introduces variety into a child's environment. It expands his horizons and experiences beyond the home. Nursery school supplements the home; it is not a substitute for the home experiences which a child and his parents need.

The longer the day for children in group care, the more the program should try to incorporate a homey atmosphere. Both at home and at school, children need opportunities to solve real problems—to learn to cope with one's self, with other children, with adults, with natural environment (the outdoors), and man-made environment (furniture, stairs, etc.).

The church kindergarten is similar to the nursery school. However, a child is usually enrolled for half-day sessions throughout the five-day week. The program is structured with definite physical skills and mental achievements built into its goals. Any church considering a kindergarten needs to be aware of the curriculum offered in public school kindergartens. Church kindergartens should achieve the same educational goals as the secular kindergarten, adding goals pertaining to spiritual knowledge and behavior.

The church kindergarten is limited to children who are four or five years of age. Like the church nursery, the kindergarten has special concern for the spiritual growth of the children it serves. Its faculty members, in addition to having teacher certification, should be dedicated Christians. Its curriculum provides opportunities for worship and other experiences that help broaden a young child's spiritual understanding.

The church day-care center has a less structured program than either the nursery school or kindergarten. Its sessions are five days a week, from early morning till late afternoon, to accommodate the working hours of parents. Though few day-care centers are able to do so, there should be some consideration for school-age children who need supervision before or after school. When possible, these children should come to the church facilities for free play and planned activities.

Reasons for Day-Care Programs

What are some of the reasons for day-care centers? In 1970, there were 16,600 licensed day-care centers, according to the US Department of Health, Education, and Welfare, plus numerous unlicensed facilities. But it is estimated that only about 625,000 children were enrolled in these centers. A report, "Windows on Day Care," compiled by the National Council of Jewish Women in 1972, indicates that only about 10 percent of the six million children under the age of six with working mothers are in *licensed* day-care centers. Many of these children are cared for by older children, a neighbor, a relative, or in an *unlicensed* facility. An unlicensed facility often makes little attempt to maintain standards of health and hygiene, to say nothing of offering the children experiences that are mentally and physically stimulating.

There is no doubt that the need for adequate day care can scarcely be overestimated. But in addition to what the secular day-care center offers, the church can reach both the child and the parents with spiritual truth. However, the local church must decide whether child care is a ministry it wishes to undertake. The answer cannot be a simple yes or no. Churches operating day-care centers indicate that there are benefits to the church. But these benefits should be regarded as by-products and not motivating factors for establishing a day-care center. The underlying reason for providing child care should be a ministry to meet crucial human needs in the name of Christ.

What are the by-product benefits to the church? One benefit is stronger ties with church families whose children are cared for in the center. Another benefit is a greater Christian influence in the community. One denomination has estimated that 17 percent of the children enrolled in child care eventually came into the church, bringing their families.

Whatever child-care program is undertaken, the ministry should be regarded as an integral part of the church's total program in the same sense as that of the Sunday school or youth program. Not only must the child care program have facilities and staff, it should also have the united prayer support and interest of the church!

Basic Considerations for a Child Care Program

What are some basic considerations for a child-care program? Though additional criteria for evaluating child-care programs appear elsewhere in this chapter, eight basic guidelines are listed here to provide an overview of specifications and considerations for child care:[2]

1. The ratio of children to teacher should be as follows:
   For two-year-olds, three children per teacher
   For three- and four-year-olds, five children per teacher
   For five- and six-year-olds, seven children per teacher
2. Space should include 75 square feet outdoors and 35 square feet indoors for each child.
3. Safety and hygiene considerations should include fire protection, adequate heating and ventilating, lighting, protection from safety hazards, liability insurance, first-aid equipment, clean kitchen facilities and toilets (at least one toilet and wash basin for every 15 children).
4. A medical report for each enrolled child should be required.
5. Both indoor and outdoor play apparatus should include blocks and other toys; raw materials for creative expression—wood, sand, clay, crayons, and paints; an ample supply of books, records, and homemade or manufactured rhythm band instruments.
6. The educational program should have understandable and measurable goals, adapted to the age groups served.
7. Teachers should be well-adjusted personalities with the necessary educational background. They should hold to the same basic beliefs as the church which administers the program.
8. The church child-care center should be especially concerned about parental involvement. If the church neglects communication with parents, it weakens its ministry to parents.

The establishment of child-care centers has hardly met the need for early childhood education. The 1970 White House Conference on Children put child care at the top of the list of sixteen "overriding concerns."[3] Many children not in child care centers are left to fend for themselves. It is not farfetched to assume that a significant percentage of these children will some day require rehabilitative services, whether by a probation officer, social worker, or psychiatrist. Good care now may reduce costs in the future.

Day care involves children at the most impressionable time of their lives. Caroline Chandler, a medical doctor, recognizes the importance of these early years. She says,

> The early years are important years because on them rests the entire span from childhood to old age. During early childhood, development comes about through two processes—maturation and learning. Although learning can be accelerated by people and things in the child's environment, the steps in maturation can be neither telescoped nor skipped. All children go through the same pattern of development even though there may be wide variation in the rate of development among individual children. This holds true for physical and emotional (or personality) development.[4]

Because early childhood years are important, a child must have the best environment possible. For many children, this is the child-care center. Educators are increasingly endorsing day care because of the benefits to the children themselves. Ideally, the mother creates the preconditions for the development of human intelligence, the foundation on which public school education builds. However, not all mothers have the time or inclination for doing this properly, and even those who are expert may need some help. The mothers who would welcome help may find it in the church nursery school or kindergarten.

The need for adequate child care is undebatable! However, the local church must do more than recognize the general need. The church must see its own vision, determine its own dedication, and declare its own involvement.

Does the local church care about day care? The alert and progressive local church cares about day care, because through an adequate program the church can accomplish these goals: (1) guide the child's physical, intellectual, emotional, social, and spiritual growth, (2) make better use of buildings and facilities during the week; (3) reach families for Christ and church membership. Through day care, families will be reached that would never open their doors (and hearts) for any other reason.

The Southern Baptist denomination has sponsored church kindergartens for a number of years. In the early 1970s, they had 1,715 known kindergartens. The estimated total number of children attending church preschools was 95,470. Of that number, only 17.5 percent were children whose parents were church members. In addition to the kindergarten program, the denomination reported 258 known day-care programs.

The Church of the Nazarene denomination, another group seeing the day-care center as an opportunity to reach unchurched families, surveyed its day-care ministries. The survey indicated that one out of every sixty children enrolled became affiliated with the local church.

In the Scripture Press Ministries survey of church day-care centers and nursery schools (referred to earlier), 50 percent of the pastors whose churches did not have a program were interested in starting child care.

Characteristics of a Good Program

What characterizes a good child care program? Consideration for the physical, mental, emotional and spiritual needs of the young child is more important than church facilities or even the opportunities of counseling with parents. A good child-care program must be geared to the needs and potential development of young children. Though originally designed to care for only the physical needs, current child-care programs seek to become interested in the *whole child.*

Any church contemplating child care must meet state and local regulations. Information is available from each state's Department of Children and Family Services at the state capital or through a regional office. Regulations will specify minimum standards. Some states will also provide budget guides for day-care centers. A state budget guide will suggest the necessary items to be purchased on a limited budget. Other helpful publications, such as suggested menus and lists of noncost or low-cost materials to equip the center, may be obtained.

The following items must be adequate before a church considers opening a day-care center:

Space: Is there space for running about freely for active play and still other space where quiet play may go on undisturbed, both indoors and out?

Hygiene: Is there adequate and approved fire protection? Are heating facilities adequate and officially approved? Is there protection against drafts?

Equipment: Are there large pieces of apparatus to climb? Are there ample raw materials that will stimulate the child's initiative and self-expression?

Personnel: Are there enough teachers both to guide the group and to take care of individual children's needs?

Methods: Is each child helped to gain increasing power in concept development? Instead of always being shown or told, is he encouraged to use materials creatively? Does the teacher realize that patterns to follow or models to copy usually hamper creativity?

Attitudes: Are the teachers well adjusted? Do they realize that human feelings are important? Do they give children a feeling of adequacy, stability, and belonging, without showing favoritism?

> Without question the intangibles for every nursery school or child care center program depend on the quality of the staff—particularly the director. He creates the atmosphere in which the children live and breathe and have their being.
>
> There are clues by which the effects of the "intangible atmosphere" on the children can be measured. Just watch them. Are they absorbed in their activities? Do they behave like people or like puppets awaiting orders? Are their faces alive and expressive or bored and listless? Is there a natural hum or normal activity and conversation or is there the enforced quiet that waits for a pin to drop with a loud clang? Are questions being asked, heard, and honestly answered? Are children feeling good about themselves? Are they valued as persons or only as automatons? Have they opportunities to experiment, make mistakes, use their own best judgment as well as improve their skills and their controls? Is their feeling of independence being encouraged? May they express individual differences or is there always only one right way—the teacher's? Can minds and bodies and feelings stretch themselves or are they kept too neatly confined by expectations of convenient conformity?[5]

A Typical Day

What are the qualifications for workers in a church-sponsored center? State certification regulations change. Therefore, it is advisable to check on current standards. However, some qualifications do not change. Love and concern are important factors, but mere affection is not enough. Some government-sponsored day-care centers have received criticism because of the affection displayed by the workers. The attitude of these workers is: "You poor deprived child. Your mommy can't be with you. So you may do whatever you want to make up for it." These workers are not expressing genuine love for the child. If they were, they would work to give him their love while making him a self-reliant and self-respecting individual in his particular set of circumstances or environment.

Because each member of the staff has a direct or indirect influence on each child, it is important that staff members respect each other and respect the children. Each staff member must consider the child's well-being as most important. In addition to education and experience, every worker in a church-sponsored child-care center should use the following personal checklist.

1. I am dependable and consistent with the children.
2. I practice patience, love, and understanding.
3. I learn from the children and other sources.
4. I know the Bible and bring its concepts into the curriculum.
5. I do my best to be physically attractive.
6. I am available to the children, meaning I respond with curiosity, enthusiasm, and enjoyment, as the need demands.
7. I enjoy children and have a growing understanding of them.
8. I know the world in which each preschooler lives—his family, home, and his activities away from the church.
9. I regularly attend courses or read books helpful to my work.
10. I realize that I will never get to the place where I know all the answers.

Qualifications for Workers

What is a typical day like in a child-care program? The daily schedule differs for each type of child-care facility, depending on the length of the day, climate, building arrangements, the children's ages, and the abiliites and interests of both the children and the staff. The program suggested here is for a day-care center operating for a full day. Nursery schools and church kindergartens could follow a similar schedule. However, the church kindergarten would include more structured activities with less emphasis on choice of activity or outdoor play. Both the nursery school and kindergarten would be in session from about nine o'clock till noon or from one o'clock to three-thirty.

If the day-care center operates only a half day, its basic program would follow the suggested program for either the morning or afternoon session. A morning day-care center would begin as does the full day program. However, it would end with a fifteen-minute period planned to prepare the children for going home. The following is a suggested schedule for a full-day day-care center:

7:30- 9:00 admission, morning health inspection, toileting period, if necessary
breakfast, if this is a regular part of the program
choice of activity—for example, dramatic play in the housekeeping corner; quiet play, such as working puzzles, using crayons, stringing beads, looking at books, block building; active play with indoor climbing equipment; easel painting; caring for small pets and plants

9:00- 9:30 morning juice, usually a social sit-down period

9:30-10:30	outdoor play (In inclement weather portable outdoor apparatus may be brought indoors.)
10:30-10:45	clean-up, toileting, washing
10:45-11:30	stories, music, conversation periods
11:30-11:45	rest or quiet period
11:45-12:15	noon meal
12:15-12:30	preparation for nap, toileting, washing, undressing
12:30- 2:30	nap
2:30- 3:00	dressing, afternoon snack
3:00- 4:00	choice of activity and perhaps some planned activities—music, stories, games
4:30- 5:30	indoor or outdoor play and preparation for going home.

Curriculum

What are some possibilities for a curriculum? The curriculum for the church-sponsored child-care center would have spiritual emphases not found in the secular program. These would include more learning experiences planned to develop concepts about biblical truths. Children would have opportunities to hear both Bible stories and modern stories that emphasize Christian beliefs. Prayer would be used whenever it seemed to fit into the conversation—thanksgiving for good times and God's gifts; petition for family and personal needs; and thanks before snacks and meals. Some of the songs, rhymes, finger plays, and other teacher-directed activities would focus on spiritual truth. Creative handwork would be more than mere fun or development of skills.

Currently, child-care staffs seem to be writing their own curriculums, adapting from a variety of published sources—both secular and religious. (Some of the religious sources are listed in the bibliography.) But there is a need for publishers to produce curriculum guides for church-sponsored child care centers. Some denominations have established curriculum guidelines, such as the following.

1. Surround a child with Christian love—both in materials and attitudes.
2. Use many opportunities to point a child to God:
   Thank God before snacks and meals.
   In conversation, express appreciation for God's goodness in weather, new clothing and experiences, new babies and pets. A child's discovery of God's handiwork in nature usually provides an opportunity to direct his thinking to the Creator and Sustainer of the universe.
3. Stories, songs, poems, and action rhymes which are not Bible stories must never be contrary to Christian beliefs. The Bible stories used

should be coordinated with those used in Sunday school and other church agencies.

4. The curriculum and daily program must meet the following needs of the child:
   a) The need for a sense of security—of feeling liked and cared for as he is; of feeling that he knows what is expected of him and that he can depend on the adults around him
   b) The need for a sense of adequacy—of feeling that he can do what is expected of him and that he can make a contribution to others—children and adults.
   c) The need for a sense of belonging—of feeling that he is accepted as part of the child care group or as a part of a small group.
   d) The need to discover and express individuality in the way a child uses materials—of feeling that he can often express his own ideas in the way he responds to and uses materials.

How should a church begin a day-care program? Halbert suggests that the following steps be taken by the study committee of a church interested in beginning a day-care center, nursery school, or kindergarten.[6]

1. Survey the needs of the church and community.
2. Survey the attitudes and interests of church members to discover their feelings toward a weekday ministry.
3. Contact agencies for information about zoning regulations, building requirements, enrollment levels, tuition, policies.
4. Evaluate the church's facilities in light of state requirements and the standards agreed on by the committee.
5. Study the community, agencies, and groups now providing this service.
6. Prepare a tentative financial plan that shows income sources and expenses.
7. Submit the information and a recommendation to the church.

The study committee or day-care board should perform the following duties to begin the school and when the school is in operation.[7]

1. Determine policies and procedures for operating and administering the program.
2. Determine staff qualifications and enlist personnel to direct and teach in the program.
3. Lead in complying with legal and licensing requirements.
4. Organize efforts to involve church members and parents.
5. Lead in an aggressive public relations program to keep church members informed and educated about activities and happenings in the school.

6. Review reports and records regularly to insure proper operation of the center.
7. Oversee the financial position and budget of the center.
8. Make regular reports and recommendations to the church about the work and activities of the program.
9. Coordinate the program with other preschool ministries of the church.

Summary

The local church should be interested in child care because it helps fulfill the Great Commission. The local church has the special resources to meet the need of a child for identity and discovery of authenticity as a person. The church is in a position to guide the child's fresh curiosity about all of life to the One who made and controls all of life. It is only the church that proclaims the living Christ as man's Redeemer. And it is in knowing Him that even a young child can find meaning and reality in life.

The Nazarene denomination emphasizes four *C*s as necessary to begin and sustain a day-care center:

1 Conviction that there is a real need to reach those outside of Christ
2. Compassion and longing to do something about the need
3. Cooperation among church members to do their share or to support paid personnel
4. Consistency in maintaining the work once begun

A church that sees child care as a fruitful ministry must begin with these four *C*s. Then certification or licensing, equipment, personnel, and curriculum fall into their proper places as means to make Christ known to young children.

NOTES

1. *Church Sponsored Day Care Centers and Nursery Schools* (Glen Ellyn, Ill.: Scripture Press, 1971), p. 6.
2. Adapted from *Some Ways of Distinguishing a Good School or Center for Young Children* (Washington, D.C.: National Assn. for Education of Young Children).
3. Kathryn Close, "Selecting Priorities at the White House Conference on Children," *Children* 18 (March-April, 1971), 42.
4. Caroline Chandler, "The Importance of the Early Years," in *Early Childhood—Crucial Years for Learning* (Washington, D.C.: Association for Childhood Education, 1971), p. 3.
5. Cornelia Goldsmith, "Begin Early," *Childhood Education* 40 (March, 1966): 344.
6. Adapted from William H. Halbert, Jr., "Weekday Early Education Committee: What Is It? How Does It Work?" *Church Administration* 15 (Dec., 1972): 16.
7. Ibid.

FOR FURTHER READING

A Creative Guide for Preschool Teachers. Racine, Wis.: Western, 1966.

Adams, Ruth J. *The Kindergarten How-To-Do-It Book.* Minneapolis: Denison, 1962.

A Lap To Sit On . . . and Much More. Washington, D.C.: Assoc. for Childhood Ed. Int., 1966.

Barry, James C., and Treadway, Charles F. *Kindergarten Resource Book.* Nashville: Broadman, 1965.

Church Sponsored Day Care Centers and Nursery Schools. Glen Ellyn, Ill.: Scripture Press, 1971.

Early Childhood: Crucial Years for Learning. Washington, D.C.: Assoc. for Childhood Ed. Int., 1966.

Evans, E. Belle, and Sain, George E. *Day Care for Infants.* Boston: Beacon, 1972.

Gilliland, Anne Hitchcock. *Understanding Preschoolers.* Nashville: Convention, 1969.

Green, Arthur S. *The Kindergarten Arts and Crafts Book.* Minneapolis: Denison, 1962.

Halbert, William H. Jr. *Church Weekday Early Education Director's Guide.* Nashville: Convention, 1972.

Hammond, Sarah Lou. *Good Schools for Young Children.* New York: MacMillan, 1963.

Hemphill, Martha. *Weekday Ministry with Young Children.* Valley Forge, Va.: Judson, 1973.

Hoover, F. Louis. *Art Activities for the Very Young.* Worcester, Mass.: Davis, 1961.

Hutchens, Elizabeth G. "The Future of Preschool Education." *Church Administration* June, 1969.

Huttar, Leora W. *Jack and Jill Stay for Church: How to Lead a Churchtime Nursery.* Chicago: Moody, 1965.

Implications of Basic Human Values for Education. Washington, D.C.: Assoc. for Childhood Ed. Int., 1964.

Johnson, L. Ted. "Serving Christ and Community Through Nursery School or Day Care Center," *The Standard* 59 (March, 1969): 25, 26.

LeBar, Mary E. *Wonder Programs for 4s and 5s, Yearbook 1.* Wheaton, Ill.: Scripture Press, 1972.

———. *Wonder Programs for 4s and 5s: Yearbook 2.* Wheaton, Ill.: Scripture Press, 1973.

Newbury, Josephine. *Nursery-Kindergarten Weekday Education in the Church.* Richmond: Knox, 1960.

Robison, Helen F. and Spodek, Bernard. *New Directions in the Kindergarten.* New York: Columbia U., Teachers College Press, 1967.

Tobey, Kathrene McLandress. *The Church Plans for Kindergarten Children.* Philadelphia: Westminster, 1959.

Wetzel, V. Robert. "Ways a Christian Preschool Serves the Community." *Leader Guidebook* 72 (April-June, 1971): 3-6.

Part VI

WORKING WITH EXCEPTIONAL CHILDREN

25

Teaching Gifted Children

Charles T. Smith

SPECIAL EDUCATION for the intellectually gifted dates back to at least the seventh century before Christ. Nebuchadnezzar, the great Babylonian king, had besieged and crushed the city of Jerusalem, deporting many of its citizens. He ordered the chief of his officials to bring some of the sons of Israel, including members of the royal family and of the nobles to serve in his palace. In order to qualify, they were to be those "in whom was no defect, who were good looking, showing intelligence in every branch of wisdom, endowed with understanding, and discerning knowledge, and who had ability for serving in the king's court" (Dan 1:4, NASB). Once selected, these candidates entered a vigorous three-year education program involving the "literature and language of the Chaldeans" (Dan 1:4, NASB). Daniel and his three friends became the king's top pupils.

HISTORY OF EDUCATION FOR THE GIFTED

History reveals definite efforts to educate the gifted and to utilize their talents. Over 2000 years ago, in ancient Greece, Plato advocated that young children of superior intellect be selected for education in specialized forms of science, philosophy, and metaphysics. The survival of Greek democracy was seen by Plato to be contingent on the eventual use of these superior citizens in leadership roles in the state.[1]

In the sixteenth century, special efforts were promoted by Suleiman the Magnificent to identify the gifted Christian youth in the Turkish empire and educate them in Islam, philosophy, science, art, and war. Surveillance of the population at regular intervals led to the selection and education of a large group of superior individuals who, after one generation, made the Ottoman Empire a great power in science, art, culture, and war.[2]

CHARLES T. SMITH, M.R.E., is Minister to Children at the College Avenue Baptist Church, San Diego, California.

In the seventeenth century, the bishop Comenius made frequent reference to the special education of students with exceptional aptitudes for learning. He advocated financial aid to those bright students from poor homes.[3]

Thomas Jefferson, early in the eighteenth century, proposed that the state of Virginia "strengthen its natural aristocracy of virtues and talents by establishing rigorously selective tests in the grammar schools through which 'the best geniuses will be raked from the rubbish annually' and sent to William and Mary College at public expense."[4]

During the nineteenth and twentieth centuries, little organized effort was made in Europe and the United States to select the gifted children for special education. In Europe, secondary schools and universities were generally keyed to educate those of higher social class and family influence from which the more intelligent were believed to come. Now there is a growing trend to base such education on the academic achievement and interests of the children.[5]

The United States has concentrated its efforts on the education of all children, through mass education procedures, believing that all men are created with equal potential and thus worthy of equal educational opportunities. Until recently, however, special educational provisions for gifted children (such as special classes and programs) did not receive wide public support. The present interest in the education of the gifted is due to a number of national and international situations: (1) the sharp conflict of ideology between nations; (2) the knowledge explosion; and (3) complaints about the place of the gifted child in the American educational system.[6]

Identifying the Gifted Child

There are various opinions among educators as to what constitutes a gifted child. Many use the word *gifted* synonymously with "high IQ" (intelligence quotient—the ratio between mental age, determined by tests, and chronological age). Others believe that the use of intelligence tests as the sole measure of giftedness is inadequate. They point out that intelligence tests fail to measure sufficiently a broad range of cognitive abilities (convergent thinking rather than divergent is the main emphasis, thus nullifying the creative abilities) and cannot adequately account for school achievement and academic performance (a child with a high IQ may do poorly in school, and one with a low IQ may do well).[7]

A Broader Definition of Giftedness

Sometimes individuals are thought to be gifted due to the extent of their proficiency in music, art, drama, or mechanics, and many other areas, as opposed to strict academic giftedness. For this reason, the National Society for the Study of Education defined giftedness thus: "A talented or gifted child is one who shows consistently remarkable performance in any worth-while line of endeavor. Thus, this definition includes not only the intellectually gifted but also those who show promise in music, the graphic arts, creative writing, dramatics, mechanical skills, and social leadership."[8] But Kirk points out that this definition is based solely on performance rather than on potential development; it excludes the underachieving gifted child and the one who uses his abilities in socially unacceptable channels.[9]

Sumption and Luecking define the gifted as "those who possess a superior central nervous system characterized by the potential to perform tasks requiring a comparatively high degree of intellectual abstraction or creative imagination or both."[10] Most studies have established a substantial relationship between creativity and intellectual aptitude, though a few have supported the creativity-intelligence distinction.[11]

The first definition is broad, allowing for achievement in any area; while the latter considers the potential to achieve. Perhaps Neff's eclectic definition is best since it combines the best of both aspects: "The gifted person is one whose performance, or potential to perform, in worth-while human endeavors requiring a comparatively high degree of intellectual abstraction and/or creative imagination is consistently remarkable."[12]

IQ—THE FINAL MEASURE OF GIFTEDNESS

Despite the current efforts to depend less on IQ in identifying the gifted, most schools and educators continue to rely on standardized intelligence tests, due primarily to the fact that there are few other measuring devices. Kirk admits that superior intelligence is only one way of determining success and achievement but believes it still remains the basic ingredient of what is called giftedness. For practical purposes, he narrows giftedness to a few general terms: "*superior ability to deal with facts, ideas, or relationships,* whether this ability comes from high IQ or a less well-defined creativity." He then proceeds to refer to those with special aptitudes (mechanical, artistic, musical, physical, linguistic, social) as talented, rather than gifted. He realizes that there is considerable overlapping between those who are talented and those who are gifted; the very talented may also be intellectually gifted.[13]

When IQ is used for identifying giftedness, authorities set different standards, ranging from an IQ of 115 to an IQ of 180 and above.[14] Keller defines the academically talented as those with IQ's of 116 and above (Binet test), constituting 20 percent of the school population. Among this group are "most of the creatively talented, many of the psychosocially talented and a good portion of the kinesthetically talented."[15] Federal education officials list two gifted levels. The gifted are those with IQs of 132, and they comprise approximately 3 percent of the school population. The highly gifted are those with IQs of 148, and they comprise only 1 percent of the school population.[16] Kirk prefers to make the standard for giftedness higher, beginning with IQs above 148. "Superior" children are those with IQs from 116 to 132, and the "very superior" have IQs ranging from 132 to 148.[17]

Causes of Giftedness

FAMILY BACKGROUND AND INFLUENCE

According to Keller, there is a growing resource of information on gifted children. They tend to come from small families (frequently the first child), from well-educated and productive parents (30 percent of children from gifted parents are also gifted), from high socioeconomic background (40 percent do not need college scholarships), from certain ethnic-cultural origins (first are English, German, and Jewish families), and from particular religions (first Jews, then Protestants, and then Catholics).[18]

Mounting evidence points to the strategic role of the parents and family in the development of gifted children. "Considering that most persons concerned about raising the intellectual level of Americans concentrate on improving the schools, this may well be the most significant oversight in American education."[19] Pressey points up the importance of early training and postulates that "a practical genius is produced by giving a precocious, able youngster early encouragement, intensive instruction, continuing opportunity as he advances, a congruent stimulating social life, and cumulative success experiences."[20]

On the other hand, undue parental pressure on children to learn and succeed may be harmful to children; intellectual growth depends largely on intellectual readiness, intrinsic motivation, and an accepting, encouraging environment.

HEREDITY VERSUS ENVIRONMENT

Heredity as well as environment has an impact on intellectual ability. Jensen has concluded that about 80 percent of intelligence is determined by heredity, while others estimate that the inherited factor is only from 25 to 45 percent.[21] In a congressional report by the United States Commissioner of Education, the inherited factor rates high. "Various estimates of the proportions of intelligence variance due to heredity and environment, based on twin studies over a twenty year period, ascribe from sixty to eighty percent to heredity. All of the researchers agree that some part of the variance must be attributed to the effect of the environment in which children are reared."[22]

The preschool years are particularly important in the development of intelligence. Bloom believes that half of a seventeen-year-old's mental ability is developed in his first four years of life.[23] Furthermore, it is said that in Bloom's analysis of major studies, he concluded, "The greatest impact on IQ from environmental factors would probably take place between the ages of 1 and 5, with relatively little impact after age 8."[24]

These facts have become part of the rationale for public and private thrusts in preschool education.

Characteristics of Gifted Children

Although no two gifted children are alike, they do tend to possess certain characteristics that distinguish them from other children. Observant teachers will be able to spot these characteristics or abilities both in and out of the classroom.

GENERAL CHARACTERISTICS

According to a recent study on the education of mentally gifted minors (based on 132 IQ as the beginning of giftedness), such children are likely to possess the following abilities:

1. They learn to read earlier and with greater comprehension. Kindergarten teachers need to discover which of their pupils already read, and arrange curriculum accordingly.
2. They learn basic skills faster and need less practice. If parents and teachers persist in teaching the gifted child at the same speed and with the same amount of repetition as a normal child, the advanced one will become bored, careless, and lose his motivation.
3. They can understand abstract ideas that other children at the same age level cannot.
4. They pursue interests beyond the usual limitations of childhood.
5. They can comprehend implications and nuances which other children need to have explained to them. Gifted ones pick up more information and do so faster.
6. They can take responsibility at an earlier stage in life and assume it more naturally.
7. They can maintain much longer concentration periods. They often become immersed with the facts and content of a subject for its own interest, not because it was presented entertainingly.
8. They can express thoughts readily and communicate with clarity in one or more areas of talent.

9. They read widely, quickly, and intensely in one subject or in many areas.

10. They have seemingly limitless energy to expend.

11. They can manifest creative and original verbal or physical responses.

12. They employ a more complex processing of information than the average child their age.

13. They can respond and relate well to peers, parents, teachers, and adults who likewise function easily in the higher-level thinking processes, depending upon a balance in their emotional adjustment.

14. They can have many projects going, particularly at home, so that they are either busily occupied or looking for something to do.

15. They often assume leadership roles because the innate sense of justice that is often noticeable in them, and youth gives them strength to which other young people respond.[25]

There are some additional characteristics which may also evidence themselves in the gifted child. He may have a highly developed sense of humor and creative wit. His nonconformity may be a troublesome characteristic to his parents and teachers and is generally related to his highly original and creative nature. Socially the gifted child may find himself in a dilemma, wanting to be loved and share love, but being critical, snobbish, and even intolerant of others with less talent. Nevertheless, he is often found to be cheerful, thoughtful, sympathetic, generous, and conscientious.[26]

In physique and general health, the gifted child surpasses the best standards for American children.[27] Coupled with his excellent physical development is his superior muscular coordination (though his handwriting may be poor anyway).[28]

One of the activities he enjoys is collecting things, frequently of an unusual or complicated nature (stamps, butterflies, chemicals, archaeological artifacts). His hobbies are numerous and precocious when compared to those of children the same chronological age.[29]

RELIGIOUS CHARACTERISTICS

Neff, writing from a religious perspective, adds the following general characteristics:

1. The gifted child has an earlier and greater degree of religious development. By reading over the general characteristics of gifted children, it is necessary only to transfer them into a Christian education setting to see the type of pupil the parent and the Sunday school teacher has to teach. His ability to learn and understand the Bible and its abstract doctrinal concepts and principles for living is great. The gifted student will begin earlier to ask searching questions about the universe, the purpose for life,

the reason for creation, the effects of man's fall, the means of salvation, the destiny of man, the nature of angelic creatures, the nature of God and the Trinity, and questions on ethical principles, problems and solutions. His higher intelligence provides the need and reason for earlier religious instruction. And the higher the intelligence, the greater the demand for such Christian teaching.[30]

Monroe states that a child's ability to understand abstract concepts (which is basic to understanding theological concepts) depends on (1) his innate mental ability; (2) the nature of his environment; and (3) his particular pattern in rate of growth.[31]

It is obvious that the gifted child will understand abstract theological concepts (i.e., Jesus is the same as God, or Jesus had to die to obtain our salvation) much sooner than the normal child, due to his exceptional intellectual ability.

2. Neff's second characteristic of a gifted child is a reasoning ability that allows him to perceive subtle relationships and to observe inconsistencies. It is this quality that makes the gifted child seem so adult-like. His early use of the words *like* and *as* indicate his ability to generalize (a process resulting in the use of similes and metaphors as he sees similarities and makes comparisons).[32] After the father of a bright four-year-old read from a Bible storybook the story of David and Goliath, the daughter, with all sincerity, asked, "Daddy, did God like David to kill Goliath?" The question was loaded. Only recently had the mother exhorted her not to hit other children in the neighborhood. The child was confronted with an apparent conflict in morality that perplexed her. The father's explanation failed to satisfy her, so she repeated the question two more times. The gifted child will be quick to note subtle relationships and point up any inconsistencies.

3. The gifted child has a highly developed moral and spiritual awareness with the unusual ability to translate this into conduct. The gifted child's interest in religious things coincides with his mental age rather than his chronological age. Therefore, when he reaches the mental age of about twelve, according to Hollingworth, he is ready for full admittance to religious participation (church doctrinal orientation and active church membership).[33]

Therefore, an understanding of the gospel of Christ and personal response to it in conversion will logically accompany the gifted child's early spiritual awareness. It is probable that this decision will easily precede the child's twelfth year, depending on the nurture received and readiness factors other than intellect. His spiritual maturity in understanding and behavior are likely to set him apart from his peers and may result in social separation—something to be guarded against.

4. The gifted child has a tendency toward self-criticism and moral anxiety. The gifted child's keen insight, critical judgment, knowledge, and unusual ability to make evaluations have both good and bad points. With his sense of moral values developing earlier than other children, he becomes disturbed (e.g., a preschooler watching a boxing match on TV with his father) over the mistreatment of others and may accept personal responsibility, even guilt, for group actions. The gifted child tends to set high standards for himself, his family, and his church group. He may become disillusioned with the group if they fail to measure up to his standards.[34]

5. The gifted child searches for purpose and meaning in life. He seeks a reason for being and exerts considerable energy to accomplish something of real worth. It is Neff's conviction that in the religious realm, this quest for meaning generally turns out to be a baffling and frustrating experience. The child becomes confused by unacceptable answers to his questions about God, bored with the traditional methods of Christian instruction, disgusted over the inconsistencies, frustrated over his own unresolved spiritual conflicts, and senses guilt because of injustices. Soon a feeling of alienation from God sets in, due to his lack of appropriate, harmonized, theological information.[35]

The gifted child's search for eternal purpose becomes stalled, and he often rejects Christianity. In time he either becomes involved in some fanatical endeavor or lives out his life in meaningless, unfulfilled existence. Only a few are fortunate enough to be guided into a constructive and reasonable faith in God.[36] The challenge of meeting the gifted child's need for purpose and meaning in life within existing structures of Christian education is one to which the Christian teacher should forthrightly and intelligently respond.

Education of the Gifted

After the Soviet Union launched Sputnik, national interest was created for the special education of the gifted children in the United States. At that time, the prevalent idea was the acceleration of federally sponsored education programs for the gifted. Soon special provisions were being made to adapt the school program to the abilities of the gifted children, including "1) accelerating, enriching, or grouping children, 2) devising a curriculum suitable to children with high abilities, and 3) utilizing appropriate instructional procedures."[37]

Organizational Procedures

The first of these provisions relates to the organizational procedures commonly used in providing an appropriate learning environment for gifted students in public schools.

Acceleration. A method frequently employed is known as acceleration, which involves stepping up the learning pace for the gifted student. Acceleration takes on several forms: (1) early admission to kindergarten or the first grade; (2) skipping grades; and (3) telescoping grades.

Frequently acceleration involves the early admission of children to kindergarten or the first grade. Intellectual readiness of pupils for such a step is determined by individually administered IQ tests, and social readiness is determined by interviews with school officials and observation of the children in informal group play. Early admission has the value of adapting to the readiness of children and providing a greater likelihood that the entrant will pursue an undisturbed course in elementary school; further acceleration is rarely necessary.[38]

A second form of acceleration is skipping grades, which involves completely eliminating one grade of school. Gold believes there is little justification for skipping grades, since it is employed as the simplest solution to the obvious boredom of a bright child. Initially, skipping is a challenge to the child, but soon the problem repeats itself and demands more skipping, and may eventually place the child out of reach of his friends and in a class where he is the smallest pupil.[39] Kirk disagrees and cites research that demonstrates that "children who have skipped grades have shown social, educational, and vocational adjustment superior or comparable to that of equally intelligent nonaccelerates."[40]

A third form of acceleration is telescoping grades, which enables gifted children to cover the same material provided in a regular curriculum but in a shorter time.[41] The nongraded elementary class is a good example. For some three years, children remain in a basic group (either primary or intermediate) and are helped to make individual progress toward specific, individual, learning goals. If academic progress leads to an early completion of the class (in two years rather than three), promotion from the ungraded class may occur.[42] Pupils are frequently grouped according to ability within a class or placed in separate classes for brighter learners.[43]

Enrichment. The second organizational procedure involves providing special opportunities for the gifted student to broaden and deepen his interests and insights through many activities and experiences within the regular school class or program. *Enrichment* has been tried through the following procedures: (1) challenging children in regular grades with additional reading assignments and outside class activities; (2) grouping children within the class for activities that fit their abilities and interests; (3) employing a special teacher who helps identify the gifted, assists the regular teachers in the instruction of their gifted pupils, counsels these children regarding their study activities, and holds some special study seminars with them; and (4) encouraging the maintenance of high standards in the instruction of the gifted.[44]

According to Gallagher, enrichment has often failed to meet educational anticipations due to the additional work required of the teacher. Special assignments must be worked out for the gifted child on top of those already required for the rest of the class. The teacher must also be well oriented in advanced subject matter to provide effective student guidance. Furthermore, appropriate methods of stimulating the high-level concept realization and productive thinking capable of the gifted students again strains the teacher's knowledge.[45] The use of assistant teachers or teacher's aides especially oriented to meet some of these special enrichment needs may be one way to bring about greater success.

Grouping. Another organizational procedure used in teaching the gifted involves grouping them in one of the following ways: (1) within regular classrooms (for academic subjects); (2) in special sections for the study of academic subjects (e.g., English, science, mathematics, and social studies); (3) in modified special classes (special instruction with other gifted students as a part of each school day); (4) in special classes (progressing from grade to grade but with a special curriculum adapted to their interests and abilities); and (5) in special schools (separate institutions for the gifted). The first two provisions are the most widely accepted, while the last three are more controversial.[46]

"The fundamental argument for such grouping rests on the belief that it drastically reduces the wide variation in achievement found in a heterogeneous group."[47] But Burns and Johnson contend that research does not support the practice of sectioning bright pupils into classrooms for the purpose of attaining a homogeneous learning group. They point out that the achievement differences between a normal group of students and a gifted group is not of a significant magnitude to have a practical influence in the classroom. Every group of students has high, average, and low achievers (the bright child may be in any of these categories) in any particular achievement area. "If ability grouping based upon intelligent quotient is to be used with pupils of average to very superior ability, the justification for such grouping will have to depend on reasons other than homogeneity of achievement."[48]

Glasser believes that keeping classes grouped heterogeneously rather than homogeneously has at least three advantages: (1) they eliminate early segregation of various types of students; (2) they keep communication open between the potential student failures and the successful students; (3) the faster learners can help motivate and assist the slower ones.[49]

Glasser contends that virtually all subjects are easily and best taught in mixed groups. The heterogeneous class will succeed except when there is a great disparity in reading levels accompanied by behavior disturbances. Homogeneous reading groups are then employed, meeting about one and one-half hours each day. These groups are evaluated at least twice a semester so that rapidly progressing students may be moved on to a more advanced group.[50]

IMPLICATIONS FOR CHRISTIAN EDUCATION

The Christian day school generally follows the organizational procedures commonly practiced in public education, and the Sunday school may follow in a somewhat similar way. If a particular child is entering kindergarten or the first grade early, he will obviously do so in the graded Sunday school program. The same procedure will follow if he skips a grade.

If the child is in a nongraded primary or intermediate class, he may be placed in his chronological age Sunday school department or class or an older department or class that fits his level of social and intellectual maturity. Since the child is in Sunday school only an hour a week, his sense of social acceptance and comfort is of significance. Therefore, teachers should be careful not to accelerate him to a group where he is hindered in developing friendships.

Group-graded departments of children will offer a child contact with his peers and also the opportunity to progress, according to his ability, with children who are older. In this case, teachers must be alert to the fact that the gifted child should be encouraged to go to an older class or group that fits his ability or to choose a learning activity that challenges his interest and capabilities.

Closely graded departments may have as much as a four-year span of abilities represented among their one-year chronologically grouped pupils. Care should be given in placing the gifted child among students with whom he can successfully work and learn; a capable teacher is of paramount importance.

Enrichment is a logical means of keeping the bright child challenged in the Sunday school, but the department superintendent and teacher are the key to its success. Additional activities and assignments may be initiated by the pupil or suggested by the teacher. Independent work or collaboration with other students in researching and completing certain creative, Bible-learning activities will certainly be a productive procedure to follow.

Such small group collaboration may represent ability grouping within a graded department or class, similar to that which Glasser recommends, when a homogeneous grouping proves unsatisfactory. For example, the gifted child who is six years old may already be reading on a third grade level. He may therefore have to work independently or in collaboration with one or more pupils who are able to read well. But the worship, music, and discussion activities will generally suit both the gifted and the average child.

Special classes or modified classes for superior and gifted children may be put to use either on Sunday or during the week for educational purposes. No church should feel locked into a heterogeneous grouping of children if particular needs may be better met in a more homogeneous grouping. Churches that are running a two- to three-hour Sunday morning educational schedule may find the modified special class fits perfectly into their schedule. Gifted and superior-ability students may meet together for forty-five minutes to an hour with an able teacher for special studies utilizing library resources for research, exploring Bible subjects of interest to them.

CURRICULUM PROCEDURES WITH GIFTED CHILDREN

The discussion of the characteristics of gifted children and organizational procedures in providing adequately for their education has already provided some insight into the type of curriculum and instructional approach needed.

The curriculum plan must fit the gifted child's needs and capabilities. Kirk suggests five ways the elementary school curriculum may be expanded for the gifted. These ideas can be adapted easily into the church educational program.

Exploring structure and principles. First, there needs to be an emphasis on the gross structure and basic principles of subject content rather than on mere facts. Gifted elementary students will particularly benefit from understanding the underlying scheme—structure, ideas, theories—of the subjects they study. Once this underlying scheme has been found, the advanced students will be more freely motivated to absorb new knowledge and grasp the specific facts of the field. Gifted students are able to handle the theoretical aspects of the various fields of knowledge and in a sense emulate the scientist in the investigation of the phenomena behind the product.[51]

The gifted child will become bored if his teachers only tell the familiar Bible stories and do not give him opoprtunity to explore the entire background of a particular event and to find and investigate the biblical principles behind God's actions. The preadolescent pupil may want to compare the ethical teachings of the Old Testament with the New Testament, explore the geological evidence for a worldwide flood, or search out the theories on the origin of the Bethlehem star. The Bible itself may be a wonder to this child, and he may want to examine the evidences for its validity. His curiosity—even his doubts—must never threaten the teacher but serve to motivate further study and instruction.

Searching the method as well as the facts. Second, there needs to be an emphasis on the methods used to gain information rather than on the information itself. Again, the student is to act as a scientist in his exploration of assigned problems, using plans of operation provided by his teacher. Explanations by the teacher on cause and effect are to be avoided, since the objective in his approach is for the student to discover these relationships on his own.[52]

As the gifted child is led in the study of the Bible, he may soon desire an understanding of how the Bible was written, including information about the authors of the various books, dates the books were composed, how they became canonized, and how they have been preserved. A simplified study of the Dead Sea Scrolls may be particularly appreciated by the gifted student. The study of elemental biblical hermeneutics may even interest the older elementary student. The exploration of biblical manners and customs and archaeology may also prove an effective study for the students who wish to know how biblical people lived, worked, and traveled, and how such information sheds light on our understanding of Scripture.

Capitalizing on interests and readiness. Third, there needs to be an emphasis on being aware of the interests and readiness of the gifted child. Frequently the child asks questions and expresses interest in discussing subjects which parents and teachers may feel he is totally unprepared to understand. But the gifted child is able to understand concepts traditionally reserved for high school students when he is taught them in a simplied form. Bruner advocates this approach in his "spiral curriculum," in which children are taught and then retaught in an expanded form the great issues, principles, and values of society in a manner consistent with their form of thought and frame of reference.[53]

The Jewish fathers practiced this principle in the instruction of their children through the annual feasts (i.e., Passover, Pentecost, Atonement, Tabernacles). Their small children would not understand the deep significance of the Passover lamb or the symbolism of the Day of Atonement. But each year their understanding was deepening, and, for the bright Jewish child, a comprehension of the abstract meaning of these concrete observances was increasing each time they were experienced.

Sunday school teachers will be presenting significant biblical personages and events to their children which the gifted child will have comprehended at a much younger age. Each coverage should bring something new to light for the students, and the gifted child will soon explore the stories to their depths. The teacher should be alert to each child's interests and readiness to further explore biblical doctrines and subjects and be able to guide him in following these interests to his intellectual satisfaction and for his Christian nurture.

Expanding content, depth, and breadth. Fourth, there needs to be an emphasis on expanding the depth and breadth of the curriculum. Special classes for the gifted tie directly into meeting this need, but regular class enrichment is certainly a key means of expanding subject content for the gifted student. Enrichment may be accomplished either through additional reading and assignments in a subject (breadth), or through a more intensive study of some aspect of the curriculum (depth) rather than a superficial approach to it.[54]

Christian education within the church program must be characterized by flexibility in approach to studying the Bible. Teachers who have a gifted child in their group should be prepared to lead him more deeply or broadly in the subjects, issues, and people of the Scriptures. In studying events in the life of the apostle Paul, the gifted child may wish to trace Paul's life from beginning to end or concentrate on one aspect of his life, such as his strict Jewish upbringing and training as a Pharisee. If the gifted child is expected to be content with studying the same material and in the same fashion as the other students, boredom is sure to result.

Using resource persons. Fifth, there needs to be an emphasis on using special teachers or resource persons to assist in meeting the far-flung interests of the gifted child. It is frequently necessary to call such persons into the class or send the gifted pupil or group to such persons to gain futher information and guidance. Team teaching is sometimes used to provide instruction in specific areas by competent teachers. Academic guidance may also be provided through a special teacher who is able to ascertain a gifted pupil's interests and abilities and direct him into a challenging and need-fulfilling area of study.[55]

Those who are teaching a gifted child will find using resource persons to be particularly rewarding when they reach the limitations of their own knowledge in a technical, theoretical, doctrinal, historical, or philosophical area of student inquiry. Admitting one's lack of knowledge in an area and then calling on others (the pastor, education director, seminary student, adult teacher) for special assistance will help hold the gifted child's interest and satisfy his budding curiosity and hunger for spiritual knowledge and guidance.

Older preschool as well as elementary gifted students can ask some profound questions and launch out into some heavy subjects. Such inquiries may be converted into learning activities, placing the pupils in the exploratory learning role and directing them to the persons who may provide just the information needed. At times, the pupils should be led to share their discoveries with the entire class or department for the group's stimulation and benefit.

INSTRUCTIONAL PROCEDURES WITH GIFTED CHILDREN

A broad range of instructional procedures needs to be employed in teaching the gifted child including the use of (1) creative teaching principles; (2) creative teaching methods and activities; and (3) flexible groupings and scheduling. These procedures will be discussed as they relate to Christian education.

Creative teaching principles. When the teaching of the gifted child is approached in ordinary, traditional ways, pupil dissatisfaction may result. More progressive or creative principles must be employed, which lead to the direct involvement of the pupil in satisfying learning experiences. Some of the important principles are as follows:

1. The gifted child must be presented with a constant intellectual challenge both at school and at home.
2. The gifted child must be exposed to large bodies of knowledge.
3. The gifted child's curriculum should be characterized by breadth, depth, and flexibility.
4. The gifted child requires adequate time for exploration of knowledge and critical thinking.
5. The gifted child's independence, originality, and creative expression in learning must be encouraged and utilized.
6. The gifted child must have the freedom to initiate or suggest learning ideas and activities and choose the specific activities he desires to pursue.
7. The gifted child learns easier with less repetition, drill, and routine.
8. The gifted child must have a receptive learning environment that assists him in meeting his needs of affection, independence, approval, and self-esteem.
9. The gifted child must be stimulated to further study to avoid underachievement and to realize fully his potential.
10. The gifted child needs guidance in the rational and creative use of his knowledge.
11. The gifted child must have his individual achievements oriented socially and spiritually.
12. The sum total of the gifted child's learning experiences must fit his religious as well as general characteristics.

Creative teaching methods and activities. It is quite obvious that the effective teaching of the gifted child will require a greater variety of methods; the standard methods (storytelling, flannelgraph, discussion, workbook activity, memory work) will not by themselves fit the principles already outlined. Many of the traditional methods result in more teacher activity than pupil activity; this is just the opposite of what is needed.

There are some ten categories of creative methods which may serve as avenues of learning for the gifted child: (1) art (painting, clay modeling, etc.); (2) writing; (3) drama (pantomime, role playing, picture posing); (4) group vocals; (5) interviewing (biblical and contemporary persons); (6) music; (7) map study; (8) construction (tabernacle, Palestinian home), (9) learning games and puzzles; and (10) research (field trips, using resource books and visual aids).

The preschool child will find art, construction, music, and puzzle activities particularly useful. The various interest centers in his Sunday school class may contain the materials necessary for good learning. A book rack may contain books with more detailed Bible story pictures and captions which the older, bright preschooler may be able to read. An easel and paints may provide the child with tools necessary for painting pictures of Bible events or people. Play dough or clay may be the means of "making" his church or the bread and fishes Jesus used to feed the people. Puzzles should naturally be more complicated than those used with the gifted child's peers. While the child is physically engaged, he will be more fluent in conversation with his teachers about God's world, church, book, people, and acts.

Enrichment of the children's curriculum will also be facilitated through the use of creative methods. Bible stories and correlated music will naturally accompany the Bible learning activities that the children suggest and/or choose. Any one of the avenues or methods may serve as a challenging approach, if it leads to the impression and expression of an appropriate breadth and depth of Bible knowledge. The gifted child will participate earlier in creative writing activities and research than the average child, due to his rapidly developing vocabulary (i.e., writing contemporary versions of Bible stories, diaries of Bible personalities, Bible times newspapers using the Bible and other resource books for important information). His contributions in art, modeling, and construction activities will be more detailed and complicated. His research projects (using books, cassette tapes, programmed materials) will be particularly rewarding to him and with guidance, his factual findings may be worked into a game form to be used by his peers.

Flexible groupings and scheduling. Flexibility of approach is essential in dealing with the varied differences in individual needs, interests, backgrounds, and aptitudes in the average class. In such an environment, the gifted child is more free to investigate and pursue his interests. Furthermore, the entire class or department may benefit considerably from special reports and presentations by the gifted child.[56]

If a church is following the plans the major Sunday school curriculum publishers recommend for preschool education, adequate flexibility in groupings and schedule is generally provided. Children are free to roam from group to group as they participate in interest centers of their choice, each stressing some aspect of the Bible story and theme. Teachers at each center guide the informal participation of the children and may enrich the learning activity for the gifted child. These children may desire to stay with an activity for a longer period, pursuing the subjects in greater detail with the teacher.

On the middle and older children's level, traditional plans and schedules do not generally provide the flexibility desired for the gifted child. Children are placed for thirty to forty-five minutes in permanent class groups in which each child is expected to participate in the same teacher-led experiences. When few, if any, learning activity options and choices are provided, a sterile atmosphere for the gifted child exists.

Plans that are most conducive to the gifted child include temporary groupings of pupils (those which only last as long as a unit of study, usually a month), which are organized around Bible learning activities chosen by the pupils. This arrangement allows the gifted child's interest and curiosity to be channeled into an area of study which he may suggest or be led into according to his ability. Such activities may either be individualized (something frequently preferred by the gifted child) or carried on with a group of pupils who may represent a wide range of intellectual capabilities (where the gifted child may spearhead the study and indirectly assist in teaching the slower students).

The type of learning activity will generally determine how successfully the gifted child may collaborate with slower pupils. Does the activity challenge his abilities? Does it tap his curiosity or interests? Do they include study procedures and skills that both the average and gifted child can perform on their own level? Is the nature of the activity such that it constitutes a meaningful learning experience both for the average and gifted pupil? Frequently the gifted child will enjoy doing the technical research necessary for the construction of a model of the tabernacle, while other children may enjoy gathering the materials and making the objects that will go into this project. Thus, collaborative learning between a wide range of student abilities is possible.

THE TEACHER OF GIFTED CHILDREN

The teacher is the key figure in the Christian education of the gifted. He is not only the trusted and wise guide and advisor but a model of intellectual interest and achievement. His basic role is to stimulate intellectual interest in Bible study and to structure effective learning experiences, rather than being merely a conveyor of facts and information. His approach and methods are flexible and creative rather than authoritarian and traditional. He maintains a positive attitude in teaching that encourages the creativity and spontaneity of the gifted in learning.

The best teacher for gifted children will not necessarily be the most learned and educated, but the one who has the ability to stimulate the gifted pupil to maximum achievement.

The teacher's qualifications which assist in accomplishing this end will include the following, some of which are adapted from Hildreth's discussion of this subject:[57]

1. He is enthusiastic about God and His Word, and possesses a vital, growing relationship with Christ and the body of Christ.
2. He possesses a healthy emotional, mental, and social state of being with which the gifted child may identify.
3. His training includes not only experience in creative teaching but a broad range of subject knowledge, including a competent grasp of Bible doctrine, history, and customs.
4. He understands and loves children and possesses a keen knowledge of the gifted child's general and spiritual characteristics.
5. He has the ability to discern the special interests and talents of the gifted (musical, artistic, mechanical, etc.) and is likely to arouse and utilize them in the teaching-learning process.
6. He has the ability to manage teaching in a small group as well as on an individual basis.
7. He encourages original thinking and intelligent problem solving.
8. He possesses skill in listening to children's questions and helping them seek out answers.
9. He is skilled in the techniques of intelligent conversation, questioning, and answering.
10. He develops a meaningful relationship with the gifted child and his parents and assists the parents in meeting the intellectual and spiritual needs of their children.

The training of the gifted child will include the normal orientation and experience necessary for regular Christian day school or Sunday school teachers. Additional preparation will be necessary in the areas already discussed in this chapter. Furthermore, the educational resources and supplies which are so vitally related to the enrichment or acceleration of the gifted child's Christian education must be available and employed by the teacher.

THE CHURCH'S ROLE IN TEACHING THE GIFTED

It is the local church's responsibility to make adequate provisions for the Christian education of gifted children. In the average-size church, the number of gifted children will be small, and, as a result, they may constitute an overlooked minority. Yet these children offer a great deal of promise in their contributions to Christianity in its mission in the world.

The following are suggested steps which the church should follow in carefully planning and developing a ministry to the gifted. First, the church should determine the need in the church and in the community by the following procedures: (1) it should discover who the gifted ones are; (2) it should gather information from teachers and parents which may reveal the giftedness of a particular child; (3) it should consult with public school officials as to which children score in the upper 5 or 10 percent of pupils of a particular age (those who gather this information must keep it in strict confidence); (4) it must not administer intelligence tests; (5) it should seek to identify the gifted by uncovering their talents.

Second, the church should institute a program for gifted children, using the following guidelines: (1) it should study the effectiveness of the education presently being provided for gifted children in the elementary or church school; (2) it should determine the acceleration or enrichment needed; (3) it should evaluate the teacher changes or adjustments required; (4) it should seek out the teachers most suited to teach gifted children and approach them for this ministry; (5) it should prepare the teachers through regular training procedures, extra curriculum study, and observation of gifted children in classroom learning activity; (6) it should determine the suitability of the regular church curriculum and decide what enrichment and special groupings will be necessary; (7) it should accumulate educational resource materials needed for enrichment utilizing the church and public library; (8) it should follow the educational procedures most suited to the gifted in order to fully meet their intellectual-spiritual needs; (9) it should guide the gifted children in the constructive, Christian-oriented use of their abilities and talents; (10) it should work closely with the parents of gifted children, realizing that God has given them the primary responsibility for the Christian nurture of their children.

The challenge which faces both the churches and parents in the Christian education of their gifted children must be intelligently and enthusiastically responded to. Far too little attention has been given to the life of the gifted to make any claim that they are being adequately provided for. The God-given abilities and talents of this exceptional group must be conserved and developed through special Christian education.

NOTES

1. Samuel A. Kirk, *Educating Exceptional Children,* 2d ed. (Boston: Houghton Mifflin, 1972), p. 105.
2. Ibid., pp. 105-106.
3. Gertrude H. Hildreth, *Introduction to the Gifted* (New York: McGraw-Hill, 1966), p. 42.
4 Ibid., p. 43.
5. Kirk, p. 106.
6. Ibid., pp. 106-107.
7. Jacob W. Getzels and Philip W. Jackson, *Creativity and Intelligence* (New York: John Wiley and Sons, 1962), pp. 2-3.
8. *Education for the Gifted:* Fifty-Seventh Yearbook of the National Society for the Study of Education (Chicago: U. Chicago, 1958), 2:19.
9. Kirk, p. 108.
10. Sumption and Luecking, quoted in Kirk, p. 108.
11. *Education of the Gifted and Talented,* Report to the Congress of the United States by the U.S. Commissioner of Education (Washington, D.C.: U.S. Gov. Printing Office, 1972), p. 20.
12. Herbert B. Neff, *Meaningful Religious Experiences for the Bright or Gifted Child* (New York: Association, 1968), p. 29.
13. Ibid., pp. 109-110.
14. Kirk, p. 109.
15. William P. Lineberry, ed., *New Trends in the Schools* (New York: Wilson, 1967), p. 47.
16. Ibid.
17. Kirk, p. 113.
18. Lineberry, p. 48.
19. Ibid., p. 48.
20. Kirk, p. 114.
21. Cassidy, Robert, "Can Our Schools Survive?" *Parent's Magazine* 48 (May, 1973): 10-14.
22. *Education of the Gifted and Talented,* p. 18.
23. Lineberry, p. 133.
24. *Education of the Gifted and Talented,* p. 24.
25. *Education of Mentally Gifted Minors* (Sacramento, Calif.: California State Department of Education, 1971), pp. 11-12.
26. Neff, pp. 42-43.
27. Kirk, p. 124.
28. Neff, pp. 41-42.
29. Ibid.
30. Neff, pp. 57-58.
31. Doris Monroe, *Integrative Review of Research Relating to Concept Development in Children* (Nashville: Baptist Sunday School Board, 1964), pp. 69-71.
32. Neff, p. 40.
33. Ibid., pp. 37-38.
34. Ibid., pp. 37-38, 43-44.
35. Ibid., p. 59.
36. Ibid., pp. 59, 60.
37. Kirk, p. 135.
38. Milton J. Gold, *Education of the Intellectually Gifted* (Columbus, Ohio: Merrill, 1965), p. 336.
38. Ibid.
40. Kirk, p. 136.
41. Ibid.
42. Gold, p. 337.
43. Hildreth, p. 290.
44. Kirk, p. 139.
45. James J. Gallagher, *Teaching the Gifted Child* (Boston: Allyn & Bacon, 1964), pp. 80, 82, 83.
46. Kirk, pp. 140-141.
47. Paul C. Burns and A. Montgomery Johnson, *Research in Elementary School Curriculum* (Boston: Allyn & Bacon, 1970), p. 478.

48. Ibid., p. 480.
49. William Glasser, *Schools Without Failure* (New York: Harper & Row, 1969), pp. 88-89.
50. Ibid., p. 91.
51. Kirk, p. 146.
52. Ibid., pp. 146-147.
53. Ibid., p. 147.
54. Ibid., p. 148.
55. Ibid., pp. 148-149.
56. Ralph L. Pounds and Robert L. Garretson, *Principles of Modern Education* (New York: Macmillan, 1962), p. 231.
57. Hildreth, pp. 531-33.

FOR FURTHER READING

Bruner, Jerome S. *The Process of Education.* Cambridge, Mass.: Harvard U., 1960.

Dunn, Lloyd M., et al., eds. *Exceptional Children in the Schools.* New York: Holt, Rinehart, & Winston, 1963.

Fleigler, Louis A., ed. *Curriculum Planning for the Gifted.* Englewood Cliffs, N.J.: Prentice-Hall, 1961.

Freehill, Maurice F. *Gifted Children: Their Psychology and Education.* New York: Macmillan, 1961.

Gowan, John C. and Demos, George D. *The Education and Guidance of the Ablest.* Springfield, Ill.: Thomas, 1964.

Hill, Mary Broderick. *Enrichment Programs for Intellectually Gifted Pupils.* California Project Talent, publication no. 4. Sacramento, Calif.: California State Dept. of Ed., 1969.

Hollingworth, Leta. *Children Above 180 IQ.* New York: Harcourt, Brace & World, 1942.

Kemp, Charles F. *Church: The Gifted and the Retarded Child.* St. Louis: Bethany, 1958.

Martinson, Ruth A. *Special Programs for Gifted Pupils.* California State Department of Education bulletin, vol. 31, no. 1, January 1962. Sacramento: California State Dept. of Ed., 1962.

Piaget, Jean. *Language and Thought of the Child.* 3d ed. New York: Humanities, 1959.

Robeck, Mildred C. *Acceleration Programs for Intellectually Gifted Pupils.* California Project Talent, publication no. 3. Sacramento: California State Dept. of Ed., 1968.

Strang, Ruth. *Helping Your Gifted Child.* New York: Dutton, 1960.

Sumption, Merle R., and Luecking, Evelyn. *Education of the Gifted.* New York: Ronald, 1960.

Torrance, E. Paul. *Gifted Children in the Classroom.* New York: Macmillan, 1965.

26

Teaching Mentally Retarded Children

Roberta L. Groff

EVERY YEAR approximately 130,000 babies are born in the United States with some degree of mental retardation. In Canada, approximately 17,000 babies each year are born retarded. In both countries, 3 percent of the population are retarded. In the US, this is 6½ million people—*twice* as many as those who are affected by blindness, polio, cerebral palsy, and heart disease *combined.*

In the past, churches have lacked concern, care, and programming for the mentally retarded and their families. However, in the last decade or so, churches, as well as the general public, have awakened to the fact that mental retardation is a serious problem. A growing spate of literature is being written on the Christian education of the retarded, and an increasing number of churches are developing classes for retardates. These teaching programs include Sunday school classes, weekday programs, after-school instruction, vacation Bible school, and resident and day camps.

The needs of the retarded person are the needs which motivate us all. He longs to love and to be loved. He longs for warmth, home, friends. He suffers bewilderment, frustrations, hurts, and pains. These indicate his needs as a person. The term *retarded* tells us that his ability to satisfy these needs will be slow in developing.

The church can help meet the spiritual needs of retarded children in a way that no community program can possibly do. A concerned parent has suggested two specific ways in which local churches can minister to retardates. First, churches, realizing that the retarded are individuals for whom Christ died, can provide classes in Sunday school and vacation Bible school and boys and girls weekday activities for the retarded. Second,

---

ROBERTA L. GROFF, M.A., is Principal of the Horizon School for Exceptional Children, Didsbury, Alberta, Canada, and Professor of Christian Education, Mountain View Bible College, Didsbury.

churches can show concern for each retardate's family members. Brothers, sisters, grandparents, and other relatives are deeply affected by the discovery that a child in their family has mental retardation. The parents of the mentally retarded have heavy burdens. The church can share in these burdens through the gift of understanding. All members of the family need to know that their church and their minister care for them in this additional burden which they carry.[1]

Historical Background

Jacob Rodrigues Pereire, Jean Marc Itard, Johann Jacob Guggenbuhl, Edward Seguin, Samuel Howe, and Marie Montessori belong in the roster of pioneers who have made valuable contributions to the study of mental retardation and the care and training of the retarded.

Ancient history records that the retarded were known as "defectives." Wealthy Romans kept a "fool" in the household as an amusement for guests. Later they became playthings for princes.[2] Retarded persons received the worst treatment during the Reformation; many Reformers regarded them as something less than human, void of a soul.[3]

In 1799, a boy, believed to be around the age of twelve, was captured in the forest of Aveyron, France. This boy, whom they called Victor, revealed more animal characteristics than human. He lacked speech, selected his food by smell, and in general did not respond like a human being. Jean Marc Itard felt that Victor (called the "wild boy of Aveyron") was an example of a completely untutored human being and that, with proper training, this boy could respond as a human being. Itard was successful in getting the boy to control his actions and to read a few words. Itard's method of teaching was "repeated rewarding trials." Although he felt his experiment was a failure, educators are recognizing his methods as important in teaching mentally retarded children.

Edward Seguin (1812-1880), continued the search for methods of training retardates. He established the first public residential facility in France for the mentally retarded and did extensive writing relating to the care, treatment, and curriculum for the retarded. His philosophy of education is not too different from many principles advocated today. He emphasized education of the whole child, individualized instruction, the importance of rapport between student and teacher, and the principle of beginning with needs and concerns of the child before proceeding to the unknown.

During our century, Marie Montessori and Ovide Decroly have built on the work of Itard and Seguin. These researchers all worked on sensory-motor development of the brain because of their conviction that all learning comes through the senses.

The first step taken in the United States toward providing care for the retarded was the introduction of a bill in the Massachusetts legislature in 1846 providing for the establishment of a state asylum for "idiots." This bill was defeated, but, as an outcome, an experimental school for teaching "idiots" was opened in Massachusetts in 1848. Other states followed, and the nineteenth century witnessed a promising begining of scientific work on behalf of the mentally retarded. Educational programs were developed, state institutions were established, and social responsibility was recognized.

Definition

Current definitions of mental retardation are numerous. Most of them are valid because they cover some aspect of the condition.

Dybwad called mental retardation "a condition which originates in the developmental period and is characterized by markedly subaverage intellectual functioning, resulting in some degree of social inadequacy."[4]

According to the American Association on Mental Deficiency, retardation is "a group of conditions which renders the individual unable to compete in ordinary society because of impaired or incomplete mental development."[5] Simply stated, mental retardation is the result of injury to or disease of the brain either before, during, or after birth.

The terms referring to the mentally retarded vary according to historic precedent as well as to the physical, emotional, and social implications. Some terms for the least serious retardation are *marginally independent, feebleminded, moderate,* and *educable* (meaning they can benefit from some education and eventually hold jobs under supervision). More severely mentally handicapped persons have been termed *semidependent, imbecile, trainable retarded* (meaning they can be taught self-care). Terms for the more seriously retarded persons are *idiot, custodial, nursing care, defective, low-grade,* and *dependent.*

Causes

Retardation is no respecter of persons. Retardates are born to average, brilliant, and dull parents alike, and into highly educated families as well as illiterate families. More than two hundred causes have been identified. Generally, they can be classified as (*a*) heredity; (*b*) prenatal, perinatal, and postnatal trauma; and (*c*) social-cultural factors.[6] Pediatricians estimate that more than 90 percent of mental retardation occurs in the prenatal stage.[7] Such genetic factors as defects in endocrine functioning, blood incompatibilities, and virus illnesses in pregnant women are also suspected as contributing to mental retardation.

Injury at birth also causes brain damage. For example, when oxygen is accidentally cut off during the birth process, some brain cells are killed.

Retardation results when the dead cells happen to be those controlling the intelligence.

Postnatal causes of retardation fall into three groups: acute illnesses, traumatic events, and progressive disorders which were not recognized at an early age.[8] Any illness which produces a long-lasting high fever can cause brain damage, as can severe head injuries and convulsions. Some other factors include nutritional deprivation and metabolic disturbances. Toxic agents may poison the brain cells and prevent their functioning.

Classification

Mental retardation is a broad category which includes persons who are functioning at numerous levels of efficiency. It means that intelligence and physical growth are subaverage to some degree.

In the realm of persons with normal intelligence, we assign the levels of average, above average, and genius. So retardates have similar levels, known in the descending order as educable, trainable, and those requiring custodial care. Schools use these categories as general guidelines for assigning retarded children to given classrooms.

We have suggested that an enormous number of factors contribute to classifying the level of a retarded person. Not everyone in the field agrees as to how those factors should be classified. As a result, the several national organizations use slightly differing classifications.

The American Association on Mental Deficiency classifies measured intelligence of the retarded into five categories: borderline, mild, moderate, severe, and profound. The American Psychiatric Association puts the retarded into three groups: mild, moderate, and severe. "Mildly retarded" would include individuals with an IQ in the 75 to 85 range; "moderately retarded" includes those in the 50 to 75 range, and "severely retarded" designates those in the 0 to 50 range.[9] This classication, however, tends to lead to oversimplification of a complex problem. Within each of these levels there is a wide range of abilities, especially among the severely retarded.

The National Association for Retarded Children suggests this classification: marginal dependent (or educable), semidependent (or trainable), and dependent (or custodial or nursing). The marginal dependent (or educable) are those in the IQ range of 50 to 75. They are persons who have learning difficulties in the regular grades.[10] The semidependent (or trainable) have been defined as having an IQ from 30 or 35 to 50 or 55. The dependent (or custodial or nursing) retardates are those with IQs below 30. These individuals are totally dependent, and many of them require nursing care throughout life.

Characteristics

The mentally retarded can be identified by a definite set of mental, physical, social, and emotional characteristics. Each person, of course, does not possess every characteristic. But each one does have learning problems to varying degrees. In addition, the mentally retarded have poor language communication skills, physical handicaps and illnesses, lack of motivation, limited experiences, and behavior problems. Some other general characteristics are listed below:[11]

TRAINABLE RETARDED

Physical: Can have oddly shaped skulls; can be mongoloid and epileptic, some have cerebral palsy; tend to have smaller physiques and growth abnormalities in height and weight; may have dazed conditions, odd body and facial mannerisms, excessive fondling of others and unusual emotional states[12]

Mental: Have poor reasoning, ineffective use of language, inability to think abstractly, low concentration level, lack of motivation; have trouble carrying a task to completion; lack imagination and creativity; IQ is between 30 and 50

Social: Have almost no motivation or ability to create giving attachments or to mingle inoffensively with more normal persons; with consistent reinforcement, can be taught acceptable social behavior

Emotional: Are quiet and introverted; sometimes loud and physically offensive; possess little motivation outside of their own needs and are sometimes oblivious even to their own needs

EDUCABLE RETARDED

Physical: Are more like normal children physically than mentally, socially, or emotionally; have poorer motor coordination and higher incidence of sight, speech, and hearing difficulties

Mental: Have limited vocabulary and poor reasoning ability; IQ ranges between 50 and 75

Social: Can attain good social adjustment and be self-directive to some degree, that is, to their own satisfaction; family and community may be dissatisfied with a retardate's ability to mix intelligently, which, in turn, engenders further negative social and interpersonal behavior

Emotional: Bear the same traits as listed above for trainables; however, some retarded persons have good emotional health within the limits of their handicap, especially if they come from homes where they have been totally accepted and loved

Learning

Researchers have found no evidence that the retarded learn by a process different than the way normal persons learn. Retardates assimilate information by the same mechanical means. But since they have incurred mechanical damage known as brain injury, they do not take in the same impressions as others. Normal persons learn as they react to their environment through sight, touch, taste, hearing, and smell. But in retardates, brain damage has blocked or dulled some of the senses. All retarded persons have the added emotional handicap of knowing that their learning and behavior differ from those around them. They see and feel their own clumsiness and incoordination, but they are powerless to help themselves.[13]

Along with dulled sensory perception, the retarded have limited use of logic and reasoning because their thinking does not pass easily from the concrete, see-and-feel world to the abstract. For example, trainables cannot grasp the abstract meaning of numbers and thus cannot come to the deductive conclusion involved in telling time. When no logical, reasoning, thought-building process is involved in a learning procedure, the person will likely succeed if all other positive factors (including a comfortable, secure environment and approving, undemanding teachers) are provided.

Another adjustment concerns the language the teacher uses. He must be overly conscious that learning success for mentally retarded students depends on how well he speaks in words they can understand. The effective teacher begins at the language level of the students, works at that level, and then slowly introduces new words.

The retarded child cannot be expected to wait with his question. His learning must be immediate and spontaneous; he needs much preacademic learning. In church-related teaching situations, children need to learn to follow directions, to sit still, to communicate with others. The Sunday school teacher must continually repeat instructions as well as lesson points. The retarded child must practice even minor things before he can perform them well. This is especially true of the trainable pupil. In fact, he can excel at tasks he learns by rote. Teachers should allow him to distribute papers, books, and supplies. They must be prepared to reward the student who has successfully completed a task with something pleasurable, even her own smile. No endeavor should go unrecognized.[14]

Religious Consciousness

The ability of the retarded to have spiritual awareness and to become spiritually regenerated has been questioned by some educators, and some have denied it completely. However, this denial places retarded persons below the level of human beings. Another attitude intimates that the retarded need carry no spiritual responsibility because they are "heaven's very special children," and thus are instruments of an unusual mission for God.[15] Some sincerely believe that the retarded are beyond spiritual experience and responsibility. However, in some cases, this view may simply be an excuse to justify withholding religious education. The rationale some follow is this: the retarded can't understand anyway, so why try at all?

As a result of her experience in teaching mentally retarded children and adults, the author is very reluctant to deny their basic human nature. Evidence of this fact was recorded by one of the early researchers. Edward Seguin wrote that mentally retarded persons "have a moral nature. No one who has had the happiness of ministering to them will deny" that.[16]

As the retarded should not be considered religiously unaware, neither should they be labeled spiritually irresponsible. Responsibility always depends on mental and physical age. We do not expect the child who is a Christian to handle adult spiritual problems. But we do teach him simpler concepts and expect some spiritually motivated behavior from him. So it is with mentally retarded persons; some will achieve greater knowledge and responsibility than others. If the mental age is six years, then all functioning—including spiritual—will likely be at that level. Mary Theodore concurs:

> A severely retarded person with mental age from three to seven, has a limited concept of goodness and wickedness. He can absorb some moral training, but his degree of responsibility will be small. He fails to see implications and foresee consequences of his actions.[17]

Religious Concepts

The ability of a retarded person to grasp spiritual concepts depends entirely on his mental age. Jesus, God, the Holy Spirit, sin, death, forgiveness, and eternal life are primarily abstract concepts. Retarded children and adults, particularly at the trainable level, are able to think only in the here-and-now, feel-and-touch world. Thus the paramount consideration is not to debate their spiritual consciousness and responsibility but to discover the degree to which their knowledge and responsibility can extend. The degree differs with every retardate, as it does with the normally intelligent person.

The author feels that the opportunity for salvation is important for the retarded, especially if he ever does reach or go beyond the (mental) age of accountability. The consequences are too great not to present salvation. While it is true that some of the retarded are manipulated into religious experiences, others have made intelligent decisions for God. The following is the simple, scriptural formula for discussing God's plan of salvation.

1. Most mentally handicapped can understand some degree of right and wrong, that everyone has done wrong things and that he himself has done wrong things. These displease God or make Him unhappy (Ro 3:23).

2. The result of wrong behavior is being put away from God forever; but if we are sorry for our sin, He will take us to His home in heaven (Ro 6:23). If the retarded person does understand sin or wrongdoing, he must ask forgiveness, though it be in the very simplest terms.

3. God took punishment for his sin when He allowed men to kill His Son by nailing His body to a cross. Christ died because He loved us so much and didn't want God to punish us (Jn 3:16).

4. The retarded person should respond and can respond when his mental capacity permits. He must be sorry for his sin and come to the point where he can say with his mouth and feel in his heart, "Jesus is my Friend. He died to take my sin away" (Ro 5:8).

The Teacher of the Mentally Retarded

The success of the church teaching situation for the retarded comes in direct proportion to the ability of its teacher. Certain competencies—spiritual, social, and emotional—are necessary if his work with the retarded is to prove effective. As a priority, the special education teacher must be a Christian in order to accomplish spiritual results. He must have patience, respect for and sensibility to human need,[18] plus love for the student who is "different."

Leaders in the church's special educational program should have professional competence in addition to Christian character. The teacher needs a good working knowledge of mental deficiency or at least familiarity with learning disorders. No teacher will ever be effective unless he works from a basic knowledge of learning problems.[19]

He must be patient. His classroom atmosphere should be informal but have established routines. He must be creative, able to present lessons with a variety of methods, thereby more nearly meeting the needs of individual students.

To the following checklist of attitudes, every teacher and worker with the retarded should give prayerful and careful consideration.[20]

1. Am I comfortable with this person? The ideal teacher of the retarded is relatively free of the fear which would prohibit him from being relaxed with the retardate. Many retarded persons have offensive and annoying mannerisms. The teacher becomes attached to the retarded both because of and in spite of their imperfections.

2. What are my feelings toward him? Do my feelings change? A person

may seem perfectly comfortable with the retarded and yet never experience a change of attitude about them. Some of us see the retarded as a group that never grows or matures in any way. Teachers must recognize the humanity of the retarded and be willing to provide them with learning opportunities.

3. Can I accept the pupil where he is and not show irritation at his efforts to learn? The effective teacher combines patience with a sensitivity to the needs of each student. One cannot teach the retarded as a group, for each pupil manifests his learning problems differently within the large framework of disorders.

4. Am I rigid in my approach? No retarded youngster is able to respond to an unbending, unaccommodating attitude from his teacher. Flexible methods and expectations are necessary in order to have an ideal learning situation.

5. Am I satisfied with him? The honest teacher will ask himself, "Does the quantity and quality of the student's learning growth show that I am doing my job?" Because the work of retardates always falls behind the norm of children his age, the teacher's goal is always twofold: that learning and ego-building will take place. He must pattern learning tasks in such a way that the pupil succeeds and thereby feels good about himself.

6. Can I set limits? This involves two things: establishing clear behavioral bounds, and determining the goal for a given learning experience. Students must learn the behavior they can and cannot use. Sometimes the teacher must bodily move an unwilling child, or actually make him do something. These pupils need a structured learning situation, a given task which they can successfully complete through predetermined and precise steps.

7. Have I been careful to discuss his problems at an appropriate time? The retarded person's feelings go as deeply as anyone else's. Some problems need to be discussed with him privately. Others should be dealt with in his absence, and some may need to be shared in the presence of others. In any situation, the best type of counseling for the betterment of the individual should be given.

8. Do I feel and express my love to him?

9. Can I help fellow church members understand retardation and the need to extend social acceptance to the mentally retarded?

Teaching Methods

STORYTELLING

Storytelling is one of the world's oldest artistic forms. Retarded children love stories because they help kindle their meager imagination. Also stories help mold ideas. Intelligent choice of stories plus expertise in telling them will assist the retarded in understanding healthy moral behavior. Such concepts as "Thou shalt not steal" take root in the mind far more easily when the teacher uses a story rather than a lecture. Bible characters become human, and children see that Bible people faced problems similar to ours. They thought about stealing and lying. They did these things, but God forgave them and is also willing to forgive us.

"Whatever the teacher tells the trainable pupil, he accepts as true; therefore he accepts fairy tales just as he does Bible stories, for he can make no distinction between the real and the unreal, between fact and fancy, or between Cinderella and David and the giant."[21] The teacher must explain the difference every time he tells a story.*

Those who teach retarded children should use visual aids abundantly. The spoken word alone leaves a clouded impression on the retarded, so the use of visual aids to supplement the spoken word is of utmost importance. Flannelgraph is an excellent visual aid. Lap flannelboards are effective in helping children learn Bible stories. Each child should have his own board to use. Lap flannelboards can be made by covering sturdy cardboard boxes (with hinged lids) with contact paper and covering the lid with flannel material. Children can cut figures from magazines and papers and create their own visualized story. Flash cards, records, strips, and show-'n'-tell records and filmstrips are other effective audio and visual aids.[22]

ROLE PLAYING

Students will grasp differing roles more easily if they can perform them. For example, children learn something about the role of father or mother by acting out that role. Almost any kind of experience can become the subject for role playing. It may bring about controlled, emotional releases to the child. It can give him an opportunity to learn the art of social cooperation. And it can help reinforce concepts he has learned.

In using role playing with the retarded, start with something very simple. For example, have all the children pretend to gather baby Moses in their arms, put him in his basket, and place him in the water. Do not attempt any role-play situation until a story is clear in the children's minds.

PUPPETRY

Puppetry has great value for use with the mentally handicapped. It helps them become cooperating members of a group and to adjust socially to their peers. Through a puppet, the child assumes a new identity. The teacher thus gains a new understanding of any behavior maladjustments. If the retarded have little or no speech ability, they can be taught to act

*For more on storytelling, see chaps. 13 and 14.

out recorded stories with puppets.† The teacher can use puppets to tell a story, to lead a song, to ask a child to cooperate, to teach a memory verse.

MUSIC

Although music is effective in teaching any child, it is of particular value in the teaching of the mentally retarded. Learning experiences can be made more pleasant if the teacher associates them with the use of music. Through music, children hear of God's love and can verbally and emotionally respond to it. What children are learning becomes more permanent in their minds if they are able to sing about it.

Music has a calming effect on the retarded child. Soft, slow music may calm a group of excitable children. Conversely, stirring music may stimulate an unresponsive child into class participation. Joyful music may bring happiness to an unhappy child. It can also be an aid in developing the sense of hearing.[23]

Perry suggests other values that music may have for the retarded. It can—

set a mood;
provide a tool for learning ideas;
enhance social growth because they learn to do something together such as singing or clapping;
stimulate physical coordination because they can march or keep time in other ways;
stimulate spiritual growth because they hear spiritual ideas in the words of songs and can be led into worship.[24]

Perry suggests the following criteria for selecting music. It must—

have a simple melody, no longer than twelve measures with a limited and repetitious range of notes;
have familiar, interesting words, not baby talk;
have a clear rhythm with prominent beats;
have slow tempo because the retarded need more time to pronounce words;
have a definite Christian message;
meet a wide range of needs within the class.[25]

Record and cassette players are valuable means for developing the retarded child's appreciation and awareness of music. Many retarded persons have difficulty with sound discrimination; thus records can help

†A catalog of puppets, scripts, and backdrops for use in Christian education can be obtained from Higley Press, P.O. 2470, Jacksonville, Fla. 32200.

refine their hearing sense. Teachers can use this tool with a group or with individuals.

The rhythm band is a good means of encouraging social growth in retarded children. They realize that though each one has a different instrument, no one instrument is more important than the other. They also learn cooperation by realizing that they cannot always play the instrument they desire.[26] (See chap. 18 also.)

CRAFTS

Craft activities for the retarded need to be selected carefully if they are to serve their designated purpose. Each activity chosen should reinforce the lesson and help meet the teaching aim. Any craft project must be explained carefully to the students with regard to the process and the end result. When students understand the end result, they will work toward it in methodical, slow steps. Teachers must analyze the steps beforehand and explain each step clearly. Otherwise, students may become confused and give up.

Molloy suggests these criteria for selecting crafts. They must—

be useful to the child;
be simple enough to be learned with directed instruction and practice;
have an added degree of difficulty in successive crafts which will teach a new manual skill;
be interesting to the child.[27]

In Sunday school, crafts usually cannot be put to optimum use because of limited time. However, churches with weekday or extended sessions for the retarded can make better use of crafts. (See chap. 15 also.)

SUMMARY

Ten years ago there were virtually no special church-sponsored classes for the retarded. Today Christian educators are recognizing this long-neglected ministry and are opening their arms in love for these children. It is a wide open door, and if entered, will bring enrichment to many lives. The teacher, helper, and director of the activities will have his life enriched by knowing and responding to the needs of these children and their families. Parents and families of the retarded will be strengthened through the knowledge that the church cares, and the children will understand the love of God through the love and concern of the church.

Christian education of the retarded calls for skill. Conferences and workshops on ministering to the retarded will help teach a congregation about mental retardation, about community services available for the retarded, and about the learning potential of the retarded.

The pastor and congregation working together can be a real force in reaching the mentally retarded and their families for Christ.

NOTES

1. Dorothy L. Hampton, "Retarded Children and Christian Concern," *Christianity Today* 8 (Jan. 31, 1964): 12-14.
2. Leo Kanner, *A History of the Care and Study of the Mentally Retarded* (Springfield, Ill.: Thomas, 1964), pp. 5-6.
3. Ibid., p. 7.
4. Gunnar Dybwad, *Challenges in Mentally Retarded* (New York: Columbia University, 1964), p. 3.
5. Edward L. French and J. Clifford Scott, *Child in the Shadows* (New York: Lippincott, 1960), p. 40.
6. Bernard Faber, *Mental Retardation: Its Social Context and Social Consequences* (Boston: Houghton Mifflin, 1968), p. 6.
7. Harriet E. Blodgett, *Mentally Retarded Children: What Parents and Others Should Know* (Minneapolis: U. Minnesota, 1971), p. 15.
8. Ibid., p. 18.
9. Louis Rosenzweig and Julia Long, *Understanding and Teaching the Retarded Child* (Darien, Conn.: Educational Pub., 1960), p. 12.
10. Ibid., p. 13.
11. Adapted from John W. Howe and Thomas W. Smith, *Characteristics of Mentally Retarded Children,* (County Superintendent of Schools, Los Angeles Board of Education, Bulletin No. 3, 1950).
12. *Exceptional Children in the Schools,* ed. Lloyd M. Dunn (New York: Holt, Rinehart, & Winston, 1963), p. 141; and Harry J. Baker, *Introduction to Exceptional Children* (New York: Macmillan, 1959), p. 261.
13. *Mental Retardation,* ed. Alfred E. Baumeister (Chicago: Aldine, 1967), p. 185.
14. Ibid., p. 191.
15. Parents sometimes hold this view, such as is described by Dale Evans Rogers in her book *Angel Unaware* (Westwood, N.J.: Revell, 1953).
16. Edward Seguin, *Idiocy and Its Treatment by the Physiological Method* (New York: Columbia, 1907), p. 47.
17. Mary Theodore, *The Challenge of the Retarded Child* (Milwaukee: Bruce, 1959), p. 153.
18. Elmer L. Towns and Roberta L. Groff, *Successful Ministry to the Retarded* (Chicago: Moody, 1972), p. 61.
19. Ibid.
20. Bernice Baumgartner, *Helping the Trainable Mentally Retarded Child* (New York: Columbia U., 1967), pp. 77-78.
21. Towns and Groff, pp. 77-78.
22. An 8mm. Stori-Strip Projector may be purchased from Gospel Light Publications, Glendale, California 91204. Show 'n' Tell records and filmstrips on Bible stories, produced by General Electric, can be purchased from David C. Cook Publishing Company, Elgin, Illinois 60120, or from a GE dealer. For more on visuals and audio aids, see chap. 16.
23. Natalie Perry, *Teaching the Mentally Retarded Child* (New York: Columbia University, 1960), p. 93.
24. Ibid.
25. Ibid., pp. 159-61.
26. For additional information on music for retarded children, consult these sources: Bernice W. Carlson and David R. Ginglend, *Play Activities for Retarded Children* (Nashville: Abingdon, 1961); David R. Ginglend and Winifred E. Stiles, *Music Activities for Retarded Children* (Nashville: Abingdon, 1965); Doris Driggers Monroe, "Music Has Charms for the Retarded, Too," *Church Training* 1 (Nov., 1971): 36-41; Ferris and Jennet Robins, *Educational Rhythmics for Mentally and Physically Handicapped Children* (New York: Association, 1968).
27. Julia S. Molloy, *Trainable Children* (New York: Day, 1961), p. 334.

FOR FURTHER READING

Books and Articles

Agee, J. Willard. "The Minister Looks at Mental Retardation." *Pastoral Psychology* 13 (Sept., 1962):12-22.

Bauer, Charles E. *Retarded Children Are People.* Milwaukee: Bruce, 1964.

Baumgartner, Bernice. *Helping the Trainable Mentally Retarded Child.* New York: Columbia U., 1967.

Blodgett, Harriet E. *Mentally Retarded Children: What Parents and Others Should Know.* Minneapolis: U. Minnesota, 1971.

Bogardus, LaDonna. *Christian Education of Retarded Children and Youth.* Nashville: Abingdon, 1963.

Buck, Pearl S. *The Gifts They Bring.* New York: Day, 1965.

Carlson, Bernice W., and Ginglend, David R. *Play Activities for the Retarded Child.* Nashville: Abingdon, 1961.

Carpenter, Robert D. *Why Can't I Learn?* Glendale, Calif.: Gospel Light, 1972.

Doll, G. L. "Church and the Handicapped Child." *Christianity Today* 9 (Feb. 26, 1965): 15-19.

Egg, Marie. *Educating the Child Who Is Different.* New York: Day, 1968.

———. *When a Child Is Different.* New York: Day, 1960.

French, Edward L., and Scott, J. Clifford. *Child in the Shadows: A Manual for Parents of Retarded Children.* New York: Lippincott, 1960.

Hahn, Hans R., and Raasch, Werner H. *Helping the Retarded to Know God.* St. Louis: Concordia, 1969.

Kemp, Charles F. *The Church: The Gifted and the Retarded Child.* St. Louis: Bethany, 1957.

Monroe, Doris D. *A Church Ministry to Retarded Persons.* Nashville: Convention, 1972.

Organizing Religious Classes for Mentally Retarded Children. St. Louis: Lutheran Church (Missouri Synod), n.d.

Palmer, Charles E. *The Church and the Exceptional Person.* Nashville: Abingdon, 1961.

Perry, Natalie. *Teaching the Mentally Retarded Child.* New York: Columbia U., 1960.

Peterson, Sigurd D. *Retarded Children: God's Children.* Philadelphia: Westminster, 1960.

Sieving, Hilmar A., ed. *The Exceptional Child and the Christian Community.* River Forest, Ill.: Lutheran Educ. Assoc., 1950.

Rosenzweig, Louis, and Long, Julia. *Understanding and Teaching the Dependent Retarded Child.* Darien, Conn.: Educational Publ., 1960.

Schultz, Edna. *They Said Kathy Was Retarded.* Chicago: Moody, 1963.

Stair, Ernest R. "Religion and the Handicapped Child." *Religious Education* 62 (1968): 352-54.

Stubblefield, Harold W. *The Church's Ministry in Mental Retardation.* Nashville: Broadman, 1965.

Theodore, Mary. *The Challenge of the Retarded Child.* Milwaukee: Bruce, 1959.

Thomas, Janet K. *How to Teach and Administer Classes for Mentally Retarded Children.* Minneapolis: Denison, 1968.

Towns, Elmer L., and Groff, Roberta L. *Successful Ministry to the Retarded.* Chicago: Moody, 1972.

Your Child and the Mentally Retarded. Nashville: Baptist Sunday School Board. n.d.

Welborn, Terry, and Williams, Stanley. *Leading the Mentally Retarded in Worship.* St. Louis: Concordia, 1973.

Wood, Andrew H. *A Manual for Reaching Retarded Children for Christ.* Union Grove, Wis.: Shepherds, n.d.

Journals on Mental Retardation or Including Articles on the Subject

American Journal of Mental Deficiency. 5201 Connecticut Avenue, N.W., Washington, D.C. 20015.

American Journal of Public Health. 1015 Eighteenth Street, N.W., Washington, D.C. 20036.

Church Training. 127 Ninth Ave., North, Nashville, Tenn. 37203.

Exceptional Children. 1411 S. Jefferson Davis Hwy., Arlington, Va. 22202.

Journal of Educational Psychology. 1200 Seventeenth St., N.W., Washington, D.C. 20013.

Journal of Religion and Health. 16 East 34th St., New York, N.Y. 10016.

Mental Retardation. 5201 Connecticut Ave., N.W., Washington, D.C. 20002.

Mental Retardation News. 910 17th St., N.W., Washington, D.C. 20006.

Pastoral Psychology. Manhasset, N.Y. 11030.

Today's Health. 535 N. Dearborn St., Chicago, Ill. 60610.

Other Sources of Information

Association for Childhood Education International. 3615 Wisconsin Avenue, N.E., Washington, D.C. 20016.

Canadian Association for Retarded Children. 4700 Keele St., Downsview, Ontario.

Child Study Association of America. 9 East 89th Street, New York, New York 10028.

National Association for Retarded Children. 910 17th St., N.W., Washington, D.C. 20006.

National Education Association. 1201 Sixteenth St., N.W., Washington, D.C. 20006.

Public Affairs Pamphlets. 22 East 38th St., New York, N.Y. 10016.

U.S. Department of Health, Education, and Welfare. Washington, D.C. 20025.

Films and Filmstrips

Mentally Retarded: Educable. Audio-Visual Center. Indiana University. Bloomington, Indiana 47401. Twenty-nine-minute film, black and white.
Mentally Retarded: Trainable. Audio-Visual Center. Indiana University. Bloomington, Indiana 47401. Twenty-nine-minute film, black and white.
New Experiences for Mentally Retarded Children. Film Production Service. Virginia Department of Education. Richmond, Va. 23216. Thirty-one-minute film, black and white.
Christ's Love Unfolds for All Children. Concordia Publishing House. 3558 S. Jefferson Ave., St. Louis, Mo. 63118. Filmstrip with 33⅓ rpm record.

Sources of Lesson Materials

Abingdon Press. 201 Eighth Ave., South, Nashville, Tenn. 37203.
Concordia Publishing House. 3558 S. Jefferson St., St. Louis, Mo. 63118.
John Knox Press. 801 E. Main St., Richmond, Va. 22309.
Milwaukee County Association for Retarded Children. 1426 W. State St., Milwaukee, Wis. 53233.
Shepherds, Inc. P.O. Box 1261, Union Grove, Wis. 53182.
Sunday School Board. Southern Baptist Convention. 127 Ninth Ave., North, Nashville, Tenn. 37203.

27

Teaching Other Exceptional Children

Paul W. Cates

For many years, the secular world has concerned itself with helping and teaching exceptional children, those children handicapped by blindness, hearing and speech difficulties, other physical limitations, emotional disturbances, or behavior disorders. Comparatively little has been done, however, in churches to minister spiritually to these youngsters with special needs. Happily, a growing number of Christian leaders are awakening to the opportunities of giving these children a *Christian* education through the work of the local church.

Who Is the Exceptional Child?

There have been many attempts to define the term *exceptional children.* The term has been used when referring to a particularly gifted child or to a child with exceptional talent. It has also been used of the deviant or atypical child. In educational literature, the term has generally been accepted to include both the handicapped and the gifted.

In this chapter, the exceptional child is a child who deviates from the average or normal child and is deficient in mental characteristics, sensory ability, neuromuscular or physical characteristics, social or emotional areas, communication abilities, or a combination of these, to such an extent that he requires modifications of teaching practices, with special facilities and services to assist him in developing to his maximum capacity.

Some other types of exceptional children are discussed in chapters 25 and 26. In this chapter, we shall discuss visually handicapped children, speech handicapped children, auditory handicapped and deaf children,

---

Paul W. Cates, Ph.D., former Director of the DePaul University Psychological Education Clinic, Chicago, Illinois is now doing private consultant work with Psychological Service Associates.

physically handicapped children, emotionally disturbed children, and children with behavior disorders.

Table 27.1. indicates the approximate number of handicapped children in the United States as reported in 1969 and 1970 by the Bureau of Education for the Handicapped.[1]

TABLE 27.1

NUMBER OF HANDICAPPED CHILDREN IN THE UNITED STATES

TYPE OF HANDICAP	FISCAL YEAR 1968	FISCAL YEAR 1969
Mentally retarded	1,503,000	1,360,737
Hard of hearing and deaf	286,200	316,456
Speech impaired	2,141,600	2,180,589
Visually handicapped	75,800	66,679
Emotionally disturbed	800,000	767,108
Crippled	305,400	192,662
Other health impaired (including learning disabilities)	759,900	1,089,817
Multihandicapped	89,100	35,918
National total	5,961,000	6,009,966

VISUALLY HANDICAPPED CHILDREN

"Among all living creatures, man is the most eye-minded. Nothing does he treasure more than the apple of his eye."[2]

Educational procedures rely heavily on the sense of vision. *Blindness* covers a fairly wide range of visual defects and refers to severe limitations either in the sharpness of sight or in the size in area which can be seen at one time. A blind person may be able to distinguish only large objects or he may be able to read only the largest print, or he may see only things in a tiny circle straight ahead of him. He would not have enough sight to serve him for the ordinary activities of life for which sight is essential. The blind child lacks an extremely important group of learning experiences, those which depend on sight.

DEFINITIONS AND CLASSIFICATIONS

The complexity of visual impairment according to varying dimensions is likened to the complexity of the human organism. Visually handicapped children can be classified on the basis of the physical measurements of visual acuity and narrowness of the visual field, or the use that is made of the visual sense modality for learning.

The 1966 Fact Book National Society for the Prevention of Blindness defined the blind as follows:

a. Blindness is generally defined in the United States as visual acuity for distance vision of 20/200 or less in the better eye with best correction; for visual acuity of more than 20/200 if the widest diameter of field of vision subtends an angle no greater than 20 degrees.
b. The partially seeing are defined as persons with a visual acuity greater than 20/200 but not greater than 20/70 in the better eye with correction.[3]

However, recent data have resulted in a revision in terminology. For educational purposes, Kirk suggests two definitions: the visually impaired, which refers to those who can learn to read print; and the blind, who cannot read print, but who need instruction in braille.[4]

It had been noted that children with the same degree of given visual defect may have different visual abilities on clinical tests, in terms of learning. Of the 14,225 children who were registered with the American Printing House for the Blind, the following data was compiled: 3 percent of the children were classified as legally blind with 20/200 vision. Yet 82 percent of them could read print; only 12 percent could read braille; 6 percent could read both; 7 percent could recognize hand movements at close distance. Of the total group, 24 percent were educationally blind and read braille only; 66 percent of legally blind had some residual vision; and a large proportion of these could read print.[5]

ASSESSMENT OF VISUAL PROBLEMS

It has been stated in textbooks that total blindness is relatively easy to recognize and detect in a child by one year of age; however, it is the less severely handicapped youngster who is much more difficult to identify.

The following are indications of visual difficulty.

1. Strabismus: inability of one eye to attain binocular vision with the other because of imbalance of the muscles of the eyeball; nystagmus; squint
2. How the child uses his eyes: tilting of the head, holding objects close to the eyes, rubbing and squinting of eyes, displaying sensitivity to bright light, and rolling the eyes
3. Inattention to visual objects and visual tasks
4. Awkwardness in games requiring eye-hand coordination
5. Avoidance of tasks that require eye work
6. Affinity to tasks that require distance vision
7. Any complaints about inability to see
8. Lack of normal curiosity in regard to visually appealing objects.

When a teacher observes these indications of visual difficulty in a child in his group, he should suggest to the parents that the child's eyes should be tested. The most generally accepted single test for visual acuity is the Snellen Test, used to detect nearsightedness, some degrees of astigmatism, higher degrees of farsightedness, and other eye conditions which cause a blurred or imperfect image. A better instrument is one of the ortho-raters such as the Keystone Telebinocular, which has been determined to be 57 percent effective. The final determination should be made by either an ophthalmologist or optometrist who can accurately diagnose and assess the degree or kind of visual handicap.

CAUSES OF BLINDNESS

The American Foundation for the Blind and the National Society for the Prevention of Blindness listed these causes of blindness: prenatal origin, 61 per cent; infectious disease, 16.8 percent; cause undetermined or not specified, 9.4 percent; injuries, 7.6 percent; tumors, 3.8 percent; general disease, 1.2 percent; and poisoning, 0.2 percent.[6]

Studies of students in schools for the blind show a shift in causes. The most significant item is the decrease of infectious diseases, due to improved programs for prevention of gonorrheal ophthalmia and syphilis.[7]

Retrolental fibroplasia accounted for a large proportion of blind children between 1940, 1952, and 1953, and since that date, the incidence has dropped abruptly due to better control of oxygen.[8]

The National Society for the Prevention of Blindness estimated the total number of blind persons in this country to be 400,000. This includes 2,780 under the age of five; 36,230 between ages five and twenty; and 360,440 over the age of twenty.[9]

Among visually handicapped children, national attention has been given primarily to the legally blind, and less concern has been shown to partially seeing children.

Several studies have been conducted by Bateman and Tilman to compare visual handicaps to reading and psycho-linguistic abilities.[10] The visually handicapped person has adjustment problems if he perceives that others have a poor attitude toward his problem.

GENERAL EDUCATION OF THE VISUALLY HANDICAPPED

The majority of visually handicapped children in local day schools are assigned to a regular grade according to their age and level of academic achievement. The general goal or objectives of education are the same for visually handicapped children as for seeing children, even though the procedures of attaining these goals are achieved by modifying instructional materials and providing special teaching procedures.

Most visually handicapped children can attend regular kindergarten in communities without much difficulty. In the activities of listening to stories, show and tell, and other oral activities, the blind child is not at a disadvantage. Church workers should keep this in mind if they have visually handicapped children in their classes.

SPECIAL EDUCATION OF THE VISUALLY HANDICAPPED

Lowenfield gives the following principles for teaching blind children:

1. Individualize the instruction as much as possible.
2. Use materials that can be touched and manipulated.
3. Unify the instruction in which knowledge about a total situation is related to experience.
4. Give additional stimulation to expand horizons, develop imagery, and widen environment.
5. Provide opportunity for self-activity.[11]

The American Bible Society Braille Bible can be used effectively with the visually handicapped. The exceptional person as well as the normal one needs Jesus Christ and the church. Through participation in the worship and instruction of the church, children who are blind may come to know and love the Lord Jesus and to have their lives enriched. The church too will benefit through increased understanding and compassion.

THE USE OF CREATIVE MUSIC

Music can help blind children develop the sheer joy of sharing, by singing and listening to his fellow peer group. Music can create security and stimulation of thought and helps develop their understanding of God's Word and message. Music can also provide oportunities for mental, spiritual, and social growth. (See also chap. 18.)

THE USE OF CREATIVE ARTS

The use of crayons, paper, pencils, blunt scissors, and tubes of watercolors can all help a blind child express what he feels inside. These expressions and feelings help him indicate and share his individuality. Many times when a child cannot verbalize adequately, he can express himself through creative activities. Although his work will need further guidance than the child with sight, it will allow him to express himself and show his individual talents in ways that might not be expressed by a normal child. It also helps the child become aware of the world around him. These crafts should be of interest to the child and should be a step toward learning about God and life in its fullest. (See also chap. 15.)

ROLE PLAYING

Role playing can help the child become familiar with and remember events, ideas, and situations which we have told them in Bible stories, incidents in homes, and other situations. Any experience can be acted out, even those from real-life situations that the child has experienced during the preceding week. Role playing helps the child develop control, and it can help a frustrated child act out certain behavior characteristics that are not acceptable in other forms. It also gives the teacher an opportunity to understand his individual needs. Creative playacting and pantomimes may also be used with the blind.

Speech Handicapped Children

Speech is defective when it draws unfavorable attention to itself, whether through unpleasant sound, inappropriateness to age level, interference with communication, or maladjustment on the part of the person speaking. To be normal, speech should permit the undistracted interchange of verbal language, be free from grimaces, phonemic misarticulation, and unnatural and unusual voice qualities, speaking rates, and rhythm. Vocabulary and sound usage should be adequate and appropriate for the age level, and speech should be delivered in logical, syntactical order. Speech patterns, such as the Southern drawl, Eastern twang, Midwestern nasality, and foreign accents are not regarded as defective speech, despite phonemic and international peculiarities.

RELATION OF SPEECH DEFECTS TO OTHER DISABILITIES

Disabilities in the communication processes may be in speech, language, reading, writing, or spelling. Sometimes a learning disability in one function is correlated with retardation in other areas; in other cases, the learning disability is specific to one area only.

Kirk says that since the child with defective speech may be found in any group of exceptional or otherwise normal children, he may be at either end of the extremes: he may possess a high IQ or a low IQ; he may be severely handicapped in motor skills or have good coordination; he may hear exceptionally well or be hard of hearing; he may be well adjusted or emotionally and socially disturbed; he may have normal vision or be blind; he may have a well-built body or suffer from multiple physical handicaps.[12]

Van Riper, Kirk, Travis, and others agree to this grouping of speech defects: (1) articulation disorders; (2) voice disorders; (3) stuttering; (4) retarded speech development; (5) cleft palate; (6) cerebral palsy; (7) impaired hearing; and (8) aphasia and related areas. Assuming a total population of 40,000,000 children between the ages of five and twenty-one years, it is estimated that 5 percent are handicapped by speech difficulties.[13]

ARTICULATORY DISORDERS

Articulatory disorders are those deviations which involve substitutions, omissions, distortions, and additions of phonemes. These difficulties may occur as the articulators (tongue, teeth, lips, palates, jaws) modify the flow of air sounds from the larynx by changing their positions and contacts. Such labels as *lisping, lolling,* and *baby talk* are common forms of articulatory defects.

The teacher must work closely and carefully with the parents and classmates in order to motivate a child with such a disorder without upsetting the total classroom atmosphere. Since many stutterers are victims of interruptions, rejections, frustration, and hostility, the teacher can help eliminate these feelings through patience and understanding. He should allow the child to breathe correctly and get enough time to speak. Other classmates should be kind enough to cooperate. Of course, referral to a speech therapist may be necessary.

DELAYED SPEECH

Some children speak through grunts and gestures; others speak copiously. Some do not want to talk, and they fail to acquire normal speech.[14]

Some children do not develop speech as expected at their age level, or they develop only partial understanding of language or vocal expression.

This retardation of speech development has been classified as delayed speech. The causes of delayed speech include these: (1) hearing loss; (2) mental retardation; (3) emotional disturbances; (4) environmental deprivation; (5) cerebral dysfunction; (6) glandular irregularities; and (7) the intangible "congenital aphasia."

SPEECH DEFECTS ASSOCIATED WITH HEARING LOSS

Hearing losses, mild or severe, have been associated with delay in speech development or with inadequate speech. Surveys of speech handicapped children in schools reveal a greater frequency of children who have speech defects and hearing losses.

SPEECH DEFECTS ASSOCIATED WITH CLEFT PALATE

To understand why cleft palates occur, one must know something of the development of the embryo.[15] The speech disorder with cleft palate and lip is caused by failure of the bone and tissue of the palates to fuse during the first thirteen weeks of pregnancy. There are three major problems involved: clefts of propalate, clefts of the palate, and clefts of both propalate and palate. "Persons having unrepaired cleft palate and lip deformity exhibit a severely nasal voice or hoarse quality and a wide range of articulation disorders.[16]

The cerebral palsied child may show a number of defects in every aspect of speech. His voice may be affected in many ways: poor quality, breathiness, harshness, nasality, weakness in intensity, slowness, jerky rhythm, or faulty articulation.

SPEECH DISORDERS ASSOCIATED WITH CEREBRAL PALSY

"The cerebral-palsied person is above all else a human being with an injured neuromuscular system who lacks motor control. He is a person with a personality, who strives and feels like others."[17]

With speech problems, there should be a deemphasis on the disability. Poor speech habits may cause a child to desire silent reading rather than to share auditorily with his classmates. He should be given opportunities to show his expertise through other channels. If he is provided with a special channel, such as a visual presentation, he can share all things that he can make for the class through arts and crafts. Many children with speech defects seem to be able to communicate much more freely through the media of music because of its rhythmical flow. The teacher should be aware that this child, who is intent and worried about his speech, may be ignoring the meaning the teacher is trying to bring to the lesson. His speech defect may interfere with his rate and inability to phrase things correctly. His articulatory disorders may result in misunderstandings and may cause reading to be unpleasant for him and something to avoid. His lessons should be short, concise, and meaningful.

The correction of speech impairments require full attention. This can be done in different ways.

1. Because of the child's difficulty in this area, parents may tend to overprotect him and to do too much for him. Sometimes his speech is strained and inadequate partly because people do not give the child the opportunity to try. His vocal musculature should be exercised when this situation occurs. It is necessary to acquire the cooperation of everyone involved and to motivate speech through unstressful experience and exercise.

2. Sometimes the teacher or parent must alleviate as soon as possible the unacceptable behavioral patterns that some of these children have acquired, such as drooling or a tongue hanging from an open mouth. The child should be taught to swallow correctly, to close the mouth, and keep the tongue inside. The cooperation of everyone is required, especially the parents, since they are in daily and hourly contact with their own child.

3. Language is auditory. By explorative experience and the need for verbal expression, the child needs experiences in motor activities. Since speech is a motor activity, it is necessary to use what speech specialists call a multiple sense modality approach, the use of auditory, visual, and

kinesthetic senses in the production of speech. These children do not speak unless they are motivated to speak. One of the problems with children that have speech problems is how to help them realize their need for improving their speech. Through their own efforts and exercises, they can correct inappropriate tongue and jaw movements or breathing requiring unpressured concentrated attention.

Teachers in the church who display genuine love to and concern for children with these needs will find that both the children and their parents will respond with appreciation. Here is opportunity to evidence the patience, kindness, and selflessness of God-given love (1 Co 13:4-5).

Auditory Handicapped and Deaf Children

A deaf child is one in whom the residual hearing is not sufficient to enable him to understand speech and develop language successfully, even with a hearing aid, without specialized instruction. Two definitions of a deaf child are noted: (1) medically, a deaf child has a hearing loss approaching an average of seventy or eighty decibels or greater, across the speech range in the better ear without a hearing aid; (2) educationally, a deaf child has a hearing loss approaching an average of sixty or sixty-five decibels across the speech range in the better ear without a hearing aid, and is unable to develop language successfully, even with a hearing aid, without special education.

A hard-of-hearing child is one whose hearing, although defective, is functional with or without a hearing aid, but whose hearing loss causes a language deficit, rendering him unable to make full use of the regular school experience without special services.

Prevalence of Hearing Loss

Several studies have been conducted on the prevalence of defective hearing. It is difficult to estimate the rate of occurrence, due partly to the method of testing, the criteria used by the investigator, the community, and other factors.

Since 1850, the American Annals of the Deaf has compiled figures on the population of children with impaired hearing. These figures revealed the incidence is higher in males than females.[18]

Causes of Deafness in Young Children

Although deafness may be either inherited or acquired, most auditory disorders found in infants and very young children are inherited. Sometimes a physical defect of the outer or middle ear may cause the trouble, but usually congenital disorders of hearing are due to damage to inner ears. The organ of hearing may be malformed or absent, or the hearing nerve or auditory brain center may be damaged. Cerebral palsy, mental retardation, or birth injuries may cause a disturbance of the perception of speech, and so the child reacts as though he is deaf. Another cause of infant hearing loss and other possible complications is German measles contracted by the mother during her pregnancy.

Acquired deafness results after birth. It may come from incompatibility of the Rh factor of the parent. Though this cause is congenital, the trouble develops after the child is born. Deafness may also be caused by illness or accidents. Some of the illnesses include meningitis, encephalitis, jaundice, mumps, and other less common diseases. In fact, any childhood disease causing an extremely high fever may result in damage to the inner ear. Damage from scarlet fever is less common than it was some years ago. These diseases cause deafness only if they attack the hearing structure of the ear, the auditory nerve, or the central nervous system. Then the results may be either deafness or defective hearing.

SYMPTOMS OF HEARING DEFICIENCIES

Teachers and parents should be familiar with certain symptoms of hearing difficulty. An alert parent may detect an auditory disorder in his child as early as three months. Something may be wrong when the baby is not soothed by the parent's voice or when he fails to turn his head in the direction of sound. Other symptoms are inattention, no "startle" reflex, inability to use or understand words, excessive use of gestures, the use of vision or touch to gain understanding of his environment. Also, the baby may be hard to waken. Older children with hearing deficiencies may be slow in speaking or may talk in toneless speech without inflection. Because such a child cannot communicate easily with adults, he may throw temper tantrums to relieve himself of bottled-up feelings and emotions. Another symptom of an auditory disorder is that the hard-of-hearing or deaf child usually plays too hard. He is overactive and almost violent in playing. A child with hearing difficulties is frequently inattentive, turns his head toward the speaker, and cups his hand behind one ear. He may ask that questions be repeated. At home, when he listens to radio or television, he may have the volume exceptionally loud. He may also complain of a ringing or buzzing in his ear.

Some symptoms of deafness can be due to other causes, such as emotional disturbance, mental retardation, a brain injury, or a brain condition called aphasia. An aphasic child can hear sounds and language and may learn to read, but he cannot verbalize. If he has motor aphasis, he can be taught to speak. If he has sensory aphasia, his word memory is impaired and he cannot ordinarily be taught to speak, though occasionally other parts of the brain may take over and function for the damaged area.

The specialized curriculum for the deaf or hard of hearing should emphasize the development of communication through vision and residual hearing.

As the normal child learns to speak, the teacher can recognize a series of stages. His gurgling turns into babbling. Later he may even repeat the sounds that he hears. This is a stage of imitation. The deaf child, though, cannot hear his own babbling, and it soon stops. He does not hear the words around him and, therefore, neither imitates nor attaches meaning to them. If he learns to speak, it must be by other routes that are tedious, less efficient, and that involve a tremendous amount of time. Possible ways for the child to learn are special training through the sense of touch and vibration, the use of visual aids, kinesthetic cues or auditory stimulation, and visible speech.

Hard-of-hearing children are generally educated and belong in the church environment with his peers but should be given specific helps in auditory training, reading, and speech training.

Deaf children are those born without hearing or who have lost their hearing before acquiring speech and language. Three interrelated aspects currently in use in educating the deaf are: (1) oral approach; (2) combined approach (finger spelling and oral); (3) simultaneous approach (oral communication, finger spelling, language of signs). Because of the handicap in speech and language, most deaf children are two to five years behind in academic subjects. In actual life, deaf adults are employed in all types of work not requiring hearing, ranging from professional to unskilled labor, with the majority holding semiskilled and skilled jobs. They are considered satisfactory employees.

Other Physical Handicaps

Cerebral palsy is a condition in which the major component is neuromotor disability arising from brain maldevelopment, damage, or dysfunction.[19]

Muscular dystrophy is rarely diagnosed before the child is due to walk. The disease causes the voluntary muscle fibers to degenerate. These muscles are replaced by fatty tissue, causing the child to become progressively weaker.[20]

Spina bifida is a congenital defect in the development of the spine, associated with abnormality of its nerve contents. Most of the cases of spina bifida involve protrusion of the coverings on the spinal cord together with neural tissue through bone defect. The protrusions of the neural tissue paralyzes the lower extremities in varying degrees, along with the muscles which control retention capabilities of the bladder and bowel.[21]

Cystic fibrosis is a lethal, inherited disease. Only about 50 percent of the victims live past the age of ten; 80 percent of those die before twenty. Cystic fibrosis affects the mucus producing glands of the body, so that ducts are blocked to the pancreas, preventing the flow of the enzymes needed to properly digest food in the intestines. A thick mucus is produced in the lungs, which often leads to infection.[22]

Rheumatoid arthritis can cause great pain and deformity to its young victims. Also known as Still's disease, the effect is the destruction of linings of the joints of the body.

Epilepsy is a condition manifesting itself by spasmodic and recurrent convulsion states. These seizures are a temporary impairment of loss of consciousness related to the electrical activity of the area of the brain involved.[23]

Aphasia is the inability to express and/or understand language symbols and is the result of some defect in the central nervous system rather than the result of a defect in the peripheral speech mechanism, ear or auditory nerve, defect in general intelligence, or severe emotional disturbance.[24]

Hyperkinetic impulse disorder is poor behavioral control and a learning dysfunction in an otherwise physically well, mentally alert child.

CURRENT TRENDS

Previously cerebral palsy was thought of in terms of children who had devastating physical handicaps and required lifelong care. Now it is recognized that the majority of these children have moderate or mild physical defects and with proper help can improve sufficiently to participate in clinic schools, public school systems, and specialized vocational rehabilitation programs. Today the important area of concern is for better methods to enhance learning abilities, vocational aptitude, and psycholinguistic skills.[25]

There is agreement that the general outlook for people with epilepsy is a bright one. Knowledge and interest in epileptic children has increased dramatically since the 1940s. Diagnostic and theraupeutic techniques have made great advances in this relatively short period of time. It is currently estimated that about 50 percent of all epileptics, with the aid of medication, have their seizures completely removed. Thirty percent can have their seizures reduced to the extent that they can function as normally as any other person. Nonetheless, because the social image of the epileptic has not yet caught up with scientific fact, epileptics still may have difficulty in finding jobs, obtaining life insurance, or being accepted by their peers.[26]

By the use of proper educational techniques, asphasic children too can often look forward to normal, productive lives.[27]

PERSONAL ADJUSTMENT

Physically handicapped children will need much guidance if they are to be helped with their special problems. Handicapped children may experience one or more of these personality adjustment problems:

Overprotection on the part of parents may produce an overinhibited or dependent personality.
Some may become hypersensitive or shy or exhibit other types of withdrawn behavior.
Parents may reject the child. This rejection will often cause the child to give up.
Physical handicaps tend to reduce a child's range of activities, leading to frustration.
Anger, particularly in younger children, will be evident because of the restriction of bodily movement.[28]

With respect to adjustment of handicapped and nonhandicapped children to general social situations, their parents and peers, Cruickshank reported these conclusions: (1) Handicapped children show real interest in comparing themselves with others in an effort to determine their standings with others; (2) Handicapped children indicate greater dissatisfaction with adults and adult society than do non-handicapped children; (3) Handicapped children frequently indicate a desire to be treated like other children rather than as children with handicaps.[29]

Several factors influence how a child with epilepsy views himself: his family's attitude toward the seizures and himself; the impressions and reactions he encounters in school and with his friends, as he realizes he is different from others; and repeated trips for medical attention, constant medication and possible limited participation in activities which other children enjoy freely.[30]

With the passage of time this child may develop painful self-consciousness and social awkwardness. He may either retaliate with bitterness and anger or retreat into a state of withdrawal. His parents' feelings of helplessness, guilt, perplexity, and shame may be conveyed to him in the form of hostility, rejection, segregation from siblings, and restrictions from family and community activities.

Some of the provisions for the handicapped within the church can be loading platforms, ramps, and elevators for wheelchairs. People with braces and crutches need wide corridors, hand rails, and toilet facilities within easy access to all rooms.

Emotionally Disturbed Children

An emotionally disturbed child can be defined in terms of the effect of the child's behavior on himself and/or other people. He can be described as a "trouble-maker," "socially maladjusted," "delinquent," or "neurotic." Stated differently, an emotionally handicapped child is a child whose behavior deviates from a "normal child" so that it interferes with his mental growth and development.

The emotionally handicapped can be classified into four categories: (1) conduct disorder, referred to as "unsocialized, aggressive or psychopathic behavior," (2) personality problems—neurotic or overinhibited; (3) inadequate and immature—children who are rated sluggish, lazy, preoccupied, and daydreamers; and (4) delinquent—persons whose misbehavior is a relatively serious legal offense which is inappropriate for his level of maturity.

CHARACTERISTICS

Attempts to find a type of maladjustment characteristic of all children with emotional disabilities have failed completely. Among children with learning problems, one can find a few who are emotionally healthy, some who are very inhibited, and some with neurotic symptoms. Children with emotional problems may be identified as withdrawn, immature, overly dependent, excessive daydreamers, excitable, restless, lacking in self-confidence, easily distracted, or unable to get along with peers.

CAUSES AND PREVALENCE

Factors which perpetuate behavior disorders may arise from early home experiences. Many studies have shown that parents' inconsistencies in discipline or their rejection of or hostility toward their children are positively correlated with conduct disorders in those youngsters. Influences from the community also help determine the course of a child's social and emotional development. Factors in the home and the community are reflected in the school. Many schools seek to compensate for the detrimental influences of the home and community on the mental health of children.

The US Office of Education reports that approximately two percent of all school children are emotionally disturbed.[31] The prevalence of emotional disorder depends on the diagnostician and the meaning that is attached to the disorder.

Almost every city or county of an appreciable size has some kind of mental health or child guidance clinic. Also, adult mental hygiene clinics and family service organizations can help parents and family members lessen the plight of the emotionally disturbed child. Another resource is the guidance service program in schools, which assist normal as well as emotionally disturbed children. Residential treatment centers are of more recent origin than guidance clinics and usually are for the seriously disturbed child.

Adults working with children in local churches need to be sensitive to symptoms in children that point to emotional disturbances. Those workers should discuss these problems with the children's parents and discuss remedial action. Concerned teachers will not hesitate to give ample love to children with these needs.

Behavior Disorders in Children

Children with behavior disorders are those who are hyperactive, explosive, erratic, or uninhibited in behavior. The child who is continually in motion, blows up easily, and is readily distracted from the task at hand by outside stimuli is exhibiting behavior disorders.

TYPES OF BEHAVIOR DISORDERS

1. *Hyperactivity* includes excessive movement, constant shifting of feet, tilting of chairs, tapping of pencils, or rustling of papers. Some hyperactive children are unaware of their excessive movement and must be made to realize the disturbance they create.

2. *Distractibility* is the child's inability to give normal attention to the events and circumstances that surround him. Instead of attending to the consequential for a proper period of time, various events and objects are attended to fleetingly, irrespective of their relevance to immediate circumstances.

3. *Disinhibition* is the inability of a child to control his thought processes. Any past experiences, despite their inappropriateness, interrupt and disturb the process.

4. *Perseveration* is undue attention to an insolated phenomenon without regard to its importance, pertinence, or suitability. Even after an experience is no longer of consequence, possible detrimental attention continues inflexibility. This perseveration may entail either external or internal aspects of the experience.

STRATEGIES FOR DEALING WITH CHILDREN WITH BEHAVIOR DISORDERS

1. *Hyperactivity.* When children are seated at a table for group work in Sunday school or other church agencies, the hyperactive child should be given only those materials (such as paper and crayons) that he needs at

the moment. Other materials should be kept from him so that he is not tempted to be manipulating them. Hyperactives need large-muscle activities, such as acting out stories, singing action songs, and doing finger plays and action poems. Working with play-dough helps quiet overly active bodies. Sometimes a teacher may quietly ask a hyperactive child to help the teacher in certain activities. A teacher may sit or stand behind the hyperactive child and place a hand or only a finger on his shoulder as a cue to stop the movement. Eventually he will internalize the "feel" of this on his back and begin to gain the essential inner control.

2. *Distractibility*. The distractible child finds the average schoolroom overly stimulating and therefore is unable to perform to the best of his ability. The environment should be arranged so that he can work most successfully. The room should be free from excessive visual stimulation with the wall painted a plain soft color and exhibits kept to a minimum.

3. *Disinhibition*. Some disinhibited children, due to their inability to control their ideation, make irrelevant remarks. They think of something that cannot wait. Learning to postpone reactions is a part of maturation, but many children with behavior disorders find this a difficult pattern to establish. Disinhibition can be reduced by establishing routine both at home and at school. When a child knows the general pattern and sequence of events to be expected, his behavior is less impulsive and better organized.

4. *Perseveration*. To remedy this problem, first analyze the situations in which it occurs. Often it increases as the child fatigues; therefore, the routine should provide for quiet rest periods. When perseveration is on a particular object, the objects may need to be removed. When perseveration pertains to a certain type of action the teacher frequently uses the single word *stop*. Sometimes it is necessary to stop him physically by holding his hand; at other times, it is sufficient to raise a finger.

It should be emphasized that not all children with psychoneurological learning disabilities exhibit the behavior disorders symptoms discussed above. Many organize sensory experiences successfully and enjoy normal stimulation in the classroom; controls are necessary only for those who cannot. Children's workers in the church should observe the following suggested guidelines and practices:

1. They should identify the youngster needing help in the classroom.
2. They should provide help within the classroom by upholding the dignity of every child.
3. They should adjust the curriculum as necessary to help meet the needs of exceptional pupils.

4. They should consider providing special classes for children with certain needs.
5. They should work closely with the parents of children with special needs.

A ministry with exceptional children can be a rewarding challenge. Because of the varied needs in exceptionality, special training and facilities may be necessary. However, perhaps even more basic to a fruitful ministry is a loving concern for people with special needs and a vision to do something to meet those needs through individual and group encounter.

NOTES

1. Bureau of Education for the Handicapped, *Better Education for the Handicapped,* Annual Reports for fiscal years 1968 and 1969. Washington, D.C.: 1969, p. 4; 1970, p. 4.
2. Arnold Gesell, Frances Ilg, and Glenna Bullis, *Vision—Its Development in Infant and Child* (Darien, Conn.: Hafner, 1970), p. 3.
3. National Society for the Prevention of Blindness Fact Book (1966).
4. Samuel A. Kirk, *Educating Exceptional Children,* 2d ed. (Boston: Houghton Mifflin, 1972), p. 293.
5. American Printing House for the Blind, *One Hundred and First Report.* (Louisville, Ky.: American Printing House for the Blind, 1969).
6. American Foundation for the Blind and the National Society for the Prevention of Blindness.
7. *Blind and Partially Seeing Children in Illinois* (Chicago: Commission for Handicapped Children, 1951), p. 22.
8. Kirk, p. 301.
9. National Society for the Prevention of Blindness Fact Book (1966).
10. Kirk, p. 318.
11. B. Lowenfield, as quoted in Kirk, pp. 333-34.
12. Kirk, p. 74.
13. Midcentury White House Conference, "Speech Disorders and Speech Correction," *Journal of Speech and Hearing Disorders* 17 (June 17, 1952): 129-37.
14. Charles Van Riper, *Speech Correction—Principles and Methods* (Englewood Cliffs, N.J.: Prentice-Hall, 1963), pp. 102-103.
15. Wendell Johnson, et al., *Speech Handicapped Children* (New York: Harper, 1956), p. 331.
16. Kirk, p. 95.
17. Lee Edward Travis, *Handbook of Speech Pathology* (New York: Appleton-Century-Crofts, 1957), p. 552.
18. Kirk, p. 269.
19. Erick Denhoff and Henry Novack, "Syndromes of Cerebral Dysfunction: Medical Aspects that Contribute to Special Education," in *Methods in Special Education,* ed. R. L. Haring and Norris G. Schiefelbusch (New York: McGraw-Hill, 1967), p. 360.
20. Dwayne Peterson, "Children with Physical Disabilities and Multiple Handicaps," in *Education for the Exceptional Child,* ed. William Gearheart (Scranton, Pa.: Intext Educational Publishers, 1972), p. 251.
21. Ibid., p. 252.
22. Ibid., p. 253.
23. Peter Miller, *The Child with Epilepsy in Your School* (Chicago: Illinois Epilepsy League, 1956), p. 4.
24. M. McGinnis, F. Kleffner, and H. Goldstein, *Teaching Aphasic Children* (Washington, D.C.: Volta Bureau), p. 1.
25. Denhoff and Novack, p. 352.

26. Charles Kram, "Epilepsy in Children and Youth," in *Psychology of Exceptional Children and Youth,* ed. William M. Cruickshank (Englewood Cliffs, N:J.: Prentice-Hall, 1963), p. 390.
27. McGinnis, Kleffner, and Goldstein, p. 2.
28. Velma Morton, "Basic Problems in Guidance of the Exceptional," in *Special Education for the Exceptional,* ed. Merle Frampton and Elena Gall (Boston: F. Porter Sargent, 1955), p. 132.
29. William M. Cruickshank, "Psychological Considerations with Crippled Children," in *Psychology of Exceptional Children and Youth,* ed. William M. Cruickshank (Englewood Cliffs, N.J.: Prentice-Hall, 1963), p. 336.
30. Kram, p. 386.
31. U.S. Office of Education, Bureau of Education for the Handicapped, Washington, D.C.

FOR FURTHER READING

Visually Handicapped Children

Baker, Harry. *Introduction to Exceptional Children.* Detroit: MacMillan, 1950.

Bishop, Virginia. *Teaching the Visually Limited Child.* Springfield, Ill:: Thomas, 1971.

Jones, Reginald, L. *New Directions in Special Education.* Boston: Allyn & Bacon, 1970.

Kerby, C. E. "Cause of Blindness in Children of School Age." *The Sight-Saving Review* 28 (Spring, 1958):10-21.

Kirk, Samuel A. *Educating Exceptional Children.* Boston: Houghton Mifflin, 1962.

Speech Handicapped Children

Johnson, Wendel; Brown, Spencer J.; Curtis, James F.; Edney, Clarence; and Keaster, Jacqueline. *Speech Handicapped Children.* New York: Harper, 1956.

Kirk, Samuel A. *Educating Exceptional Children.* 2d ed. Boston: Houghton Mifflin, 1972.

Palmer, Charles E. *Speech and Hearing Problems.* Springfield, Ill.: Thomas, 1961.

"Speech Disorders and Speech Correction," *Journal of Speech and Hearing Disorders* Vol 17. Midcentury White House Conference, June 17, 1952.

Travis, Lee Edward. *Handbook of Speech Pathology.* New York: Appleton-Century-Crofts, 1957.

Van Riper, Charles. *Speech Correction–Principles and Methods.* Englewood Cliffs, N.J.: Prentice-Hall, 1963.

Auditory Handicapped Children

Bender, Ruth. *The Conquest of Deafness.* Cleveland: Western Reserve U., 1970.

Goodhill, V. *Pathology, Diagnosis and Therapy of Deafness.* New York: Appleton-Century-Crofts, 1959.

Kirk, Samuel A. *Educating Exceptional Children.* Boston: Houghton Mifflin, 1972.

Myklebust, Helmer R. *The Psychology of Deafness.* 2d ed. New York: Grune & Stratton, 1964.

Sataloff, Joseph. *Hearing Loss.* Philadelphia: Lippincott, 1966.

Other Kinds of Physically Handicapped Children

Alesevich, Eugene. "Physical Defects and Learning Abilities." In *The Slow Learner,* ed. Joseph Roucek. New York: Philosophical Library, 1969.

Carpenter, Robert D. *Why Can't I Learn?* Glendale, Calif.: Gospel Light, 1972.

Clark, Matt. "Troubled Children: The Quest for Help." *Newsweek* 83 (April 8, 1974): 52-56, 58.

Cruickshank, William M. "Psychological Consideration with Crippled Children." In *Psychology of Exceptional Children and Youth,* 3d ed., ed. William M. Cruickshank. Englewood Cliffs, N.J.: Prentice-Hall, 1971.

Denhoff, Eric, and Novack, Henry. "Syndromes of Cerebral Dysfunction: Medical Aspects that Contribute to Special Educational Methods." In *Methods in Special Education,* ed. Norris G. Haring and R. L. Schieflbusch. New York: McGraw-Hill, 1967.

Hill, Charles H. "Helping the Learning Disabled Child." *Moody Monthly* 74 (Jan., 1974):5, 55-58.

Kram, Charles. "Epilepsy in Children and Youth." In *Psychology of Exceptional Children and Youth,* 3d ed., ed. William M. Cruickshank. Englewood Cliffs, N.J.: Prentice-Hall, 1971.

Miller, Peter. *The Child with Epilepsy in Your School.* Chicago: Illinois Epilepsy League, 1956.

Peterson, Dwayne. "Children with Physical Disabilities and Multiple Handicaps." In *Education of the Exceptional Child,* ed. William Gearheart, Scranton, Pa.: Intext Educational Publ., 1972.

Weiner, Florence. *Help for the Handicapped Child.* New York: McGraw-Hill, 1973.

Emotionally Disturbed Children

Asquith, Melrose; Barton, Clifford; and Donaher, Robert. "I Have an Emotionally Disturbed Child in My Classroom." *Grade Teacher* 85 (April, 1968): 77-81, 127.

Hewett, Frank M. *The Emotionally Disturbed Child in the Classroom.* Boston: Allyn & Bacon, 1971.

Haring, Norris G. and Phillips, E. Lakin. *Educating Emotionally Disturbed Children.* New York: McGraw-Hill, 1962.

Children With Behavior Disorders

Dunn, Lloyd M. *Exceptional Children in the Schools.* Chicago: Holt, Rinehart & Winston, 1966.

Children With Learning Disabilities

Cruickshank, William M., and Johnson, G. Orville. *Education of Exceptional Children and Youth.* 2d ed. Englewood Cliffs, N.J.: Prentice-Hall, 1967.

Lerner, Janet W. *Children with Learning Disabilities.* Boston: Houghton Mifflin, 1971.

McCarthy, James A., and McCarthy, Joan F. *Learning Disabilities.* Boston: Allyn & Bacon, 1970.

Myklebust, Helmer R. *Progress in Learning Disabilities.* New York: Grune & Stratton, 1968.

Patterson, Uretha. "Children with Specific Learning Disabilities." In *Methods in Special Education,* ed. Norris G. Haring and R. L. Schiefelbusch. New York: McGraw-Hill, 1967.

Part VII

WORKING WITH CHILDREN BEYOND THE CHURCH

28

The Role of the Home in Childhood Education

Gene A. Getz

The Home Is Basic in Childhood Education

The Scriptures reveal that the home is basic in childhood education. However, it is important to emphasize that this does not mean that the church or Christian school is unnecessary. Parents in today's world would be naive indeed to say that they can do the job alone. The demands, pressures, and influences in our twentieth-century culture prohibit parents from drawing that conclusion. Parents need support and help in the Christian nurture of their children as perhaps never before.

Why does the Bible place a strong emphasis on the home in the Christian nurture of children? Generally speaking, the answer lies in the fact that there are certain learning experiences that children can have at home which are almost impossible to get in any other setting—church or school.

The Home Provides a Natural and Spontaneous Environment

It is almost impossible to reconstruct the home environment in any other setting. The home provides "wall-to-wall," twenty-four-hour-a-day experiences. The family is normally a small unit of people (which varies from culture to culture), including all age levels, who eat together, play together, travel together, and sleep under the same roof. Even communal structures are difficult to maintain on a long-term basis when more than one family unit lives together. And in our Western culture, in-laws in the same house often create serious problems.

The naturalness of the home environment is well illustrated in Deuteronomy 6, in which Moses prepared the Israelites for entering the prom-

---

Gene A. Getz, Ph.D., is Associate Professor of Pastoral Theology at Dallas Theological Seminary, Dallas, Texas, and Pastor of the Fellowship Bible Church, Dallas, Texas.

ised land. After wandering for forty years in the wilderness because of their sin, they were then ready to settle down in Canaan.

Moses warned parents in Israel regarding their own relationship to God: "And you shall love the LORD your God with all your heart and with all your soul and with all your might. And these words, which I am commanding you today, shall be on your heart" (Deu 6:5-6, NASB). Then Moses instructed parents to teach the Word of God to their children. He indicated *when* and *where* and *how* this is to take place: "when you sit in your house and when you walk by the way and when you lie down and when you rise up" (Deu 6:7, NASB).

At least three things become obvious from this passage.

1. Parents need *more than head knowledge* about the Bible. In order for them to impart the Word of God effectively to their children, the truths of the Bible must first permeate the parents' lives. An ability to quote Scripture and to teach doctrine to our children is not enough! More important than what we say about God to our children is what we are in their presence. Parents who love God with their whole heart, soul and energy will become obvious examples of Christian truth and virtue.

2. Effective teaching in the home must also involve *more than a period of instruction.* It must *happen* naturally and spontaneously—when we are seated at the table eating or in the family room watching television. It may occur when we are walking through the woods or even around the block. It may happen when we tuck the children into bed at night or when we awaken them in the morning.

3. The Word of God *must permeate the total atmosphere of the home.* Christ must be the center of every activity—whether we are in serious discussion or enjoying happy moments together building block houses, wrestling, biking, swimming, or eating out. Some of the most natural opportunities for teaching biblical truths happen in the regular activities of daily living, and if we pass them by, they may never occur again. What's more, these parent-child opportunities happen *only* in the home—not at school or in church. In the home, the realities of life are obvious—where we *are* what we *really* are—both as parents and children.

THE HOME PROVIDES AN OPPORTUNITY FOR POSITIVE PARENTAL EXAMPLES

Marshall McLuhan's theme, "the medium is the message," is more than a twentieth-century truism. It is doubtful that McLuhan himself understood the profound biblical implications of this observation—a conclusion which he built on communication phenomena in our contemporary culture.

From Old Testament days until now, God designed the home to be one of the more significant illustrations of this concept. *A godly home becomes a message in itself.* This is the thrust of Deuteronomy 6.

How were men to recognize Christians and who they were? Jesus explained it: "By this all men will know that you are My disciples, if you have love for one another" (Jn 13:35, NASB).

How were men to know that Jesus Christ was the Son of God? Again Jesus said it clearly when He prayed that we "may all be one; even as Thou, Father, art in Me, and I in Thee . . . that they may be perfected in unity, that the world may know that Thou didst send Me" (Jn 17:21, 23).

The very love and unity in the body of Christ itself becomes the message of Christ. The medium (the functioning body) was to *become* the message to the world.

God designed the home so that children could learn by example. Their value system is to emerge in the context of dynamic Christian living, where father and mother demonstrate biblical realities. As children observe their father loving their mother as "Christ loved the church" and as children see their mother submitting to their father as "the church is to be subject to Christ," they are learning biblical truth by direct experience. This is far more meaningful than mere verbalization.

The lesson is clear. If we want our children to "love as Christ loved," we must not just *tell* them to "love as Christ loved." Rather we must "love as Christ loved." If we want them to pray, *we* must pray. If we want them to be kind to others, *we* must be kind to others. If we want them to share their faith, *we* must share *our* faith. If we want them to read their Bibles, we must read *our* Bibles.

As will be shown in more detail later, God made children with a natural tendency to become what their parents are. J. A. Hadfield, a psychologist who has spent much of his life studying the development and growth patterns of children, has made a rather stunning statement. "We see," he says, "that it is by a perfectly natural process that the child develops standards of behavior and a moral sense. So that *if you never taught a child one single moral maxim, he would nevertheless develop moral—or immoral—standards of right and wrong by the process of identification.*"[1]

This is a profound statement indeed. But it is not so surprising when we look at what Scripture says about the home. Students of human behavior—secular though they may be—have discovered through the process of observation many notions that correlate either partially or totally with biblical truth.

Take the observations of psychologists and psychiatrists regarding the father image. Unknowingly they have confirmed to a great extent the importance of reflecting Christ in our parental life-style. For whether we recognize it or not, a child's view of God is very often his view of his parents—especially of his father.

I am reminded of a rather jolting statement by one of my own daughters when she was about four years old. "God," she said, "is my heavenly daddy." At that point in her life, her view of God was her view of me—a rather sobering thought indeed!

The father image, of course, is of particular significance in Scripture, and this is not without design. God the Father is desirous that children grow up with a correct view of who He really is and what He is really like. Thus Paul instructs fathers, "Do not provoke your children to anger; but bring them up in the discipline and instruction of the Lord" (Eph 6:4, NASB). And again, "Fathers, do not exasperate your children, that they may not lose heart" (Col 3:21, NASB). Bruce Narramore states the following:

> My experience in counseling neurotic adults has invariably shown that their image of God has been colored by negative experiences with parents, God's representatives on earth. This is not to say that biblical teachings on God's character failed to influence our spiritual relationships, they certainly do. *But negative emotional reactions stemming from childhood interfere with our ability to apply biblical knowledge.* Think of your own Christian experience. Haven't you sometimes feared a vengeful God or felt He didn't understand? Have you had difficulty believing God's will was best for you? Have you resented God's direction or discipline? Most of these feelings are emotional hangovers from childhood experiences.
>
> In a real sense God has given us a divine opportunity to shape our children's lives for time and for eternity. It is beautiful to realize we can actually teach our children the love and character of God. It is awesome to know that our own hang-ups can drive wedges between our precious children and God, the Creator of the universe.[2]

The Early Years Are the Crucial Years

James R. Dolby, a Christian psychologist, states: "I concur with those who say that the first year of life is the most important year in a person's existence. During this year he learns whether the world is cruel or comfortable; he learns that he is a separate entity apart from the world of stimuli outside him. This year is the foundation on which all personality rests."[3]

Unfortunately some Christians have interpreted a statement of this nature to mean that man cannot change nor can he be a responsible human being. Man *can* change, and man *can* become a responsible individual through the power of the indwelling Christ. And I might add that man can change without remembering and understanding all that has happened in his past life. He can forget the past and move on.

But man can never be made over completely in his emotional and physical life. In fact, the Bible teaches that the effects of the sins of the fathers is sometimes seen in the third and fourth generation of children (Num 14:18). Though this may have specific reference to Israel and God's judgment on them, the principle inherent in these words of Scripture is verified again and again in today's world. An immature and carnal parent produces immature and carnal offspring who in turn produce immature and carnal offspring.

The early years, then, are the crucial years, and, of course, the home provides the context for the early years. Pine underscores this fact in this striking statement: "If a child's educational achievements depend so heavily on what he learned before the age of six, the home—not the school—emerges as the major educational institution in the land."[4]

Mature psychological development in a child provides the foundation on which mature spiritual development takes place. For example, the greatest psychological need of a child during his first year of life is for security and love. An environment that is filled with uncertainties, adult disagreements, and impatience, creates insecurity for a child. Children in the first year of life need exposure to parents who are truly manifesting the fruit of the Spirit—"love, joy, peace, patience, kindness, goodness, faithfulness, gentleness, self-control" (Gal 5:22-23). The human being who manifests these characteristics makes the child's environment a *secure* place for him to grow in and to develop. In turn, a secure environment enables a child to develop those personality traits that prepare the way for biblical teaching and learning.

A child begins to learn biblical truth the moment he is born, but mainly at the nonverbal and emotional (affective) level. Here is an excellent example of McLuhan's statement that "the medium is the message." The environment in which a child lives *is* the Christian message itself. And if the environment radiates love and security, he immediately picks up these "signals"— though mainly at the subconscious level. His personality is being formed. The foundations are being laid for an acceptance of the biblical message at the conscious level. Conversely, if the environment reflects hostility, uncertainty, and insecurity, the foundations are being laid for a rejection of the biblical message at the conscious level.

A profound proverb reads, "Train up a child in the way he should go, Even when he is old he will not depart from it" (Pr 22:6).

This verse has often been quoted as a promise that parents can claim in rearing their children. Unfortunately we often miss the significance of this verse, for it probably means, "Train up a child according to his way"—that is, "according to the natural bent of his personality."

Franz Delitzsch translates: "Give to the child instruction to his way: So he will not, when he becomes old, depart from it." He then comments as follows: "The instructions of youth, the education of youth, ought to be conformed to the nature of youth; the matter of instruction, the manner of instruction, ought to regulate itself according to the stage of life, and its peculiarities; the method ought to be arranged according to the degree of development which the mental and bodily life of the youth has arrived at."[5]

Anyone who has worked with children to any extent recognizes that they go through various stages or phases in their development. This, of course, is verified by numerous volumes on the subject of child development. It was even said of Jesus Christ that He, as a child, "kept increasing in wisdom and stature, and in favor with God and men" (Lk 2:52, NASB).

It is vitally important for parents to understand the natural phases of childhood development and to train up their children "according to their way." When parents work *against* rather than *with* these natural phases, unfortunate results often occur. In fact, children have been known eventually to reject everything their parents stand for because of this violation.

SPECIFIC PHASES

There are various approaches to describing the phases of early child development from ages one through three or four. The following, adapted from Hadfield, are graphic and realistic. Though they originate in the psychological literature, they seem to correlate very significantly with biblical concepts.[6]

Self-display. A two-year-old child who calls attention to himself is naturally moving from the security of the first year to the exploration of the second year. Self-display appears naturally and innately.

However if the child becomes extensive in his "showing off," he is doing so because of insecurity and lack of attention. To snub him or to punish him only aggravates his problem. A "limelight" child at the age of two needs attention—not negative and disciplinary—but personal and positive attention.

CURIOSITY AND EXPLORATION

A child of two is also naturally curious. He has an innate desire to explore. Consequently, he needs an environment that is conducive to this need.

Parents who overly restrict him and force him into an unnatural role are working against his natural God-created tendencies. This is the way he learns, and this is the way he develops a healthy personality. Unfortunately our present culture has created an environment in many homes that works against the child rather than with him. Our living rooms are filled with "thou-shalt-not-touch" items which create frustration for a two-year-old. As much as possible, he needs an environment that allows him freedom to move about, to play, to touch. All of this is forming a foundation for continued and future exploration and interest in biblical truth at the cognitive level. Research shows that healthy interest and motivation to learn in later life is very much related to the full expression of this need during these early years.

IMITATION

The natural capacity to imitate comes into full force between one and two years of age. *What* the child imitates comes from his environment. It is a subconscious process, unrelated to his power to reason, and *is far more effective than verbal teaching.*

Parents must be living models of Jesus Christ with this age. Children naturally and spontaneously imitate another person's behavior. They reflect either bad habits or our good habits. If we act in impatient ways, they reflect impatience. If we are selfish, they reflect selfishness. If we are insecure, they reflect insecurity. If we constantly strike out, they learn to strike back.

Fortunately and unfortunately, they also imitate other children. This means that parents should attempt to create an environment where older children do not take advantage of younger children and set bad examples. For instance, a four-year-old who constantly hits a two-year-old teaches him to strike at others.

When teaching a two-year-old, then, it is important to teach biblical truth by example as well as by formal teaching. A child who is growing and developing in an environment that reflects the fruit of the Spirit learns to reflect these personality traits, even though he is too young to understand and comprehend biblical doctrine didactically.

SELF-WILL

The most misunderstood phase in child development is the self-will phase. It is a particularly difficult phase for Christians because of their view of the biblical doctrine regarding the "old nature."

There is no doubt that every child is born into this world with a sin nature. This sin nature is the capacity to serve sin and self. As a child matures and develops, this capacity is greatly affected by environmental conditions. If the child is in an environment that is characterized by Christian attributes, he tends to take on the same characteristics, even apart from conversion. If he is in an atmosphere that is characterized by non-Christian attributes, he tends to take on these characteristics.

Christians frequently make the mistake of classifying the old nature as a full-blown manifestation of sin. We do this because we see the child through adult eyes (our own adult perspective and what is true in our own adult lives). We often interpret the biblical reference to the degenerative manifestation of the sin nature in adult people as being applicable to small children from birth. We tend to classify every manifestation of anger in a child in the same category as if an adult lost his temper. Every manifestation of self-centeredness is classified as the same type of manifestation as it also appears in our adult lives. Every evidence of interest and curiosity in his sexual nature is sometimes classified as a manifestation of the same thing we see in mature sinning adults. To many Christians, these characteristics in a child are proof positive that man is a sinner by nature.

Actually this is an inaccurate interpretation of child behavior—physically, psychologically, and spiritually. The old nature in a child is not synonymous with being a "practicing and mature sinner." Rather it is a capacity that causes an individual to become a "practicing sinner." How we as parents and teachers handle these natural characteristics just described has a great deal to do with how quickly a child develops spiritual problems.

The self-will phase is a natural phase in a child of two. It is biological as well as psychological. He is learning to cope with his world—including people. It is important for Christian parents to distinguish this phase from what the Bible classifies as the "old nature." Functionally speaking, it helps to preserve this biblical concept until the child's personality is organized, coordinated, and harmonized at about age four. This capacity seems to come into full fruition at this time, that is, unless we misunderstand the self-will period and begin to work against it. If we do, the imitation capacity takes over, and the natural process of anxiety, anger, aggression, fear, and insecurity begin a premature manifestation of sin problems.

Christian parents then must understand the self-will period in a two-year-old. It must be channeled and directed—not broken. A child needs to learn to cope with his world but in appropriate ways. If he has the right behavioral models, combined with understanding adults, he will move naturally into the suggestibility phase around age two-and-a-half or three—a phase where he *naturally* desires to be like his parents.

SUGGESTIBILITY

If a child does not naturally begin to develop traits that are more cooperative around two-and-a-half to three years, then his self-will phase may be extending into the suggestibility phase. This means that the child's parents have probably "worked against" the self-will phase rather than "with it."

Parents need to understand what has happened. To continue to force and repress the child who is engaged in this struggle will only cause the self-will phase to continue to extend itself into later years, producing an anxious and perhaps aggressive and angry personality. Herein lie the roots to some very significant spiritual and psychological problems which may appear in later life.

How do you teach a child from two-and-a-half to three? How do you get him to respond? Remember that a normal child of this age will usually *imitate* what you do but tends *not* to do something *if you tell him to.* In other words, the best way to teach kindness, cooperation, respect, and reverence toward God and the Bible is to demonstrate these characteristics in our own lives as parents.

Remember too that a child of two-and-a-half to three detects "verbal" and "life" contradictions very quickly. He will reject "words" and "do what you do" if the two are not in harmony. You do not have to tell a child of this age to "do what you do" and "not as you say." He will follow your examples automatically.

IDENTIFICATION

The next phase in the child's development is identification—the tendency to "take over" the personality of a parent. The three-year-old may say, "I'm Daddy mowing the lawn," or, "I'm Mommy washing the dishes," or, "I'm Teacher telling a story."

Since a child normally identifies with those he loves and admires, it is important for parents to establish a relationship with him that reflects security and a feeling af comfortableness. The more a child is attracted to a parent or a teacher, the more he will want to be like him.

Again, this underscores the importance of adults being the right behavioral model. The more the adult exemplifies Jesus Christ, the more the child will reflect these same traits, even though he may not be able to understand fully Christian truths.

This process can also be dangerous. All adults have weaknesses. We all have strengths which may not suit the temperament and innate capacities of the child. Therefore, it is important to expose children to a variety of behavioral models—both adults and children—who also exemplify Christian virtues. Significantly, God designed a natural context in which this can happen—the family. It takes two persons to bring a child into the world. Thus the child has two personalities with which he identifies from birth. Also, it seems logical that the more children there are in a family, the more opportunity an individual child has to mix with a variety of personalities in close range and to incorporate into himself those characteristics and interests most suited to his or her temperament. This is why it is sometimes true that an only child or the first child has difficulties.[7]

Fortunately, a child is not locked in to bad identifications, and he can change rather quickly if he is exposed on a regular basis to people who exhibit positive characteristics. The key term here is *regular basis,* and it is the home that provides the context for this exposure at close range on a consistent basis.

EGO IDEAL

Between the ages of three and four, a child begins to move toward developing a well-organized personality. Adults begin to see duality in his personality, self-consciousness, self-criticism, self-control, and the development of the will.

From a biblical perspective, this is an extremely important age. It is at this time that the biblical doctrine regarding the "old nature" becomes very significant. The Adamic nature begins to become a force in the child's life, a force which a child does not understand but one which Christian parents *must* understand. The child naturally and normally begins to be pulled internally in two directions—to imitate what is good and to imitate what is bad.

If a child has felt the necessary security of the first year and has had good behavioral models in the second, and if we have handled the self-will phase with understanding and discretion, the child will find it rather easy to continue to conform to positive examples in his life.

Conversely, if we have violated the natural bent of the child in his early years, the child will have a much more difficult time responding to certain norms. He is now at an age when he begins to scrap the personality of the parent and keep the character of the parent. He is now becoming his own person. He is shedding the aspects of identification and is establishing within himself guiding principles. Put another way, he no longer says, "I am a kind, gentle, and unselfish man like Daddy"; rather, he says, "I am a kind, gentle, and unselfish boy."

Since a child between three and four has a capacity for self-consciousness, he also has a capacity for self-criticism. He can now develop very strong feelings of shamefulness. He can also feel stupid, selfish, and clumsy.

This has significant implications for Christian parents. Very quickly, we can develop a morbid self-consciousness in a child by confronting him with adult concepts of sin and degeneration. He feels guilt naturally, especially if an adult whom he admires often "says so." When a relatively good child from a Christian home becomes obsessed with feelings of shame and unworthiness, he has, no doubt, been inappropriately exposed to the concept of sin. He has developed an overly sensitive conscience.

This type of problem in a child is often reflected by unusual criticism of others—both children and adults. The child may try to pull others down to his own level. He may also project his own self-criticism on others and feel they are perpetually criticizing him. When in a group, he may also develop ideas of reference, that is, he may feel that the scolding of a group of children by a teacher is a direct reference to himself.

This is not to say that we should not deal with the concept of sin. But it does mean that we must deal with it at a child's level, not an adult level. In fact, a child of four is very cognizant of tendencies to do wrong things, even without being verbally reminded. He is very much aware of the natural inner struggle that begins to emerge in his personality. If he has developed normal personality patterns, he is ready to understand clearly the positive aspects of the gospel—that Jesus Christ desires to be his Saviour from sin.

As a child grows through the school years, patterns of acceptable or unacceptable behavior continue to develop more fully. If a positive foundation has been laid carefully in his earlier years, the child may be more inclined toward positive attitudes and behavior in accord with the Word of God through parental example.

Guiding Children Ages Four Through Seven

A child between ages four and seven needs an adult who understands his *individuality*. He has all the "ingredients" of a grownup. His personality is organized, and he can make judgments. He feels independent and has a new sense of power and self-assurance. He now has a will in the *true* sense of the word. He responds naturally to rivalry. His imagination is very keen—so much so that he confuses fact and fiction.

If a child's environment has been proper, as described in the previous sections, he may now be ready for conversion. A child of four or five can, with clear understanding, invite Jesus Christ to be his Saviour. Since he is aware of sin, he can make his decision in the light of his *need* for a Saviour.* True, his understanding is limited and immature, but one who works closely with children can testify to their ability to grasp their need for salvation. The gospel need not be presented with great force and condemnation; rather, a simple story of another child inviting Christ to be his Saviour can ignite in the heart of a child his need to do so himself.

A child from four to seven is capable of understanding biblical truth. Parents can encourage children in this age group to memorize Scripture,

*For more on this subject, see chap. 11, "Evangelism of Children."

listen to appropriate biblical stories, and learn basic doctrine. These biblical truths must be taught at their level of understanding, must be visualized whenever possible, and must be integrated into activities that are normal and natural to him.

Guiding Children Eight Through Twelve

Normally, children in this age group move from *individuality* and self-centeredness to *socialization* and group interest. They are generally healthy, have keen minds, are more goal oriented than before, like to collect things, and are extroverted. They do not outwardly show too much concern for adults, but they are concerned about their peers and about being a part of the group. They will respond to authority but do so more quickly when they choose to do so. Their interest in play, hobbies, and games is at an all-time high.

Since children from eight to twelve tend to put adults in a secondary place in their thinking, it is wise to avoid authoritarian attitudes in discipline and control. They want to be treated more as adults than children. Understand, of course, they *are* children—and down deep they know this too—but they are struggling toward maturity. If they are involved in setting boundaries for themselves, they will more willingly abide by the rules. In fact, they may be harder on themselves than an adult may be.

Children of this age are capable of learning significant portions of Bible doctrine, of memorizing Scripture easily. And they respond enthusiastically to well-presented biblical accounts reflecting heroism, bravery, and courage.

Children in this age level are capable of assimilating many facts without regard to application. Therefore parents must help their children relate Scripture to life. Parents must be careful, however, that they do not cause a child to expect more from his life than he can give—causing excessive guilt. But he must be taught to integrate truth into his life.

Again this can best be done in the activities he likes best. Natural sports provide unlimited opportunities for biblical *input* as well as application. Since games are organized and have rules, they reflect essential elements of balanced living. Consequently, they provide unique opportunities for life-related learning. Also, their behavior at play reflects their homelife and their deepest needs. For example, a child who is unusually hostile while at play (beyond normal aggressiveness) may be repressed at home, or he may be insecure and unsure of himself because of lack of direction and control at home.

Though children during this age level have keen minds, they must still be motivated to learn. Old methods and approaches in biblical teaching may not hold interest too long for the "Sesame Street" generation. Much biblical truth is not naturally exciting to an eight- to twelve-year-old. But there is nothing more important. The god of this world is bent on crowding out the most essential things from children's lives. Christian leaders and educators in the twentieth century must decide which one to follow and lead children to follow. In many cases, complacency already reflects that decision.

The Church Working with the Home

Parents have a significant, irreplaceable role in nurturing their children in the things of God. Fortunately, however, this monumental task need not be carried on without assistance. The alert local church can do much to support and aid parents in their role of child training by following these three suggestions:

First, the church should *provide training for parents on how to understand and rear their children.* Many fathers and mothers are not as aware as they should be of the concepts discussed in the preceding pages of this chapter. For example, they are not sufficiently sensitive to the power of nonverbal communication in the life of a small child. Furthermore they do not see the significant correlation between proper psychological development and spiritual development. Also many do not understand the natural phases through which all children develop—their natural bent.

Second, the church must *provide the home with a program of Christian education that supplements and supports parents in their task of child nurture.* Today there is a strong movement to place Christian education back in the home, "where," they say, "it belongs." Though this emphasis is good in some respects, it is also dangerous, for it tends to overlook or unduly minimize the role of the local church.

On the one hand, we *do* need to put Christian education back in the home. There are some aspects of Christian education—some basic aspects—that only the home can implement.

But there are also aspects of Christian education of children that most parents cannot handle alone. Our culture has created so many competitive forces and demands on the home that it is almost impossible for the average parent to provide all that a child needs in the way of Christian nurture.

Unfortunately, in our zeal to provide this Christian nurture in the church, we have gone to the other extreme—developing curriculum, multiplying agencies, and giving parents the impression that the church has the answer for the Christian education of their children. Many parents—already overly pressured with demands on their time—have gladly relinquished their child nurture responsibility to the church.

The answer, of course, is that we need *both* child nurture in the home and child nurture in the church. There are certain objectives the church cannot achieve. The home, with its natural and spontaneous environment, its father and mother figures, its wall-to-wall experience, is basic to effective Christian education.

But there are also certain objectives that parents have difficulty achieving alone. For example, a well-trained staff of teachers in a well-equipped classroom can provide a quality experience in learning and applying Bible content that would be very difficult for parents to duplicate.

The home, then, needs the church in the nurture of its children. But it needs a supplementary and supportive program—not one that competes or encourages parents to relinquish their own responsibilities.

Third, the church needs to *provide a program of Christian education that incorporates biblical principles of child nurture.* In the Bible, child nurture is described in the context of an informal, warm, and accepting atmosphere. Also in Bible times, parents were the primary teachers. Learning was individualized within the context of small, closely knit family units. And learning took place in a variety of ways.

These biblical realities translated into principles provide us with some significant guidelines for carrying out Christian education of children in the local church. Teachers and others who work with the young should carefully consider the following questions regarding the use of biblical principles:

1. Is the learning environment in our Sunday schools and other agencies warm and accepting, creating an informal climate for learning? Or is the atmosphere formal, cold, and academic?
2. Are our children exposed to husband-and-wife teams who can function not only as teachers but as parental substitutes—demonstrating the same qualities of exemplary life as dedicated Christian parents?
3. Is learning individualized, and does it take place in small, closely knit groups that simulate family units? Or is it a larger group process, where individual children are lost in the mass?
4. Does learning happen in a variety of ways—visually, verbally and through active involvement—using a variety of media and techniques? Or is it a process that consists of one basic approach—"listening" to a teacher "talk"?

There is much, then, that the church can do to assist parents in Christian education. The challenge, however, is to help parents truly function as parents, to supplement but not to replace the home, and to utilize biblical teaching-learning principles with children.

The Home Working with the Church

Christian education is a two-way street. The home needs the church, but also it is true that the church needs the home.

A local church cannot adequately meet its objectives with children without *specific* support from Christian homes. What are some ways by which the home can help the church in the Christian education of children?

First, parents should not expect the church to solve problems that can only be effectively solved at home. For example, a discipline problem at home must be solved at home. The church should not be expected to do it.

Second, parents can cooperate with teachers and workers in solving discipline problems, in doing homework, and in applying Christian truths.

Third, parents can encourage their children to become involved in the Christian education program. They can get them to church on time. They can talk about the importance of Sunday school and church. They can pray together for their teachers and pastor. They can encourage their children to prepare their lessons. They can encourage Bible reading and memorization of verses.

Fourth, parents can encourage the workers in their church who minister to their children. Parents can invite them to dinner, pray for them, talk with them about their children, and express appreciation to them.

Summary

In summary, then, it must be restated that the Bible clearly focuses on the home as basic to childhood education. It provides a natural and spontaneous environment for Christian learning. God has created the family structure to provide parental behavioral models for children to emulate, models that in themselves provide basic doctrinal input regarding God and what He is like.

How important for parents to become more and more like Jesus Christ—in their relationship as husband and wife, in their relationship with their children, as well as in their relationship with other people—both Christians and non-Christians.

How important, too, for parents to understand the natural phases of child development, so that they can work with the natural way of the child rather than against it.

As parents and teachers work cooperatively, as church and home complement each other in their roles, the task of educating children in spiritual living will become far more effective than is otherwise possible.

NOTES

1. J. A. Hadfield, *Childhood and Adolescence* (Baltimore: Penguin, 1962), p. 134. Hadfield's italics.
2. Bruce Narramore, *Help! I'm a Parent* (Grand Rapids: Zondervan, 1972), pp. 13-14. Narramore's italics.
3. James R. Dolby, *I, Too, Am Man* (Waco, Tex.: Word, 1969), p. 78.
4. Maya Pines, *Revolution in Learning: The Years from Birth to Six* (New York: Harper & Row, 1967), p. 52.
5. Franz Delitzsch, *Biblical Commentary on the Proverbs of Solomon* (Grand Rapids: Eerdmans, 1950), pp. 86-87.
6. J. A. Hadfield has outlined various places in his book *Childhood and Adolescence,* which, in my opinion, correlate significantly with biblical precepts.
7. A first child often has difficulties also because of the insecurity faced by parents with their first child. Parents also tend to try too hard with the first. They want to produce the perfect child. The more relaxed the parents are with their child, the more the child is relaxed.

SELECTED BIBLIOGRAPHY

Adams, Jay E. *Christian Living in the Home.* Nutley, N.J.: Presbyterian and Reformed, 1972.

Anderson, Robert H., and Shane, Harold. *As the Twig Is Bent: Readings in Early Childhood Education.* Boston: Houghton Mifflin, 1971.

Brandt, Henry R. *Keys to Better Living for Parents.* Chicago: Moody, 1962.

Brandt, Henry R., and Dowdy, Homer E. *Building a Christian Home.* Wheaton, Ill.: Scripture Press, 1960.

Bye, Beryl. *Teaching Our Children the Christian Faith.* London: Hodder & Stoughton, 1965.

Deal, William S. *Counseling Christian Parents.* Grand Rapids: Zondervan, 1970.

Dobson, James. *Dare to Discipline.* Wheaton, Ill.: Tyndale, 1970.

Dodson, Fitzhugh. *How to Father.* Los Angeles: Nash, 1973.

———. *How to Parent.* Los Angeles: Nash, 1970.

Dolby, James R. *I, Too, Am Man.* Waco, Tex.: Word, 1969.

Drakeford, John W. *The Home: Laboratory of Life.* Nashville: Broadman, 1965.

Edens, David, and Edens, Virginia. *Why God Gave Children Parents.* Nashville: Broadman, 1966.

Evans, Laura Margaret. *Hand in Hand: Mother, Child and God.* Westwood, N.J.: Revell, 1960.

Feucht, Oscar E., ed. *Family Relationships and the Church.* St. Louis: Concordia, 1970.

———. *Helping Families Through the Church.* Rev. ed. St. Louis: Concordia, 1971.

Gangel, Kenneth. *The Family First.* Minneapolis: HIS International, 1972.

Getz, Gene A. *The Christian Home in a Changing World.* Chicago: Moody, 1972.

Ginott, Haim G. *Between Parent and Child.* New York: MacMillan, 1965.

Hadfield, J. A. *Childhood and Adolescence.* Baltimore: Penguin, 1962.

Hendricks, Howard, *Heaven Help the Home.* Wheaton, Ill.: Scripture Press, 1973.

Heynen, Ralph. *The Secret of Christian Family Living.* Grand Rapids: Baker, 1965.

Krumboltz, John D., and Krumboltz, Helen B. *Changing Children's Behavior.* Englewood Cliffs, N.J.: Prentice-Hall, 1972.

LeBar, Lois E. *Family Devotions with School-Age Children.* Westwood, N.J.: Revell, 1973.

Lee, Mark W. *Our Children Are Our Best Friends.* Grand Rapids: Zondervan, 1970.

Matthews, Charles A. *The Christian Home.* Cincinnati: Standard, n.d.

Narramore, Bruce. *A Guide to Child Rearing.* Grand Rapids: Zondervan, 1972.

———. *Help! I'm a Parent.* Grand Rapids: Zondervan, 1972.

Narramore, Clyde M. *How to Succeed in Family Living.* Glendale, Calif.: Regal, 1968.

———. *How to Understand and Influence Children.* Grand Rapids: Zondervan, 1957.

Scudder, C. W. *The Family in Christian Perspective.* Nashville: Broadman, 1962.

Small, Dwight H. *Design for Christian Marriage.* Westwood, N.J.: Revell, 1959.

Tournier, Paul. *To Understand Each Other.* Richmond, Va.: Knox, 1962.

Wagemaker, Herbert. *Why Can't I Understand My Kids?* Grand Rapids: Zondervan, 1973.

Zuck, Roy B., and Getz, Gene A., eds. *Ventures in Family Living.* Chicago: Moody, 1971.

29

The Role of the Christian Day School

Roy W. Lowrie, Jr.

In the broad spectrum of Christian education, the vigorous growth of Christian day schools is among the more significant developments during recent years. Many new schools are starting, and many existing schools are growing.

The Christian day school is not designed to replace the church or the home. Instead it seeks to supplement the responsibility of the church and the home. Because the Christian school and the evangelical church each adheres to a biblical philosophy of life, they seek to teach in harmony. By contrast, the non-Christian school and the evangelical church do not believe the same philosophy of life. The church teaches a philosophy of life based on revelation from God, whereas the non-Christian school rejects revelation and teaches a philosophy based on man's reason. The result is confusion for students, as they hear widely divergent teachings at church and in school.

The Christian day school also seeks to work cooperatively with the Christian home. The school reinforces the home as the biblical directives and admonitions to parents are exercised by the teachers. During the school day, teachers stand in the place of parents.

Educational Philosophy and Purpose

To comprehend the Christian day school, its biblical basis must be examined, for the school justifies its existence from the Bible. The reasoning is this: if the Bible is true, education—to be true—must be based on the Bible. To put it another way, since there is a revelation from God, a school

---

Roy W. Lowrie, Jr., Ed.D., is Headmaster of the Delaware County Christian School, Newton Square, Pennsylvania, and Executive Director of the National Association of Christian Education Administrators.

should be based on that revelation and not on the reason of natural man. To exclude the Bible from the philosophical foundation of a school is to present a false, distorted, and invalid education. The fear of the Lord is the beginning of wisdom and of knowledge.

The following statements of educational philosophy, purpose, and objectives are typical of Christian day schools:

1. God is the Creator and Sustainer of all things and the source of all truth.
2. God maintains control over His entire universe.
3. Because of sin, man tends to omit God and thus fails to relate himself and his knowledge to God, the Source of all wisdom.
4. Regeneration is by faith in Jesus Christ. True meanings and values can be ascertained only in the light of His person, purpose, and work.
5. God has revealed Himself in a general way in His created universe and in a specific way in the Bible.
6. The home, the church, and the school should complement each other, promoting the student's spiritual, academic, social, and physical growth.
7. The teacher stands in the place of the parents, the place of authority and responsibility.
8. God has given differing abilities to each student. It is the teacher's responsibility to challenge each child according to his ability and to seek to teach him at his academic level.
9. The Christian is not to be conformed to the world, but must accept his responsibility and his role in our democratic society.
10. The student's home, church, and school experience should be a preparation for a life of fellowship with God and of service to man.
11. The prayer of a righteous man has a powerful effect in the education of a child.

The purpose of Christian day schools is to provide a sound academic education integrated with an evangelical Christian view of God and the world. The Bible is specific in stating the principles which underlie Christian education. St. Paul presented a comprehensive principle when he wrote of Christ, "For by him were all things created, that are in heaven, and that are in earth. . . . And he is before all things, and by him all things consist" (Col 1:16-17). And the writer of the fourth gospel said, "All things were made by him; and without him was not any thing made that was made" (Jn 1:3).

There is an important difference between the Christian and the non-Christian viewpoints on a given subject. Even though knowledge is factually the same for both, no subject can be taught in the totality of its truth if the Creator is ignored or denied. Knowledge is purified by the recognition of God's place in it. No other approach to education can be entirely God honoring, for parents and children.

Christian parents are responsible for the education of their children; and that education includes the counsels of God revealed in His world as well as those revealed in His Word. These parents want their children to be educated at home *and* at school with the consciousness that all truth is God's truth, including history and geography, science, music, and the arts, and that Jesus Christ is to be central in all learning and living.

Specific Objectives

The Christian day school has numerous objectives in common with public schools and with other independent schools, although the Christian school sees these common objectives from the biblical perspective. It should be noted, however, that the Christian day school has distinctive objectives which cannot be reached in the public schools, and which are not accepted by other independent schools. To illustrate, the first ten objectives in the following list are distinctive to the Christian day school, while the last ten objectives would also be accepted by public and by other independent schools:

1. To teach that the Lord Jesus Christ is the Son of God who came to earth to die for our sins
2. To teach the necessity of being born again by the Spirit of God by receiving the Lord Jesus Christ
3. To teach that growth in the Christian life depends on fellowship with God through reading the Bible, prayer, and service
4. To teach that the Bible is the Word of God and that it is practical and important
5. To teach the application of biblical ethics and standards of morality to every part of life
6. To teach students to manifest fairness, courtesy, kindness, and other Christian graces
7. To stress the urgency of world missions
8. To teach students to get along with non-Christians and with Christians who hold differing views
9. To relate the various subject matter areas with the truth of the Bible
10. To teach that God is the Creator and Sustainer of the universe and of man
11. To teach students to apply themselves to their work and to fulfill their responsibilities
12. To teach students to work independently and cooperatively

13. To teach students to think for themselves and to stand up for their personal convictions in the face of pressure
14. To develop the students' creative skills
15. To help develop the students' appreciation of the fine arts
16. To help the students develop effective communication skills
17. To teach the knowledge and skills required for future study or for occupational competence
18. To help students develop discretion in physical and mental recreation
19. To help students appreciate their national heritage and the current problems facing their country and the world
20. To show students their present civic responsibility and to prepare them for adult responsibility as citizens of their nation.

Pros and Cons of the Christian School

Arguments favoring Christian day schools include the following: (1) teachers are born-again, dedicated, not merely holding a job; (2) parents have high interest in the education of their children; (3) exceptionally good relationships exist between the school and the home; (4) it provides a good student-teacher ratio for instruction; (5) in general, students do not have serious learning or behavior problems; (6) unity is felt within the faculty; (7) good relationships exist between the faculty and the administration; (8) enough problems arise that God must be sought and trusted daily; (9) the opportunity is given to learn from the Bible daily; and (10) academic work is integrated with the Bible.

Arguments against Christian day schools include the following: (1) facilities are inadequate or inferior; (2) programs are restricted, especially in music and athletics; (3) students are too sheltered; (4) students and teachers should be in other schools as witnesses; (5) the school is for students who cannot do well in other schools; (6) teachers are not highly qualified; (7) finances are too meager to provide quality education; (8) principals are not highly trained; (9) faculty and administrative turnover is excessive; and (10) money spent on the school should go to foreign missions.

Since each Christian day school is independent, apart from a few which are in a system, each must be considered on its own merits and limitations determined. Sweeping generalizations about the schools should be heard with caution.

Statistical Data

Each year the Board of Parish Education of the Lutheran Church, Missouri Synod of St. Louis, Missouri, compiles statistics on nonpublic elementary and secondary schools, and publishes them in mimeographed form. The following tables show the status of selected schools, kindergarten through eighth grade, for 1966 and for 1971.

TABLE 29.1

Protestant Schools, Kindergarten Through Eighth Grade

Name	Schools		Teachers		Students	
	1966	1971	1966	1971	1966	1971
American Lutheran Church	56	50	273	394	6,183	6,996
Church of the Lutheran Conference	9	11	19	35	402	413
General Conference of Seventh Day Adventists	1,002	911	2,887	3,037	46,727	51,181
General Council of the Assemblies of God	24	42	163	287	2,811	5,364
Los Angeles Baptist City Mission Society	28	24	206	229	4,522	4,571
Lutheran Church in America	15	18	132	149	2,227	3,601
Lutheran Church–Missouri Synod	1,339	1,176	6,439	6,577	159,564	146,352
Mennonite Christian Day Schools	262	61	405	211	10,592	4,047
National Association of Christian Schools	185	313	2,004	3,022	26,932	47,680
National Union of Christian Schools	243	262	2,380	2,027	54,271	49,971
Wisconsin Evangelical–Lutheran Synod	228	252	926	1,075	24,931	26,420
Totals	3,391	3,122	15,834	17,043	339,162	346,596

Similar information from the same source shows the status of selected Protestant nonpublic high schools, grades 9 through 12, for 1966 and for 1971, as reported in Table 29.2.

TABLE 29.2

PROTESTANT NONPUBLIC HIGH SCHOOLS

NAME	SCHOOLS		TEACHERS		STUDENTS	
	1966	1971	1966	1971	1966	1971
Church of the Lutheran Confession	1	1	3	9	41	43
General Conference of Seventh Day Adventist	32	38	416	560	5,035	9,496
General Council of the Assemblies of God	2	3	9	27	105	490
Los Angeles Baptist City Mission Society	1	1	15	28	176	530
Lutheran Church–Missouri Synod	25	27	620	691	11,435	12,543
Mennonite Christian Day Schools	8	10*	83	151*	1,067	1,836*
National Association of Christian Schools	72	147	526	1,200	5,976	9,753
National Union of Christian Schools	35	46	253	665	7,556	13,550
Wisconsin Evangelical–Lutheran Synod	8	9	141	130	2,641	3,054
Totals	184	282	2,066	3,461	34,032	51,295

*Statistics are for 1970, not for 1971 as others.

Several general conclusions seem warranted from these tables: (1) most Christian day schools are elementary schools, not high schools; (2) Christian day schools tend to be small in enrollment compared to public schools; (3) although most of these schools are growing, some are declining; (4) the National Association of Christian Schools grew the most during this five-year period.

Patterns of Organization

The three main organizational patterns for Christian day schools are listed and described as follows:

1. *The parent-society school.* This school is started by a group of parents, perhaps with interested friends or relatives, who form a legal corporation for the purpose of operating the school. To be eligible for membership in the society of corporation, a person must subscribe to the school's doctrinal platform and make a minimum financial contribution annually. The corporation, frequently called the school society, elects a board of trustees from among the society members. Since society members must agree to the school's doctrinal platform, dissidents do not get on the board. The board is responsible for operating the school.

The school property belongs to the society. Typically, the great majority of corporation members are parents; thus this organization is often called a parent-controlled school. Only parents who fulfill the requirements for membership, however, belong to the corporation. It is possible, then, to be a school parent and not a corporation member. Only corporation members vote on school matters.

2. *The church-related school.* This school is owned and operated by a local church. It is governed by one of the existing church boards, or, more likely, a new board, with some representation from present boards, is established to operate the school. Facilities are used jointly by the church and by the school and are owned by the church.

This type is also called a parochial school. Most Christian day schools established recently are in this group. There are fewer state regulations on this type because of the favored position which the church has with the state. In recent years, some parent-controlled schools have had court cases with the state, while similar schools owned by local churches were not involved in litigation.

3. *The privately-owned school.* This school is owned and operated by an individual, by a family, or by a group of people. It may or may not have a board. If it has a board, that board is usually advisory only, for the school is really run by the owner or owners. Unlike the first two types, this school may be a proprietary school. Property belongs to the owner. Policies, procedures, and standards are established by the owner.

Each organizational pattern has advantages and disadvantages. Since organizational structure has lasting consequences, it is important for steering committees of proposed schools to investigate organizational patterns carefully. Whatever the organizational pattern, the essentials for quality education are the same for any Christian day school.

Essentials for Quality Christian Education

Christian school administrators accept the responsibility to operate sound academic schools. To put it simply, no child should have to take an academic penalty to get a Christian school education. A second-rate education based on the true philosophy of life is unacceptable.

The following essentials for quality education are each important; thus no attempt has been made to rank them in order of importance: (1) a primary desire to see God honored through the education offered to children and young people; (2) a clear understanding of the philosophy, purposes, and objectives of the Christian day school; (3) a principal or headmaster with leadership ability who is qualified spiritually, academically, biblically, and administratively to be the chief administrator; (4) a school board which works vigorously within clearly defined responsibilities; (5) a qualified faculty, born again, trained in the academic field for which each is hired, trained in Bible; (6) a low turnover rate in the faculty and in the administration; (7) a program of prayer by faculty, students, teachers, parents, and board which permeates the entire school program; (8) a financial stability which provides operational and capital improvement funds; (9) a selected student body whose educational needs can be met by the school; (10) a large enough enrollment to keep teachers from being spread too thin, for too many lesson preparations are required when several grades are combined in the same classroom; (11) adequate salaries to allow teachers and administrators to work without constant worry about the financial status of their families; (12) complete trust that God will do everything that He has promised in His Word, and the willingness to take steps of faith by individuals and by the corporate school body.

The main essential for quality education is the teacher. Buildings and equipment are necessary, but are secondary. Some of the qualifications for teachers and for administrators will now be considered.

Qualifications for Teachers and Administrators

Christian day schools need teachers who are spiritually qualified. Teachers must be born again persons to whom God has given the gift of teaching, who find their natural place in the classroom with children. They must have preparation in Bible and a continuous desire to study God's Word.

Teachers must be able to lead students to Christ, be sensitive to the leading of the Holy Spirit, and be wholesome, exemplary Christians. Their own faith must be lively and growing as they experience God in their personal lives. They must know how to pray and how to ask in faith for the wisdom that is from above.

Other qualifications include these: self-disciplined, conscientious, hard-working, respectful of authority, able to function as a team worker, healthy, possessing a sense of humor, patient, enduring, happy, not a murmurer, evidencing the fruit of the Spirit, and walking in the Spirit.

Christian day schools need teachers who are academically qualified, well trained and competent in the content of the subjects they teach and in varied methods of instruction. Teachers also need an understanding of child growth and development. They must be willing to continue their education, earning at least the master's degree. Academic qualifications are essential because the quality of instruction will affect about sixty years of the child's subsequent life, if the Lord tarries. A Christian day school should never offer a contract to a teacher to work in an area for which he is not trained.

To be properly prepared for teaching, Bible college graduates need training in academic subject areas, while graduates of other colleges need training in Bible. Since the school purposes to integrate a sound academic education with the Christian view of God in the world, both academic and Bible training are essential. There are no shortcuts. This preparation takes time, usually more than four years.

Christian day school principals should meet all the spiritual and academic qualifications for teachers plus at least three years of teaching experience before becoming principals. Additional qualifications for principals include the following: (1) the spiritual gift of administration; (2) leadership ability; (3) graduate study in school administration, preferably in Christian school administration; (4) courage; (5) vision; (6) endurance; (7) the ability to work with adults as well as with children; (8) fiscal responsibility; and (9) the qualifications of 1 Timothy 3:2-6, even though the school is not a church.

The greatest need in the Christian day school movement today is qualified principals. Men and women are needed to train for administration to lead these schools to become strong institutions, spiritually and academically.

Schools need teachers and principals for whom the Christian day school is their life ministry and not a stepping stone to another job, not a means of working a husband through seminary or graduate school, not one of two jobs. God is raising up teachers and principals who are planting their lives in this field of Christian service. Some are beginning teachers; others are experienced teachers and principals who are being called out of other school systems into God's school system, where Jesus Christ and the Bible are central in every aspect.

Curriculum

Christian day schools give serious attention to curriculum development, for they are academic schools, not vacation Bible schools which operate for nine or ten months. Students take the same standardized achievement tests that are given to students from other schools. Christian school graduates compete for college entrance just like anyone else and are accepted on the basis of their educational preparation.

Bible instruction has a central place in the curriculum. Most other subjects are taught at the same grade level as the other schools in the community to facilitate the transferring of students in and out of the school. The Christian day school has complete control, however, in the choice of books and materials for each subject. This is an important factor in curriculum development.

The difference in Christian day schools is not so much in the subjects offered, but in the way in which these subjects are taught from the Christian perspective. Frank Gaebelein, headmaster emeritus of the Stony Brook School, expresses it in this way, "All truth is God's truth." This refers not only to the Bible but to all academic truth. All truth is ultimately from God.

A current trend in Christian day schools is to develop a curriculum which is Christian in actual content. It appears that this trend may grow. New materials are being developed, although slowly. The development of these materials is difficult because the Christian day schools are independent and do not agree on what constitutes a Christian curriculum. This is analogous to evangelical churches which do not agree on what constitutes the proper Sunday school curriculum.

The schools are careful to fulfill any curriculum requirements of the department of education in the state in which the school is located.

Buildings and Equipment

The days of Mark Hopkins sitting on a log with his student are gone. Christian day school buildings do not have to be luxurious, but they should meet recognized standards for good school buildings from the standpoint of room sizes, health, safety, and sanitation. Outdoor play space should also meet recognized standards for that size school. Schools must obtain whatever legal permits are required in that community for use of the buildings as a day school.

Schools held in existing buildings which were not designed for day school use have problems. Some of these problems can be resolved, others cannot. It is often difficult to operate a school in facilities not designed for children's use.

Some churches are building their Christian education facilities according to day school specifications. Facilities are shared by the school and by the church, thus gaining efficient use of the property. This is an encouraging trend. In this approach, care must be taken to provide proper outdoor play areas.

When schools build new facilities, the recognized planning principle is this: determine the school's program, then design the plant for that program.

Equipment for Christian day schools should be sufficient in variety, quantity, and quality for the school to accomplish its stated objectives. Schools must achieve the financial stability required for the annual purchase of equipment and supplies. Because a school is Christian does not mean that it can get by with inadequate buildings, insufficient equipment, or sparse supplies. There is a relationship between facilities, equipment, and the quality of education offered by a school, whether or not that school is Christian.

Role of the Church

The school sees its work as supplemental to the evangelical church, but the church does not often feel that way about the school. This is unfortunate and may be due to the following reasons: (1) the school may attract money away from the church; (2) division may occur in the church because of the school; (3) there may be misunderstanding of the philosophy and objectives of the school.

The role of the church in a church-related school is clearly illustrated in the Norfolk (Va.) Christian School, which is sponsored by the Tabernacle Church. Church membership and fellowship depend on relationship and fellowship with Christ, not on enrollment in that church's school. The Tabernacle Church teaches the sovereignty of God over every aspect of life, including education, and teaches Christian family living, with the result that many parents send their children to the school. The church and the school work harmoniously in their programs for the growth of the students and of the parents.

The role of the church to the other kinds of Christian schools includes the following: (1) prayer; (2) financial help; (3) student enrollment; (4) encouragement and understanding.

Regardless of organizational structure, all Christian day schools are serving within the body of Christ, His church. It should be recognized that the whole body of Christ profits when any child or young person receives an education in which Jesus Christ is central. Believers do not choose a church home on the basis of the preacher's degrees, the architecture, or the equipment of the building, but on the truth of the preaching of the church. Similarly, churches should recognize that a school should be chosen in the same way, and should help support Christian day schools exhibiting high standards. Many churches are indifferent and some are even negative toward these schools. But these attitudes appear to be changing as the times become more evil.

The schools must do a better job of interpreting themselves to the churches and not become defensive, uncommunicative. Strong bonds need to be built between the churches and the schools. They are not to be competitors.

An Evaluation

The Christian day school is a testimony to God's name in elementary and secondary education. Every major court decision in the past decade has gone against allowing Bible reading and prayer as religious exercises in tax-supported schools. Even with electives in philosophy of religion and the Bible as literature, public schools are far from being Christianized. Christian schools are the answer to the dilemma of education.

New schools need time to become established, to purchase property, to develop a strong faculty, to become accredited. This often takes years, during which the school is open to criticism. There is much hope, however, because the schools are based on the true foundation, the Bible, which foundation is lacking in other schools, regardless of their buildings or reputations.

The need for Christian day schools will undoubtedly increase noticeably in this decade. It is apparent that the enemy is coming into education like a flood, and it is equally obvious that the Lord will raise up His standard in education too. As older teachers retire from public schools during this decade and are replaced by beginning teachers who do not accept the life values and standards of their predecessors, public schools will change radically and quickly. This trend has already started.

To serve God as a Christian day school teacher or principal is a worthy use of one's life. There are many positions open now, and there will be in the future. These schools offer an unusual opportunity to affect children and young people for God.

FOR FURTHER READING

Armerding, Hudson, ed. *Christianity and the World of Thought.* Chicago: Moody, 1968.

Benson, Warren S. "A History of the National Association of Christian Schools, 1947-1972." Ph.D. dissertation, Loyola University of Chicago, 1974.

Billings, Robert J. *A Guide to the Christian School.* Hammond, Ind.: Hyles-Anderson, 1971.

Blum, Virgil. *Freedom of Choice in Education.* New York: Macmillan, 1958.

Byrne, Herbert W. *A Christian Approach to Education.* Grand Rapids: Zondervan, 1961.

Clark, Gordon H. *A Christian Philosophy of Education.* Grand Rapids: Eerdmans, 1946.

Course of Study for Christian Schools. Grand Rapids: National Union of Christian Schools, 1947.

Fakkema, Mark. *Christian Philosophy.* Chicago: Christian Schools Service, 1952.

Fuller, Edmund, ed. *Christian Idea of Education.* New Haven, Conn.: Yale U., 1957.

Gaebelein, Frank E. *Christian Education in a Democracy.* New York: Oxford U., 1951.

———. *The Pattern of God's Truth.* New York: Oxford U., 1953.

Gordon, Rosalie. *What's Happened to Our Schools?* New Rochelle, N.Y.: America's Future, 1956.

Kievel, Paul A. *The Christian School: Why It Is Right for Your Child.* Wheaton, Ill.: Scripture Press, Victor Books, 1974.

Kraushaar, Otto. *American Nonpublic Schools.* Baltimore: John Hopkins U., 1972.

Lockerbie, Bruce D. *The Way They Should Go.* New York: Oxford U., 1972.

Lowrie, Roy. *Christian School Administration.* Wheaton, Ill.: National Association of Christian Schools, 1966.

———. *Your Child and the Christian School.* Wheaton, Ill.: National Association of Christian Schools, 1967.

Rafferty, Max. *Suffer Little Children.* New York: Devin-Adian, 1962.

Rushdoony, Rousas. *The Messianic Character of American Education.* Philadelphia: Presbyterian & Reformed, 1963.

Van Til, Cornelius. *The Dilemma of Education.* Nutley, N.J.: Presbyterian & Reformed, 1956.

Worrell, Edward. *Restoring God to Education.* Wheaton, Ill.: Van Kampen, 1950.

Zuck, Roy B. *Let's Be Logical.* Wheaton, Ill.: National Association of Christian Schools, n.d.

Index

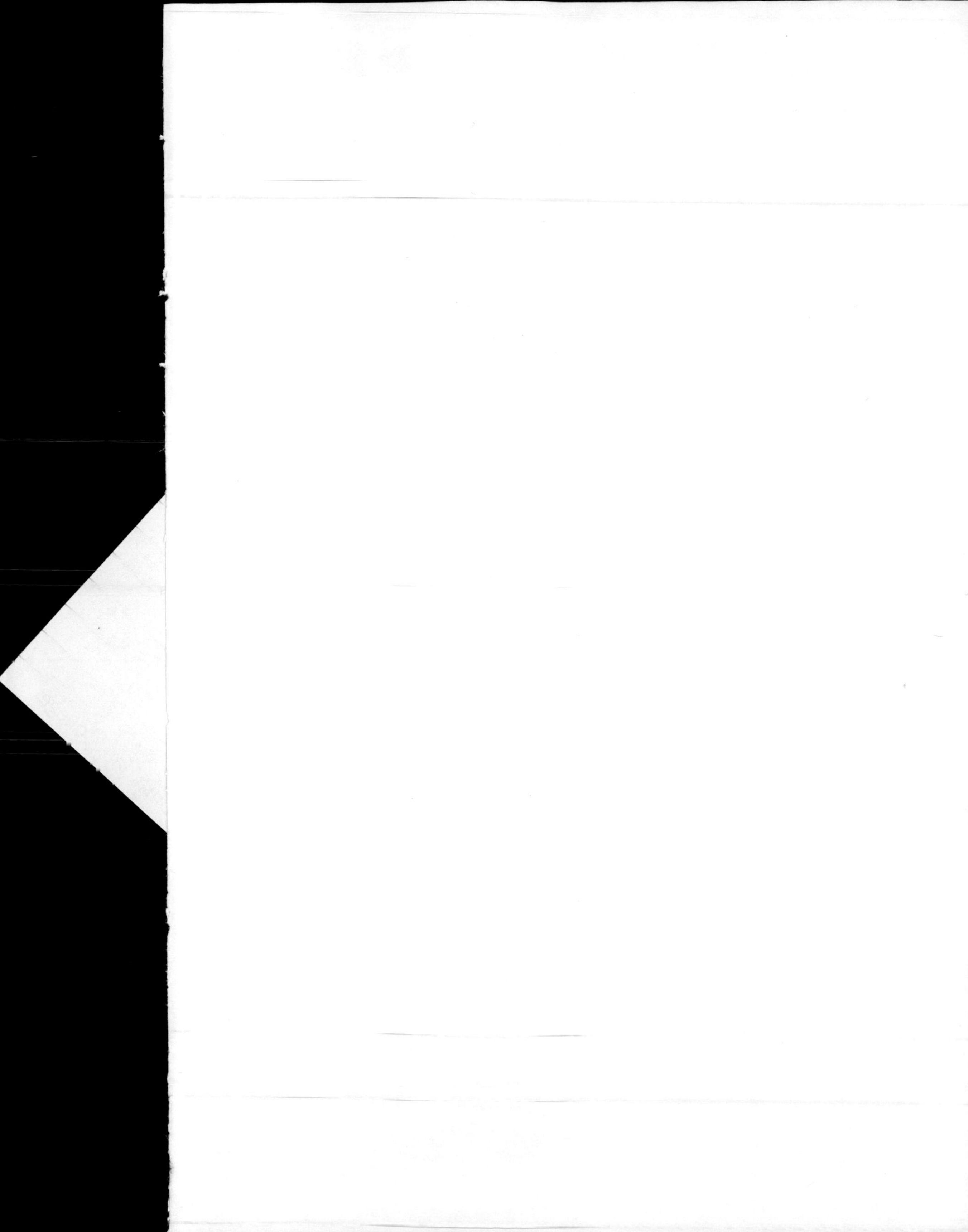

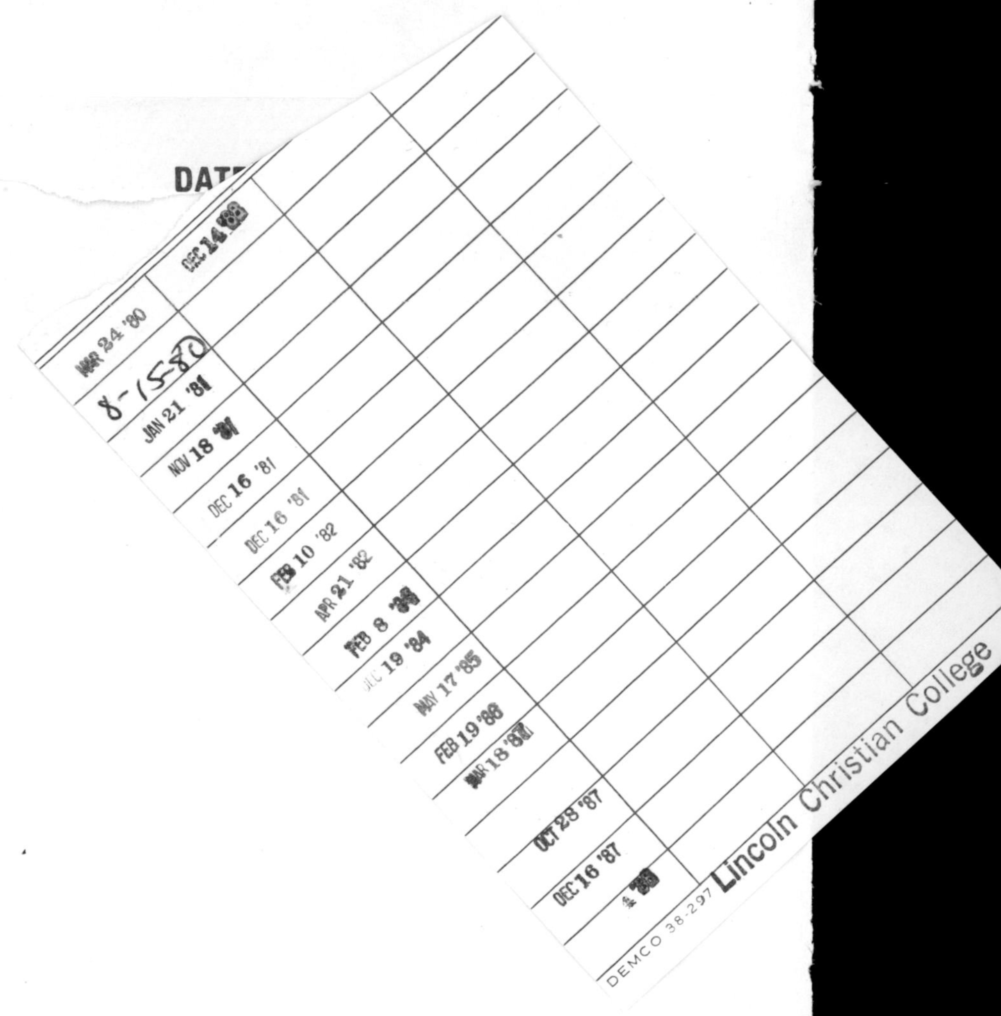
DATE
MAR 24 '80
8-15-80
JAN 21 '81
NOV 18 '81
DEC 16 '81
DEC 16 '81
FEB 10 '82
APR 21 '82
FEB 8 '83
DEC 19 '84
MAY 17 '85
FEB 19 '86
MAR 18 '87
OCT 28 '87
DEC 16 '87
DEC 14 '88
DEMCO 38-297
Lincoln Christian College